C000171781

STREET ATLAS
County Durham and Teesside

First published in 1996 as *'Durham'* by

Philip's, a division of
Octopus Publishing Group Ltd
2-4 Heron Quays, London E14 4JP

Third colour edition 2004
First impression 2004

ISBN-10   0-540-08672-X (spiral)
ISBN-13   978-0-540-08672-6 (spiral)

© Philip's 2004

OS Ordnance Survey®

This product includes mapping data licensed
from Ordnance Survey® with the permission of
the Controller of Her Majesty's Stationery Office.
© Crown copyright 2004. All rights reserved.
Licence number 100011710.

Printed and bound in Spain
by Cayfosa-Quebecor

Contents

Digital Data

The exceptionally high-quality mapping found in this atlas is available as digital data in TIFF format, which is easily convertible to other bitmapped (raster) image formats.

The index is also available in digital form as a standard database table. It contains all the details found in the printed index together with the National Grid reference for the map square in which each entry is named.

For further information and to discuss your requirements, please contact Philip's on 020 7644 6932 or james.mann@philips-maps.co.uk

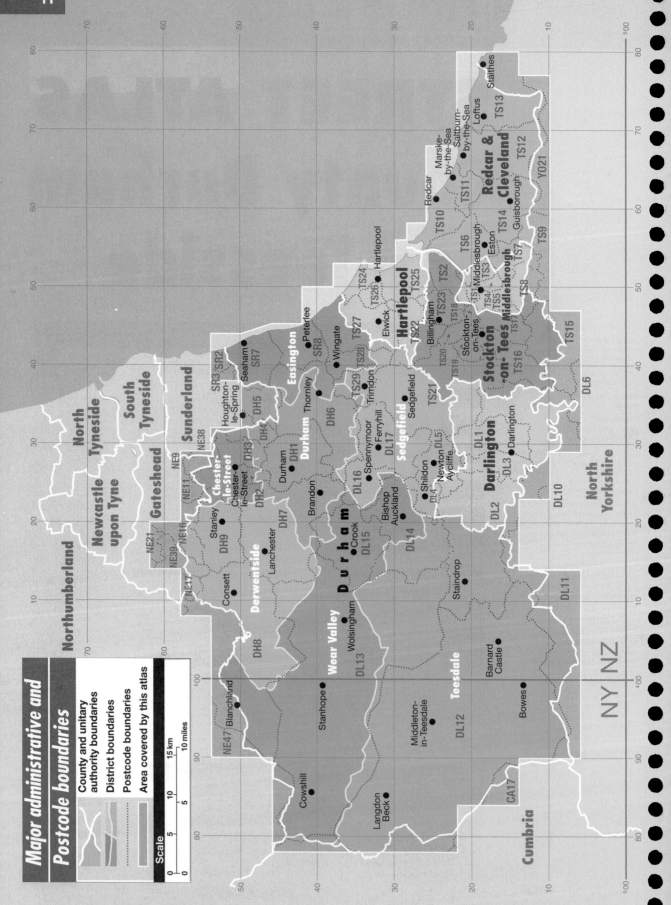

Major administrative and Postcode boundaries

County and unitary authority boundaries
District boundaries
Postcode boundaries
Area covered by this atlas

Scale
0   5   10   15 km
0   5   10 miles

Northumberland

North Tyneside

South Tyneside

Newcastle upon Tyne

Gateshead

Sunderland

NE9

NE11

NE38

NE21

NE39

NE16

NE17

NE47

Derwentside

Consett

Stanley

Lanchester

DH9

DH7

DH8

Chester-le-Street

Chester-le-Street

DH3

DH2

DH4

DH5

Houghton-le-Spring

SR2

SR3

Seaham

SR7

Durham

Durham

DH1

DH6

Brandon

Crook

DL15

Wolsingham

DL13

Wear Valley

Stanhope

Cowshill

Langdon Beck

DH16

Easington

Peterlee

SR8

Thornley

Wingate

TS27

TS28

TS29

Trimdon

Spennymoor

Ferryhill

DL17

Sedgefield

Sedgefield

TS21

Bishop Auckland

Shildon

Newton Aycliffe

DL5

DL4

DL14

DL16

Staindrop

Barnard Castle

Bowes

Middleton-in-Teesdale

DL12

Teesdale

Durham

Elwick

Hartlepool

Hartlepool

TS24

TS26

TS25

TS22

TS23

TS19

TS20

TS18

Billingham

TS2

Stockton-on-Tees

Stockton-on-Tees

TS16

TS17

TS1

TS4

TS5

TS3

Middlesbrough

Middlesbrough

TS8

TS6

Eston

TS14

TS7

Guisborough

TS9

Redcar

TS10

TS11

Marske-by-the-Sea

Saltburn-by-the-Sea

Loftus

Staithes

TS13

Redcar & Cleveland

TS12

YO21

Darlington

Darlington

DL1

DL3

DL2

DL6

DL10

DL11

North Yorkshire

CA17

Cumbria

NY NZ

Motorway with junction number	
Primary route – dual/single carriageway	
A road – dual/single carriageway	
B road – dual/single carriageway	
Minor road – dual/single carriageway	
Other minor road – dual/single carriageway	
Road under construction	
Tunnel, covered road	
Rural track, private road or narrow road in urban area	
Gate or obstruction to traffic (restrictions may not apply at all times or to all vehicles)	
Path, bridleway, byway open to all traffic, road used as a public path	
Pedestrianised area	
Postcode boundaries (DY7)	
County and unitary authority boundaries	
Railway, tunnel, railway under construction	
Tramway, tramway under construction	
Miniature railway	
Railway station (Walsall)	
Private railway station	
Metro station (South Shields)	
Tram stop, tram stop under construction	
Bus, coach station	

Acad	**Academy**	Inst	**Institute**	Recn Gd **Recreation Ground**
Allot Gdns	**Allotments**	Ct	**Law Court**	
Cemy	**Cemetery**	L Ctr	**Leisure Centre**	Resr **Reservoir**
C Ctr	**Civic Centre**	LC	**Level Crossing**	Ret Pk **Retail Park**
CH	**Club House**	Liby	**Library**	Sch **School**
Coll	**College**	Mkt	**Market**	Sh Ctr **Shopping Centre**
Crem	**Crematorium**	Meml	**Memorial**	TH **Town Hall/House**
Ent	**Enterprise**	Mon	**Monument**	Trad Est **Trading Estate**
Ex H	**Exhibition Hall**	Mus	**Museum**	Univ **University**
Ind Est	**Industrial Estate**	Obsy	**Observatory**	W Twr **Water Tower**
IRB Sta	**Inshore Rescue Boat Station**	Pal	**Royal Palace**	Wks **Works**
		PH	**Public House**	YH **Youth Hostel**

■ The small numbers around the edges of the maps identify the 1 kilometre National Grid lines
■ The dark grey border on the inside edge of some pages indicates that the mapping does not continue onto the adjacent page

Ambulance station	
Coastguard station	
Fire station	
Police station	
Accident and Emergency entrance to hospital	
Hospital (H)	
Place of worship	
Information Centre (open all year)	
Parking, Park and Ride (P) (P&R)	
Post Office (PO)	
Camping site, caravan site	
Golf course	
Picnic site	
Important buildings, schools, colleges, universities and hospitals (Prim Sch)	
Built up area	
Woods	
Water name (River Medway)	
River, weir, stream	
Canal, lock, tunnel	
Water	
Tidal water	
Non-Roman antiquity (Church)	
Roman antiquity (ROMAN FORT)	
Adjoining page indicators and overlap bands (87) (228) The colour of the arrow and the band indicates the scale of the adjoining or overlapping page (see scales below)	

Enlarged mapping only

Railway or bus station building	
Place of interest	
Parkland	

The scale of the maps on the pages numbered in blue is 5.52 cm to 1 km • 3½ inches to 1 mile • 1: 18103	0 ¼ ½ ¾ 1 mile / 0 250 m 500 m 750 m 1 kilometre
The scale of the maps on pages numbered in green is 2.76 cm to 1 km • 1¾ inches to 1 mile • 1: 36206	0 ¼ ½ ¾ 1 mile / 0 250m 500m 750m 1kilometre
The scale of the maps on pages numbered in red is 11.04 cm to 1 km • 7 inches to 1 mile • 1: 9051	0 220 yards 440 yards 660 yards ½ mile / 0 125m 250m 375m ½ kilometre

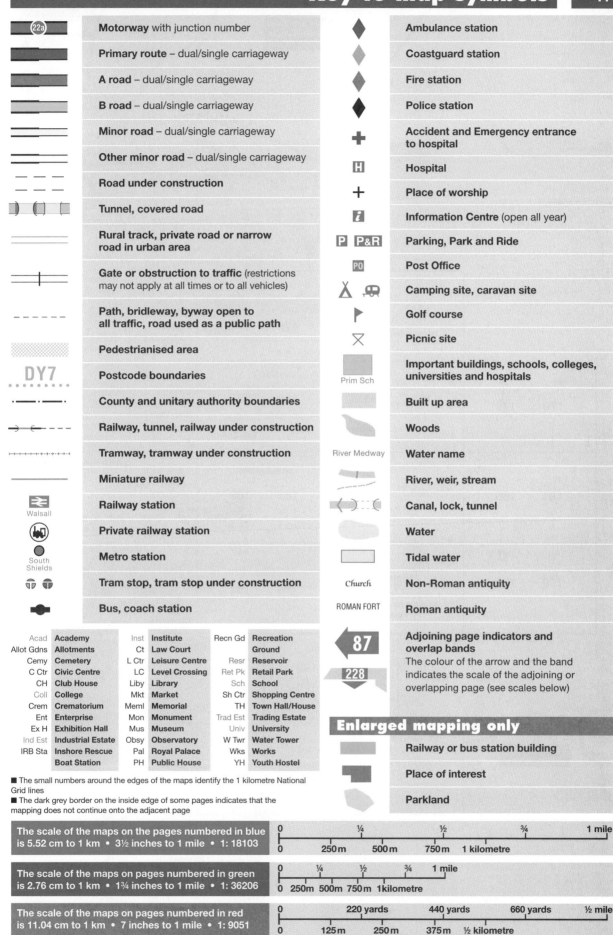

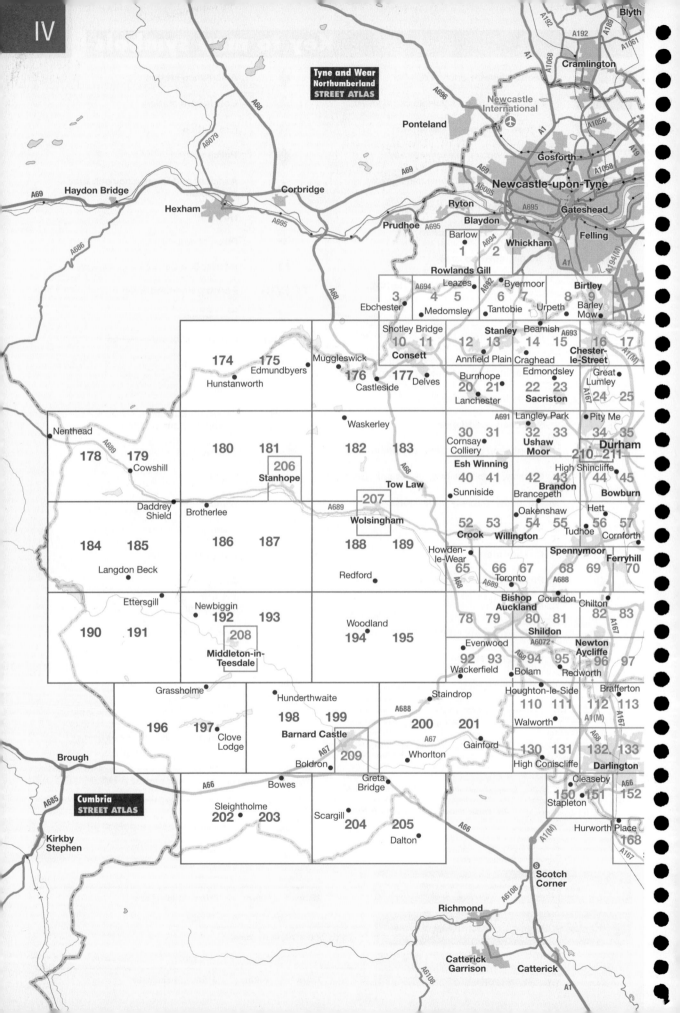

Tyne and Wear Northumberland STREET ATLAS

Blyth

Cramlington

Ponteland

Newcastle International

Gosforth

Newcastle-upon-Tyne

Haydon Bridge

Corbridge

Hexham

Prudhoe

Ryton

Blaydon

Gateshead

Whickham

Felling

Barlow 1 | 2

Rowlands Gill

Ebchester 3 | 4 Leazes 5 | 6 Byermoor 7 | 8 Birtley 9

Medomsley Tantobie Urpeth Barley Mow

Shotley Bridge 10 | 11 | Consett 12 | Stanley 13 | Beamish 14 | 15 | Chester-le-Street 16 | 17

174 | 175 Muggleswick 176 | 177 Delves | Annfield Plain Craghead | 20 | 21 | 22 | 23 | 24 | 25

Edmundbyers Castleside | Burnhope Edmondsley Great Lumley

Hunstanworth | Lanchester | Sacriston

Nenthead | Waskerley | Langley Park Pity Me

178 | 179 180 | 181 182 | 183 | 30 | 31 | 32 | 33 | 34 | 35

Cowshill 206 Stanhope | Cornsay Colliery Ushaw Moor | Durham

Esh Winning | High Shincliffe | 210 211

Daddrey Shield Brotherlee 207 Tow Law 40 | 41 | 42 | 43 | 44 | 45

184 | 185 186 | 187 Wolsingham | Sunniside Brancepeth Brandon | Bowburn

Langdon Beck | 188 | 189 Crook Willington | 52 | 53 | 54 | 55 | Oakenshaw | Hett | 56 | 57 | Cornforth

Redford | Howden-le-Wear | Tudhoe | Spennymoor | Ferryhill

Ettersgill Newbiggin 192 | 193 | Woodland | 65 | 66 | 67 | 68 | 69 | 70

190 | 191 208 Middleton-in-Teesdale 194 | 195 Toronto | Bishop Auckland Coundon Chilton | 82 | 83

78 | 79 | 80 | 81 | Shildon | Newton Aycliffe

Grassholme Hunderthwaite Staindrop | Evenwood | 92 | 93 | 94 | 95 | 96 | 97

196 | 197 198 | 199 200 | 201 | Wackerfield Bolam Redworth | Houghton-le-Side | 110 | 111 | 112 | 113 | Brafferton

Clove Lodge Barnard Castle 209 Whorlton Gainford | Walworth | 130 | 131 | 132 | 133 | Darlington

Brough Boldron | Greta Bridge | High Conscliffe | Oleaseby

Bowes | Stapleton | 150 | 151 | 152

Cumbria STREET ATLAS

Sleightholme 202 | 203 Scargill 204 | 205 Dalton | Hurworth Place 168

Kirkby Stephen | Scotch Corner

Richmond

Catterick Garrison | Catterick

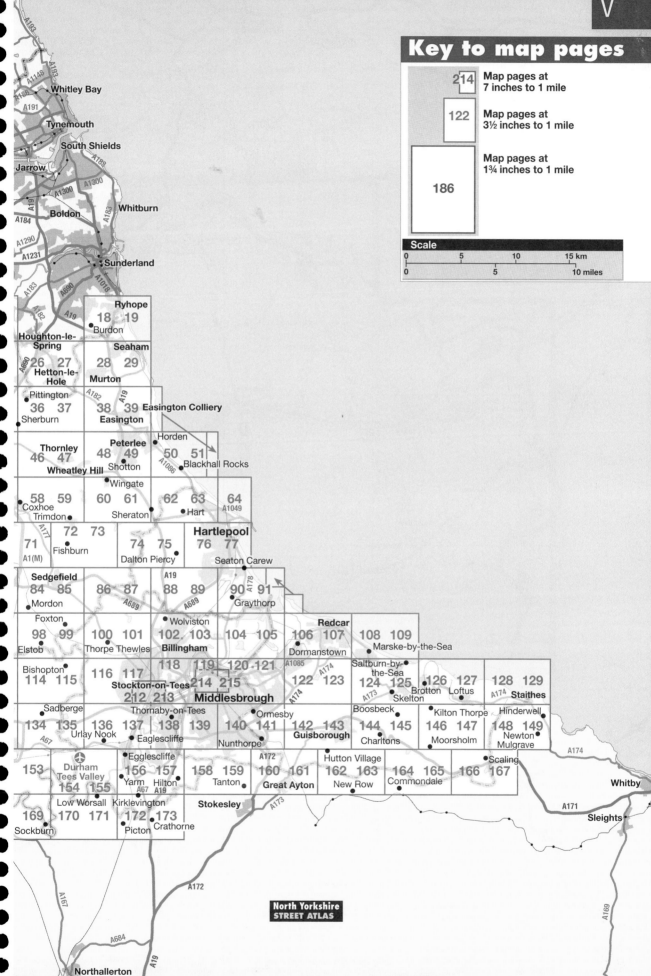

V

Key to map pages

214	Map pages at 7 inches to 1 mile
122	Map pages at 3½ inches to 1 mile
186	Map pages at 1¾ inches to 1 mile

Scale

0 ... 5 ... 10 ... 15 km
0 ... 5 ... 10 miles

Whitley Bay
Tynemouth
South Shields
Jarrow
Boldon
Whitburn
Sunderland

Ryhope
18 19
Burdon
Houghton-le-Spring
Seaham
26 27 28 29
Hetton-le-Hole
Murton
Pittington
36 37 38 39 Easington Colliery
Sherburn
Easington
Horden
Thornley
Peterlee
46 47 48 49 50 51
Wheatley Hill
Shotton
Blackhall Rocks
Wingate
58 59 60 61 62 63 64
Coxhoe
Trimdon
Sheraton
Hart
72 73 74 75 76 77
71
Fishburn
Hartlepool
Dalton Piercy
Seaton Carew
Sedgefield
84 85 86 87 88 89 90 91
Mordon
Graythorp
Foxton
Wolviston
Redcar
98 99 100 101 102 103 104 105 106 107 108 109
Elstob
Thorpe Thewles
Billingham
Dormanstown
Marske-by-the-Sea
Bishopton
Saltburn-by-the-Sea
114 115 116 117 118 119 120 121 122 123 124 125 126 127 128 129
Stockton-on-Tees
214 215
Brotton
Loftus
Staithes
Skelton
212 213
Middlesbrough
Sadberge
Thornaby-on-Tees
Ormesby
Boosbeck
Kilton Thorpe
Hinderwell
134 135 136 137 138 139 140 141 142 143 144 145 146 147 148 149
Urlay Nook
Eaglescliffe
Nunthorpe
Guisborough
Charltons
Moorsholm
Newton Mulgrave
Egglescliffe
Hutton Village
Scaling
153 156 157 158 159 160 161 162 163 164 165 166 167
Durham Tees Valley
Yarm
Hilton
Tanton
Great Ayton
New Row
Commondale
Whitby
154 155
Low Worsall
Kirklevington
Stokesley
Sleights
169 170 171 172 173
Sockburn
Picton
Crathorne

North Yorkshire STREET ATLAS

Northallerton

Scale

0 .... 5 .... 10 km

0 .. 1 .. 2 .. 3 .. 4 .. 5 miles

Hartlepool Bay

ol Hartlepool

Seaton Carew

A689

Greatham

Graythorp

ly

Tees Bay

en

ley

A178

South

Haverton Hill

Port Clarence

REDCAR

Coatham

Dormanstown

Marske-by-the-Sea

A174

Saltburn-by-the-Sea

A1085

166

A1053

South Bank

Grangetown

Kirkleatham

Lazenby

Yearby

New Marske

Skinningrove

Middlesbrough

Wilton

Upleatham

Brotton

Boulby

Eston

Normanby

Dunsdale

Skelton

Carlin How

Loftus

A174

Staithes

B1380

Park End

Ormesby

North Skelton

Kilton Thorpe

Easington

Port Mulgrave

ddles-

A174

242

Redcar and

Guisborough

Boosbeck

Margrove Park

Lingdale

Stanghow

Liverton

Roxby

Hinderwell

Runswick Bay

Newton Mulgrave

Runswick Bay

Kettleness

Goldsborough

bugh

A1043

Marton

6

A171

Hutton Gate

Charltons

Cleveland

Moorsholm

Ellerby

A174

Lythe

Sandsend

Coulby Newham

Munthorpe

Hutton Village

B1366

9

Res.

Scaling

East Barnby

Mickleby

West Barnby

East Row

Dunsley

Whitby

Sal

on

Hemlington

Newton under Roseberry

329

Scaling Dam

Scaling Res.

Ugthorpe

Newholm

Newby

B1292

A172

Great Ayton

Little Ayton

New Row

Commondale

B1266

A171

13

Aislaby

Briggswath

Ruswarp

B1410

Stainsacre

er

Tanton

Stokesley

A173

Easby

Kildale

Danby

Stonegate

299

Sleights

Ugglebarnby

Sneaton

B1416

ame

ridge

Battersby

Castleton

Ainthorpe

Houlsyke

Lealholm

Egton

Grosmont

Sneatonthorpe

A171

Kirkby

Great Broughton

Ingleby Greenhow

Westerdale

Low Garth

Street

Glaisdale

Egton Bridge

Esk Valley

Littlebeck

Carlton in Cleveland

B1257

Faceby

Esk

A169

435

433

Beck Hole

Goathland

norlton

432

Flask

by

Urra

454

Seave Green

Chop Gate

404

COCKAYNE RIDGE

401

Cockayne

Wake Lady Green

404

299

420

Church Houses

19

Fangdale Beck

B1257

Thorgill

Rosedale Abbey

20

Pickering Forest

Langdal Forest

Low Mill

Seph

Cropton Hartoft End Forest

Stape

A169

Dove

Lastingham

Levisham

TOLL

Lar

Hawnby

Gillamoor

Fadmoor

Hutton-le-Hole

Spaunton

Newton-on-Rawcliffe

Lockton

Staindale Forest

248

Rye

Old Byland

Rievaulx

Pockley

Beadlam

Cropton

Low Dalby

Dalby Forest

le

Cold Kirby

Scawton

Helmsley

A170

Nawton

Welburn

Kirkbymoorside

13

Keldholme

Sinnington

Wrelton

Aislaby

Middleton

stonecliffe

Wombleton

Kirkby Mills

Great Edstone

Marton

Pickering

A170

Ellerburn

n-under-

Harome

Normanby

Cost

Thornton-le-Dale

Wilton

Allerston

B1415

s

14

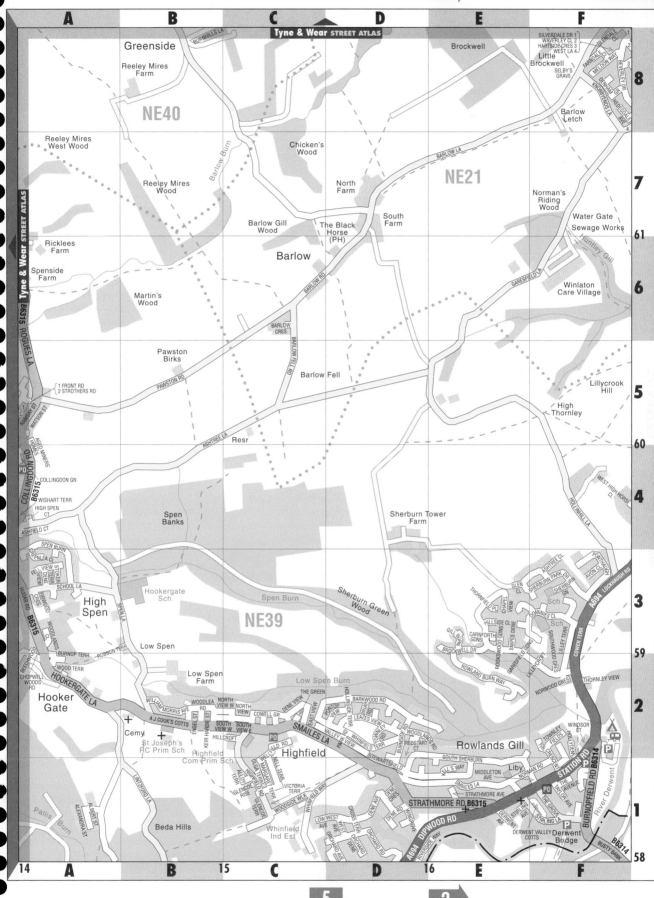

Tyne & Wear STREET ATLAS

Greenside

Reeley Mires Farm

NE40

Reeley Mires West Wood

Reeley Mires Wood

Ricklees Farm

Spenside Farm

Martin's Wood

Barlow Gill Wood

Chicken's Wood

North Farm

The Black Horse (PH)

Barlow

South Farm

Brockwell

Little Brockwell

SILVERDALE DR 1
WAVERLEY CL 2
HARTSIDE CRES 3
WEST LA 4

Selby's Grave

Barlow Letch

NE21

Norman's Riding Wood

Water Gate Sewage Works

Winlaton Care Village

Lillycrook Hill

High Thornley

Pawston Birks

Barlow Fell

1 FRONT RD
2 STROTHERS RD

PAWSTON RD

ASHTREE LA

Resr

BARLOW FELL RD

BARLOW CRES

WEST HIGH HORSE CL

HOLMHILL LA

Spen Banks

Sherburn Tower Farm

Spen Burn

Sherburn Green Wood

High Spen

NE39

Hookergate Sch

Low Spen

Low Spen Farm

Low Spen Burn

Hooker Gate

HOOKERGATE LA

Chopwell Woods Rd

Beda Hills

WILLIAM MORRIS AVE

A J COOK'S COTTS

St Joseph's RC Prim Sch

Cemy

Highfield Com Prim Sch

Highfield

THE GREEN

DENE VIEW

EAST VIEW

Whinfield Ind Est

Rowlands Gill

STRATHMORE RD B6315

A694 DIPWOOD RD

RIVERSIDE WAY

Derwent Bridge

Derwent Valley Cotts

River Derwent

B6314

BUSTY BANK

STATION RD

BURNOPFIELD B6314

A694 LOCKHAUGH RD

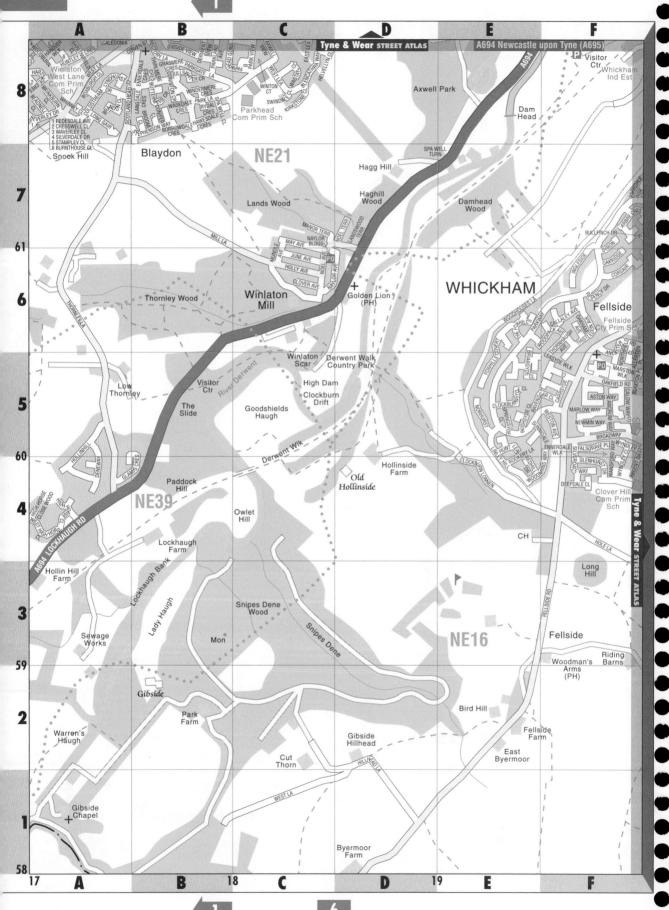

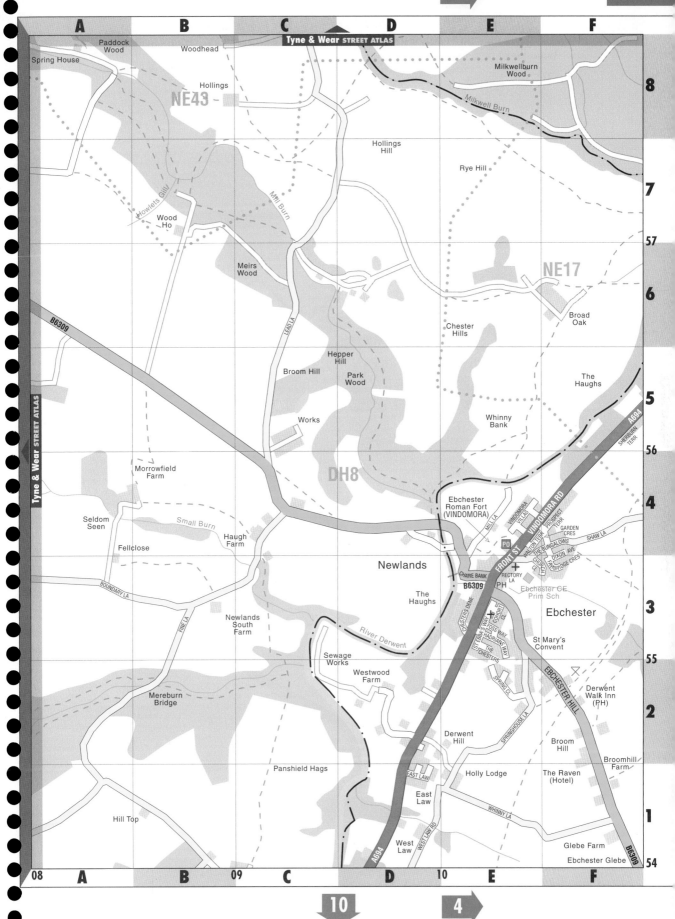

Tyne & Wear STREET ATLAS

Tyne & Wear STREET ATLAS

NE43

NE17

DH8

Paddock Wood
Spring House
Woodhead
Hollings
Milkwellburn Wood
Milkwell Burn
Hollings Hill
Rye Hill
Howlets Gill
Wood Ho
Mill Burn
LEADLA
Meirs Wood
Broad Oak
Chester Hills
The Haughs
Hepper Hill
Broom Hill
Park Wood
Whinny Bank
Works
B6309
SHERBURN TERR
A694
Morrowfield Farm
Small Burn
Ebchester Roman Fort (VINDOMORA)
MILL LA
VINDOMORA VILLAS
VINDOMORA RD
WALTON TERR
PROSPECT TERR
GARDEN CRES
SHAW LA
THE BUNGALOWS
DIXON AVE
CHURCH
HARBRIDGE CRES
Seldom Seen
Haugh Farm
Fellclose
Newlands
PO
FRONT ST
RECTORY LA
Ebchester CE Prim Sch
Ebchester
BOUNDARY LA
CHARE BANK
PH
B6309
The Haughs
CHESTERS DENE
St Mary's Convent
Derwent Walk Inn (PH)
Newlands South Farm
FINE LA
River Derwent
ST EBBA'S WAY
FOSS WAY
HADRIANS WAY
COHORT CL
THE CHESTERS
EBCHESTER HILL
Sewage Works
Westwood Farm
SPRING CL
Mereburn Bridge
Derwent Hill
SPRINGHOUSE LA
Broom Hill
Broomhill Farm
Panshield Hags
EAST LAW
Holly Lodge
The Raven (Hotel)
Hill Top
East Law
A694
WEST LAW RD
WHINNY LA
Glebe Farm
West Law
Ebchester Glebe
B6309

4

4

10

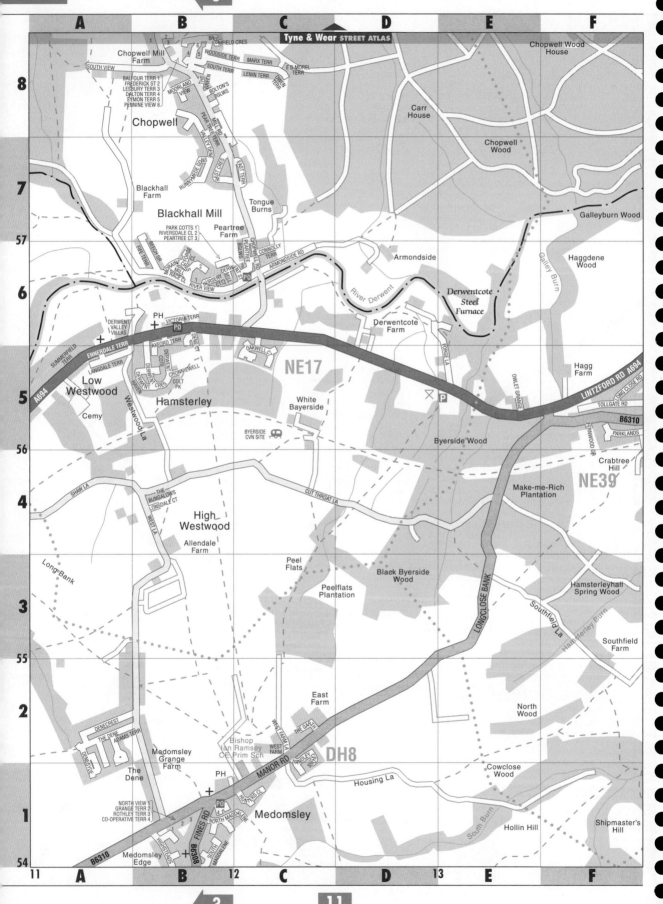

A   B   C   D   E   F

8

Chopwell Mill Farm
SOUTH VIEW
BALFOUR TERR 1
FREDERICK ST 2
LESBURY TERR 3
DALTON TERR 4
SYMON TERR 5
PENNINE VIEW 6
MOORLAND VIEW
THE GREEN
BOLTON'S BGLWS
WOODSIDE TERR
MARX TERR
LENIN TERR
E D MOREL TERR
OWEN TERR
SOUTH TERR
BR 2
CMFIELD CRES

Chopwell

Chopwell Wood House

Carr House

Chopwell Wood

7

Blackhall Farm

Blackhall Mill

Tongue Burns

Galleyburn Wood

57

PARK COTTS 1
RIVERSDALE CL 2
PEARTREE CT 3
Peartree Farm
CONNOLLY TERR
PEARTREE BGLWS
CHOPWELL RD
ARMONDSIDE RD

Armondside

Haggdene Wood

FIFE TERR
BEECH LA
MORAINE FORGE
MILL RACE CL
MILL ST
DERWENT ST
NURSERY
RIVER VIEW
PO

Derwentcote Steel Furnace

6

DERWENT VALLEY VILLAS
PH
VICTORIA TERR
PO
River Derwent

Derwentcote Farm

Galley Burn

SUMMERFIELD TERR
ENNERDALE TERR
A694
LANGDALE TERR
AXFORD TERR
DERWENT CL
DERWENT CRES
CRONNIEWELL
COLT PK
DENE CT
OAKWELL CT

NE17

FORGE LA

Hagg Farm

LINTZFORD RD A694
LONG CLOSE RD

5

Low Westwood

Hamsterley

Cemy

White Bayside

OWLET GRANGE

TOLLGATE RD

B6310

WESTWOOD LA
BYERSIDE CVN SITE

Byerside Wood

NE39

FERNWOOD GR
PARKLANDS

56

SHAW LA
THE BUNGALOWS
LONSDALE CT
WEST LA

CUT THROAT LA

Make-me-Rich Plantation

Crabtree Hill

4

High Westwood

Allendale Farm

Peel Flats

Black Byerside Wood

Hamsterleyhall Spring Wood

Long Bank

Peelflats Plantation

LONGCLOSE BANK

SOUTHFIELD LA

Hamsterley Burn

3

55

Southfield Farm

East Farm

North Wood

2

DENECREST
THE DENE
ADAMS TERR
DENESIDE

Medomsley Grange Farm

WEST FARM LA
THE GARTH
WEST FARM

Bishop Ian Ramsey CE Prim Sch

DH8

Cowclose Wood

Housing La

The Dene

PH

MANOR RD
RIDLEY SQ

1

NORTH VIEW 1
GRANGE TERR 2
ROTHLEY TERR 3
CO-OPERATIVE TERR 4
FINES RD
PO
NORTH MAGDALENE
HUNTERS CL

Medomsley

South Burn

Hollin Hill

Shipmaster's Hill

54

B6310

Medomsley Edge
SOUTH MAGDALENE
HUNTERS CLOS
B6308

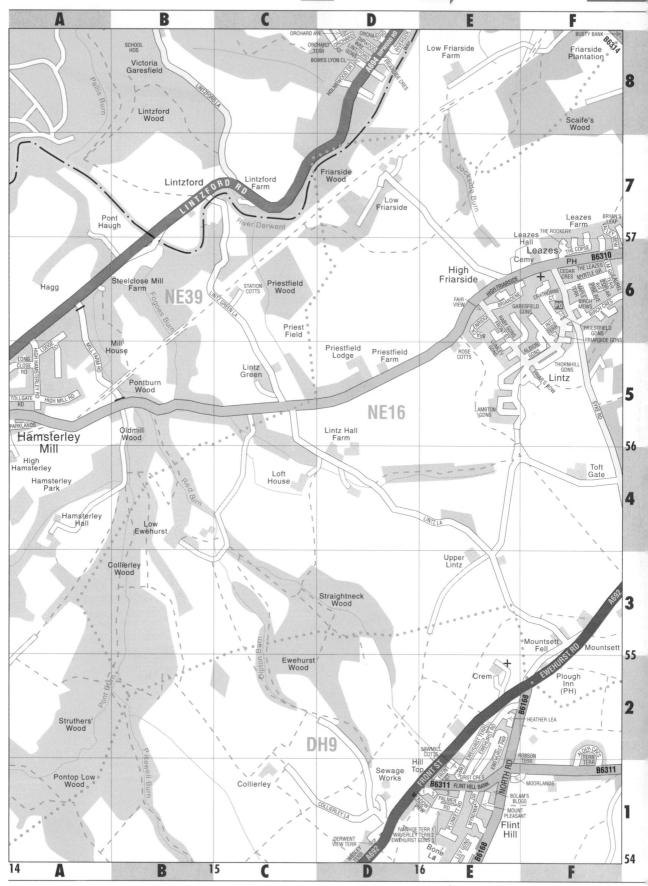

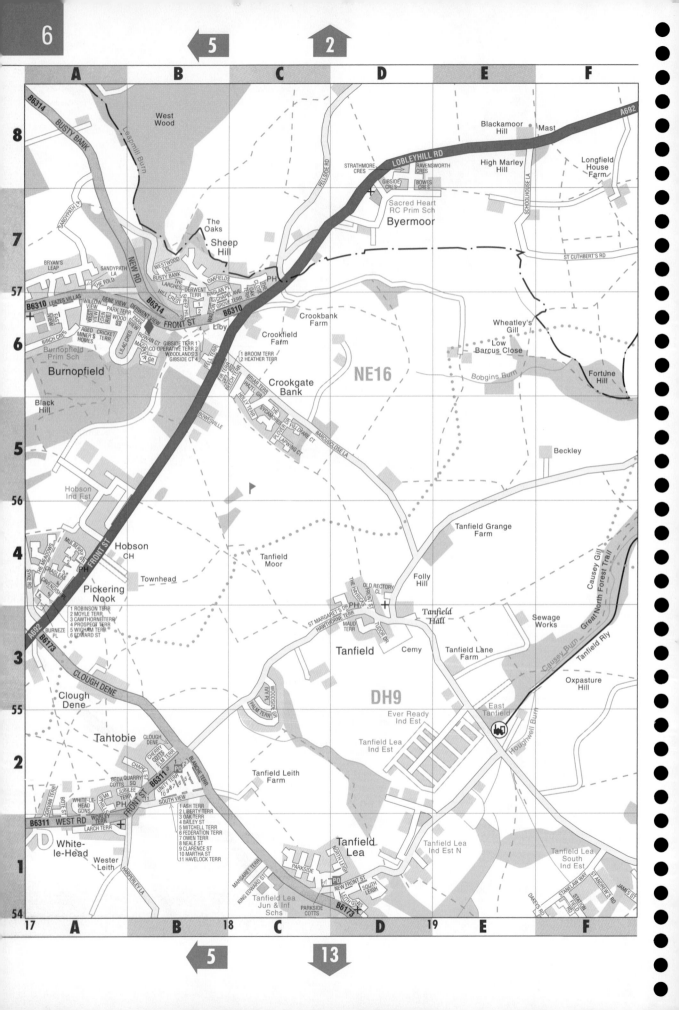

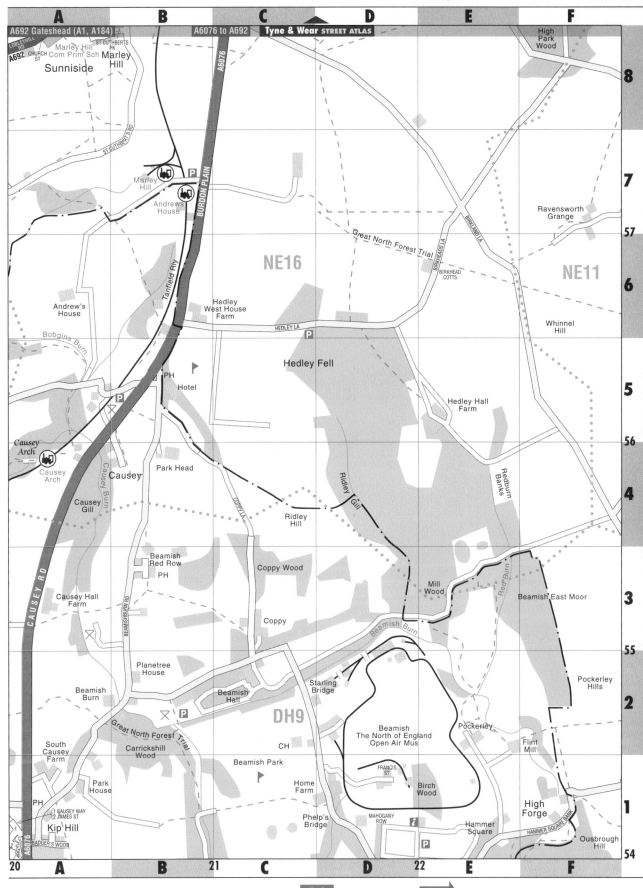

A692 Gateshead (A1, A184)   A6076 to A692   **Tyne & Wear** STREET ATLAS

A   B   C   D   E   F

LOBLEYHILL RD
A692
St Cuthberts Com Prim Sch
CHURCH ST
ST CUTHBERTS PK
Sunniside   **Marley Hill**
Marley Hill

High Park Wood

8

Marley Hill
Andrews House

BURDON PLAIN

A6076

7

St Cuthbert's Rd

57

Great North Forest Trail

BIRKLAND LA

Ravensworth Grange

NE16

BIRKHEADS LA
BIRKHEAD COTTS

NE11

6

Andrew's House

Tanfield Rly

Hedley West House Farm

HEDLEY LA
P

Whinnel Hill

Bobgins Burn

PH
Hotel

Hedley Fell

Hedley Hall Farm

5

P

Causey Arch

Causey Burn

Causey   Park Head

COPPY LA

Ridley Gill

56

Redburn Banks

Causey Gill

Ridley Hill

4

Beamish Red Row
PH

Coppy Wood

Mill Wood

Red Burn

Beamish East Moor

BEAMISHBURN RD

Causey Hall Farm

Coppy

Beamish Burn

3

CAUSEY RD

55

Planetree House

Starling Bridge

Pockerley Hills

2

Beamish Burn

Great North Forest Trail

Beamish Hall
P

DH9

Beamish
The North of England Open Air Mus

Pockerley

Flint Mill

South Causey Farm

Carrickshill Wood

CH

FRANCIS ST

Beamish Park

Home Farm

Birch Wood

High Forge

Park House

1 CAUSEY WAY
2 JAMES ST

Phelp's Bridge

MAHOGANY ROW

Hammer Square

HAMMER SQUARE BANK

1

PH

Kip Hill

A6076
BADGER'S WOOD

P

Ousbrough Hill

54

20   A   B   21   C   D   22   E   F

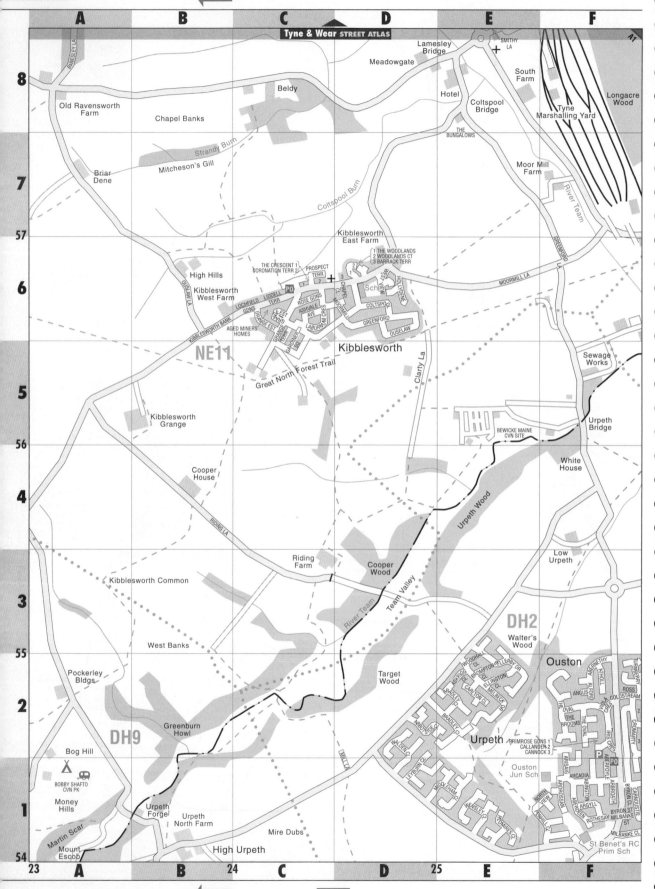

Tyne & Wear STREET ATLAS

NE11

DH9

DH2

Kibblesworth

Ouston

Urpeth

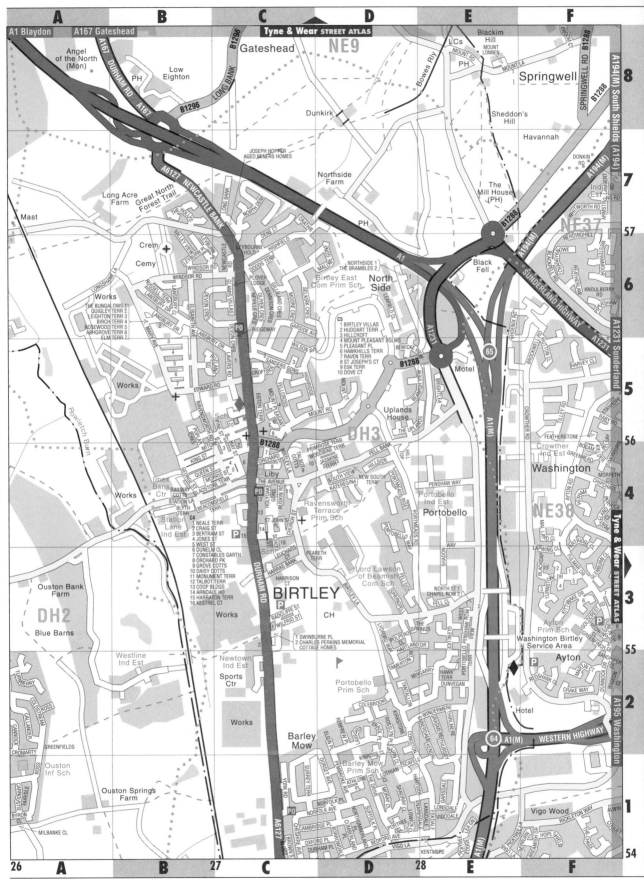

Map grid references (top and bottom): A B C D E F

Vertical grid references: 8 7 57 6 5 56 4 3 55 2 1 54

Bottom numbers: 26 A B 27 C D 28 E F

A1 Blaydon
A167 Gateshead
Gateshead
NE9
Springwell
A194(M) South Shields (A194)
SPRINGWELL RD
B1288

Angel of the North (Mon)
Low Eighton
A167 DURHAM RD
A167
PH
B1296
LONG BANK
B1296
Dunkirk
Joseph Hopper Aged Miners Homes
Northside Farm
PH
Bowes Rly
Blackim Hill
L Cs
Mount Rd
Mount La
Sheddon's Hill
Havannah
The Mill House (PH)
Donkin Rd
A194(M)
Ind Est
Whitworth Rd
Armstrong
Lambert

A6127 NEWCASTLE BANK
Great North Forest Trail
Long Acre Farm
Mast
Crem
Cemy
Long Bank
North Lane
Dene Ct
Crathie
Highfield
Leybourne Hold
North Side
Birtley East Com Prim Sch
A1
Black Fell
B1288
Sunderland Highway
NE37
Heronkeld
Rowe
Blackfell Rd
Heatherlaw
Knoulberry Rd
Parshaw
A1231 Sunderland
A1231

Works
THE BUNGALOWS 1
QUIGLEY TERR 2
LEIGHTON TERR 3
BIRCH TERR 4
ROSEWOOD TERR 5
ASHGROVE TERR 6
ELM TERR 7
Works

Valley Tilbury Pl
Leyburn Pl
The Holts
Russell Terr
Lansbury Dr
Lansbury Ave
Elisabeth Terr
Lansbury Dr
Mary Ave
Windsor Rd
Windsor Rd
Glamis Villas
Levon Cres
Devon Cres
Rutland
Ravensworth Rd
PO
Ridgeway
Neville Cres
Oliver Cres
Dodds Terr
Plover Lodge
Dennison Cres
Gilliland Cres
Moore Cres
Garside Ave
Selkirk Cres
Wilson Ave
Sanders Gdns
Crofts
3
4
5
6
7
Malds
Svid
NORTHSIDE 1
THE BRAMBLES 2
C5
1 BIRTLEY VILLAS
2 HUDDART TERR
3 HILLCROFT
4 MOUNT PLEASANT BGLWS
5 PLEASANT PL
6 HAWKHILLS TERR
7 RAVEN TERR
8 ST JOSEPH'S CT
9 ESK TERR
10 DOVE CT
Bewicke Rd

Rowletch Burn
Works
Sch
Poplar
Ravensworth Rd
Mitchell
King St
Queen St
Morris St
Gladstone Terr
Garden St
B1288
B1288
Orchard La
Birtley La
Eaton Terr
Mount Pleasant
Mount Rd
Mount Rd
Fellcross
Highside
Primrose Terr
Woodbine Terr
Jasmine Terr
South View
Katere gina
New South Terr
South View
Fell Bank
Hillside
DH3
The Uplands
Uplands House
Top
Hill
Leamed Cl
Leamed Cl
A1231
A1(M)
Crowther Rd
Tilley Rd
Raby Rd
Harvey Cl
Phoenix Rd
Brockwell Ct
Hutton Cl
Featherstone
Bolam Cl
Crowther Ind Est
Greenhead
Washington
NE38
Stanhope
Morpeth
Chipchase

Imex Bsns Ctr
Works
Railway Cotts
Station La
Blyth Terr
Station Lane Ind Est
C4
1 NEALE TERR
2 CRAIG ST
3 BERTRAM ST
4 JONES ST
5 WEST ST
6 DUNELM CL
7 CONSTABLES GARTH
8 ORCHARD PK
9 GROVE COTTS
10 DAISY COTTS
11 MONUMENT TERR
12 TALBOT TERR
13 COOP BLDGS
14 ARNDALE HO
15 HARRATON TERR
16 KESTREL CT
Beaconsfield Terr
Holyoake
Gibbs
Ruskin Rd
The Avenue
Liby
PO
St John's
Church St
Leuchars Cl
Harras Bank
13
14
15
16
P
St John's Ct
Ravensworth Terrace Prim Sch
Peareth Terr
Portobello
Portobello Ind Est
Portmeads Rd
Portmeads Rise
Penshaw Way
Shadon
Way
Hart
Portobello Way

Ouston Bank Farm
DH2
Blue Barns
Durham Rd
Harrison Ct
BIRTLEY
P
Radcliffe St
Wilfrid St
CH
1 SWINBURNE PL
2 CHARLES PERKINS MEMORIAL COTTAGE HOMES
Birtley La
Lord Lawson of Beamish Com Sch
NORTH ST 1
CHAPEL ROW 2
Fell Cl
The Springs
Glenlee
Springwell
Lydmond Way
Polperro
West View
Penshaw Row
Lapwing Dr
Kittiwake Dr
Ayton Prim Sch
Washington Birtley Service Area
P
Ayton
Goldcrest Rd
Dunlin Dr
Wrekenton
Greenfinch Cl

Westline Ind Est
Newtown Ind Est
Sports Ctr
Works
Portobello Prim Sch
Colebrooke
Kingstone
Portobello Ter
Mingarry
Hawk Terr
Dunvegan
Hotel
Redshank Cl
Crake Way
Martin Ct
Sandpiper
Dunnock Ct

Turnberry
Colstream
Ross
Callander Ct
Cannock
Cromarty
Greenfields
Ouston Inf Sch
Carruthers
Fairisle
Byron
Cl
Milbanke Cl
Ouston Springs Farm
Barley Mow
York Rd
A6127
PO
Surrey Terr
Norfolk Cl
Norfolk Ave
Cambridge Pl
Cheshire Ave
Oxford Pl
Durham Pl
Renfrew
Elgin
Kinross Cl
Dorset Ave
Athlone
The Drive
Pembroke Ave
Borrowdale
Vigo La
Portree
Bedford Ave
Barley Mow Prim Sch
Lothian
Scafell
Saturn
Coniston
Windermere
Thirlmere
Ennerdale
Thursby
Garsdale
Lonsdale
Kentmere
Vigodale
Eskdale
Lowick Ct
Lodge
Naresdale
Leghall
Vigo Wood
Rickleton Way
The Chase
Alwin
A195 Washington
A1(M)
WESTERN HIGHWAY
64
65
Motel
A194(M)
North Side

F3
1 WHEATEAR CL
2 FIELDFARE CL
3 STONECHAT CL
4 CORMORANT CL
5 PLOVER CL
6 WHITETHROAT CL
7 GLENHOLME CL
8 TEAL CL
9 WREN CL

Grid columns: A B C D E F
Grid rows: 8 7 53 6 5 52 4 3 51 2 1 50

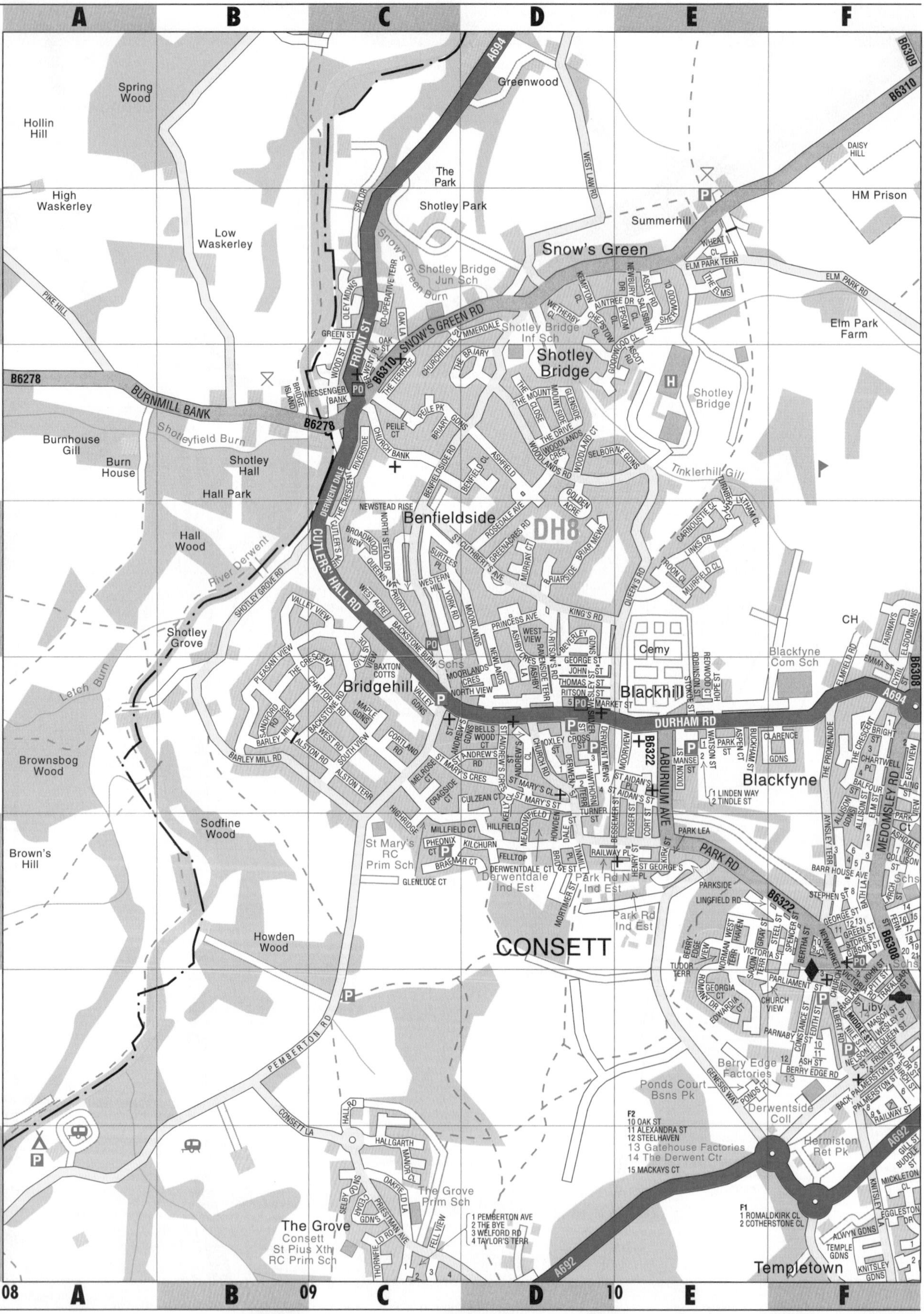

Major place labels:

Spring Wood · Greenwood · Hollin Hill · High Waskerley · Low Waskerley · The Park · Shotley Park · Summerhill · HM Prison · Daisy Hill · Snow's Green · Shotley Bridge Jun Sch · Shotley Bridge Inf Sch · Elm Park Terr · Elm Park Rd · Elm Park Farm · Snow's Green Burn · Shotley Bridge · Shotley Bridge · Burnmill Bank · B6278 · B6310 · Burnhouse Gill · Burn House · Shotley Hall · Hall Park · Shotleyfield Burn · Benfieldside · DH8 · Tinklerhill Gill · Hall Wood · River Derwent · Shotley Grove · Letch Burn · Cutlers Hall Rd · Bridgehill · Blackhill · Cemy · Blackfyne Com Sch · CH · Brownsbog Wood · Brown's Hill · Sodfine Wood · Howden Wood · Durham Rd · Blackfyne · St Mary's RC Prim Sch · Derwentdale Ind Est · Park Rd Ind Est · Park Rd · CONSETT · Parkside · Lingfield Rd · Pemberton Rd · Consett La · Hallgarth · The Grove Prim Sch · Ponds Court Bsns Pk · Berry Edge Factories · Berry Edge Rd · Derwentside Coll · Hermiston Ret Pk · Medomsley Rd · B6308 · B6322 · A692 · A694 · B6309 · The Grove · Consett St Pius Xth RC Prim Sch · Templetown

Index (bottom):

Index boxes on map:

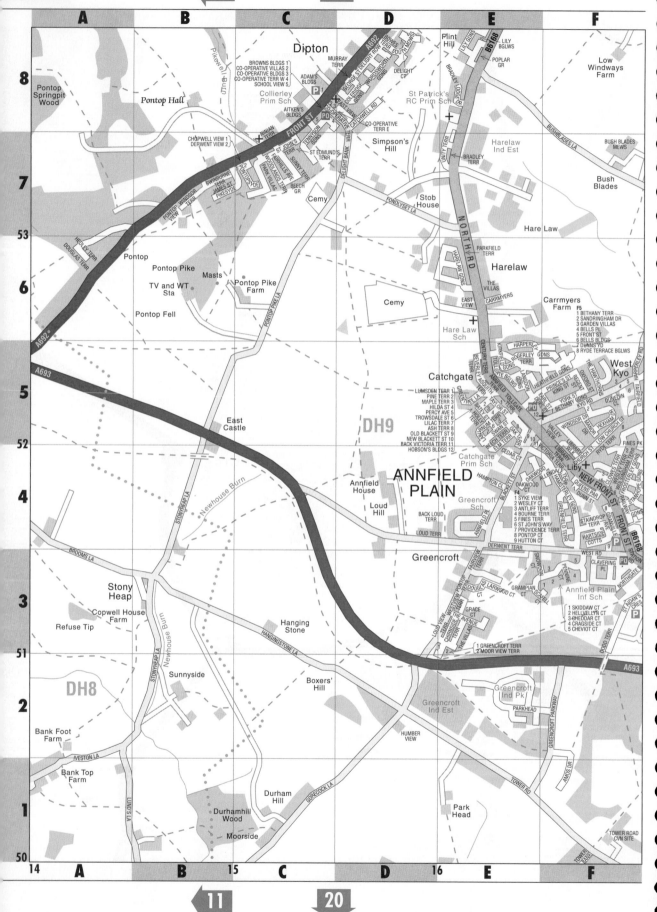

A B C D E F

8

7

53

6

5

52

4

51

2

1

50

14 A B 15 C D 16 E F

Dipton

Pontop Springpit Wood

Pontop Hall

BROWNS BLDGS 1
CO-OPERATIVE VILLAS 2
CO-OPERATIVE BLDGS 3
CO-OPERATIVE TERR W 4
SCHOOL VIEW 5

Collierley Prim Sch

MURRAY TERR
ADAM'S BLDGS
AITKEN'S BLDGS
P

St Patrick's RC Prim Sch

DELIGHT CT
Plint Hill
LILY GDNS
LILY BGLWS
B6168
POPLAR GR

Low Windways Farm

CHOPWELL VIEW 1
DERWENT VIEW 2

Simpson's Hill

Harelaw Ind Est

BUSHBLADES LA

BUSH BLADES MEWS

Bush Blades

HEDLEY TERR
DOUGLAS TERR
Pontop

Cemy

Stob House

BRADLEY TERR
UNITY TERR
NORTH RD

Parkfield TERR

Hare Law

Pontop Pike
Masts
TV and WT Sta
Pontop Pike Farm

Pontop Fell

Cemy

HARELAW GDNS
EAST VIEW
CARRMYERS
THE VILLAS

Harelaw

Carrmyers Farm

F5
1 BETHANY TERR
2 SANDRINGHAM DR
3 GARDEN VILLAS
4 BELLS PL
5 FRONT ST
6 BELLS BLDGS
7 DUNNS YD
8 RYDE TERRACE BGLWS

A692

A693

East Castle

Hare Law Sch

Catchgate

LUMSDEN TERR 1
PINE TERR 2
MAPLE TERR 3
HILDA ST 4
PERCY AVE 5
TROWSDALE ST 6
LILAC TERR 7
ASH TERR 8
OLD BLACKETT ST 9
NEW BLACKETT ST 10
BACK VICTORIA TERR 11
HOBSON'S BLDGS 12

West Kyo

DH9

Annfield House

Loud Hill

BACK LOUD TERR

LOUD TERR

ANNFIELD PLAIN

Catchgate Prim Sch

Greencroft Sch

DERWENT TERR

F4
1 SYKE VIEW
2 WESLEY CT
3 ANTLIFF TERR
4 BOURNE TERR
5 FINES TERR
6 ST JOHN'S WAY
7 PROVIDENCE TERR
8 PONTOP CT
9 HUTTON CT

WEST RD

HARTSIDE COTTS

B6168
FRONT ST

NEW FRONT ST

P

BROOMS LA
STONYHEAP LA
Newhouse Burn

Stony Heap

Copwell House Farm
Refuse Tip

HANGINGSTONE LA

Hanging Stone

Greencroft

FAIRVIEW
SNOWDON CT
GRACE CT
LARWOOD CT
GRAMPIAN CT
SCAFELL

PENNINE
Annfield Plain Inf Sch

1 SKIDDAW CT
2 HELLVELLYN CT
3 CHEDDAR CT
4 CRAGSIDE CT
5 CHEVIOT CT

ST ADAM'S CRES
P

DH8

Sunnyside

Bank Foot Farm

IVESTON LA

Bank Top Farm

GORECOCK LA

Boxers' Hill

1 GREENCROFT TERR
2 MOOR VIEW TERR

A693

Greencroft Ind Pk
PARKHEAD

Greencroft Ind Est

HUMBER VIEW

Durham Hill
Durhamhill Wood

Moorside

Park Head

TOWER RD

GREENCROFT PARKWAY

TOWER ROAD CVN SITE
TOWER PARK

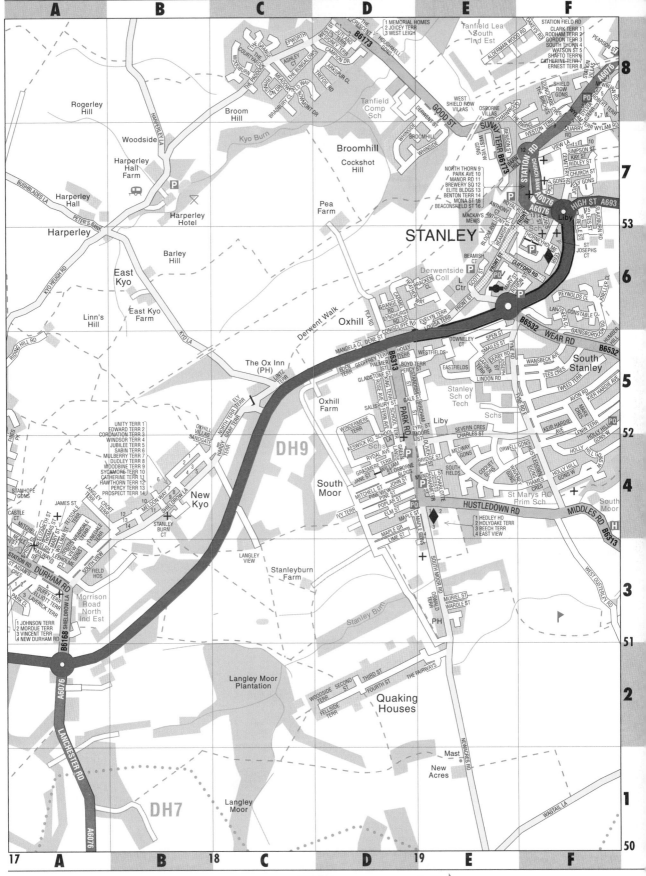
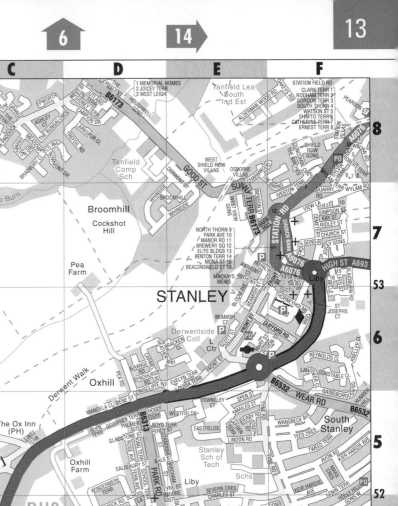

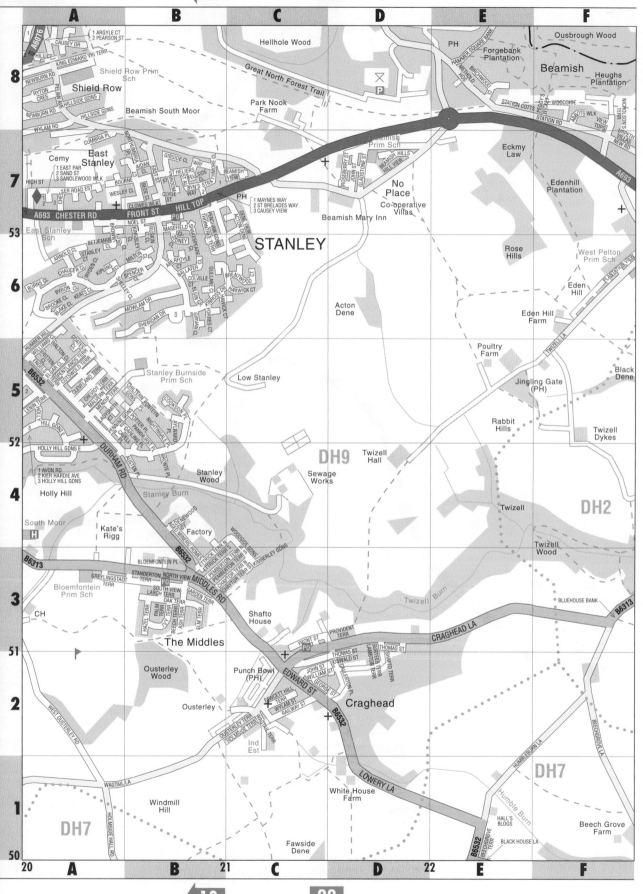

A B C D E F

8
7
53
6
5
52
4
3
51
2
1
50

DH9
Weather Hill
Urpeth Common
Urpeth South Farm
Sandy Fords
1 INSTITUTE TERR E
2 INSTITUTE TERR W
3 AVONDALE HO
Perkinsville
Recn Gd
LYNE CL
TWEED CL
WANSBECK DR
OUSTON LA
LYNE CL
FRONT ST
GADLEY DR
BRECON PL
COURTNEY DR
GARRIGLCH DR
ARUNDEL WLK
Rabbit Hills
High Handenhold
STONY LA
NEW RD
CO-OPERATIVE SYDNEY ST TERR
ARTHUR ST
LAUREL CRES
BAYTREE TERR
LILAC GDNS
URPETH TERR 5 4
VICTORIA TERR
SOUTH VIEW
2 3
EXFIELD
GREENS BANK
SUMMERFIELD
TWIZELL LA
PO
ORCHARD CL
PH
EDEN CROFT
West Pelton
1 THE FAIRWAYS
2 ROSEMOUNT
1 ST PAUL'S TERR
2 WEST VILLAS
Moss Close Farm
ELM AVE
OAK TERR
THE PARADE
THE PARADE
CHURCH RD
HEATHMEADS
VICTORIA TERR
Cemy
PREBEND ROW
THORNTONS CL
THORNTON GR
KING'S LA
MOSSWIN
GREENACRES
FAIRFIELD
SANDYFORD PL
SANDYFORD
MIDDLEFIELD
KINGSWAY VILLAS
FRONT ST
HARLAW
P
IVYWAY
NYLTON TERR
CONSTANCE ST
ERNEST ST
BARBARY CL
WHELDON TERR
1 THE AVENUE
2 WHELDON TERR
Liby
Pelton Com Prim Sch
BRACKENBEDS
A693
PELTON LA
PELTONIA
SOUTH VIEW
FIELDSIDE
SOUTHFIELD
VICARAGE
GRANGE
THE GARTH
ELWIN ST
ELWIN PL
BRACKENBEDS
CH
Grange Villa
STONE ROW
QUEEN'S ST
EAST ST
WEST ST
BERT'S
PINE ST
GRANGE CT
CORONATION TERR
Lowsing Hills
PO
CO-OPERATIVE TERR
NEWBRIDGE BANKS
Pelton Lane Ends
GRETA ST N 1
GRETA ST S 2
BEAMISH CT 3
AGED MINERS HOMES 4
PELTON MEWS
HOLYOAKE ST
ALEXANDRA ST
PROVIDENT ST
INDUSTRIAL ST
EDWARD ST
Roseberry Prim Sch
HARE'S BLDGS
PELTON LA
Roseberry Villas
Newfield Terr
PH
NORTH VIEW
PO
SOUTH VIEW
Newfield
DH2
Roseberry Sports & Com Coll
Newfield Farm
Great North Forest Trail
PELTON HOUSE FARM EST
STATION LA
J CHARLES ST
Bernard Terr
Recn Gd
SPRINGFIELD TERR
ROSE TERR
HAWTHORNE TERR
PARK VIEW
BATTLE GN
STATION HOS
Pelton
Hare Law
WILLIAM ST
Front St
FRONT ST
STATION HOS
Stella Gill Ind Est
The Bottoms
Grange Plantation
Twizell Burn
NEW GRANGE TERR 1
PLUNKETT TERR 2
MILLER GDNS 3
2
1
GRANGE TERR
DUNSANY TERR
FELLROSE CT
CRAGHEAD RD
Pelton Fell
GLENSIDE TERR
BURNTHOUSE BANK
B6313
PELTON FELL RD
BLUEHOUSE BANK
Wearholme
Tribley Cotts
Hett Hills
Hett Hills
BEAMISH VIEW
The Moorings (PH)
GARDINER CRES
VALLEY RD
BRIARWOOD AVE
FERNDENE AVE
MILTON TERR 1
SHAKESPEARE TERR 2
MASEFIELDS 3
WORDSWORTH AVE
BYRON AVE
RUSKIN AVE
CHENLEY AVE
RODGE PL
WHITEHILL CRES
TENNYSON
SHELLEY GDNS
SHELLEY CT
WHITEHILL FELL RD
Whitehill Farm
Rabbit Banks
SMYTHWAITE
BRAINWOOD DR
AUCKLAND
DOVECOTE FARM
White Hall Farm
Tribley Farm
Cong Burn
ASHGROVE 1
BANK'S HOLT 2
SUMMERFIELDS 3
CLOVERHILL 4
ELMWOOD 5
OAKFIELD 6
POPPYFIELDS 7
FONGLEY
HEATHFIELD
LONG DALE
GILL BURNS
WEST DR
RED DR
DOVECOTE DR
Broomyholm Plantation
Broomy Holm
DH7
WALDRIDGE LA
ACCOMMOOR
MEADOW DR
West Farm
LESBURY CL
NORTON
Little Burn
Congburn Plantation
Dene Cotts
The Waldridge Tavern (PH)
CHESTER ST
WALDRIDGE RD
OAK ST
POPLAR ST
PINE ST
OLIVE ST
LIME ST
CEDAR ST
DRONFIELD CL 1
ELSDON CL 2
SHILLMOOR CL 3
FENWICK CL
FALSTONE DR
CRASTER
FLOQ CL
FLEETHAM CL
BRANDON CL
EMBLETON DR
Waldridge
BRECKBROVE LA

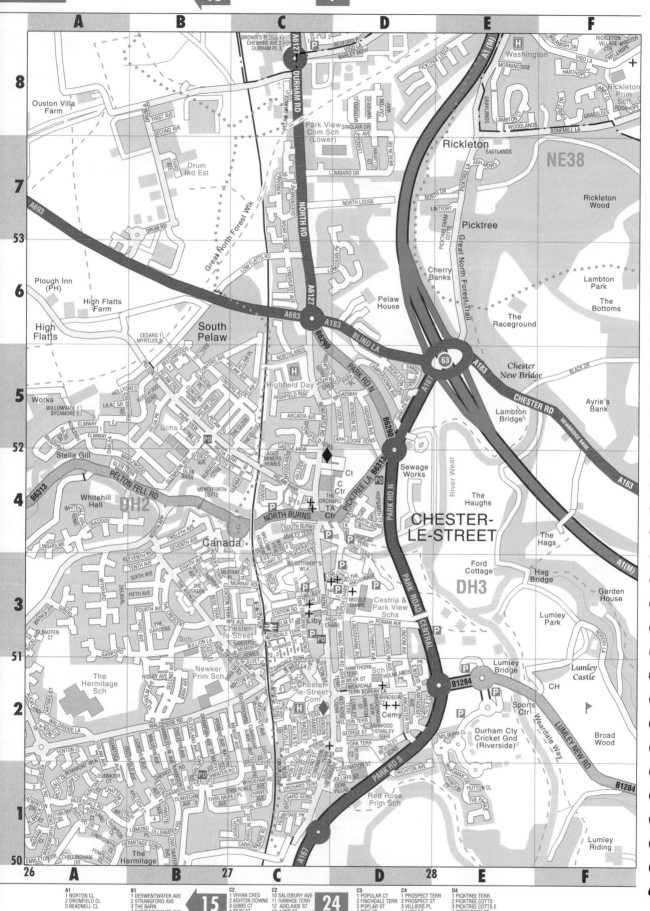

A1
1 NORTON CL
2 DRONFIELD CL
3 BEADNELL CL

B1
1 DERWENTWATER AVE
2 STRANGFORD AVE
3 THE BARN
4 BASSENTHWAITE AVE

C2
1 VIVIAN CRES
2 ASHTON DOWNE
3 GIBBS CT
4 REAY CT
5 PENTLAND CT
6 LAWSON CT
7 RIDDELL CT
8 HEMEL ST
9 THOMAS ST

C2
10 SALISBURY AVE
11 IVANHOE TERR
12 ADELAIDE ST
13 LYNN ST
14 ROBERTSON ST
15 VICTORIA PL

C3
1 POPULAR CT
2 FINCHDALE TERR
3 POPLAR ST
4 PINE ST
5 VICTOR ST
6 ALBERT ST

C4
1 PROSPECT TERR
2 PROSPECT ST
3 VILLIERS PL
4 LUCY ST
5 MORNINGSIDE CT

D4
1 PICKTREE TERR
2 PICKTREE COTTS
3 PICKTREE COTTS E
4 GREENBANK ST
5 RIVER TERR
6 PICKTREE MEWS

15
24

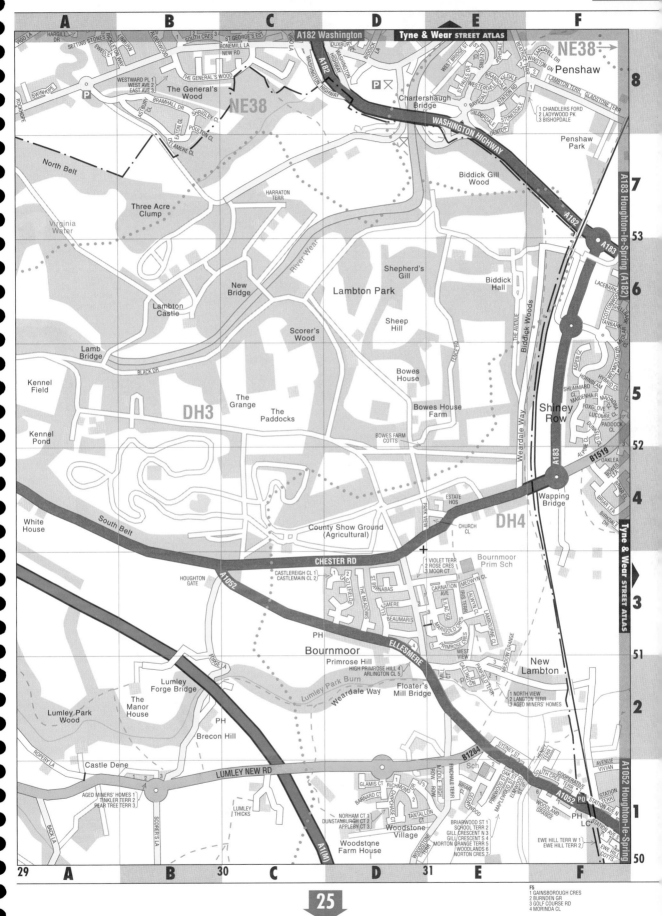

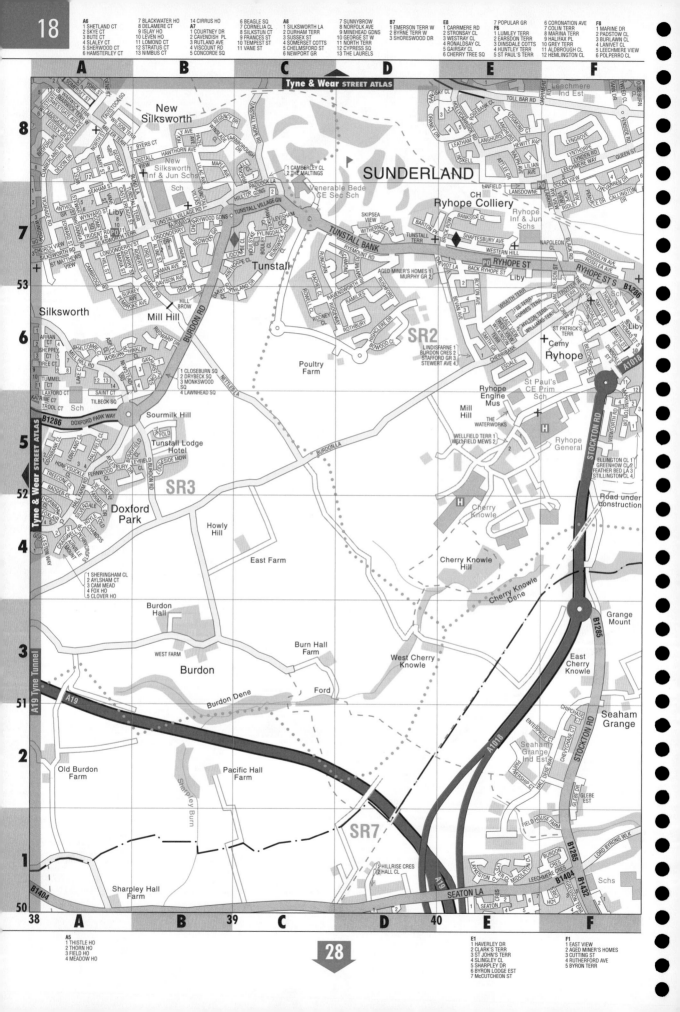

A1018 Sunderland

Ryhope
Nook

1 TOLL BAR RD
2 MARINE DR
3 TOLL BAR HO
4 LEECHMERE WAY
5 QUEEN ST
6 LADOCK CL
7 POLPERRO CL

Maiden's
Flat

SALTERFEN RD
SALTERFEN LA

Road under construction

RYHOPE RD

BYONY TCH
ATHELSTAN
RIGG
CLIFF RD
PO TER
CLIFF
TERR

CLIFF
VIEW

SEAHAM RD

Halliwell Banks

THE VILLAGE

B1287

1 FLORALIA AVE
2 GREY TERR
3 GORDON TERR
4 KILBURN CL
5 SOUTH FARM
6 ERNEST TERR
7 RICHARDSON TERR
8 FAWCETT TERR
9 THOMPSON TERR
10 CRANSTON PL
11 ROBSON PL
12 ARTHUR ST
13 MOIR TERR
14 CHARLES ST
15 JOHN ST

STATION RD
SCOTLAND

GROUNDRY AVE
SEA VIEW
GEORGE

BREWER TERR
ETHEL TERR

FEATHER BED
ARTHUR
AVE

ATHOL GDNS
REGENT RD

MARVILLE W
MARVILLE

FEATHER BED LA

SR2

Pincushion

Road under construction

Ryhope Dene
House
(Convent)

Ryhope Dene

SR7

Hall
Farm

Seaham
Hall

BYRON'S
CT

LC

LORD BYRONS WLK

Seaham Dene

NEW DR

PROMENADE

P

B1287

1 BURNWAY
2 NEWLANDS RD W
3 NEWARK CRES
4 NAVENBY CL

WOODLANDS
SEAHAM RD

P

NORFOLK
CL

BURNHALL DR

ROCHAMBY
NORTON AVE

1 SUTHERLAND ST
2 EMBANKMENT RD

STONEYCROFT WAY 1
ROCKINGHAM CL 2

NORTH RD
RUNSWICK
DR

THE
CASTLEREAGH
HOMES

Seaham
Sch

Northlea

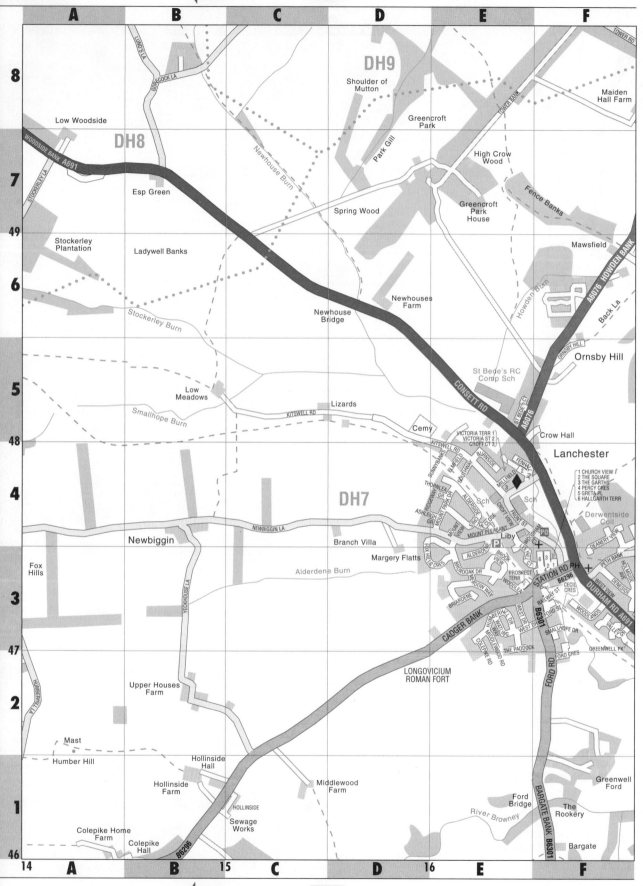

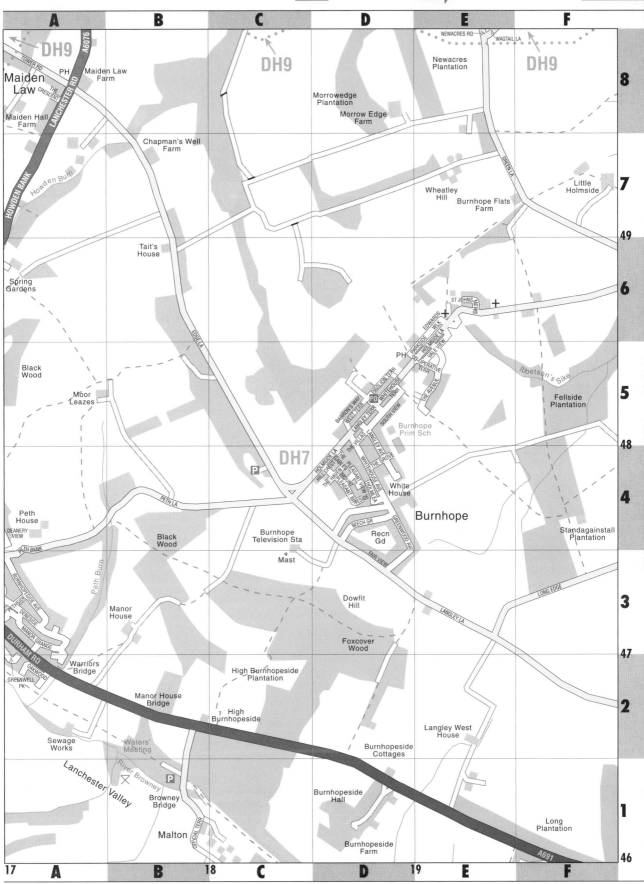

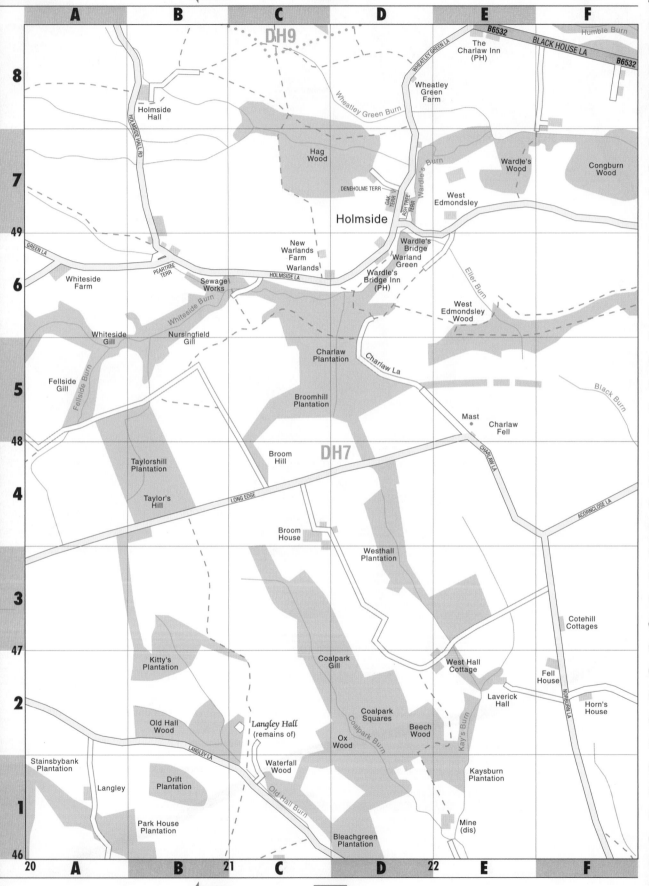

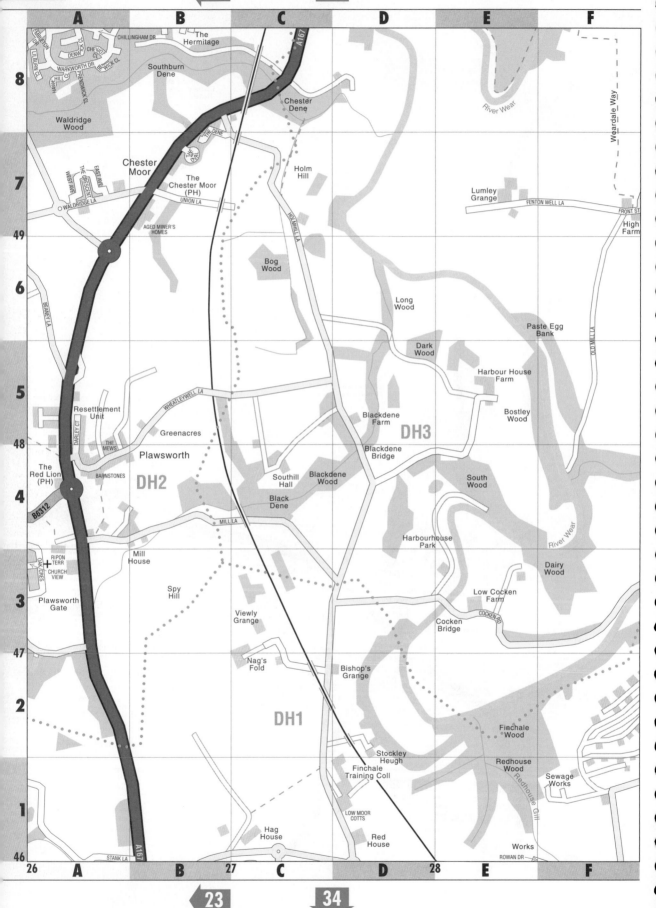

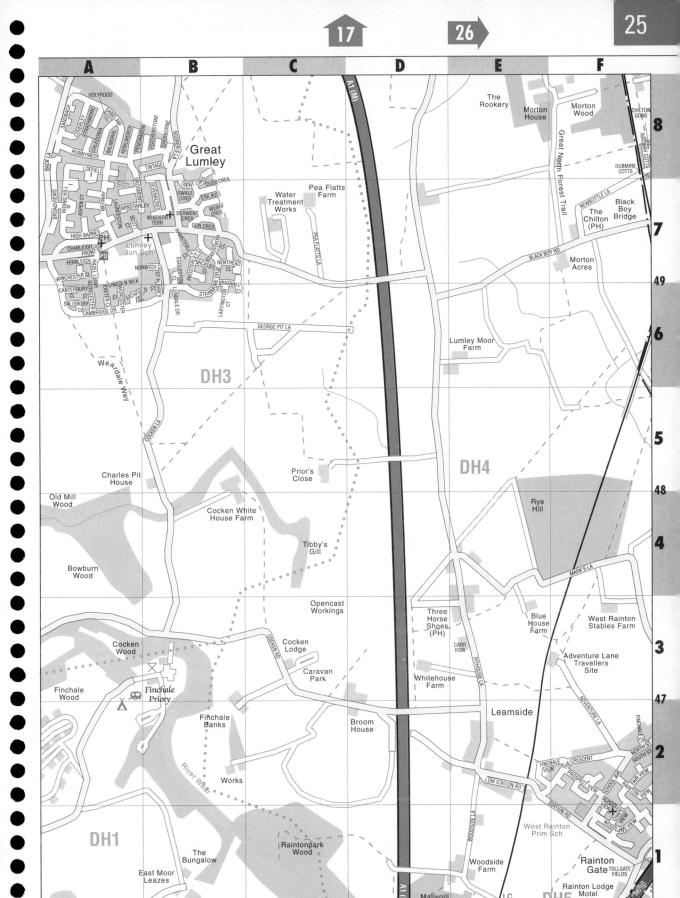

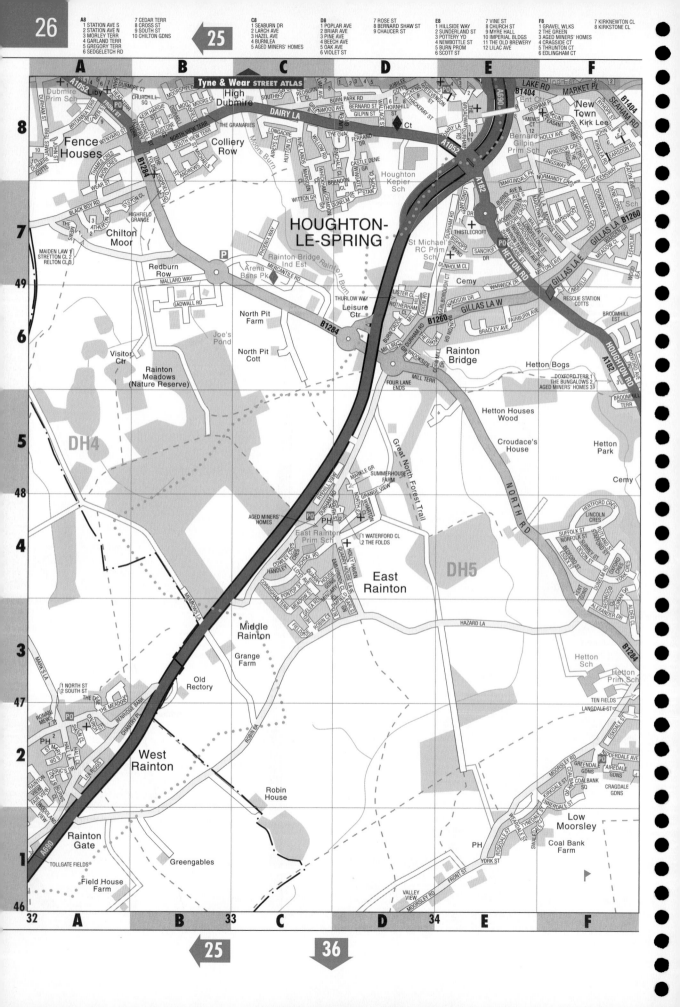

Tyne & Wear STREET ATLAS

B1404

Warden Law

Mast

The Copt Hill (PH)

CH

Low Moors

High Sharpley

SEAHAM RD
QUEENSWAY
B1404
B1260
GILLAS LA

BURDON AVE
STATION AVE
WARDEN GR
WOOD LEA
COPTLEIGH
LEEHOLME

Copt Hill

The Moors

Rough Dene Burn

Sharpley Plantation

49

BROOMHILL EST
Eppleton Prim Sch
Broom Hill
DOXFORD TERR
ELMFIELD

Low Downs

BYER SQ
BYER ST
DENE ST
LOW DOWNS RD
COLLINGWOOD ST
LINDSAY ST
HARRY ST
JANE ST
MAUDLIN ST

LOW DOWNS SQ

High Downs

GREEN LA
SALTERS LA

South Sharpley

6

Wind Farm

Windmill Hill

NORTH LA

HEATHER DR
LOUVAIN TERR W
Cemy

BALL'S GN
MARK GN
OSWALD RD
CHURCH RD
ALL SAINTS CR / ALCON WAY
QUEEN ST
WILLIS ST
REGENT
HIGH DOWNS SQ
DOWNS TERR
LADY ST
GEORGE ST
PRINCESS GDNS
NICHOLAS ST
THOMAS ST
BLOSSOM ST
EPPLETON TERR
EPPLETON TERR E
PERCY ST
EPPLETON ROW
EPPLETON EST

Eppleton Quarry (dis)

Hetton Downs

Downs Pit La

Great Eppleton

Great North Forest Trail

SR7

48

DH5

ST CUTHBERT'S CL
ST BEDE'S CL
EDWARD ST
BARRINGTON CT
BARRINGTON TERR
AYLESFORD
CHAPEL ST
FAIRY ST
CAROLINE ST
SCOTT ST
UNION ST
BARNES ST
GARDEN ST
SOUTH MARKET ST
MARKET ST
VICTORIA ST
VICTORIA ST E
VICTORIA ST W
SUMMERFIELD
MOSSOM ST
IRWIN ST

HETTON-LE-HOLE

Hetton Lyons Country Park

CARRHOUSE LA

Carr House Farm

Carr House Plantations

4

HOUGHTON RD
HOUGHTON RD W
WOODLEA CL
Liby
P
Sports Ctr
WELFARE RD
BARNARD
MOORSLEY RD
PARK VIEW
THE QUAY
OFFICE PL
BURN LA
HOLLOWDENE
RECTORY RD
STATION VIEW
SPRINGWELL TERR
FRONT ST
JOHN ST
JOHN ST
RICHARD ST
PAVILION TERR
1 PEMBERTON ST
2 RAILWAY ST
3 STEPHENSON CL
STATION RD N
THE AVENUE

Hetton Lyons Park

Bracken Hill

Rye Hill

SALTERS LA

3

TEN FIELDS
THE CRESCENT
SATTERDALE ST
LANGDALE ST
BEDALE ST
ROCHDALE ST
LUNESDALE ST
CHANDALE GDNS
MARDALE AVE
LYNESDALE ST
BORROWDALE ST
NIDDERDALE AVE
DEEPDALE ST
LAMBTON DR
NORTH RD
B1284
STATION RD
FOUR LANE ENDS
STATION AVE
LOGAN ST
WEAR ST
1 BACK CORONATION TERR
2 CORONATION TERR
LEE TERR
PARKGATE

Hetton Lyons Ind Est

47

COLLIERY LA
B1285

Hetton Lyons Prim Sch
MOORHOUSE GDNS
HETTON MOOR TERR

LYONS COTTS
THE LYONS
Lyons

Grotto Plantation

Orchard Hill

Murton Moor Farm
B1285

2

CASTLE CL
PHIM RD
CLASPATH RD
BAILEY ST
CROSSGATE
CASTLE WAY
GILSGATE RD
WHITE GATES
LILYWHITE TERR
STAGNER TERR
WALTER TERR
DERWENT ST
CALDEW CRES
LYONS AVE
BELT CRES
BOWES AVE
HORNSEY TERR

White Hill

Eppleton Hall

Constitution Hill

REDHILLS WAY
BELMONT RISE
ELVET ST
PETH GN
LYONS ST
NEIL ST
PEMBERTON BANK
MART'S SIDINGS
HART'S SIDINGS

1 JUBILEE HO
2 TOWER CT
3 ELEMORE LA
4 THE LAWNS

MURTON LA

Hetton Moor Farm

Murton Moor

1

HORNSEY CRES 1
FREDERICK TERR 2
LAWSON TERR 3
SMITH'S TERR 4
CAMPBELL TERR 5
GIRVAN TERR 6
GIRVAN TERR W 7

BANK
STORE
BRICK GARTH
JUBILEE
HIGH ST
A182
PO
Liby
NORTH VIEW
Cemy
THE POPLARS
WILLOW CRES

DH6

46

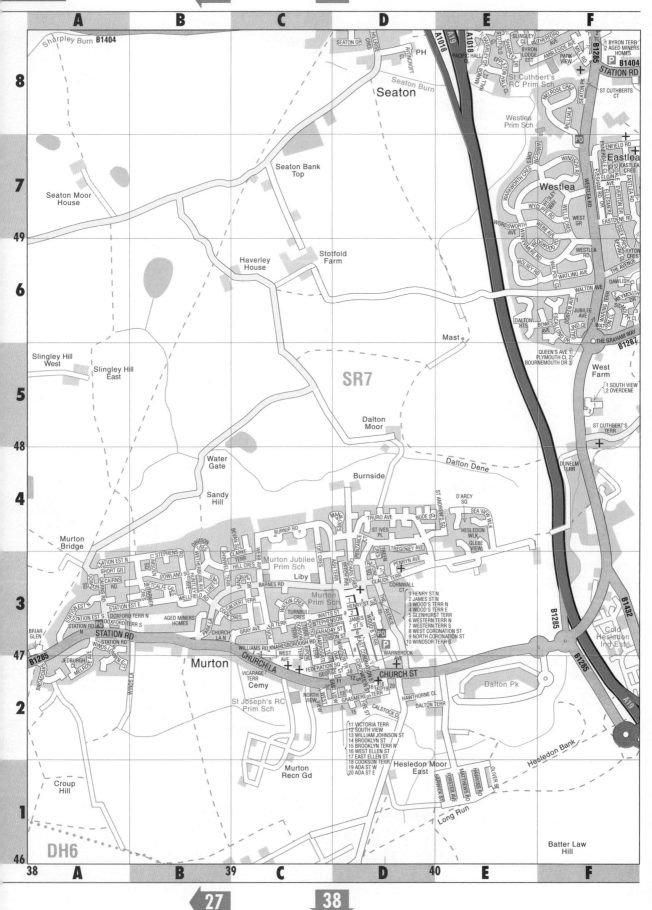

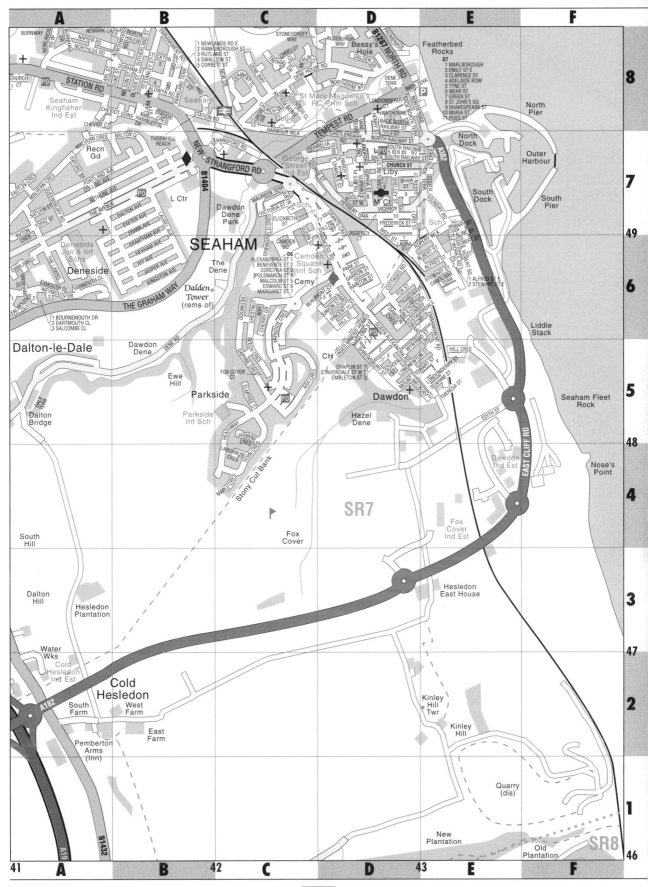

	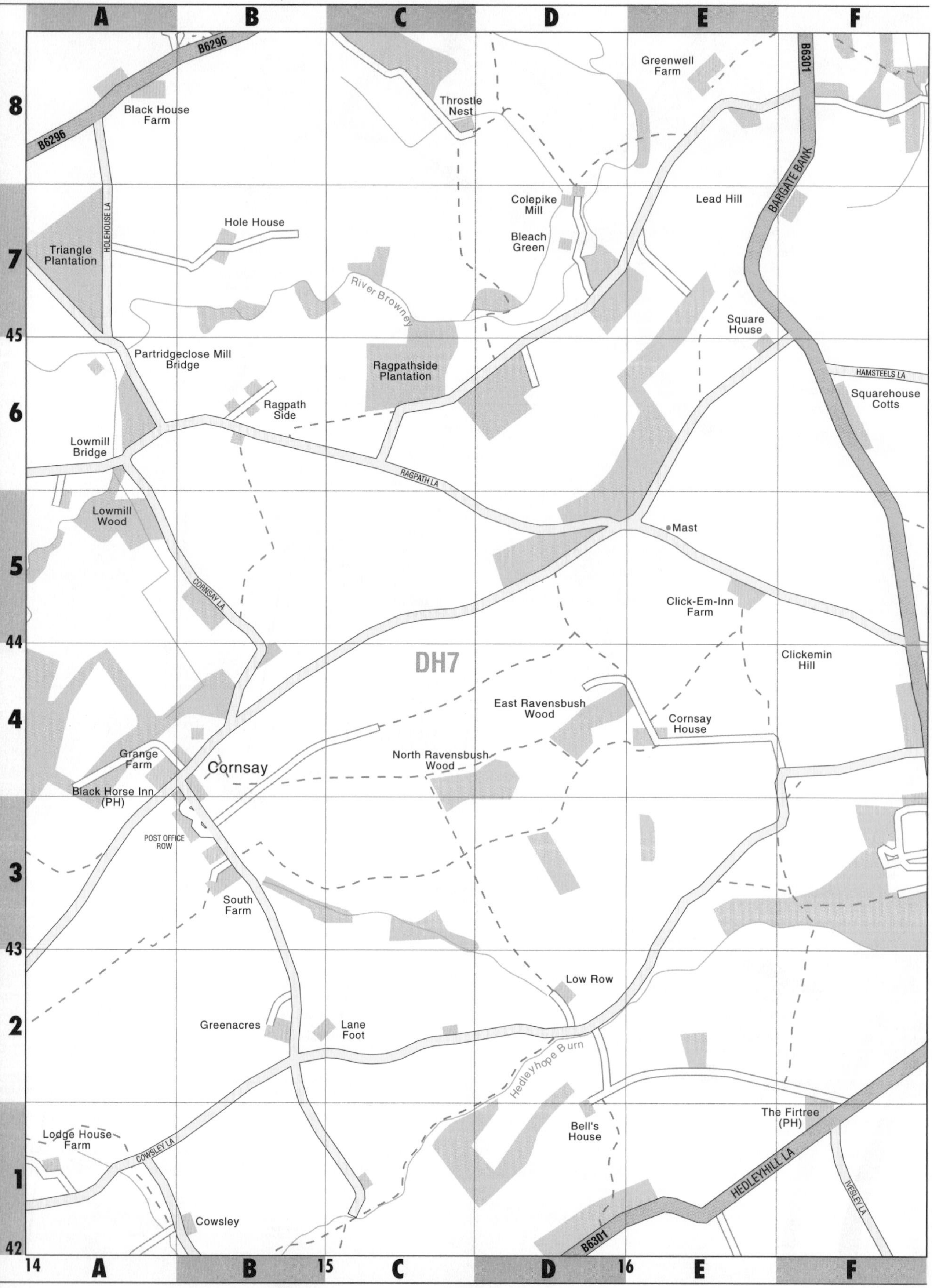 A	B	C	D	E	F

8 B6296

Black House Farm

Greenwell Farm

Throstle Nest

B6296

Holehouse La

7 Triangle Plantation

Hole House

Colepike Mill

Lead Hill

Bleach Green

Bargate Bank

B6301

River Browney

45

Partridgeclose Mill Bridge

Square House

Ragpathside Plantation

Hamsteels La

6 Ragpath Side

Squarehouse Cotts

Lowmill Bridge

Ragpath La

5 Lowmill Wood

Mast

Cornsay La

Click-Em-Inn Farm

44

Clickemin Hill

DH7

4 East Ravensbush Wood

Cornsay House

Grange Farm

North Ravensbush Wood

Cornsay

Black Horse Inn (PH)

3 Post Office Row

South Farm

43

Low Row

2 Greenacres

Lane Foot

Hedleyhope Burn

The Firtree (PH)

Lodge House Farm

Bell's House

1 Cowsley La

Hedleyhill La

Ibsley La

Cowsley

B6301

42

| 14 | A | B | 15 | C | D | E | 16 | F |

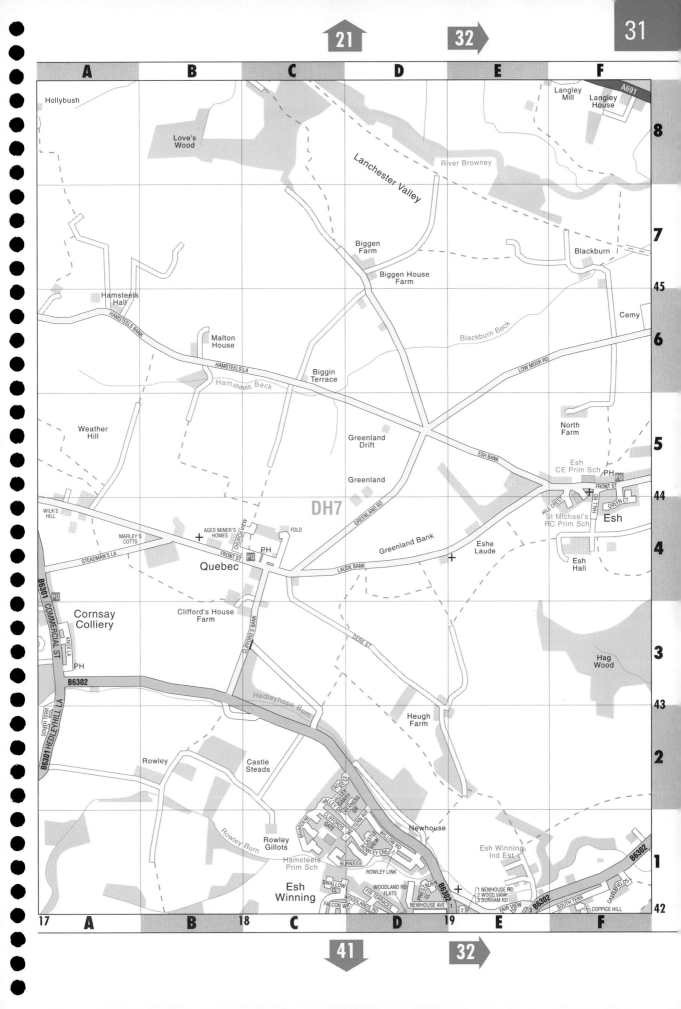

A   B   C   D   E   F

8

A691
Castleways Bridge
Parkhouse Cottages
Langley La
Parkhouse Villas
Lane Ends Bridge
Bleachgreen Burn
Newlands
Norburn La
Park View
Front St
B6312
A691

Langley Park Ind Est
Stobilee Farm
Wall Nook
River Browney
Wallnook Bridge
Blackcliff Hill

7

Hedley's Wood
D'Arcy St 1
Railway St 2
Logan St 3
George St 4
Durham St 5
Langley St 6
Wood View
Wallnook La
The Firs
The Centurion (PH)

Riverside Ind Est
Diggerland
P
1 Dean St
2 Hawthorne Terr

45

Lambton St 1
Rutherford Ct 2
Clifford St 1
Finings St 2
North View 3
Finings Ave 4
Dales
Brownie Ct
Oak St
Elm St
Bridge St
Paints
12 13
1 Lime Terr
2 Laurel Terr

Davis Cres
The Haven
Garden Ave
Dowbank
Hazelwood C
South View
Linden
Irene
Park Dr
Park Cl
Esh Hillside

Cemy
Stringer Terr
The Crescent
Low Moor Rd
Hospital Rd
Cherrytree Dr
Beech Ct
Malten Terr
Ivy Terr
Springwell
Eastern Ave
Crossways
Hilltop View

6

Willow Cl
Cedar Ct
Eldon Cl
Aldridge Rd
Ramshaw
Phoenix Cl
Elm Ave
Appleton
Harrington Cl
Hilton Cl
Downing
Marlewood
Langley Park Prim Sch
L Ave
East
Clere

C6
1 Church St
2 Quebec St
3 Brown's Terr
4 Lilian Terr
5 Lloyds Terr
6 Rose Terr
7 Midhill Cl
8 Aged Miners Homes
9 Springwell Cl
10 Esh Terr
11 Thomas St
12 Ash St
13 Larch Terr

Langley Park

Hill Top

5

Groove Bank
Front St
Hilltop
The Board Inn (PH)
Hilltop Quarry (dis)

Consett Terr

44

Low Esh Farm
The Rookery

DH7
College Rd
Mill House
Ushaw Park

4

Ushaw Farm
Ushaw Coll
Park Wood

Fortypence Plantation
Farm Plantation
East Lodge

3

Hag Wood
Sports Gnd

Hagg House Farm
Farhill Plantation
F2
1 Walton's Bldgs
2 Cock's Cottages
3 Bannerman Terr
4 White House Ave
5 Hunter Ave
6 Flass Terr
7 Flass Ave
8 High View

East Flass
Deerness View
Joyce Terr
Ladysmith Terr
Cockhouse Farm
Whitehouse La

43

Broadgate Road
Broadgate Farm
COCKHOUSE LA
Welby Dr
Ushaw Terr
Dale St
Arthur St
Hall Ave

2

Flasshall La
Flass Lodge
P
Temperance Terr
B6302

Flass Hall
River Deerness
Ushaw Moor Inf Sch
Ushaw Villas
Ushaw Moor
Station Rd
Highfield Terr
Middlefield Terr
Broom La

Flass Terr

B6302
Sewage Works
Ragg Path Wood
Hare Holme Farm
Deerness Valley
P
Sports Gnd

1

42

20   A   B   21   C   D   22   E   F

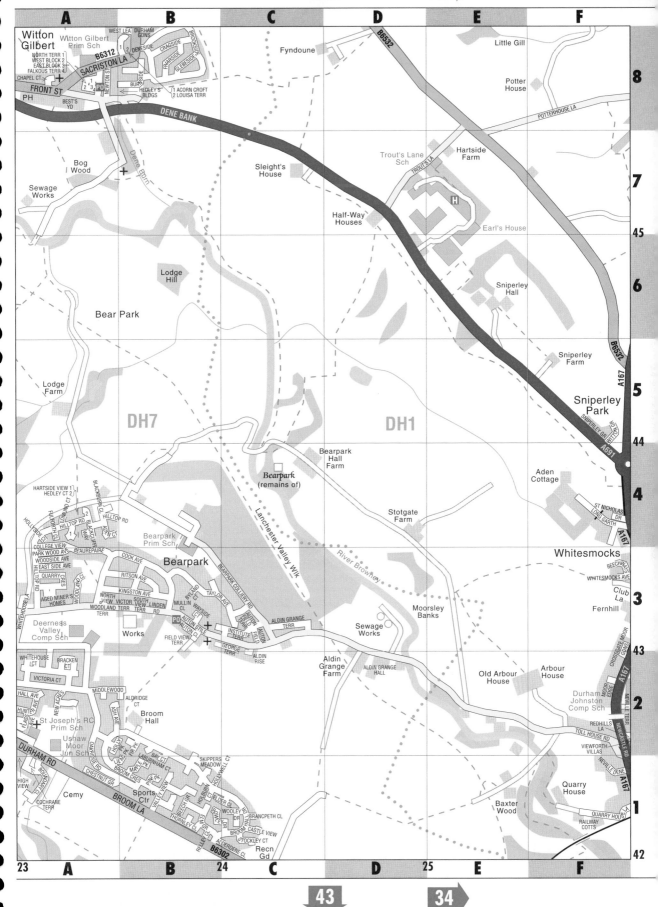

Witton Gilbert
WEST LEA · DURHAM GDNS
BROOKSIDE
CRAGSIDE
FRIARSIDE · GLEBESIDE
Witton Gilbert Prim Sch
NORTH TERR 1
WEST BLOCK 2
EAST BLOCK 3
FALKOUS TERR 4
CHAPEL CT
B6312
SACRISTON LA
NEWTON ST
DENESIDE
BURN
HEDLEY'S BLDGS
1 ACORN CROFT
2 LOUISA TERR
FRONT ST
PH
BEST'S YD
PO

DENE BANK

Fyndoune
B6532
Little Gill

Potter House

POTTERHOUSE LA

Sleight's House
Half-Way Houses
Trout's Lane Sch
TROUT'S LA
Hartside Farm
Earl's House
H

Bog Wood
Dene Burn
Sewage Works

Lodge Hill

Sniperley Hall

Bear Park

Sniperley Farm

Lodge Farm

DH7

DH1

Sniperley Park
SNIPERLEY GR
A167
A691
B6532

Bearpark Hall Farm

Bearpark (remains of)
Lanchester Valley Wlk

Aden Cottage

Stotgate Farm
River Browney

ST NICHOLAS DR
LONG GARTH
A167

Whitesmocks
BEECHCROFT
WHITESMOCKS AVE

HARTSIDE VIEW 1
HEDLEY CT 2
BLACKBURN CL
HILLTOP RD
ADEN CL
Bearpark Prim Sch
COLLEGE VIEW
PARK WOOD AVE
WOODSIDE AVE
EAST SIDE AVE
QUARRY
AGED MINER'S HOMES
HOLLISIDE
FULTHORPE
EDMUND CT
HILLTOP RD
BLACKCLIFFE WAY
HILLTOP RD
BEAUREPAIRE
COOK AVE
RITSON AVE
NORTH VIEW
VICTOR SOUTH TERR
LINDEN RD
MULLIN CL
RYLAND WAYSIDE
TAYLOR AVE
KINGSTON AVE
WOODLAND TERR
Bearpark
BEARPARK COLLIERY RD
AUTON FIELD
ALDIN GRANGE TERR
Moorsley Banks
Club La
Fernhill

WHITEHOUSE LA
Deerness Valley Comp Sch
Works
PO
AUTON STILE
INSTITUTE TERR
GEORGE TERR
FIELD VIEW TERR
ALDIN RISE
Sewage Works
Aldin Grange Farm
ALDIN GRANGE HALL
Old Arbour House
Arbour House
CROSSGATE MOOR
A167

WHITEHOUSE LCT
BRACKEN CT
VICTORIA CT
HALL AVE
NEW ACRES
HUNTERS
FLASS
MIDDLEWOOD
ALDRIDGE CT
ASH AVE
Broom Hall
St Joseph's RC Prim Sch
Ushaw Moor Jun Sch
NEVILLE DENE
MOOR EDGE
Durham Johnston Comp Sch
REDHILLS LA
TOLL HOUSE RD
VIEWFORTH VILLAS
NEWCASTLE RD

DURHAM RD
BOULEVARD
CHESTNUT GR
OAKRIDGE RD
BROOM CRES
BROOM PK
MAPLE PK
FIR PK
LABURNHAM CT
BAY CT
VALLEY VIEW
SKIPPERS MEADOW
Baxter Wood
Quarry House
QUARRY HOUSE LA
RAILWAY COTTS
A167

HIGH VIEW
Cemy
COCHRANE TERR
Sports Ctr
THORNLEY CL
ELM CL
BEECH GR
HOLBURN
ELDER CL
WOOLEY CL
ROWLEY CL
BRANCEPETH CL
BROOM CASTLE VIEW
ALDERDENE CL
STOCKLEY CT
Recn Gd
BROOM LA
B6302

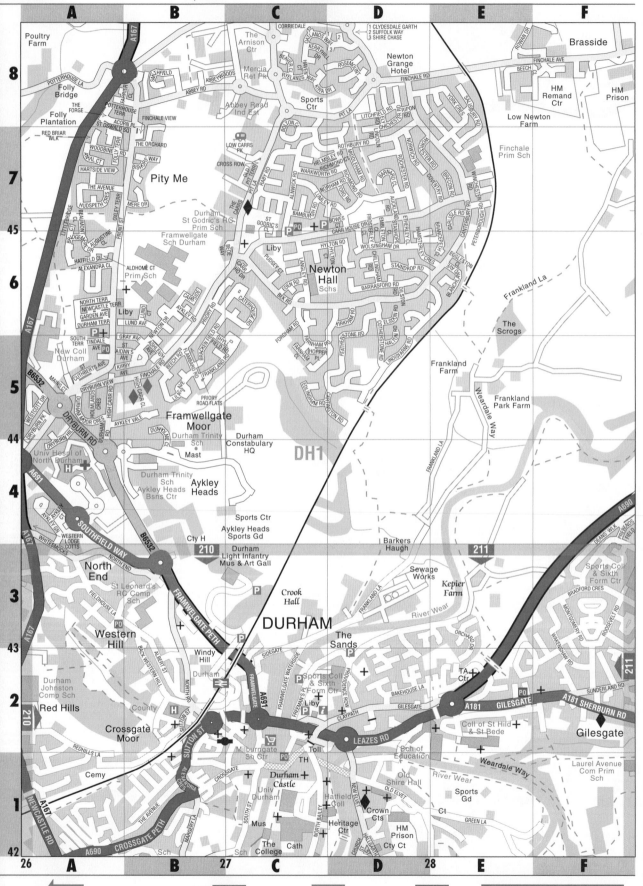

35
26

A | **B** | **C** | **D** | **E** | **F**

Pitfield House

Homer Hill Farm

High Moorsley

Valley View

High Moorsley Farm

DH5

Great North Forest Trail

MOORSLEY RD

PITTINGTON RD

Cobbler's Hill

Quarryhouse Wood

STATION RD

Pittington Hill

Hillside Farm

PITTINGTON LA

PH

Coronation Cres

FRONT ST

HIGH ST

ELEMORE LA

Low Pittington

1 WELLINGTON ST
2 HILLSIDE GROVE
3 GRAHAM TERR
4 HALLGARTH VIEW

LADY'S PIECE LA

ELEMORE ST

ST LAWRENCE RD

NEWBY LA

NORMAN TERR

ST LAWRENCE

ST JOHN'S RD

PO

Willow Garth

PRIORS GRANGE

GLEN'S FLATS

ELIZABETH CT

High Pittington

The Moor

Horseshoe Wood

Pittington Prim Sch

HALLGARTH LA

SOUTH END

Coldwell Burn

MANOR VIEW

CHURCH VALE

COALFORD LA

Sewage Works

DH6

White's Wood

Hallgarth Farm

Hallgarth

Hallgarth Manor (Hotel)

MOOR VIEW

Littletown

Dog Kennel Bank

CROSS ST

PLANTATION AVE

Pittington Bridge

Coalford Beck

Littletown Farm

Littletown House

Duke of York (PH)

Hastings House

Stand Bridge

LITTLETOWN LA

FORSTER AVE

PARK HOUSE GDNS

Sherburn Village Prim Sch

COOKSHOLD LA

Cook's Hold Farm

Saw Mill

Black Banks

GEORGE ST

NELSON TERR

HALL ST

SNODS

MILFORD PL

WHALTON CL

MELTON AVE

Sherburn

1 CHASE CT
2 KINNOCK CL
3 HALLGARTH VILLAS
4 BROADVIEW VILLAS

Sherburn Hill

WEST VIEW

BANNERMAN TERR

NORTH VIEW

SOUTH VIEW

KELL CRES

JUBILEE CRES

EAST VIEW

JUBILEE CRES

High House Farm

ALSTON WLK

B1283

PEART CL

CHAPEL CT

NEWBY

FRONT ST

SOUTH ST

LOCAL AVE

WESLEY TERR

Sherburn Hill Prim Sch

THE CROFT

PO

FRONT ST

PINDERS WAY

MILL LA

AGED MINERS HOMES

PALATINE VIEW

PH

B1283

1 CO-OPERATIVE VILLAS
2 BRIGHTON TERR
3 DURHAM LA

32 | 33 | 34

A | **B** | **C** | **D** | **E** | **F**

42 43 44 45 7 8

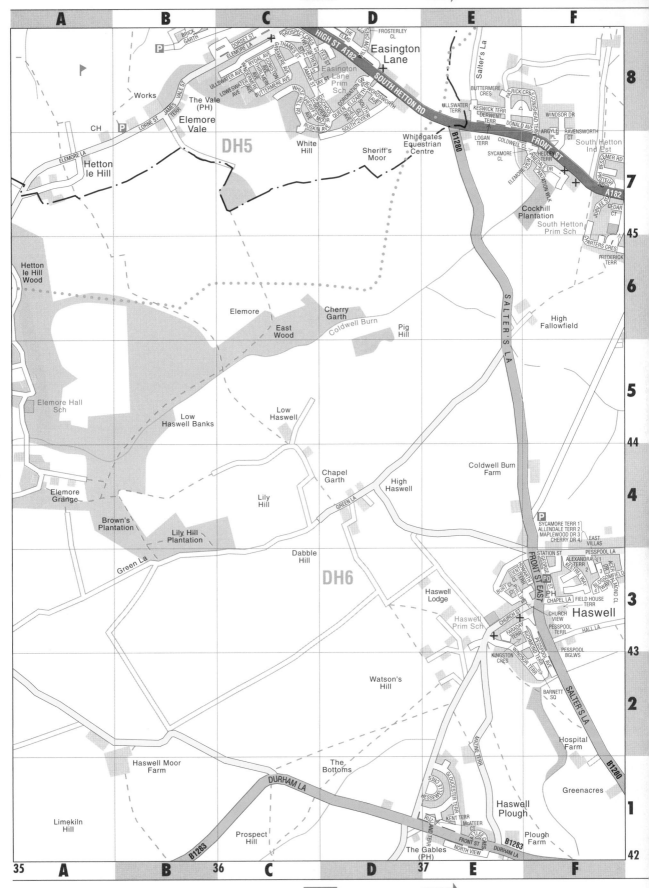

A   B   C   D   E   F

8   7   45   6   5   44   4   43   2   1   42

35   36   37

DH5

DH6

Works
CH
The Vale (PH)
Brick Garth
Elemore Vale
Hetton le Hill
White Hill
Sheriff's Moor

High St A182
Easington Lane
Easington Lane Prim Sch
South Hetton Rd
Frosterley Cl
The Elms
Whitegates Equestrian Centre

Salter's La
Buttermere Cres
Prick Cres
Conished Terr
Ullswater Terr
Keswick Terr
Derwent Terr
Donald Ave
Windsor Dr
Argyle Pl
Ravensworth Ct
South Hetton Ind Est
Logan Terr
Coldwell Cl
Sycamore Cl
Hedley Terr
Chester Dr
Elemore View
Plantation Walk
Cockhill Plantation
South Hetton Prim Sch
Bessemer Rd
Pasteur
Prospect
A182
Jubilee St
Cedar Ct
Quarters Cres
Frederick Terr

Hetton le Hill Wood

Elemore
East Wood
Cherry Garth
Coldwell Burn
Pig Hill
High Fallowfield

Salter's La

Elemore Hall Sch
Low Haswell Banks
Low Haswell
Coldwell Burn Farm

Elemore Grange
Brown's Plantation
Chapel Garth
Lily Hill
High Haswell
Green La
Lily Hill Plantation

Green La
Dabble Hill
Haswell Lodge

Sycamore Terr 1
Allendale Terr 2
Maplewood Dr 3
Cherry Dr 4
East Villas
Pesspool La
Station St
George Rd
Alexandra Terr 1
Kestrel Way
Crossomfield Way
Richmond Cl
Front St
Den Burn Cl
Burt Ct
PH
Chapel La
Field House Terr
Church View
Church Terr
Pesspool Terr
Haswell Prim Sch
Faraday Terr
Richmond Terr
Pesspool Ave
Hall La
Haswell
Kingston Cres
Windsor Ave
Pesspool Bglws
Barnett Sq
Salter's La

Watson's Hill
Hospital Farm

Haswell Moor Farm
The Bottoms
Durham La
Greenacres

Limekiln Hill
Prospect Hill
B1283
Hessewk
Gloucester Terr
Kent Terr
McAtter Ct
Rutland Terr
North View
Clee Cres
Front St
Durham La
Haswell Plough
Plough Farm
The Gables (PH)
B1280

A B C D E F

8

SR7

East Batter Law
Farm

Little Coop
House Farm

West Batter Law
Farm

7

South Hetton
Ind Est

BESSEMER RD

1 FREDERIOK TERR
2 ROSE COTTS
3 FALLOWFIELD TERR

A182 FRONT ST

PH

South
+Hetton

Coop House
Wood

HAWTHORN

CORONATION SQ

GRASMERE
TERR

WINDERMERE RD

WEST LA

Coop Hill

45

QUIN
SQ

CHAPTERS CRES

EBRE DALE GDNS

GREENCROFT

PARKLANDS
GR

THE
BUNGALOWS

BEVIN SQ

COTTS

PO

BRYDON CRES

PALMER ST

PHILIP ST

JAMESON ST

AMELAINE CRES

MATTHEWS CRES

OAKWOOD DR

MATTHEWS DR

ASHWOOD DR

FORSTER CRES

GREGSON TERR

VICARAGE
CL

Carr's
Farm

Great Coop
House Farm

Round Hill

Hallfield

6

Low Fallowfield

North Hill

West Moor
House Farm

Milestone Hill

Milestone
House

5

DH6

Duncombe
Moor

44

4

Holy Cross
Farm

Junction House
Farm

A19

PESSPOOL LA

CHESTNUT DR

Cove Holes

Rymer's Moor

SR8

Bridge Hills

A182 HALL WLKS

3

Pesspool
Hall

HALL LA

Low Ling Close

Loaning Burn

Cow Close
Farm

Calf Close
Farm

B1283

DURHAM LA

Kippering
Banks

Holmlea

43

Mawson's Hill

2

High Ling
Close

Moor House
Farm

Mast

Quarry
(dis)

Pesspool
Wood

Pesspool Dene

1

B1280 SALTER'S LA

Tuthill
House

DURHAM LA

Sandy
Carrs

Westmoor
Farm

North West
Ind Est

KITCHING RD

HACKWORTH RD

MILL HILL

42

B1283

Tuthill Bridge

38 A B 39 C D 40 E F

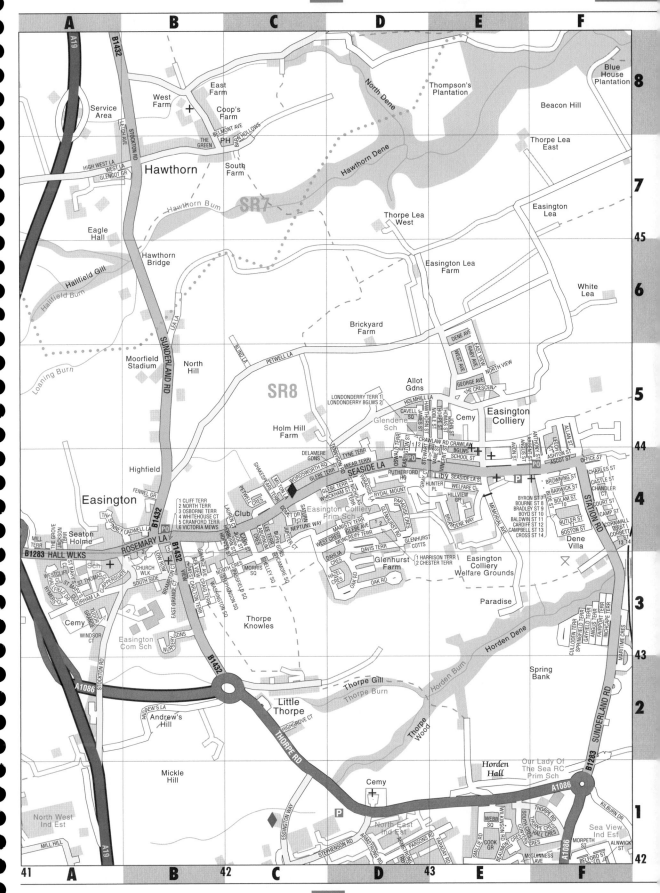

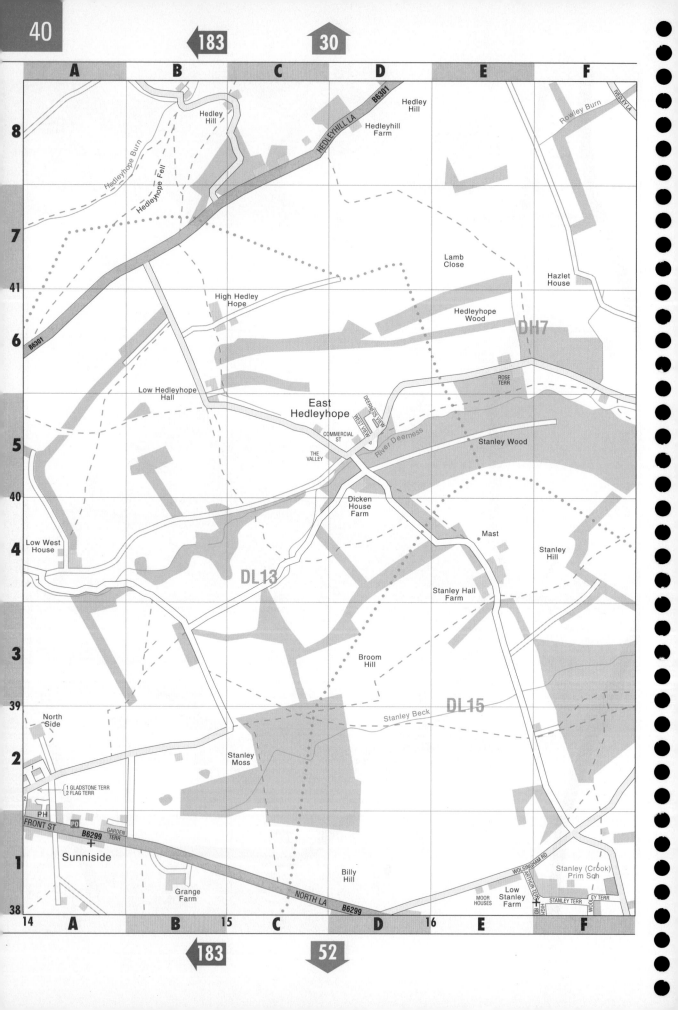

183
30

A B C D E F

8

7

41

6

B6301

HEDLEYHILL LA
B6301

Hedley Hill

Hedleyhope Burn

Hedleyhope Fell

Hedley Hill

Hedleyhill Farm

Lamb Close

Rowley Burn

HESLEYLA

Hazlet House

Hedleyhope Wood

DH7

High Hedley Hope

Low Hedleyhope Hall

East Hedleyhope

DEERNESS VIEW
WEST VIEW

COMMERCIAL ST

THE VALLEY

River Deerness

ROSE TERR

Stanley Wood

5

40

4

Low West House

DL13

Dicken House Farm

Mast

Stanley Hill

Stanley Hall Farm

3

Broom Hill

DL15

39

Stanley Beck

North Side

2

Stanley Moss

1 GLADSTONE TERR
2 FLAG TERR

PH

FRONT ST
PO
B6299
GARDEN TERR

Sunniside

1

Grange Farm

NORTH LA
B6299

Billy Hill

WOLSINGHAM RD
ARTHUR TERR

Stanley (Crook) Prim Sch

MOOR HOUSES

Low Stanley Farm

STANLEY TERR

HIGH RD

EY TERR
WOOD

38

14 A B 15 C D 16 E F

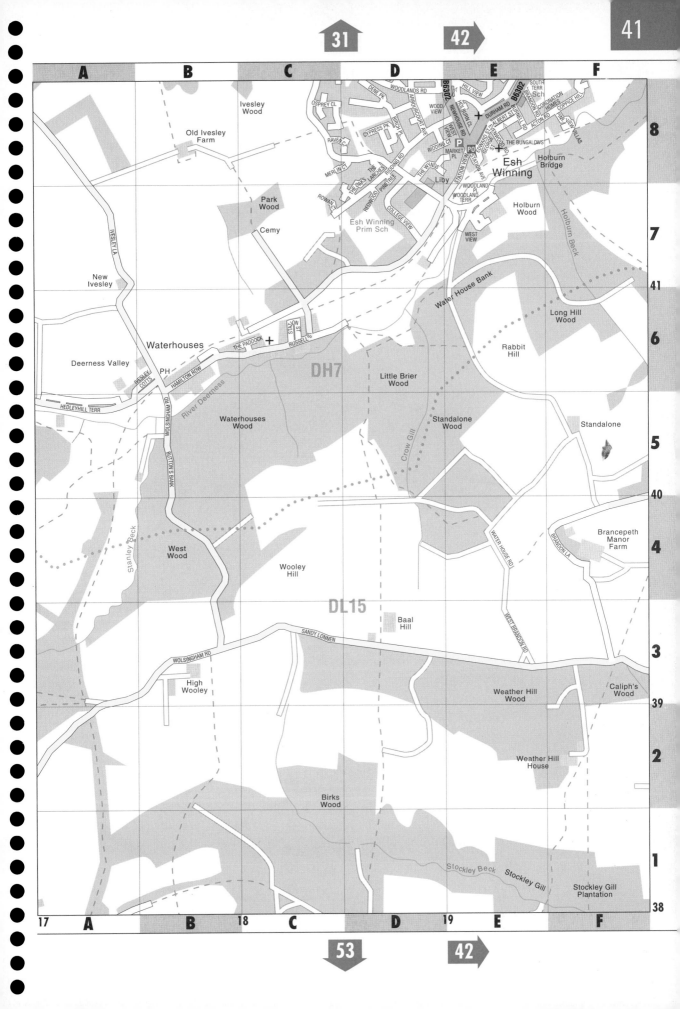

41
32

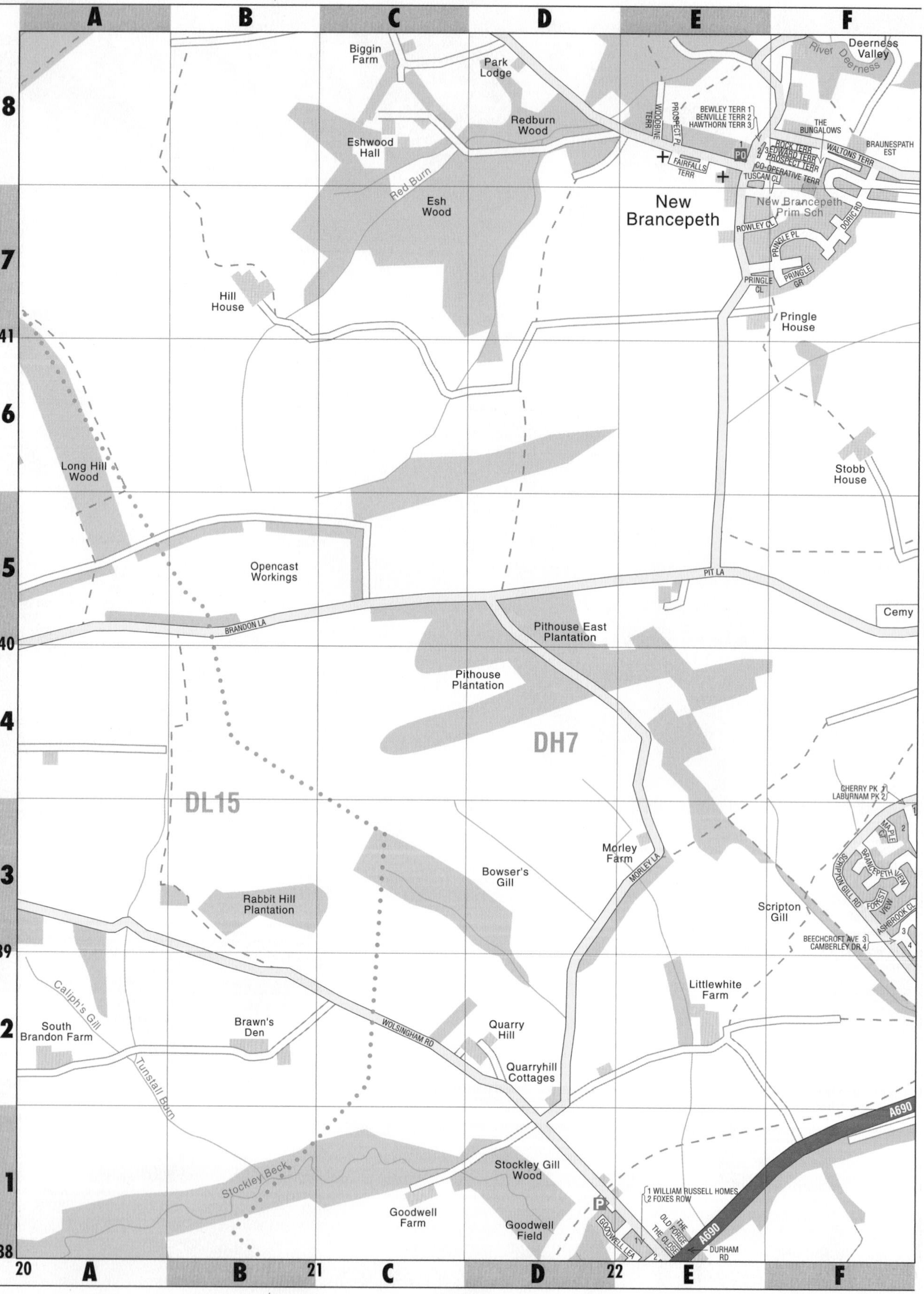

A B C D E F

8

7

41

6

40

5

4

DH7

DL15

3

39

2

1

38

20 A B 21 C D 22 E F

41
54

Biggin Farm
Park Lodge
Redburn Wood
Eshwood Hall
Esh Wood
Red Burn
Hill House
Long Hill Wood
Opencast Workings
BRANDON LA
Pithouse East Plantation
Pithouse Plantation
Rabbit Hill Plantation
Bowser's Gill
Morley Farm
MORLEY LA
Scripton Gill
Caliph's Gill
South Brandon Farm
Brawn's Den
Tunstall Burn
WOLSINGHAM RD
Quarry Hill
Quarryhill Cottages
Littlewhite Farm
Stockley Beck
Goodwell Farm
Stockley Gill Wood
Goodwell Field
New Brancepeth
New Brancepeth Prim Sch
Pringle House
Stobb House
Cemy
PIT LA
A690
DURHAM RD

For full street detail of the highlighted area see pages 210 and 211.

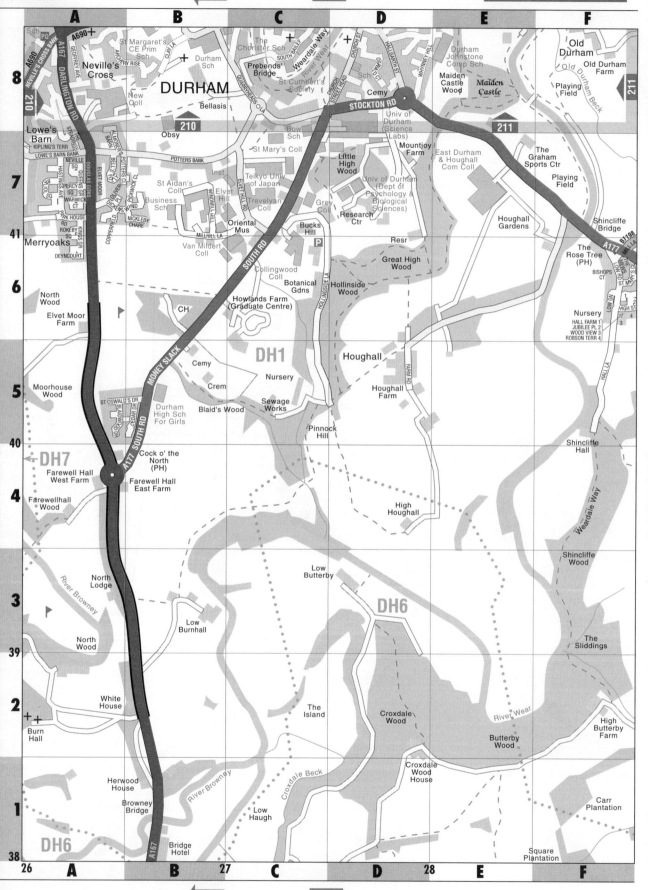

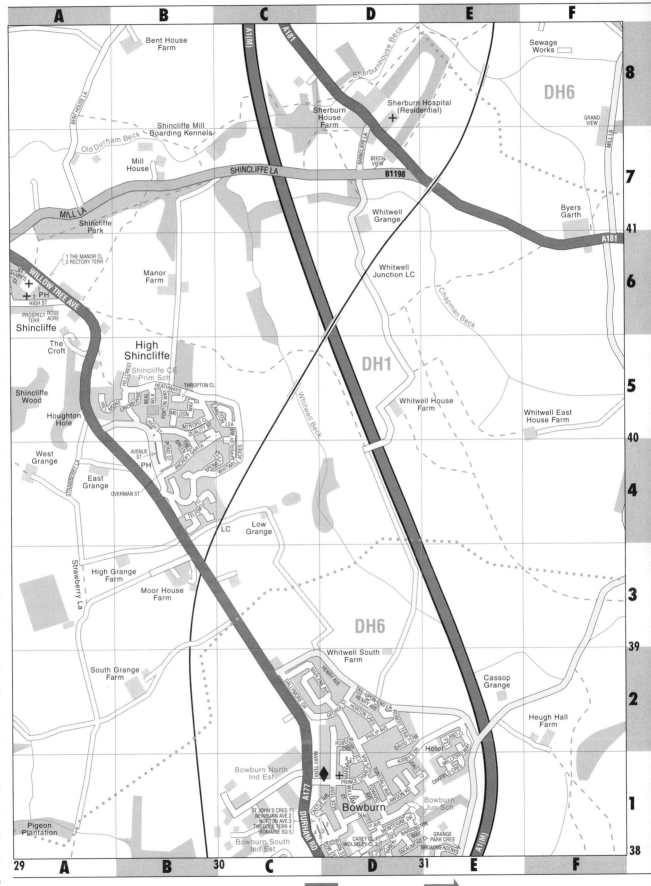

A B C D E F

8

DH6

Sewage Works

Bent House Farm

Sherburnhouse Beck

Sherburn House Farm

Sherburn Hospital (Residential)

Shincliffe Mill Boarding Kennels

GRAND VIEW

MILL LA

Old Durham Beck

7

SHINCLIFFE LA

Mill House

SHINCLIFFE LA

B1198

BEECH VIEW

Byers Garth

MILL LA

Shincliffe Park

Whitwell Grange

41

A181

1 THE MANOR CL
2 RECTORY TERR

WILLOW TREE AVE

Whitwell Junction LC

Chapman Beck

6

ST MARY'S CL

PH

Manor Farm

HIGH ST

PROSPECT TERR   ROSE ACRE

Shincliffe

DH1

Whitwell Beck

The Croft

High Shincliffe

Shincliffe CE Prim Sch

Whitwell House Farm

5

Shincliffe Wood

HILLCREST
LINDISFARNE
BEAL WLK
FOXTON WAY
HEATHWAYS
THROPTON CL
WAY
MELDON
LANGTON
LEA
APPERLEY AVE

Whitwell East House Farm

Houghton Hole

HIGH ST
MITFORD CL
QUALITY ST

40

West Grange

AVENUE ST
THE GREEN
POND CL
WHITWELL
ACRES

PH

East Grange

ANCROFT GARTH

SPCM CL

4

OVERMAN ST

Strawberry La

TELFOR

LC

Low Grange

High Grange Farm

Moor House Farm

3

DH6

South Grange Farm

Whitwell South Farm

39

Cassop Grange

2

Pigeon Plantation

DALTYMORE DR

HENRY AVE
MARLENE AVE
GEORGE ST
TAIT-UPON-END LA
HENRY AVE
HORTON CRES
ROBERT TERR
PHILIP AVE
DAVID TERR

Heugh Hall Farm

Hotel

S'LAND CL

MILLFORD WAY

KIRBY'S DR

ROBSON CRES

OAKFIELD CRES

Bowburn North Ind Est

MARY TERR

DURHAM RD

A177

CASTLE AVE
PRINCE CHARLES AVE
TUNSTALL AVE
JONES CL
Bowburn Jun Sch

Bowburn

GRANGE PARK CRES

1

ST JOHN'S CRES 1
NEWBURN AVE 2
NORTON AVE 3
TWEDDLE TERR 4
ROMAINE SQ 5

BEDE TERR
MARGARET CL
EDWARD ST
SAYERS CL
LAWSON RD
MONTEIGNE DR
BARRINGTON WAY
BEAUMONT CL
BROADMEADOWS

CAREY CL 1
WOLSELEY CL 2

Bowburn South Ind Est

A1(M)

38

29 A B 30 C D 31 E F

45
36

A B C D E F

8

7

41

6

5

40

4

3

39

2

1

38

32 A B 33 C D 34 E F

B1283

GEORGE ST
CHURCHILL TERR

DURHAM LA B1283

Crime Rigg
Farm

Crime Rigg
Quarry

CRIME RIGG BANK

WOODSIDE

SOUTH AVE

RECTORY
VIEW

CHURCH
VILLAS

Shadforth Beck

CHURCH LA

Shadforth

Hill House
Farm

Long Myers
Farm

Sherburn Beck

NORTH SIDE

BRIDGE CT

GEORGE SQ

CHARE LA

PH

A181

SOUTH SIDE

DENE CT

OLIVER CRES

DH1

Running
Waters

Three Horse Shoes
(PH)

DH6

Shadforth Dene

Chapman
Bridge

Strawberry Hill
Farm

Witch Hill

Witch Hill
Quarry

SILENT BANK

Old Cassop

Chapman Beck

Cassop Moor

Cassop
Farm

A181

Dene House
Farm

Cassop Vale

Victoria Inn
(PH)

DENE VIEW

Sewage
Works

FRONT ST.

PO

HIGH CROSS ST.

LYNN CRES.

The Heather Lad Inn
(PH)

LUKE AVE

B6291

Cassop

Quarrington Quarry

Cemy

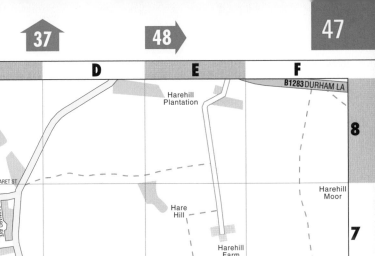

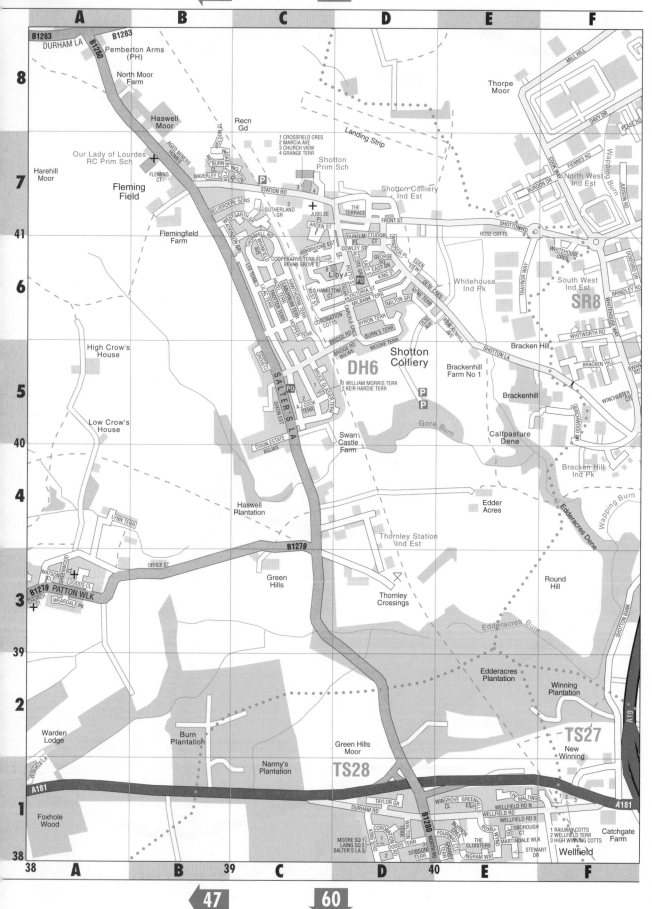

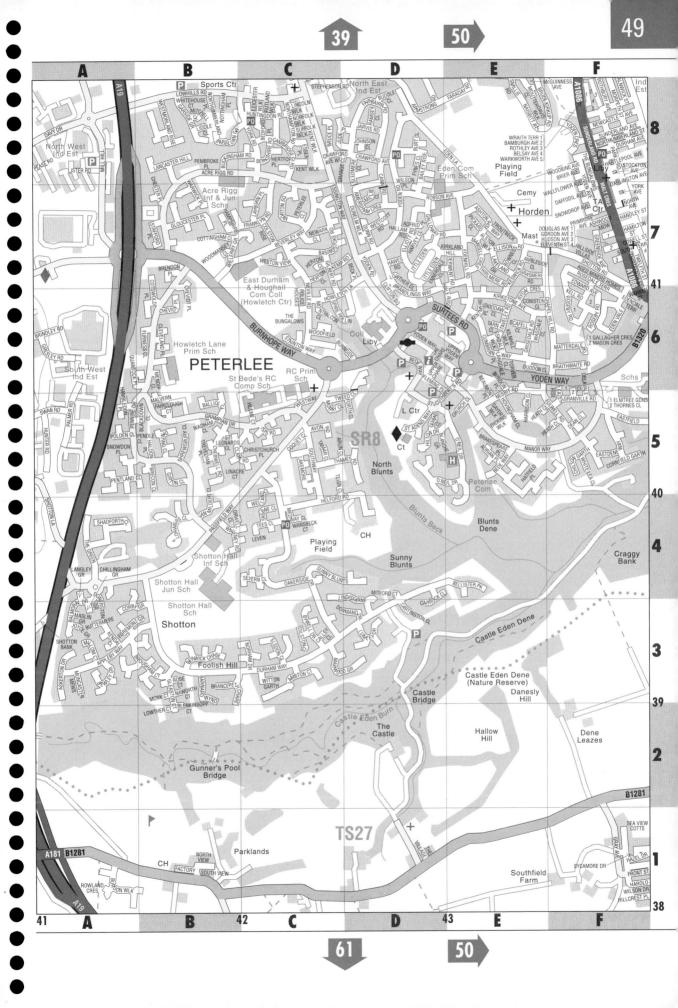

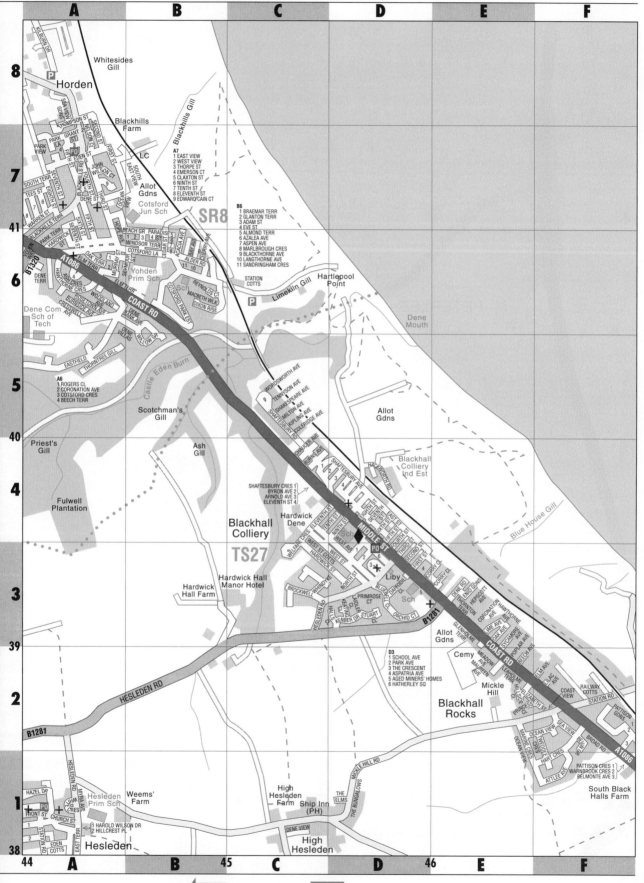

A   B   C   D   E   F

8 Horden
Whitesides Gill

Blackhills Gill
Blackhills Farm
LC

A7
1 EAST VIEW
2 WEST VIEW
3 THORPE ST
4 EMERSON CT
5 CLAXTON CT
6 NINTH ST
7 TENTH ST
8 ELEVENTH ST
9 EDWARD CAIN CT

7 Allot Gdns
Cotsford Jun Sch
SR8

B6
1 BRAEMAR TERR
2 GLANTON TERR
3 ADAM ST
4 EVE ST
5 ALMOND TERR
6 AZALEA AVE
7 ASPEN AVE
8 MARLBROUGH CRES
9 BLACKTHORNE AVE
10 LANGTHORNE AVE
11 SANDRINGHAM CRES

41 Yohden Prim Sch
Sch

STATION COTTS
Hartlepool Point
Limekiln Gill

6 Dene Terr
COAST RD
Dene Com Sch of Tech
Dene Mouth

Eastfield
Thorntree Gill

A6
1 ROGERS CL
2 CORONATION AVE
3 COTSFORD CRES
4 BEECH TERR

Castle Eden Burn

Scotchman's Gill

WORDSWORTH AVE
TENNYSON AVE
SHAKESPEARE AVE
MILTON AVE
SHAFTESBURY RD
KIPLING AVE
COLERIDGE AVE

Allot Gdns

40 Priest's Gill
Ash Gill
CHAUCER AVE
BURNS AVE
SHAFTESBURY AVE
HACKWORTH RD
Blackhall Colliery Ind Est

4 Fulwell Plantation

SHAFTESBURY CRES 1
BYRON AVE 2
ARNOLD AVE 3
ELEVENTH ST 4

Blackhall Colliery
Hardwick Dene
Hardwick Dene

Blue House Gill

TS27
WELFARE CRES
WEST ST COTTS
WEST ST
WEST AVE
MIDDLE ST
PO

3 Hardwick Hall Farm
Hardwick Hall Manor Hotel
BROCKWELL
WINDY AVE
NORTH ST
HESLEDEN PL
HILLS
PRIMROSE CT
KEATING AVE
KENBER DR
STUART CL
LADLEY CL
DAFFODIL CL
ORCHID CT
Liby
Sch
DENE RD
CORRY CL
ENID GDNS
THORNTON AVE
HEPSCOTT AVE
CORONATION AVE
HAWTHORNE AVE
B1281
Allot Gdns
GLENHOLME TERR
COAST RD
LIME AVE
SYCAMORE AVE
POPLAR AVE
BEECH AVE

39

D3
1 SCHOOL AVE
2 PARK AVE
3 THE CRESCENT
4 ASPATRIA AVE
5 AGED MINERS' HOMES
6 HATHERLEY SQ

Cemy
MEADOW AVE
MARNEN AVE
ELM AVE
LILAC AVE
ELIZABETH ST
LEAMFIELD TERR
HILLSIDE
PRINCESS CL
COAST VIEW
RAILWAY COTTS

2 HESLEDEN RD
Blackhall Rocks
Mickle Hill
OCEAN VIEW
SEA VIEW
MARINE CRES
HART CRES
BERLIN
BROAD RD
STATION RD
PATTISON GDNS
A1086

B1281

MICKLE HILL RD
ATTLEE AVE

PATTISON CRES 1
WARNBROOK CRES 2
BELMONTE AVE 3

1 HAZEL DR
MYRA AVE
Hesleden Prim Sch
Weems' Farm
High Hesleden Farm
Ship Inn (PH)
THE ELMS
THE BUNGALOWS
South Black Halls Farm

PO
FRONT ST
CHURCH ST

1 HAROLD WILSON DR
2 HILLCREST PL

DENE VIEW

38 STATION RD
EDEN COTTS
Hesleden
High Hesleden

44   A   B   45   C   D   46   E   F

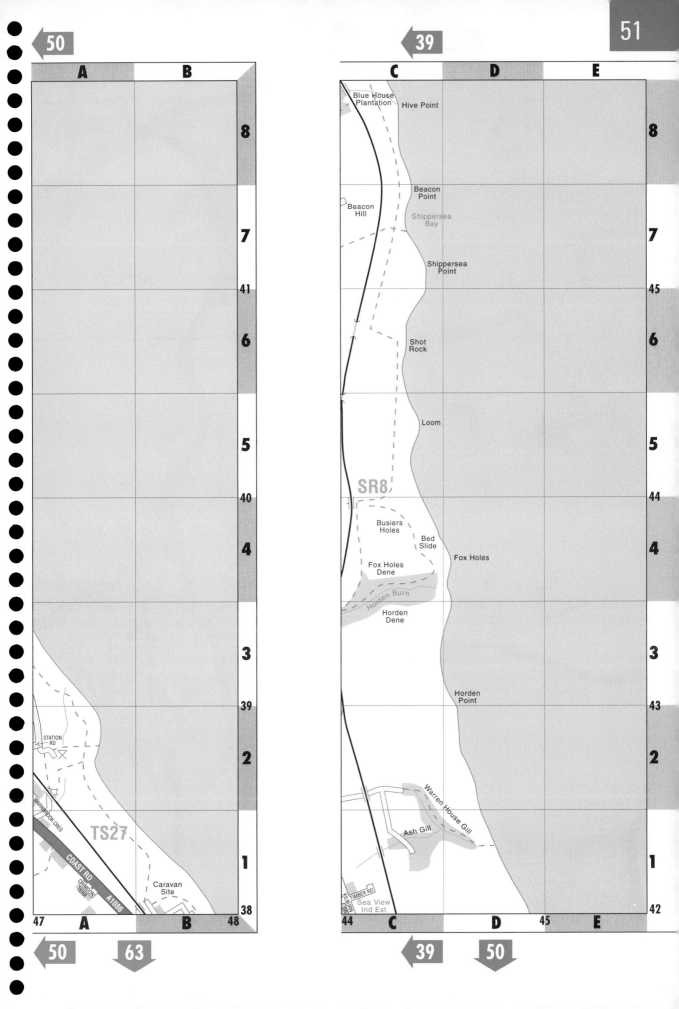

8

7

41

6

5

40

4

3

39

2

1

38

Blue House
Plantation
Hive Point

Beacon
Point

Beacon
Hill
Shippersea
Bay

Shippersea
Point

8

7

45

6

Shot
Rock

5

44

Loom

SR8

4

Busiers
Holes
Bed
Slide
Fox Holes

3

Fox Holes
Dene

Horden Burn

Horden
Dene

2

Horden
Point

43

1

42

STATION
RD

WARMBROOK CRES

TS27

COAST RD
CARMDON
TERR
A1086

Caravan
Site

Warren House Gill

Ash Gill

TIMBER RD
KILBURN
Sea View
Ind Est

47   A   B   48

44   C   D   45   E

A B C D E F

8

7

37

6

36

5

4

3

35

2

1

34

DL13

DL15

B6299

NORTH LA

Stanley Crook

Heights of Alma

ALMA TERR

HIGH HILL

JOBSON TERR

WOOLEY TERR

Recn Gd

WELL BANK B6298 BILLY HILL

HILL TERR

MOUNT PLEASANT

CO-OPERATIVE TERR

FRANCIS ST

CHAPEL ST

B6299

WILSON ST

BLACK RD

RESERVOIR TERR

RAILWAY TERR

White Lea Farm

WHITE LEA RD

Old White Lea Farm

Old White Lea Cottage

ARTHUR PIT COTTS

WHITE LEA RD

Peases West Prim Sch

STANLEY WAY

WEST TERR

ALBERT TERR

Billy Row

PO

INSTITUTE TERR

Low Albert Terr

Billy Row Gn Peases West

North Roddymoor Farm

Dun Cow Inn (PH)

IVY CRES
CHESTNUT GR

POPLAR TERR

ELM GDNS

MYRTLE GR

RODDYMOOR

OAK GDNS

HIGH TERR

DALE TERR

EAST TERR

RODDYMOOR RD

TEMPERANCE TERR

Billy Hall Farm

Roddymoor

Roddymoor Farm

FIRE AND RESCUE STATION COTTS

CRAIG LEA RD

Craig Lea

Red House Farm

RODDYMOOR RD

West Roddymoor

Comrie House

STEELS HOS

PEASEHOLM BGLWS

Peases West Sports Ctr

Farrers Arms (PH)

Allot Gdns

Crook Beck

WHITWELL TERR

SWINGFIELD

MALTON

THOMAS

PERCY ST

RYAN AVE

Hartside Prim Sch

CHURCH HILL

St Cuthbert's RC Prim Sch

MOWN MEADOWS RD

Middle Mown Meadows

Low Mown Meadows

West End Villas

COMMERCIAL ST

CHURCH ST

George Terr

SANDRINGHAM RD

WHEATBOTTOM

CO-OPERATIVE TERR

Five Hos

Cold Knot

HIGH WEST RD

WEST RD

Libys

Crook Bsns Ctr

EMMERSON ST

LINTON TERR

High Woodfield West

High Woodfield East

Woodfield Hill

KINGSLEY DR

TREVELYAN PL

FIELDING CT

AUSTEN WAY

WESTFIELD DR

HAMSTERLEY CL

SATLEY CL

COLLIERY CT

Crook Prim Sch

Macdonald Ind Est

Castle Close Ind Est

BEECHBURN PK

CONISTON CRES

DERWENT AVE

GRASMERE DR

ENNERDALE DR

GASKELL WAY

BRONTE CT

SHERIDAN DR

SHELLEY CL

BYRON CT

LONGFELLOW CT

WORDSWORTH CL

THISTLEFLAT RD

HEATHER LA

FERN VALLEY

BURHOPE CL

PROSPECT RD

Pennine Ct

INSTITUTE TERR

CORONATION TERR

PLANTATION TERR

HARPERLEY TERR

THE GROVE

A68

Fir Tree

PO

Redmires Farm

Fox Covert Plantation

The Greenhead (Hotel)

GREEN HEAD

White House Farm

High Farm

CROOK

PROSPECT RD

NEW RD

B6298

Crook (Beechburn) Ind Est

BROOKSIDE COTTS

INGLEROCK CL

High Beechburn

Greenhead

Fold House Farm

THE HOLLIN

A689

Low Beechburn

RUMBY HILL

WATERGATE LA

Watergate Lane Farm

E4
1 WATERLOO CL
2 FLANDERS WAY
3 NELSON ST
4 CALVERT ST
5 MORAVIAN ST
6 WHITFIELD ST
7 VICTORIA ST
8 ROSEMOUNT TERR

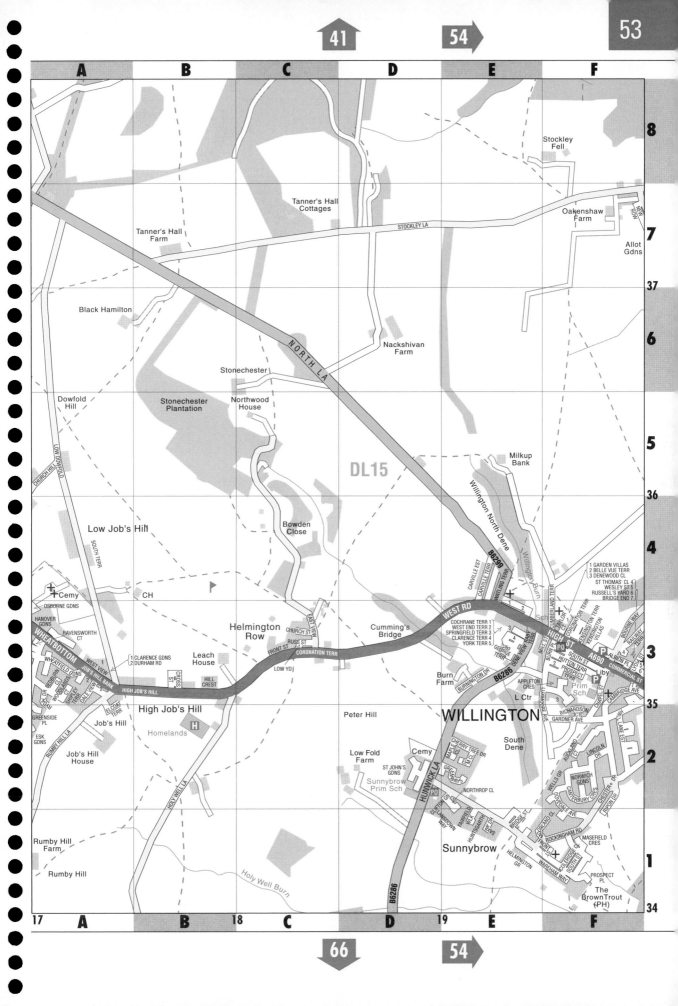

A   B   C   D   E   F

8
Stockley Fell

7
Tanner's Hall Cottages
STOCKLEY LA
Oakenshaw Farm
NEW ROW
Tanner's Hall Farm
Allot Gdns

37

6
Black Hamilton
NORTH LA
Nackshivan Farm

Dowfold Hill
Stonechester
Northwood House
Milkup Bank

5
Stonechester Plantation
DL15
Willington North Dene
Willington Burn

36

Low Job's Hill
SOUTH TERR
Bowden Close
CARVILLE EST
CARVILLE TERR
WHITLING TERR
B6298
1 GARDEN VILLAS
2 BELLE VUE TERR
3 DENEWOOD CL
ST THOMAS' CL 4
WESLEY ST 5
RUSSELL'S YARD 6
BRIDGE END 7

4

Cemy
CH
WEST RD
COCHRANE TERR 1
WEST END TERR 2
SPRINGFIELD TERR 3
CLARENCE TERR 4
YORK TERR 5

HANOVER GDNS
OSBORNE GDNS
RAVENSWORTH CT
Helmington Row
CHURCH VIEW
EAST VIEW
Cumming's Bridge
CORONATION TERR
KENSINGTON TERR
CUMBERLAND TERR
3

WHEATBOTTOM
WHEATFIELD GDNS
WEST VIEW
1 CLARENCE GDNS
2 DURHAM RD
Leach House
RUSS ST
FRONT ST
CORONATION TERR
Burn Farm
HIGH ST
A690
RAILWAY
COMMERCIAL ST
ALBION PL
BOURNE WAY
Liby

BEDBURN
WOODLANDS
SUPLEY TERR
DALE VIEW
JOB'S HILL BANK
CROSS ST
HILL CREST
LOW YD
BURNINGTON DR
B6286
APPLETON CRES
L Ctr
Prim Sch
35

GREENSIDE PL
ESK GDNS
Job's Hill
DELCOT TERR
HIGH JOB'S HILL
High Job's Hill
Homelands H
Peter Hill
WILLINGTON
RICHARDSON ACTE
GARDNER AVE
LINCOLN CL
CAMBRIDGE AVE

Job's Hill House
RUMBY HILL LA
Cemy
CHERRY TREE DR
MAPLE CL
South Dene
NORWICH GDNS
CHESTER DR
2

Low Fold Farm
St John's GDNS
Sunnybrow Prim Sch
HUNWICK LA
GREENWAY
NORTHROP CL
BRIDGE ST
ROCKINGHAM RD
MASEFIELD CRES

Rumby Hill Farm
CLIFTON
LANSDOWN WAY
HUNTSGARTH
FAIRFIELD WLK
HELMINGTON GR
WAREHAM WAY
1

Rumby Hill
Holy Well Burn
B6286
Sunnybrow
PROSPECT PL
The Brown Trout (PH)

34

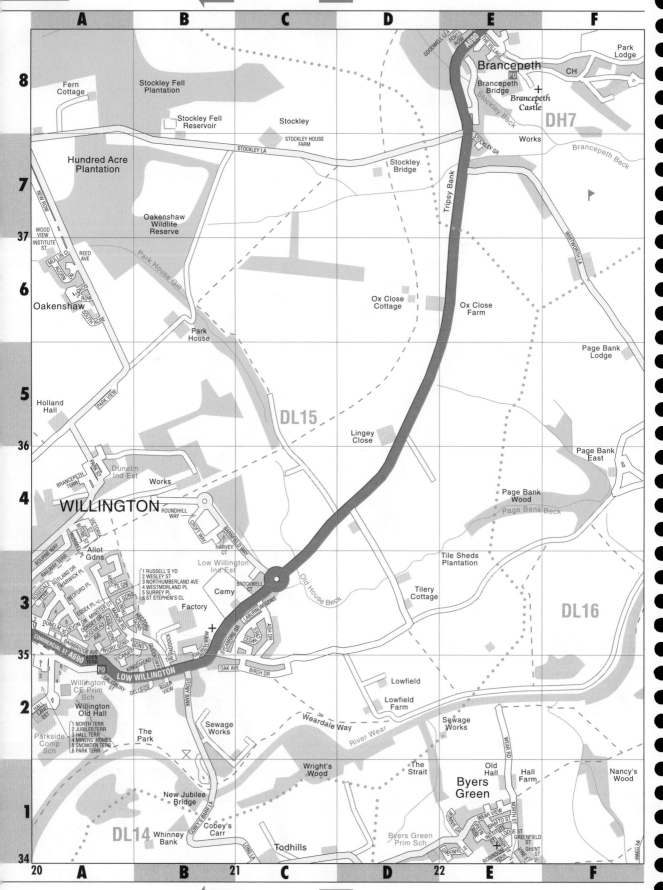

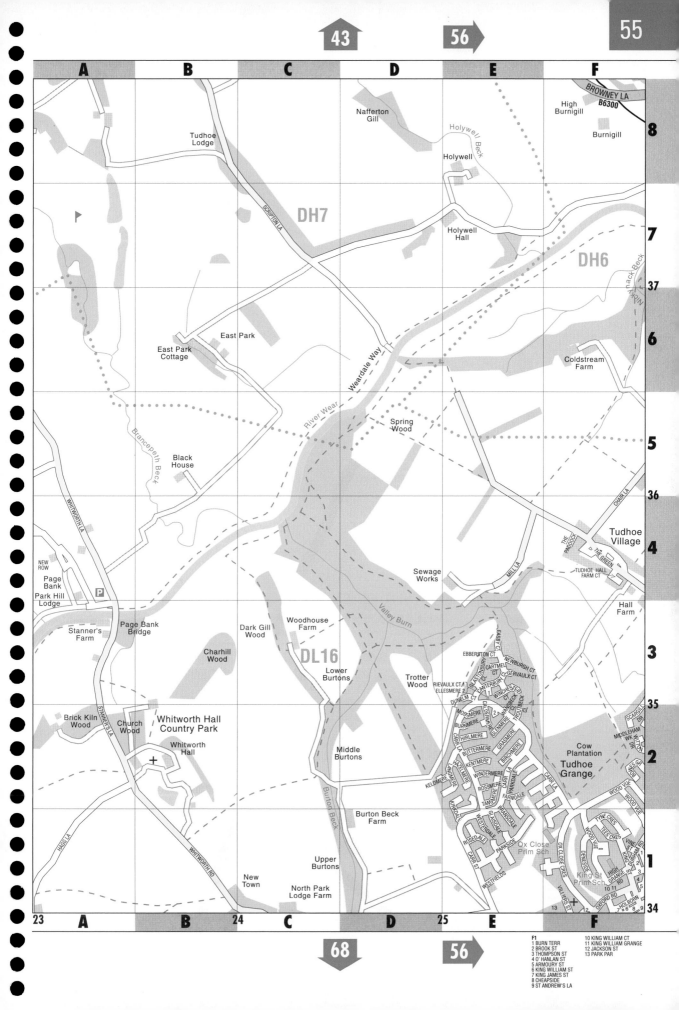

55
44

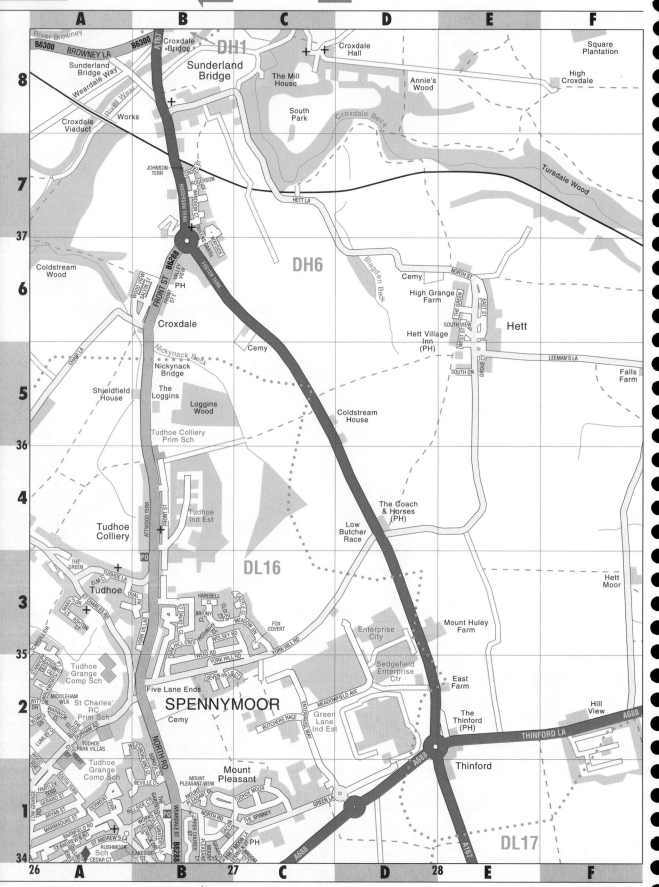

A B C D E F

8

SLATER PL 1
THE LEASES 2
Bowburn South Ind Est
LC
Wellsprings Bsns Ctr
PO
Liby
A177
DURHAM RD
ASH TERR
DURHAM
TONG ST
STEADINGS LA
CLARENCE ST
CAMBRIDGE TERR
CROW TREES LA
LAMB'S PL
OXFORD RD
RUNCIE PL
DURLE
DURHAM RD
WALKER'S
WYLAM ST
BROADMEADOWS
Bowburn Inf Sch
NEVILLE TERR
LANSDOWNE CRES
GRANGE PARK CRES
A1(M)
Grey Gables
HEUGH HALL ROW

Cemy

7

Peat Edge
Durham Service Area
A688
61
B6291
A177
SOUTHLANDS
PARK AVE
37

6

Bowburn Beck
Sewage Works
Tursdale House
Hett Mill
LC
PARK ALE
PARKFIELD
PARK HILL
PARK VILLAS
NEWTON VILLAS
HOLME ST
HOLLY DOCK
WESTLANDS
WYLAM PE
CLARENCE
ST MARY'S TERR
CLARENCE VILLAS
The Kicking Cuddy (PH)

5

LEEMAN'S LA
Tursdale Beck
Cornforth Moor Farm
DH6
Four Mile Bridge
BRIDGE END
WEST TERR
COMMERCIAL RD
COMMERCIAL RD W
WEST PAR
CORONATION TERR
CORONATION TERR
BASIC COTTS
36
B6291

4

Broom Hill Farm
Tursdale Bsns Pk
Tursdale
RAMSAY ST
SCHOOL ST
The Willows Farm
Coxhoe
Recn Gd
P
PETTERSON DALE
CHURCH ST
WILLOW CL
LANDSDOWNE RD
LINDEN GR
LINDEN TERR
WEL FARM
CO-OPERATIVE TERR 1
LUMLEY TERR 2
BARKER'S BLDGS 3
GARDEN TERR 4

3

Tursdale Junction
TURSDALE AGED MINE WORKERS WAR MEMORIAL HOMES
A688 TERR
Brandon Hill Farm
Wayside Cott
A177
THINFORD RD
THINFORD RD
East Pasture House
MEADOW CL
MEADOW VIEW
KENMIR'S BLDGS
Coxhoe Prim Sch
CONFORTH LA
VICTORIA TERR
SCHOOL AVE
GLADSTONE TERR
ASHBOURNE DR
ASHBOLINE TERR
BOGMA AVE
CONFORTH LA
A177
35

2

THINFORD LA
Cemy
BRIDGE ST
THINFORD ST
PINE RD
Metal Bridge
Brandon House
Sewage Works
LYNN LINK
CRES
A1(M)
RAILWAY TERR
THE GREEN
BRIDGE RD
PH

1

Cookson's Green
DL17
CORNFORTH BY-PASS
VERDUN TERR
CORONATION TERR
MAUGHAN ST
ELVET CL
THRISLINGTON
READING ST
SPRING ST
THE OAKS
STATION RD
BARRATT WAY
BEECH ST
OSWALD CL
CUTHBERT RD
HIGH ST
PALM
SYCAMORE RD
BIRCH RD
MAPLE GR
CEDAR TERR
JOSEPH HOPPER TERR
Liby
VICARAGE
THE GROVE
WINDSOR RD
WEST VIEW
MIDDLEHAM RD
RAISBY TERR
GLEBE VILLAS
WYNDSOR RD
West Cornforth Prim Sch
Cornforth
Quarry
PO
ROBERTS SQ
POPLAR TERR
P
34

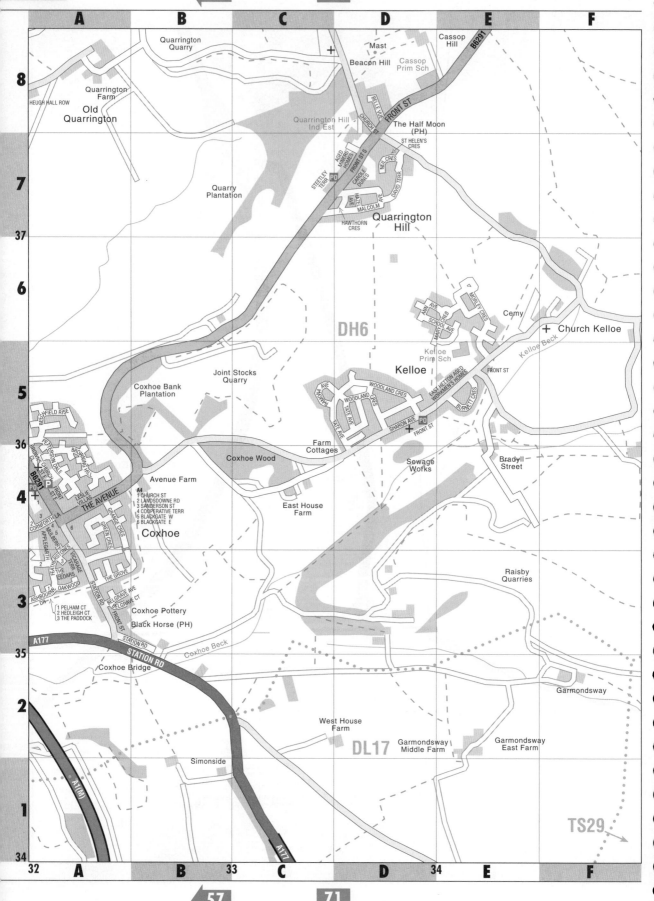

A177

A1(M)

A177

Old Quarrington

Quarrington Farm

HEUGH HALL ROW

Quarrington Quarry

Quarry Plantation

Mast
Beacon Hill

Cassop Hill

Cassop Prim Sch

B6291

FRONT ST

BELLE VUE

CHURCH ST

Quarrington Hill Ind Est

STEETLEY TERR
PO

AGED MEMBERS HOMES

FRONT ST S

NEIL CRES

ST HELEN'S CRES

The Half Moon (PH)

CAROLE DUKES

DAVID TERR

HAZEL AVE
MALCOLM AVE

HAWTHORN CRES

Quarrington Hill

Joint Stocks Quarry

Coxhoe Bank Plantation

DH6

AMY AVE
SCHOOL AVE
MARY CRES

MURSLEY CRES

Cemy

Church Kelloe

Kelloe Prim Sch

Kelloe Beck

Kelloe

FRONT ST

EAST HETTON AGED WORKMEN'S HOMES

FARADAY AVE

WOODLAND CRES

WOODLAND CRES

TATE AVE

TATE AVE

SHARON AVE
PO
FRONT ST

BURNETT CRES

Coxhoe Wood

Farm Cottages

Sewage Works

Bradyll Street

Avenue Farm

BEECHFIELD R/SE

PETERSON DALE

BROWNS CHURCH SHOP

B6291

CORNFORTH LA

LESLIE VILLAS

THE AVENUE

BROWNING HILL

GRANGE CRES

GREEN CRES

A4
1 CHURCH ST
2 LANSDOWNE RD
3 SANDERSON ST
4 COOPERATIVE TERR
5 BLACKGATE W
6 BLACKGATE E

East House Farm

Coxhoe

Raisby Quarries

MULBERRY RD

FEATHERSTONE TERR

VICARAGE TERR

THE CEDARS

OAKWOOD

ASHBOURNE DR

STATION RD

BELGRAVE AVE

BELGRAVE CT

THE GROVE

1 PELHAM CT
2 HEDLEIGH CT
3 THE PADDOCK

FRONT ST

Coxhoe Pottery

Black Horse (PH)

STATION RD
STATION RD

Coxhoe Beck

Coxhoe Bridge

Garmondsway

West House Farm

DL17

Garmondsway Middle Farm

Garmondsway East Farm

Simonside

TS29

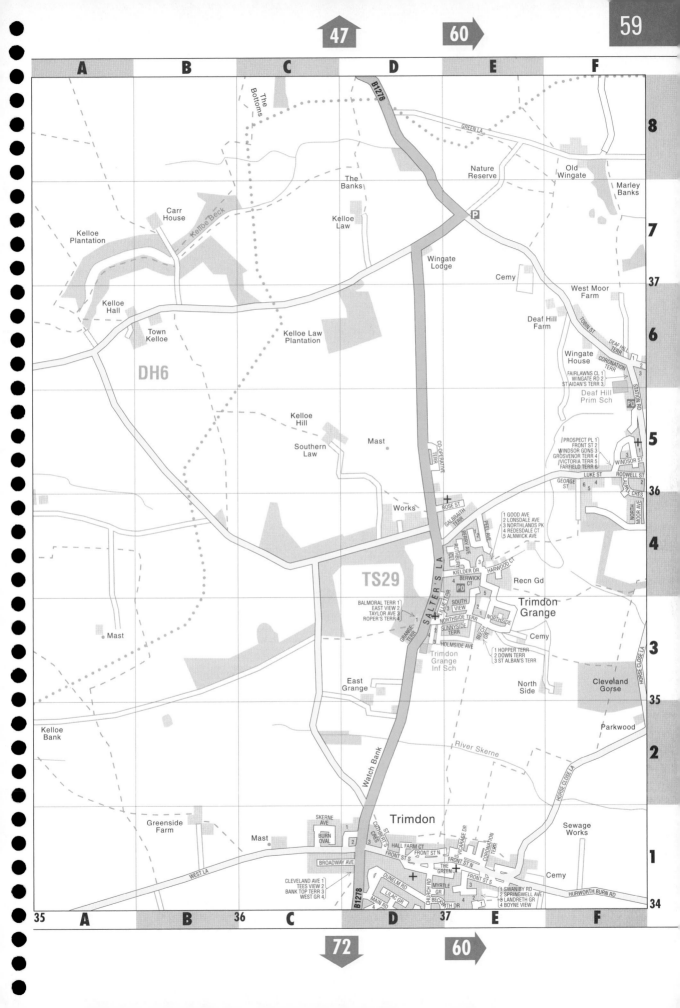

A   B   C   D   E   F

8

GREEN LA

The Bottoms

B1278

Nature Reserve

Old Wingate

Marley Banks

The Banks

Kelloe Law

Carr House

7

Kelloe Plantation

Kelloe Beck

Wingate Lodge

Cemy

West Moor Farm

37

Kelloe Hall

Deaf Hill Farm

6

Town Kelloe

Kelloe Law Plantation

DH6

Wingate House

Deaf Hill TERR

TOBIN ST

CORONATION TERR

FAIRLAWNS CL 1
WINGATE RD 2
ST AIDAN'S TERR 3

Deaf Hill Prim Sch

STATION RD

PO

Kelloe Hill

Southern Law

Mast

CO-OPERATIVE TERR

PROSPECT PL 1
FRONT ST 2
WINDSOR GDNS 3
GROSVENOR TERR 4
VICTORIA TERR 5
FARFIELD TERR 6

WINDSOR ST

RODWELL ST

5

GEORGE ST

LUKE ST

LAUREL CRES

36

Works

ROSE ST

GALBRAITH TERR

1 GOOD AVE
2 LONSDALE AVE
3 NORTHLANDS PK
4 REDESDALE CT
5 ALNWICK AVE

NORTH MOOR AVE

TS29

SALTER'S LA

BERRY AVE

ROTHBURY DR

PEEL AVE

KIELDER DR

HARWOOD CT

Recn Gd

4

BERWICK CT

PO

SOUTH VIEW

Trimdon Grange

BALMORAL TERR 1
EAST VIEW 2
TAYLOR AVE 3
ROPER'S TERR 4

NORTHSIDE TERR

NORTHSIDE

SUNNYSIDE TERR

GRANGE TERR

BECK

Cemy

HOLMSIDE AVE

Trimdon Grange Inf Sch

1 HOPPER TERR
2 DOWN TERR
3 ST ALBAN'S TERR

3

East Grange

North Side

Cleveland Gorse

HORSE CLOSE LA

35

Kelloe Bank

Parkwood

Watch Bank

River Skerne

2

Greenside Farm

HORSE CLOSE LA

Mast

SKERNE AVE

BURN OVAL

Trimdon

Sewage Works

1

BROADWAY AVE

CHISER'S CRES

FRONT ST S

HALL FARM CT

FRONT ST N

VICARAGE DR

CORONATION TERR

FRONT ST N

THE GREEN

FRONT ST N

FRONT ST S

Cemy

HURWORTH BURN RD

WEST LA

CLEVELAND AVE 1
TEES VIEW 2
BANK TOP TERR 3
WEST GR 4

B1278

MAIN RD

DUNELM RD

LILAC GR

CHURCH RD

BECK

MYRTLE GR

KEITH DR

1 SWANIBY RD
2 SPRINGWELL AVE
3 LANDRETH GR
4 BOYNE VIEW

34

35   A   B   36   C   D   37   E   F

DH6

TS27

A B C D E F

8

CUMMINGS SQ 1
FORSTER SQ 2
WILLIAMSON SQ 3

SNAITH TERR

VICARAGE EST

KING'S RD

CORONATION RD

NATTRESS
TERR

CARADOC RD

B1280

1 HOWDEN GDNS
2 ARMSTRONG AVE

QUIN CRES
PARTRIDGE
TERR

SALTERS LA

DAWSON
RD

GRAY SQ

BRUCE CRES

NEW CROSS
ROW

NORTH ROW

NORTH RD

GULLY RD

Wingate Grange
Farm

QUEEN'S RD

FOREST GATE

Pickering Hill

WOODLAND VIEW

NORTH RD E

Wingate
Jun Sch

Wellfield
Com Sch

MOOR LA

Wingate

Beech
House

7

Wingate Grange
Ind Est

Cemy

Liby

Wingate
Inf Sch

37

Low Grange
Farm

FRONT ST S

Tilery
Farm

6

BICKERTON ST

CHAPEL ST CHAPEL CT

MARKET CRES

JOHNSON ST

HADRIAN
CT

STATION RD

PO

FRONT ST

RODBRIDGE
STATION

P
PARK

ROWLANDS TERR 1
GLADSTONE TERR 2

LAKE VIEW

LAKE BANK TERR

CHURCH ST

TOWNEND CT

St Mary's
RC Prim Sch

St AIDAN'S
TERR

Deaf
Hill

WATSON CRES

BEECH GR

ASH
GR

WOOD VIEW

DORMAND CT

DORMAND
VILLA

MALVERN
CRES

RYDALE
CT

RUSSELL CRES

MAY CRES

LILAC
CRES

BRACKENHILL CT

FERNDALE CT

BEACHDALE

MILBANK TERR

CRAVEN'S BLDGS

MARGARET TERR

WINGATE RD

SYCAMORE
CRES

LABURNUM
AVE

SPRINGDALE

LABURNUM
CRES

Station Town

NEWHOLME EST

4

5

HOLME LEA
TERR

NATTRESS TERR

PURVIS TERR

Welfare
Park

Rodridge Cottage
Farm

BURN VALLEY GDNS 1
BRIDGE TERR 2
ELLERBOURNE TERR 3
HEATON TERR 4

COMMERCIAL
ST

DINSLEY
DR

36

TS29

West
Woodburn

TS28

LAWSON
ST

ST PAUL'S RD

PARK RD

Langdale Oval

Trimdon Colliery

Dyke House
Farm

Langdale

Beaumont
Nursery

Bridgefield
Farm

B1280

HOGG ST

LOW DYKE ST

4

Woodlands
Close

Langley Beck

Hurworth
Bryan

3

HORSE CLOSE LA

35

2

Park Ho

White Hurworth
Farm

Hurworth Burn

1

River Skerne

Hurworth Burn
Resr

34

HURWORTH BURN RD

38

A

B

39

C

D

40

E

F

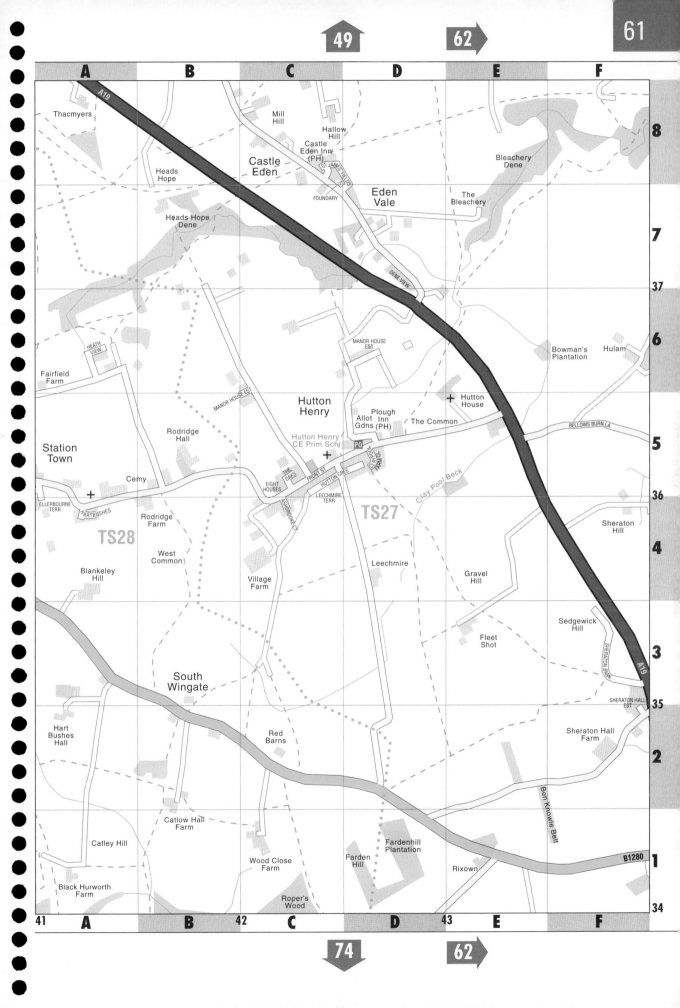

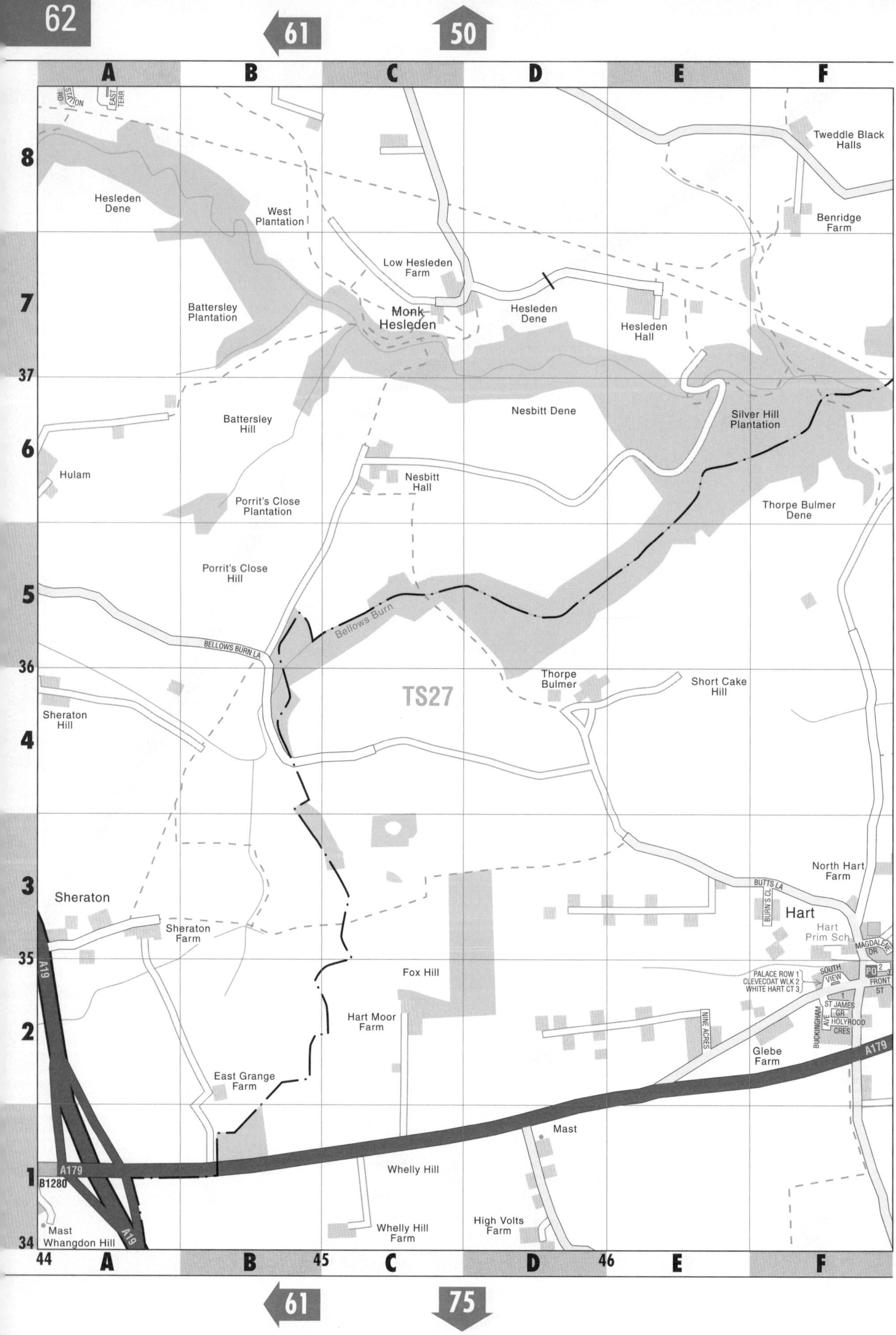

A B C D E F

8

Tweddle Black
Halls

Hesleden
Dene

West
Plantation

Benridge
Farm

7

Battersley
Plantation

Low Hesleden
Farm

Monk
Hesleden

Hesleden
Dene

Hesleden
Hall

37

Battersley
Hill

Nesbitt Dene

Silver Hill
Plantation

6

Hulam

Porrit's Close
Plantation

Nesbitt
Hall

Thorpe Bulmer
Dene

Porrit's Close
Hill

5

Bellows Burn

BELLOWS BURN LA

Bellows Burn

TS27

Thorpe
Bulmer

Short Cake
Hill

36

Sheraton
Hill

4

North Hart
Farm

3

Sheraton

Sheraton
Farm

BUTTS LA

BURN'S CL

Hart

Hart
Prim Sch

MAGDALENE DR

35

A19

Fox Hill

PALACE ROW 1
CLEVECOAT WLK 2
WHITE HART CT 3

SOUTH
VIEW

PO

FRONT
ST

2

Hart Moor
Farm

NINE ACRES

ST JAMES
GR

HOLYROOD
CRES

BUCKINGHAM AVE

Glebe
Farm

A179

East Grange
Farm

Mast

1

A179

Whelly Hill

High Volts
Farm

B1280

Whelly Hill
Farm

34

Mast
Whangdon Hill

A19

44 A 45 B C 45 D 46 E F

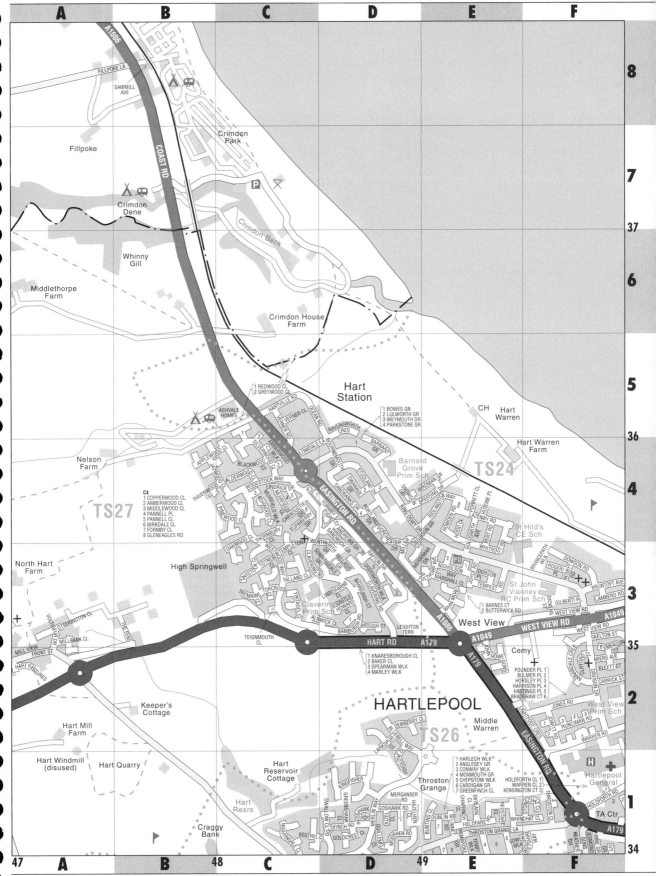

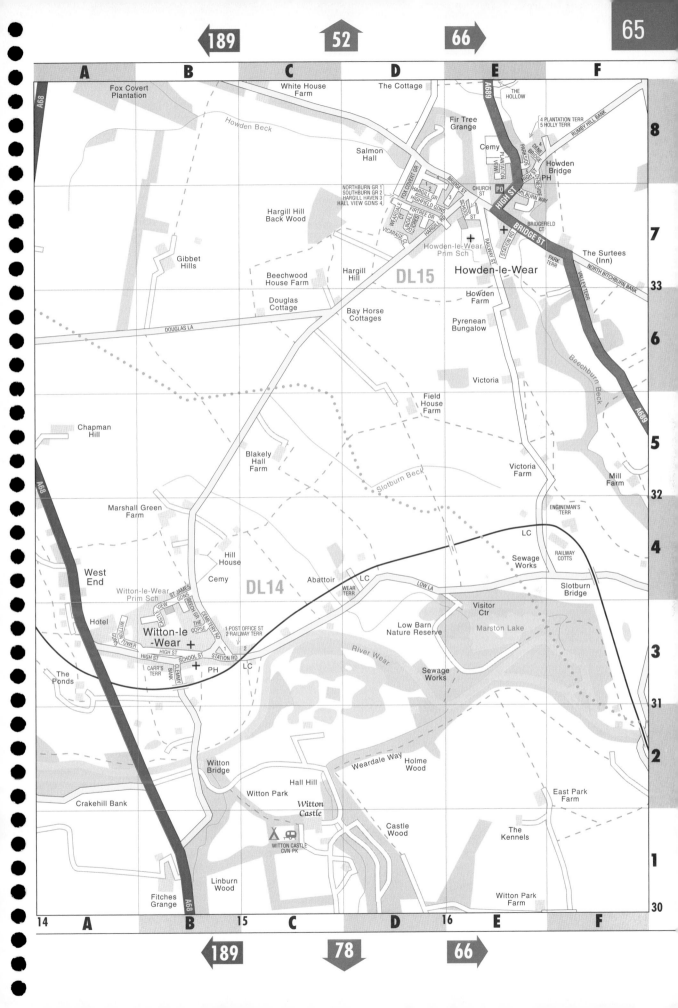

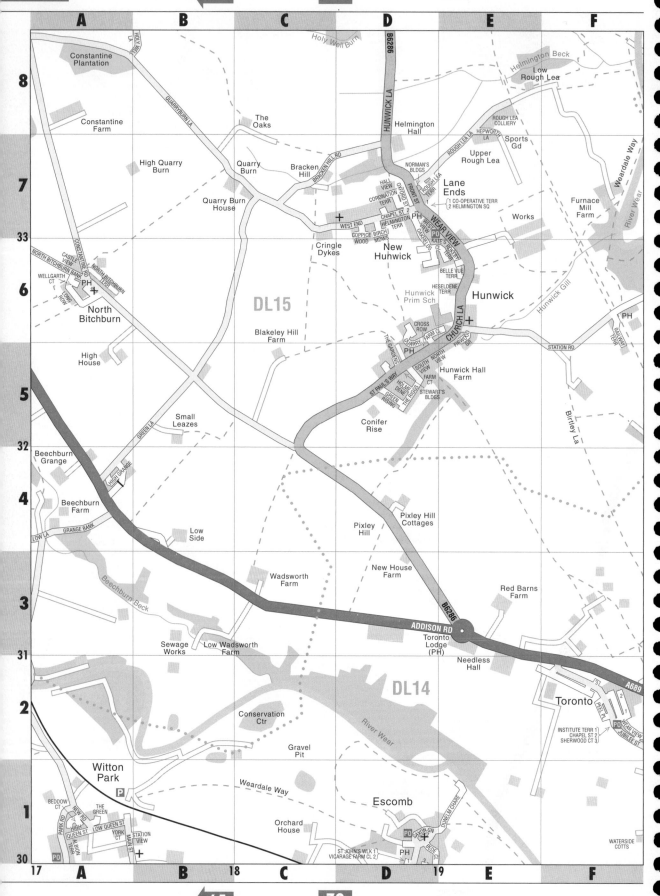

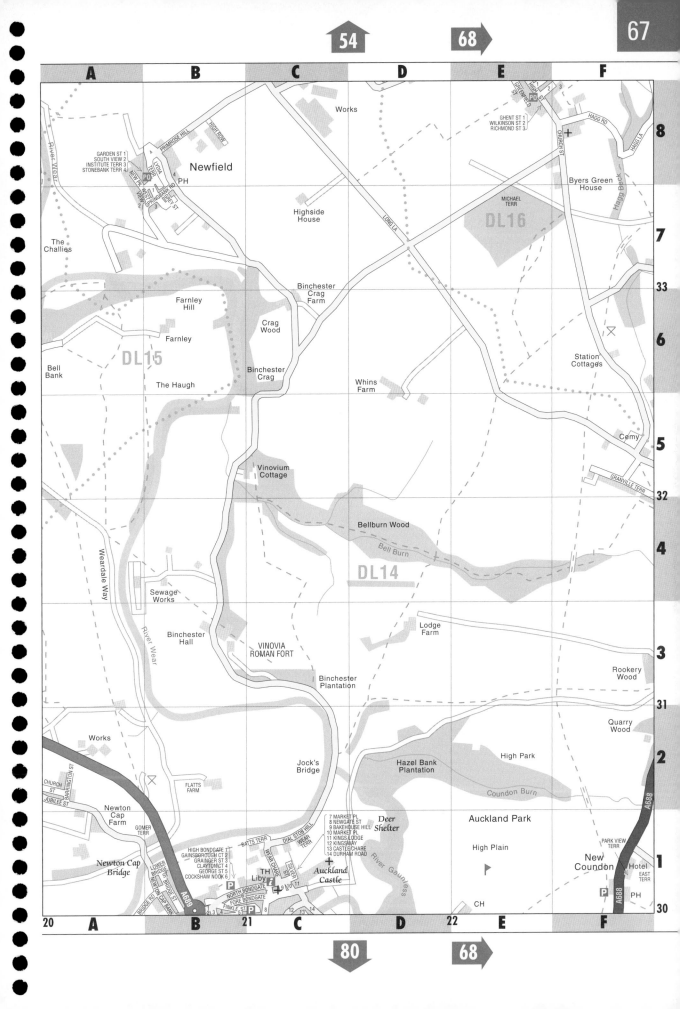

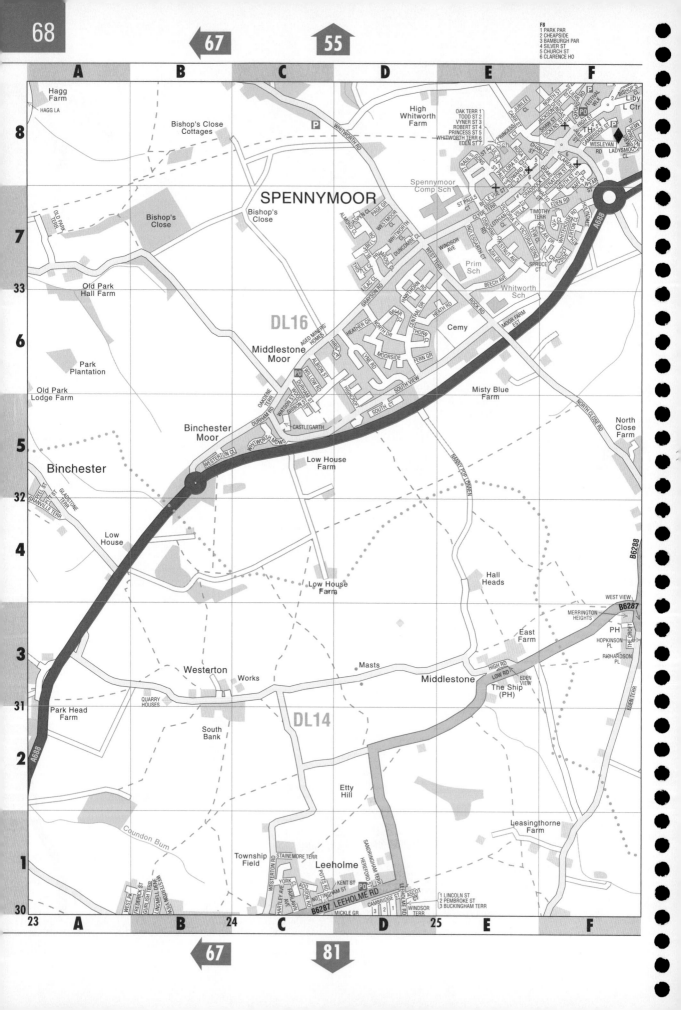

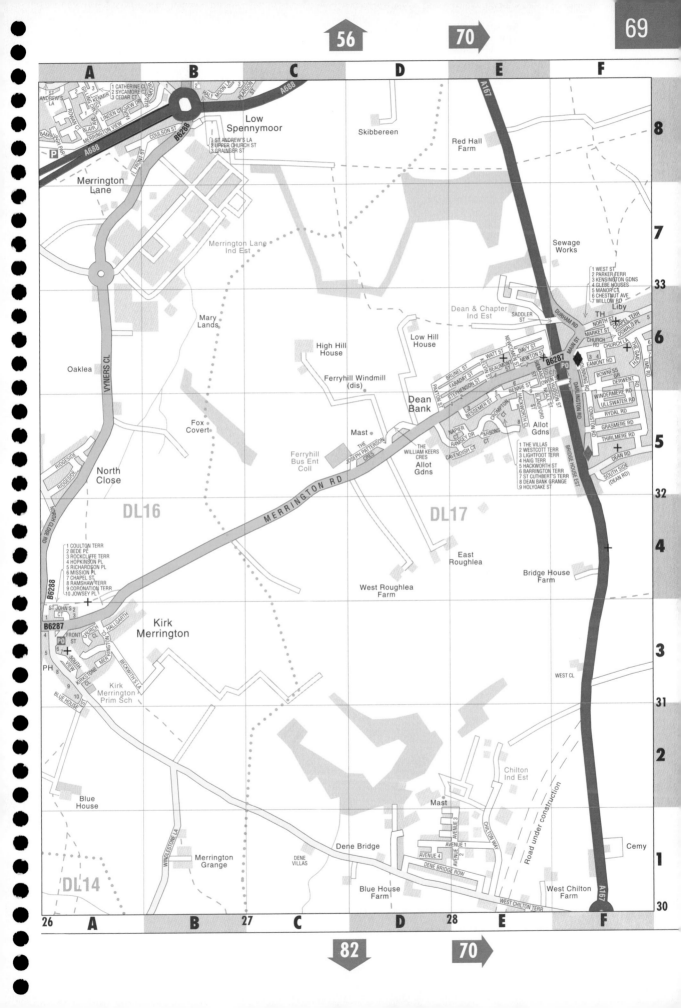

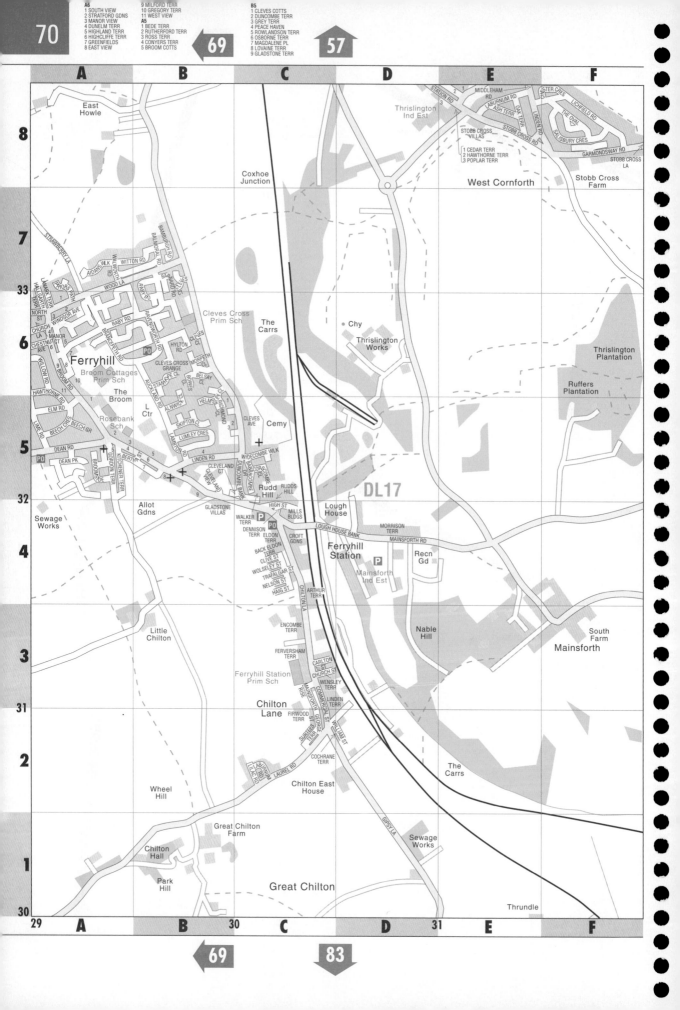

69
57
69
83

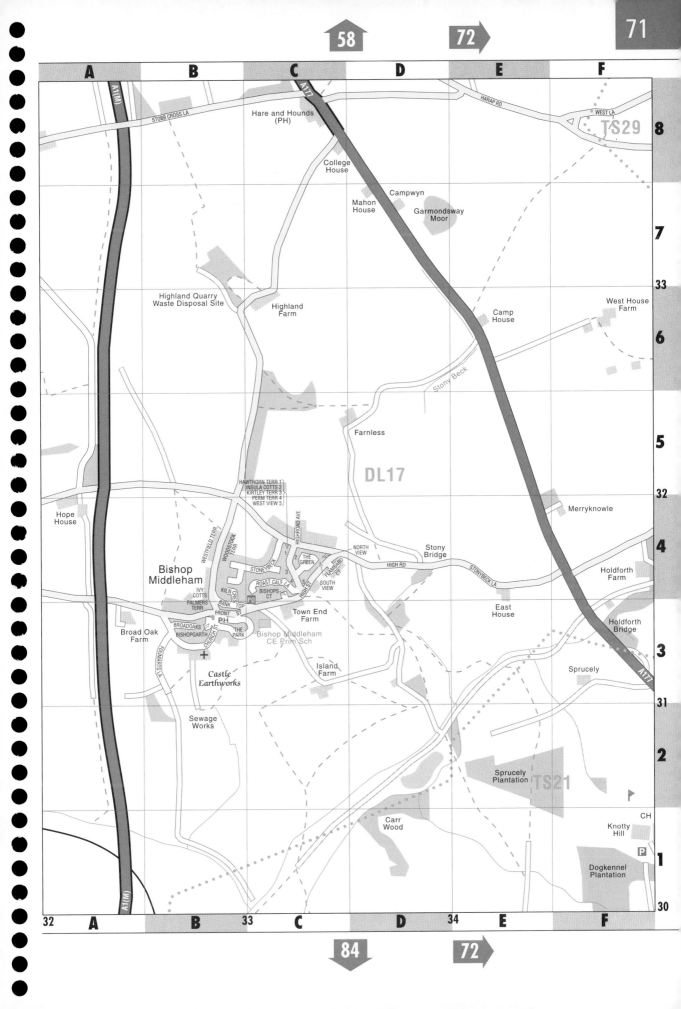

71 59

A B C D E F

8

West La

Catley Hill House

Trimdon House

WEST GR

B1278

S MINE CRES

MAIN RD

CHURCH RD

PO
Liby

BOYNE VIEW

SWAINBY RD

Trimdon

ROSEBERRY RD

MANOR CL 1
HOPE CL 2
HURWORTH CL 3
WOODLAND CL 4
BRIAR GR 5
BECKWITH DR 6

WYNYARD RD

Trimdon
Village
Inf Sch

HART VIEW

HARAP RD

Harap Hill

CHISHOLM RD

WINDSOR SQ

HALLGARTH RD

ELWICK VIEW

Trimdon
Jun Sch

7

Trimdon House Farm

NEWLANDS RD

GREENBANK RD

MEADOW RD

CARRSIDE RD

TS29

St William's
RC Prim Sch

Trimdon
Cottage

33

South Moor Farm

West Carrside Farm

Carr Side Covert

6

DL17

Hope House

5

BEVERIDGE CL

ST MARKS RD

ST BEDE AVE

CATHERINE RD

1 CLERVAUX TERR
2 PARK VIEW
3 BRECKON TERR
4 ALHAMBRA TERR

SALVIN TERR

STOBART TERR

ELDERBERRY MEWS

SCORFIELD

FISHBURN TERR

HARBINSON RD

SALTER'S RD

EAST VIEW

Fishburn
Prim Sch

GREENSIDE

HARAP RD

Galley Law Farm

LITTLE THORNTON

WEST TERR

FRONT ST

SOUTH VIEW

PO

PH

AGED MINERS HOMES

POPLAR CRES

Recn Gd

32

Fishburn Ind Est

SYCAMORE RD

BUTTERWICK RD

WALDEN TERR 5
MAUGHAN TERR 6
REGENT TERR 7
CHAYTOR TERR 8
CLEVELAND VIEW 9
PRUDHOE AVE 10
CORONATION AVE 11
ELDON TERR 12

SALTER'S LA

MOORSIDE CRES

DAGDALE RD

HUTTON CL

MILLFIELD RD

BRIDGE VIEW

4

Sewage Works

HEATHERDENE RD

BEECHWOOD RD

SPRINGFIELD RD

SYCAMORE RD

MILLFIELD ROAD W

BROCKWELL CL

SALTER'S LA

Three Horse Shoes Inn
(PH)

P

STONE CROSS

Fishburn

3

Lizards Farm

Fishburn Bridge

TS21

Mill House

Bridge House

BUTTERWICK RD

31

A177

Sewage Works

Weterton House Farm

River Skerne

Butterwick Bridge

2

WELLGARTH MEWS

ST LUKES CRES

WINTERTON COTTS

Weterton House

Redcar Beck

TURNPIKE WLK

MILLCLOSE WLK

Cemy

WINTERTON COTTS

1

HOMESTALL

FARIFIELD
MANOR
MEADOW
HILL

WINTERTON AVE

PASTURE FIELD

Howle Hope

The Brocks

30

B1278

Works

Firtree Hill

35 A 36 B C 37 D E F

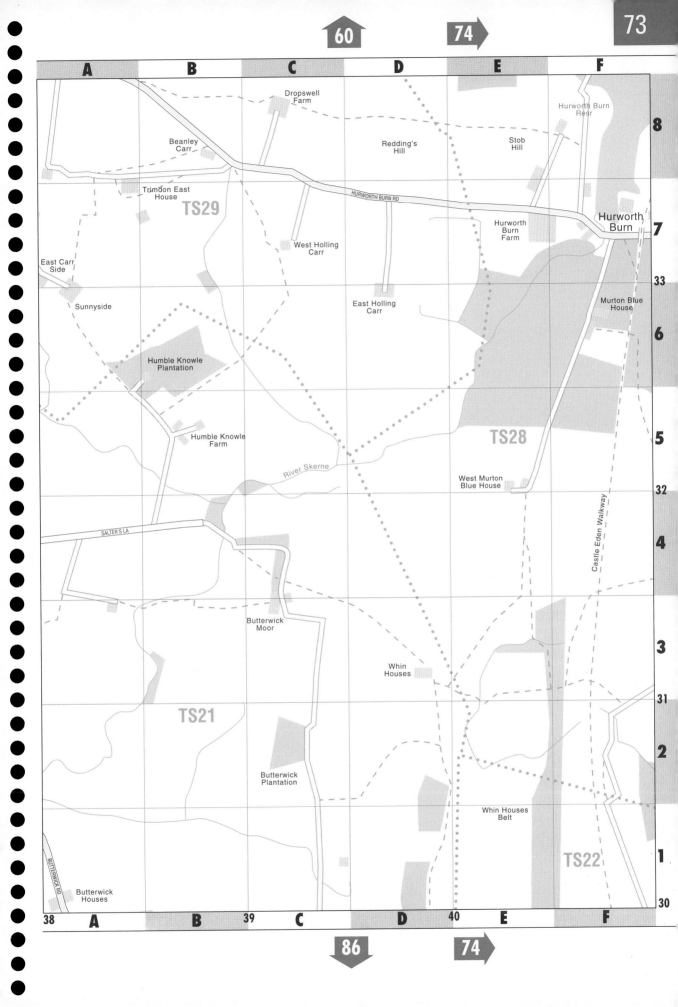

A B C D E F

8
7
33
6
5
32
4
3
31
2
1
30

Dropswell
Farm

Hurworth Burn
Resr

Beanley
Carr

Redding's
Hill

Stob
Hill

Trimdon East
House

TS29

HURWORTH BURN RD

Hurworth
Burn

Hurworth
Burn
Farm

West Holling
Carr

East Carr
Side

Murton Blue
House

Sunnyside

East Holling
Carr

Humble Knowle
Plantation

TS28

Humble Knowle
Farm

River Skerne

West Murton
Blue House

Castle Eden Walkway

SALTER'S LA

Butterwick
Moor

Whin
Houses

TS21

Butterwick
Plantation

Whin Houses
Belt

TS22

BUTTERWICK RD

Butterwick
Houses

38 A B 39 C D 40 E F

73
61

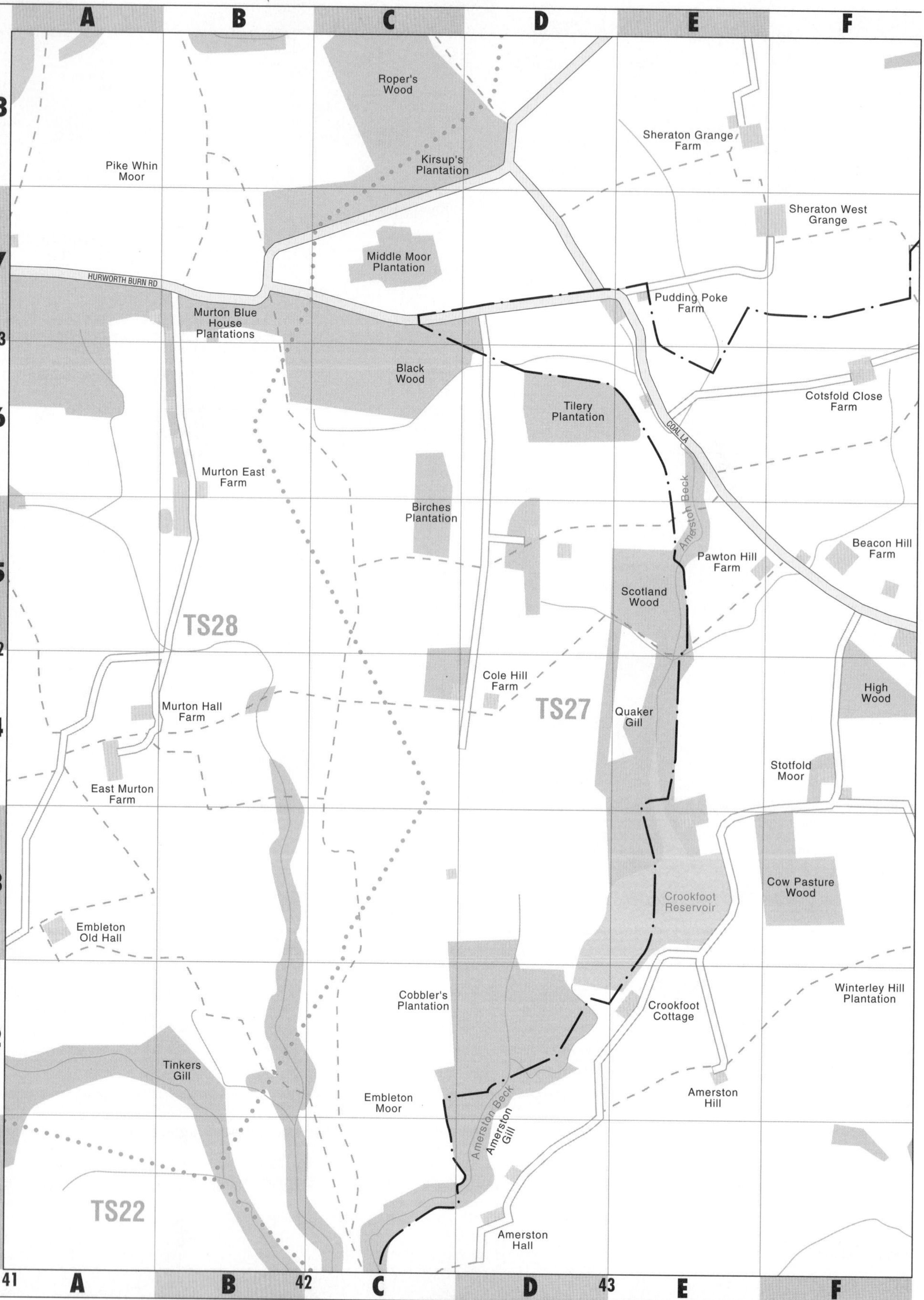

A B C D E F

8

Roper's Wood

Sheraton Grange Farm

Pike Whin Moor

Kirsup's Plantation

Sheraton West Grange

7

HURWORTH BURN RD

Middle Moor Plantation

Pudding Poke Farm

Murton Blue House Plantations

33

Black Wood

Cotsfold Close Farm

6

Tilery Plantation

COAL LA

Murton East Farm

Birches Plantation

Amerston Beck

Beacon Hill Farm

Pawton Hill Farm

5

Scotland Wood

TS28

32

Cole Hill Farm

Murton Hall Farm

TS27

Quaker Gill

High Wood

4

Stotfold Moor

East Murton Farm

3

Crookfoot Reservoir

Cow Pasture Wood

Embleton Old Hall

31

Cobbler's Plantation

Crookfoot Cottage

Winterley Hill Plantation

2

Tinkers Gill

Embleton Moor

Amerston Beck

Amerston Gill

Amerston Hill

1

Amerston Gill

TS22

30

41 A B 42 C D 43 E F

73
87

Amerston Hall

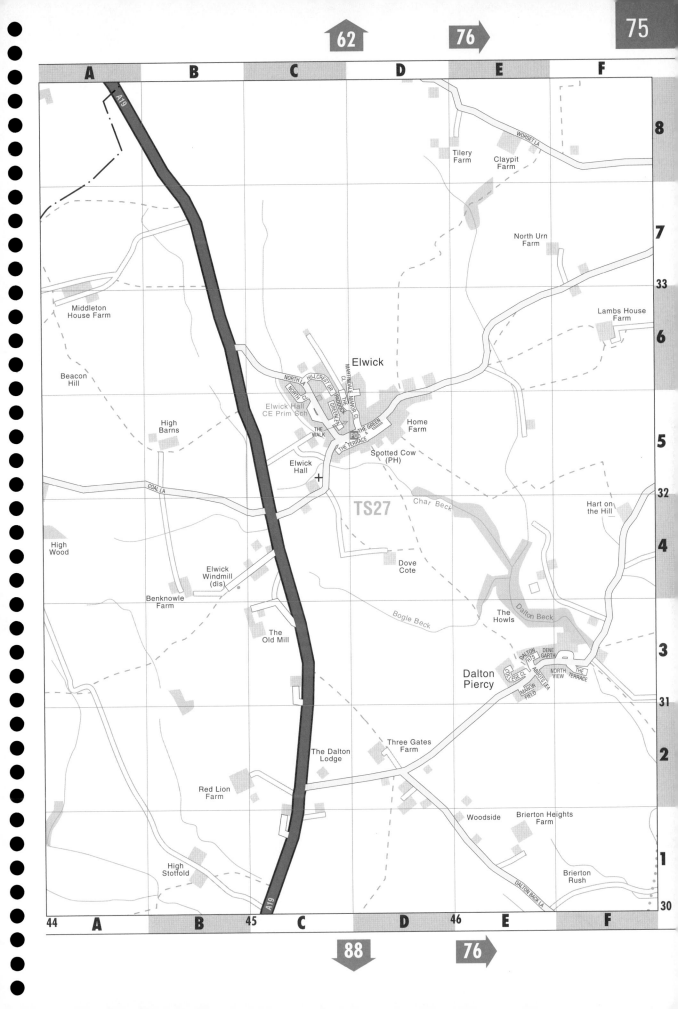

A B C D E F

8

7

33

6

5

32

4

3

31

2

1

30

Tilery Farm

Claypit Farm

WORSET LA

North Urn Farm

Middleton House Farm

Lambs House Farm

Beacon Hill

Elwick

High Barns

NORTH LA
HILLCREST GR
NORTH CL
MARINDALE
MANOR CL
THE PADDOCK
THE GREEN CM

Elwick Hall CE Prim Sch

Home Farm

THE WALK
THE GREEN
PO
THE TERRACE

Elwick Hall

Spotted Cow (PH)

COAL LA

TS27

Char Beck

Hart on the Hill

High Wood

Dove Cote

Elwick Windmill (dis)

Benknowle Farm

The Howls

Dalton Beck

Bogle Beck

The Old Mill

Dalton Piercy

DALTON LA'S
CGE CL
DENE GARTH
MANOR FIELD
ABBOTS LA
NORTH VIEW
THE TERRACE

Three Gates Farm

The Dalton Lodge

Red Lion Farm

Woodside

Brierton Heights Farm

High Stotfold

Brierton Rush

DALTON BACK LA

A19

44 A B 45 C D 46 E F

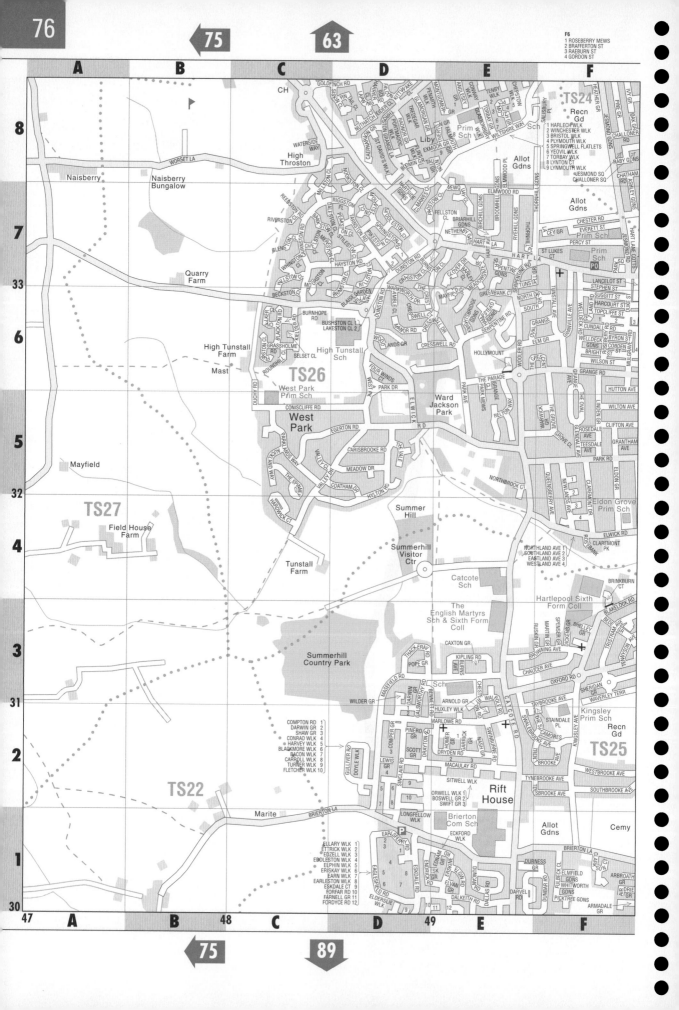

77
64
90

A6
1 SLATER ST
2 HAWKRIDGE ST
3 BROOK ST
4 CHRISTOPHER ST
5 GROSVENOR ST
6 LABURNUM ST

7 STRAKER ST
8 MORTON ST
9 ALBANY CT
10 HARTLEY ST
11 HARTLEY CL
12 HUNTER ST
13 GROSVENOR GDNS

14 HUTTON CT
15 ST JOSEPH'S CT
A7
1 PRESTON ST
2 ERNEST WLK
3 BLAKE WLK
4 HOPPS ST

A8
1 JESMOND EST
2 WILLOW WLK
3 CEDAR WLK
4 CHALLONER SQ
5 CHATHAM SQ
6 RABY SQ

B6
1 TEES ST
2 MIDDLETON GRANGE LA
3 SWAINSON PL
4 WESLEY SQ
5 UPPER CHURCH ST

B7
1 MAPLETON RD
2 BREWARD WLK
3 MASON WLK
4 POTTER WLK
5 HERBERT WLK
6 LYNNFIELD RD

7 STUART ST

C6
1 CHURCH SQ
2 CENTRAL BLDGS
3 STATION APP
4 AVONDENE FLATS
5 SCARBOROUGH ST
6 JERSEY ST

7 BRITANNIA CL

C5
1 BRUNSWICK ST
2 ANDREW ST
3 NEWHAVEN CT
4 WHITBY GR
5 HUCKELHOVEN CT
6 FASTNET GR
7 ST ABBS WLK
8 ST BEES WLK
9 LAMBTON ST
10 MUSGRAVE WLK
11 BURBANK CT
12 LIZARD WLK
13 LONGSCAR WLK
14 SPURN WLK
15 GOODWIN WLK
16 DUNDAS ST

DARLINGTON ST 1
THROSTON ST 2
BACK THROSTON ST 3
NUNS ST 4
PRIORY CT 5
GLADSTONE ST 6
THE LAWNS 7
SUNNISIDE 8
ABBEY ST 9
GROVES ST 10
ST MARY ST 11
ST MARY ST 12
VICTORIA ST 13
FRIENDSHIP LA 14
SANDWELL CHARE 15
FRIARAGE GDNS 16
VICTORIA PL 17
MANNERS ST 18
RABY ST 19
REGENT SQ 20
BEDFORD ST 21
LONDONDERRY ST 22
CROFT TERR 23
ANCHOR CT 24

1 SPINNAKER HO
2 ANCHOR HO
3 MARITIME CL
4 ADMIRAL WAY
5 CAPTAINS WLK
6 CAPSTAN HO
7 FLEET HO
8 FLOTILLA CL
9 PILOT HO
10 MERCHANT HO
11 CHART HO
12 MAYFLOWER CL
13 SCHOONER CL
14 TRIDENT CL
15 DUNLIN HO
16 OSPREY HO
17 KINGFISHER HO
18 COMPASS HO
19 FULMAR HO

1 STAITHES CT
2 MUSGRAVE ST
3 ST ANN'S CT
4 ST CATHERINE'S CT
5 HILDA WLK
6 MAINSFORTH FLATS

1 OYSTERMAN HO
2 JARSLING HO
3 REEF HO
4 CLOVE HITCH HO
5 BOWLINE HO
6 JACKSONS LANDING

1 WINTER CL
2 FAULDER WLK
3 BOWNESS CL

1 ARDROSSAN CT
2 ALFORD CT
3 ALNESS GR

Bottom indexes:

A4
1 ELWICK GRANGE
2 FLAXTON CT
3 ELWICK CT
4 GRASMERE ST

A5
1 MITCHELL ST
2 ALDERSON ST
3 CAMPION ST
4 BENSON ST
5 BENTLEY ST

B3
1 ST AIDAN'S ST
2 LEAMINGTON DR
3 WESTMORELAND ST
4 ALVERSTONE AVE
5 WORCESTER GDNS

B4
1 BATHGATE TERR
2 THOMPSON ST
3 WESTMORELAND ST
4 MOYNE GDNS
5 LONSDALE CT
6 VICARAGE CT
7 THE MALTINGS
8 RUSSELL WLK
9 NORTHAMPTON WLK

10 NOTTINGHAM WLK
11 CUMBRIA WLK
12 NORTHUMBERLAND GR
13 NORTHUMBERLAND RD
14 WESTMORLAND WLK
15 SHROPSHIRE WLK

B5
1 STOTFOLD ST
2 JOHNSON ST
3 JUBILEE HO
4 GAINFORD ST
5 GILL ST
6 YORK FLATLETS
7 BREWERY ST

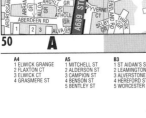

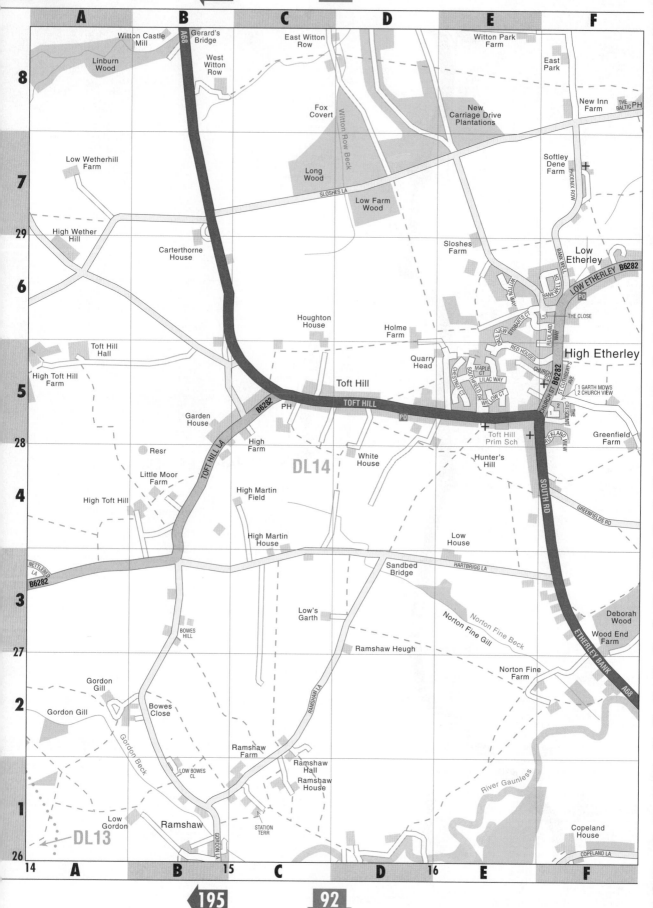

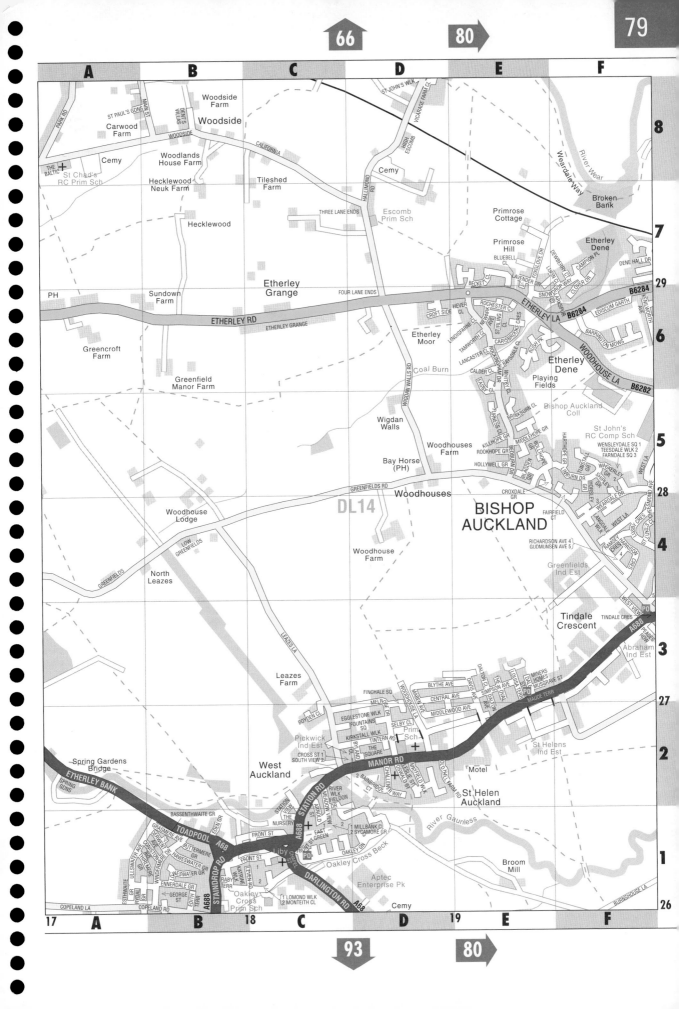

A B C D E F

8
7
29
6
5
28
4
3
27
2
1
26

St Paul's Gdns
Woodside Farm
Woodside
Carwood Farm
Main St
Dent's Villas
Park Rd
Woodside
California
Cemy
The Baltic
St Chad's RC Prim Sch
Woodlands House Farm
Hecklewood Neuk Farm
Tileshed Farm
Hecklewood
Three Lane Ends
St John's Wlk
Vicarage Farm Cl
High Escomb
Cemy
Escomb Prim Sch
Weardale Way
River Wear
Broken Bank
PH
Sundown Farm
Etherley Grange
Four Lane Ends
Etherley Rd
Etherley Grange
Primrose Cottage
Primrose Hill
Bluebell Cl
Dewberry Cl
Foxglove Dr
Campion Pl
Etherley Dene
Dene Hall Dr
B6284
Becket Cl
Lavender Cl
Snowdrop Cl
Etherley La
B6284
Ediscum Garth
Kenilworth Ave
Greencroft Farm
Hever Cl
Croft Side
Rochester Cl
Newark Cl
Lindisfarne Cl
Stirling
Carisbrooke Ct
Barrington Mdws
Woodhouse La
B6282
Greenfield Manor Farm
Etherley Moor
Coal Burn
Wigdan Walls Rd
Tamworth Cl
Lancaster Cl
Calder Cl
Rockingham Cl
Easby Rd
Pinkers Ct
Rush Pk
Brinkburn Cl
Etherley Dene
Playing Fields
Bishop Auckland Coll
Killhope Gr
Rookhope Gr
Hollywell Gr
Middlehope Gr
Bollihope
Lingen
Harthope Gr
St John's RC Comp Sch
Wensleydale Sq 1
Teesdale Wlk 2
Farndale Sq 3
Wasserley Gr 1
Shirley Gr 2
Tunstall
Hornsey Gr
Tilburn Dr
West La
Wigdan Walls
Bay Horse (PH)
Woodhouses Farm
Croxdale Gr
28
Weardale Dr
Angdal Wlk
West La
Libby Cres
Greenfields Rd
Woodhouses
DL14
BISHOP AUCKLAND
Fairfield Ct
Richardson Ave 4
Gudmunsen Ave 5
Ramsey Cres
Harrison Cres
St Luke's Cl
Chesmond Ave
Woodhouse Lodge
Low Greenfields
Woodhouse Farm
Greenfields Ind Est
Westview
P O
Greenfields
North Leazes
Tindale Crescent
Tindale Cres
A688
Eags Row
Abraham Ind Est
3
Leazes La
Leazes Farm
Dalton Cl
Davis Ave
The Oval
Simpson Ave
Leslie St
Dalton St
Miners Homes
Musgrave St
Maude Terr
Blythe Ave
Central Ave
Middlewood Ave
20
St Helens Ind Est
27
Finchale Sq
Boyden Cl
Melrose Dr
Woodhouse La
Maben Ave
Egglestone Wlk
Fountains Sq
Kirkstall Wlk
Selby Cl
Tintern Rd
Prim Sch
Pickwick Ind Est
Cross St 1
South View 2
Briar
The Square
Mayfield Wlk
Oswald St
Old Hall Farm Pk
Motel
St Helens Ind Est
2
West Auckland
Manor Rd
Leslie St
Challey Way
St Helen Auckland
Spring Gardens Bridge
Etherley Bank
Spring Gdns
Bassenthwaite Gr
Eden Gr
Toadpool
A68
Station Rd
Front St
Station View
The Nursery
River Wlk
Meadow View
Arnold St
East Green
Oakley Gn
Millbank Cl 1
Sycamore Gr 2
Bainbridge Ct
River Gaunless
Broom Mill
1
Grasmere Ave
Derwent Gr
Coniston Gr
Hawkshead Gr
Thirlmere Gr
Windermere Gr
Buttermere Gr
Hawes Water Gr
Ullswater Ave
Ennerdale Gr
Rydal Gr
Esthwaite Gr
George St
Edith Terr
A688
Staindrop Rd
Raby Terr
Katrine Wlk
Front St
Libby Chapel
P O
Oakley Cross Beck
Oakley Cross Prim Sch
1 Lomond Wlk
2 Monteith Cl
Darlington Rd
A68
Aptec Enterprise Pk
Cemy
Burkshouse La
Copeland La
Copeland Rd
26

17 A B 18 C 19 D E F

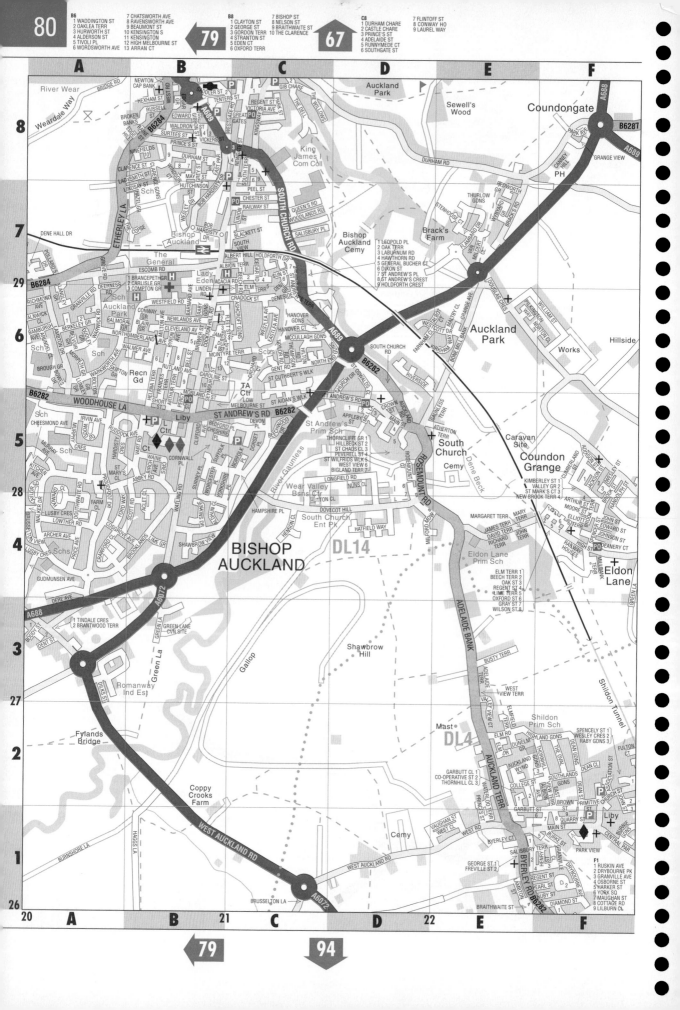

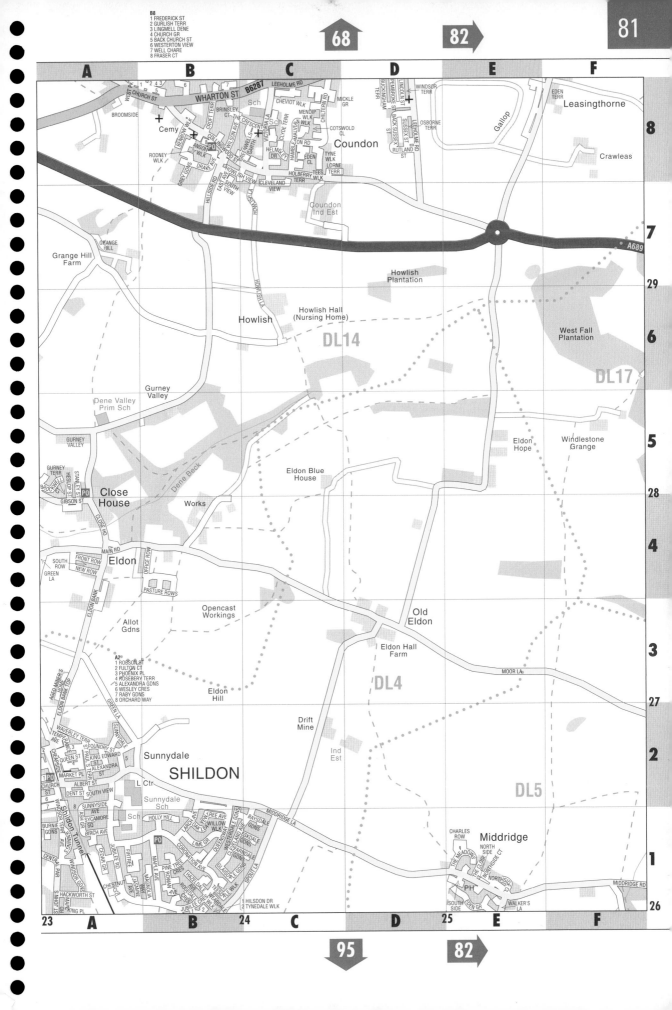

B8
1 FREDERICK ST
2 GURLISH TERR
3 LINGMELL DENE
4 CHURCH GR
5 BACK CHURCH ST
6 WESTERTON VIEW
7 WELL CHARE
8 FRASER CT

A   B   C   D   E   F

WEST PK
WHARTON ST
B6287
LEEHOLME RD
BROOMSIDE
Cemy
BRINSLEY CT THE CRESCENT
Sch
CHELTON RD
CHELTFAN RD
MICKLE GR
LINCOLN ST
WINDSOR TERR
EDEN TERR
Leasingthorne
Coundon
Crawleas

Gallop
8

Coundon Ind Est
A689
7

Grange Hill Farm
Grange Hill
Howlish Plantation
29

Howlish
Howlish Hall (Nursing Home)
West Fall Plantation
6

DL14
DL17

Gurney Valley
Dene Valley Prim Sch
5

Gurney Valley
Eldon Hope
Windlestone Grange

Gurney Terr
BROCKWELL
Close House
Eldon Blue House
Dene Beck
Works
28

SOUTH ROW
FRONT ROW
NEW ROW
Eldon
OFFICE ROW
MAIN RD
4
GREEN LA
PASTURE ROWS
ELDON BANK

Allot Gdns
Opencast Workings
Old Eldon
3

A2
1 ROBSON ST
2 FULTON CT
3 PHOENIX PL
4 ROSEBERY TERR
5 ALEXANDRA GDNS
6 WESLEY CRES
7 RABY GDNS
8 ORCHARD WAY
Eldon Hall Farm
Eldon Hill
MOOR LA
DL4
27

Drift Mine
Ind Est
Sunnydale
SHILDON
2

WAVERLEY TERR
FOUNDRY ST
QUEEN ST
KING EDWARD ST
PAUL'S TERR
MARKET PL
ALBERT ST
DENT ST
SOUTH VIEW
Sunnydale Sch
L Ctr
SUNNYSIDE AVE
MIDDRIDGE LA
DL5

HOLLY HILL
Middridge
CHARLES ROW
NORTH SIDE
NORTHSIDE CT
1

Shildon Tunnel
BIRCH AVE
HACKWORTH ST
1 HILSDON DR
2 TYNEDALE WLK
SOUTH SIDE
PH
WALKER'S LA
MIDDRIDGE RD
26

23   A   B   24   C   D   25   E   F

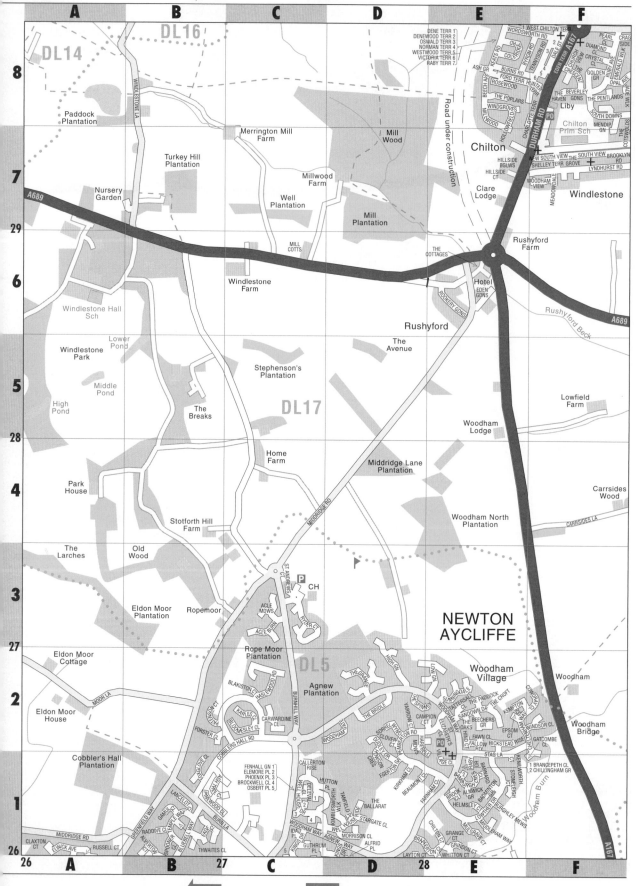

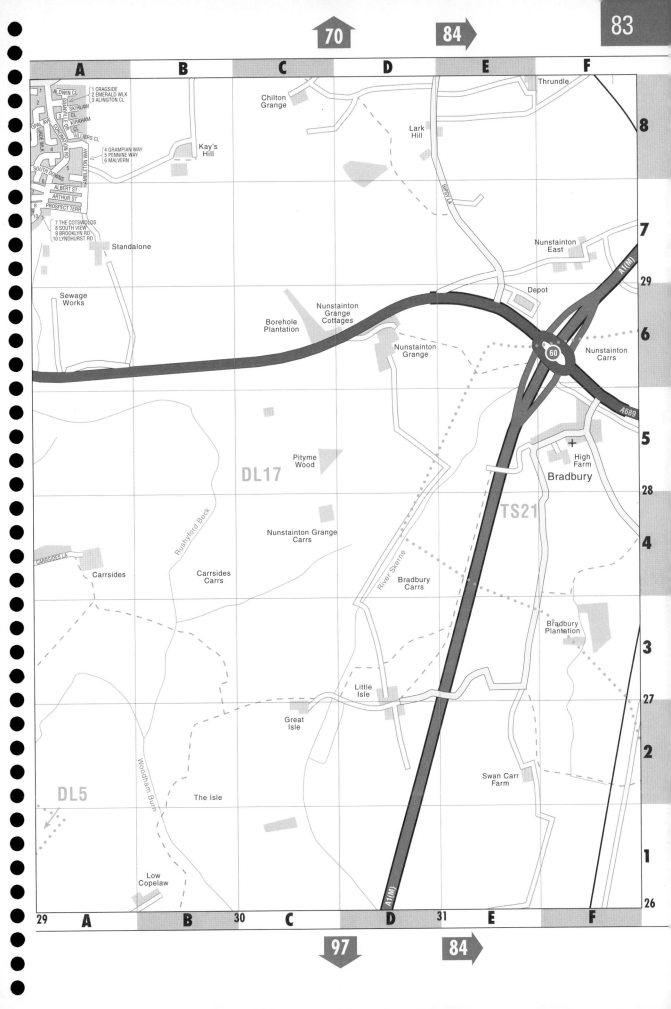

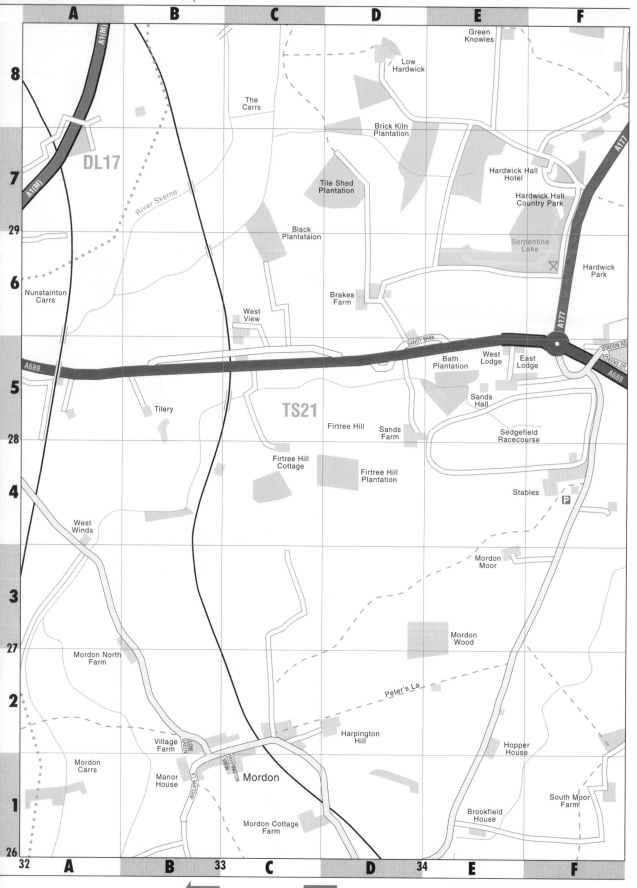

83
71

A   B   C   D   E   F

8

DL17

7

29

6

Nunstainton
Carrs

5

28

4

West
Winds

3

27

Mordon North
Farm

2

Peter's La

Village
Farm

Mordon
Carrs

Manor
House

Mordon

1

Mordon Cottage
Farm

26

32   A   B   33   C   D   34   E   F

River Skerne

The
Carrs

Low
Hardwick

Green
Knowles

Brick Kiln
Plantation

Tile Shed
Plantation

Black
Plantataion

Brakes
Farm

West
View

Tilery

TS21

Firtree Hill

Sands
Farm

Firtree Hill
Cottage

Firtree Hill
Plantation

Hardwick Hall
Hotel

Hardwick Hall
Country Park

Serpentine
Lake

Hardwick
Park

SANDY BANK

Bath
Plantation

West
Lodge

East
Lodge

Sands
Hall

Sedgefield
Racecourse

Stables

Mordon
Moor

Mordon
Wood

Harpington
Hill

Hopper
House

Brookfield
House

South Moor
Farm

A689

A1(M)

A177

STATION RD

QUEENS DR

A689

AYCLIFFE LA

HARPINGTON VIEW

LOW GREEN

83
98

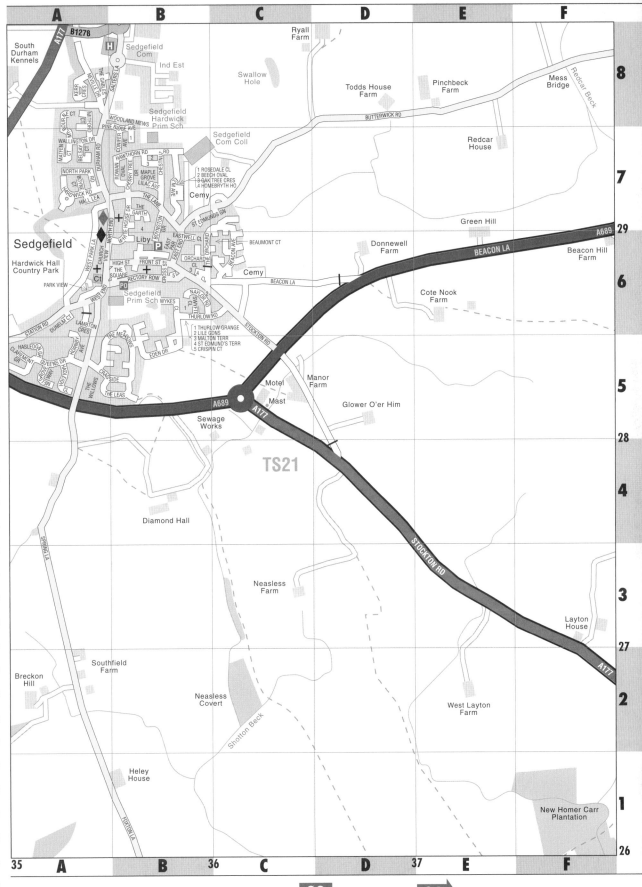

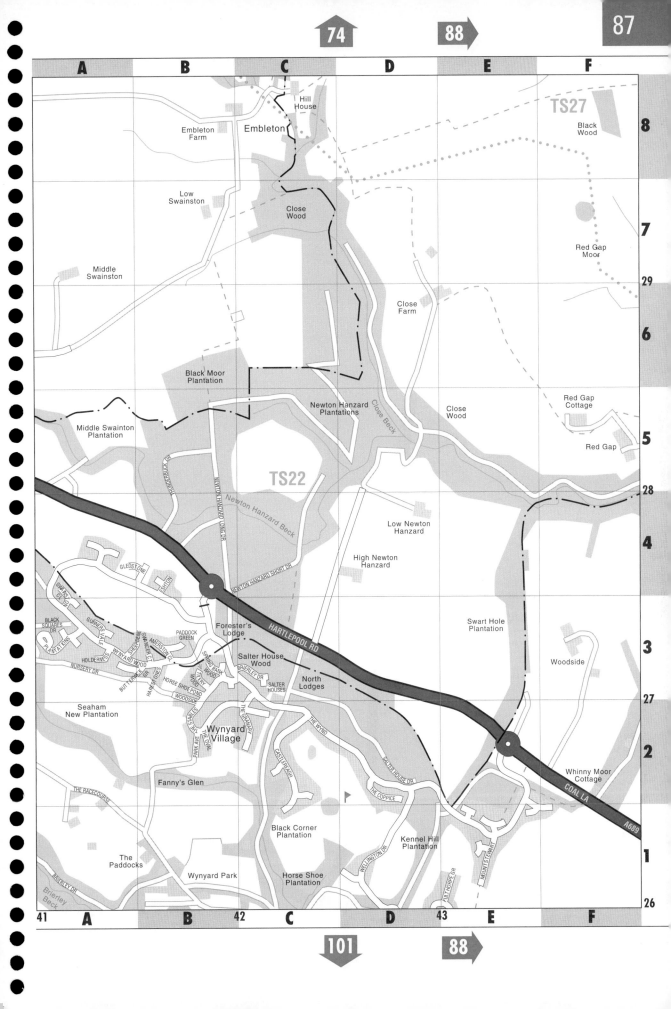

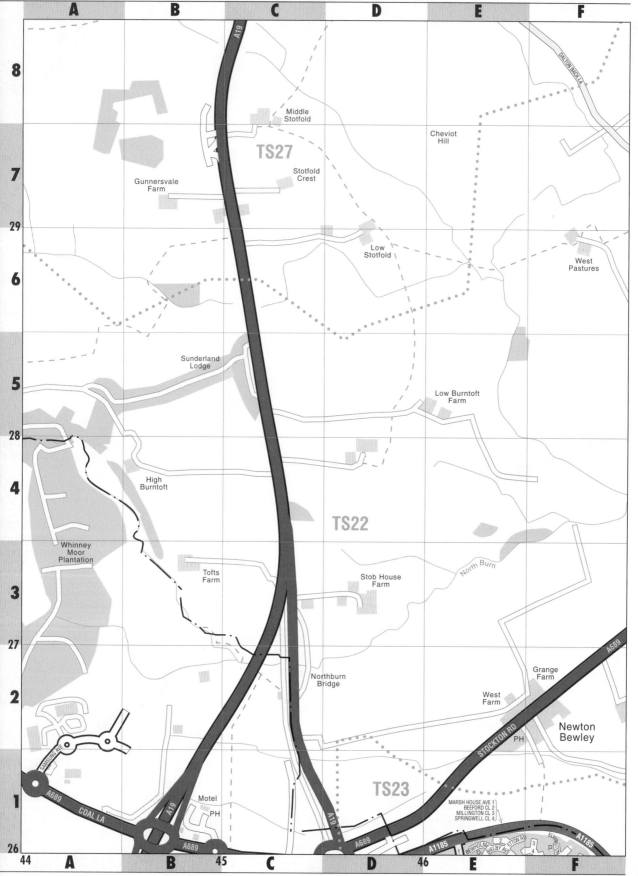

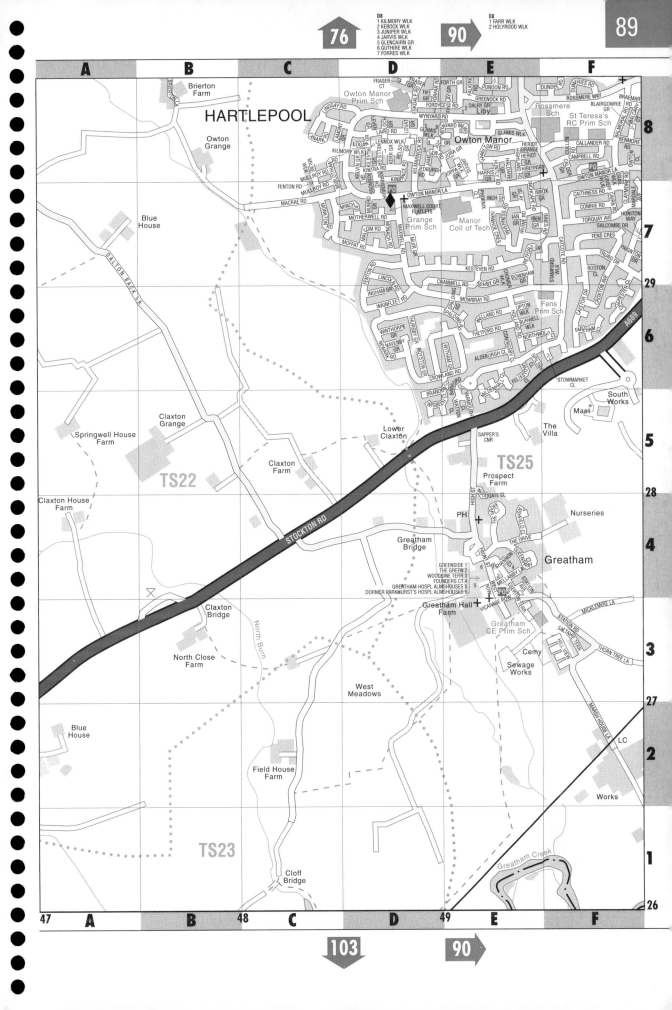

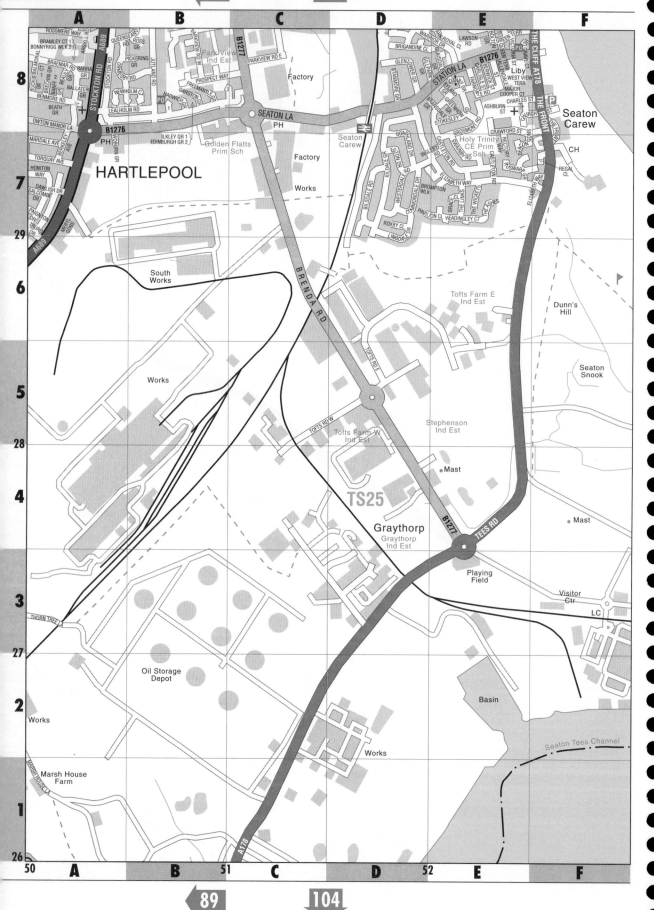

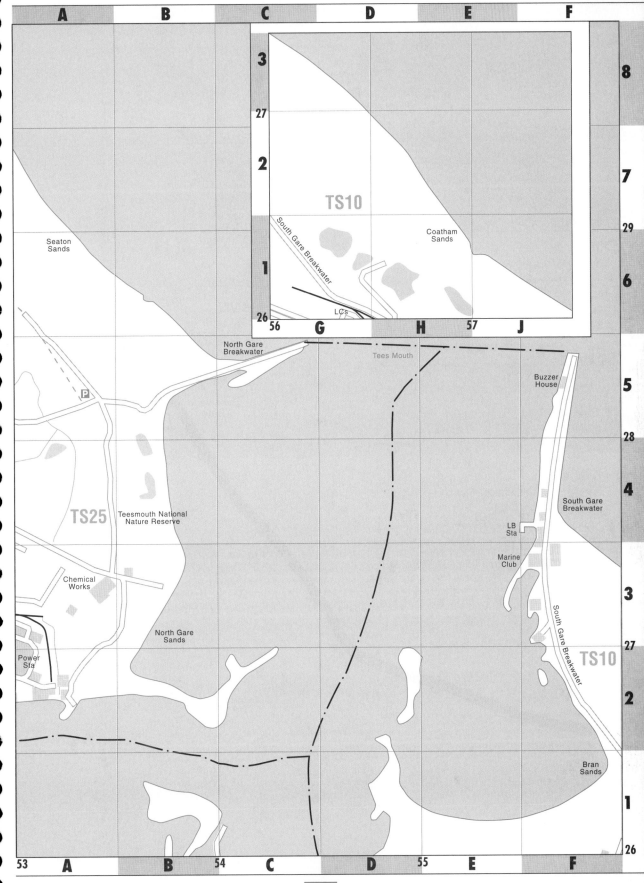

A B C D E F

8
27
2
7
29
1
6
26

TS10

South Gare Breakwater

Coatham Sands

56 G H 57 J

North Gare
Breakwater

Tees Mouth

Buzzer
House

5

28

4

Seaton
Sands

P

TS25

Teesmouth National
Nature Reserve

LB
Sta

South Gare
Breakwater

Marine
Club

Chemical
Works

North Gare
Sands

South Gare Breakwater

TS10

27

Power
Sta

2

1

Bran
Sands

26

53 A B 54 C D 55 E F

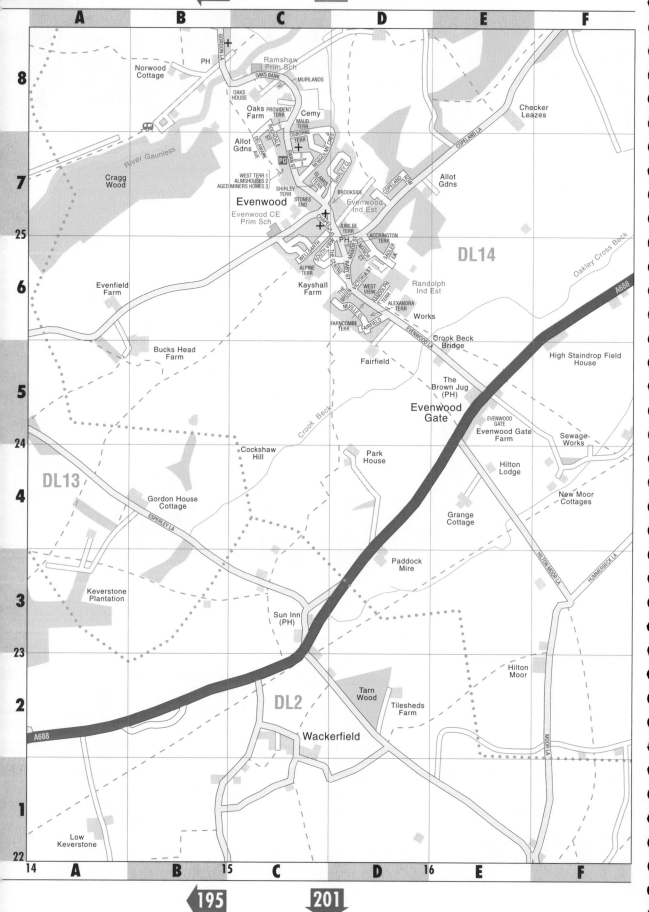

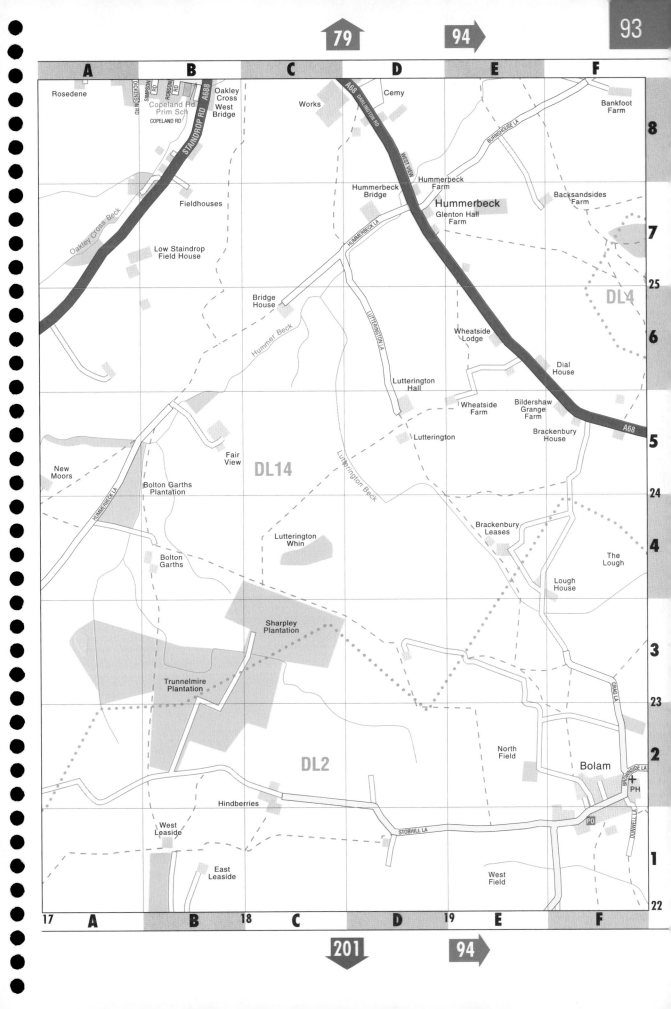

A B C D E F

Rosedene

DICKENSON RD
SIMMONS RD
ROBSON RD
Copeland Rd
Prim Sch
COPELAND RD
STAINDROP RD A688

Oakley
Cross
West
Bridge

Works

A68 DARLINGTON RD

Cemy

Bankfoot
Farm

8

WEST VIEW

BURNSHOUSE LA

Fieldhouses

Hummerbeck
Bridge

Hummerbeck
Farm

Hummerbeck

Backsandsides
Farm

HUMMERBECK LA

Glenton Hall
Farm

7

Oakley Cross Beck

Low Staindrop
Field House

25

DL4

Bridge
House

Hummer Beck

LUTTERINGTON LA

Wheatside
Lodge

6

Dial
House

Lutterington
Hall

Wheatside
Farm

Bildershaw
Grange
Farm

A68

5

Lutterington Beck

Lutterington

Brackenbury
House

Fair
View

DL14

Brackenbury
House

New
Moors

Bolton Garths
Plantation

Lutterington
Whin

Brackenbury
Leases

24

The
Lough

4

HUMMERBECK LA

Bolton
Garths

Lough
House

Sharpley
Plantation

3

Trunnelmire
Plantation

CRAG LA

23

North
Field

Bolam

2

DL2

BROWNSIDE LA

+
PH

Hindberries

DUNWELL LA

West
Leaside

STOBHILL LA

PO

1

East
Leaside

West
Field

22

17 A B 18 C D 19 E F

93
80

A
B
C
D
E
F
8
7
25
6
5
24
4
3
23
2
1
22
20
21
22
DL14
HAGGS LA
Brusselton Farm
Brusselton
Low West Thickley Farm
SOUTH TERR
OLD ENGINE HOS
BRUSSELTON LA
A6072
Works
Timothy Hackworth Prim Sch
B6282 BYERLEY RD
MIDDLETON RD
RICHMOND CL
CHAPEL ST
Furnace Pit Ind Est
Hackworth Ind Pk
SOUTH ST
SCOTT ST
B6282
THE MALLARDS
F8
1 RUSKIN AVE
2 OXFORD ST
3 WINDSOR CT
4 ADELAIDE ST
5 MADDISON ST
6 STRAND ST
7 STATION ST
8 RAILWAY TERR
9 REDWORTH RD
Brusselton Wood
DL4
High West Thickley
Redmires Farm
Mast
Hill Top
Mast
High Side Farm
DL14
A68
Bildershaw
Widehope Farm
Newbiggin Farm
Newbiggin East
Todd Fall Farm
Royal Oak
Royal Oak Farm
Moor House
Newbiggin Moor
CORNER BANK LA
RED HOUSE LA
NEWBIGGIN LA
B6275
Primrose Farm
Trout Farm
STONY BANK
DL2
Corner Beck
White House Farm
HIGHSIDE RD
Toy Top
Brown Side
Toytop Plantation
Toytop Farm
WHITE HOUSE LA
PARK HOUSE LA
Halliwell Beck
BROWNSIDE LA
Fowler House
Houghton Bank
Legs Cross
Legg's Cross Farm
Sunnydale Farm
South Moor Farm
Ox Close Farm
Mount Pleasant
High House Farm
HOUGHTON BANK LA
Bellow Banks Hill
Dunwell Field
B6275
A68

93
110

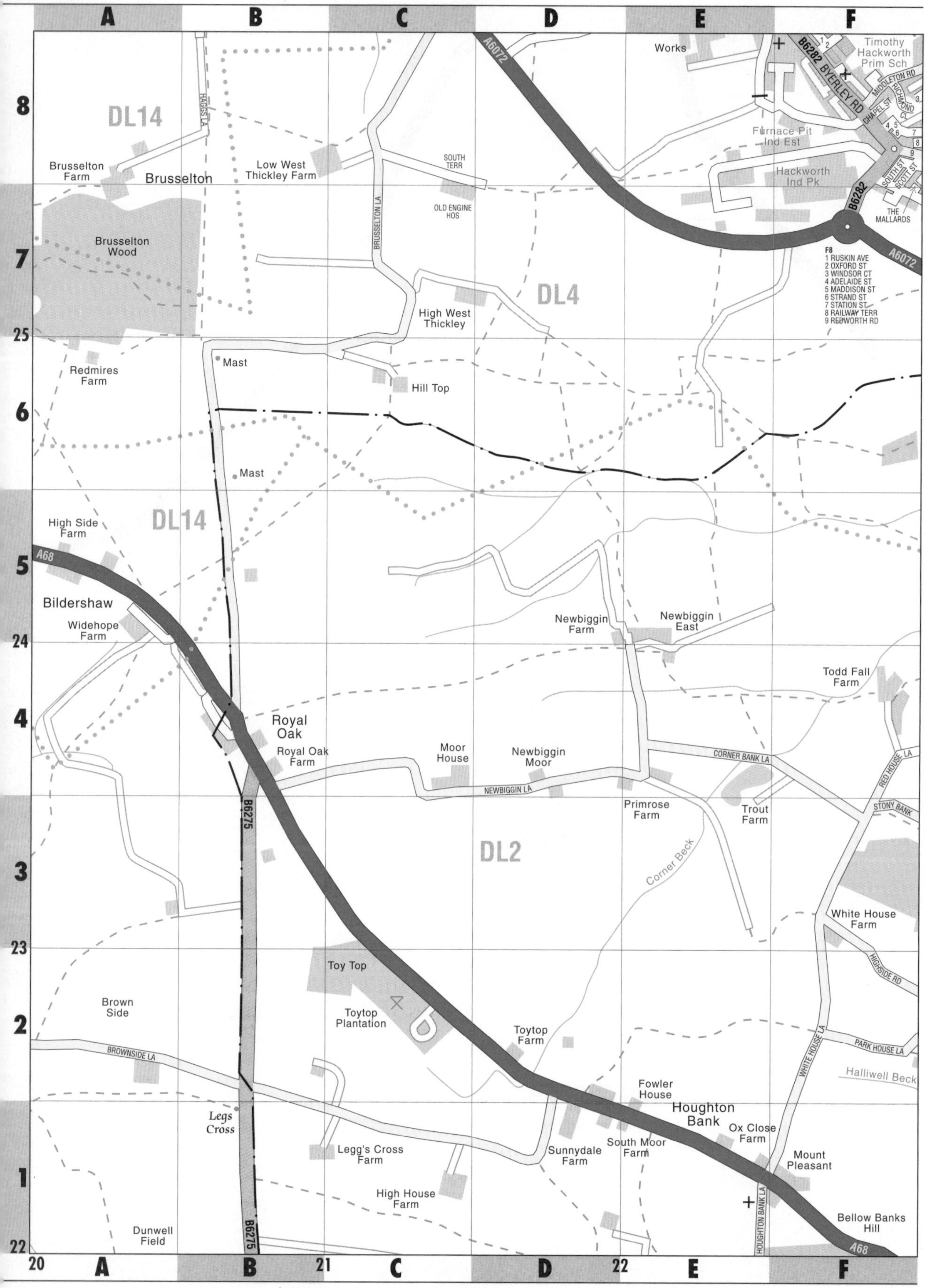

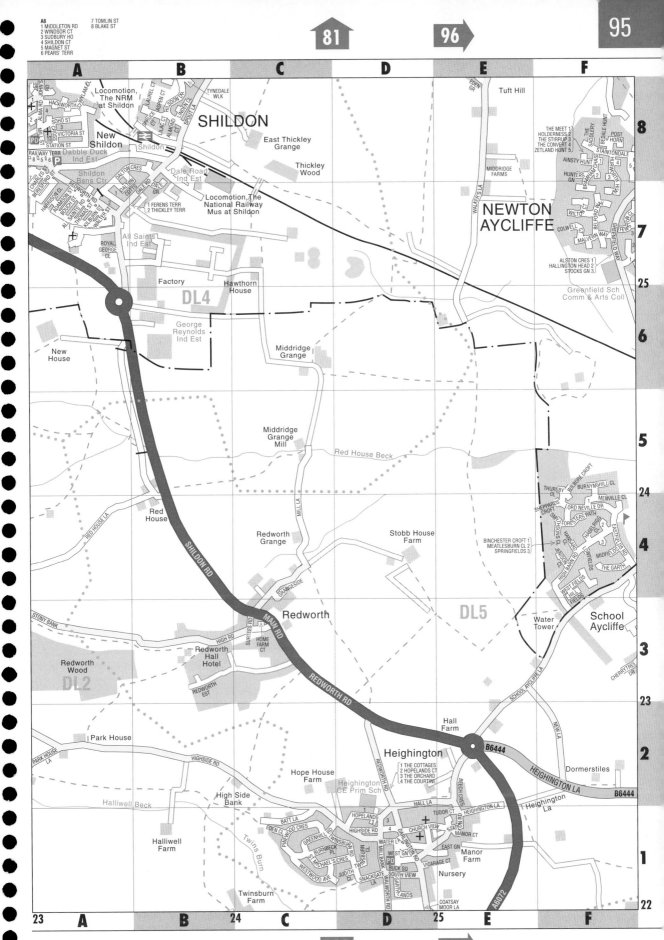

A8
1 MIDDLETON RD
2 WINDSOR CT
3 SUDBURY HO
4 SHILDON CT
5 MAGNET ST
6 PEARS' TERR
7 TOMLIN ST
8 BLAKE ST

SHILDON

New Shildon

Locomotion, The NRM at Shildon

East Thickley Grange

Thickley Wood

Dabble Duck Ind Est

Shildon Bsns Ctr

Dale Road Ind Est

Locomotion, The National Railway Mus at Shildon

1 FERENS TERR
2 THICKLEY TERR

All Saints Ind Est

ROYAL GEORGE CL

Factory

Hawthorn House

DL4

George Reynolds Ind Est

New House

Middridge Grange

Red House Beck

Middridge Grange Mill

SHILDON RD

MILL LA

Red House

Redworth Grange

Stobb House Farm

DL5

NEWTON AYCLIFFE

Tuft Hill

EDEN GR

WALKER'S LA

MIDDRIDGE FARMS

THE MEET 1
HOLDERNESS 2
THE STIRRUP 3
THE CONVERT 4
ZETLAND HUNT 5.

THE SADDLERY

POST HORN

BEDALE HUNT

STAINTONDALE

AINSTY HUNT

HUNTERS GN

BRANHAM CHASE

HURWORTH

BELFORD WY

WILTON CT

COLWELL

MALVERN WAY

GREENFELD WAY

FEWS

ALSTON CRES 1
HALLINGTON HEAD 2
STOCKS GN 3.

Greenfield Sch Comm & Arts Coll

THURSBY CL

WILLMORE CROFT

BURNYNGHILL CL

SHEPPARDS CROFT

ORD NEVILLE DR

MENVILLE CL

FORESTERS PATH

SMITHSONS CL

HANSARD

HASELRIGG

EASTFIELDS RD

HIGH BARN RD

JENISON CL

LINFIELDS

MIDFIELDS

THE GARTH

WEST FIELDS

HILL FIELDS

BINCHESTER CROFT 1
MEATLESBURN CL 2
SPRINGFIELDS 3

Water Tower

School Aycliffe

CHERRYTREE DR

SCHOOL AYCLIFFE LA

NEW LA

Redworth

MAIN RD

SURTEES RD

HIGH RD

HOME FARM CT

REDWORTH RD

GRANGESIDE

STONY BANK

RED HOUSE LA

Redworth Wood

DL2

Redworth Hall Hotel

REDWORTH EST

Park House

PARK HOUSE LA

HIGHSIDE RD

Halliwell Beck

Halliwell Farm

High Side Bank

Hope House Farm

Heighington CE Prim Sch

REDWORTH RD

Heighington

1 THE COTTAGES
2 HOPELANDS CT
3 THE ORCHARD
4 THE COURTINE

Hall Farm

B6444

HEIGHINGTON LA

B6444

Dormerstiles

Heighington La

Twins Burn

Twinsburn Farm

Halliwell Farm

EDEN CL

BATT LA

PINEWOOD CRES

GREENHILL RD

BURNBECK PL

ST MICHAEL'S CRES

WESTWOOD AVE

JUDITH CL

HOPELANDS

TWINSBURN RD

HIGHSIDE RD

MILLBANK

SNACKGATE LA

WATER LA

SOUTH VIEW

TWIN CL

WALWORTH RD

BUCK SQ

WEST GN

PO

GARTH LANDS

DARLING RD

CHURCH VIEW

HALL LA

TUDOR CT

STATION RD

EAST GN

VICARAGE CT

MANOR CT

Nursery

Manor Farm

COATSAY MOOR LA

A6072

BEECH CRES

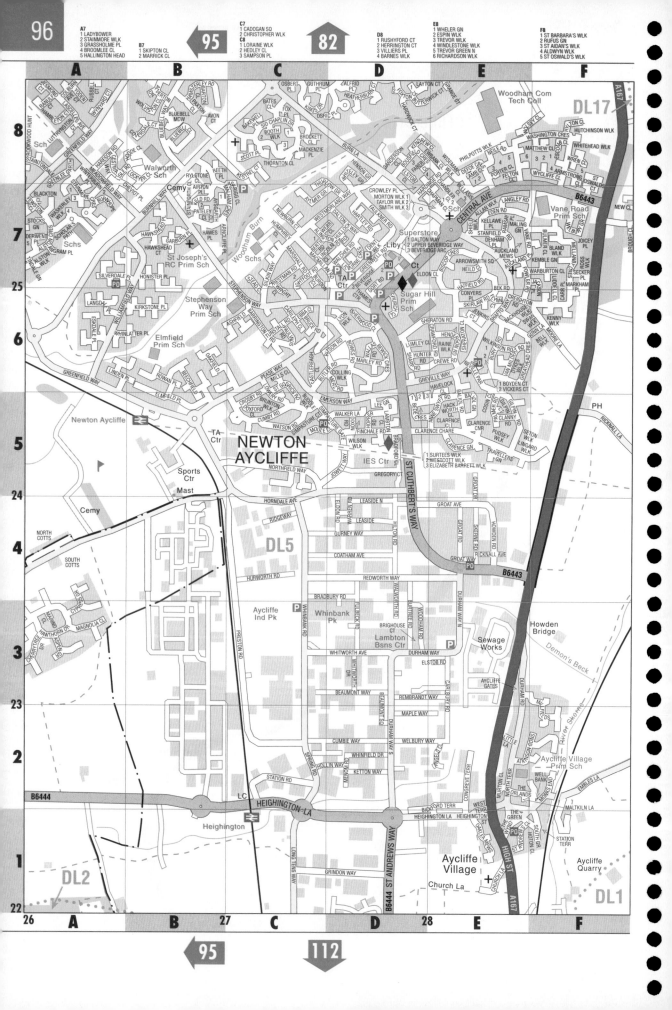

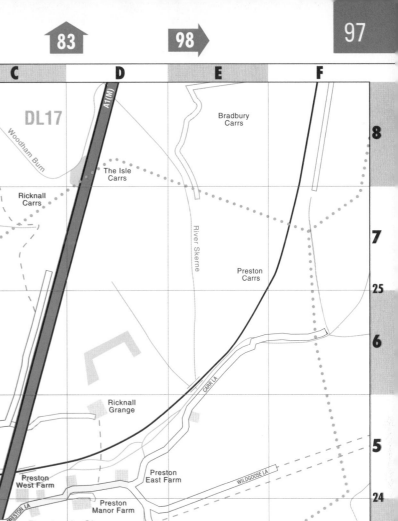

A   B   C   D   E   F

8

DL17

Woodham Burn

Bradbury
Carrs

The Isle
Carrs

Ricknall
Carrs

River Skerne

7

25

Preston
Carrs

YORK RD

BECK CO

CEDAR DR

Aycliffe Young
Peoples Centre

6

High
Copelaw

DL5

Ricknall
Grange

CARR LA

Ricknall
Lane End

5

Ricknall Mill
Farm

Blacksmiths Arms
(PH)

Preston
West Farm

Preston
East Farm

WILDGOOSE LA

24

PRESTON LA

Preston
Manor Farm

Preston-le-Skerne

LEGHALL LA

4

Heworth
House

RICKNALL LA

TS21

3

Rye Close
Farm

Lea
Hall

23

HEIGHINGTON LA

Preston
Tilery

EMBLES LA

Graham's
Wood

GREEN LA

The
Sycamores

2

Whinfield
House

LODGE LA

Preston
Lodge

Aycliffe
Quarry

High
Clump

LIME LA

DL1

1

SALTERS LA

Oat Hill
Farm

A1(M)

High
Grange

High
House

22

DL17

Mordon Carrs

Mordon Lodge

Croftlands

Boghall Plantation

Mordon South Side

LC

Bog Hall Farm

Hope House Farm

Howe Hills Plantation

West View

Stillington Moor

Howe Hills Farm

Stillington Beck

High Grindon

TS21

Merton Grange

Elstob Beck

BLEACH HOUSE BANK

Oaklea

North Farm

Elstob

ELSTOB LA

Elstob Hall

Grindon La

Elstob Cottage

Elstob Hill Farm

Elstob Hill

Grindon Lane Wood

Stainton Covert

Stainton Hill House

Lea Close Farm

Whinny Hill

Great Stainton

Kings Arms (PH)

BACK LA

GLEBE RD

Town Farm

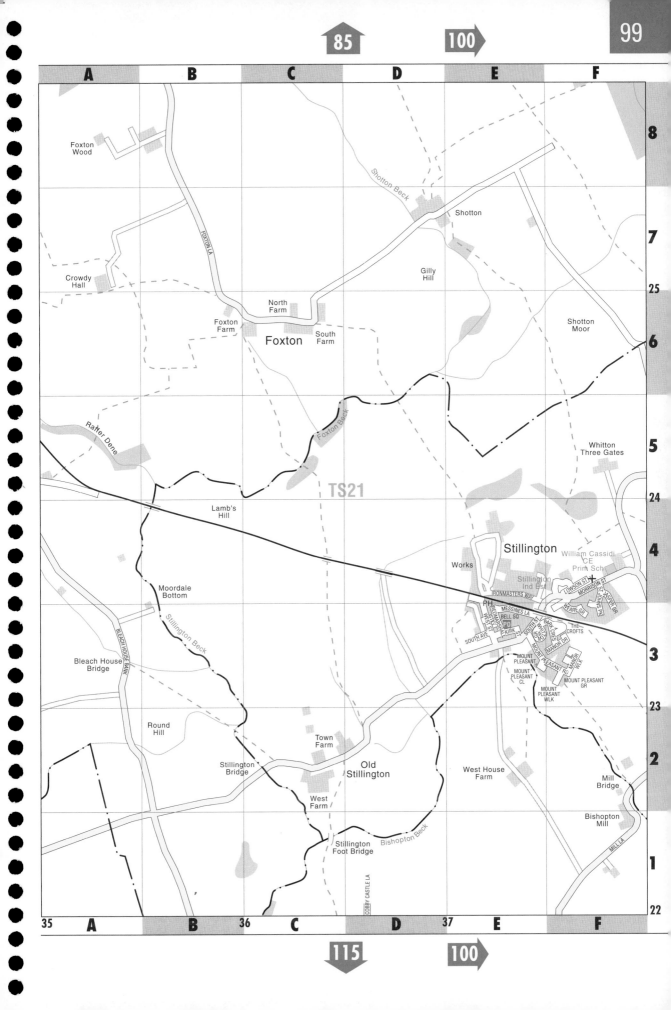

A B C D E F

8

7

25

6

5

24

4

23

2

1

22

Foxton Wood

FOXTON LA

Crowdy Hall

North Farm

Foxton Farm

South Farm

Foxton

Shotton Beck

Shotton

Gilly Hill

Shotton Moor

Rafter Dene

Foxton Beck

Whitton Three Gates

TS21

Lamb's Hill

Stillington

William Cassidi CE Prim Sch

Works

Stillington Ind Est

IRONMASTERS WAY

Moordale Bottom

Stillington Beck

BLEACH HOUSE BANK

Bleach House Bridge

Round Hill

Town Farm

Old Stillington

Stillington Bridge

West Farm

Stillington Foot Bridge

Bishopton Beck

West House Farm

Mill Bridge

Bishopton Mill

MILL LA

COBBY CASTLE LA

PH

MESSINES LA
BELL SQ
PO
PRESBYTERIAL KIRK
WEST ST
SOUTH ST
WHITTON CL
SOUTH AVE
PARK CRES
MANOR DR
MANOR WLK
THE CROFTS
LOWSON ST
MORRISON ST
ST JOHNS PK
SASPER GR
WEARE GR
MOUNT PLEASANT
MOUNT PLEASANT RD
MOUNT PLEASANT CL
MOUNT PLEASANT GR
MOUNT PLEASANT WLK

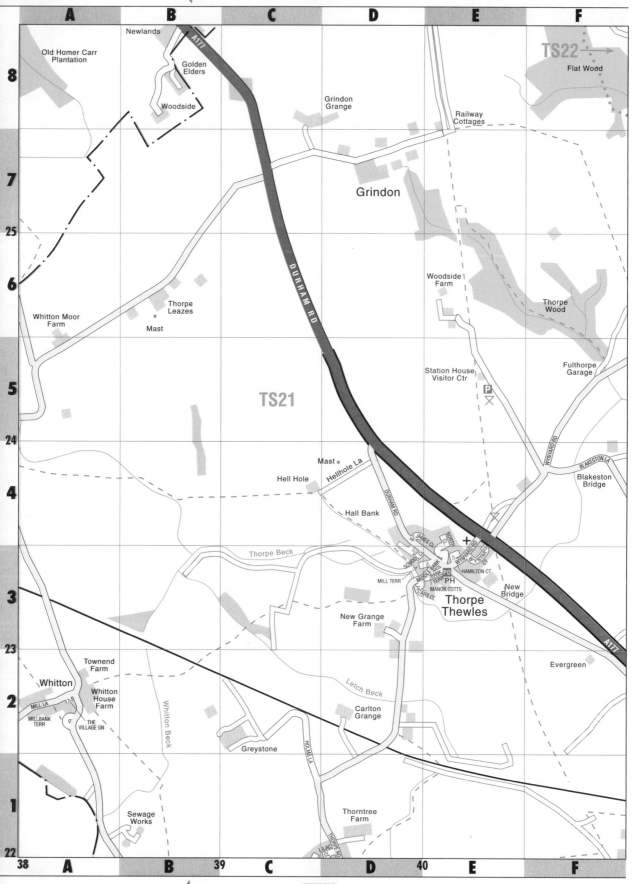

8

BRIERLEY DR
Fulthorpe Glen
Eagle Bridge
Wynyard Hall
The Kennels
Lion Bridge
FULTHORPE GR
WELLINGTON DR
FORESTERS CL
BRANTOFT
EAGLE BRIDGE
LANNIGATE CL
LION BRIDGE CL
EMBLETON
CH

Wynyard Woodland Park
Mon
Swancar Pond

7

Sewage Works
Dog Bridge
Wash Plantation
Parkside Manor
Warren Lodge
Aranvale
Warren Farm
Bradley Farm
Parkside Lodge
WYNYARD RD
TS22
P

25

Fulthorpe
Bottle Hill Wood
Ship Dene
Golden Gates
Hurle House
Corner's Plantation
Wilmire House

6

White House Farm

Bottle Hill
Thornley Hill

5

Blakeston Hall
Thorpe Beck
Viewly Hill

24

TS21
Wolviston Mill

4

Thorney Close Farm
Newclose Farm

Low Middlefield Farm
West Newlands Farm
TS20

3

Middlefield Farm
North Plantation
Brookdale Farm

23

Howden Hall
Howden House
White House Farm
STOCKTON-ON-TEES
Calf Fallow Farm
CALF FALLOW LA

2

PH

High Middlefield
BLAKESTON LA
North West Junction
White House Plantation
Hornleys
LC
Rec Gd
NORTHUMBERLAND GR
WESTMORLAND GR

DURHAM RD
LC
ROSSLARE RD 1
REYNOLDSTON AVE 2
RAMPSIDE AVE 3
REDBROOK AVE 4
SYON GDNS
CANTSBURY RD
LYNMOUTH RD
KENLEY GDNS
ASHVILLE AVE
MARQUIS GR
GRANTHAM RD
WHITFIELD RD
CUMBERLAND GR
RIPLEY RD

CHELSEA GDNS
CORBY LODGE
JUNCTION RD
B1274

1

Blakeston Com Sch
TS19
NORTON JUNCTION COTTS
WOLSEY
EGERTON CL
H
Nuffield
THE GLEBE
BRENKLEY
GARFORTH CL
BRAMLING CL
BIRDSALL
WHINFLOWER DR
FOSTON CL
FULTHORPE RD

A177
B1274
RAGLAN CT
RUNFOLD CL
RADFORD CL
RADPATH LA
ROSTREVOR AVE
ROSENEATH AVE
BARFORD CL
DRAYCOTT CL
SEAHAM
MAPLETON DR

22

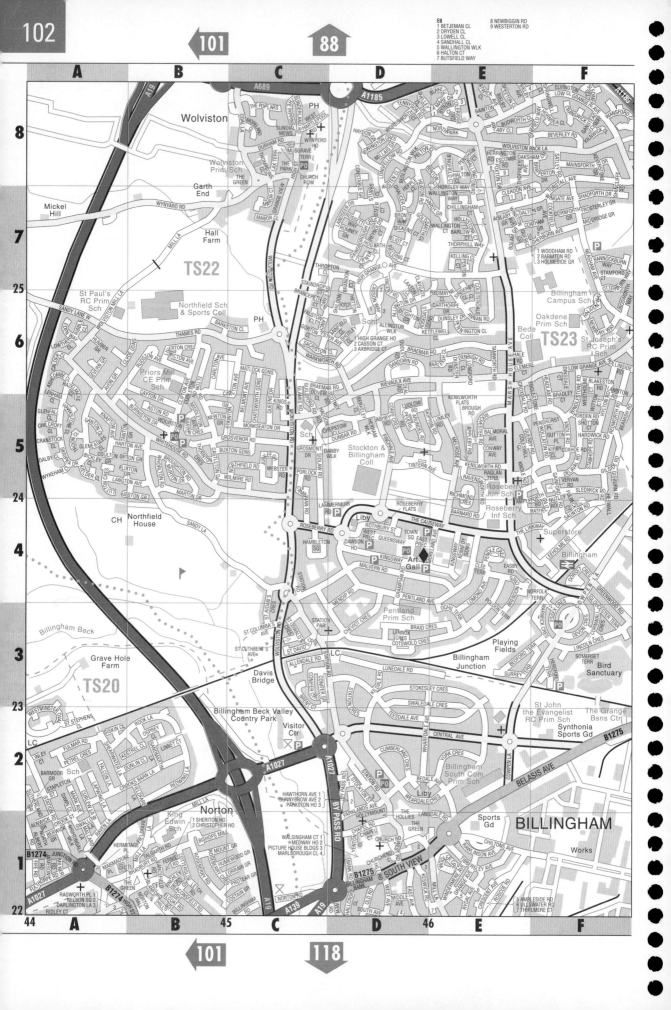

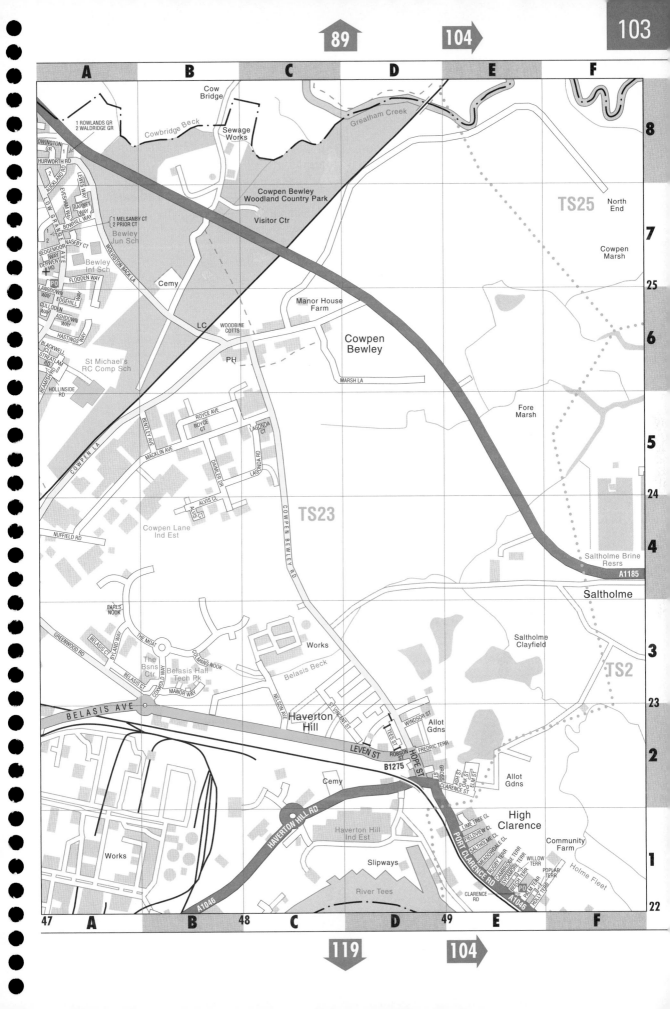

← 103   90

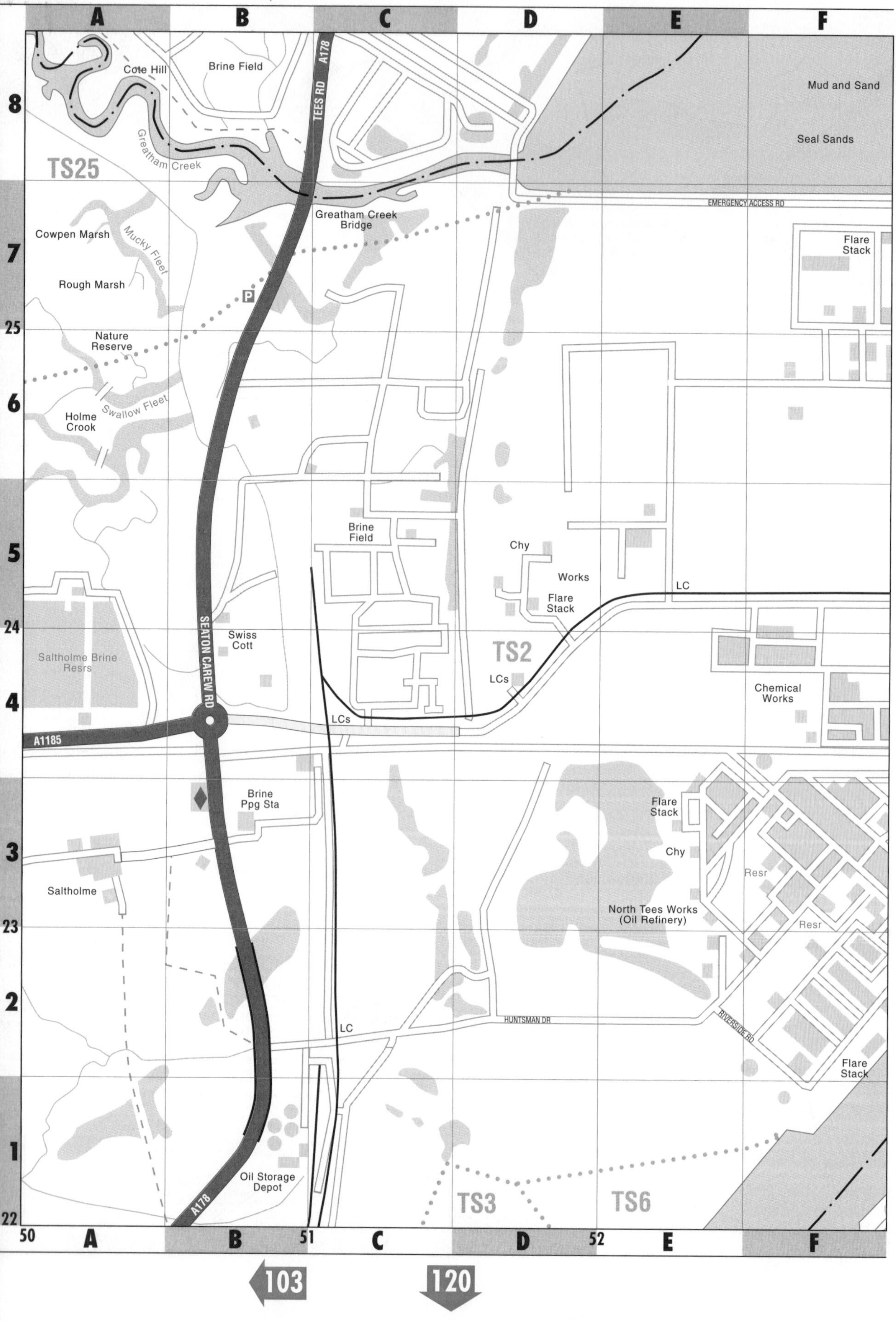

A   B   C   D   E   F

8

TS25

Cote Hill

Brine Field

Mud and Sand

Seal Sands

Greatham Creek

TEES RD A178

Greatham Creek Bridge

EMERGENCY ACCESS RD

7

Cowpen Marsh

Mucky Fleet

Flare Stack

Rough Marsh

P

25

Nature Reserve

Swallow Fleet

6

Holme Crook

5

Brine Field

Chy

Works

Flare Stack

LC

SEATON CAREW RD

24

Swiss Cott

TS2

LCs

Chemical Works

Saltholme Brine Resrs

4

A1185

LCs

3

Saltholme

Brine Ppg Sta

Flare Stack

Chy

Resr

23

North Tees Works (Oil Refinery)

Resr

2

LC

HUNTSMAN DR

RIVERSIDE RD

Flare Stack

1

A178

Oil Storage Depot

TS3

TS6

22

50   A   B   51   C   D   52   E   F

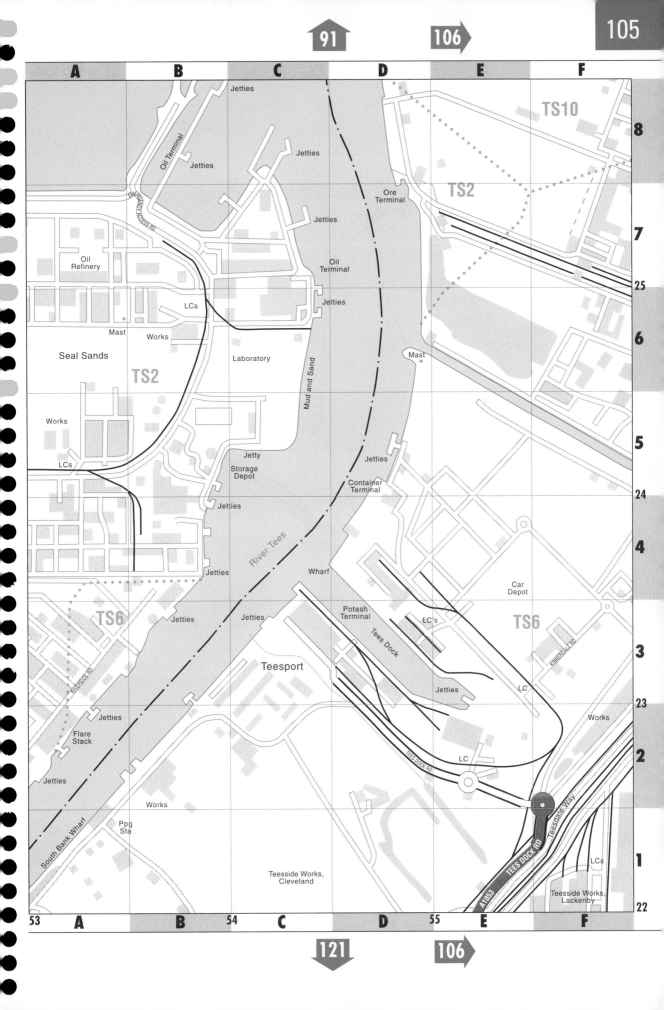

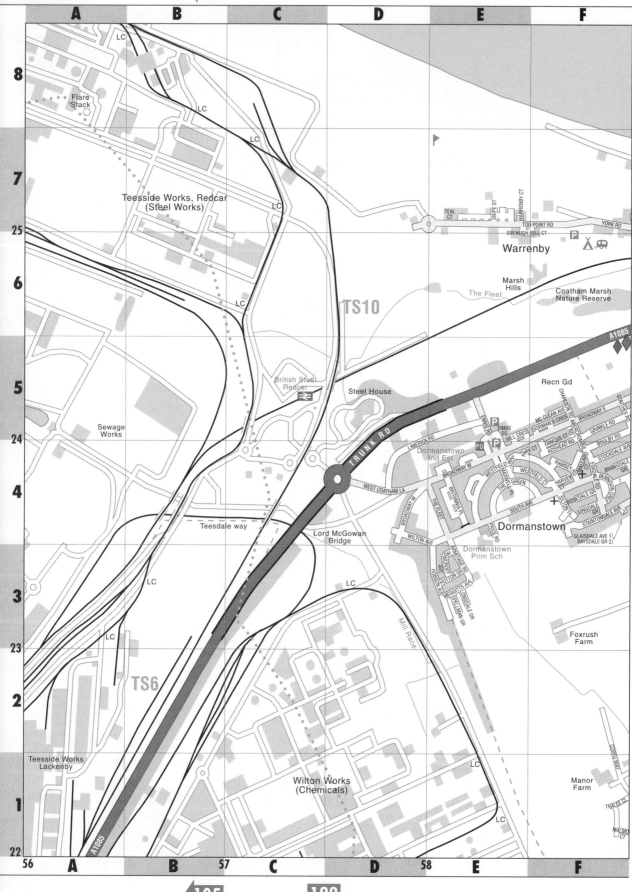

8

7

25

6

5

24

4

3

23

2

1

22

A B C D E F

Flare
Stack

Teesside Works, Redcar
(Steel Works)

LC

LC

LC

LC

LC

TS10

British Steel
Redcar

Steel House

Sewage
Works

Teesdale way

LC

LC

TS6

Teesside Works
Lackenby

Lord McGowan
Bridge

Wilton Works
(Chemicals)

LC

LC

LC

LC

Mill Race

Warrenby

TEAL
CT

SNIPE ST

WARRENBY CT

TOD POINT RD

SIR HUGH BELL CT

YORK RD

Marsh
Hills

The Fleet

Coatham Marsh
Nature Reserve

A1085

Recn Gd

TRUNK RD

WEST COATHAM LA

ENNIS RD

ENNIS
SQ

LIMERICK RD

BROADWAY W

Dormanstown
Ind Est

MC CLEAN AVE
DORMAN'S CRES
CHARLTON RD
ABERCROMBY RD
BROADWAY E
STAITHES RD
HILL CRES
FAWCUS CT
ADSHEAD RD
GRINKLE RD
BOULBY RD
RAMSEY
HARVEY
MAXWELL RD
WESTFIELD CT
WESTFIELD WAY
PARK CT
WESTFIELD
ESDALE RD
STOCKDALE RD
BRANSDALE
BEANLDS CRES
ROSEDALE GR
UPGDALE
GR
STAINTONDALE AVE

THE GREEN
BRITANNIA PL
SOUTH AVE
SILTON
THE FLEET

WILTON AVE

BROADWAY W

PRIDE RD

Dormanstown
Prim Sch

ARMITAGE RD
WALDROP
HUTTON GR
HOBSON AVE
SPELLMAN GR
CONSDALE GR
MEGGITTS AVE
TRALEE CL
CAVENDISH RD

Dormanstown

GLAISDALE AVE 1
BAYSDALE GR 2

Foxrush
Farm

Manor
Farm

COSBY WAY

TRALEE CL

MALMO
CT

A1085

108

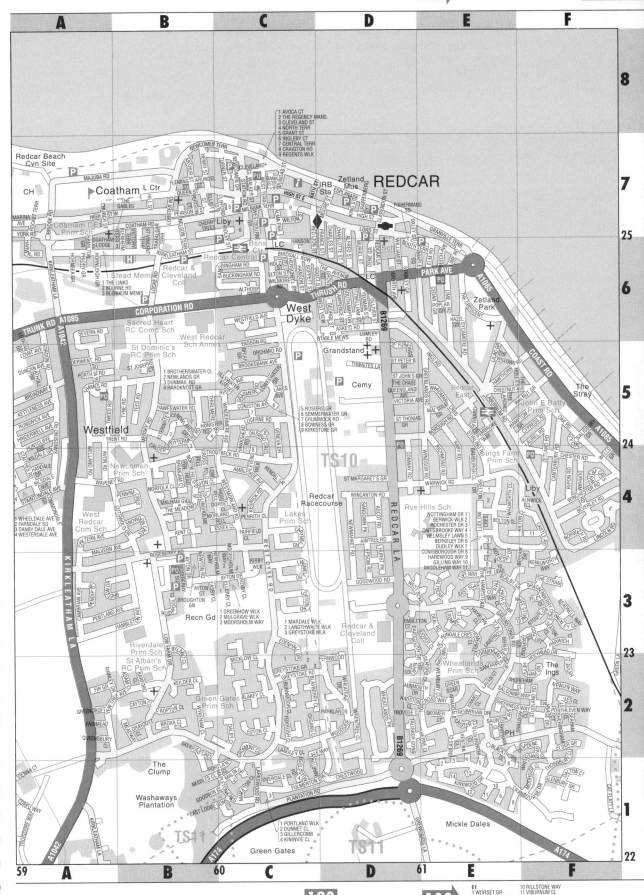

123
108

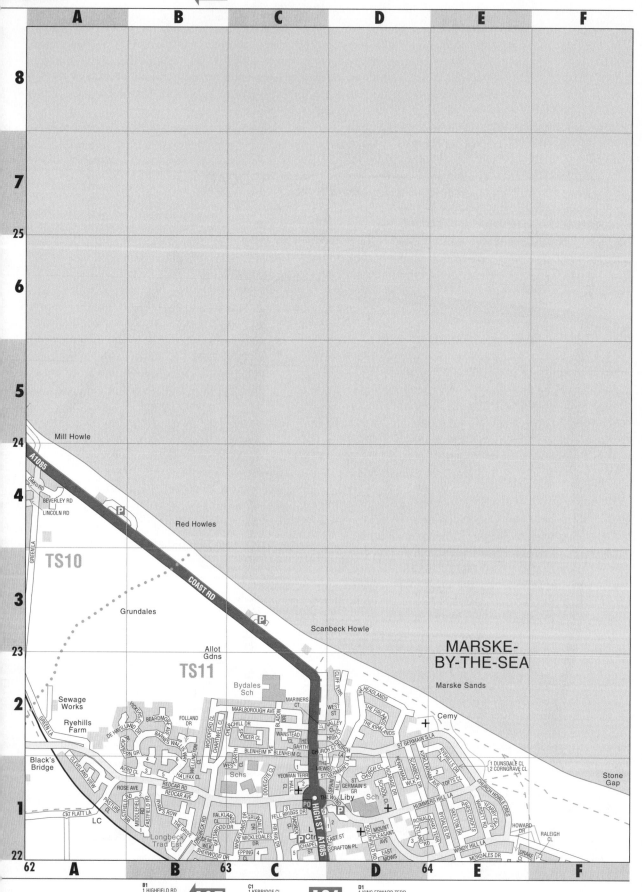

MARSKE-BY-THE-SEA

TS10

TS11

Mill Howle

Red Howles

Grundales

Scanbeck Howle

Marske Sands

Allot Gdns

Bydales Sch

Sewage Works

Ryehills Farm

Black's Bridge

Longbeck Trad Est

Cemy

Stone Gap

B1
1 HIGHFIELD RD
2 NORTHFIELD RD
3 SPITFIRE CL
4 LANCASTER DR
5 LYSANDER CT
6 BRABAZON DR

107

C1
1 KERRIDGE CL
2 ST MARK'S CL
3 GREENACRES CL
4 INGLEWOOD AVE
5 CHAPEL CL
6 ADELAIDE PL

124

D1
1 KING EDWARD TERR
2 THE CRESCENT
3 FITZWILLIAM CL

	A	B	C	D	E	F	
							8
							7
							25
							6
							5
							24
							4
							3
							23
							2
			Saltburn Sands				1
TS11							22
65	A	B 66	C	D 67	E	F	

201
94

A68

8

Houghton-le
-Side

Blue House
Farm

Side Hill

Hillside
Farm

Manor
House

Bolam
Grange

B6275

Kitching's
Plantation

Houghton
Grange

Great Boldearns
Hill

7

Sandforth
Moor

21

Ling
Plantations

6

Houghton
Plantation

Grimshaw
Hill

BLIND LA

Ling Beck

Ling
Bridge

HOUGHTON LA

Covertside

Dobinson's
Rush

5

East Limekiln
Banks

Denton Grange
Moor

Hopper's
Plantation

SUMMERHOUSE BACK LA

20

Banks
Cottage

Limekiln
Banks

DL2

Denton Grange
East

4

Denton Grange
West

Tenement Beck

Willow
Beds

Stripe
Plantation

Wry Nook
Plantation

North
Farm

Bow
Bridge

3

Summerhouse

Glebe
Farm

PH

PO

B6279

19

THE
GRANGE

Denton Hall Farm

RABY
COTTS

Denton Hall

The
Grange

Summerhouse Beck

Denton

Tomtit
Wood

2

DENTON
CROSS ROADS

NEW LA

DENTON HALL
COTTS

Castle
Farm

Kilnfield
Plantation

Ruffley
Hill

1

B6275

B6279

18

201
130

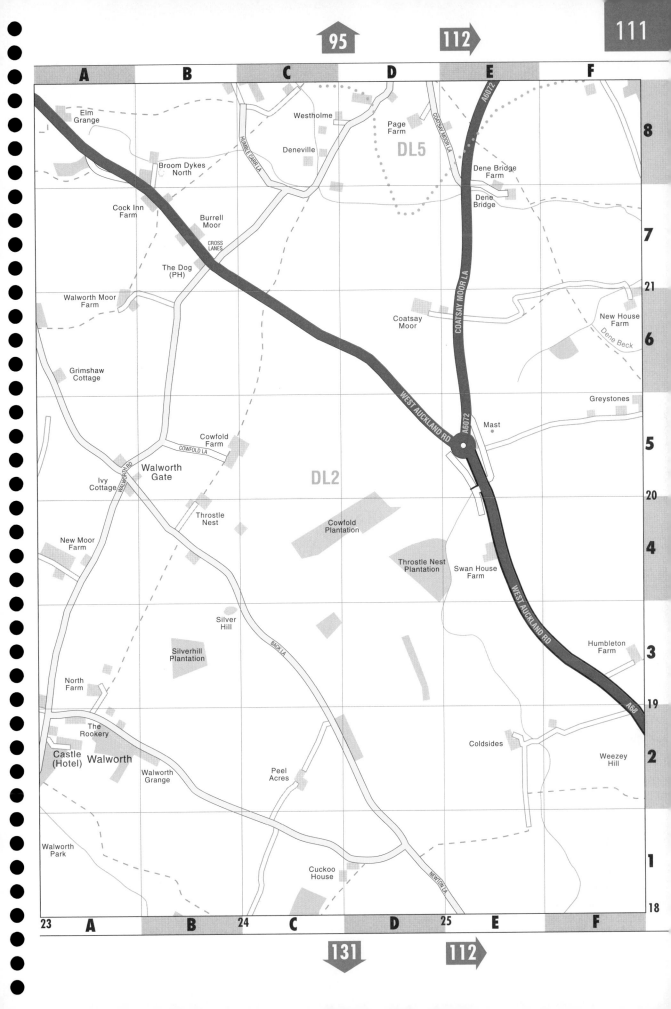

111
96

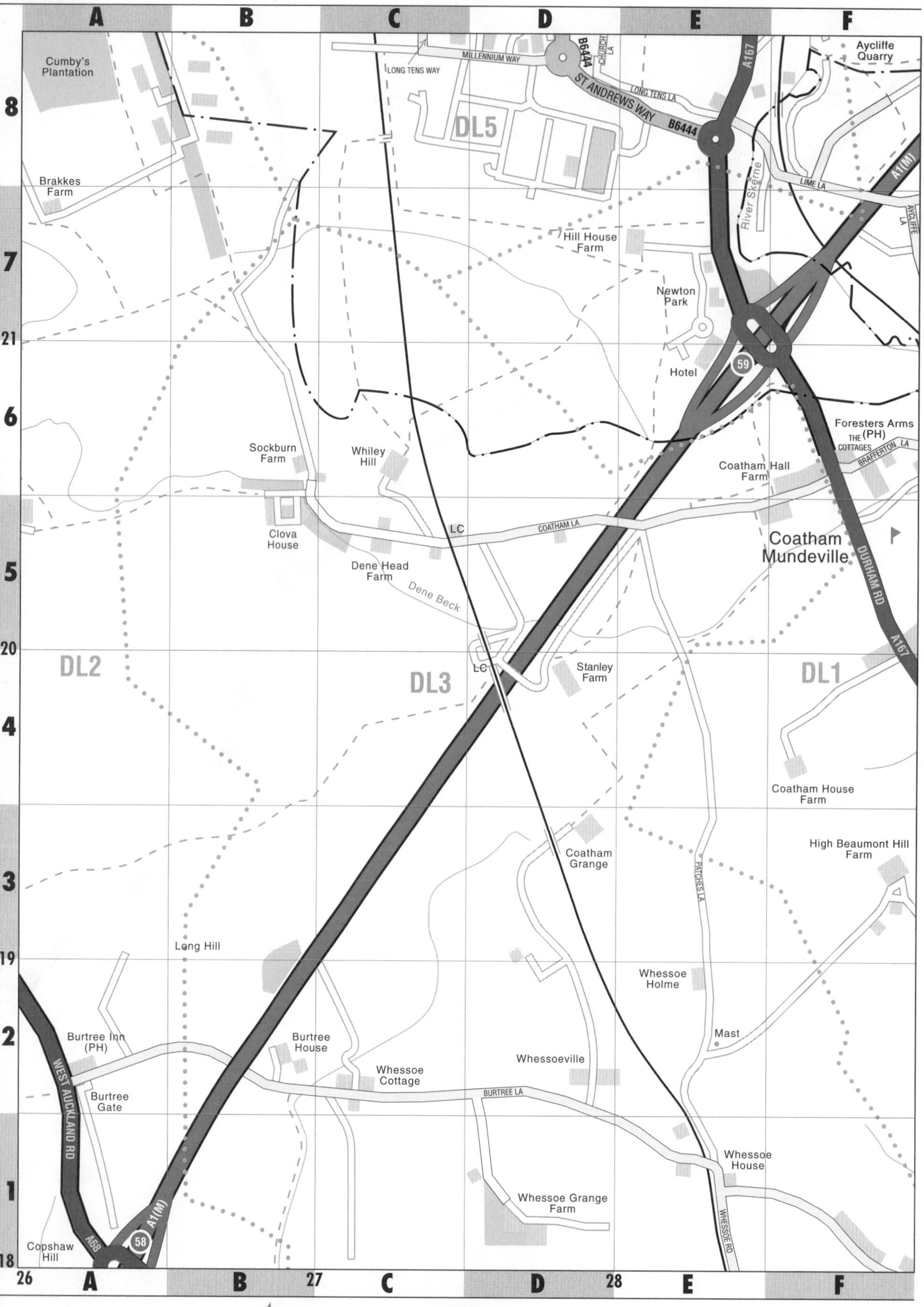

A   B   C   D   E   F

8

Cumby's
Plantation

DL5

B6444

Aycliffe
Quarry

St Andrews Way

Long Tens Way

Millennium Way

Long Tens La

B6444

A167

Brakkes
Farm

A1(M)

River Skerne

Lime La

Aycliffe

7

Hill House
Farm

Newton
Park

21

Hotel

59

6

Foresters Arms
(PH)
THE
COTTAGES

Brafferton La

Sockburn
Farm

Whiley
Hill

Coatham Hall
Farm

Clova
House

LC

Coatham La

Coatham
Mundeville

5

Dene Head
Farm

Dene Beck

Durham Rd

20

DL2

LC

DL3

Stanley
Farm

DL1

A167

4

Coatham House
Farm

3

Coatham
Grange

High Beaumont Hill
Farm

Patches La

19

Long Hill

Whessoe
Holme

Mast

2

Burtree Inn
(PH)

Burtree
House

Whessoeville

West Auckland Rd

Burtree
Gate

Whessoe
Cottage

Burtree La

Whessoe
House

1

A68

58

A1(M)

Whessoe Grange
Farm

Whessoe Rd

18

Copshaw
Hill

26   A   27   B   C   27   D   28   E   F

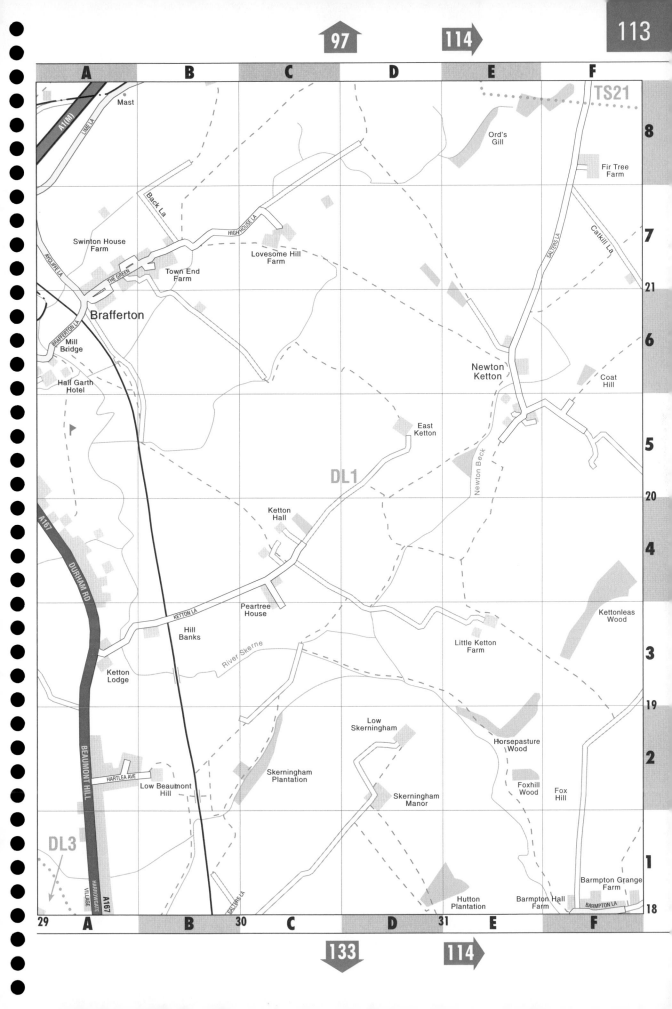

A   B   C   D   E   F

TS21

Mast

A1(M)

LIME LA

8

Ord's
Gill

Fir Tree
Farm

Back La

HIGH HOUSE LA

SALTERS LA

Catkill La

7

Swinton House
Farm

Lovesome Hill
Farm

THE GREEN

Town End
Farm

21

ANGLIFFE LA

Brafferton

BRAFFERTON LA

Mill
Bridge

Newton
Ketton

6

Coat
Hill

Hall Garth
Hotel

East
Ketton

Newton Beck

5

DL1

20

A167

DURHAM RD

Ketton
Hall

4

KETTON LA

Peartree
House

Kettonleas
Wood

Hill
Banks

River Skerne

Little Ketton
Farm

3

Ketton
Lodge

19

Low
Skerningham

Horsepasture
Wood

2

BEAUMONT HILL

HARTLEA AVE

Low Beaumont
Hill

Skerningham
Plantation

Skerningham
Manor

Foxhill
Wood

Fox
Hill

DL3

1

HARROWGATE
VILLAGE

A167

SALTERS LA

Barmpton Grange
Farm

Hutton
Plantation

Barmpton Hall
Farm

BARMPTON LA

18

29   A   B   30   C   D   31   E   F

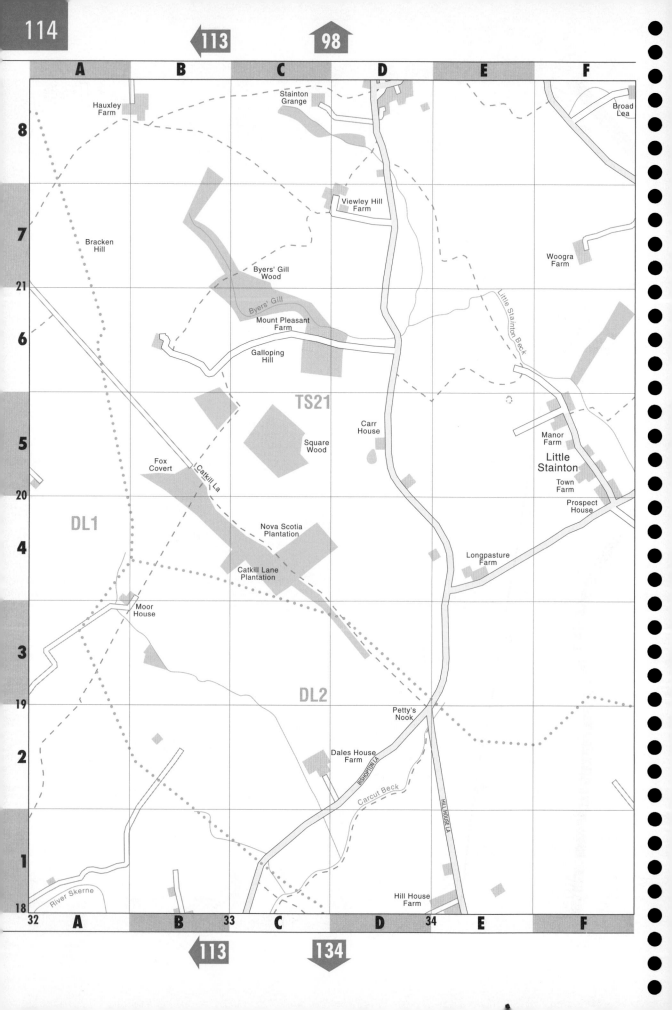

A   B   C   D   E   F

8

Hauxley
Farm

Stainton
Grange

Broad
Lea

7

Bracken
Hill

Viewley Hill
Farm

Woogra
Farm

21

Byers' Gill
Wood

Byers' Gill

6

Mount Pleasant
Farm

Galloping
Hill

Little Stainton Beck

TS21

Carr
House

Little
Stainton

Manor
Farm

5

Square
Wood

Town
Farm

Fox
Covert

Catkill La

20

DL1

Nova Scotia
Plantation

Prospect
House

4

Catkill Lane
Plantation

Longpasture
Farm

Moor
House

3

DL2

19

Petty's
Nook

2

Dales House
Farm

BISHOPTON LA

HILL HOUSE LA

Carcut Beck

1

18

River Skerne

Hill House
Farm

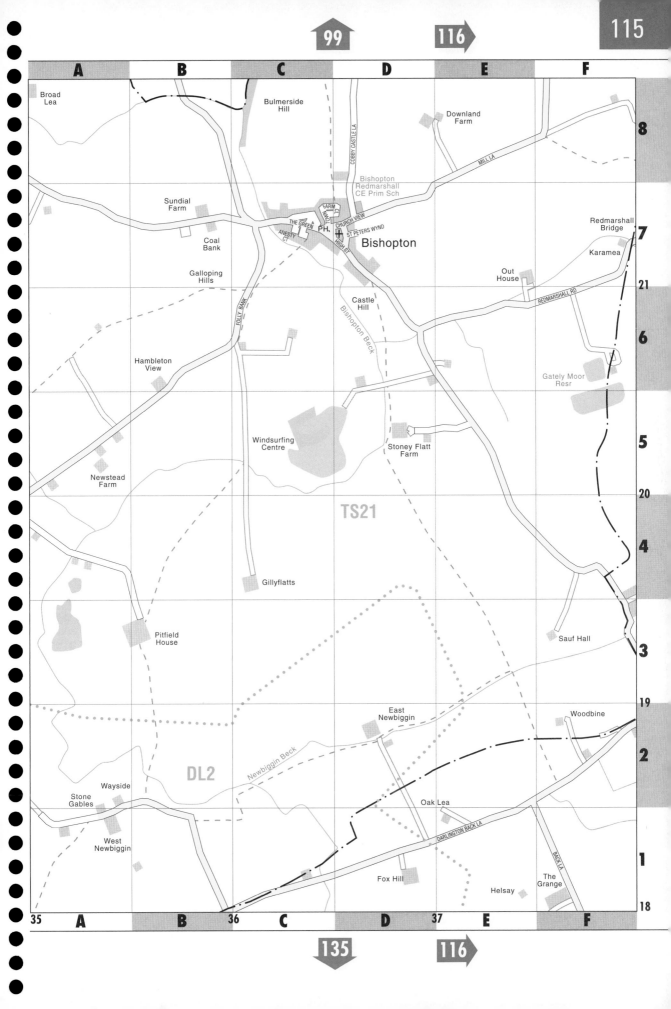

115 100

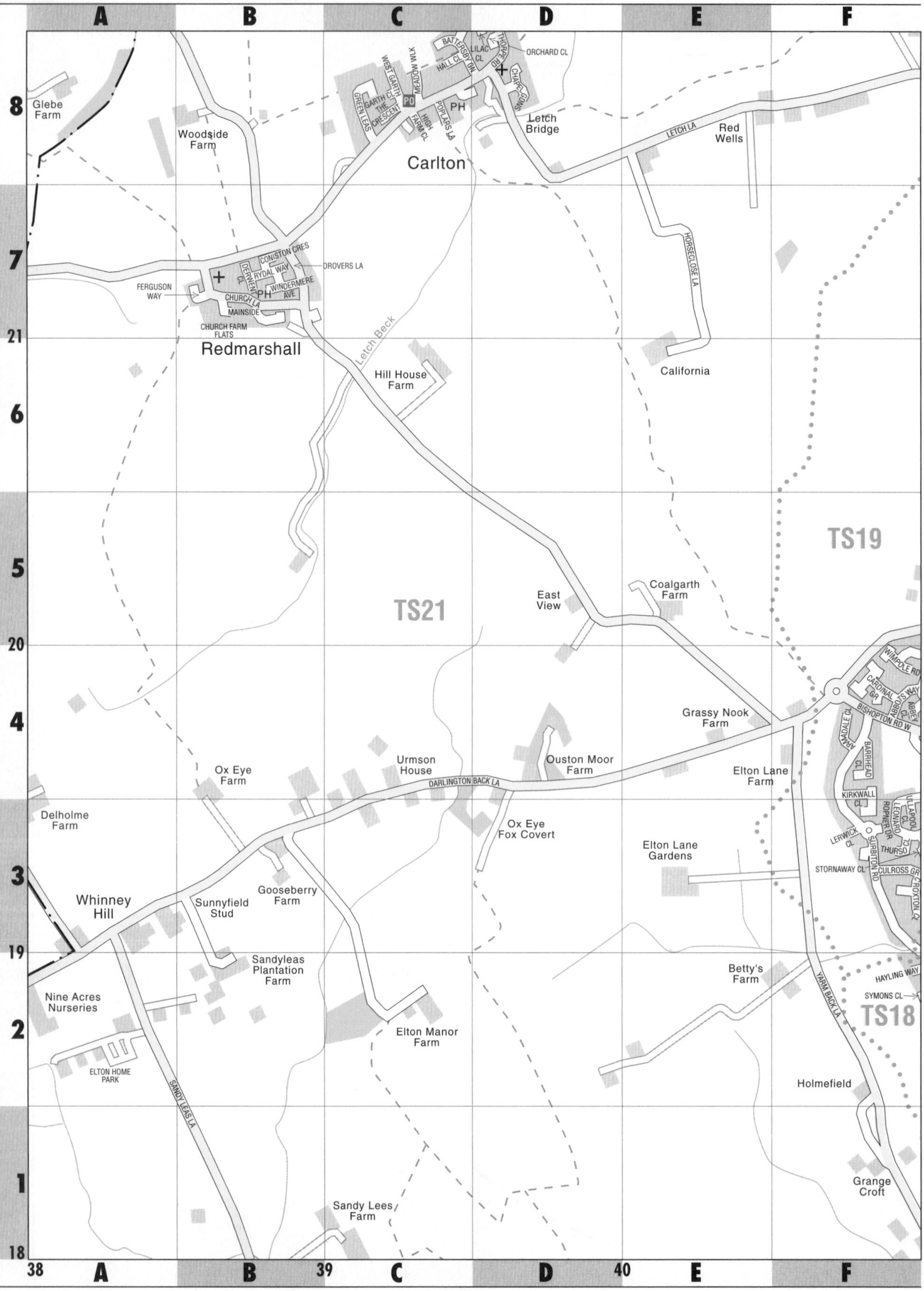

A B C D E F

8

Glebe Farm

Woodside Farm

WEST GARTH
THE CRESCENT
GREEN LEAS
MEADOW WK
WM WOODFM WK
POPLARS LA
HIGH HENN CL
BATTERSBY DR
HALL GT
LILAC CL
THORPE DR
CHAPEL DRNS
ORCHARD CL

PO
PH

Letch Bridge

Carlton

LETCH LA
Red Wells

7

FERGUSON WAY

CONISTON CRES
RYDAL WAY
DERWENT WAY
CHURCH LA
MAINSIDE
PH
WINDERMERE AVE
DROVERS LA

CHURCH FARM FLATS

Redmarshall

HORSECLOSE LA

21

Hill House Farm

California

Letch Beck

6

TS19

5

East View

Coalgarth Farm

TS21

20

Grassy Nook Farm

4

Ox Eye Farm

Urmson House

DARLINGTON BACK LA

Ouston Moor Farm

Elton Lane Farm

WHIMPLE RD
CARDINAL GR
ASHBY
BISHOPTON RD W
ARMADALE
SOMERBY
CROSBY CT
LS WAY
BARRHEAD CL

Delholme Farm

Ox Eye Fox Covert

Elton Lane Gardens

KIRKWALL CL
LERWICK CL
ULLAPOOL
LEONARD
ROPNER DR
THURSO
STORNAWAY CL
CULROSS GR
CROYTON CT
SURBITON RD

3

Whinney Hill

Sunnyfield Stud

Gooseberry Farm

19

Sandyleas Plantation Farm

Betty's Farm

HAYLING WAY
SYMONS CL

Nine Acres Nurseries

TS18

2

ELTON HOME PARK

SANDY LEAS LA

Elton Manor Farm

YARM BACK LA

Holmefield

1

Grange Croft

Sandy Lees Farm

18

38 A B 39 C D 40 E F

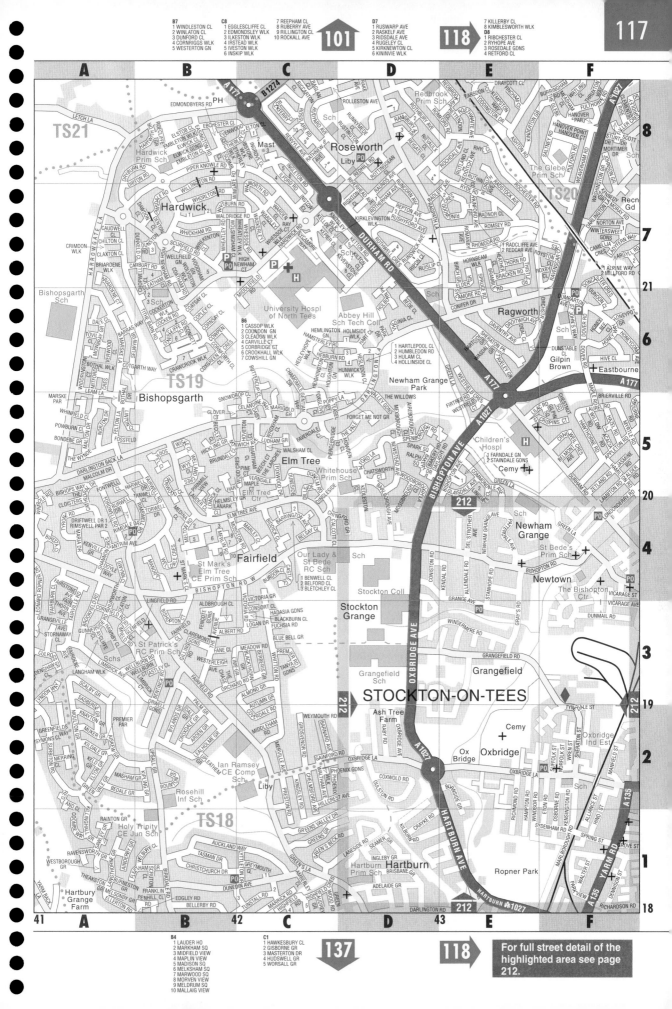

B7
1 WINDLESTON CL
2 WINLATON CL
3 DUNFORD CL
4 CORNRIGGS WLK
5 WESTERTON GN

C8
1 EGGLESCLIFFE CL
2 EDMONDSLEY WLK
3 ILKESTON WLK
4 IRSTEAD WLK
5 IVESTON WLK
6 INSKIP WLK

7 REEPHAM CL
8 RUBERRY AVE
9 RILLINGTON CL
10 ROCKALL AVE

101

D7
1 RUSWARP AVE
2 RASKELF AVE
3 RIDSDALE AVE
4 RUGELEY CL
5 KININVIE WLK

7 KILLERBY CL
8 KIMBLESWORTH WLK

118

D8
1 RIBCHESTER CL
2 RYHOPE AVE
3 ROSEDALE GDNS
4 RETFORD CL

B4
1 LAUDER HO
2 MARKHAM SQ
3 MIDFIELD VIEW
4 MAPLIN VIEW
5 MADISON SQ
6 MELKSHAM SQ
7 MARWOOD SQ
8 MORVEN VIEW
9 MELDRUM SQ
10 MALLAIG VIEW

C1
1 HAWKESBURY CL
2 GISBORNE GR
3 MASTERTON DR
4 HUDSWELL GR
5 WORSALL GR

137

118

For full street detail of the highlighted area see page 212.

A8
1 GILPIN HO
2 ANSTEY HO
3 RAGWORTH PL
4 CAMERON ST
5 NEWBY CL
6 COLPITT CL
7 SUMMERHOUSE SQ

B7
1 HARLAND PL
2 CHAPMAN ST
3 HOLLY ST
4 WRIGHTSON ST
5 CHESTERTON CT
6 OAKLANDS AVE
7 WESTLANDS AVE

117

B8
1 FOX ALMSHOUSES
2 PICTON PL
3 MALDEN RD
4 BEACONSFIELD RD
5 MAYBRAY KING WLK
6 RIDLEY MEWS

102

B8
7 SMIRKS YD
8 THORP MEWS
9 DRAGON CT
10 MILL MEADOW CT

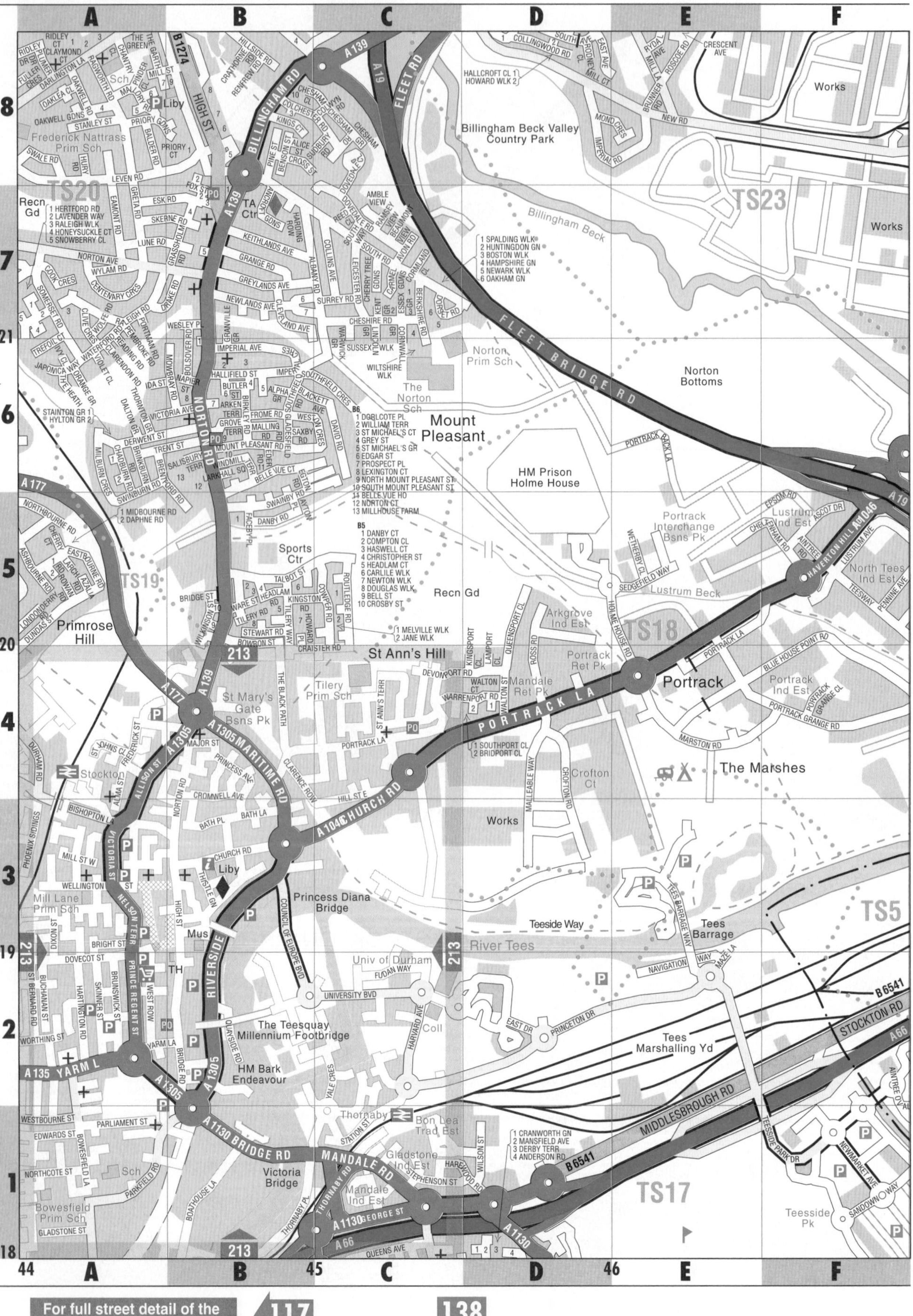

For full street detail of the highlighted area see page 213.

117
138

For full street detail of the highlighted area see pages 214 and 215.

F1
1 PALLADIUM BLDGS
2 CROFTON AVE
3 HAWTHORNE AVE
4 ROSECROFT AVE

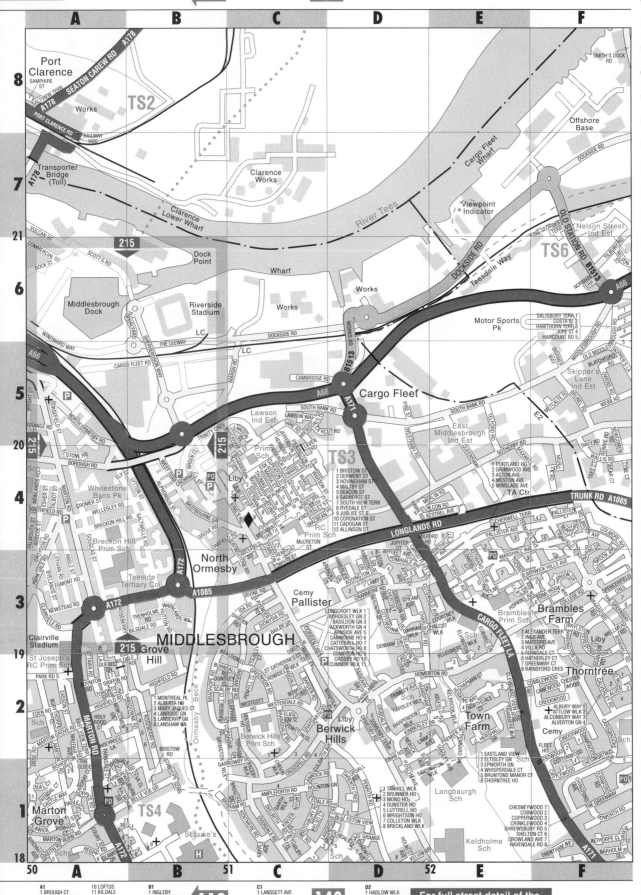

119 104

A B C D E F

8 Port Clarence
SAMPHIRE ST
SALTVIEW TERR
Works
TS2
Clarence Works

7 Transporter Bridge (Toll)
RAILWAY HOS
Clarence Lower Wharf
River Tees
Cargo Fleet Wharf
Viewpoint Indicator
Offshore Base
SMITH'S DOCK RD
DOCKSIDE RD

21 VULCAN ST
COMMERCIAL ST
SCOTT'S RD
215
Dock Point
Wharf
DOCKSIDE RD
Teesdale Way
OLD STATION RD B1513
Nelson Street Ind Est
TS6

6 Middlesbrough Dock
Riverside Stadium
LC
Works
Works
WORKS RD
DOCKSIDE RD
Cargo Fleet
Motor Sports Pk
SALISBURY TERR 1
COSTA ST 2
HAWTHORN TERR 3
AIRE ST 4
HARCOURT RD 5
Skipper's Lane Ind Est

5 BRIGHT ST
A66
WINDWARD WAY
THE LEEWAY
CARGO FLEET RD
LC
CAMBRIDGE RD
A66
B1513
A171
SOUTH BANK RD
East Middlesbrough Ind Est

20 GRANGE RD
215
ELSTONE RD
BOROUGH RD
NORTH ORMESBY RD
TRINITY CRES
215
Lawson Ind Est
SOUTH BANK WAY
TS3
1 BRISTOW ST
2 DERWENT ST
3 HOVINGHAM ST
4 MALTBY ST
5 DEACON ST
6 SADBERGE ST
7 SOUTH VIEW TERR
8 RYEDALE ST
9 JUBILEE ST.S
10 CORONATION ST
11 CADOGAN ST
12 ALLINSON ST
1 PORTLAND HO
2 GRIMWOOD AVE
3 ASTON AVE
4 WESTON AVE
5 WINSLADE AVE
TA Ctr

4 Whitestone Bsns Pk
Breckon Hill Prim Sch
RC Prim Sch
McCreton
TRUNK RD A1085
LONGLANDS RD
PALLISTER AVE

3 Teeside Tertiary Coll
A172
A1085
North Ormesby
Cemy Pallister
1 ALEXANDER TERR
2 INGS AVE
3 MATFORD AVE
4 VILLA RD
5 FERNDALE CT
6 HATHERLEY CT
7 GREENWAY CT
8 RAINSFORD CRES
Brambles Farm
Brambles Prim Sch
Liby

19 Clairville Stadium
St Joseph's RC Prim Sch
215
Grove Hill
MIDDLESBROUGH
1 LONGCROFT WLK
2 BORDESLEY GN
3 BASILDON GN
4 ACKWORTH GN
5 ARNSIDE AVE
6 CAMBORNE HO
7 CATTERALL HO
8 CHATSWORTH HO
9 COMPTON HO
10 CROSBY RD
11 CUMNOR WLK
Thorntree

2 MARTON RD
HOLY ROOD
1 MONTREAL PL
2 ALBERTA HO
3 MARY JAQUES CT
4 LANROOD GN
5 LANBERRY GN
6 LANSHAW GN
Berwick Hills Prim Sch
Berwick Hills
Liby
Town Farm
1 ALBURY WAY 1
2 ATTLOW WLK 2
3 ALCONBURY WAY 3
4 ALVERTON GN 4
Cemy
1 EASTLAND VIEW
2 ELTISLEY GN
3 EPWORTH GN
4 WHISPERDALE CT
5 BRUNTONS MANOR CT
6 THORNTREE HO

1 Marton Grove
TS4
A172
St Luke's
H
1 TANHILL WLK
2 BRUNNER HO
3 MOND HO
4 DUNSTER HO
5 LUTTRELL HO
6 WRIGHTSON HO
7 COLLETON WLK
8 BRECKLAND WLK
Langbaurgh Sch
Keldholme Sch
CHESNEYWOOD 1
COBWOOD 2
COPPERWOOD 3
CRINKLEWOOD 4
SHREWSBURY RD 5
SHELTON CT 6
CROWLAND AVE 7
RAVENDALE RD 8
A171

18
50 A 51 B C 52 D E F

A1
1 BROUGH CT
2 HEADINGHAM CL
3 SUNLEY AVE
4 BARNARD CT
5 BEECHWOOD AVE
6 BELVEDERE RD
7 ST LUKE'S COTTS
8 NEWBY
9 MALTBY
10 LOFTUS
11 KILDALE
B1
1 INGLEBY
2 FLAMBOROUGH
3 ESCOMB
4 DURHAM
5 CORBY
6 BAMBOROUGH
7 ALNWICK
8 GUISBOROUGH
9 HAREWOOD
C1
1 LANSSETT AVE
2 ROSSETT WLK
3 SAMUELSON HO
4 ASKRIGG WLK
C2
1 WESTCROFT
2 EASTCROFT
3 GILLING WLK
4 BARSBY GN
D2
1 HADLOW WLK
2 FIRSBY WLK
3 MALLING WLK
4 GATWICK GN
5 GARSDALE GN

119 140

For full street detail of the highlighted area see page 215.

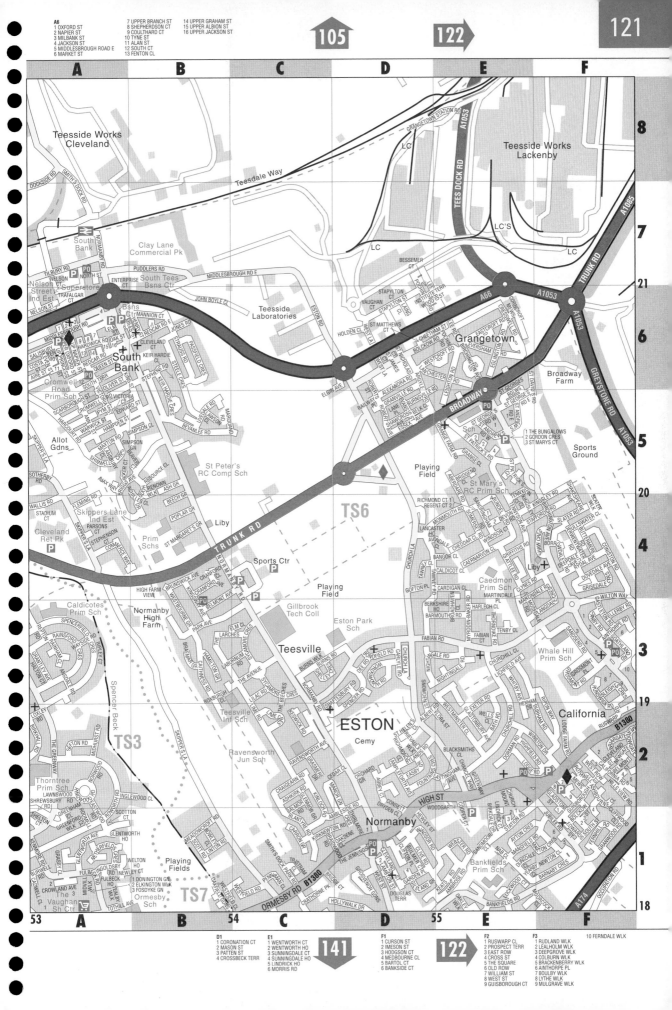

A B C D E F

8

Teeside
Works
Lackenby
LC
LC
LC

TRUNK RD

A1085

TS10

7

Wilton Works

A174

21

6

Power Sta

TS6

5

A1053

GREYSTONE RD

Resrs

North
Lodge

20

Wilton
Prim Sch

Lazenby

GRANGE EST
PARRINGTON
RD
PASTURE LA
LILAC CL
NORTH
QUEEN
CHAPEL
ST
HIGH ST
ROW

TS10

WILTON
VILLAGE

Wilton

4

LACKENBY
RD
WILTON GN
ESTON RD
TURNER PH
TERR
CHESTNUT

Wilton
Wood

Broom
Hill

CH

WILTON
CASTLE

High
Farm

A1053

A174

LAZENBY BANK RD

Lackenby

BLAKEY
WLK
1 BAYSDALE WLK
2 GLAISDALE RD
LACKENBY LA
CASBY
INGLEBY CL
KIRBY CL

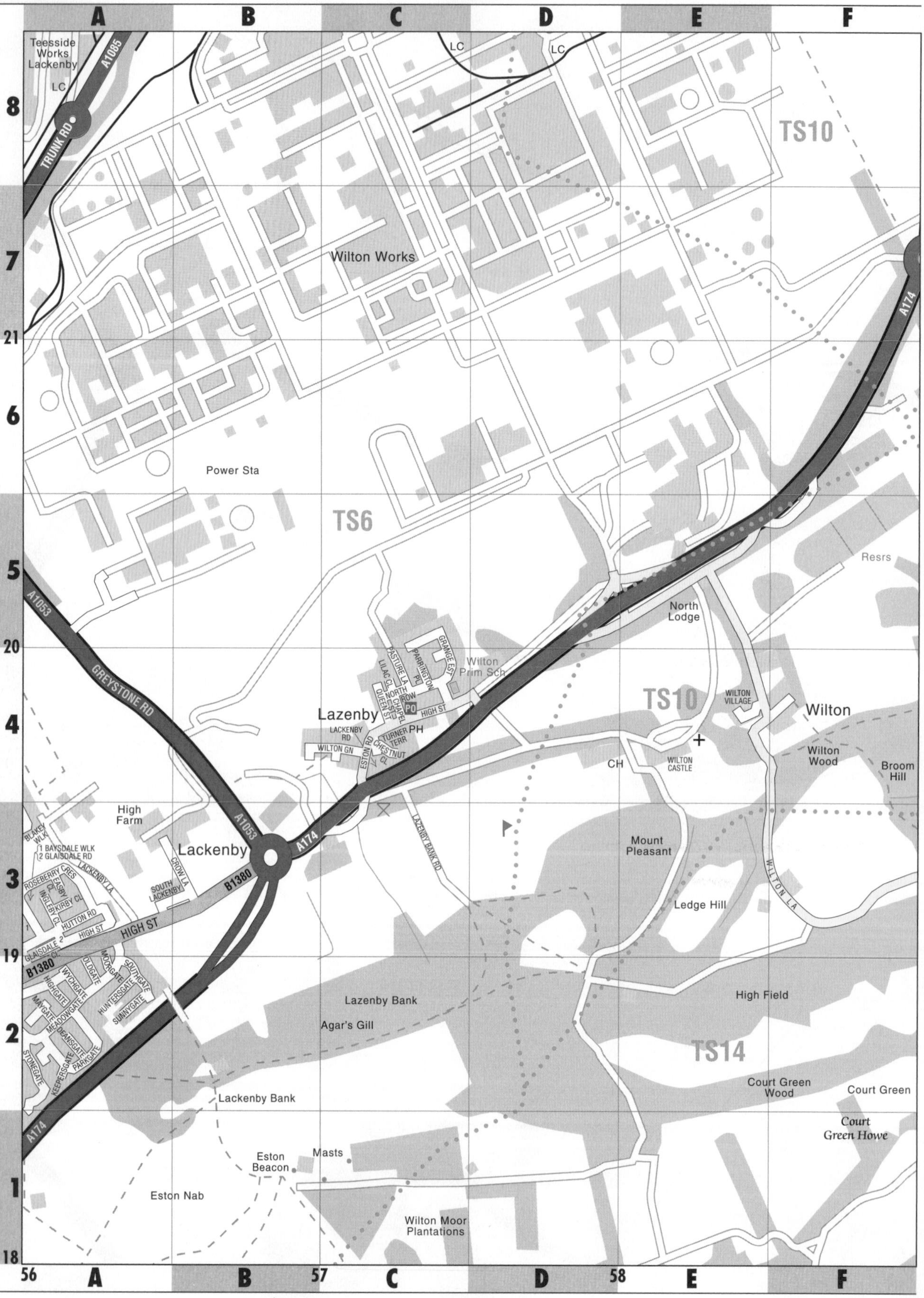

ROSEBERRY CRES

B1380

CROW LA

SOUTH
LACKENBY

Mount
Pleasant

WILTON LA

3

HUTTON RD

HIGH ST

Ledge Hill

GLAISDALE CL

B1380

HIGHGATE
WYCHGATE
MAYGATE
KEEPERSGATE
MILDRINSGATE
RAMSGATE
PARKGATE
STONEGATE
MOORGATE
SOUTHGATE
HUNTERSGATE
SUNNYGATE
MEADOWGATE

19

HIGH ST

High Field

2

Lazenby Bank

Agar's Gill

TS14

Court Green
Wood

Court Green

A174

Lackenby Bank

Court
Green Howe

Eston
Beacon

Masts

1

Eston Nab

Wilton Moor
Plantations

18

56 A B 57 C D 58 E F

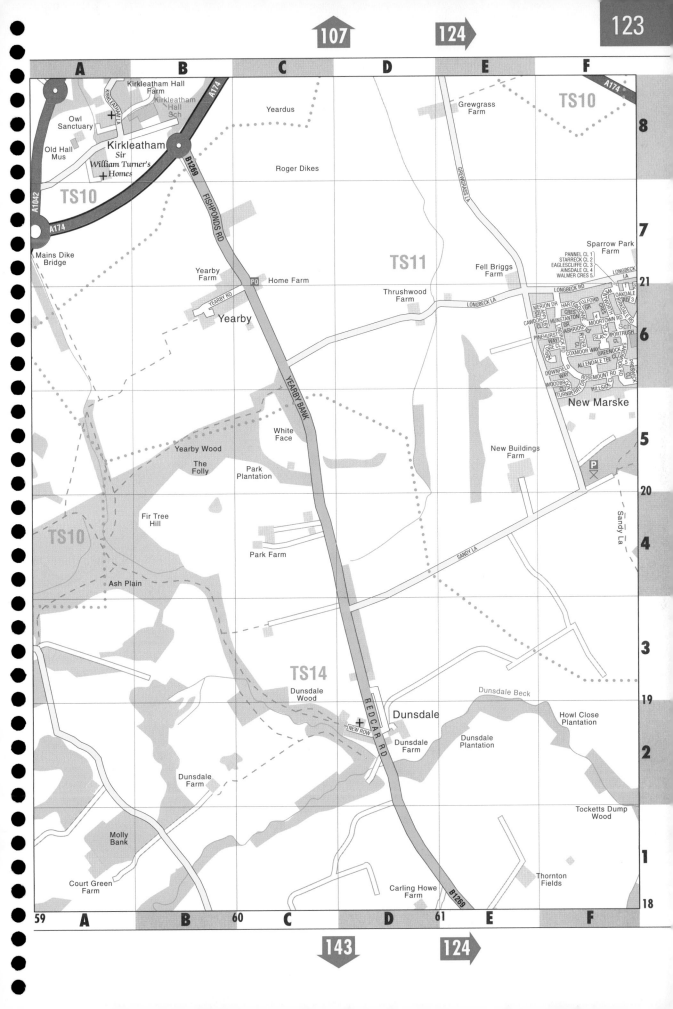

TS10

Kirkleatham Hall Farm

Owl Sanctuary

Kirkleatham Hall Sch

Old Hall Mus

Kirkleatham
Sir
William Turner's
Homes

TS10

Yeardus

Grewgrass Farm

TS10

Roger Dikes

Mains Dike Bridge

Yearby Farm

Home Farm

TS11

Fell Briggs Farm

Sparrow Park Farm

PANNEL CL 1
STARRECK CL 2
EAGLESCLIFFE CL 3
AINSDALE CL 4
WALMER CRES 5

Yearby

Thrushwood Farm

Longbeck La

Longbeck Rd

New Marske

White Face

Yearby Wood

The Folly

Park Plantation

New Buildings Farm

Fir Tree Hill

TS10

Park Farm

Sandy La

Ash Plain

Sandy La

TS14

Dunsdale Wood

Dunsdale Beck

Howl Close Plantation

Dunsdale

New Row

Dunsdale Farm

Dunsdale Plantation

Dunsdale Farm

Tocketts Dump Wood

Molly Bank

Court Green Farm

Carling Howe Farm

Thornton Fields

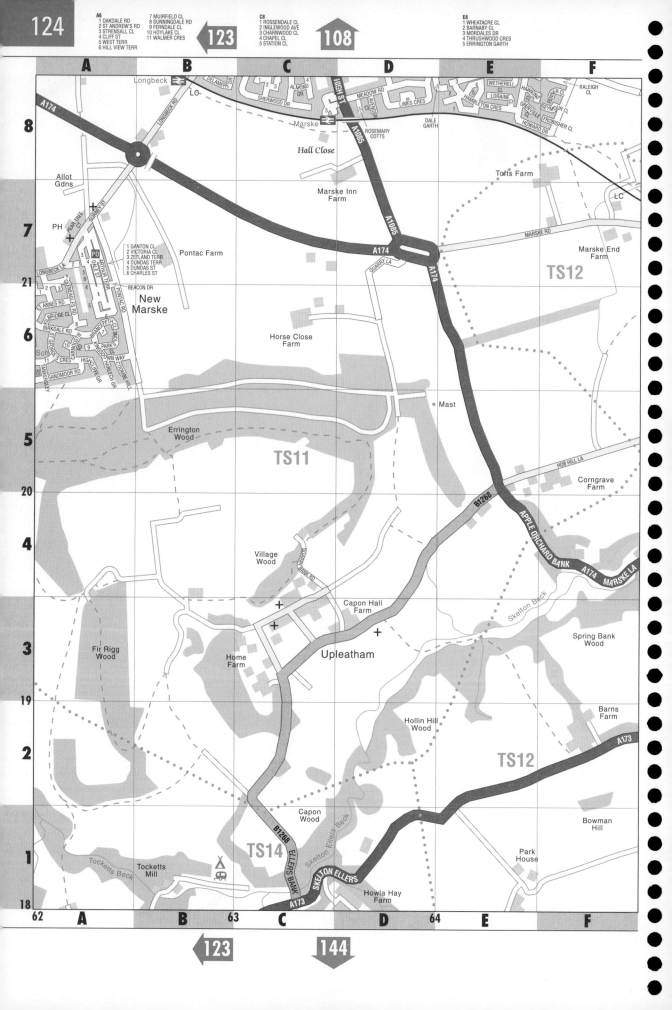

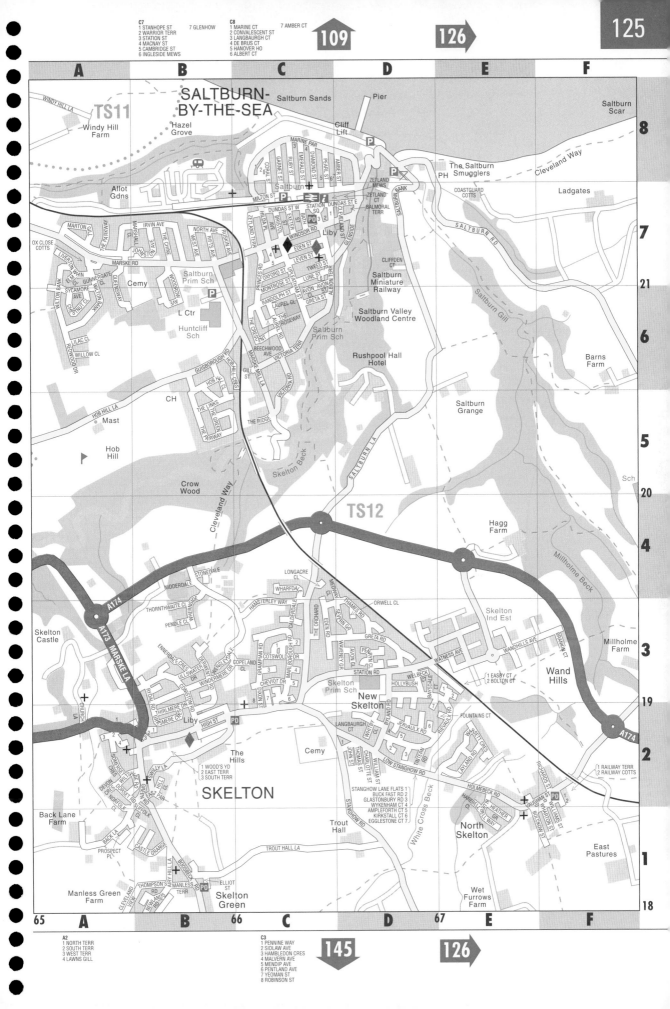

125

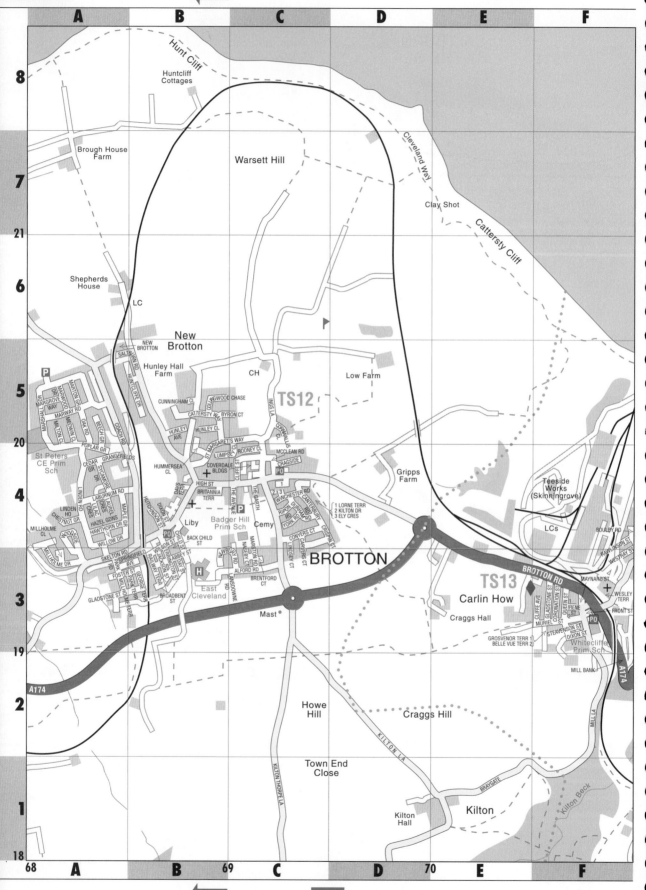

125

146

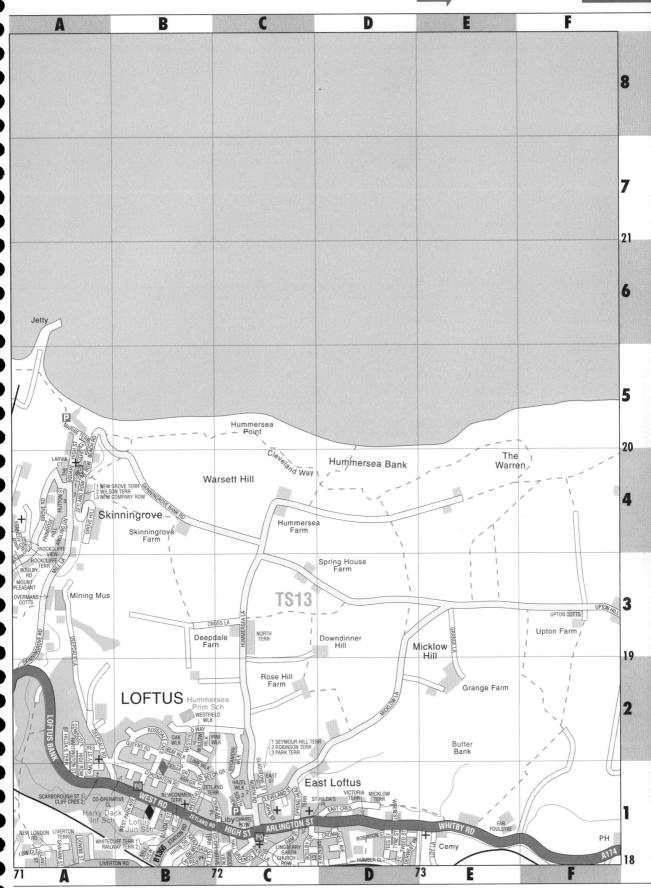

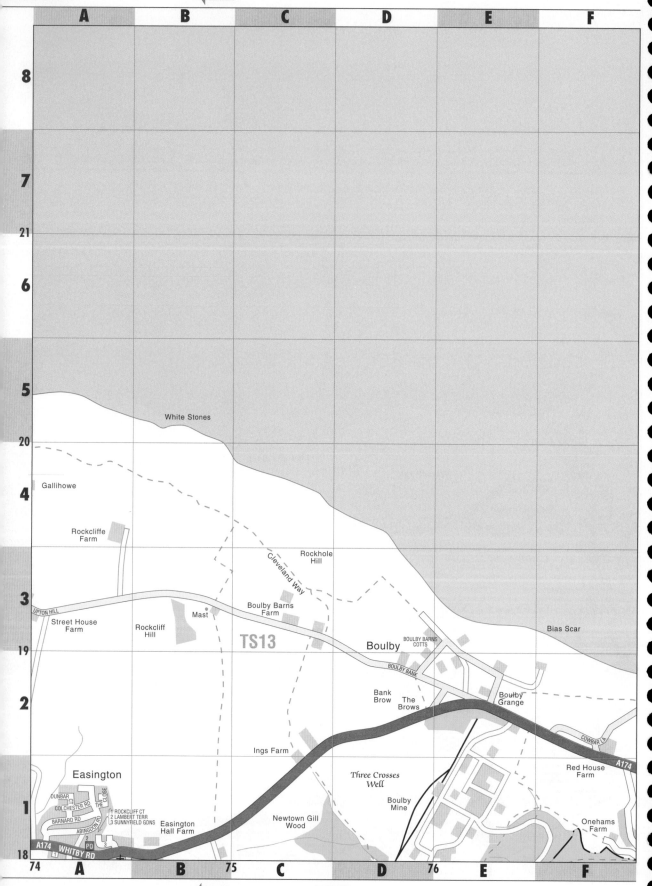

A B C D E F

8

7

21

6

5

White Stones

20

4

Gallihowe

Rockcliffe
Farm

Rockhole
Hill

Cleveland Way

3

UPTON HILL

Street House
Farm

Rockcliff
Hill

Mast

Boulby Barns
Farm

TS13

BOULBY BARNS
COTTS

Boulby

Bias Scar

19

BOULBY BANK

2

Bank
Brow

The
Brows

Boulby
Grange

COWBAR LA

Ings Farm

Three Crosses
Well

Red House
Farm

A174

1

Easington

DUNBAR
COLCHESTER RD
BARNARD RD
ABINGDON RD
THE CLOSE
1 ROCKCLIFF CT
2 LAMBERT TERR
3 SUNNYFIELD GDNS

Easington
Hall Farm

Newtown Gill
Wood

Boulby
Mine

Onehams
Farm

18

A174

WHITBY RD

74

A

B

75

C

D

76

E

F

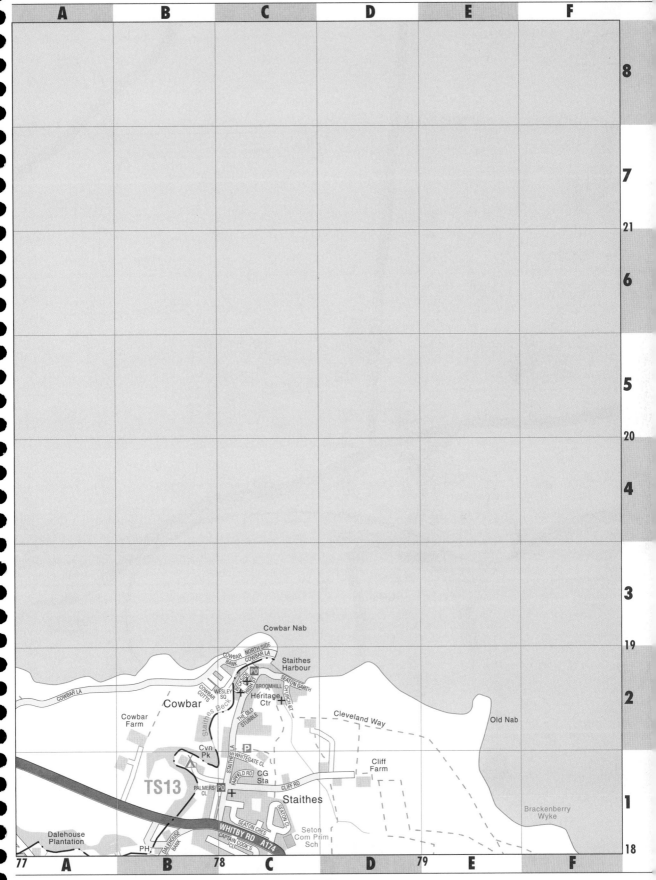

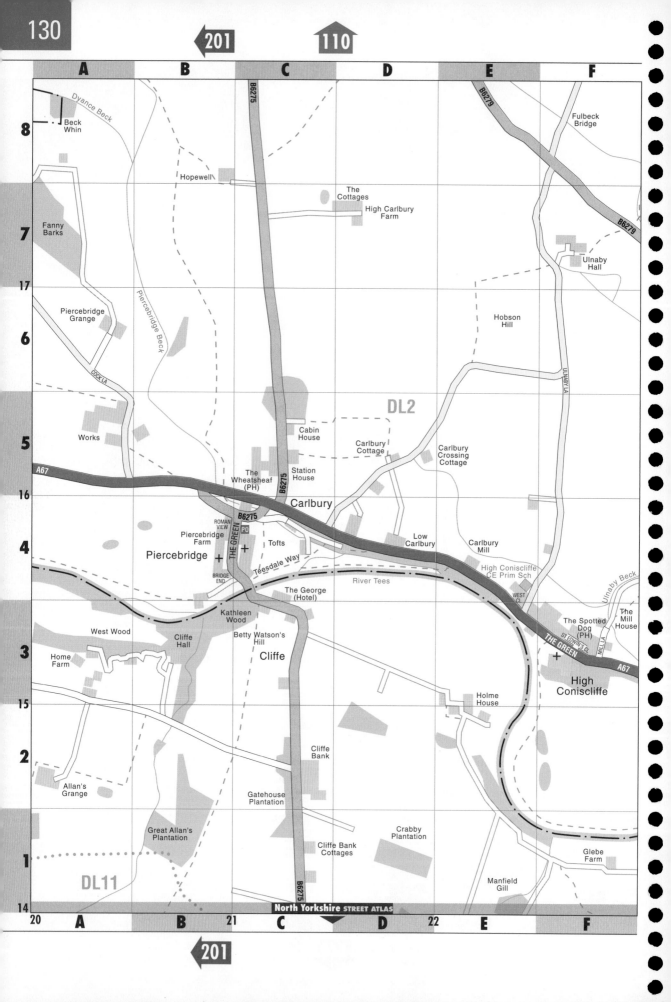

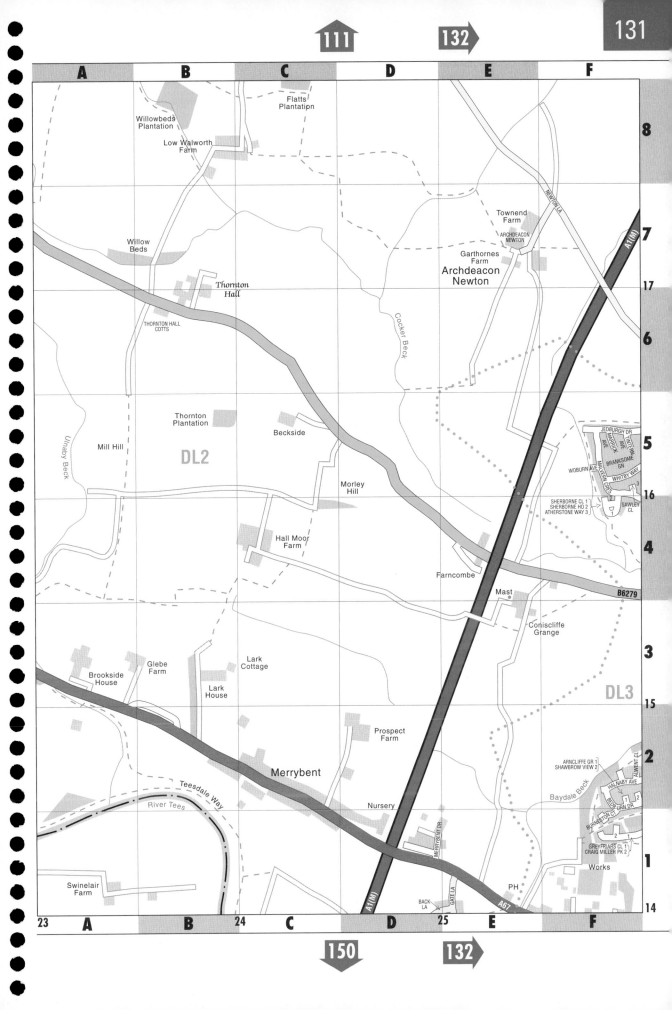

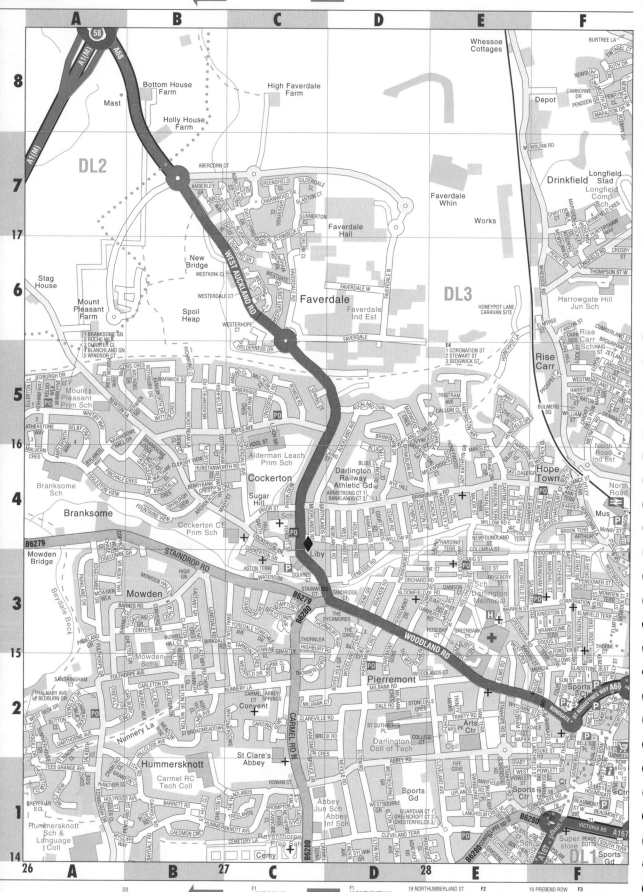

D3
1 HEATHERWOOD GR
2 THE HAWTHORNS
3 THE CEDARS

F1
1 EAST RABY ST
2 GARSDALE CT
3 BUCKDEN CT
4 ARCADIA CT
5 POST HOUSE WYND
6 BUCKTON'S YD
7 CLARK'S YD
8 EAST ROW
9 CHURCH ROW

F1
10 BAKEHOUSE HILL
11 HORSE MARKET
12 MARKET PL
13 BLACKWELLGATE
14 HOUNDGATE MEWS
15 CHANCERY LA
16 ST AUGUSTINE'S CT
17 LARCHFIELD HO
18 HOGARTH CT

19 NORTHUMBERLAND ST
20 WELLINGTON COURT MEWS
21 SOUTH ARDEN ST
22 FEETHAMS
23 FEETHAMS S
24 OAKLEA CT

F2
1 KING ST
2 GRACE CT
3 UPPER ARCHER ST
4 TEMPERANCE PL
5 UNION ST
6 QUEEN ST
7 CROWN ST
8 WINSTON ST
9 PROSPECT PL

10 PREBEND ROW
11 PRIESTGATE
12 CORNMILL CTR
13 ASHFIELD CT

F3
1 MARBURN PL
2 MELVILLE ST
3 WESTBROOK TERR
4 DENE PARK CT
5 CHELMSFORD ST
6 OAKLANDS TERR
7 DERWENT ST

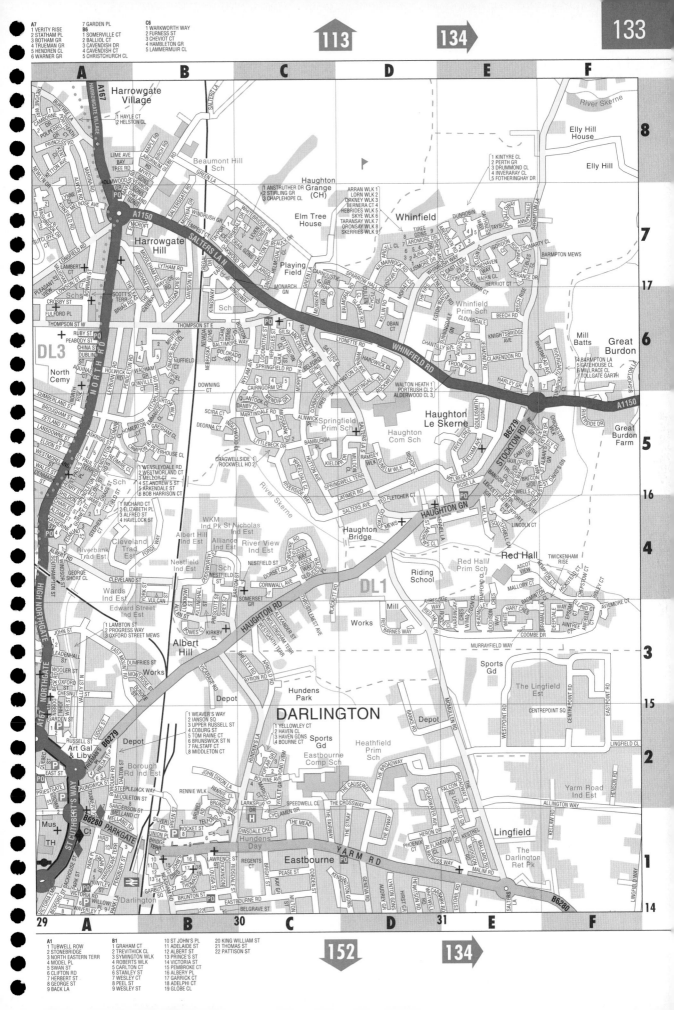

133
114

A B C D E F

8

Burdon
Hall

Burdon
Gardens

BISHOPTON LA

7

Sadberge
CE Prim Sch

Hill
Cottage

HILLHOUSE LA

NORTON BACK LA

17

Carcut Beck

Works

GOODWOOD
CL

Well House
Farm

CHAPEL RD

NORTON CRES

NORTON RD

DALE RD

THE ORCHARD 1
EAST VIEW 2
STAINTON VIEW 3
HILLSIDE TERR 4
LAUREL TERR 5
CHURCH VIEW 6
DARLINGTON RD 7

PO 3

EAST CL

2 1

6   5

ABBEY RD

Buck Inn
(PH)

STOCKTON RD

6

DL1

Village
Hall

WEST VIEW

BEACON
GRANGE PK

CHURCH
LA

MIDDLETON RD

Sadberge

A66

Beacon
Hill

Sadberge Resr
(dis)

BEACON HILL

Lea
Close

A1150

5

Little
Burdon

Bumper
Hall

16

Toft
Hill

BUESS LA

4

Sadberge Hall
Farm

Sadberge
Hall

Street House
Farm

DL2

3

The
Kennels

15

South
Burdon

Midway
Farm

2

LINGFIELD CL

LINGFIELD WAY

DUDLEY RD

Ashtree
Cottage

SADBERGE RD

Highfield
Farm

ALLINGTON
WAY

Locomotive
Sculpture

Morton Palms
Farm

GEORGE'S GATE

Allot
Gdns

The
Fighting Cocks
(PH)

1

MORTON RD

PALMS
CT

Palm
Bridge

HAXBY RD

STATION RD

1 HARPERS TERR
2 STATION TERR

A67

Yarm Road
Ind Est

WILD RD
Woodlands

H

Morton
Park

A66

Acolan
House

A67

PALM TREE
VILLAS

HEATHFIELD PK

14

32   A   B   33   C   D   34   E   F

133
153

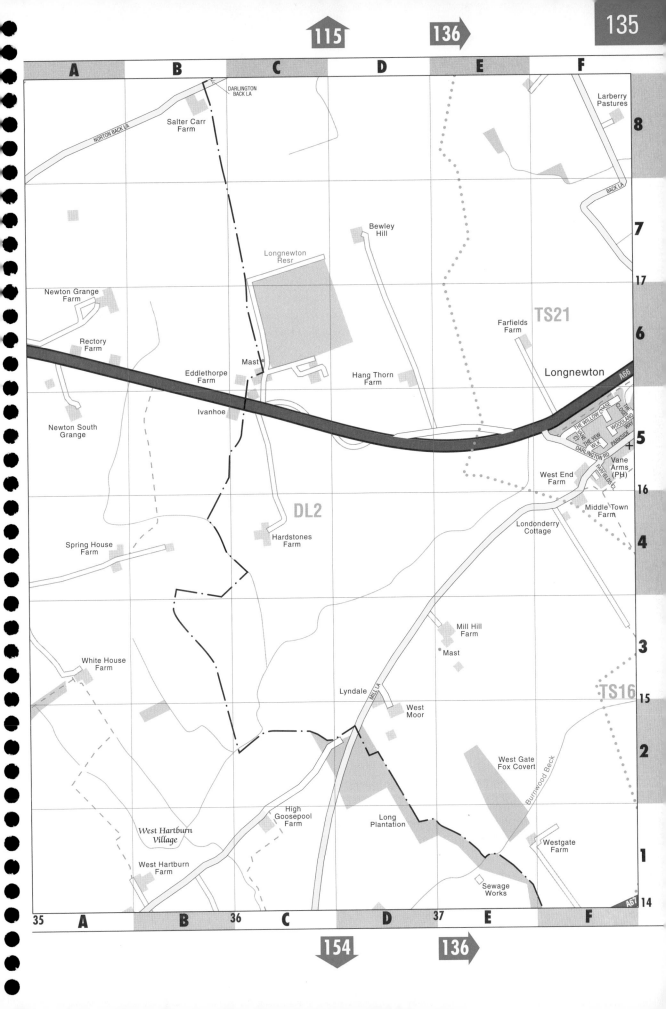

A   B   C   D   E   F

DARLINGTON BACK LA

Larberry
Pastures

Salter Carr
Farm

8

NORTON BACK LA

BACK LA

Bewley
Hill

7

Longnewton
Resr

17

Newton Grange
Farm

TS21

Farfields
Farm

6

Rectory
Farm

Longnewton

A66

Eddlethorpe
Farm

Mast

Hang Thorn
Farm

THE WILLOW CHASE
THE YEW WLK
VANE CT
WOODLAND WAY
PARKSIDE
LODGE FR

Ivanhoe

Newton South
Grange

DARLINGTON RD
FARFIELDS CL

5

Vane
Arms
(PH)

West End
Farm

DL2

16

Middle Town
Farm

Hardstones
Farm

Londonderry
Cottage

Spring House
Farm

4

Mill Hill
Farm

Mast

3

White House
Farm

Lyndale

MILL LA

15

West
Moor

TS16

West Gate
Fox Covert

2

Burnwood Beck

High
Goosepool
Farm

Long
Plantation

Westgate
Farm

West Hartburn
Village

1

West Hartburn
Farm

Sewage
Works

A67

14

35   A   B   36   C   D   37   E   F

135 116

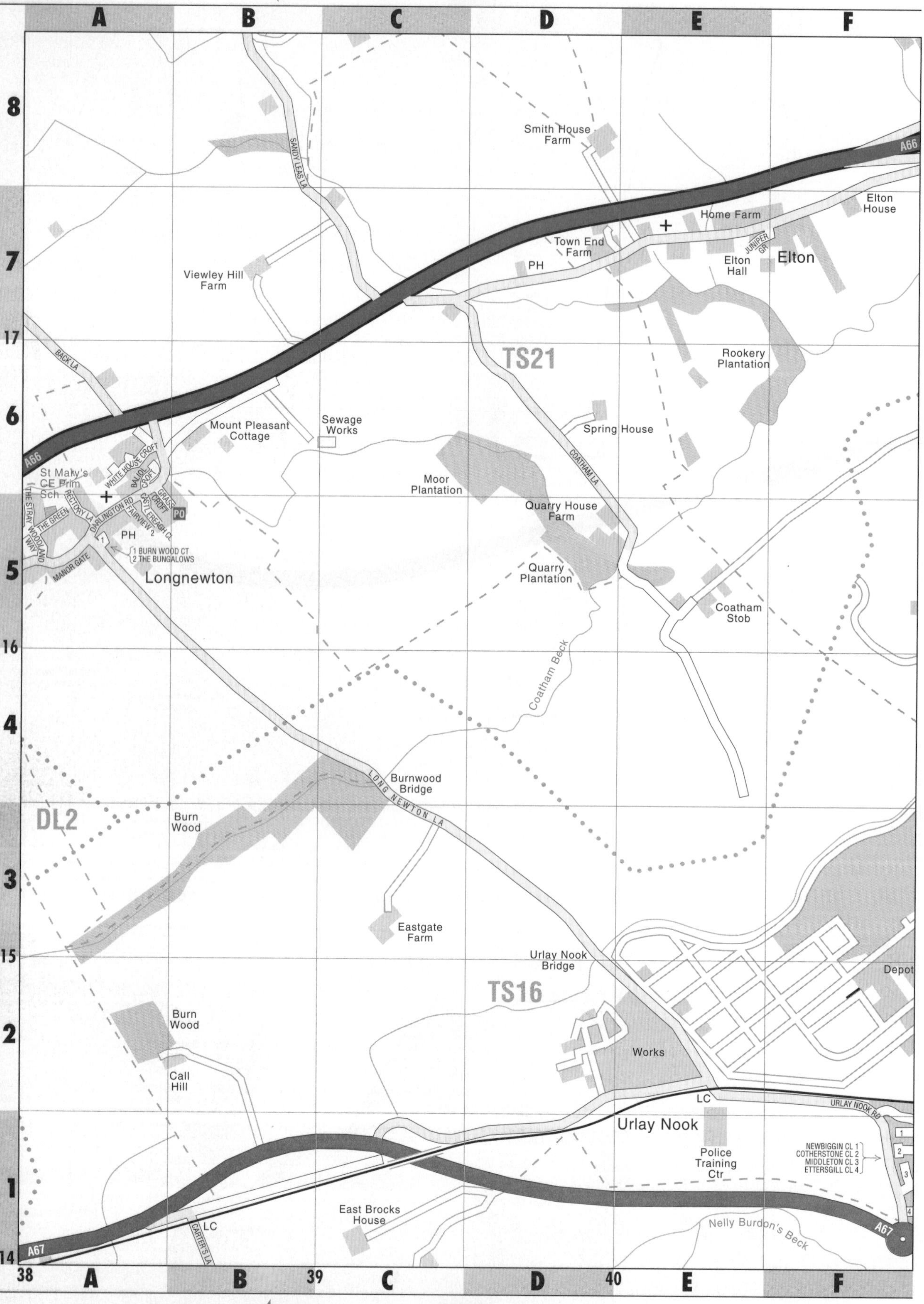

A B C D E F

8

Smith House Farm

A66

Elton House

Home Farm

7

Town End Farm

Viewley Hill Farm

PH

Elton Hall

JUNIPER GR

Elton

17

BACK LA

Rookery Plantation

TS21

6

Mount Pleasant Cottage

Sewage Works

Spring House

A66

COATHAM LA

St Mary's CE Prim Sch

WHITE HOUSE CROFT

BARON CROFT

GRASS CROFT

Moor Plantation

THE STRAY

WOODLAND WAY

THE GREEN

RECTORY LA

DARLINGTON RD

CROFT TERRACE

CL

FAIRVIEW 2

PO

Quarry House Farm

5

PH

MANOR GATE

1

1 BURN WOOD CT
2 THE BUNGALOWS

Longnewton

Quarry Plantation

Coatham Stob

16

Coatham Beck

4

LONG NEWTON LA

Burnwood Bridge

DL2

Burn Wood

3

Eastgate Farm

15

Urlay Nook Bridge

TS16

Depot

2

Burn Wood

Works

NEWBIGGIN CL 1
COTHERSTONE CL 2
MIDDLETON CL 3
ETTERSGILL CL 4

Call Hill

LC

URLAY NOOK RD

1

Urlay Nook

Police Training Ctr

1
2
3

East Brocks House

Nelly Burdon's Beck

A67

A67

14

LC

CARTER LA

LC

38 A B 39 C D 40 E F

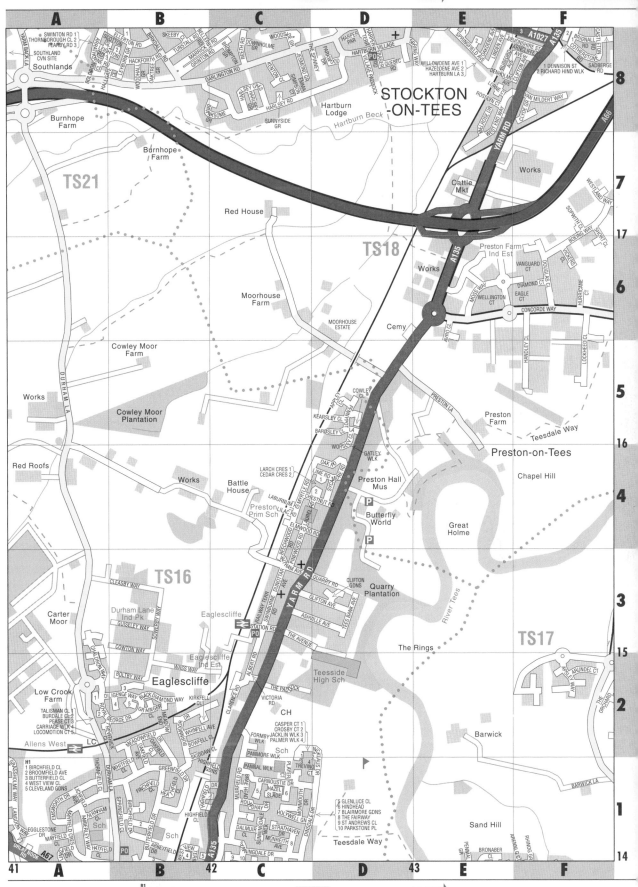

STOCKTON-ON-TEES

TS21

TS18

TS16

TS17

Preston-on-Tees

Eaglescliffe

B1
1 BIRCHFIELD CL
2 BROOMFIELD AVE
3 BUTTERFIELD CL
4 WEST VIEW CL
5 CLEVELAND GDNS

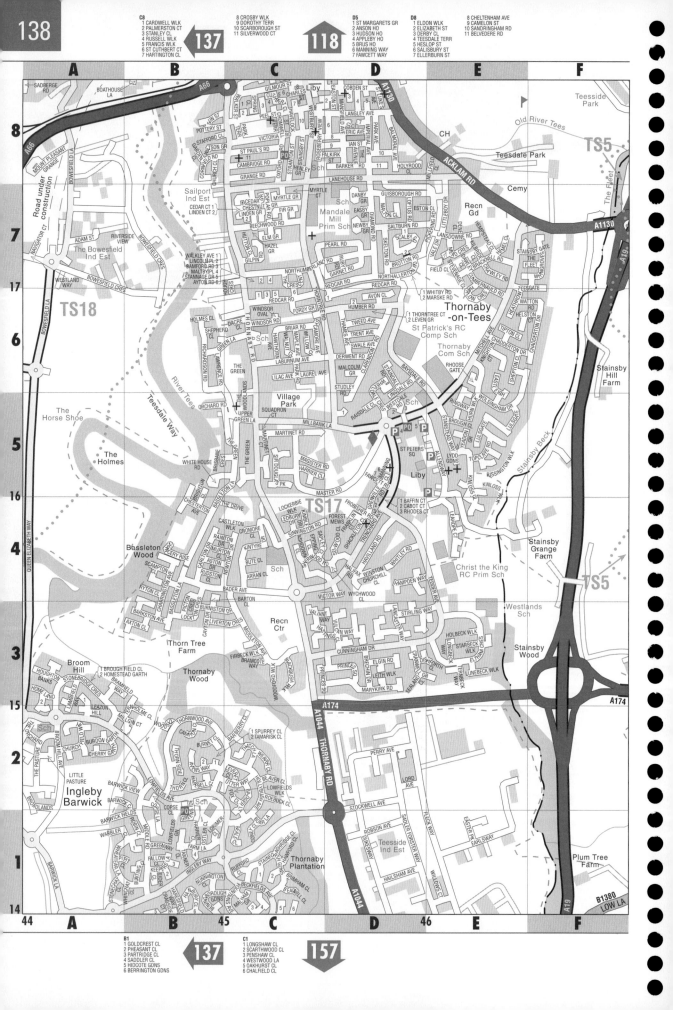

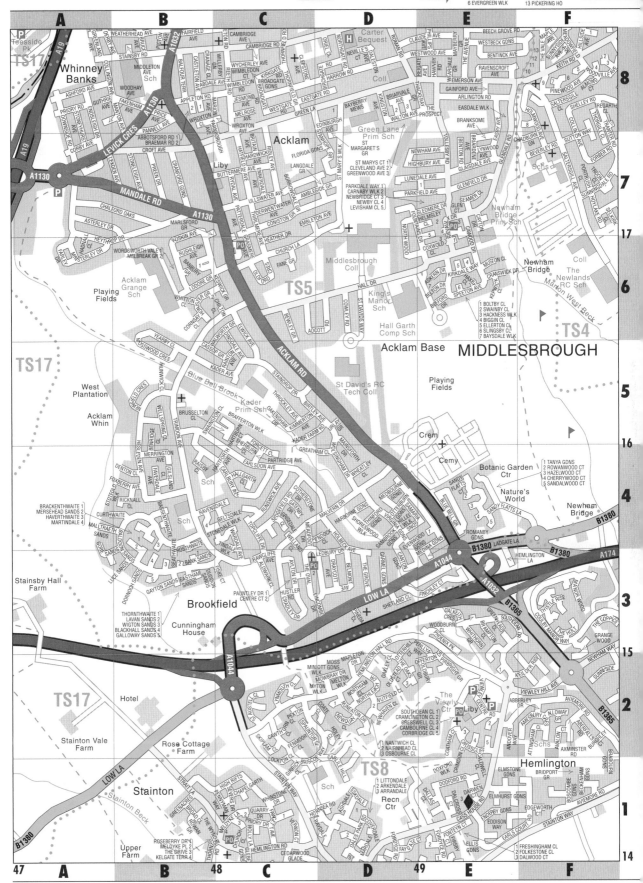

F8
1 CROSTHWAITE AVE
2 MULBERRY CT
3 KEITHWOOD CL
4 WHITEBEAM CT
5 ELDERWOOD CT
6 EVERGREEN WLK
7 LIMETREE CT
8 BROOKSIDE AVE
9 HOLLYHURST AVE
10 SWALEDALE HO
11 FROME HO
12 MOWBRAY HO
13 PICKERING HO

◄ 139   120

D8
1 KIRKLAND WLK
2 ILSTON GN
3 CORYTON WLK
4 CORSHAM WLK
5 COPLEY WLK
6 COPNOR WLK

7 CHADWELL AVE
8 CHEADLE WLK
9 CHATTON CL
10 PHYLLIS MOHAN CT
11 LUDFORD AVE
12 MARGROVE WLK
13 LANGLEY CT

E8
1 ANGLESEY AVE
2 DUNMOW AVE
3 BUSHMEAD TERR
4 ORMSTON AVE
5 ORDSALL GN
6 CHETWODE TERR

7 CROXDEN GR
8 GLASTONBURY HO
9 KEYNSHAM AVE
F8
1 ALVINGHAM TERR
2 WOBURN GR
3 SAWTRY RD

4 KIRKSTALL AVE
5 VICTORIA GDNS
6 PARK AVE N
7 SOMERVILLE AVE

MIDDLESBROUGH

TS3

TS4

TS5

TS7

TS8

Park End

Beechwood

Easterside

Tollesby

Coulby Newham

Marton

The James Cook University

St Luke's

Middlesbrough Coll

Prissick Sports Ctr

Prissick Farm

Stewart Park

Centre Lodge

Captain Cook's Birthplace Mus

Ormesby Hall

Ormesby Grange

The Park

Low Gill

Inwood Lodge

Slip Inn Bridge

Police HQ

Newham Grange Leisure Farm

Paddock Wood

Hollowfield

The King's Acad

Mast

Riding Ctr

Lingfield Prim Sch

Langdon Sq

Alderwood

MARTON RD

LADGATE LA

STOKESLEY RD

DIXONS BANK

A174

A172

A171

B1380

B1365

The Gardens

Allot Gdns

1 ABBERSTON WLK
2 GLEASTON WLK
3 GLENEAGLES CT
4 FORMBY GN
5 MUIRFIELD WAY
6 AINSDALE WAY

ASTONBURY GN 1
ALBOURNE GN 2
DIPTON GN 3
DUNBAR AVE 4
EPSOM AVE 5

ISLINGTON WLK 1
PENSBY AVE 2
WESTWICK TERR 3

LANGRIDGE CRES 1
ROSSETT WLK 2
BRIDNOR RD 3
FARNHAM WLK 4

1 PENNYMAN CT
2 HOLME CT

1 SOUTHMEAD AVE
2 RUNNYMEAD GN
3 STONOR WLK

GLAMIS GN 1
MARSDEN CL 2
BRETBY CL 3

Ridgeway TA Ctr

Parkway Ctr

Cath

F3
1 RUFFORD CL
2 HULTON CL
3 RIBBLETON CL
4 SCOTFORTH CL

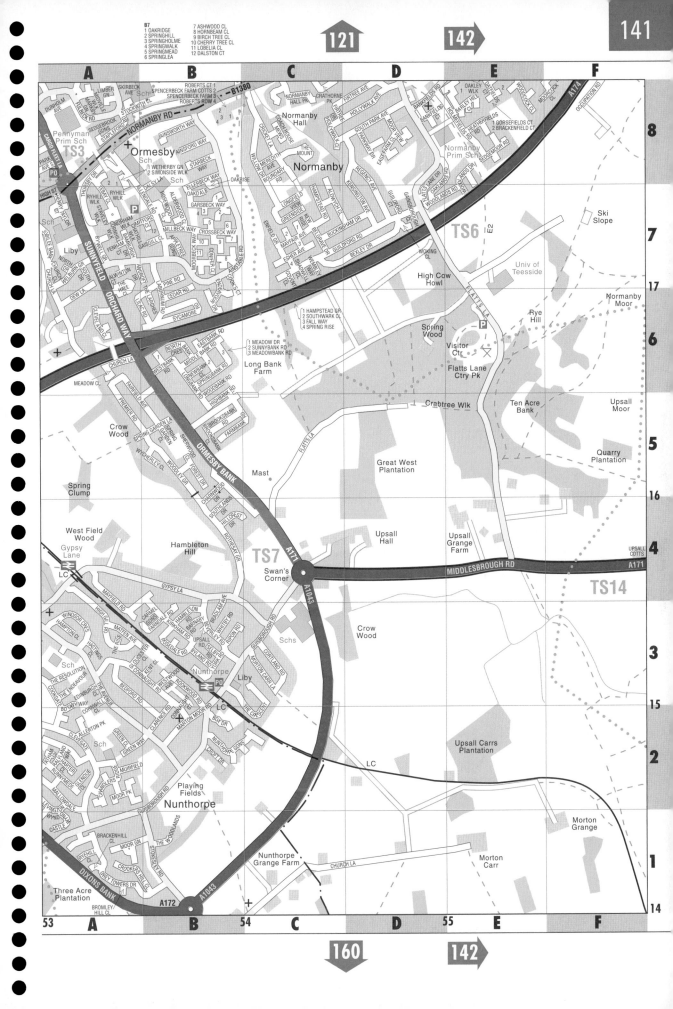

A **B** **C** **D** **E** **F**

8

TS6

Eston Moor

Wilton Moor

Harrison's
Plantation

High Court
Green

West
Banks

Moordale Beck

Carr
Pond

Moordale
Bog

High Barnaby
Farm

Poplar
Farm

7

17

Bank Field

6

Osborne
Rush

West
Hills

Cleveland Way

Claphams
Wood

Barnaby Side

Scugdale
Farm

5

16

Barnaby Side
Farm

Mill
Farm

PH

TS14

Barnaby
Grange
Farm

MIDDLESBROUGH RD

A171

Windy
Hill

Sandswath Beck

4

A171

MIDDLESBROUGH RD

A173

Hemble Hill
Farm

Stokesley Rd

Main Stell

Killing Howe

Blind La
Railway Cotts

Lowcross
Farm

Grove
Hill

3

East Upsall
Farm

Cleveland Way

Guisborough
Forest
Visitor Ctr

Pinchinthorpe

15

Boundary
Plantation

Low
Farm

Pinchinthorpe
House

2

Spite
Hall
Farm

Ward's
Belt

Garbutt's
Plantation

High
Farm

Bousdale
Farm

Bousdale
Wood

TS7

1

A173

Bousdale
Hill

14

TS9

Pinchinthorpe
Hall

56 **A** **B** 57 **C** **D** 58 **E** **F**

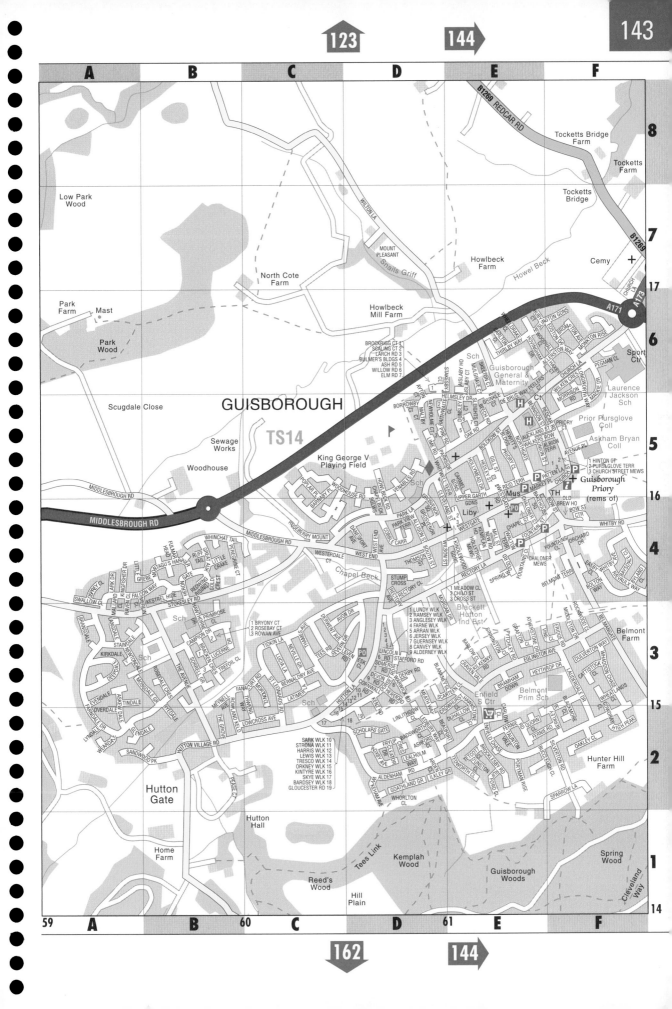

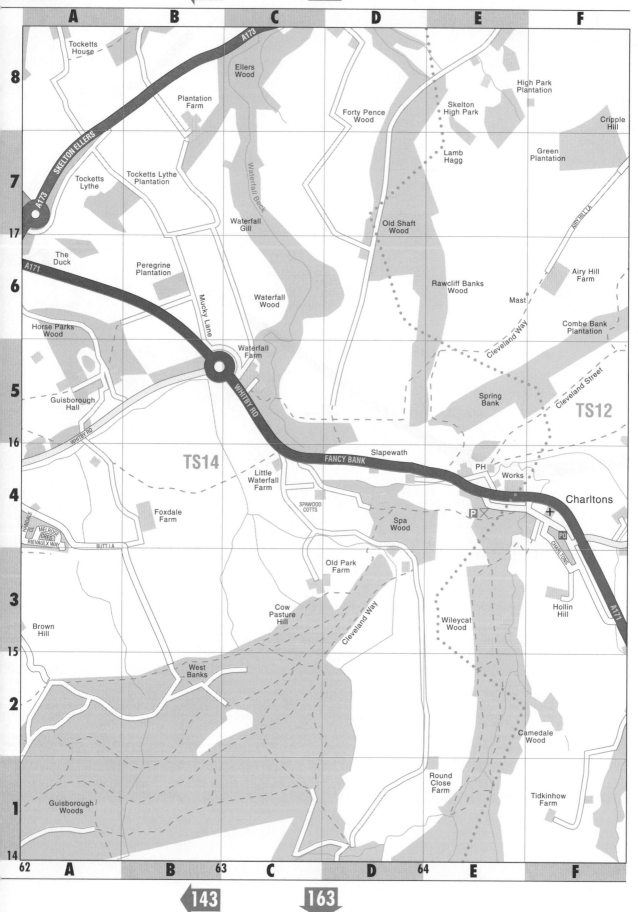

A B C D E F

8
7
17
6
5
16
4
3
15
2
1
14

Cleveland View
Newlands Rd
Airy Hill La
Cleveland Way
Boosbeck Bridge
Marleys Wood
Boosbeck Rd
Hobdale Terr
Boos Beck
Rookery Dale
Wharton Pl
Wandhill Gdns
Boosbeck
Priestcrofts
Claphow Resr
Wygrave
Claphow Whin
Claphow
Green Bank Terr 1
Chadderton Cl 2
Oxford St
Brookside
Queen St
High St
PH
Oldham Cl
Wand Hill
Oldham St
1
2
3 Shepherd Ct
4 Cross Row
5 Carney St
6 Gerrie St
7 Fenton Ct
8 Albion St
Fenton St
Oakley Rd
4
5
6
7
8
PO
Lockwood Prim Sch
Church Dr
Groundhills Farm
Hutton Wood
Combe Bank Farm
Allot Gdns
Lingdale Rd
Moorcock Row
Lingdale
Kilton La
Mutton Scalp Rd
Ricey Hill
Lingdale Head
Bellwood Ave
Wilkinson St
Wilson St
High St
Eskdale Terr
Catherine St
Scarth Cl
Pease St
Meadow Dale Ct
PO
Ind Est
Whitwell Pl
Rosedale Gdns 1
Farndale Gdns 2
Prospect Terr 3
Ivan St 4
Moordale Ct 5
Davison St
Cockburn St
Kirkbright Pl
Stanghow Rd
Kilton La
Cedarhurst Dr
Dale Terr
Beechcroft
Allot Gdns
Lingdale Prim Sch
Windsor Dr
Sandringham Rd
Balmoral Rd
TS12
Hollin
Margrove Park
Skelton Warren
Busky Dale
Seaton Hill
Seaton Terr
Low Stanghow Rd
Plantation Cotts
Low House
Margrove Heritage Ctr
Stanghow Ridge
Stanghow
Millers La
Butts Hill
Birk Brow Rd
Aysdalegate
Mast
Low Moor
P
Ridge Farm
Stanghow Firs
Kateridden Beck
Kateridden
Millers La
Plum Tree Farm
Aysdale Gate
Quarton Knoll
Swindale Farm
Woodhill Gill
Woodhill Gill Head
Lockwood Beck Farm
A171
Swindale La

65 A B 66 C D 67 E F

145
126

	A	B	C	D	E	F

8

Merry Lockwood Gill

Kilton Thorpe

KILTON THORPE LA

Cock Shots

Kilton Castle (rems of)

Greenhills Farm

Merrys Wood

KILTON LA
KILTON THORPE

Stank Ho Farm

Castle Wood

Clarkson's Wood

7

Long Moor

Kilton Hill

17

Mines (dis)

Park House Farm

6

Buck Rush Farm

Mains Wood

Long Moosholm Farm

Lodge Wood

5

TS12

TS13

Great Charles Hill

Nest Hagg Wood

16

4

Hunger Hill

Hagg Beck

MOORSHOLM LA

Hagg Wood

Throstle Nest

Liverton Mill Farm

Hagg Hill

Mill Beck

3

Stanghow Bridge

Hankills

LIVERTON MILL BANK

Red House Farm

15

Moorsholm Mill

LONG LA

North Lane Farm

Elm Heads

2

The Grange

PH

Moorsholm

Pinkney Bank Wood

1

Red Hall

RECREATION VIEW

HIGH ST

HILLOCKS LA

ASHBERRY CL
MOOR CL

Cow Close

GUISBOROUGH RD

14

SWINDALE LA

68	A	B	69	C	D	70	E	F

145
165

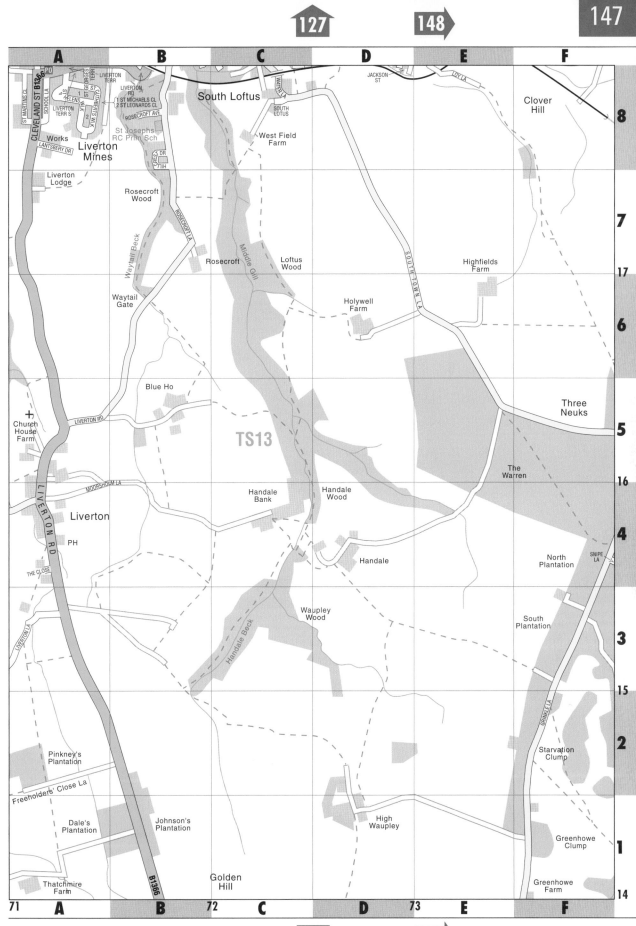

147 128

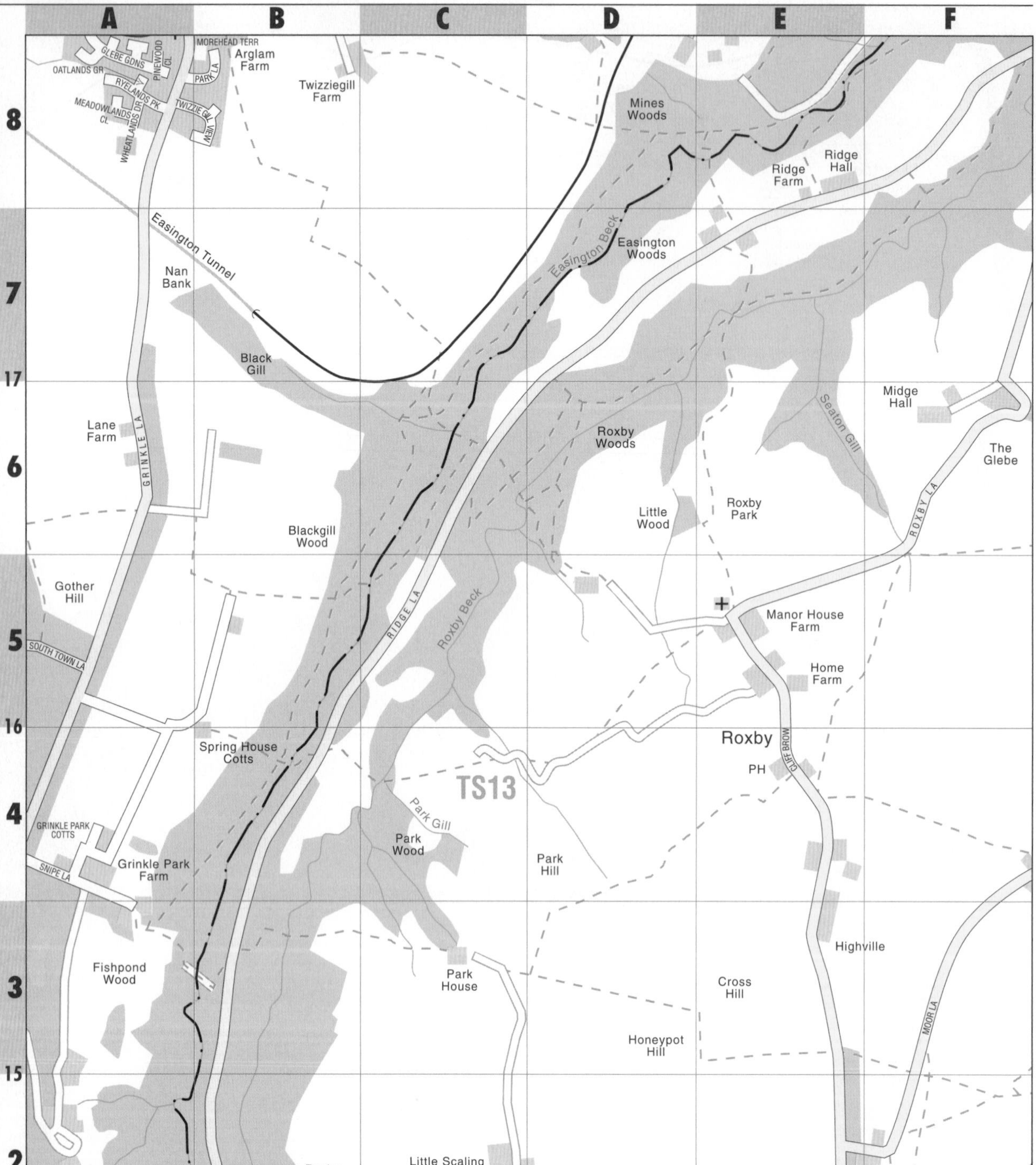

A B C D E F

8
OATLANDS GR
GLEBE GDNS
PINEWOOD
MOREHEAD TERR
Arglam Farm
PARK LA
TWIZZIE DR
WHEATLANDS DR
RYELANDS PK
MEADOWLANDS CL
Twizziegill Farm
Mines Woods
Ridge Farm
Ridge Hall

7
Easington Tunnel
Nan Bank
Easington Beck
Easington Woods

17
Black Gill

6
Lane Farm
GRINKLE LA
Blackgill Wood
Roxby Woods
Little Wood
Roxby Park
Seaton Gill
Midge Hall
The Glebe
ROXBY LA

5
Gother Hill
SOUTH TOWN LA
RIDGE LA
Roxby Beck
Manor House Farm
Home Farm

16
Spring House Cotts
Roxby
PH
CLIFF BROW

4
GRINKLE PARK COTTS
SNIPE LA
Grinkle Park Farm
TS13
Park Gill
Park Wood
Park Hill

3
Fishpond Wood
Park House
Cross Hill
Highville
MOOR LA

15
Honeypot Hill

2
Grinkle Park Hotel
Roxby Woods
Little Scaling Farm
Moor House Farm
Borrowby Moor

1
Grinkle Park
Grinkle Wood
Hag Hill
Mill

14
74 A B 75 C D 76 E F

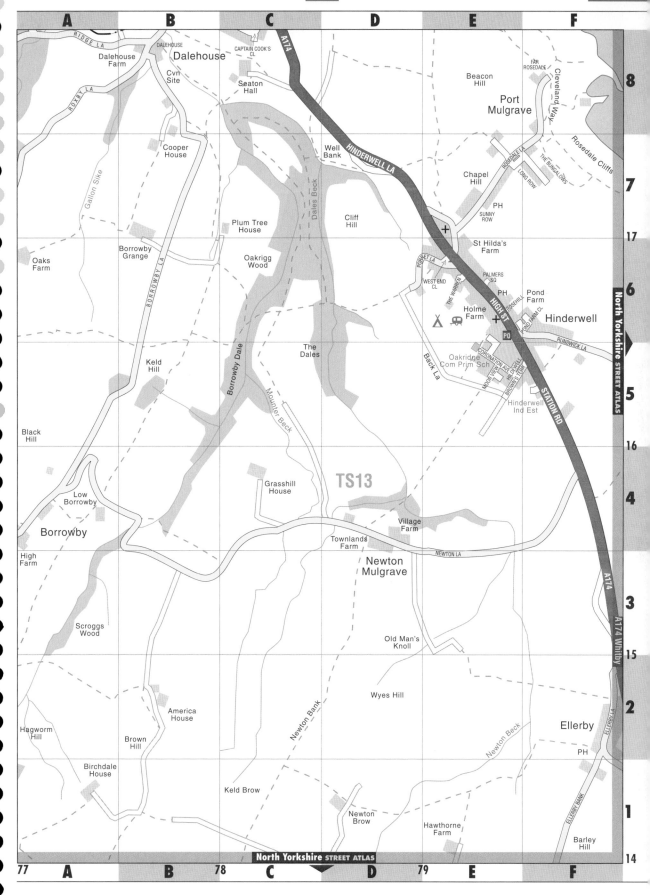

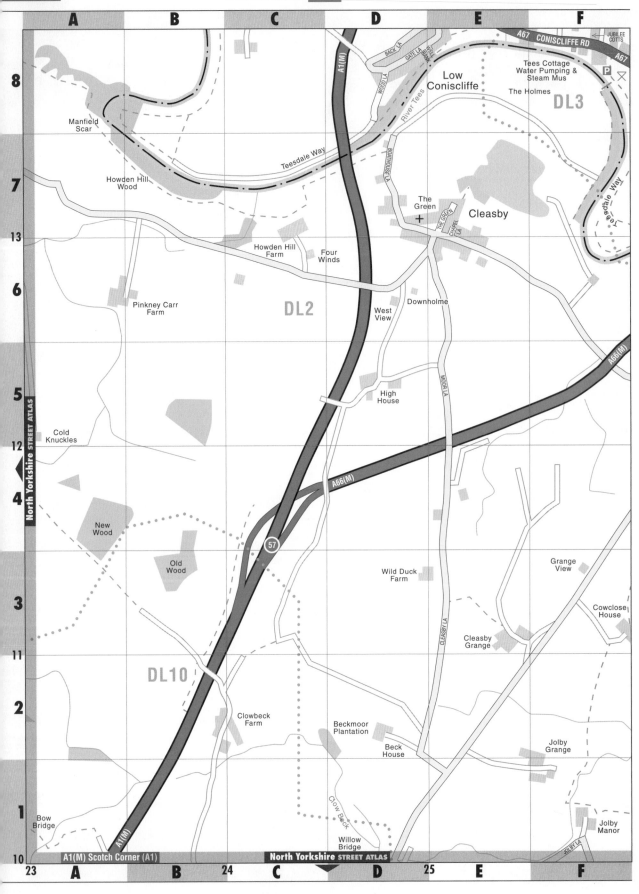

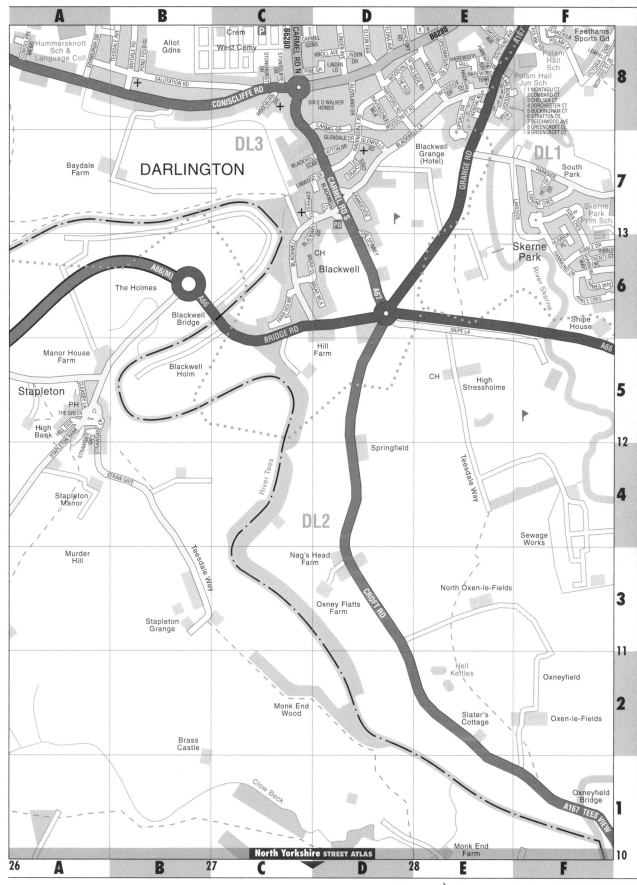

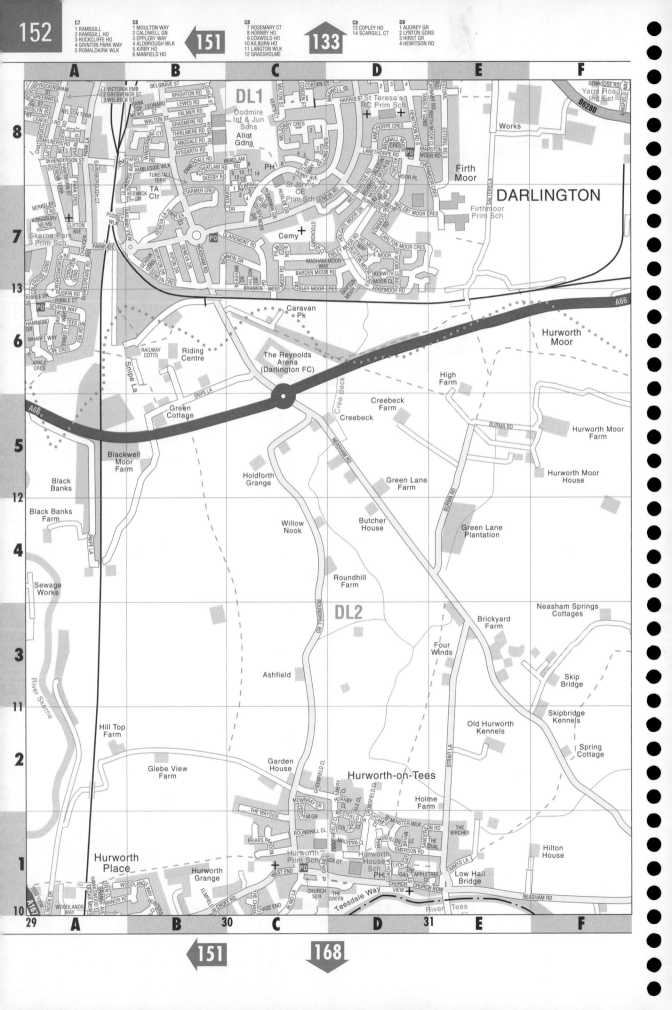

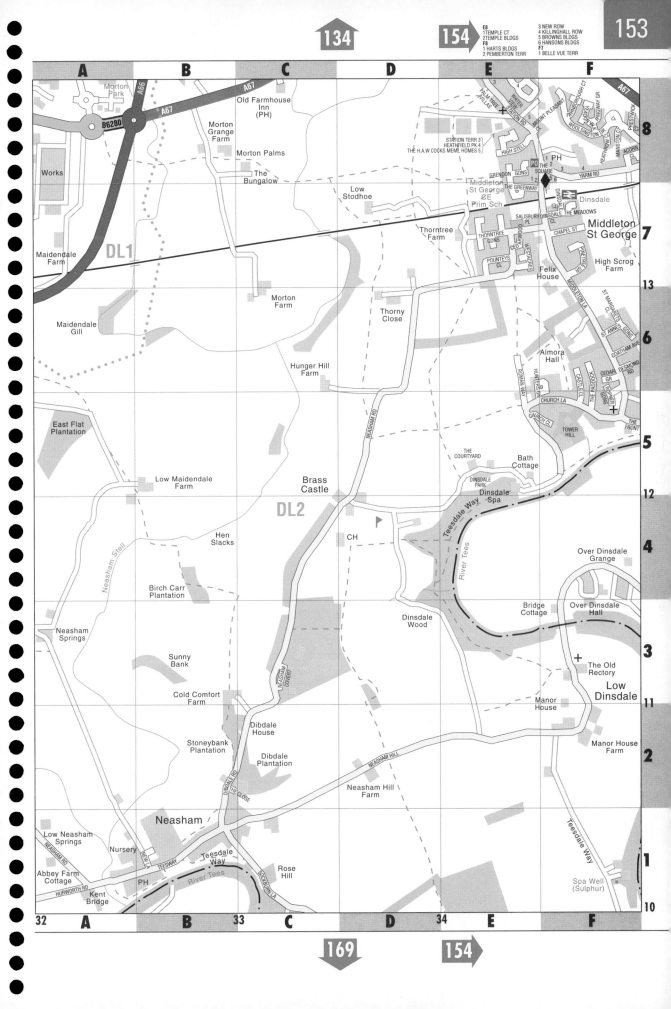

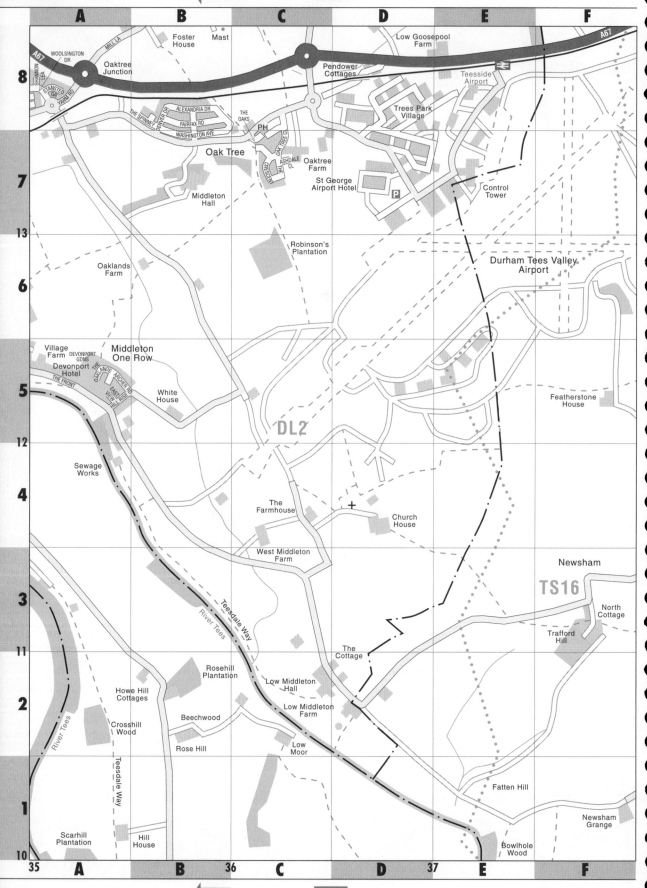

153 135

153 170

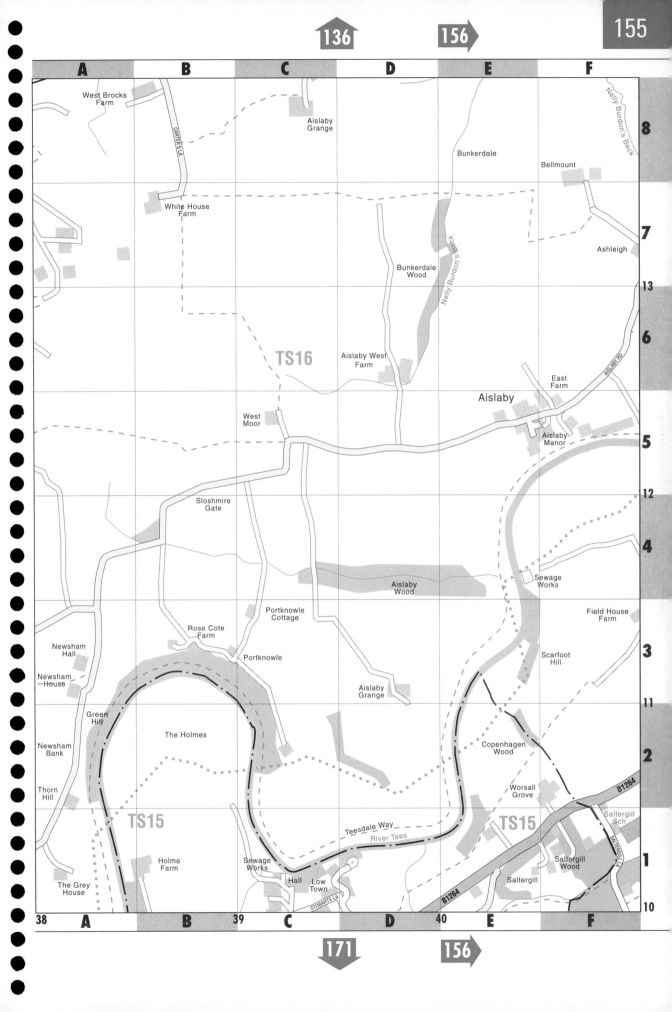

A B C D E F

8
7
13
6
5
12
4
3
11
2
1
10

West Brocks Farm

CARTER'S LA

Aislaby Grange

Bunkerdale

Bellmount

Nelly Burdon's Beck

White House Farm

Ashleigh

Bunkerdale Wood

Nelly Burdon's Beck

TS16

Aislaby West Farm

East Farm

AISLABY RD

Aislaby

West Moor

Aislaby Manor

Sloshmire Gate

Sewage Works

Aislaby Wood

Field House Farm

Portknowle Cottage

Rose Cote Farm

Scarfoot Hill

Portknowle

Newsham Hall

Aislaby Grange

Newsham House

Green Hill

Copenhagen Wood

The Holmes

Newsham Bank

Worsall Grove

B1264

Thorn Hill

Saltergill Sch

SALTERGILL LA

TS15

Teesdale Way

TS15

River Tees

Saltergill Wood

Holme Farm

Sewage Works

Saltergill

The Grey House

Hall

Low Town

B1264

STOBARTS LA

38 A B 39 C D 40 E F

155 137

155 172

B8
1 BUTTERFIELD DR
2 BUTTERFIELD GR
3 BUTTERFIELD CL
4 NEWSAM RD

TS16
TS17
TS15

Roundhill Village
White House
Betty's Close Farm
Round Hill
Ingleby Hill
River Leven
River Tees
Teesdale Way

Egglescliffe Sch
Egglescliffe CE Prim Sch
Yarm
Yarm Prep Sch
Yarm Prim Sch
Layfield Prim Sch
Conyers Sch
Levendale Prim Sch

1 RUSHMERE HEATH
2 MOOR PK
3 PRESTWICK CT
4 PORTLAND CL
5 WOODFORD GDN
6 RUTHERGLEN WLK
7 BEAUMARIS DR

1 HEADLAM TERR
2 RAILWAY COTTS
3 FLOUNDERS HO
4 MEYNELL HO

SWINBURN'S YD 1
CARLTON TERR 2
BLENAVON CT 3
TOWN HALL CT 4
FAIRFAX CT 5
DANBY WYND 6
WINGROVE 7
HAUXWELL'S BLDG 8
HIGH CHURCH MEWS 9

BRONABER CL 1
RHOBELL VIEW 2
MERIONETH CL 3

1 WINPENNY CL
2 CATERTON CL

Roselea
Holdenfields
Chameral
Spell Close Farm
HM Prison
Kirklevington Grange
Kirklevington Hall
Hall Wood
Pit Wood
Saltergill Beck
Far End Farm
Hotel
Morley Carr
Lowlands Farm
Grey Close
Holme House Farm
Nelly Burdon's Beck
Saltergill Sch
Sewage Works
Spital Flatt
The Rookery
The Friarage
The Yarm Sch
Green Lane Bridge
Old Hall
Devil's Hill
Old Station Mews

YARM RD HIGH ST THE SPITAL THIRSK RD WORSALL RD GREEN LA ALLERTON BALK
A67 A135 A1044 B1264 B1265

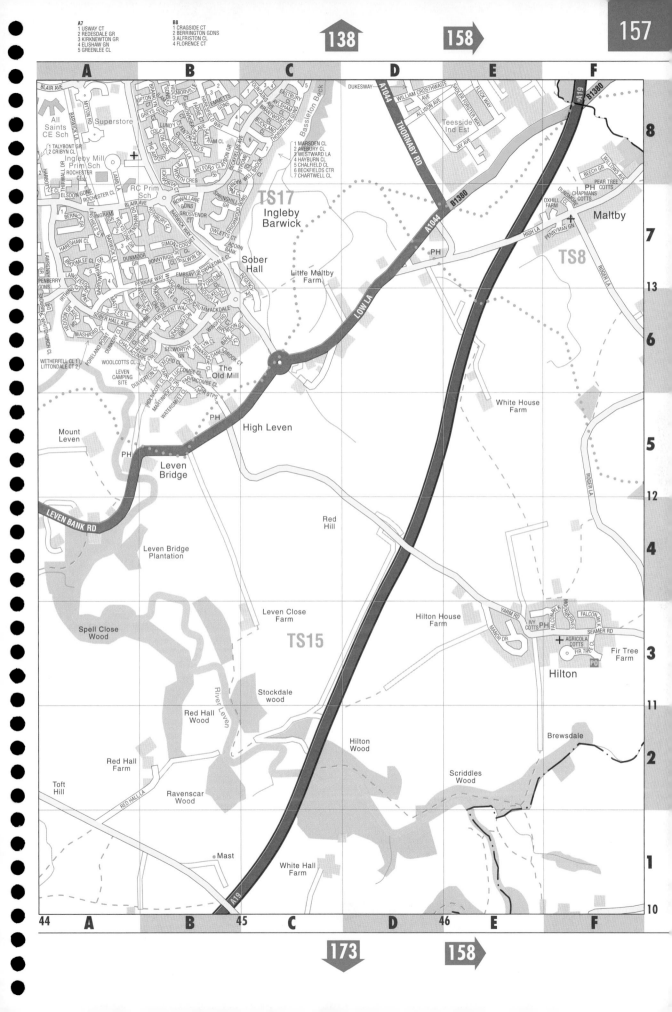

	A	B	C	D	E	F

8

THORNTON CL
THORNTON RD
THORNTON VALE
MALTBY RD
LOW FARM CL
CEDAR DR

CEDARWOOD GLADE
FARMCOTE CT
FORD
CASS HOUSE RD
STAINTON WAY
FAVERSHAM CL
HIGHDALE WAY
FORDYCE RD
FAIRFAX CT

Thornton Plantation

Grange Farm

Stainton Grange

Holme Farm

Thornton

Aspen

7

Boltonmoss Hill

Maltby Beck

Thornton Grange

13

Sleepy Hollow

SEAMER RD

TS8

Fox Covert

Maltby Farm

Low Thornton Moor

Severs' Plantation

6

Maltby Grange

ROGER LA

Thornton Moor

5

High Farm

12

Barley Flatts Wood

Coldpool

Antelope Lodge

4

High Plantation

3

ROGER LA

Greenfield

Low Fields

WELL LA

Low House Farm

The Boffins

11

TS15

Boy Hill

TS9

2

Middleton Lodge

STAINTON RD

PH

1

Seamer Grange Farm

Boy Hill Farm

HILTON RD

Seamer

THE GREEN

LECONFIELD

10

47	A		B	48	C		D	49	E		F

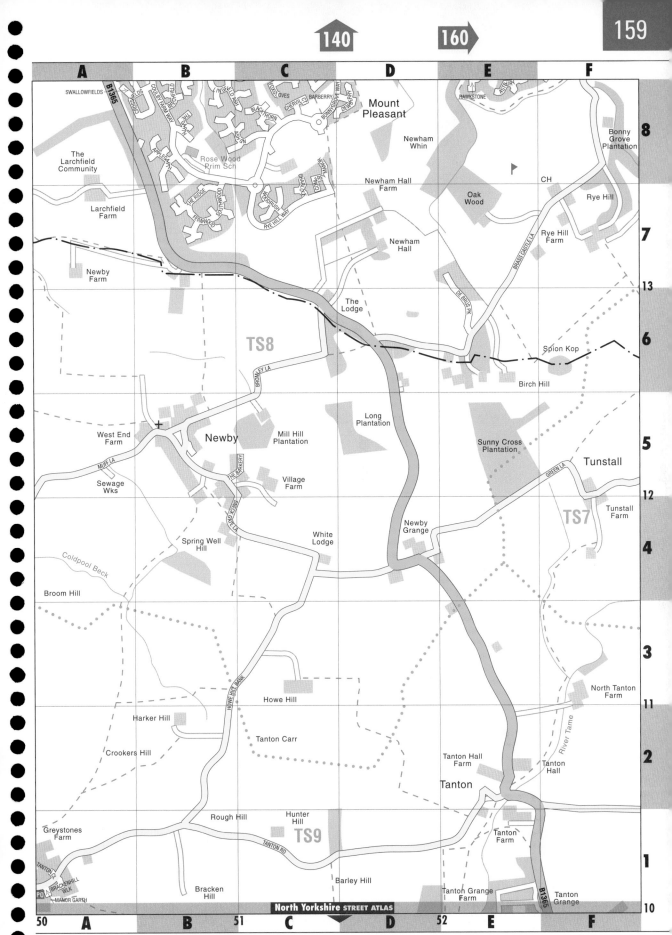

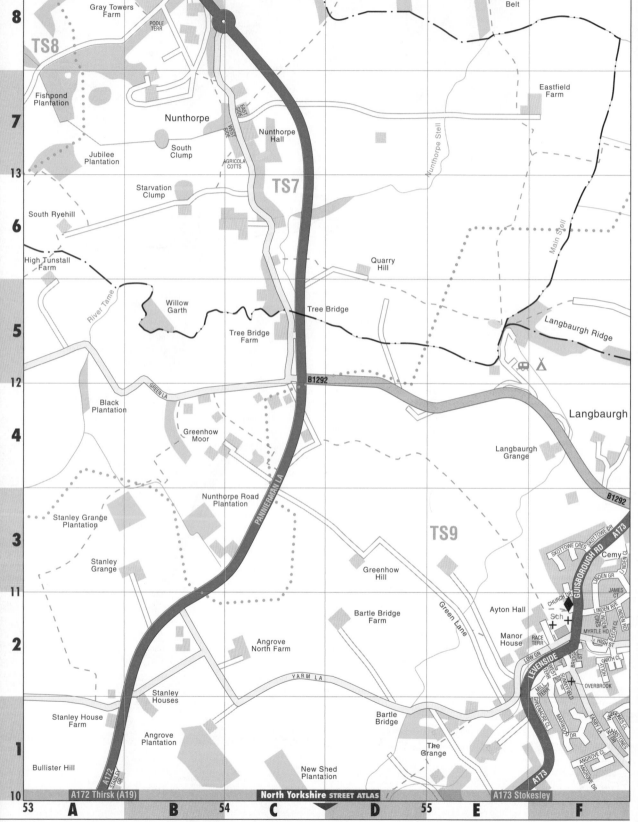

A · B · C · D · E · F

8

7

13

6

5

12

4

3

11

2

1

10

53 · A · B · 54 · C · D · 55 · E · F

TS8

Gray Towers Farm

POOLE TERR

Fishpond Plantation

Nunthorpe

Jubilee Plantation

South Clump

CHURCH LA

A172

EAST SIDE

WEST SIDE

Nunthorpe Hall

AGRICOLA COTTS

Starvation Clump

South Ryehill

High Tunstall Farm

River Tame

Willow Garth

Tree Bridge Farm

TS7

Quarry Hill

Tree Bridge

Morton Carr Belt

Eastfield Farm

Nunthorpe Stell

Main Stell

Langbaurgh Ridge

B1292

GREEN LA

Black Plantation

Greenhow Moor

Nunthorpe Road Plantation

Stanley Grange Plantation

Stanley Grange

PANNIERMAN LA

Langbaurgh

Langbaurgh Grange

B1292

TS9

Greenhow Hill

Green Lane

Ayton Hall

Manor House

Bartle Bridge Farm

Angrove North Farm

Stanley Houses

Stanley House Farm

Bullister Hill

Angrove Plantation

A172

STANLEY GR

YARM LA

Bartle Bridge

New Shed Plantation

The Grange

A173

GUISBOROUGH RD

SKOTTOWE CRES

SKOTTOWE DR

A173

Cemy

LINDEN GR

JAMES CT

LINDEN AVE

LINDEN CL

MYRTLE HO

BEECH CL

CHURCH RD

Sch

RACE TERR

HIGH ST

GARTH CL

LEVENSIDE

WEST TERR

MILL TERR

SUNNYFIELD

BRIDGE TERR

GREENACRE CT

MARWOOD DR

OVERBROOK

FABER LA

ANGROVE CL

ANGROVE DR

A172 Thirsk (A19)

A173 Stokesley

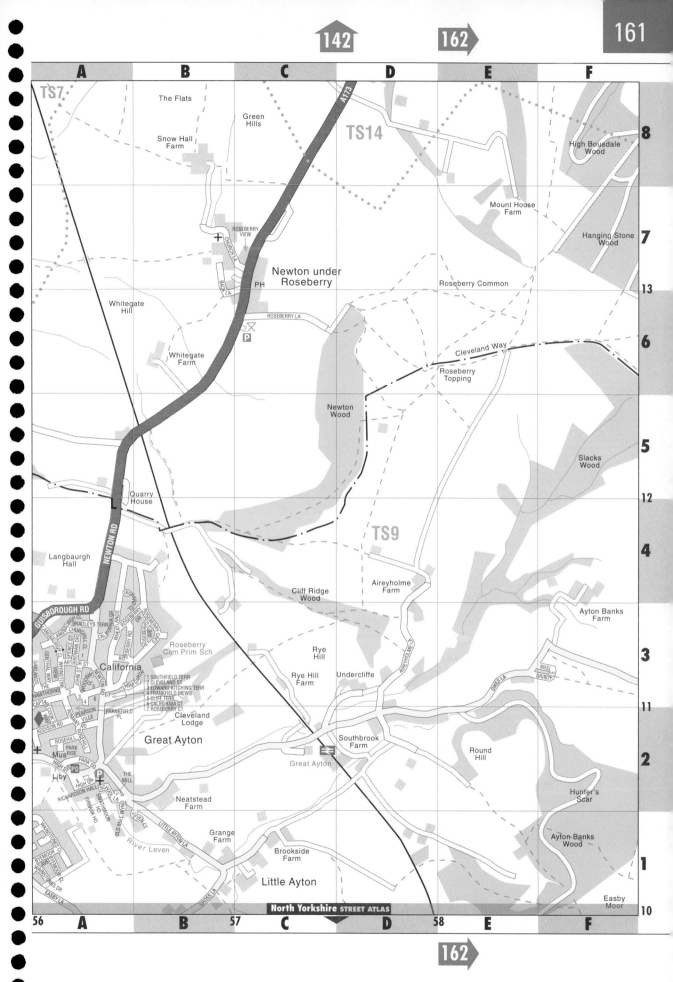

A B C D E F

TS7

The Flats

Green Hills

TS14

Snow Hall Farm

High Bousdale Wood

8

ROSEBERRY VIEW

Mount House Farm

Hanging Stone Wood

7

CHURCH LA

BACK LA

Newton under Roseberry

Roseberry Common

13

PH

Whitegate Hill

ROSEBERRY LA

Cleveland Way

6

P

Roseberry Topping

Whitegate Farm

Newton Wood

Roseberry Common

Slacks Wood

5

Quarry House

12

NEWTON RD

TS9

4

Langbaurgh Hall

Cliff Ridge Wood

Aireyholme Farm

Ayton Banks Farm

GUISBOROUGH RD

Roseberry Com Prim Sch

Rye Hill

DIKES LA

GRIBDALE TERR

3

California

Rye Hill Farm

Undercliffe

AIREYHOLME LA

1 SOUTHFIELD TERR
2 CLEVELAND ST
3 EDWARD KITCHING TERR
4 FRANKFIELD MEWS
5 CLIFF TERR
6 CALIFORNIA CT
7 ROSEBERRY CT

11

Cleveland Lodge

Great Ayton

Southbrook Farm

Round Hill

2

Mus

Great Ayton

Liby

PO

Hunter's Scar

THE MILL

RICHARDSON HALL

Neatstead Farm

Ayton-Banks Wood

1

River Leven

Grange Farm

Brookside Farm

Little Ayton

Easby Moor

10

56 A B 57 C D 58 E F

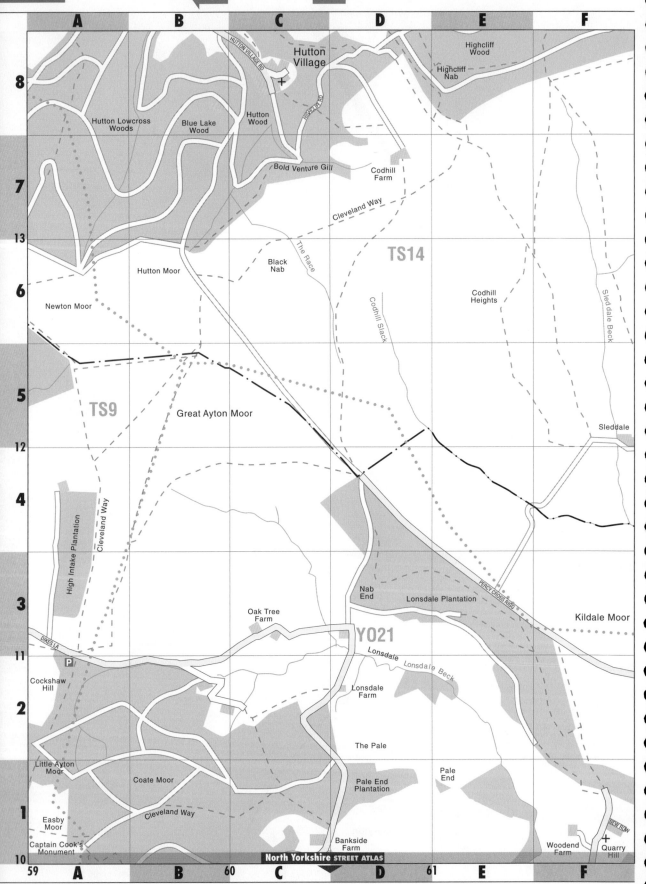

A   B   C   D   E   F

8

Hutton Village

Hutton Lowcross Woods

Blue Lake Wood

Hutton Wood

Highcliff Wood

Highcliff Nab

7

Bold Venture Gill

Codhill Farm

Cleveland Way

13

Black Nab

The Race

TS14

6

Hutton Moor

Newton Moor

Codhill Slack

Codhill Heights

Sleddale Beck

5

TS9

Great Ayton Moor

12

Sleddale

4

High Intake Plantation

Cleveland Way

PERCY CROSS RIGG

3

Nab End

Lonsdale Plantation

Kildale Moor

Oak Tree Farm

YO21

11

DIKES LA

P

Cockshaw Hill

Lonsdale

Lonsdale Beck

2

Lonsdale Farm

The Pale

Little Ayton Moor

Coate Moor

Pale End Plantation

Pale End

1

Easby Moor

Cleveland Way

Woodend Farm

NEW ROW

Quarry Hill

Captain Cook's Monument

Bankside Farm

North Yorkshire STREET ATLAS

10

59   A   B   60   C   D   61   E   F

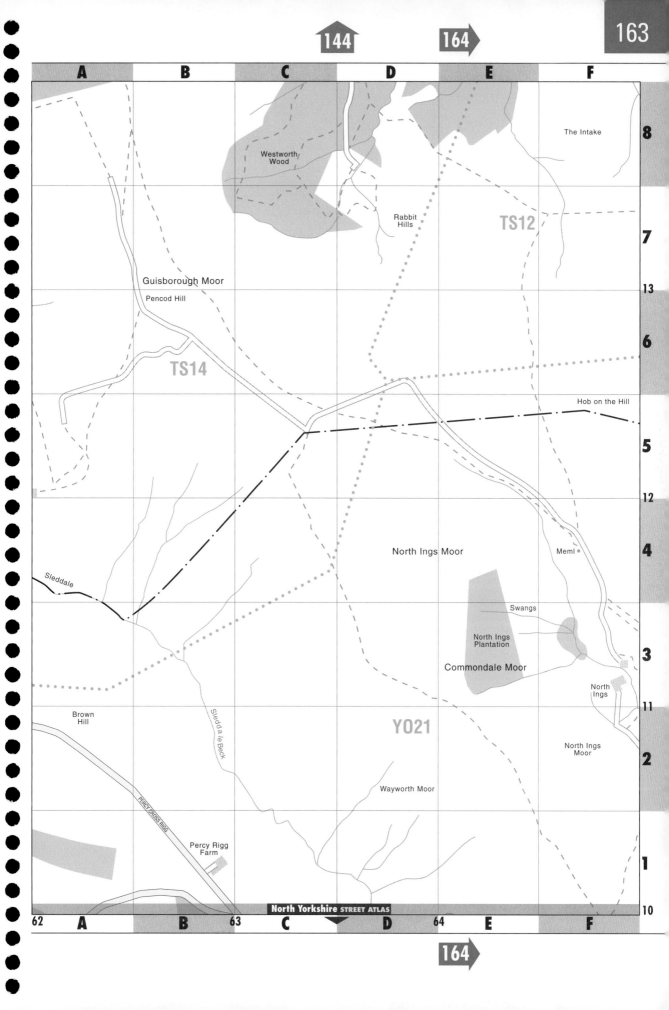

A B C D E F

8

Westworth
Wood

Rabbit
Hills

The Intake

TS12

7

Guisborough Moor

13

Pencod Hill

6

TS14

Hob on the Hill

5

12

North Ings Moor

Meml

4

Sleddale

Swangs

North Ings
Plantation

3

Commondale Moor

North
Ings

11

Brown
Hill

YO21

North Ings
Moor

2

Wayworth Moor

Percy Rigg
Farm

1

10

62 A B 63 C D 64 E F

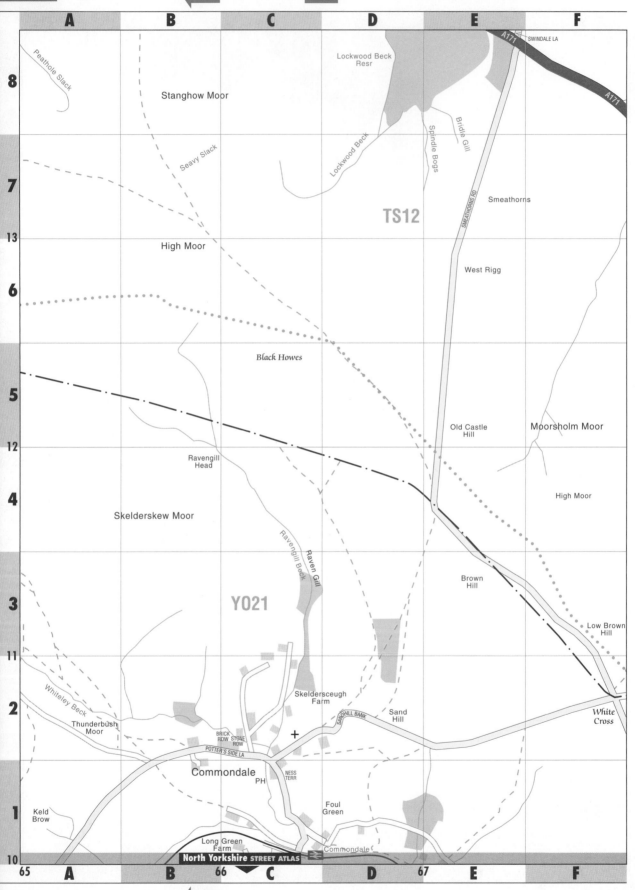

A B C D E F

8

Peathole Slack

Stanghow Moor

Lockwood Beck Resr

A171 SWINDALE LA

7

Seavy Slack

Lockwood Beck

Spindle Bogs

Bridle Gill

SMEATHORNS RD

Smeathorns

13

High Moor

TS12

West Rigg

6

Black Howes

Old Castle Hill

Moorsholm Moor

5

Ravengill Head

12

Skelderskew Moor

Ravengill Beck

Raven Gill

High Moor

4

YO21

Brown Hill

Low Brown Hill

3

Skeldersceugh Farm

SANDHILL BANK

Sand Hill

White Cross

11

Whiteley Beck

Thunderbush Moor

BRICK ROW STONE ROW

POTTER'S SIDE LA

2

Commondale

PH

NESS TERR

Keld Brow

Foul Green

1

Long Green Farm

Commondale

10

North Yorkshire STREET ATLAS

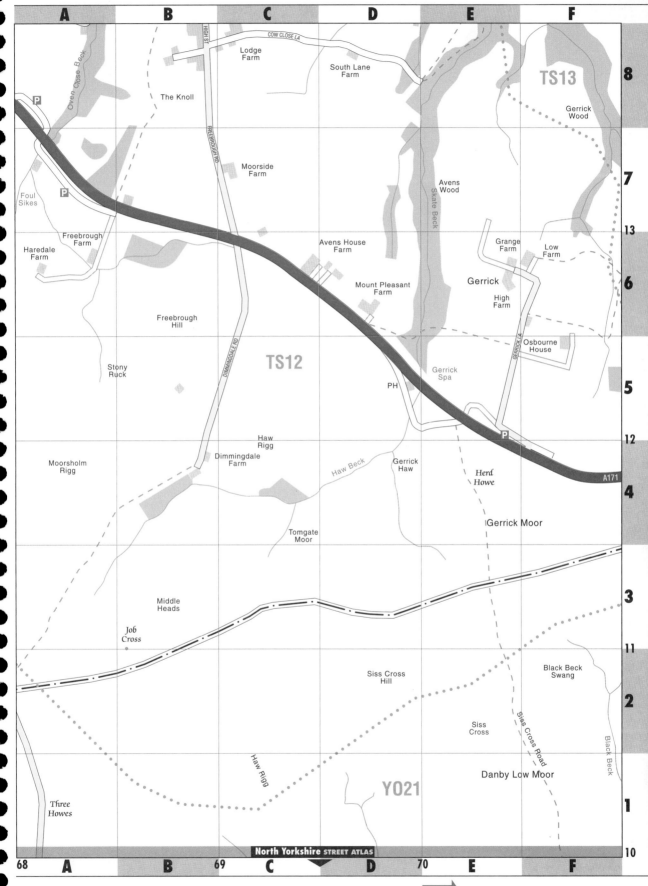

A B C D E F

Oven Close Beck

P

Foul
Sikes

Haredale
Farm

Freebrough
Farm

P

Moorsholm
Rigg

Three
Howes

The Knoll

HIGH ST

Lodge
Farm

COW CLOSE LA

FREEBROUGH RD

Moorside
Farm

Freebrough
Hill

Stony
Ruck

DIMMINGDALE RD

Haw
Rigg

Dimmingdale
Farm

TS12

Middle
Heads

Job
Cross

Haw Rigg

South Lane
Farm

Avens House
Farm

Mount Pleasant
Farm

PH

Haw Beck

Tomgate
Moor

Gerrick
Haw

Siss Cross
Hill

YO21

Skate Beck

Avens
Wood

Gerrick
Spa

Herd
Howe

Gerrick Moor

Siss
Cross

Danby Low Moor

TS13

Gerrick
Wood

Grange
Farm

Low
Farm

Gerrick

High
Farm

GERRICK LA

Osbourne
House

P

A171

Black Beck
Swang

Siss Cross Road

Black Beck

A | B | C | D | E | F

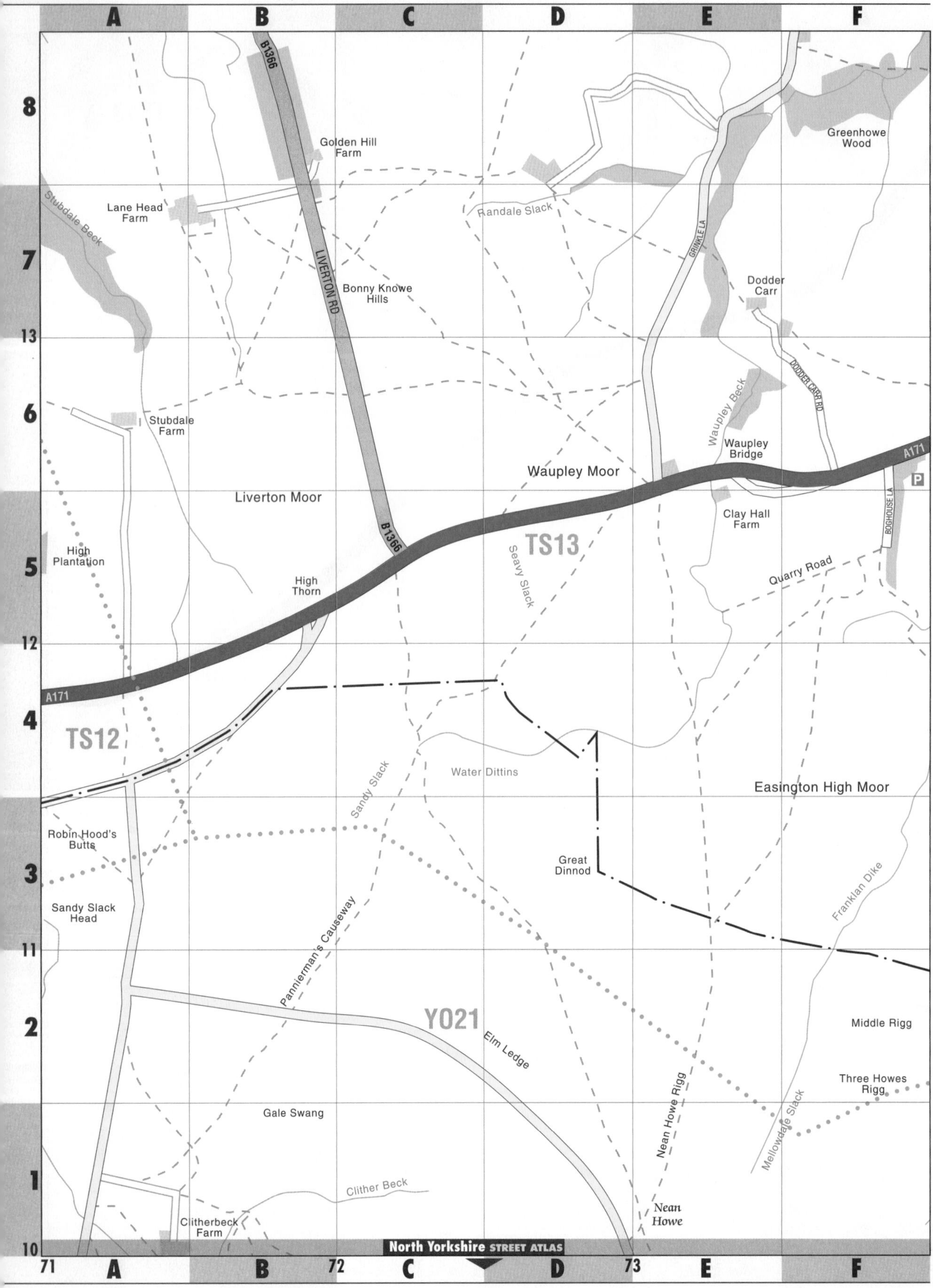

8

Stubdale Beck

B1366

Golden Hill Farm

Lane Head Farm

Randale Slack

Greenhowe Wood

7

GRINKLE LA

Bonny Knowe Hills

LIVERTON RD

Dodder Carr

13

DODDER CARR RD

6

Stubdale Farm

Waupley Beck

Waupley Bridge

A171

Liverton Moor

Waupley Moor

TS13

Clay Hall Farm

BOGHOUSE LA

P

High Plantation

Seavy Slack

Quarry Road

5

High Thorn

B1366

12

A171

4

TS12

Sandy Slack

Water Dittins

Easington High Moor

Robin Hood's Butts

Great Dinnod

Franklan Dike

3

Sandy Slack Head

Pannierman's Causeway

11

YO21

2

Elm Ledge

Middle Rigg

Nean Howe Rigg

Three Howes Rigg

Gale Swang

Mellowdale Slack

1

Clither Beck

Nean Howe

Clitherbeck Farm

10

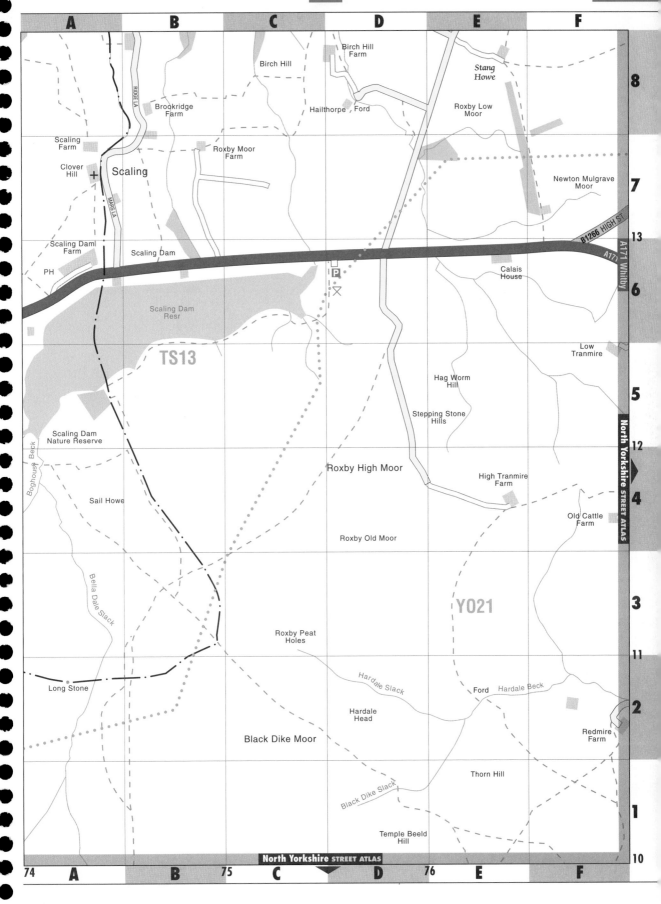

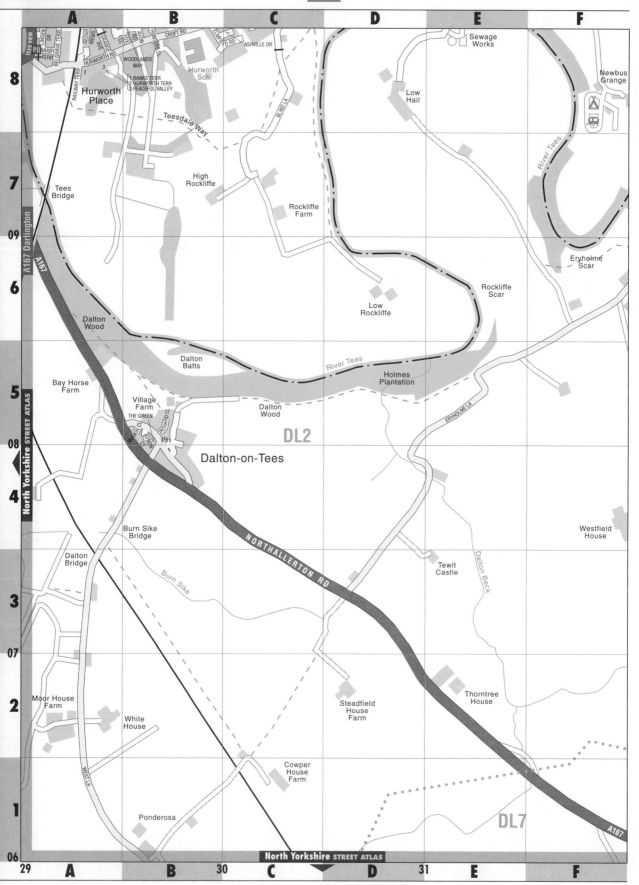

8

7

09

6

5

08

4

3

07

2

1

06

A167 Darlington

A1(M)

North Yorkshire STREET ATLAS

TEES VIEW
LINDEN
PO
BAXBY TERR
BELGRAVE TERR
RAILWAY TERR
CEDAR
GRANGE AVE
HURWORTH RD
MEWS
WOODLANDS WAY
2
3
1 BANKS TERR
2 HURWORTH TERR
3 PEACEFUL VALLEY

Hurworth Place

AVON CL
HUNTERS CL
FOX CL
CROFT RD
ELM RD
ELPRO RD
ASHVILLE DR

Hurworth Sch

BLIND LA

Teesdale Way

Tees Bridge

High Rockliffe

Rockliffe Farm

Sewage Works

Low Hail

Newbus Grange

River Tees

Eryholme Scar

Rockliffe Scar

Dalton Wood

Bay Horse Farm

Low Rockliffe

River Tees

Dalton Batts

Dalton Wood

Village Farm

THE GREEN

ORCHARD CL

MASHAM CL

BYTONS

PH

Holmes Plantation

DL2

Dalton-on-Tees

Eryholme La

Westfield House

Burn Sike Bridge

Dalton Bridge

Burn Sike

NORTHALLERTON RD

Dalton Beck

Tewit Castle

Moor House Farm

White House

WEST LA

Steadfield House Farm

Thorntree House

Ponderosa

Cowper House Farm

DL7

A167

29

A

B

30

C

D

31

E

F

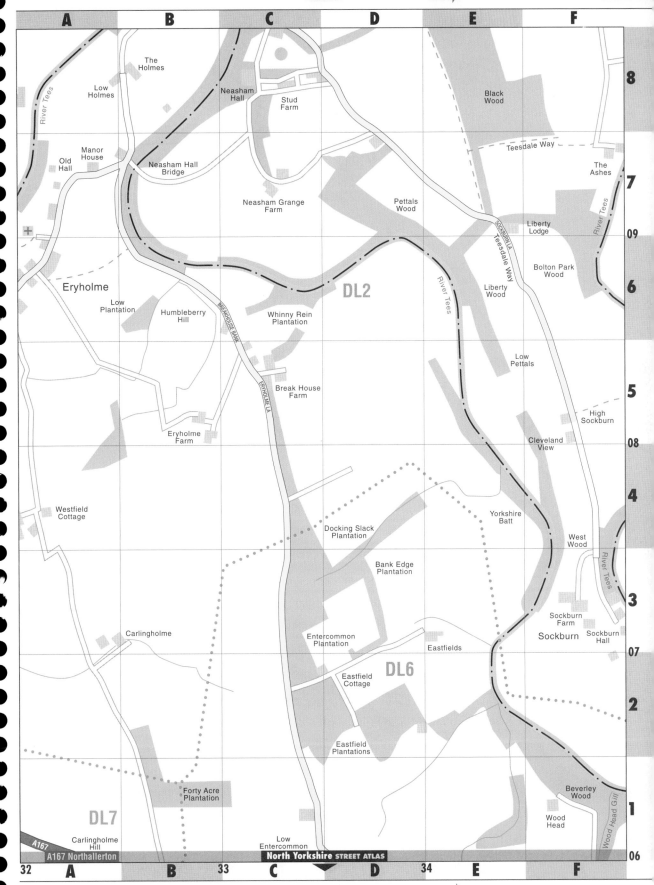

A B C D E F

8

7

09

6

5

08

4

3

07

2

1

06

River Tees

The Holmes

Low Holmes

Neasham Hall

Stud Farm

Black Wood

Teesdale Way

Old Hall

Manor House

Neasham Hall Bridge

The Ashes

River Tees

Neasham Grange Farm

Pettals Wood

Liberty Lodge

SOCKBURN LA
Teesdale Way

Eryholme

DL2

River Tees

Liberty Wood

Bolton Park Wood

Low Plantation

Humbleberry Hill

Whinny Rein Plantation

Low Pettals

BREAKHOUSE BANK

ERYHOLME LA

Break House Farm

High Sockburn

Cleveland View

Eryholme Farm

Westfield Cottage

Docking Slack Plantation

Yorkshire Batt

West Wood

River Tees

Bank Edge Plantation

Sockburn Farm

Carlingholme

Entercommon Plantation

Eastfields

Sockburn

Sockburn Hall

DL6

Eastfield Cottage

Eastfield Plantations

DL7

Forty Acre Plantation

Beverley Wood

Wood Head

Wood Head Gill

A167
A167 Northallerton

Carlingholme Hill

Low Entercommon

North Yorkshire STREET ATLAS

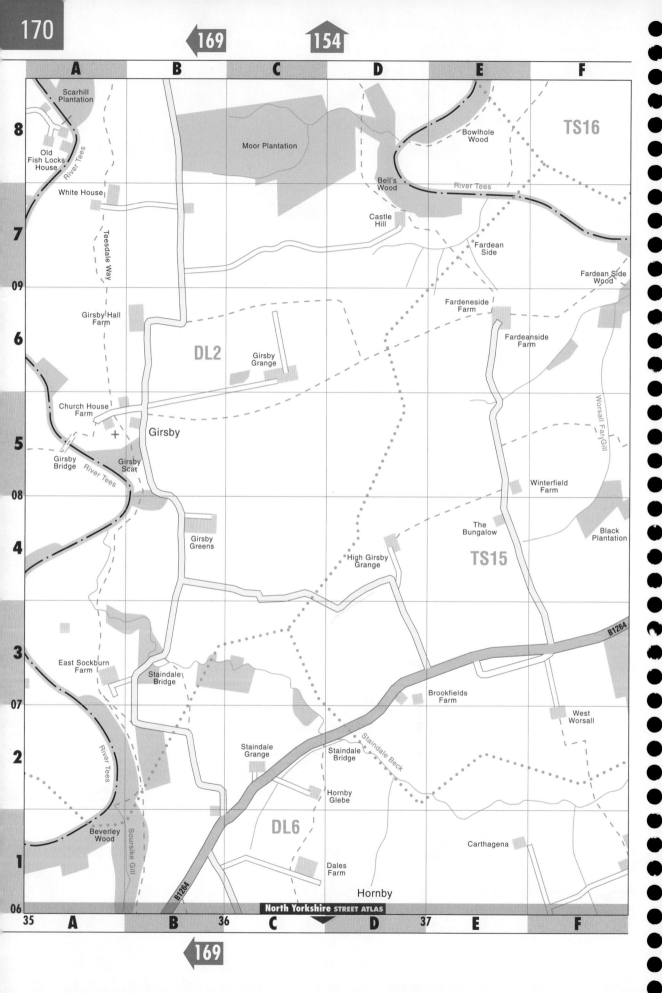

A B C D E F

8

Scarhill
Plantation

Moor Plantation

Bowlhole
Wood

TS16

Old
Fish Locks
House

White House

River Tees

Bell's
Wood

River Tees

7

Castle
Hill

Fardean
Side

Fardean Side
Wood

09

Teesdale Way

Girsby Hall
Farm

Fardeneside
Farm

6

DL2

Girsby
Grange

Fardeanside
Farm

Worsall Farm Gill

Church House
Farm

5

Girsby

Winterfield
Farm

Girsby
Bridge

River Tees

Girsby
Scar

08

The
Bungalow

Black
Plantation

4

Girsby
Greens

High Girsby
Grange

TS15

3

East Sockburn
Farm

Staindale
Bridge

Brookfields
Farm

B1264

07

River Tees

West
Worsall

2

Staindale
Grange

Staindale
Bridge

Staindale Beck

Hornby
Glebe

Carthagena

Beverley
Wood

Soursike Gill

DL6

1

Dales
Farm

Hornby

B1264

06

35 A B 36 C D 37 E F

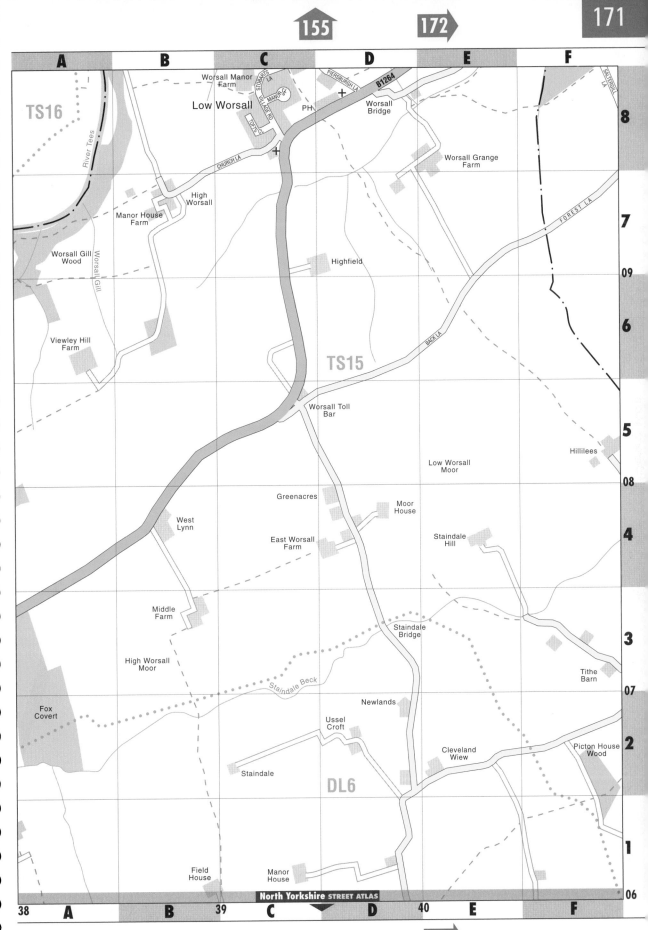

TS16

Worsall Manor Farm

Low Worsall

PH

PIERSBURGH LA

B1264

Worsall Bridge

8

SALTERGILL LA

Worsall Grange Farm

CHURCH LA

High Worsall

Manor House Farm

7

FOREST LA

Worsall Gill Wood

Worsall Gill

Highfield

09

Viewley Hill Farm

6

BACK LA

TS15

Worsall Toll Bar

5

Hillilees

Low Worsall Moor

08

Greenacres

Moor House

West Lynn

East Worsall Farm

Staindale Hill

4

Middle Farm

Staindale Bridge

3

High Worsall Moor

Staindale Beck

Tithe Barn

07

Fox Covert

Newlands

Ussel Croft

Cleveland Wiew

Picton House Wood

2

Staindale

DL6

Manor House

1

Field House

06

A B C D E F

8

Low Forest
Farm

SALTERGILL LA

The
Forest

High Forest
Farm

Grove
Platation

Grove
Farm

Manor
Farm

FOREST LA

GROVE BANK

KNOWLES CL

WEST LA

HALL MOOR CL

ASH GR

BIRCH CL

BRACE DR

PENDERS LA

ST MARTINS WAY

MAJOR CL

THE GREEN

THE STRATHMORE DR

MANOR GARTH

TOWN END

PUMP LA

A67

Kirklevington
Prim Sch

Kirklevington

Fir Tree
Farm

Knowles
Farm

7

Hill House
Farm

09

Moor House
Farm

A67 A19

6

Picton Manor

Hill
House

Sand Hills
Farm

Grange
Plantation

5

TS15

LONG LA

08

PH

LC

Grange
Farm

4

Picton House
Farm

Picton Stell
Bridge

Picton
Plantation

Glebe
Farm

Tithe Barn
Farm

Picton

RAILWAY
COTTS

Poplars
Farm

Gowsers
Plantation

YORK ST

BACK LA

3

07

KAY HOUSE LA

Four
Wynds

Kay
House

Picton Stell

A19

High
Grange

2

New Dales
Plantation

Low Flatts
Plantation

Picton
Grange

Corps House
Farm

1

Mount Pleasant
Farm

Lime
Bridge

West Moor
Farm

Mount Flatts
Farm

HAGGITT HILL LA

A19

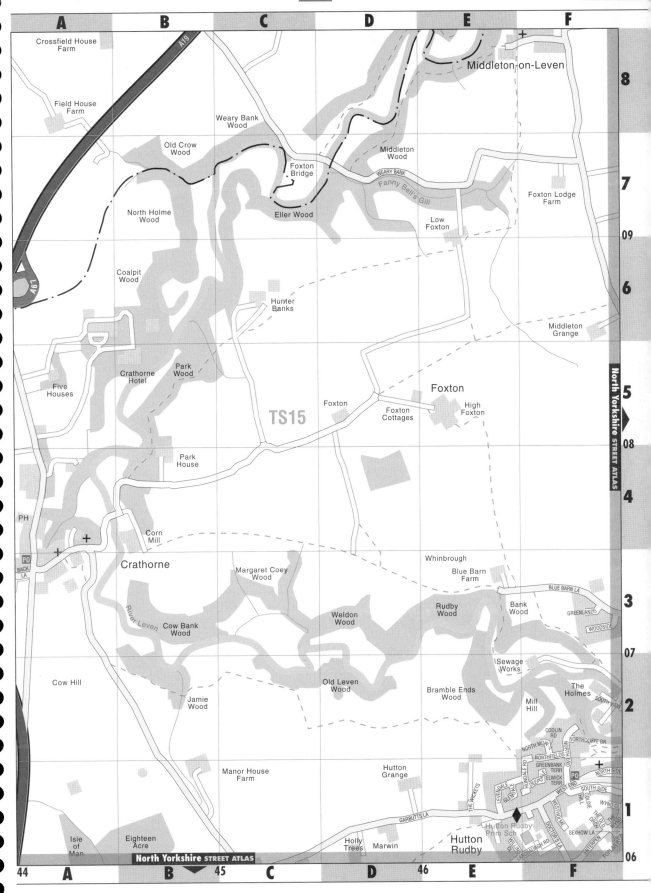

A B C D E F

8

7

09

6

5

08

4

3

07

2

1

06

44 A B 45 C D 46 E F

Crossfield House Farm

Field House Farm

A19

Weary Bank Wood

Old Crow Wood

Foxton Bridge

Middleton Wood

Middleton-on-Leven

WEARY BANK

Fanny Bell's Gill

Foxton Lodge Farm

North Holme Wood

Eller Wood

Low Foxton

Coalpit Wood

Hunter Banks

Middleton Grange

Crathorne Hotel

Park Wood

Foxton

Five Houses

Foxton

Foxton Cottages

High Foxton

TS15

Park House

PH

Corn Mill

Whinbrough

Blue Barn Farm

BLUE BARN LA

PO

BACK LA

Crathorne

Margaret Coey Wood

Rudby Wood

Bank Wood

GREENLANDS

WOODSIDE

River Leven

Cow Bank Wood

Weldon Wood

Sewage Works

The Holmes

Cow Hill

Jamie Wood

Old Leven Wood

Bramble Ends Wood

Mill Hill

SOUTH VIEW

CODLIN RD

NORTHCLIFFE GR

NORTH MDW

NORTHFIELDS

NORTH FLD

Manor House Farm

Hutton Grange

GREENBANK TERR

ELWICK TERR

DEBAR

LEVEN DALE

HUNDALE RD

GLEVEDE

THE WICKETS

DOCTOR'S LA

WEST END

NORTH SIDE

PO

SOUTH SIDE

WYND LA

WESTHOLME

COLLIE MILL

THE OLD ORCH

THE WYND

Isle of Man

Eighteen Acre

GARBUTTS LA

Holly Trees

Marwin

Hutton Rudby Prim Sch

Hutton Rudby

SEXHOW LA

WILL LA

LANGBAURGH RD

INTERPEN

FLORA LA

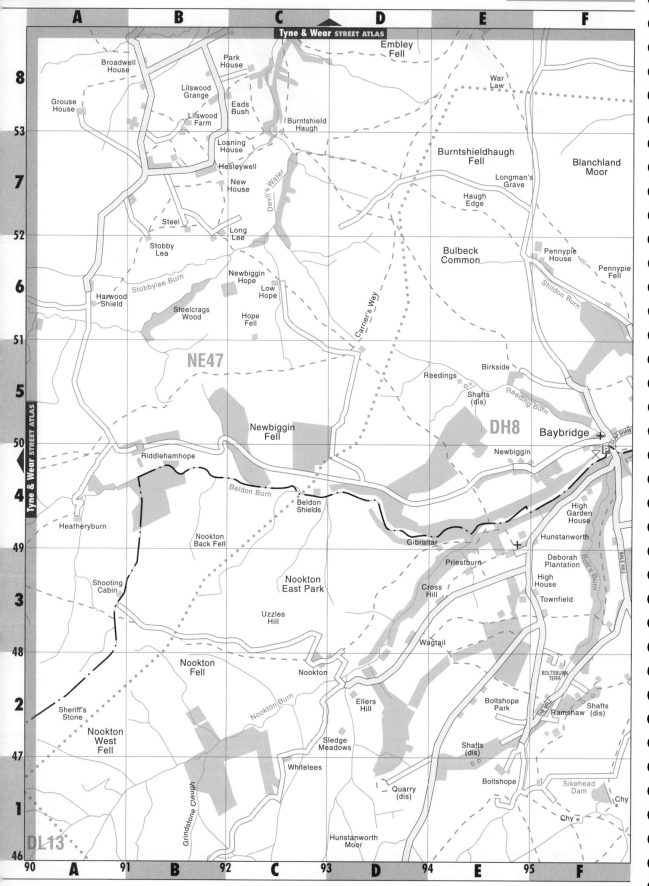

Scale: 1¾ inches to 1 mile

Embley Fell

War Law

Broadwell House

Park House

Lilswood Grange

Eads Bush

Burntshield Haugh

Grouse House

Lilswood Farm

Burntshieldhaugh Fell

Blanchland Moor

Loaning House

Longman's Grave

Hesleywell

New House

Haugh Edge

Steel

Long Lee

Bulbeck Common

Pennypie House

Pennypie Fell

Stobby Lea

Newbiggin Hope

Low Hope

Shildon Burn

Harwood Shield

Stobbylee Burn

Steelcrags Wood

Hope Fell

Birkside

Reedings

Shafts (dis)

Reeding Burn

NE47

Carrier's Way

Newbiggin Fell

DH8

Baybridge

CLAP SHAW

P

Riddlehamhope

Newbiggin

High Garden House

Beldon Burn

Beldon Shields

Gibraltar

Hunstanworth

Heatheryburn

Nookton Back Fell

Priestburn

Deborah Plantation

Boll's Burn

BALE HILL

Shooting Cabin

Nookton East Park

Cross Hill

High House

Townfield

Uzzles Hill

Wagtail

BOLTSBURN TERR

Nookton Fell

Nookton

Shafts (dis)

Sheriff's Stone

Nookton Burn

Ellers Hill

Boltshope Park

THE MILL

Ramshaw

Nookton West Fell

Sledge Meadows

Shafts (dis)

Boltshope

Whitelees

Sikehead Dam

Chy

Quarry (dis)

Chy

DL13

Hunstanworth Moor

Grindstone Cleugh

Devil's Water

176

Scale: 1¾ inches to 1 mile

0 ¼ ½ mile

0 250m 500m 750m 1 km

Tyne & Wear STREET ATLAS

NE47

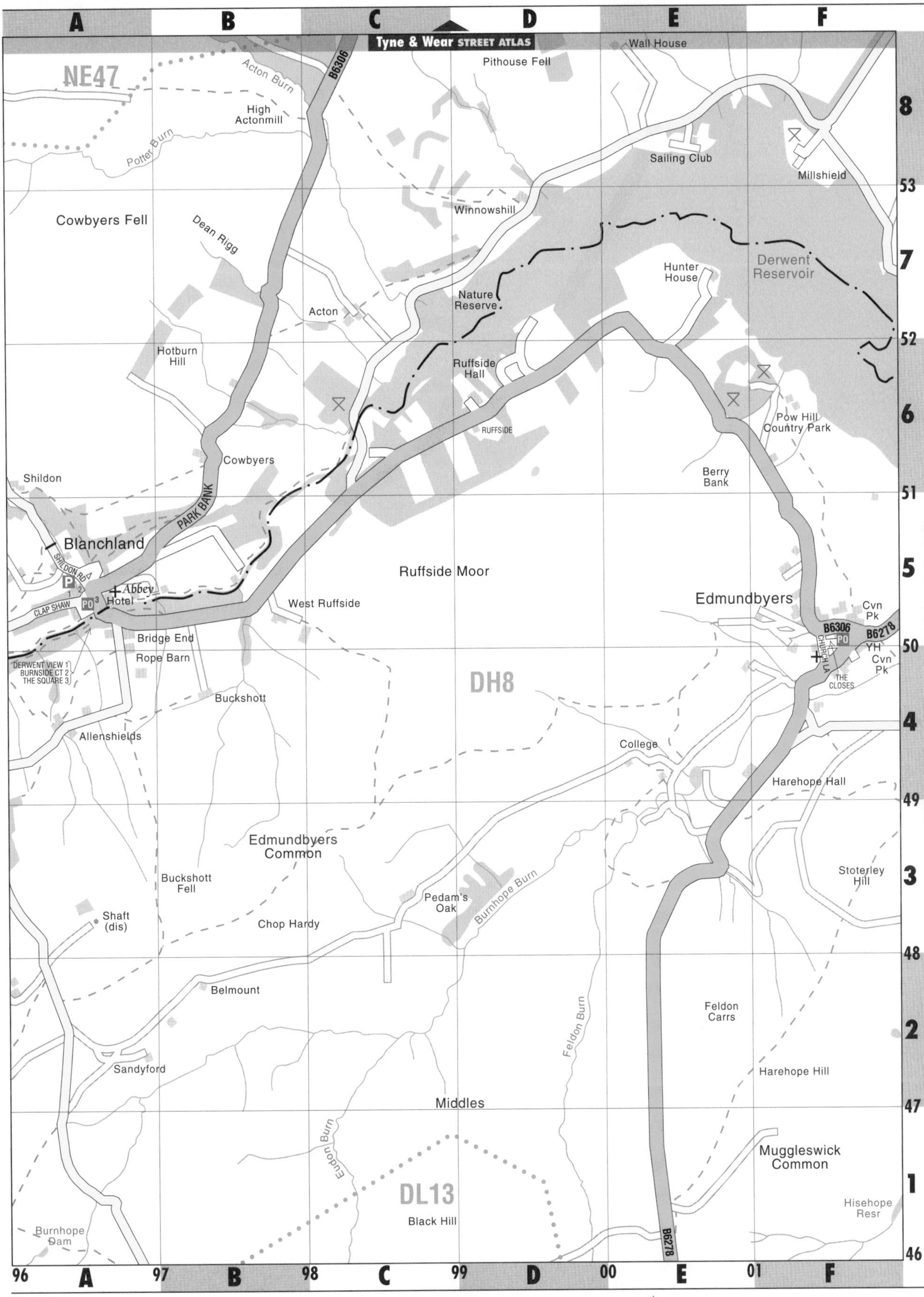

A B C D E F

8

Acton Burn

B6306

High Actonmill

Pithouse Fell

Wall House

Sailing Club

Millshield

53

Cowbyers Fell

Dean Rigg

Potter Burn

Winnowshill

Hunter House

Derwent Reservoir

7

Acton

Nature Reserve

Hotburn Hill

Ruffside Hall

52

RUFFSIDE

Pow Hill Country Park

6

Shildon

Cowbyers

RUFFSIDE

Berry Bank

51

PARK BANK

Blanchland

Ruffside Moor

Edmundbyers

B6306

Cvn Pk

B6278

5

SHILDON RD

P

Abbey

Hotel

West Ruffside

PO

YH

Cvn Pk

CHURCH LA

50

P

PO

CLAP SHAW

Bridge End

Rope Barn

THE CLOSES

DERWENT VIEW 1
BURNSIDE CT 2
THE SQUARE 3

Buckshott

DH8

College

4

Allenshields

Harehope Hall

49

Edmundbyers Common

Stoterley Hill

3

Buckshott Fell

Pedam's Oak

Burnhope Burn

Shaft (dis)

Chop Hardy

48

Belmount

Feldon Carrs

Feldon Burn

2

Sandyford

Harehope Hill

47

Middles

Muggleswick Common

B6278

Euden Burn

1

DL13

Black Hill

Hisehope Resr

Burnhope Dam

46

96 A 97 B 98 C 99 D 00 E 01 F

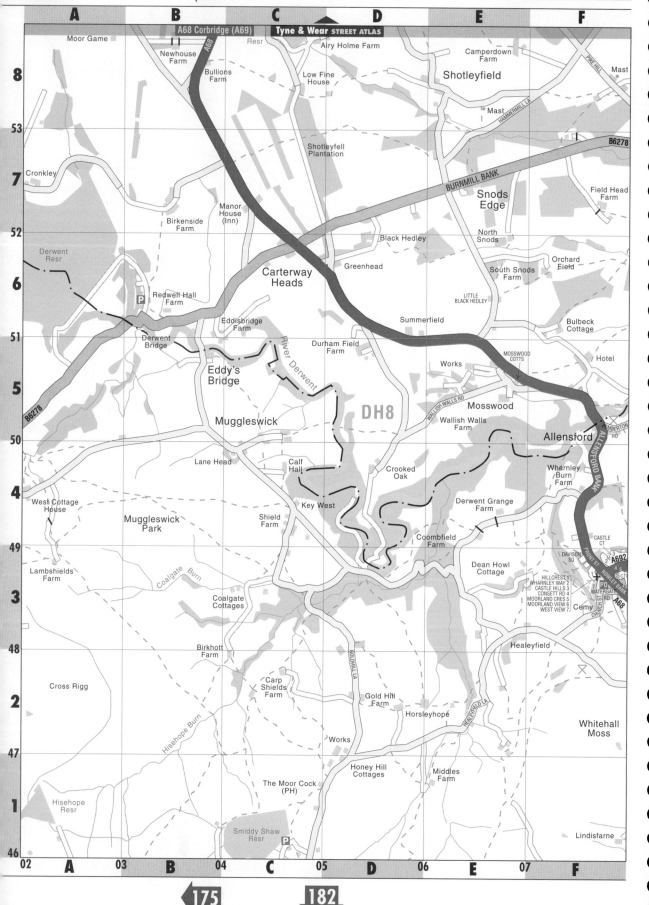

Scale: 1¾ inches to 1 mile

| 0 | ¼ | ½ mile |
| 0 | 250m | 500m 750m | 1 km |

A68 Corbridge (A69)

Tyne & Wear STREET ATLAS

Moor Game

Newhouse Farm

Bullions Farm

Airy Holme Farm

Camperdown Farm

Shotleyfield

Resr

Low Fine House

Mast

PIKE HILL

Mast

8

53

Shotleyfell Plantation

HAMMERMILL LA

B6278

7

Cronkley

BURNMILL BANK

Snods Edge

Field Head Farm

52

Birkenside Farm

Manor House (Inn)

Black Hedley

North Snods

Derwent Resr

Greenhead

South Snods Farm

Orchard Field

6

Carterway Heads

LITTLE BLACK HEDLEY

Bulbeck Cottage

Redwell Hall Farm

Summerfield

MOSSWOOD COTTS

Hotel

51

Eddisbridge Farm

Durham Field Farm

Works

Derwent Bridge

River Derwent

Eddy's Bridge

DH8

Mosswood

5

WALLISH WALLS RD

Wallish Walls Farm

Allensford

PEMBERTON RD

Muggleswick

Lane Head

Calf Hall

Crooked Oak

Wharnley Burn Farm

ALLENSFORD BANK

50

West Cottage House

Key West

Derwent Grange Farm

CASTLE CT

4

Muggleswick Park

Shield Farm

Coombfield Farm

DAVISON SQ

3

A692

Dean Howl Cottage

HILLCREST 1
WHARNLEY WAY 2
CASTLE HILLS 3
CONSETT RD 4
MOORLAND CRES 5
MOORLAND VIEW 6
WEST VIEW 7

FRONT ST

ROWLEY BANK

PO

WATERGATE RD

A68

Lambshields Farm

Coalgate Burn

Cemy

48

Birkhott Farm

Healeyfield

Cross Rigg

Carp Shields Farm

GOLDHILL LA

Gold Hill Farm

2

Hisehope Burn

Horsleyhopé

HEALEYFIELD LA

Whitehall Moss

47

Works

1

Hisehope Resr

The Moor Cock (PH)

Honey Hill Cottages

Middles Farm

Lindisfarne

46

Smiddy Shaw Resr

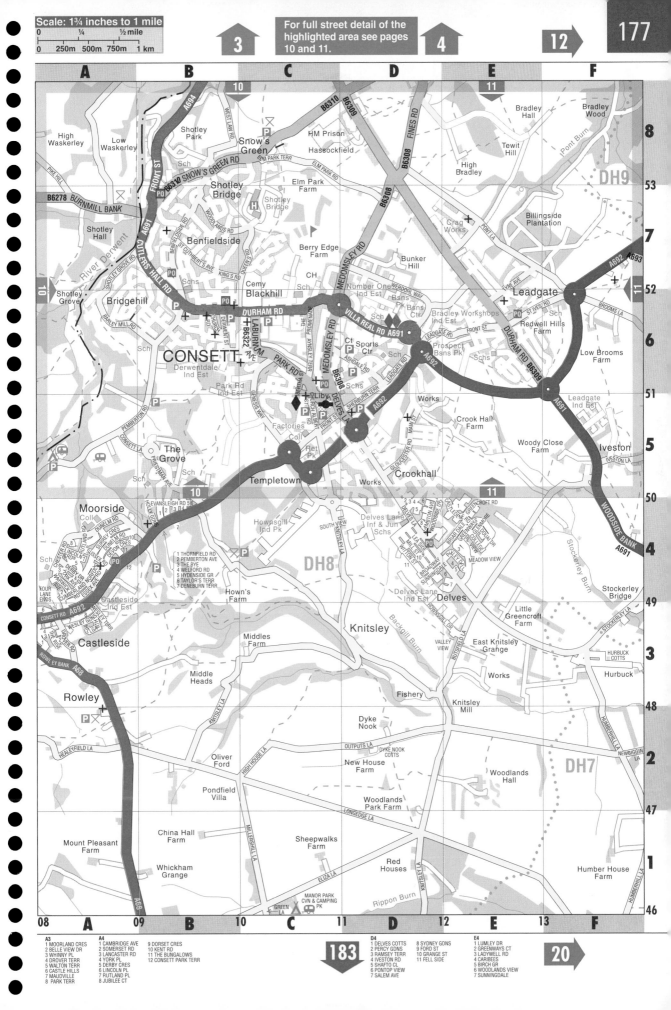

Scale: 1¾ inches to 1 mile

3 · 4 · 12 · 177

For full street detail of the highlighted area see pages 10 and 11.

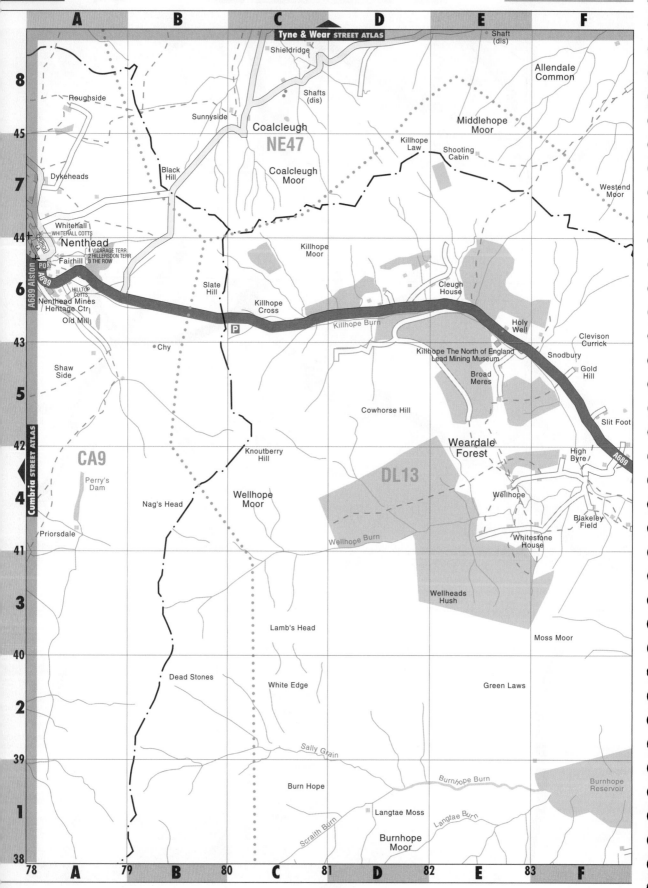

Shaft (dis)

Shieldridge

Allendale Common

Shafts (dis)

Roughside

Coalcleugh

NE47

Middlehope Moor

Sunnyside

Killhope Law

Shooting Cabin

Dykeheads

Black Hill

Coalcleugh Moor

Westend Moor

Whitehall
WHITEHALL COTTS

Nenthead

Killhope Moor

1 VICARAGE TERR
2 HILLERSDON TERR
3 THE ROW

Fairhill

Cleugh House

Slate Hill

Killhope Cross

Holy Well

Nenthead Mines Heritage Ctr

Killhope Burn

Clevison Currick

Old Mill

Killhope The North of England Lead Mining Museum

Snodbury

Chy

Gold Hill

Shaw Side

Broad Meres

Cowhorse Hill

Slit Foot

Knoutberry Hill

Weardale Forest

High Byre

A689

Perry's Dam

DL13

Wellhope

Nag's Head

Wellhope Moor

Blakeley Field

Priorsdale

Whitestone House

Wellhope Burn

Wellheads Hush

Lamb's Head

Moss Moor

Dead Stones

White Edge

Green Laws

Sally Grain

Burnhope Burn

Burnhope Reservoir

Burn Hope

Langtae Moss

Langtae Burn

Scraith Burn

Burnhope Moor

A689 Alston

Cumbria STREET ATLAS

CA9

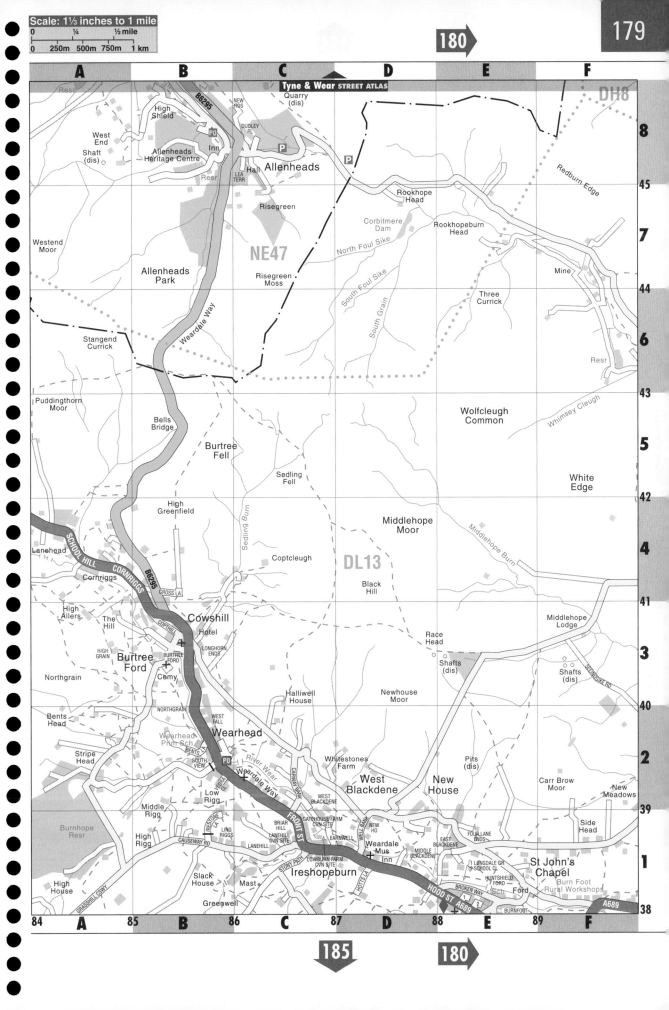

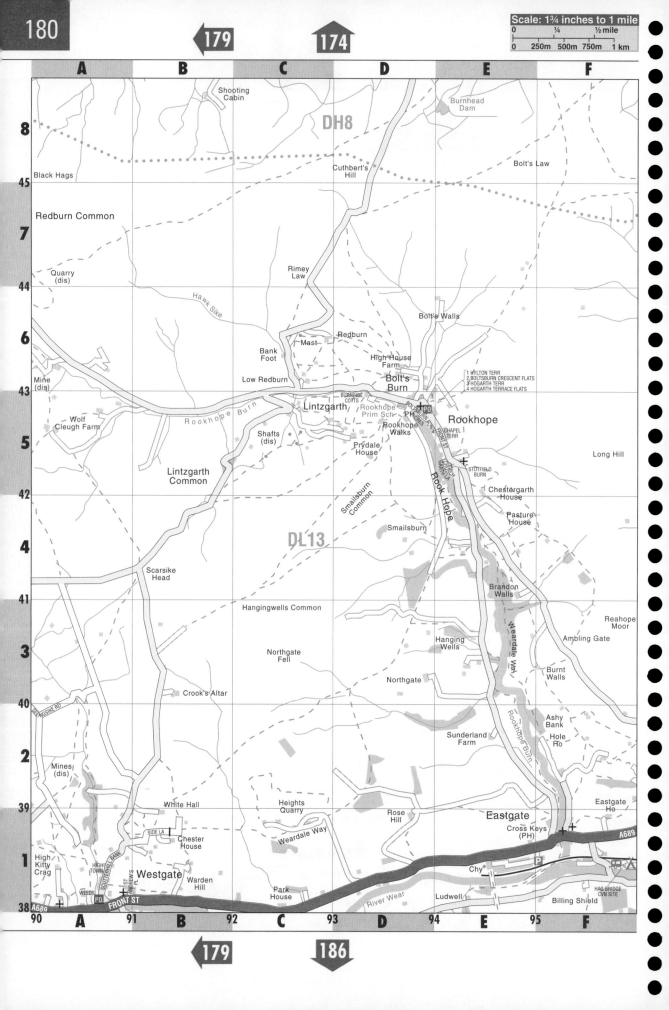

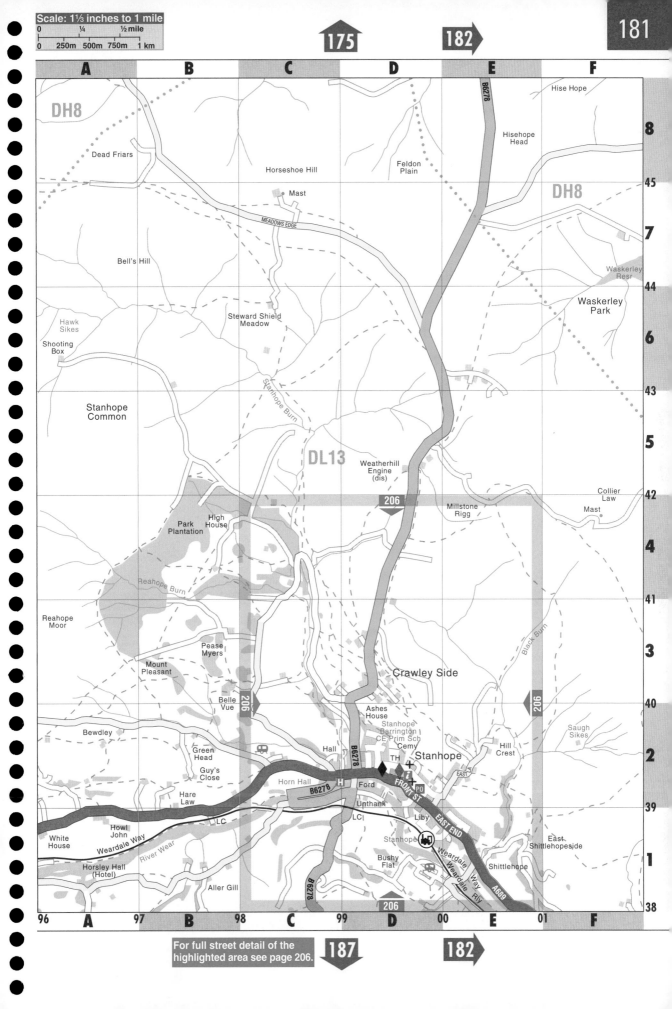

Scale: 1⅓ inches to 1 mile

0 ¼ ½ mile
0 250m 500m 750m 1 km

175
182

A   B   C   D   E   F

DH8

Hise Hope

Dead Friars

Horseshoe Hill

Feldon Plain

Hisehope Head

Mast

DH8

MEADOWS EDGE

Bell's Hill

Waskerley Resr

Steward Shield Meadow

Hawk Sikes

Waskerley Park

Shooting Box

Stanhope Burn

Stanhope Common

DL13

Weatherhill Engine (dis)

Collier Law

206

Mast

Millstone Rigg

Park Plantation

High House

Reahope Burn

Black Burn

Reahope Moor

Pease Myers

Crawley Side

206

Mount Pleasant

Belle Vue

Saugh Sikes

Ashes House

Bewdley

Stanhope Barrington CE Prim Sch

Green Head

Hall

Cemy

Stanhope

206

Hill Crest

Guy's Close

TH

EAST

Horn Hall

B6278

Ford

PO

Hare Law

FRONT ST

Unthank

LC

LC

Liby

EAST END

White House

Howl John

Weardale Way

Stanhope

Weardale Way

East Shittlehopeside

Horsley Hall (Hotel)

River Wear

Bushy Flat

Weardale Rly

Shittlehope

Aller Gill

A689

206

96   97   98   99   00   01

A   B   C   D   E   F

8
45
7
44
6
43
5
42
4
41
3
40
2
39
1
38

For full street detail of the highlighted area see page 206.

187
182

181
176

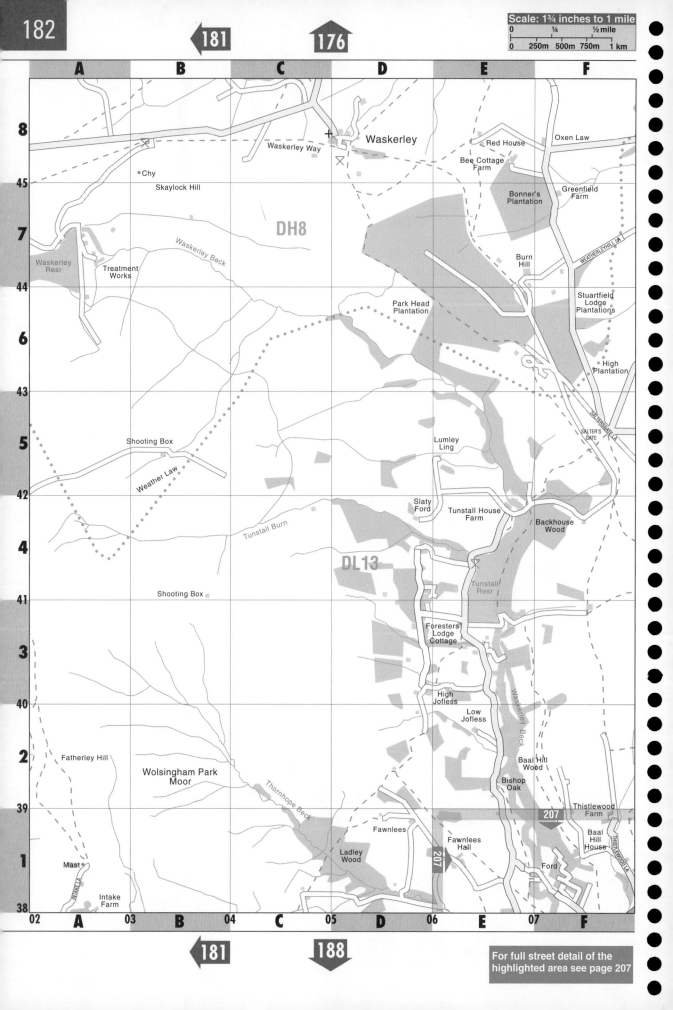

A   B   C   D   E   F

8

Waskerley Way

Waskerley

Red House

Oxen Law

Bee Cottage
Farm

45

Chy

Skaylock Hill

Bonner's
Plantation

Greenfield
Farm

7

DH8

Burn
Hill

Waskerley Beck

Stuartfield
Lodge
Plantations

Waskerley
Resr

Treatment
Works

44

High
Plantation

Park Head
Plantation

6

43

SALTERSGATE LA

SALTER'S
GATE

5

Shooting Box

Lumley
Ling

Weather Law

42

Slaty
Ford

Tunstall House
Farm

Backhouse
Wood

Tunstall Burn

4

DL13

Tunstall
Resr

Shooting Box

41

Foresters'
Lodge
Cottage

3

High
Jofless

40

Low
Jofless

Fatherley Hill

Baal Hill
Wood

2

Wolsingham Park
Moor

Bishop
Oak

Thornhope Beck

Thistlewood
Farm

39

207

Fawnlees

Baal Hill
House

1

Mast

Ladley
Wood

Fawnlees
Hall

207

Ford

INTAKE LA

Intake
Farm

38

02   A   03   B   04   C   05   D   06   E   07   F

WEATHERLEYHILL LA

THISTLEWOOD LA

181
188

For full street detail of the
highlighted area see page 207

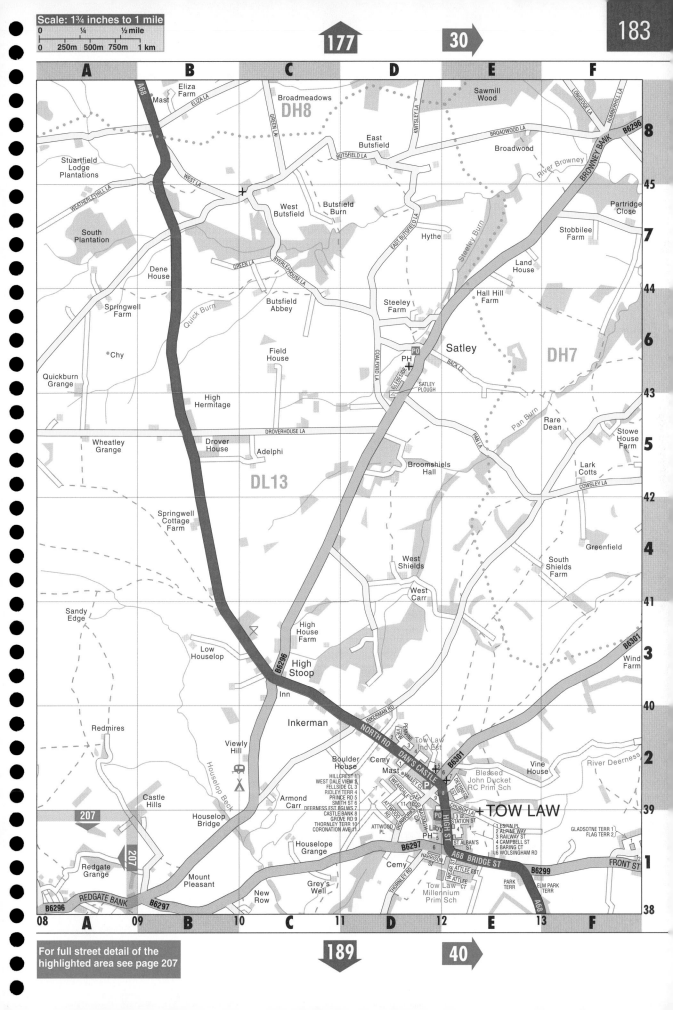

A | B | C | D | E | F

8
45
7
44
6
43
5
42
4
41
3
40
2
39
1
38

DH8

Mast
Eliza Farm
Broadmeadows
Sawmill Wood

Stuartfield Lodge Plantations
East Butsfield
Broadwood
BROADWOOD LA
Partridge Close

WEST LA
WEATHERLEYHILL LA
South Plantation
West Butsfield
Butsfield Burn
BUTSFIELD LA
Hythe
Stobbilee Farm

Dene House
GREEN LA
BYERLEYHOUSE LA
Butsfield Abbey
EAST BUTSFIELD LA
Steeley Farm
Land House

Springwell Farm
Quick Burn
Field House
Hall Hill Farm

Chy
Satley
DH7

Quickburn Grange
High Hermitage
COALFORD LA
PH
PO
GLEBESIDE LA
BACK LA
SATLEY PLOUGH

Wheatley Grange
DROVERHOUSE LA
Drover House
Adelphi
Pan Burn
Rare Dean
Stowe House Farm

DL13
Broomshiels Hall
PAN LA
Lark Cotts
COWSLEY LA

Springwell Cottage Farm
West Shields
South Shields Farm
Greenfield

Sandy Edge
West Carr

Low Houselop
High House Farm
B6301
Wind Farm

Redmires
B6296
High Stoop
Inn

Viewly Hill
Inkerman
NORTH RD
INKERMAN RD
PRIME VIEW
Tow Law Ind Est
River Deerness

Castle Hills
Boulder House
DAN'S CASTLE
Cemy
Mast
Vine House

Houselop Bridge
Armond Carr
HILLCREST 1
WEST DALE VIEW 2
FELLSIDE CL 3
RIDLEY TERR 4
PRINCE RD 5
SMITH ST 6
DEERNESS EST BGLWS 7
CASTLE BANK 8
GROVE RD 9
THORNLEY TERR 10
CORONATION AVE 11
WEARDALE CRES
ATTWOOD RD
IRONWORKS GR
NASMITH GR
PO
CHURCH LA
DEERNESS EST
Blessed John Ducket RC Prim Sch
TOW LAW

207
Redgate Grange
Houselope Grange
ATTWOOD PL
St Alban's
Liby
PH
HIGH ST
STATION ST
1 ESPLIN PL
2 ALPINE WAY
3 RAILWAY ST
4 CAMPBELL ST
5 BARING CT
6 WOLSINGHAM RD
GLADSOTNE TERR 1
FLAG TERR 2

Mount Pleasant
New Row
Grey's Well
B6297
Cemy
HARRISON
WEAR RD
ST ALBAN'S ST
BRIDGE ST
A68
ATTLEE EST
PARK TERR
B6299
FRONT ST
ELM PARK TERR

B6296
REDGATE BANK
B6297
THORNLEY RD
Tow Law Millennium Prim Sch
A68

08 | A | 09 | B | 10 | C | 11 | D | 12 | E | 13 | F

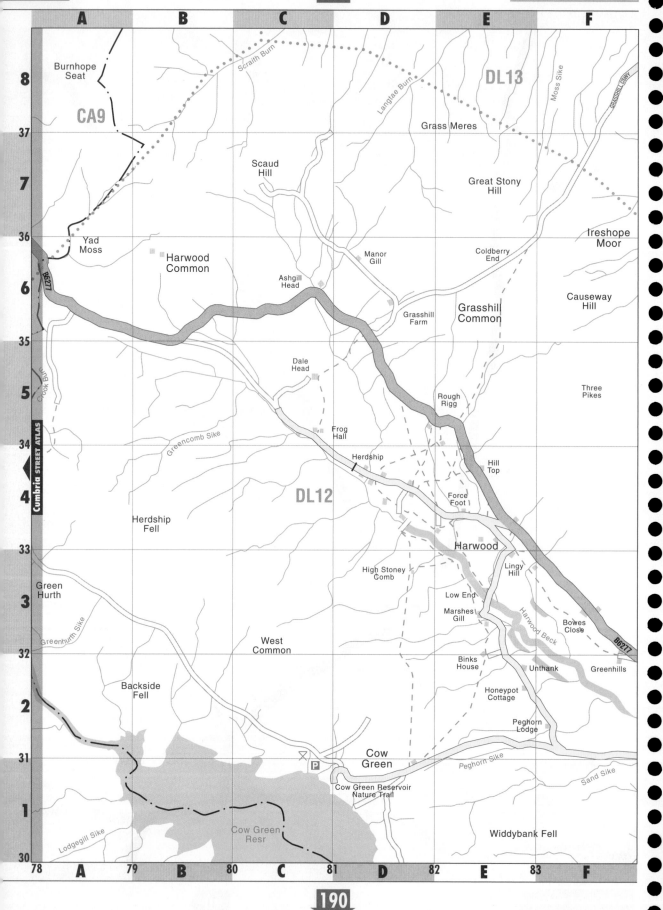

Scale: 1¾ inches to 1 mile
0   ¼   ½ mile
0   250m 500m 750m 1 km

A   B   C   D   E   F

8   Burnhope
     Seat   Scraith Burn   DL13   Moss Sike

CA9

37   Grass Meres

7   Scaud
                     Hill   Great Stony
                                                     Hill   Ireshope
36   Yad   Moor
              Moss   Harwood   Manor   Coldberry
B6277   Common   Gill   End
6   Ashgill   Grasshill   Causeway
                                     Head   Common   Hill

35   Grasshill
                                             Farm

5   Dale   Rough   Three
     Crook Burn   Head   Rigg   Pikes

34   Cumbria STREET ATLAS   Frog
                         Greencomb Sike   Hall
                                              Herdship   Hill
                                                                                Top
4   DL12   Force
                         Herdship   Foot
                         Fell   Harwood

33   Lingy
     Green   High Stoney   Hill
     Hurth   Comb   Low End   Bowes
3   Marshes   Close
     Greenhurth Sike   Gill   Harwood Beck
                                              West   B6277
32   Common   Binks
                                                             House   Unthank   Greenhills
                         Backside   Honeypot
2   Fell   Cottage
                                                                          Peghorn
                                                                          Lodge
31   Cow
                                    P   Green   Sand Sike
                                         Cow Green Reservoir   Peghorn Sike
1   Nature Trail
     Lodgegill Sike
                              Cow Green   Widdybank Fell
30   Resr

78   A   79   B   80   C   81   D   82   E   83   F

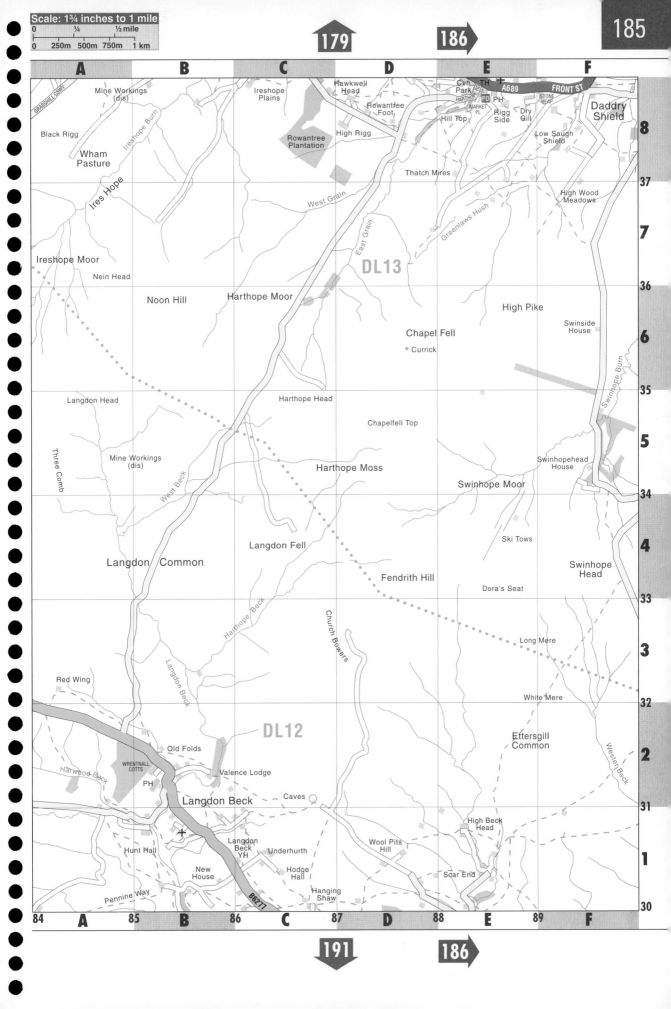

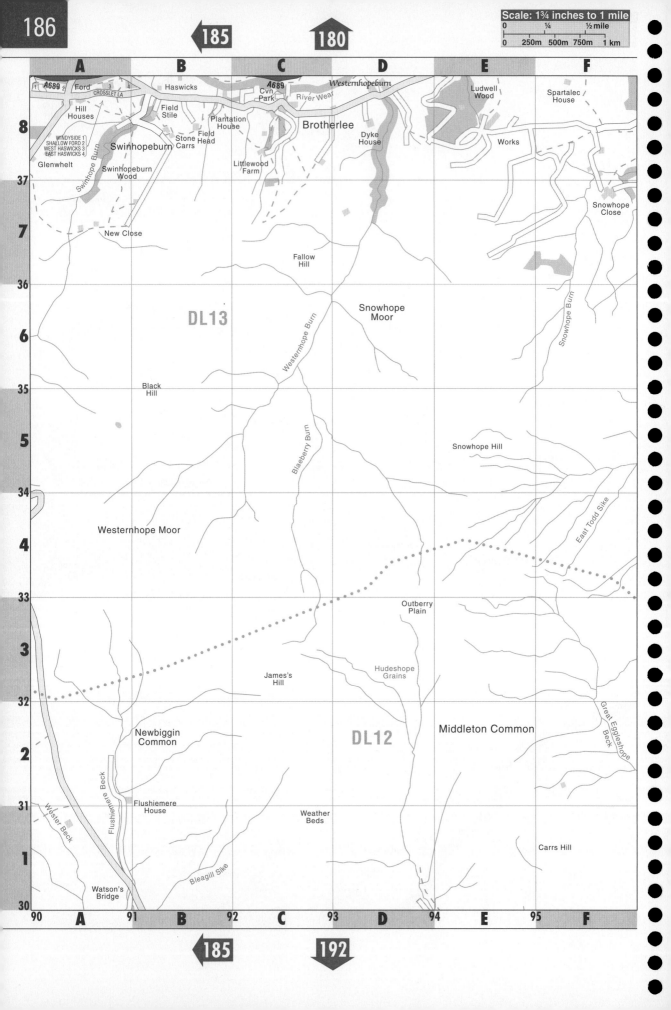

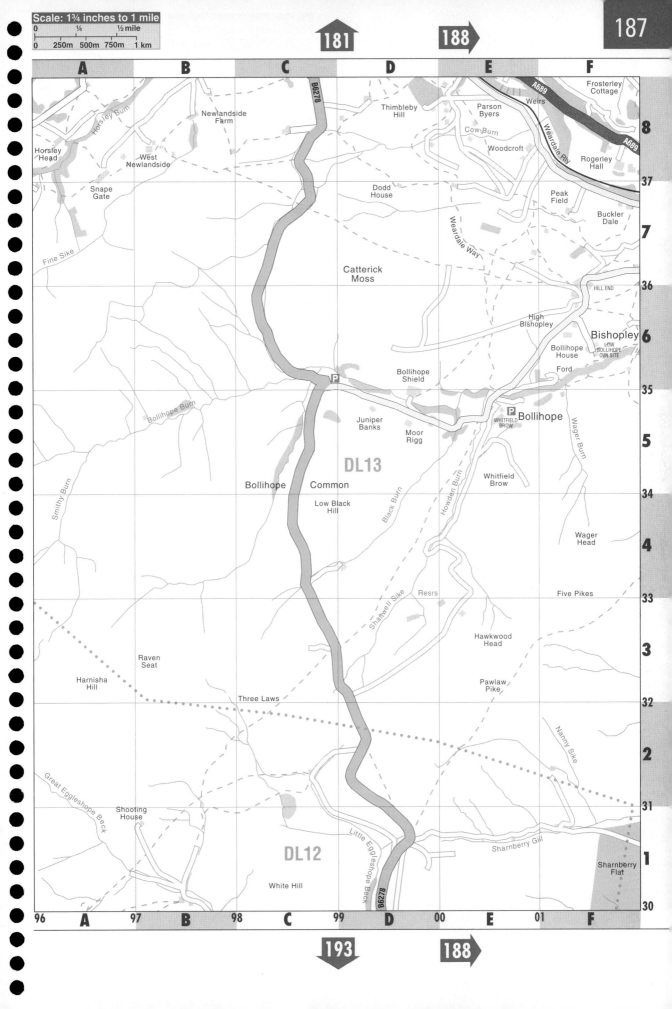

187
182

For full street detail of the highlighted area see page 207

Scale: 1¾ inches to 1 mile

0   ¼   ½ mile
0   250m 500m 750m 1 km

A   B   C   D   E   F

High Barn

Newlands Hall

Lason Field

Leazes Farm

Wolsingham
Upper Town

West Newlands

Frosterley
Cvn Pk
PH
1 STOCKLEY GR
2 STOCKLEY CRES

Hare Law

West Field House

Sch
PH
HIGH ST
A689

8

A689
WESTFIELD
KIRK RISE
P
FRONT ST
PO
HOLMEFIELD

37

MELLBUTTS BANK

River Wear

Weardale Way

LC

Wolsingham

BRIDGE END
Frosterley
Sch
BELLE VUE
NEW HOUSES
Quarry (dis)

1 WESTERN HILL
2 DENE HILL
3 THE GREEN
4 OSBORNE TERR
5 CROMER LEA
6 CROFT TERR (E)
7 CROFT TERR (W)
8 WEAR VIEW
9 GREENWELL TERR

Wks

THE BATTS

Landieu

LC

Weardale Rly LC

Holebeck House

207

Ashes House

High Wiserley

7

Coves House Farm

Towdy Potts

Friarside

WEAR BANK

36

Low Bishopley Cotts

Low Bishopley

White Kirkley

Biggins

Sunniside Farm

Spence Hill

Carr's Farm

Chatterley

6

Fine House

Harehope

Harvey Hill

East Biggins Cottage

RUSHY LEA LA

HOWLEA LA

35

207

Harthope

Lodge Wood

5

Allotment House

St John's Hall

The Lodge

Shank Wood

34

Fine Burn

Tank Wood

Ruddy Carr

4

Mine Workings (dis)

33

North Grain Beck

Doctor's Gate

Cabin Hill

3

Pikeston Fell

Quarries (dis)

32

South Grain Beck

Ayhope Beck

2

Potato Hill

North Crag Wood

31

Hamsterley Common

Redford

1

Black Hill

Brown Law

Euden Beck Cottage

Frog Wood

Sharnberry Flat

30

02   A   03   B   04   C   05   D   06   E   07   F

DL13

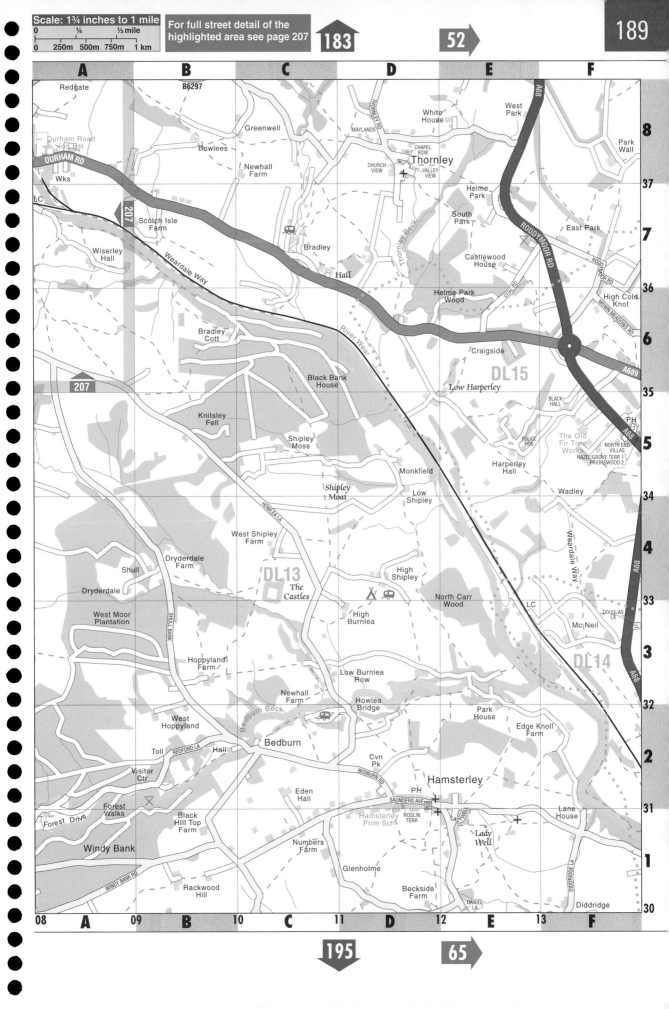

Scale: 1¾ inches to 1 mile

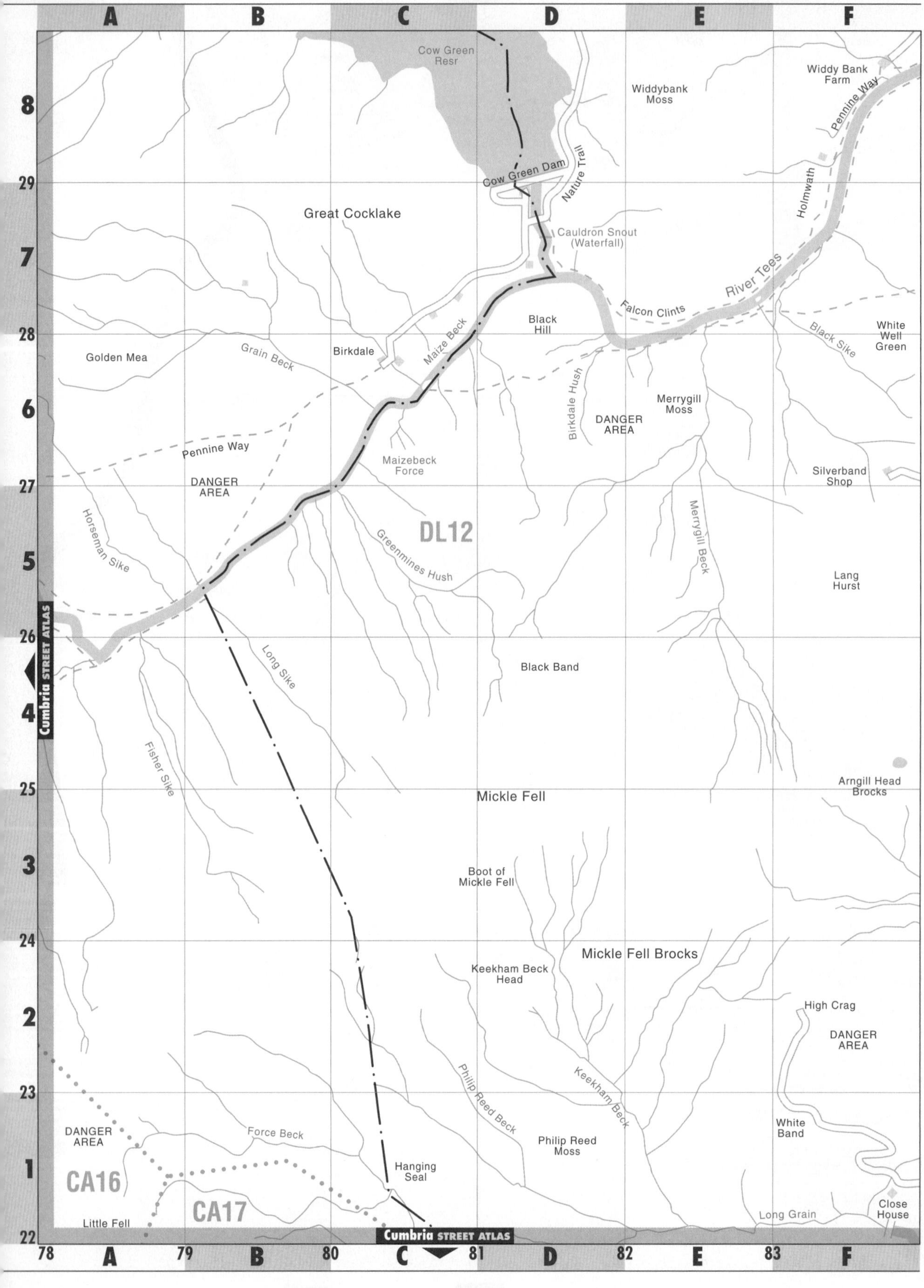

0	¼	½ mile
0	250m 500m 750m	1 km

A B C D E F

Cumbria STREET ATLAS

Cow Green Resr

Widdybank Moss

Widdy Bank Farm

Pennine Way

Cow Green Dam

Nature Trail

Holmwath

Great Cocklake

Cauldron Snout (Waterfall)

River Tees

Falcon Clints

Black Sike

White Well Green

Maize Beck

Black Hill

Golden Mea

Grain Beck

Birkdale

Birkdale Hush

Merrygill Moss

Pennine Way

Maizebeck Force

DANGER AREA

DANGER AREA

Silverband Shop

Horseman Sike

DL12

Greenmines Hush

Merrygill Beck

Lang Hurst

Long Sike

Black Band

Fisher Sike

Mickle Fell

Arngill Head Brocks

Boot of Mickle Fell

Mickle Fell Brocks

Keekham Beck Head

Philip Reed Beck

Keekham Beck

High Crag

DANGER AREA

Force Beck

Philip Reed Moss

White Band

DANGER AREA

Hanging Seal

CA16

CA17

Little Fell

Long Grain

Close House

78 A 79 B 80 C 81 D 82 E 83 F

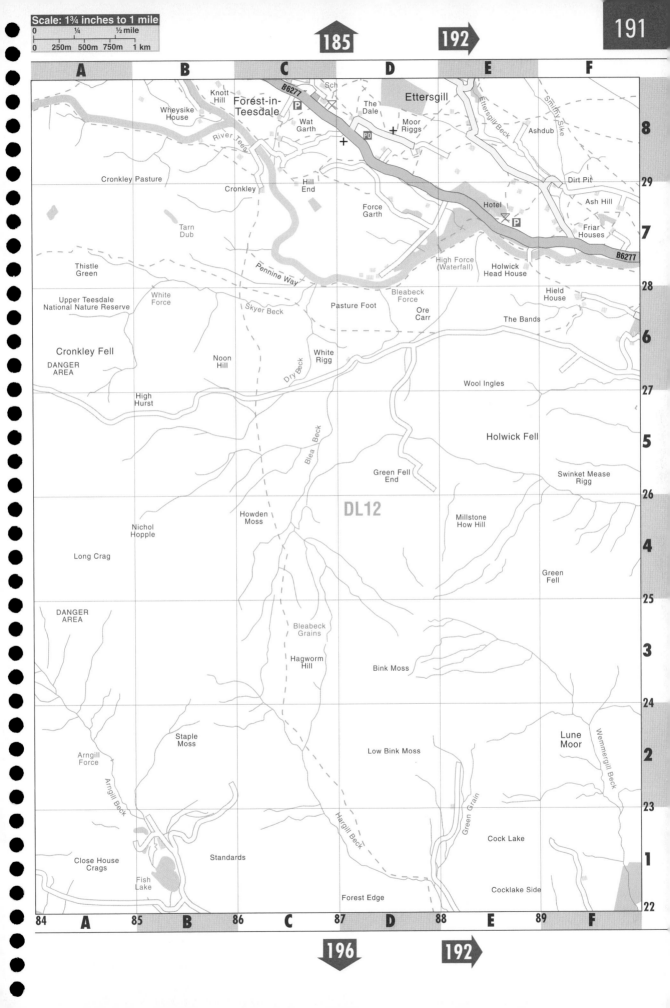

Scale: 1¾ inches to 1 mile

0   ¼   ½ mile

0   250m   500m   750m   1 km

185
192
196
192

A   B   C   D   E   F

Knott Hill
Wheysike House
Forest-in-Teesdale
B6277
Sch
The Dale
Ettersgill
Ettersgill Beck
Smithy Sike
Ashdub
Wat Garth
Moor Riggs
PO
8
River Tees
Cronkley Pasture
Cronkley
Hill End
Force Garth
Hotel
Dirt Pit
29
Ash Hill
Friar Houses
Tarn Dub
7
High Force (Waterfall)
Holwick Head House
B6277
Thistle Green
Pennine Way
Bleabeck Force
Hield House
28
Upper Teesdale National Nature Reserve
White Force
Skyer Beck
Pasture Foot
Ore Carr
The Bands
6
Cronkley Fell
Noon Hill
Dry beck
White Rigg
Wool Ingles
27
DANGER AREA
High Hurst
Blea Beck
Holwick Fell
5
Green Fell End
Swinket Mease Rigg
Howden Moss
DL12
Millstone How Hill
26
Nichol Hopple
Long Crag
Green Fell
4
25
DANGER AREA
Bleabeck Grains
Hagworm Hill
Bink Moss
3
24
Staple Moss
Low Bink Moss
Lune Moor
Wemmergill Beck
2
Arngill Force
Arngill Beck
Hargill Beck
Green Grain
23
Close House Crags
Fish Lake
Standards
Cock Lake
1
Forest Edge
Cocklake Side
22

84   A   85   B   86   C   87   D   88   E   89   F

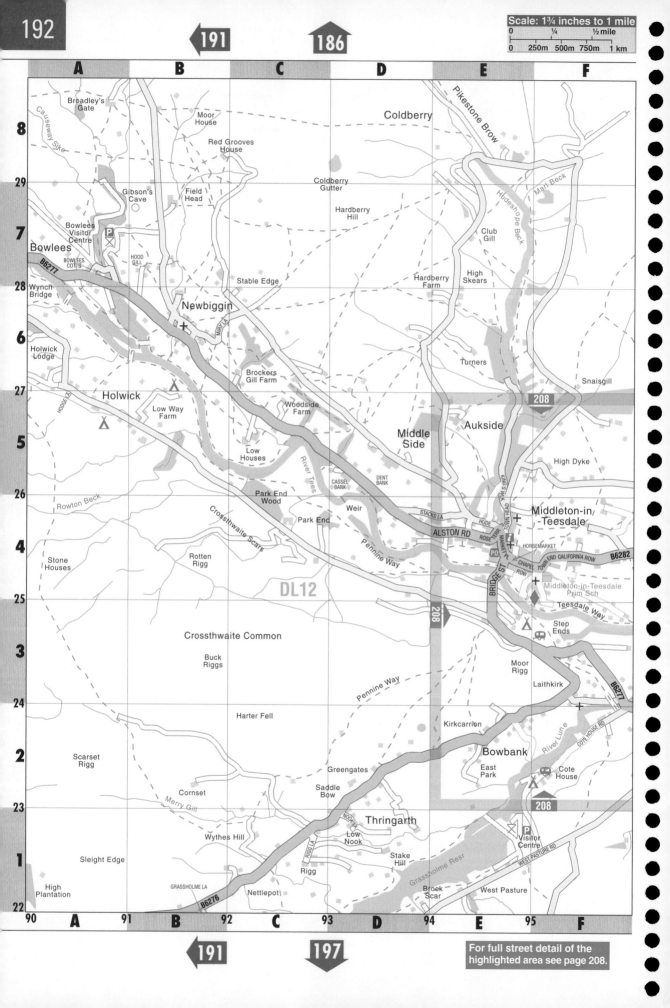

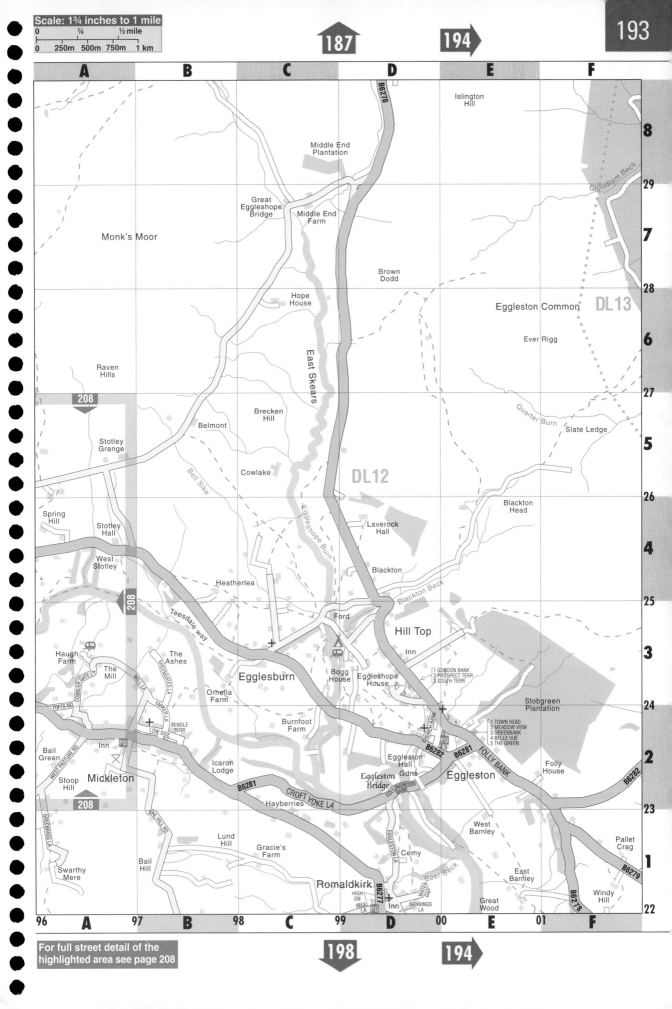

Scale: 1¾ inches to 1 mile

0   ¼   ½ mile

0   250m 500m 750m 1 km

187

194

193

A   B   C   D   E   F

B6278

Islington Hill

Middle End Plantation

8

29

Great Eggleshope Bridge

Middle End Farm

Monk's Moor

7

Brown Dodd

28

Hope House

Eggleston Common

DL13

6

East Skears

Ever Rigg

27

208

Raven Hills

Quarter Burn

Slate Ledge

5

Belmont

Brecken Hill

Bell Sike

Spring Hill

Stotley Grange

DL12

Blackton Head

26

Cowlake

Eggleshope Burn

Stotley Hall

Laverock Hall

4

West Stotley

208

Heatherlea

Blackton

Blackton Beck

25

Teesdale way

Ford

Hill Top

3

Haugh Farm

The Ashes

Egglesburn

Bogg House

Eggleshope House

Inn

1 GORDON BANK
2 PROSPECT TERR
3 SOUTH TERR

The Mill

Ornella Farm

Stobgreen Plantation

24

COBBLER GATE LA

GREENGATES LA

MILL LA

YARKER LA

LOW SIDE

BENDLE TERR

Burnfoot Farm

CHURCH BANK

1 TOWN HEAD
2 MEADOW VIEW
3 GREENBANK
4 BELLE VUE
5 THE GREEN

TOFTS RD

Bail Green

Inn

PO

Icaron Lodge

B6281

Eggleston Hall Gdns

B6282

PO

B6281

FOLLY BANK

Eggleston

Folly House

2

B6282

WEST PASTURE RD

Stoop Hill

Mickleton

208

B6281

CROFT YOKE LA

Hayberries

Eggleston Bridge

COLLINGWOOD BANK

West Barnley

23

GREENRIGG LA

BAIL HILL RD

Lund Hill

Gracie's Farm

EGGLESTON LA

Cemy

Pallet Crag

Swarthy Mere

Bail Hill

Romaldkirk

B6277

HIGH GN FELL LA

Inn

PO

SENNINGS LA

Beer Beck

WATER GAP

East Barnley

Great Wood

B6278

B6279

Windy Hill

1

22

96   A   97   B   98   C   99   D   00   E   01   F

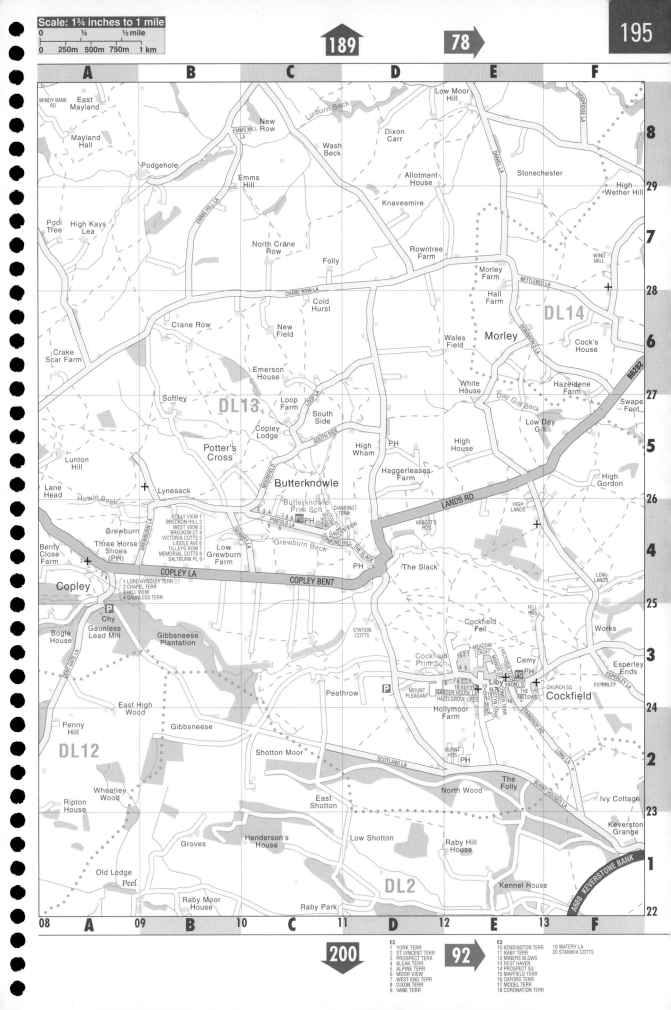

A   B   C   D   E   F

WINDY BANK RD
East Mayland
Mayland Hall
Podgehole
New Row
EMMS HILL LA
Emms Hill
Linburn Beck
Wash Beck
Dixon Carr
Low Moor Hill
DIDDRIDGE LA
Stonechester
High Wether Hill

Pool Tree
High Kays Lea
EMMS HILL LA
North Crane Row
Allotment House
Knavesmire
Rowntree Farm
DANIEL LA
Morley Farm
NETTLEBED LA
DL14
WIND MILL

Crake Scar Farm
Crane Row
Folly
New Field
CRANE ROW LA
Cold Hurst
Morley
Hall Farm
DOBINSON'S LA
Wales Field
White House
Cock's House
B6282

Softley
DL13
Emerson House
LOOP LA
Loop Farm
South Side
High House
Day Gill Beck
Hazeldene Farm
Low Day Gill
Swape Foot

Lunton Hill
Potter's Cross
Copley Lodge
MOORFIELD
South Side
SOUTH SIDE
High Wham
PH
High House
High Gordon

Lane Head
Butterknowle
Haggerleases Farm
High Lands

Howle Beck
Lynesack
GREWBURN LA
DIARRY LA
Butterknowle Prim Sch
PINFOLD LA
PO PH
DIAMOND TERR
GARDEN VIEW
LANDS RD
ABBOTT'S HOS
High Gordon

Benty Close Farm
Three Horse Shoes (PH)
FOLLY VIEW 1
BRECKON HILL 2
WEST VIEW 3
BRECKON CT 4
VICTORIA COTTS 5
LIDDLE AVE 6
TILLEYS ROW 7
MEMORIAL COTTS 8
SALTBURN PL 9
Low Grewburn Farm
Grewburn Beck
DIAMOND HILL
THE SLACK
PH
The Slack
LOW LANDS

Copley
COPLEY LA
COPLEY BENT
1 LORD HYNDLEY TERR
2 CHAPEL TERR
3 HILL VIEW
4 GAUNLESS TERR

Bogle House
P
Chy
Gaunless Lead Mill
Gibbsneese Plantation
STATION COTTS
Cockfield Fell
FELL HOS
Works

BENT GATE LA
East High Wood
Gibbsneese
Peathrow
P
MOUNT PLEASANT
Cockfield Prim Sch
MEADOW CROFT
VICTORIA RD
Cemy
PO PH
Esperley Ends
ESPERLEY

Penny Hill
Shotton Moor
SCOTLAND LA
Hollymoor Farm
GARDEN HOUSE
HAZELGROVE CRES
MANOR GR
GOMER TERR
WEST VW TERR
FRONT ST
Liby
THE FALLOWS
CHURCH SQ
Cockfield
ESPERLEY

DL12
Wheatley Wood
East Shotton
BURNT HOS
PH
North Wood
The Folly
STAINDROP RD
LONG LA
BURNT HOUSES LA
Ivy Cottage

Ripton House
Groves
Henderson's House
Low Shotton
Raby Hill House
Keverston Grange

Old Lodge Peel
Raby Moor House
Raby Park
DL2
Kennel House
A688 KEVERSTONE BANK

08   A   09   B   10   C   11   D   12   E   13   F

8 29 7 28 6 27 5 26 4 25 3 24 2 23 1 22

E3
1 YORK TERR
2 ST VINCENT TERR
3 PROSPECT TERR
4 BLEAK TERR
5 ALPINE TERR
6 MOOR VIEW
7 WEST END TERR
8 DIXON TERR
9 VANE TERR

E3
10 KENSINGTON TERR
11 RABY TERR
12 MINERS BLGWS
13 REST HAVEN
14 PROSPECT SQ
15 MAYFIELD TERR
16 OXFORD TERR
17 MODEL TERR
18 CORONATION TERR

19 WATERY LA
20 STANWIX COTTS

Scale: 1¾ inches to 1 mile
0   ¼   ½ mile
0   250m 500m 750m   1 km

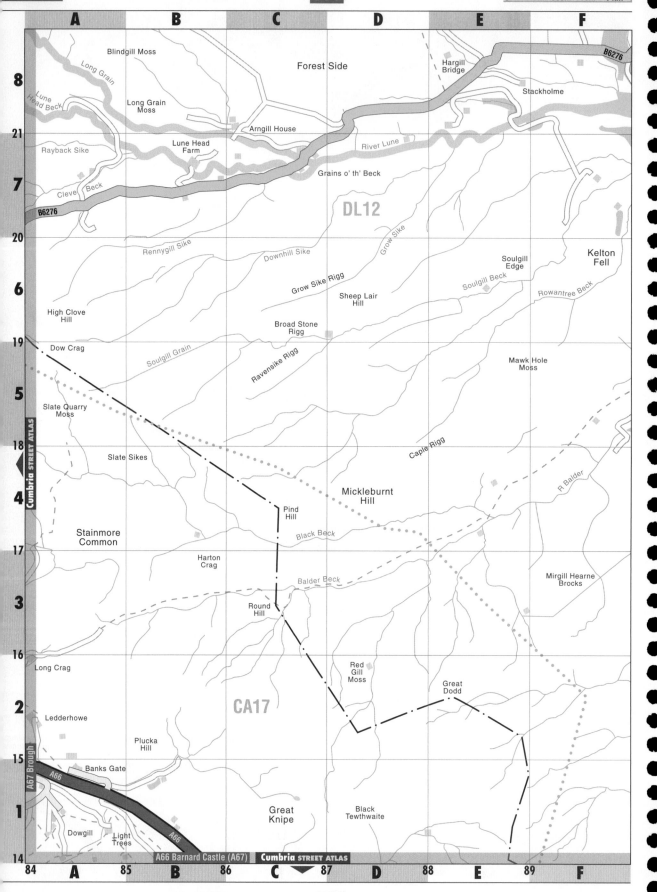

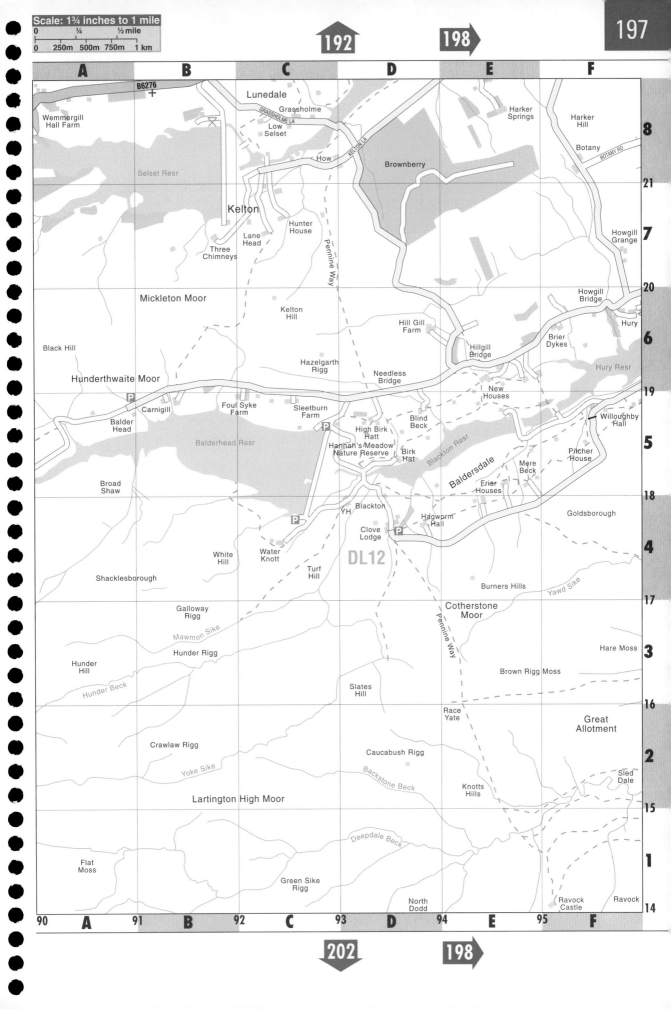

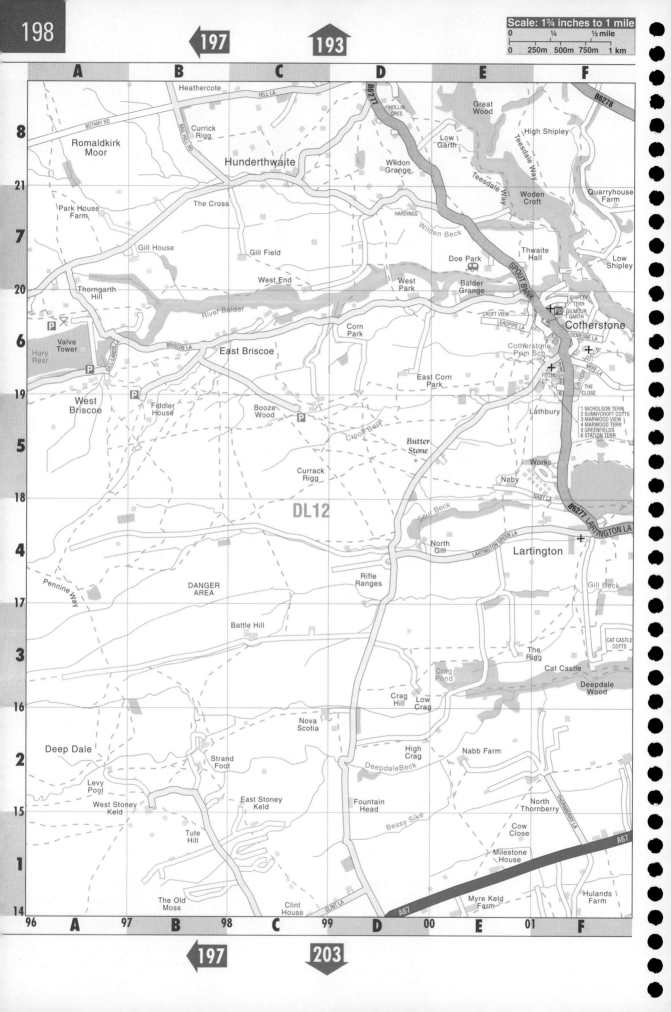

Scale: 1¾ inches to 1 mile

0	¼	½ mile
0	250m 500m 750m	1 km

A B C D E F

8

Heathercote

FELL LA

Romaldkirk Moor

BOTANY RD

BALL HILL RD

Currick Rigg

Hunderthwaite

HOLLIN CRES

B6277

Great Wood

High Shipley

Low Garth

Teesdale Way

B6278

21

Park House Farm

The Cross

Wildon Grange

Woden Croft

Quarryhouse Farm

7

HARDINGS

Wilden Beck

Teesdale Way

Thwaite Hall

Low Shipley

Gill House

Gill Field

West End

West Park

Doe Park

Balder Grange

SPOUT BANK

20

Thorngarth Hill

River Balder

CROFT VIEW

LEADPIPE LA

SHIPLEY TERR

GILMOUR GARTH

PO

Cotherstone

6

P

Valve Tower

BRISCOE LA

East Briscoe

Corn Park

Cotherstone Prim Sch

FITZHUGH CT

DEMESNE LA

3 4 5 6

MIRE LA

Larue Beck

THE CLOSE

Hury Resr

GILL LANDS LA

19

P

Fiddler House

Booze Wood

P

East Corn Park

Lathbury

1 NICHOLSON TERR
2 SUNNYCROFT COTTS
3 MARWOOD VIEW
4 MARWOOD TERR
5 GREENFIELDS
6 STATION TERR

West Briscoe

5

Crook Beck

Butter Stone

Works

Naby

Currack Rigg

NABY LA

B6277 LARTINGTON LA

18

DL12

Scur Beck

North Gill

LARTINGTON GREEN LA

Lartington

4

Pennine Way

Rifle Ranges

Gill Beck

17

DANGER AREA

Battle Hill

The Rigg

CAT CASTLE COTTS

3

Crag Pond

Cat Castle

Deepdale Wood

16

Nova Scotia

Crag Hill

Low Crag

Deep Dale

High Crag

Nabb Farm

2

Strand Foot

DeepdaleBeck

North Thornberry

THORNBERRY LA

Levy Pool

West Stoney Keld

East Stoney Keld

Fountain Head

Bessy Sike

Cow Close

15

Tute Hill

Milestone House

A67

1

The Old Moss

Clint House

GLINT LA

A67

Myre Keld Farm

Hulands Farm

14

96 A 97 B 98 C 99 D 00 E 01 F

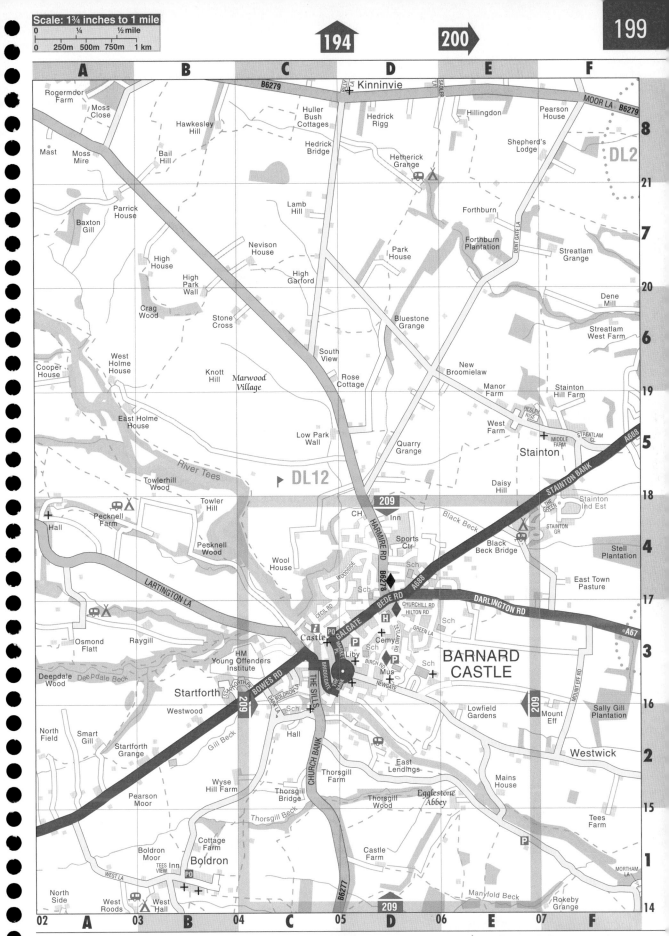

Scale: 1¾ inches to 1 mile

0   ¼   ½ mile
0 250m 500m 750m 1 km

A   B   C   D   E   F

8

21

7

20

6

19

5

18

4

17

3

16

2

15

1

14

Kinninvie

B6279

MOOR LA
B6279

Rogermoor Farm
Moss Close
Moss Mire
Mast
Baxton Gill
Parrick House
Hawkesley Hill
Bail Hill
High House
Crag Wood
High Park Wall
Nevison House
Stone Cross
Knott Hill
Marwood Village
Huller Bush Cottages
Hedrick Bridge
Lamb Hill
High Garford
South View
Rose Cottage
Hedrick Rigg
Hetherick Grange
Park House
Bluestone Grange
Hillingdon
Pearson House
Shepherd's Lodge
Forthburn
Forthburn Plantation
Streatlam Grange
Dene Mill
Streatlam West Farm
New Broomielaw
Manor Farm
Stainton Hill Farm
West Farm
Stainton
Daisy Hill
Middle Farm
Streatlam GR
DL2
DENT GATE LA
HESLEY RISE

DL12

River Tees

Cooper House
East Holme House
West Holme House
Towlerhill Wood
Towler Hill
Low Park Wall
Quarry Grange
STREATLAM CL
A688

Pecknell Farm
Hall
Pecknell Wood
Wool House
CH
Inn
Sports Ctr
Black Beck
STAINTON BANK
Stainton Ind Est
THE GREEN
STAINTON GR
Stell Plantation
Black Beck Bridge
East Town Pasture

LARTINGTON LA

209
HARMIRE RD
B6278
WOODSIDE
Sch
Sch
Sch
BEDE RD
A688
CHURCHILL RD
HILTON RD
Sch
GREEN LA
DARLINGTON RD
A67

Osmond Flatt
Raygill
CECIL RD
PO
i
Castle
GALGATE
MARKET PL
P
Cemy
ICELAND RD
Sch
Liby
BIRCH RD
P
Mus
NEWGATE
Sch
H
BARNARD CASTLE
MOUNT EFF RD
Sally Gill Plantation
Westwick

Deepdale Wood
Deepdale Beck
HM Young Offenders Institute
STAINDROP RD
209
BOWES RD
Startforth
Westwood
DARK LA
BOLDRON LA
THE SILLS
BRIDGEGATE
Sch
Sch
Hall
Gill Beck
Lowfield Gardens
209
Mount Eff

North Field
Smart Gill
Startforth Grange
Wyse Hill Farm
Thorsgill Bridge
Hall
CHURCH BANK
Thorsgill Farm
East Lendings
Thorsgill Wood
Egglestone Abbey
Mains House
Tees Farm

Pearson Moor
Thorsgill Beck
B6277
Castle Farm
209
Manyfold Beck
Mortham LA
Rokeby Grange

Boldron Moor
Cottage Farm
Boldron
TEES INN VIEW
PO
WEST LA
North Side
West Roods
West Hall

02   A   03   B   04   C   05   D   06   E   07   F

For full street detail of the highlighted area see page 209

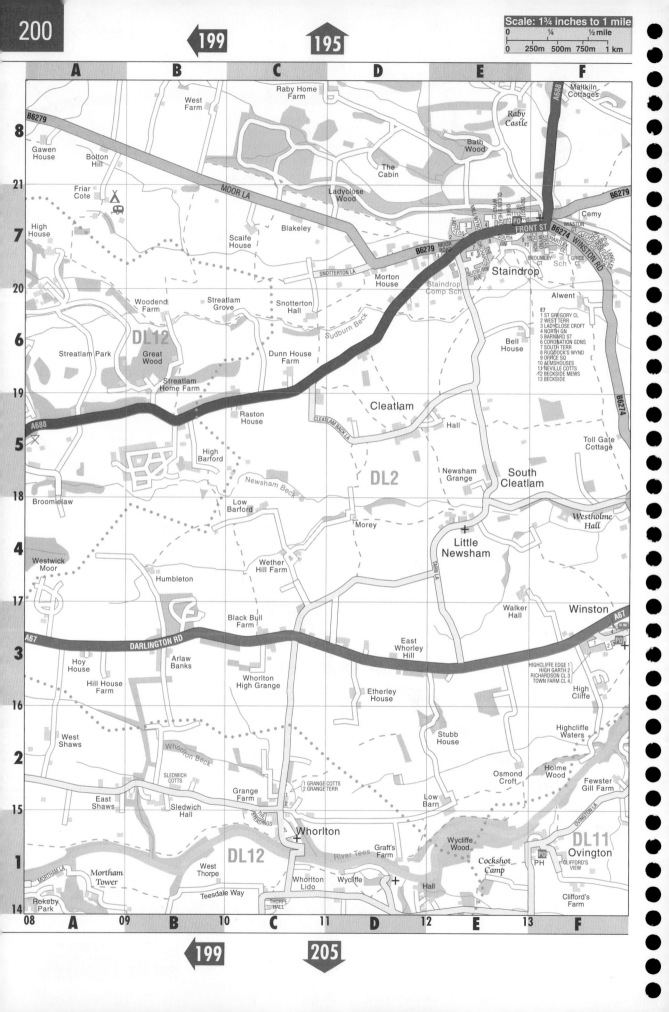

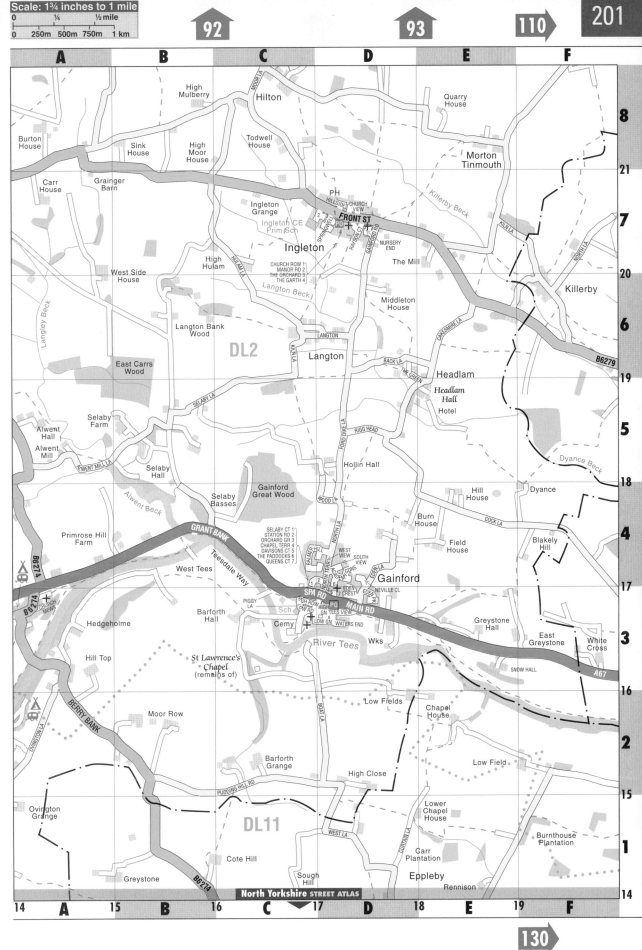

Scale: 1¾ inches to 1 mile

0   ¼   ½ mile
0 250m 500m 750m 1 km

A   B   C   D   E   F

8

Burton House

Hilton

High Mulberry

Sink House

High Moor House

Todwell House

Quarry House

21

Carr House

Grainger Barn

Morton Tinmouth

PH

Ingleton Grange

HILLSIDE   CHURCH VIEW

FRONT ST

Killerby Beck

7

Ingleton CE Prim Sch

SPRINGVILL
RAYSON CT
GAINFORD RD

PO

Ingleton

NURSERY END

The Mill

KILN LA

NORTH LA

20

West Side House

High Hulam

HULAM LA

CHURCH ROW 1
MANOR RD 2
THE ORCHARD 3
THE GARTH 4

Langton Beck

Middleton House

Killerby

6

Langton Bank Wood

KILN LA

LANGTON

CAKESMIRE LA

B6279

DL2

Langley Beck

Langton

BACK LA

THE GREEN

Headlam

19

East Carrs Wood

SELABY LA

Headlam Hall
Hotel

5

Alwent Hall

Selaby Farm

FORD DIKE LA

RIGG HEAD

Dyance Beck

Alwent Mill

ALWENT MILL LA

Selaby Hall

Hollin Hall

18

Alwent Beck

Selaby Basses

Gainford Great Wood

WOOD LA

Hill House

Dyance

COCK LA

4

Primrose Hill Farm

GRANT BANK

SELABY CT 1
STATION RD 2
ORCHARD GR 3
CHAPEL TERR 4
DAVISONS CT 5
THE PADDOCKS 6
QUEENS CT 7

NORTH LA

Burn House

Field House

Blakely Hill

17

Teesdale Way

West Tees

BALMER
HILL

WEST
VIEW
SOUTH
VIEW

EDEN LA

Gainford

NEVILLE CL

EDEN CREST
EDEN
VIEW

Greystone Hall

East Greystone

White Cross

A67

3

B6274

Hedgeholme

Barforth Hall

PIGGY LA

SPA RD

MAIN RD

Sch

HIGH ROW
LOW RD

PO
HIGH
GN TEES VIEW

WATERS END

Wks

Snow Hall

CHURCH MEWS

B6274

Hill Top

Cemy

LOW GN

River Tees

16

St Lawrence's Chapel (remains of)

Low Fields

Chapel House

OVINGTON LA

BERRY BANK

Moor Row

Low Field

2

Barforth Grange

High Close

15

DL11

PUDDING HILL RD

Ovington Grange

WEST LA

Lower Chapel House

Burnthouse Plantation

1

Cote Hill

B6274

Sough Hill

CURTAIN LA

Carr Plantation

Eppleby

Rennison

Greystone

14

A   14   B   15   C   16   17   D   18   E   19   F

Scale: 1¾ inches to 1 mile

0   ¼   ½ mile

0   250m   500m   750m   1 km

A   **B**   **C**   **D**   **E**   **F**

Black Beck

North Dodd

North Ings

Sun Dodd

Rove Gill

Pasture End

A66

A66 Brough

Key Cross

A66

Old Spital

Bowes Moor Hotel

Valley Farm

Grey Scar Farm

Spital Park

Spital Grange

Vale House Farm

Spital

Waterfall

Pennine Way

River Greta

Wytham Moor

Burnt Gill

Ay Gill

Bowes Moor

Red Gill

DL12

Stainmore Forest

Bog Tarn

The Bog

Sleightholme Beck

Sleightholme Farm

Collinson's Hill

Bog Moss

Pennine Way

SLEIGHTHOLME MOOR RD

Coney Seat Hill

White Stone Gill

Dry Gill

Frumming Beck

Rushy Moor

West Moor

Sleightholme Moor

The Disputes

Cocker

Mudbeck

Arkle Beck

LONG CSWY

Leading Stead Bottom

DL11

Broadshaw Bottom

Mirk Fell Gill

Mirk Fell

William Gill

Scollit Side

Annaside Beck

Leading Stead

Mine Workings (dis)

90   **A**   91   **B**   92   **C**   93   **D**   94   **E**   95   **F**

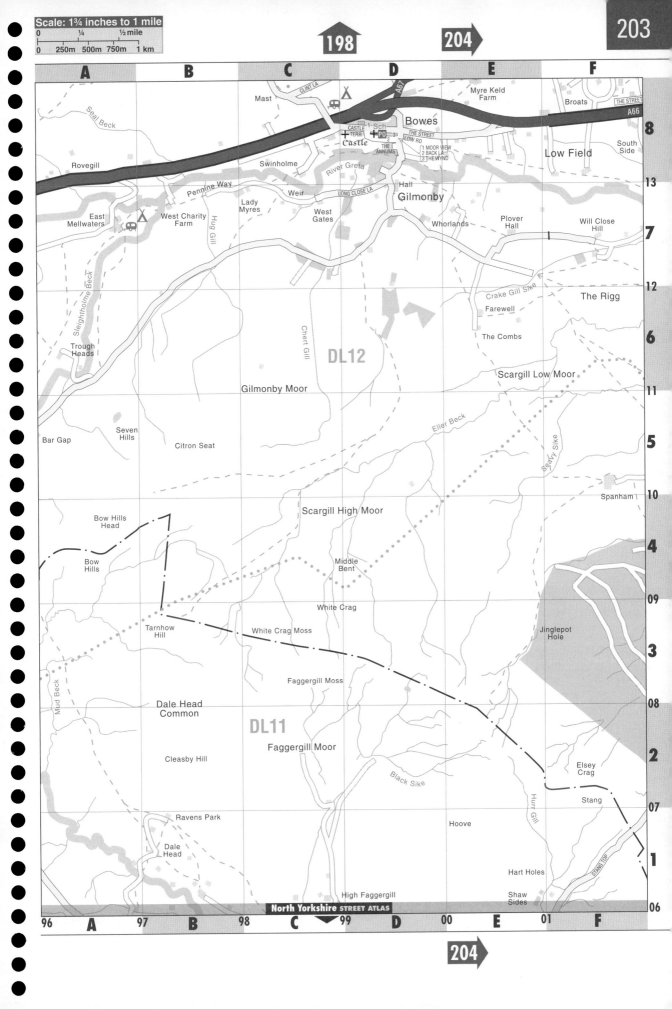

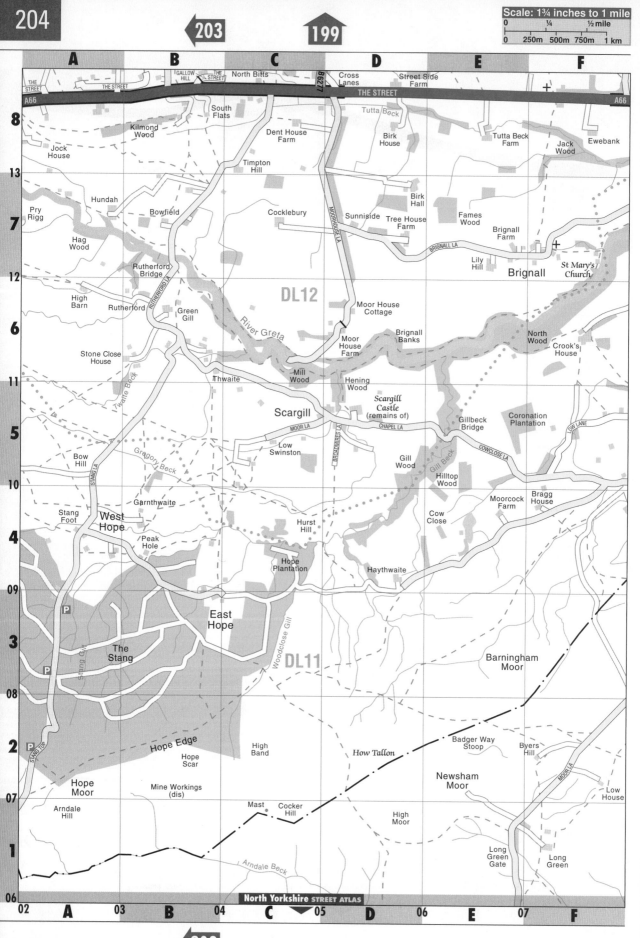

203
199

Scale: 1¾ inches to 1 mile

0   ¼   ½ mile

0   250m   500m   750m   1 km

A   B   C   D   E   F

THE STREET

GALLOW HILL

THE STREET

North Bitts

Cross Lanes

Street Side Farm

THE STREET

A66

A66

Tutta Beck

8

Kilmond Wood

South Flats

Dent House Farm

Birk House

Tutta Beck Farm

Jack Wood

Ewebank

13

Jock House

Timpton Hill

Birk Hall

Fames Wood

7

Pry Rigg

Hundah

Bowfield

Cocklebury

Sunniside

Tree House Farm

Brignall Farm

Hag Wood

Brignall La

Lily Hill

Brignall

12

Rutherford Bridge

St Mary's Church

DL12

Moor House Cottage

North Wood

Crook's House

High Barn

Rutherford

Green Gill

River Greta

Moor House Farm

Brignall Banks

6

Stone Close House

Twaite Beck

Thwaite

Mill Wood

Hening Wood

11

Scargill

Scargill Castle (remains of)

Gillbeck Bridge

Coronation Plantation

Low Lane

5

Bow Hill

Gregory Beck

Moor La

Chapel La

Cowclose La

Gill Wood

Gill Beck

Moorcock Farm

Bragg House

10

Garnthwaite

Hilltop Wood

Stang La

West Hope

Hurst Hill

Cow Close

4

Stang Foot

Peak Hole

Hope Plantation

Haythwaite

09

P

East Hope

Woodclose Gill

DL11

Barningham Moor

3

Stang Gill

P

The Stang

08

P

Hope Edge

High Band

How Tallon

Badger Way Stoop

Byers Hill

2

Stang Top

Hope Scar

Newsham Moor

Moor La

Low House

07

Hope Moor

Mine Workings (dis)

Arndale Hill

Mast

Cocker Hill

High Moor

Long Green Gate

Long Green

1

Arndale Beck

06

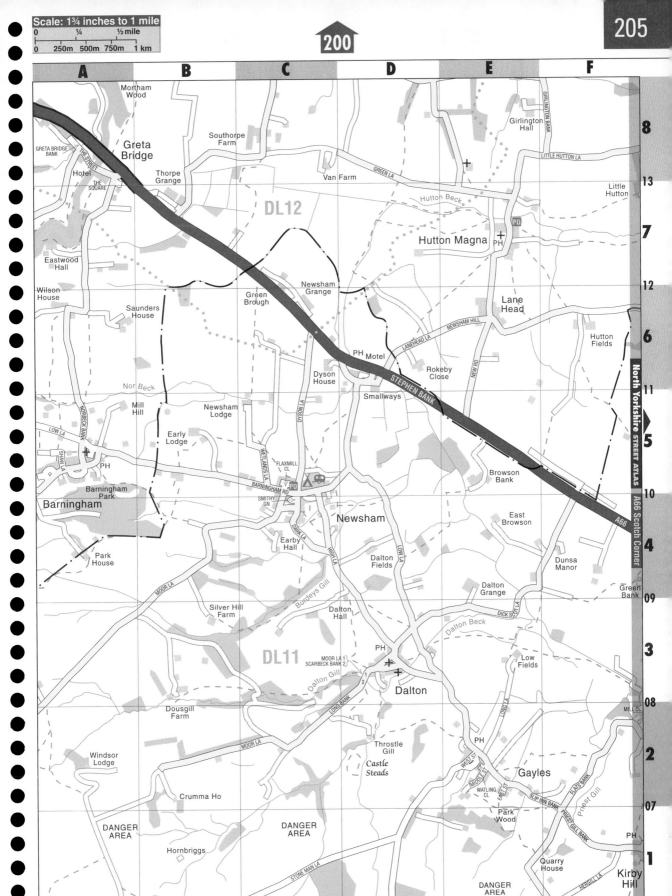

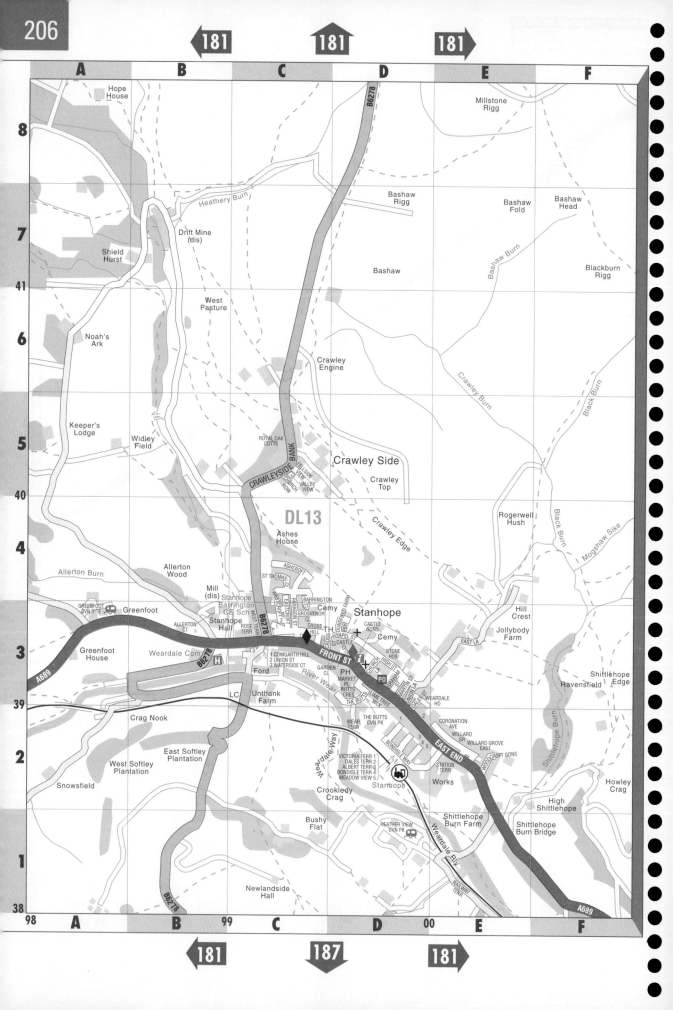

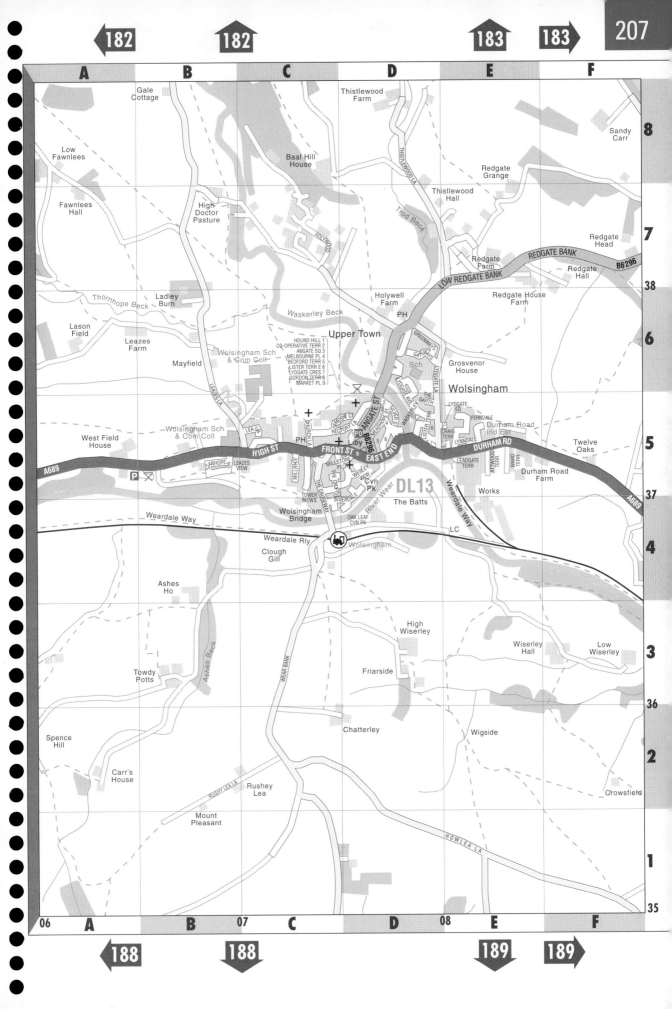

◄ 182   182   183   183 ►

A B C D E F

8
7
38
6
5
37
4
3
36
2
1
35

Gale Cottage
Low Fawnlees
Fawnlees Hall
High Doctor Pasture
Baal Hill House
Thistlewood Farm
Thistlewood Hall
Redgate Grange
Sandy Carr
Redgate Head
REDGATE BANK
Redgate Farm
Low Redgate Bank
Redgate Hall
B6296
Redgate House Farm
Thornhope Beck
Ladley Burn
Waskerley Beck
Holywell Farm
PH
Lason Field
Leazes Farm
Mayfield
Wolsingham Sch & Com Coll
Upper Town
HOUND HILL 1
CO-OPERATIVE TERR 2
ANGATE SQ 3
MELBOURNE PL 4
BEDFORD TERR 5
LISTER TERR E 6
LYDGATE CRES 7
GORDON TERR 8
MARKET PL 9
Grosvenor House
Sch
Wolsingham
West Field House
Wolsingham Sch & Com Coll
LEAZES LA
LEA GA
ANNHOPE
LEAZES VIEW
HIGH ST
PH
CHURCH LA
FRONT ST
Liby
EAST END
B6296
THE GARTH
LYDGATE SQ
FERNDALE
Durham Road Ind Est
Twelve Oaks
A689
P
MILLRACE
THE CROFTS
WESLEY VIEW
Cvn Pk
DURHAM RD
DURHAM RD
LEADGATE TERR
CRAIG TERR
LYNNDALE
ATTWOOD TERR
WARD TERR
Durham Road Farm
A689
TOWER MEWS
THE CAUSEWAY
RIVERDALE
River Wear
DL13
The Batts
Works
Wolsingham Bridge
OAK LEAF CVN PK
Weardale Way
Weardale Way
Weardale Rly
Wolsingham
LC
Clough Gill
WEAR BANK
Ashes Ho
Ashes Beck
High Wiserley
Wiserley Hall
Low Wiserley
Towdy Potts
Friarside
Spence Hill
Chatterley
Wigside
Crowsfield
Carr's House
RUSHY LEA LA
Rushey Lea
Mount Pleasant
HOWLEA LA

06 A B 07 C D 08 E F

◄ 188   188   189   189 ►

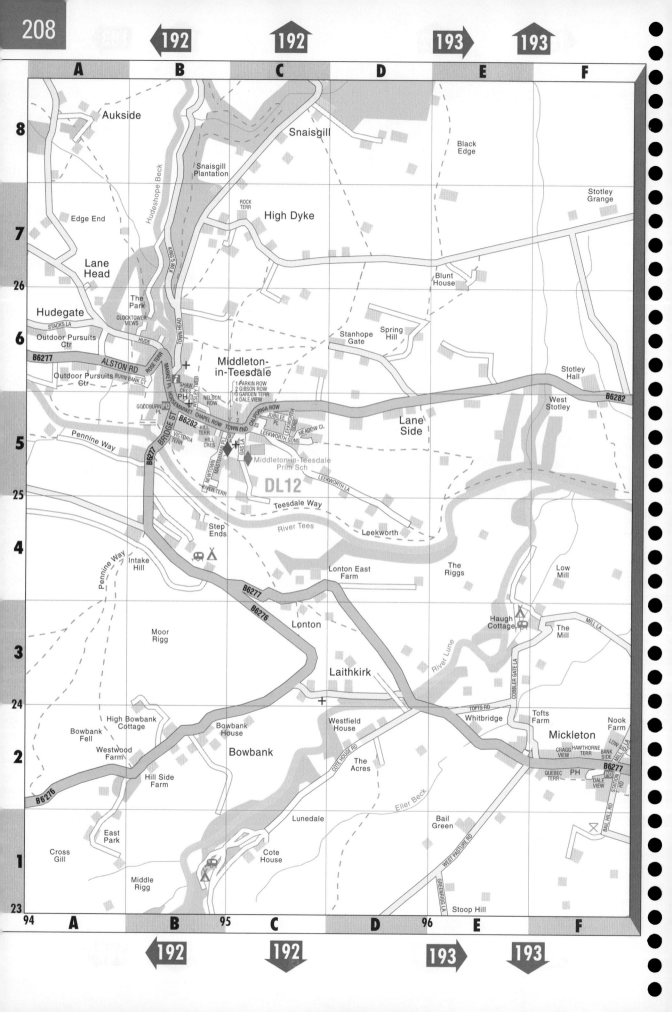

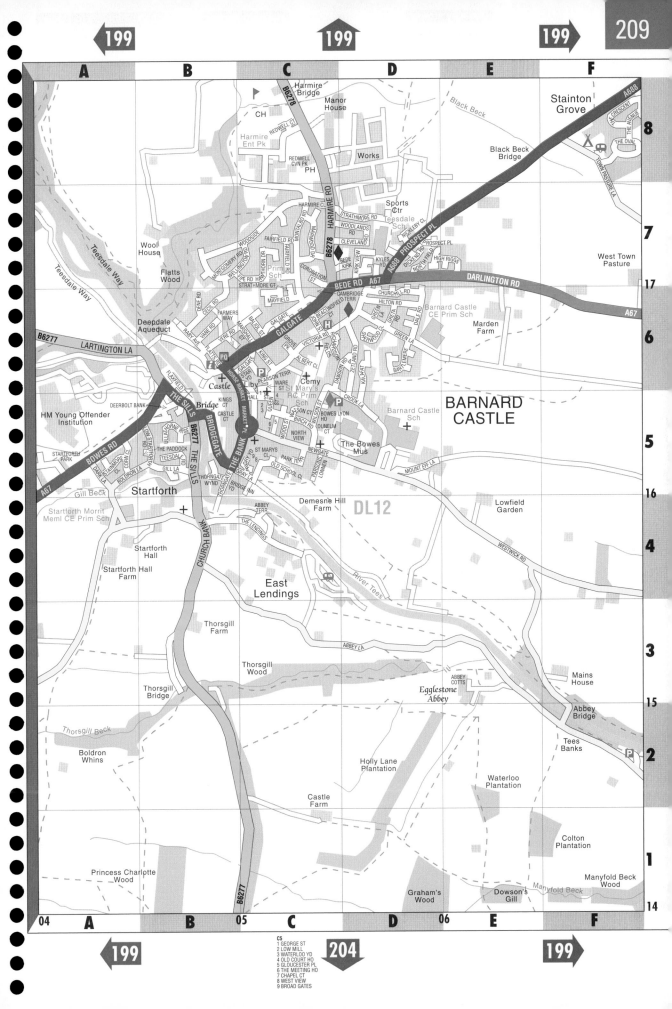

A   B   C   D   E   F

8

Stainton Grove

Harmire Bridge

Manor House

CH

B6278

Black Beck

Black Beck Bridge

Works

Harmire Ent Pk

REDWELL CT

REDWELL CVN PK
PH

Sports Ctr

Teesdale Sch

STRATHMORE RD

WOODLANDS RD

CLEVELAND

NICKLEBY CL

PROSPECT PL

A688

7

HARMIRE RD

HARMIRE CL

B6278

BEDE KIRK

KYLES

KIRK VIEW

DICKENS RD

NORTH FIELD

HIGH RIGGS

West Town Pasture

Wool House

Flatts Wood

WOODSIDE

MONTALBO RD

FAIRFIELD RD

FAIRFIELD RD

MONTGOMERY RD

WELLINGTON RD

PIE RD

HAY

Prim Sch

CORONATION ST

BEDE RD

A67

DARLINGTON RD

A67

17

Teesdale Way

Teesdale Way

STRATHMORE CT

MAYFIELD

CAMBRIDGE TERR

BEACONSFIELD RD

HILTON RD

GRETA

GREEN LA

Barnard Castle CE Prim Sch

Marden Farm

6

Deepdale Aqueduct

B6277

LARTINGTON LA

CECIL RD

RABY AVE

VANE RD

VERE RD

FARMERS WAY

BAILIOL ST

MARSHALL ST

GALGATE

GROVE

VICTORIA RD

ALBERT CL

JOHN ST

RICHARDSON RD

FIELDS

DANKSON RD

ZETLAND RD

GREEN LA

GRETA

DALE RD

KIRKWOOD CL

GREEN LA

BARTY

EMERE

BARTY CL

H

Castle

PO

Liby

HORSE MARKET

GALGATE

KING ST

STAR YD

PEARSON TERR

WARE ST

QUEEN ST

St Mary's RC Prim Sch

Cemy

CROOK LA

Barnard Castle Sch

BARNARD CASTLE

THE SILLS

BRIDGEGATE

Bridge

KINGS CT

CASTLE CT

MARKET PL

HALL

NELSON CT

WOOD ST

BIRCH RD

BOWES LYON HO

DUNELM CT

P

Barnard Castle Sch

5

DEERBOLT BANK

BOWES RD

B6277

THE SILLS

HORNE RISE

LOW STARTFORTH RD

THE PADDOCK

TEESDALE

GILL LA

THE BANK

THORNGATE

THORNGATE WYND

ST MARYS

NORTH VIEW

NEWGATE

PARK TERR

PRISCONS

LONNEN

OLD SCHOOL CL

MOUNT EFF LA

The Bowes Mus

HM Young Offender Institution

STARTFORTH PARK

DARK LA

STANMORE CL

CORFU CT

BOLDRON LA

Startforth

BRIDGE INN YD

GRAY LA

DL12

16

Startforth Morrit Meml CE Prim Sch

Gill Beck

A67

CHURCH BANK

ABBEY TERR

THE LENDINGS

Demesne Hill Farm

Lowfield Garden

WESTWICK RD

4

Startforth Hall

Startforth Hall Farm

East Lendings

River Tees

3

Thorsgill Farm

ABBEY LA

Mains House

Thorsgill Wood

Egglestone Abbey

ABBEY COTTS

15

Thorsgill Bridge

Abbey Bridge

Thorsgill Beck

Tees Banks

P

2

Boldron Whins

Holly Lane Plantation

Waterloo Plantation

Castle Farm

1

Princess Charlotte Wood

B6277

Graham's Wood

Dowson's Gill

Manyfold Beck

Colton Plantation

Manyfold Beck Wood

14

C5
1 GEORGE ST
2 LOW MILL
3 WATERLOO YD
4 OLD COURT HO
5 GLOUCESTER PL
6 THE MEETING HO
7 CHAPEL CT
8 WEST VIEW
9 BROAD GATES

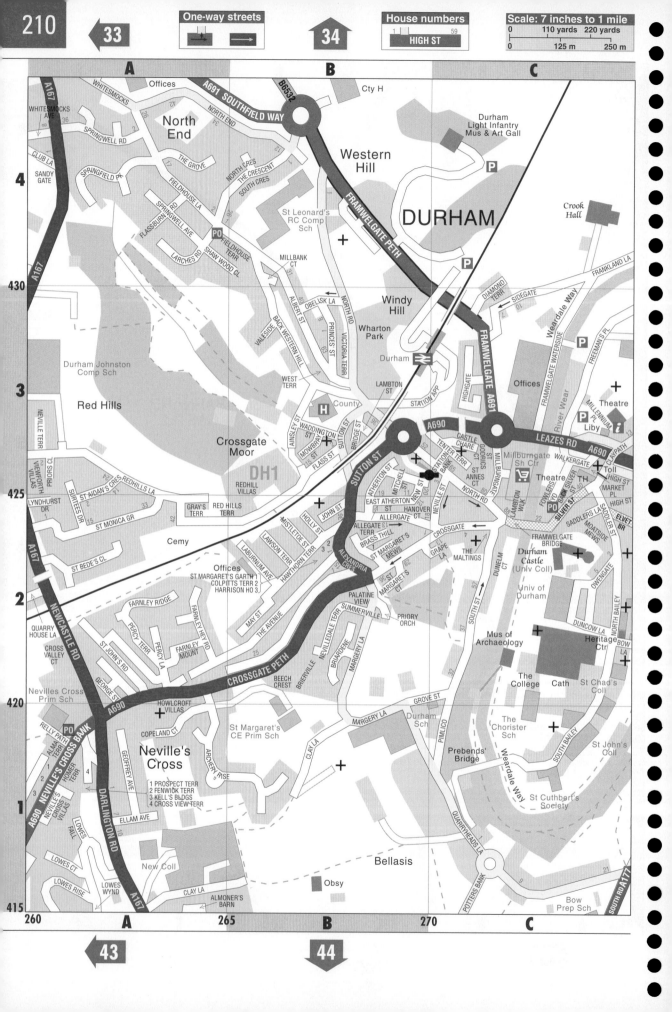

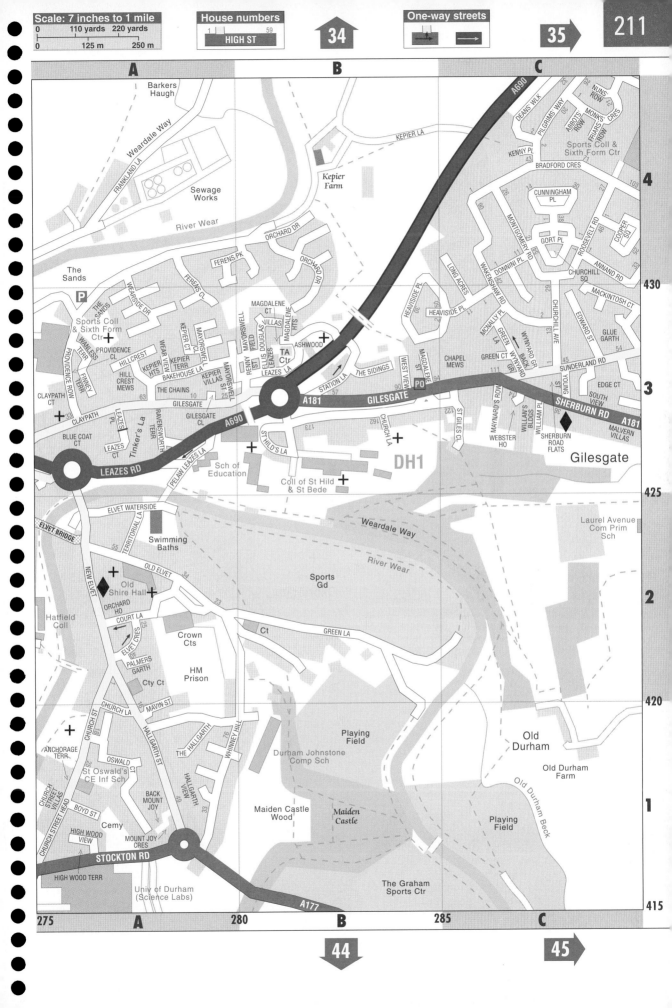

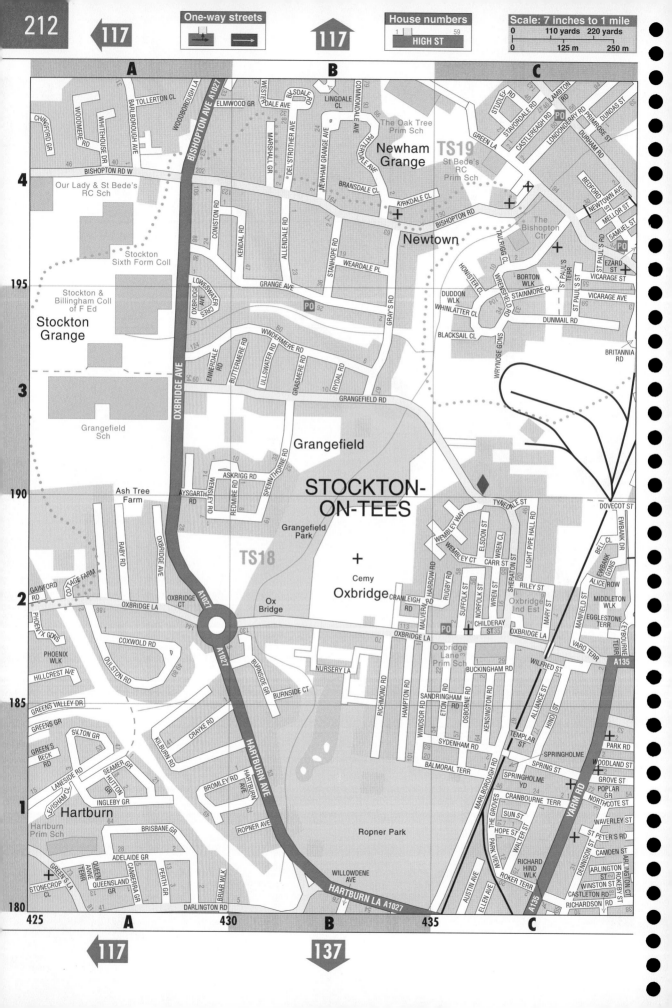

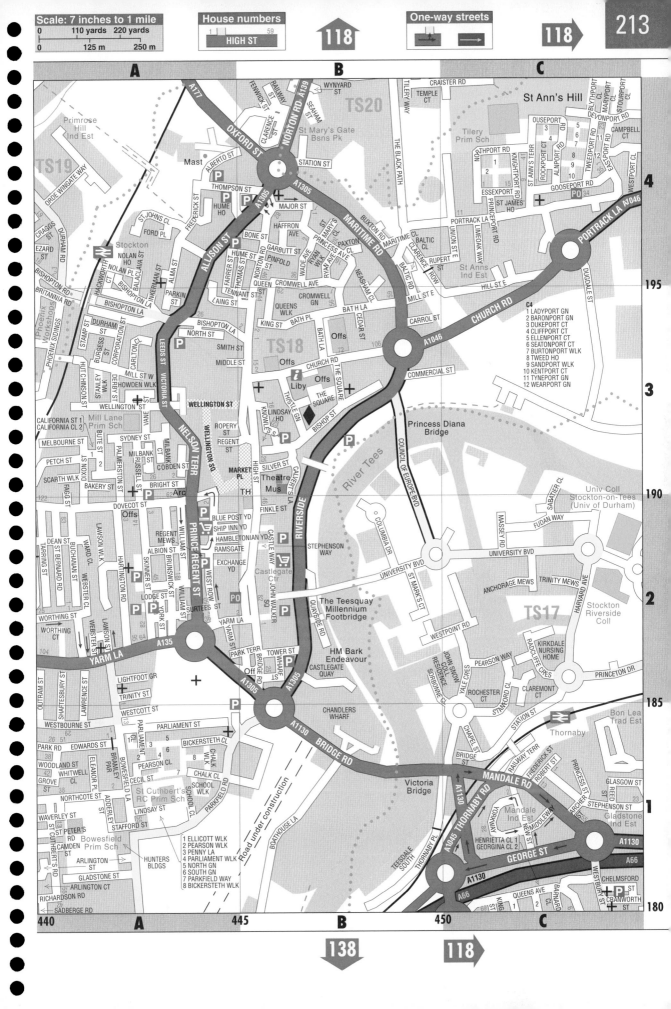

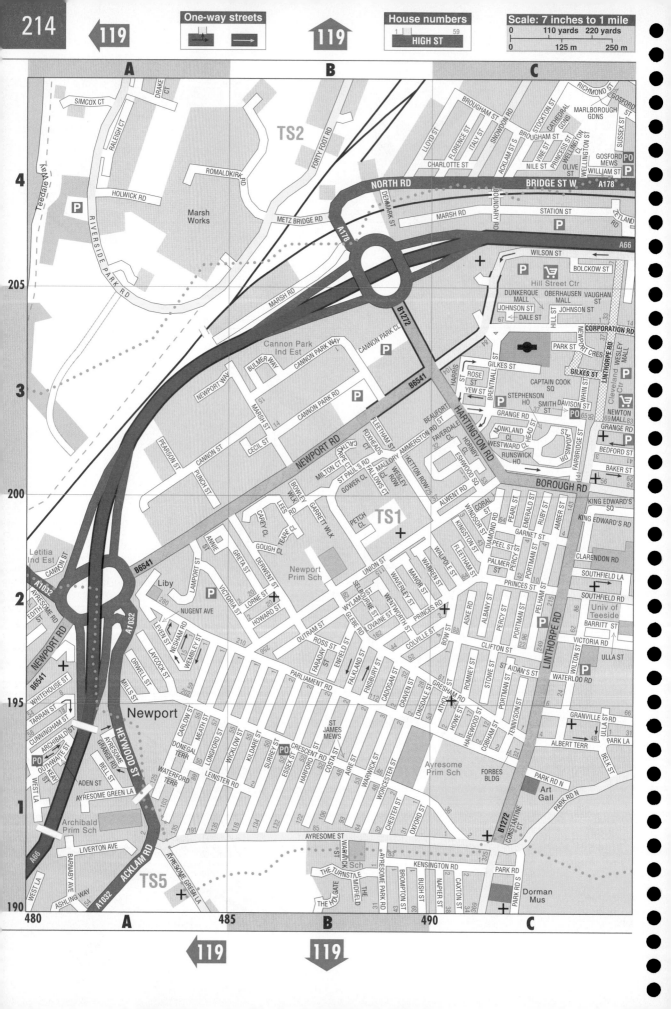

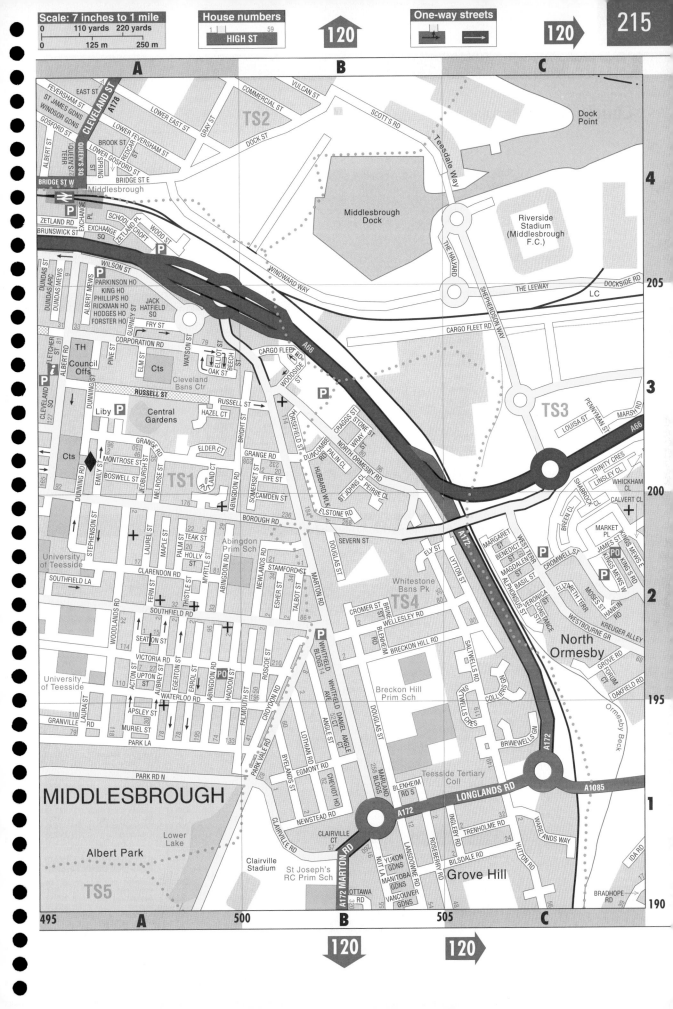

Index

Church Rd **6** Beckenham BR2..........**53** C6

Place name	**Location number**	**Locality, town or village**	**Postcode district**	**Page and grid square**
May be abbreviated on the map	Present when a number indicates the place's position in a crowded area of mapping	Shown when more than one place has the same name	District for the indexed place	Page number and grid reference for the standard mapping

Public and commercial buildings are highlighted in magenta   **Places of interest** are highlighted in blue with a star★

Abbreviations used in the index

Acad	Academy	Comm	Common	Gd	Ground	L	Leisure	Prom	Prom
App	Approach	Cott	Cottage	Gdn	Garden	La	Lane	Rd	Road
Arc	Arcade	Cres	Crescent	Gn	Green	Liby	Library	Recn	Recreation
Ave	Avenue	Cswy	Causeway	Gr	Grove	Mdw	Meadow	Ret	Retail
Bglw	Bungalow	Ct	Court	H	Hall	Meml	Memorial	Sh	Shopping
Bldg	Building	Ctr	Centre	Ho	House	Mkt	Market	Sq	Square
Bsns, Bus	Business	Ctry	Country	Hospl	Hospital	Mus	Museum	St	Street
Bvd	Boulevard	Cty	County	HQ	Headquarters	Orch	Orchard	Sta	Station
Cath	Cathedral	Dr	Drive	Hts	Heights	Pal	Palace	Terr	Terrace
Cir	Circus	Dro	Drove	Ind	Industrial	Par	Parade	TH	Town Hall
Cl	Close	Ed	Education	Inst	Institute	Pas	Passage	Univ	University
Cnr	Corner	Emb	Embankment	Int	International	Pk	Park	Wk, Wlk	Walk
Coll	College	Est	Estate	Intc	Interchange	Pl	Place	Wr	Water
Com	Community	Ex	Exhibition	Junc	Junction	Prec	Precinct	Yd	Yard

Index of localities, towns and villages

A

Acklam 139 C7
Acklam Base 139 D5
Aislaby 155 E5
Albert Hill 133 B3
Allenheads 179 C8
Allensford 176 F5
Annfield Plain 12 E4
Archdeacon Newton .131 E7
Auckland Park 80 E6
Aukside 208 B8
Aycliffe Village 96 E1
Ayton 9 F2

B

Barley Mow 9 C2
Barlow 1 C6
Barnard Castle 209 E5
Barningham 205 A4
Baybridge 174 F5
Beamish 14 F8
Bearpark 33 B3
Bedburn 189 C2
Beechwood 140 A7
Bellevue 77 C4
Benfieldside 10 C5
Berwick Hills 120 D2
Bildershaw 94 A5
Billingham 102 F1
Billy Row 52 E7
Binchester 68 A5
Birtley 9 C3
Bishop Auckland 80 C4
Bishopgarth 117 B5
Bishop Middleham ...71 B4
Bishopton 115 D7
Blackfyne 10 E4
Blackhall Colliery ..50 C4
Blackhall Mill 4 B7
Blackhall Rocks 50 E2
Blackhill 10 E4
Blackwell 151 D6
Blanchland 175 A5
Blaydon 2 B7
Bolam 93 F2
Boldron 199 B1
Bollihope 187 E5

C

California 121 F2
Canada 16 B4
Cargo Fleet 120 D5
Carlbury 130 C4
Carlin How 126 E3
Carlton 116 C8
Carrville 35 D5
Carterway Heads 176 C6
Cassop 46 F1
Castle Eden 61 C8
Castleside 177 A3
Catchgate 12 E5
Causey 7 B4
Charltons 144 F4

Boosbeck 145 C7
Borrowby 149 A4
Boulby 128 D3
Bournmoor 17 D3
Bowbank 208 C2
Bowburn 45 D1
Bowes 203 D8
Bowlees 192 A7
Bradbury 83 F5
Brafferton 113 A6
Brambles Farm 120 F3
Brancepeth 54 E8
Brandon 43 B5
Brandon Village 43 A5
Branksome 132 A4
Brass Castle 153 C5
Brasside 34 F8
Bridgehill 10 C4
Brignall 204 E7
Brookfield 139 B3
Broom Hill Hetton-le-Hole .27 A6
Broom Hill Stanley 13 D7
Broompark 43 C8
Brotherlee 186 C8
Brotton 126 D3
Burdon 18 B3
Burnhope 21 E4
Burnopfield 6 A6
Burtree Ford 179 B3
Butterknowle 195 C5
Butterwick 86 A8
Byermoor 6 D7
Byers Green 54 E1

D

Daddrey Shield 185 F8
Daisy Hill 23 B6
Dalehouse 149 B8

Chester le Street ..16 E4
Chester Moor 24 B7
Chilton 82 E7
Chilton Lane 70 C3
Chilton Moor 26 A7
Chopwell 4 B8
Church Kelloe 58 F6
Cleasby 150 E7
Cleatlam 200 D5
Cliffe 130 C3
Close House 81 A5
Clough Dene 6 A3
Coalcleugh 178 C8
Coatham 107 B7
Coatham Mundeville .112 F5
Cockerton 132 C4
Cockfield 195 F3
Cold Hesledon 29 B2
Coldpool 158 D4
Colliery Row 26 B8
Commondale 164 C1
Consett 10 D3
Copley 195 A4
Cornforth 57 E1
Cornsay 30 B4
Cornsay Colliery ...31 A3
Cotherstone 198 F6
Coulby Newham 140 A2
Coundon 81 D8
Coundongate 80 F8
Coundon Grange 80 F5
Cowbar 129 B2
Cowpen Bewley 103 D6
Cowshill 179 B3
Coxhoe 58 B4
Craghead 14 D2
Crathorne 173 B3
Crawley Side 206 D5
Croft on Heugh 77 E8
Crook 52 D2
Crookgate Bank 6 C6
Crookhall 11 B2
Crossgate Moor 210 B3
Croxdale 56 B6

E

Eaglescliffe 137 B2
Easington Loftus ..128 A1
Easington Peterlee .39 A4
Easington Colliery .39 E5
Easington Lane 37 D8
Eastbourne Darlington .133 C1
Eastbourne Stockton-on-Tees .117 F6
East Briscoe 198 C6
Easterside 140 A6
Eastgate 180 E1
East Hedleyhope 40 C5
East Hope 204 B3
East Kyo 13 B6
Eastlea 28 F7
East Loftus 127 D1
East Rainton 26 D4
East Stanley 14 A7
Ebchester 3 F3
Eddy's Bridge 176 B5
Eden Vale 61 D7
Edmondsley 23 B6
Edmundbyers 175 E5
Egglesburn 193 C3
Eggleston 193 E2
Eldon 81 A4
Eldon Lane 80 F4
Elemore Vale 37 B8
Ellerby 149 F2
Elm Tree 117 C5

Dalton 205 D3
Dalton-le-Dale 29 A5
Dalton-on-Tees 168 B4
Dalton Piercy 75 E3
Darlington 133 C2
Dawdon 29 D5
Deaf Hill 60 A5
Dean Bank 69 D5
Delves 177 D4
Deneside 29 A6
Denton 110 D2
Dipton 12 C8
Dormanstown 106 E4
Doxford Park 18 A4
Drinkfield 132 F7
Dunsdale 123 D2
Durham 210 C4

F

Fairfield 117 C4
Faverdale 132 C6
Fellside 2 F6
Fence Houses 26 A8
Ferryhill 70 A6
Ferryhill Station ..70 D4
Fir Tree 52 A1
Fishburn 72 D4
Fleming Field 48 B7
Flint Hill 5 E1
Foggy Furze 77 C2
Forest-in-Teesdale .191 C8
Foxton Hutton Rudby .173 E5
Foxton Sedgefield ..99 C6
Framwellgate 34 B5
Frosterley 188 A8

G

Gainford 201 D4
Gateshead 9 C8
Gayles 205 E2
Gerrick 165 E6
Gilesgate 211 C3
Gilesgate Moor 35 B3
Gilmonby 203 D7
Girsby 170 B5
Grangefield 212 B3
Grangetown 121 E6
Grange Villa 15 A5

Elstob 98 E4
Elton 136 F7
Elwick 75 D6
Embleton 87 C8
Eppleby 201 D1
Eryholme 169 A6
Escomb 66 D1
Esh 31 F4
Esh Winning 41 E8
Eston 121 D2
Etherley Dene 79 F6
Etherley Grange 79 C6
Ettersgill 191 D8
Evenwood 92 C7
Evenwood Gate 92 D5

A

A J Cook Terr DH6 48 C5
A J Cook's Cotts NE39 1 B2
Abberley Dr TS8 139 F2
Abberston Wlk TS4 140 A7
Abbey Cl TS19 116 F4
Abbey Cotts DL12 209 E3
Abbey Ct TS6 121 D2
Abbey Gdns DL15 54 A3
Abbey Hill Sch Tech Coll TS19 117 D6
Abbey Inf Sch DL3 132 D1
Abbey Jun Sch DL3 132 C1
Abbey La DL12 209 D3
Abbey Mews DH7 23 C2
Abbey Rd
Bishop Auckland DL14 80 B5
Darlington DL3 132 D1
Durham DH1 34 B8
Sadberge DL2 134 F6
Abbey Road Ind Est DH1 34 C8
Abbey Springs DL3 132 C2
Abbey St Brotton TS12 126 B3
Hartlepool TS24 77 F8
Abbey Terr DL12 209 C4
Abbeydale Gdns DH6 38 A6
Abbeyfield Dr TS16 137 B1
Abbeywoods DH1 34 B8
Abbots Gn DL15 54 A3
Abbots Way TS19 116 F4
Abbots Wlk DH9 14 F8
Abbots' Row DH1 211 C4
Abbotsfield Way DL3 132 B7
Abbotsford Rd TS5 139 B8
Abbotside Cl DH2 8 D2
Abbott's Hos DL13 195 D4
Abdale Ave TS5 139 B8
Aberbran Ct TS17 156 F7
Abercorn Cl [9] TS10 107 E1
Abercorn Ct DL3 132 B7
Abercrombie Rd TS10 106 F5
Aberdare Rd TS6 121 E5
Aberdeen DH2 8 F1
Aberdeen Rd
Darlington DL1 133 E7
Hartlepool TS25 77 A1
Aberdovey Dr TS16 156 C8
Aberfalls Rd TS8 139 F2
Aberfoyle DH2 8 F1
Aberfoyle Ct DH9 14 B6
Abernethy DH2 8 F2
Aberwick Dr DH2 23 F8
Abingdon Prim Sch TS1 215 A2
Abingdon Rd TS1 215 A2
Abington DH2 8 F1
Abotts Lea TS27 75 E3
Abraham Ind Est DL14 79 F3
Abridge Cl TS11 123 F6
Acacia Ave SR8 50 B6
Acacia Ct [12] TS10 107 E1
Acacia Gdns DL15 52 D4
Acacia Rd
Bishop Auckland DL14 80 B7
Stockton-on-T TS19 117 F5
Acacia St DL3 132 E4
Academy Gdns DL2 201 D4
Acclom St TS24 77 A7
Accrington Terr DL14 92 D6
Acer Dr DH6 37 F3
Achilles Cl TS6 121 B4
Acklam Grange Sch TS5 139 B6
Acklam Rd
Middlesbrough TS5 139 C5
Thornaby-on-T TS17 138 E8
Acklam St N TS2 119 E7
Acklam St S TS2 214 C4
Acklam Whin Prim Sch TS5 139 B4
Ackworth Gn TS3 120 D3
Acle Burn DL5 82 C3
Acle Mdws DL5 82 C3
Aclet Cl DL14 80 B4
Acorn Bank TS17 157 B7
Acorn Cl
Middleton St George DL2 153 F8
Sacriston DH7 23 B4
Acorn Croft DH7 33 B8
Acorn Dr DL15 54 A6
Acorn Pl Brandon DH7 43 B4
Durham DH1 34 B8
Acorn St DH2 15 B7
Acornclose La DH7 22 F4
Acre Rigg Inf & Jun Schs SR8 49 B8
Acre Rigg Rd SR8 49 B8
Acton Dene DH9 14 C7
Acton Rd DH7 41 E8
Acton St TS1 215 A2
Ada St E SR7 28 D2
Ada St W SR7 28 D2
Adam Cl TS10 107 B2
Adam St [3] Peterlee SR8 50 B6
Stockton-on-T TS18 138 A7
Adam's Bldgs DH9 12 C8
Adams Terr DH8 4 A2
Adamson St DL4 95 A7
Adcott Rd TS5 139 C6
Adderley St TS18 213 A1
Addington Dr TS3 120 D3
Addison Rd Coundon DL14 68 C1
Great Ayton TS9 161 A2
Addison Rd *continued*
Hartlepool TS24 77 B7
Middlesbrough TS5 119 D2
Toronto DL14 66 D3
Addison St
Coundon Grange DL14 80 F5
Crook DL15 52 E4
Adelaide Bank DL14,DL4 80 E3
Adelaide Gr TS18 212 A1
Adelaide Pl [6] TS11 108 C1
Adelaide Rd TS7 140 C3
Adelaide Row [4] SR7 29 D7
Adelaide St
[5] Bishop Auckland DL14 80 C8
[12] Chester le Street DH3 16 C2
[11] Darlington DL1 133 B1
[4] Shildon DL4 94 F8
Adelaide Terr DL4 80 E3
Adelphi Ct [18] DL1 133 B1
Aden Ct DH7 33 A4
Aden St TS5 214 A1
Adfrid Pl SR8 49 D7
Admiral Way TS24 77 D6
Admirals Ave TS3 120 D3
Adolphus Pl DH1 35 B2
Adolphus St W SR7 29 D7
Adrian Pl SR8 49 E5
Adshead Rd TS10 106 F4
Adstock Ave TS4 140 B7
Adventure La DH4 25 F2
Agecroft Gdns TS5 119 B1
Aged Miner's Home DL14 81 A3
Aged Miner's Homes
Bearpark DH7 33 A3
Burnopfield NE16 6 A6
Chester le Street DH2 24 B7
Hetton-le-H DH5 27 A2
[3] Houghton-le-S DH5 26 F8
Quebec DH7 31 B4
Ryhope SR2 18 E7
Sacriston DH7 23 D3
[2] Seaham SR7 18 F1
Aged Miners Homes
Chester le Street DH2 16 C4
Shotton Colliery DH6 48 B7
Wheatley Hill DH6 47 F2
Aged Miners' Homes [5] TS27 50 D3
Aged Miners' Homes
Bournmoor DH4 17 E2
Brandon DH7 43 B5
Brandon, Meadowfield DH7 43 C3
Aged Miners' Homes DH5 26 C4
Aged Miners' Homes DL14 92 C7
Aged Miners' Homes TS21 72 D5
Aged Miners' Homes DH3 17 B1
Aged Miners' Homes DH5 26 F6
Aged Miners' Homes NE39 1 A4
Aged Miners' Homes [5] DH4 26 C8
Aged Miners' Homes NE11 8 C6
Aged Miners' Homes DH2 23 F4
Aged Miners' Homes [8] DH7 32 C6
Aged Miners' Homes SR7 28 B3
Aged Miners' Homes
Pelton DH2 15 C6
Peterlee SR8 49 F7
Quarrington Hill DH6 58 D7
Aged Miners' Homes
Seaham SR7 29 D6
Seaham,Northlea SR7 28 F8
Aged Miners' Homes DH6 36 C1
Aged Miners' Homes DL16 68 C6
Aged Miners' Homes DH9 14 B4
Aged Workers Homes DL15 52 D4
Agnes St DH9 13 F7
Agnew Way DL5 82 D1
Agricola Cotts
Hilton TS15 157 F3
Mount Pleasant TS7 160 C7
Agricola Ct DL3 132 C7
Aidan Cl DH9 14 B7
Aidans Wlk DL17 70 A7
Aiden Way DH5 27 A5
Ainderby Gr TS18 117 A1
Ainderby Way TS4 140 A8
Ainderby Wlk TS24 64 B1
Ainsdale Cl TS11 123 F6
Ainsdale Way TS4 140 A7
Ainsford Way TS7 141 B8
Ainsley Gr DL3 132 C7
Ainsley St Durham DH1 210 B3
Hartlepool TS25 77 D4
Ainstable Rd TS7 141 B7
Ainsty Hunt DL5 95 F8
Ainsworth Way TS7 141 B8
Ainthorpe Cl SR3 18 B7
Ainthorpe Pl [6] TS6 121 F3
Ainthorpe Rd TS6 121 F3
Aintree Ct DL1 133 F3
Aintree Dr DH8 10 D7
Aintree Oval
Middlesbrough TS17 119 A2
Thornaby-on-T TS17 118 F2
Aintree Rd Redcar TS10 107 D4
Aintree Rd *continued*
Stockton-on-T TS18 118 F5
Airdrie Gr TS25 76 F1
Aire St
Middlesbrough TS1 214 B1
South Bank TS6 121 A6
Aireborough Cl TS19 117 D5
Airedale Gdns DH5 26 F2
Aireyholme La TS9 161 D3
Aireys Cl DH4 26 C8
Airton Pl DL5 96 B7
Airville Mount SR3 18 A4
Airy Hill La TS12 145 A8
Aiskew Gr TS19 117 A2
Aislaby Ct TS14 143 E6
Aislaby Gr TS23 102 E7
Aislaby Ho TS14 143 E6
Aislaby Rd TS16 156 A7
Aitken's Bldgs DH9 12 C8
Ajax St DL1 133 C6
Ajax Way TS6 121 A5
Alan St [11] TS6 121 A6
Albany Ct [9] TS26 77 A6
Albany Rd Marton TS7 140 C3
Stockton-on-T TS20 118 C7
Albany St TS1 214 C2
Albatross Way DL1 133 D1
Albert Cl DL12 209 C6
Albert Ct [6] TS12 125 C8
Albert Hill DL14 80 C7
Albert Hill Ind Est DL1 133 B4
Albert Mews TS1 215 A3
Albert Rd Consett DH8 10 F2
Darlington DL1 133 A4
Eaglescliffe TS16 137 C2
Eston TS6 121 D2
Middlesbrough TS1 215 A3
Stockton-on-T TS19 117 B3
Albert St
[6] Chester le Street DH3 16 C3
Chilton DL17 83 A7
Crook DL15 52 E4
[12] Darlington DL1 133 B1
Durham DH1 210 B3
Esh Winning DH7 41 E8
Hartlepool TS24 77 C5
Middlesbrough TS2 215 A4
Rowlands Gill NE39 1 A1
Seaham SR7 29 E6
Shildon DL4 81 A2
Thornley (nr Wheatley Hill) DH6 47 D4
West Pelton DH2 15 A5
Albert Terr Billy Row DL15 52 E7
Middlesbrough TS1 214 C1
Stanhope DL13 206 D2
Alberta Ho TS4 120 A2
Alberto St TS18 213 A4
Albery Pl [16] DL1 133 B1
Albion Ave DL4 80 F2
Albion Gdns NE16 5 F5
Albion Pl DL15 53 F3
Albion St Boosbeck TS12 145 C6
Spennymoor DL16 68 C6
Stockton-on-T TS18 213 A2
Albion Terr
Bishop Auckland DL14 80 C7
Guisborough TS14 143 F5
Hartlepool TS24 77 F8
Saltburn-by-t-S TS12 125 C7
Witton Park DL14 66 A1
Albourne Gn TS4 140 B6
Albury Way TS3 120 F2
Alconbury Way TS3 120 F2
Alcote Gr DH6 48 D6
Aldam St DL1 133 A4
Aldbrough Cl
[11] Ryhope SR2 18 F6
Stockton-on-T TS19 117 B3
Aldbrough Wlk [4] DL1 152 C8
Aldeburgh Cl TS25 89 E6
Aldenham Rd TS14 143 D2
Alder Cl DH5 26 F3
Alder Cres DH9 5 F2
Alder Gr DH8 11 D3
Alder Lea Cl DH1 35 A3
Alder Pk DH7 43 A3
Alder Rd Peterlee SR8 50 B6
Stockton-on-T TS19 117 F5
Alderburgh Way SR7 29 D8
Alderdene DH7 20 E3
Alderdene Cl DH7 33 B1
Aldergrove Dr TS4 140 B7
Alderlea TS7 140 F4
Alderman Leach Prim Sch DL3 132 C5
Alderman Wood Rd DH9 13 E8
Alderney Wlk TS14 143 D3
Alderside Cres DH7 20 E4
Alderson St
[4] Bishop Auckland DL14 80 B6
[2] Hartlepool TS26 77 A5
Alderwood
Coulby Newham TS8 140 B3
Washington NE38 17 B8
Alderwood Cl
Darlington DL1 133 E6
Hartlepool TS27 63 C4
Ormesby TS7 141 B7
Aldgrove Way DL3 132 E5
Aldhome Ct DH1 34 A6
Aldhun Cl DL14 80 B4
Aldin Grange Hall DH7 33 D2
Aldin Grange Terr DH7 33 C3
Aldin Rise DH7 33 C2
Aldridge Ct DH7 33 B2
Aldridge Rd TS3 140 D8
Aldwark Cl TS5 139 C3
Aldwin Cl DL17 83 A8
Aldwych Cl TS6 141 C7
Aldwyn Wlk [4] DL5 96 F8
Alexander Dr DH5 26 F3
Alexander St DL1 133 C3
Alexander Terr TS3 120 E3
Alexandra Cl DH1 34 A6
Alexandra Gdns [5] DL4 81 A2
Alexandra Rd TS6 121 D6
Alexandra St
[11] Consett DH8 10 F2
Pelton DH2 15 C6
Rowlands Gill NE39 1 A1
Shildon DL4 81 A2
Alexandra Terr
Crook DL15 52 F4
Evenwood DL14 92 D6
Haswell DH6 37 F3
Wheatley Hill DH6 47 F3
Alexandria Cres DH1 210 B2
Alexandria Dr DL2 154 B8
Alexandrina St [1] SR7 29 D6
Alford DH2 8 F2
Alford Ct TS25 77 A1
Alford La TS19 117 D5
Alford Rd TS12 126 C3
Alfred St Darlington DL1 133 A4
Hartlepool TS24 64 F1
Redcar TS10 107 D6
Seaham SR7 29 E6
Alfred St E SR7 29 E6
Alfreton Cl DH7 43 A2
Alfrid Pl DL5 96 D8
Alfriston Cl [3] TS17 157 B8
Alhambra Terr TS21 72 C5
Alice Row TS18 212 C2
Alice St TS20 118 B8
Aline St
New Silksworth SR3 18 B7
Seaham SR7 29 E7
Alington Cl DL17 83 A8
Alington Pl [3] DH1 35 A2
Alington Rd DL5 96 C7
Alison Pl TS24 64 F1
All Saints CE Sch TS17 157 A8
All Saints Dr DH5 27 A5
All Saints Ind Est DL4 95 B7
All Saints RC Prim Sch DH7 20 E4
All Saints' Rd DL4 95 A7
Allan St Darlington DL1 133 B3
Easington SR8 39 F5
Allan Wlk DL5 96 E7
Allen St DH3 16 C2
Allendale Rd
Billingham TS23 102 C3
Brandon DH7 43 C4
Ormesby TS7 141 B7
Stockton-on-T TS18 212 B4
Allendale St
Hartlepool TS25 90 E8
Hetton-le-H DH5 27 A2
Allendale Tee TS11 123 F6
Allendale Terr
Annfield Plain DH9 12 F4
Haswell DH6 37 F3
Allenheads Heritage Ctr★ NE47 179 B8
Allens West Sta TS16 137 A2
Allensford Bank DH8 176 F4
Allensway TS17 138 E5
Allerford Cl TS17 157 B6
Allergate DH1 210 B2
Allergate Terr DH1 210 B2
Allerston Way TS14 143 F6
Allerton Balk TS15 156 A3
Allerton Cl TS24 77 B8
Allerton Ct DL13 206 B3
Allerton Pk TS7 141 A2
Allerton Pl NE16 2 F5
Alliance Ind Est DL1 133 B4
Alliance St
Darlington DL3 132 F4
Hartlepool TS24 64 F1
Stockton-on-T TS18 212 C2
Allington Dr TS23 102 D6
Allington Way DL1 133 F2
Allington Wlk TS23 102 D6
Allinson St TS3 120 C4
Allison Ave TS17 157 D8
Allison Gdns DH8 10 F4
Allison St Consett DH8 10 F4
Guisborough TS14 143 D4
Stockton-on-T TS18 213 A4
Alloa Gr TS25 77 A1
Alloway Gr TS8 139 F2
Alloy Terr NE39 1 C1
Alma Par TS10 107 C7
Alma Pl DH1 35 B3
Alma Rd DL4 95 A8
Alma St Hartlepool TS26 77 A6
Stockton-on-T TS18 213 A4
Alma Terr Durham DH1 210 A1
Stanley Crook DL15 52 E8
Almond Cl Haswell DH6 37 F3
Spennymoor DL16 68 D7
Almond Ct
Middlesbrough TS4 139 F8
Shildon DL4 95 B8
Almond Gr
Marske-by-t-S TS11 124 C8
Stockton-on-T TS19 117 C3
Almond Terr [5] SR8 50 B6
Almoner's Barn DH1 44 A7
Almshouses
Evenwood DL14 92 C7
[10] Staindrop DL2 200 E7
Alness Gr TS25 77 A1
Alnmouth Dr TS10 107 D2
Alnport Rd TS18 213 C4
Alnwick [7] TS4 120 B1
Alnwick Ave TS29 59 E4
Alnwick Cl
Bishop Auckland DL14 80 A6
Chester le Street DH2 16 A1
Ferryhill DL17 70 B5
Hartlepool TS27 63 D3
Redcar TS10 107 F4
Alnwick Ct TS4 120 A1
Alnwick Gr
Newton Aycliffe DL5 82 E1
Stockton-on-T TS20 102 A1
Alnwick Pl DL1 133 C5
Alnwick Rd DH1 34 C7
Alnwick St SR8 49 F8
Alpha Gr TS20 118 B6
Alphonsus St TS3 215 C2
Alpine Cl DH4 17 F5
Alpine Ct DH2 16 C3
Alpine Terr
[5] Cockfield DL13 195 E3
Evenwood DL14 92 C6
Alpine Way
Stockton-on-T TS20 117 F7
Tow Law DL13 183 E1
Alston Cres DL5 96 A7
Alston Gn TS3 120 D3
Alston Moor Cl DL1 152 D8
Alston Rd Consett DH8 10 C4
Middleton-In-T DL12 208 A6
Alston St TS26 77 B4
Alston Terr DH8 10 C4
Alston Way DH7 43 C4
Alston Wlk
Newton Aycliffe DL5 96 A7
Peterlee SR8 49 E7
Sherburn DH6 36 A1
Althorp TS10 107 C6
Althorpe Cl TS3 120 F1
Alton Rd TS5 119 B2
Alum Waters DH7 43 A8
Alva Gr TS25 77 A1
Alverstone Ave [3] TS25 77 B3
Alverton Cl TS3 120 F2
Alverton Ct DL5 82 B1
Alverton Dr
Darlington DL3 132 C7
Newton Aycliffe DL5 96 B8
Alverton Gn TS3 120 F2
Alvingham Terr [1] TS3 140 F8
Alvis Cl TS23 103 B4
Alvis Ct TS23 103 B4
Alwent Cl DL3 131 F2
Alwent Mill La DL2 201 A5
Alwent Rd TS1 214 C3
Alwin NE38 9 F1
Alwin Cl TS17 157 B7
Alwinton Ct TS7 141 A7
Alwinton Dr DH2 16 A1
Alwyn Cl DH4 17 E3
Alwyn Gdns DH8 10 F1
Alwyn Rd DL3 133 A7
Amber Ct [7] TS12 125 C8
Amber St
Middlesbrough TS1 214 C2
Saltburn-by-t-S TS12 125 D8
Amberley Cl
Stockton-on-T TS18 117 C1
[8] Redcar TS10 107 E1
Amberley Gn TS3 120 D3
Amberley Gr DL3 132 B7
Amberley Way TS16 137 A1
Amberton Rd TS24 77 B8
Amberwood Cl [2] TS27 63 C4
Amble Cl TS26 76 D6
Amble View TS20 118 C7
Ambleside Ave
Redcar TS10 107 C4
Seaham SR7 28 F8
Ambleside Cl SR8 49 E7
Ambleside Gr TS5 139 D7
Ambleside Mews DH8 11 D4
Ambleside Rd
Billingham TS23 102 E1
Eston TS6 121 D1
Ambleside Wlk DL1 152 B8
Ambrose Rd TS6 121 E1
Amersham Cres SR8 49 D7
Amersham Rd TS3 140 D8
Amerston Cl TS22 87 B3
Amesbury Cres TS8 139 F2
Amiens Cl DL3 132 C5
Ammerston Rd TS1 214 B3
Amos Dr DH9 12 F1
Ampleforth Ave TS6 121 D2
Ampleforth Ct TS12 125 D2
Ampleforth Rd
Billingham TS23 102 F5
Middlesbrough TS3 120 C1
Ampleforth Way DL3 132 A5
Amroth Gn TS3 120 D3
Ancaster Rd NE16 2 F6
Anchor Ct TS24 77 F8
Anchor Ho TS24 77 D6
Anchor Ret Pk TS24 77 C7
Anchorage Mews TS17 213 C2
Anchorage Terr DH1 211 A1
Anchorage The DH3 16 D3
Ancroft Dr TS7 141 B7
Ancroft Garth DH1 45 B4
Ancroft Gdns TS20 118 B7
Ancrum Way NE16 2 F5
Anderson Rd TS17 118 D1
Andover Way TS8 139 E2
Andrew St [2] TS24 77 C5
Andrew Terr DH6 47 E1

Andrew's La SR8 39 B2
Andrews House Sta★ NE16 7 B7
Anesty Ct TS21 115 C7
Anfield Ct DL1 133 F3
Angate Sq DL13 207 D5
Angate St DL13 207 D5
Angel of the North (Mon)★ NE9 9 A8
Angels Cl DL5 96 E2
Angle Ct TS4 215 B1
Angle St TS4 215 B1
Anglesey Ave 1 TS3 140 E8
Anglesey Gr TS26 76 E8
Anglesey Wlk TS14 143 D3
Angling Gn TS13 127 A4
Angrove Cl
Great Ayton TS9 160 F1
Yarm TS15 156 F5
Angrove Dr TS9 160 F1
Angus DH2 8 F2
Angus Sq DH7 43 D5
Angus St Brandon DH7 43 E6
Easington SR8 39 F4
Hartlepool TS26 77 A6
Angus Terr SR8 39 F3
Anlaby Cl TS23 102 E8
Ann Ave DH6 58 D6
Ann Crook Way TS24 64 F1
Ann St 4 Consett DH8 10 F2
South Bank TS6 121 A5
Ann's Pl DH7 43 E6
Ann's Terr DL3 132 F4
Annan Rd TS23 102 E6
Annand Rd DH1 211 C4
Annandale DL1 133 E7
Annandale Cres TS24 63 F2
Annaside Mews DH8 11 D4
Anne Swyft Rd DL5 96 E5
Annfield Cl TS23 102 D6
Annfield Pl DH9 12 E4
Annfield Plain Inf Sch DH9 12 F3
Annfield Plain Jun Sch DH9 13 A3
Annfield Terr DH9 12 E5
Annie St TS1 214 A2
Annigate Cl TS22 101 E8
Annums The DL12 203 D8
Ansdale Rd TS3 121 A3
Anson Ho 2 TS17 138 D5
Anson Wlk DL14 81 B8
Anstey Ho 2 TS20 118 A8
Anstruther Dr DL1 133 B7
Anthony Ct DH9 13 E7
Anthony St Easington SR8 39 F5
Stanley DH9 13 E7
Antliff Terr 3 DH9 12 F4
Antrim Ave TS19 117 A4
Antrim Gdns SR7 29 C8
Anvil Ct DH1 34 A7
Apperley Ave DH1 45 C4
Apple Orchard Bank TS11,TS12 124 F4
Appleby Ave TS3 120 D3
Appleby Cl TS11 123 F6
Appleby Ct
Bournmoor DH4 17 D1
Crook DL15 52 E3
Appleby Gr TS24 77 B8
Appleby Ho 4 TS17 138 D5
Appleby Rd TS23 102 E5
Appleby St DL14 80 D5
Appleby Way SR8 49 A3
Appledore Gdns
Chester le Street DH3 16 D5
Edmondsley DH7 23 B7
Applegarth Coxhoe DH6 58 A3
Mount Pleasant TS8 159 B8
Appleton Cl DL3 132 F5
Appleton Cres DL15 53 F3
Appleton Rd
Middlesbrough TS5 139 B8
Stockton-on-T TS19 117 F5
Appletree Cl DL2 152 D1
Appletree Gdns TS7 141 B7
Applewood Cl TS27 63 B4
Appley Cl TS16 137 D5
Apsley St TS1 215 A1
Apsley Way TS17 137 F2
Aptec Enterprise Pk DL14 79 D1
Aquinas Ct DL3 133 A6
Arabella Cl TS24 64 E1
Arabella St TS24 64 E1
Arbourcourt Ave DH7 41 D8
Arbroath DH2 8 F1
Arbroath Gr TS25 76 F1
Arc (Theatre & Arts Ctr) TS18 213 A3
Arcadia DH2 8 F1
Arcadia Ave DH3 16 C5
Arcadia Ct 4 DL3 132 F1
Arch Ct TS24 64 C1
Archdeacon Cres DL3 132 B4
Archdeacon Newton DL2 131 E7
Archer Ave DL14 80 A4
Archer Rd DL2 154 A5
Archer St Darlington DL3 132 F2
Thornaby-on-T TS17 213 C1
Archery Rise DH1 210 A1
Archibald Prim Sch TS5 214 A1
Archibald St TS5 214 A1
Arden Cl TS14 143 D2
Arden Gr TS19 117 B2
Arden St DH6 48 C7
Ardmore Dr DL1 133 D7
Ardrossan DH2 8 F1
Ardrossan Ct TS25 77 A1
Ardrossan Rd TS25 77 A1
Arena Bsns Pk DH4 26 C7
Argent St SR8 39 F5
Argory The TS17 157 B8
Argyle Ct DH9 7 A1
Argyle Pl DH6 37 F7
Argyle Rd TS6 121 D6
Argyll DH2 8 F1
Argyll Cl DL1 133 D7
Argyll Rd Hartlepool TS25 77 A1
Marton TS7 140 C3
Stockton-on-T TS20 117 F7
Arisaig DH2 8 F1
Arisaig Cl TS16 156 C8
Ark Royal Cl
Hartlepool TS25 90 E8
Seaton Carew TS25 77 D1
Arken Terr TS20 118 B6
Arkendale TS8 139 D1
Arkendale St DL1 133 A5
Arkgrove Ind Est TS18 118 D5
Arkle Cres DL1 151 F6
Arkley Cres TS24 64 A2
Arlington Cl DH4 17 E3
Arlington Ct TS18 213 A1
Arlington Rd TS5 139 E8
Arlington St Loftus TS13 127 C1
Stockton-on-T TS18 212 C1
Stockton-on-T TS18 213 A1
Armadale TS10 107 E2
Armadale Cl TS19 116 F4
Armadale Gr TS25 76 F1
Armitage Rd TS10 106 E3
Armondside Rd NE17 4 C6
Armoury St 5 DL16 55 F1
Armstrong Ave TS28 60 E8
Armstrong Cl DL5 96 F8
Armstrong Ct DL3 132 D4
Armstrong Ind Est NE37 9 F7
Armstrong Rd SR8 49 D8
Arncliffe Ave TS18 137 F8
Arncliffe Gdns TS26 77 A5
Arncliffe Gr DL2 131 F2
Arncliffe Pl DL5 96 B7
Arncliffe Rd TS5 119 B3
Arndale Ho 14 DH3 9 C4
Arnison Ctr The DH1 34 C8
Arnold Ave TS27 50 D4
Arnold Cl DH9 14 A6
Arnold Gr TS25 76 E2
Arnold Rd DL1 133 C3
Arnold St DL14 79 C1
Arnside Ave TS3 120 D3
Arran Cl TS17 138 C4
Arran Ct
13 Bishop Auckland DL14 80 B6
Silksworth SR3 18 A6
Arran Gr TS25 77 A1
Arran Wlk Darlington DL1 133 D7
Guisborough TS14 143 D3
Arrandale TS8 139 D1
Arrathorne Rd TS18 137 A8
Arrowsmith Sq DL5 96 E7
Artemis Ct DH7 43 D4
Arthur Ave SR2 19 A6
Arthur Pit Cotts DL15 52 C7
Arthur St Beamish DH2 15 A7
Chilton DL17 83 A7
Crook DL15 52 F4
Darlington DL3 132 F4
Eldon Lane DL14 80 F4
Great Ayton TS9 161 A3
Redcar TS10 107 B7
Ryhope SR2 19 A6
Ushaw Moor DH7 32 F2
Arthur Terr
Bishop Auckland DL14 80 B5
Ferryhill DL17 70 C4
New Marske TS11 124 A7
Stanley Crook DL15 40 E1
Arun Cl SR8 49 C5
Arundel Cl DL14 80 A6
Arundel Ct TS17 137 F2
Arundel Dr DL3 132 B5
Arundel Gn TS3 120 D3
Arundel Rd
Billingham TS23 102 D5
Eston TS6 121 E4
Arundel St TS10 107 B7
Arundel Way DH7 43 C4
Arundel Wlk DH2 15 F7
Ascot Ave TS5 119 B1
Ascot Ct DL14 68 D1
Ascot Dr TS18 118 F5
Ascot Pl DH2 15 F8
Ascot Rd Consett DH8 10 E7
Redcar TS10 107 D4
Ascot St SR8 39 F4
Ascot View DL1 133 E4
Ash Ave Durham DH1 35 A1
Ushaw Moor DH7 33 A2
Ash Cres Peterlee SR8 50 A6
Seaham SR7 29 C5
Ash Dr DL15 54 C3
Ash Gn TS8 159 C8
Ash Gr Chilton DL17 82 E8
Kirklevington TS15 172 D8
Loftus TS13 127 B2
Shildon DL4 81 A1
South Bank TS6 121 B5
Spennymoor DL16 68 E7
Wingate TS29 60 A5
Ash Hill TS8 140 C1
Ash Mdws NE38 16 E7
Ash Rd TS14 143 E5
Ash St Billingham TS23 103 E2
Consett DH8 10 F2
12 Langley Park DH7 32 C6
Ash Terr
Annfield Plain DH9 12 E5
Bowburn DH6 57 D8
Cornforth DL17 70 E8
Leadgate DH8 11 D4
Murton SR7 28 D3
Tantobie DH9 6 B2
The Middles DH9 14 B3
Ash Tree Cl
Darlington DL3 132 B2
Newton Aycliffe DL5 82 B1
Ash Tree Terr DH7 22 D7
Ash Trees Sch TS23 102 D6
Ashberry Cl TS12 146 B1
Ashbourne Cl TS6 121 F2
Ashbourne Ct DH6 57 F3
Ashbourne Dr DH6 57 F3
Ashbourne Rd TS19 118 A5
Ashbrook Cl DH7 42 F3
Ashbrooke Ct TS27 61 C4
Ashbrooke Est DH6 48 C6
Ashbrooke Way TS5 119 B2
Ashburn St TS25 90 E8
Ashburton Cl TS8 140 B4
Ashby Cres DH8 10 D5
Ashby Gr TS25 89 E7
Ashby La DH8 10 D4
Ashby Rd TS23 102 D5
Ashcombe Cl TS22 102 A6
Ashcroft DL13 206 C4
Ashcroft Gdns DL14 80 C6
Ashcroft Rd DL3 151 D8
Ashdale Hemlington TS8 139 D1
Penshaw DH4 17 E8
Ashdale Cl DL2 154 C7
Ashdale Rd DH8 11 A3
Ashdown Ave DH1 35 B3
Ashdown Cl TS17 138 C4
Ashdown Way TS23 103 A6
Ashes The TS25 90 E7
Ashfield Consett DH8 10 D6
Newton Aycliffe DL5 96 C6
Ashfield Ave TS4 119 F1
Ashfield Cl TS25 89 E4
Ashfield Ct
13 Darlington DL3 132 F2
High Spen NE39 1 A4
Ashfield Terr DH3 16 D2
Ashford Ave TS5 139 A8
Ashford Cl TS14 143 D2
Ashford Dr DH7 23 B4
Ashford Gr DH6 47 E4
Ashgrove DH2 15 F2
Ashgrove Ave TS25 77 B3
Ashgrove Terr DH3 9 B5
Ashkirk Cl DH2 16 A1
Ashkirk Rd TS6 121 C2
Ashleigh DH2 16 A5
Ashleigh Ave DH1 34 B5
Ashleigh Gr DH7 20 E4
Ashley Ct DH9 13 C8
Ashley Gdns TS24 76 F7
Ashley Terr DH3 16 C4
Ashling Way TS5 214 A1
Ashmore Terr DH6 47 F3
Ashridge Cl
Ingleby Barwick TS17 138 C1
New Marske TS11 123 F6
Ashton Ct DL16 56 A3
Ashton Downe 2 DH2 16 C2
Ashton Rd TS20 117 E8
Ashton Rise
Chester le Street DH2 16 C2
Peterlee SR8 49 E7
Ashton St SR8 39 F4
Ashtree Cl NE39 1 F3
Ashtree La NE21,NE39 1 B5
Ashvale Ave NE11 8 C6
Ashvale Homes TS24 63 C5
Ashville Ave
Eaglescliffe TS16 137 D3
Stockton-on-T TS20 101 F1
Ashville Dr DL2 168 C8
Ashwood
Chester le Street DH3 16 D2
Durham DH1 211 B3
South Hetton DH6 38 A6
Ashwood Cl
Hartlepool TS27 63 C4
7 Ormesby TS7 141 B7
Ashwood Grange DH6 47 C3
Ashwood Mdw SR8 49 F7
Aske Rd
Middlesbrough TS1 214 C2
Redcar TS10 107 D6
Askern Dr TS5 139 E6
Askerton Dr SR8 49 A3
Askew Dale TS14 143 A3
Askham Bryan Coll TS14 143 F5
Askham Cl TS4 119 F1
Askrigg Cl
Newton Aycliffe DL5 96 C8
Urpeth DH2 8 E2
Askrigg Rd TS18 212 B3
Askrigg St DL1 133 A5
Askrigg Wlk 4 TS3 120 C1
Askwith Rd TS5 119 D1
Aspatria Ave 4 TS27 50 D3
Aspen Ave 7 SR8 50 B6
Aspen Cl Durham DH1 35 A3
Shiney Row DH4 17 F5
Spennymoor DL16 68 D7
Aspen Ct Consett DH8 10 E4
Great Lumley DH3 25 A7
Aspen Ct *continued*
Shildon DL4 95 B8
Aspen Dr TS5 119 F1
Aspen Gr DL5 96 A3
Aspen Rd TS16 156 B8
Aspley Cl SR3 18 A6
Asquith St DH6 47 E4
Asquith Terr DH9 12 E5
Association St DL4 80 F2
Astbury Marton TS8 140 E1
Mount Pleasant TS8 159 E8
Astbury Cl NE38 17 B8
Aster Cl TS7 140 B4
Asterley Dr TS5 139 A7
Astley Cl TS19 117 B3
Aston Ave TS3 120 E4
Aston Dr TS17 138 B4
Aston Rd TS22 102 B5
Aston Terr DL3 132 C3
Aston Way NE16 2 F5
Astonbury Gn TS4 140 B6
Athelstan Rigg SR2 19 A7
Atherstone Dr TS14 143 E3
Atherstone Way DL3 132 A5
Atherton Cl DL16 68 F7
Atherton Dr DH4 26 A7
Atherton St DH1 210 B3
Atherton Terr DL14 80 E5
Atherton Way TS15 156 A3
Athlone Pl DH3 9 D1
Athol Gdns SR2 19 A6
Athol Gr SR3 18 A7
Athol St TS1 214 C2
Atholl DH2 8 F2
Atholl Cl DL1 133 D6
Atholl Gr Hartlepool TS25 77 A1
Redcar TS10 107 A5
Atkinson Ct TS24 64 A3
Atkinson Gdns DL5 96 E2
Atkinson Gr DH6 48 B7
Atkinson Rd DH3 16 D5
Atlas Wynd TS15 156 C6
Attingham Cl TS8 139 F2
Attlee Ave TS27 50 F1
Attlee Cres DH6 37 E1
Attlee Ct DL13 183 E1
Attlee Est DL13 183 E1
Attlee Gr SR2 18 E8
Attlee Rd TS6 121 E4
Attlee Sq DH6 35 F2
Attlow Wlk TS3 120 F2
Attwood Pl DL13 183 D1
Attwood Rd DL13 183 D2
Attwood Terr
Spennymoor DL16 56 B4
Wolsingham DL13 207 E5
Atwater Cl TS15 156 D4
Atwick Cl TS23 102 E8
Aubrey St TS1 215 A2
Auckland DH2 16 A3
Auckland Ave
Darlington DL3 132 D5
Marton TS7 140 E3
Auckland Castle★ DL14 67 C1
Auckland Ct DL15 53 F2
Auckland Mews DL5 96 E7
Auckland Oval DL3 132 D5
Auckland Park Hospl DL14 80 B6
Auckland Pl DL5 96 E7
Auckland Rd
Billingham TS23 103 A8
Bishop Auckland DL14 80 D5
Durham DH1 34 D7
Ferryhill DL17 70 B6
Auckland St TS14 143 E5
Auckland Terr DL4 80 E2
Auckland View DL14 78 F5
Auckland Way
Hartlepool TS26 76 C5
Stockton-on-T TS18 117 B1
Auckland Wynd DL4 80 E2
Audrey Gr Darlington DL1 133 D1
Stockton-on-T TS18 117 C1
Augusta Cl DL1 133 E6
Augustine Cl DH1 34 A6
Austen Cl TS23 102 D8
Austen Pl DH9 14 B4
Austen Way DL15 52 C3
Austin Ave TS18 212 C1
Auton Cl DH7 33 B3
Auton Field DH7 33 C3
Auton Field Terr DH7 33 C3
Auton Stile DH7 33 B3
Autumn Gr TS19 117 C3
Avalon Ct TS8 139 F2
Avebury Cl TS17 157 C8
Avens Way TS17 138 B2
Avenue 1 DL17 69 E1
Avenue 2 DL17 69 E1
Avenue 3 DL17 69 E1
Avenue 4 DL17 69 D1
Avenue Pl TS14 143 F5
Avenue Prim Sch The TS7 141 A3
Avenue Rd TS24 77 B6
Avenue St DH1 45 B4
Avenue The
Annfield Plain DH9 12 E3
Birtley DH3 9 C4
Bournmoor DH3 17 E6
Brotton TS12 126 C4
Burnhope DH7 21 E5
Chester le Street DH2 16 B3
Consett DH8 11 A2
Coxhoe DH6 58 A4
Durham DH1 210 B2
Eaglescliffe TS16 137 C3
Avenue The *continued*
Eston TS6 121 C3
Guisborough TS14 143 B3
Hetton-le-H DH5 27 B4
Middlesbrough TS5 119 E1
Murton SR7 28 D3
Nunthorpe TS7 141 A3
Pelton DH2 15 E7
Pity Me DH1 34 A7
Redcar TS10 107 D6
Rowlands Gill NE39 1 F1
Seaham SR7 29 A7
Stainton Grove DL12 209 F8
Stockton-on-T TS19 117 B3
Thornaby-on-T TS17 138 D8
Wheatley Hill DH6 47 E3
Avenue Vivian DH4 17 F1
Aviemore Ct DL1 133 F3
Aviemore Rd TS8 139 F2
Avill Gr TS17 157 A6
Avoca Ct TS10 107 B7
Avon Cl Rowlands Gill NE39 1 F3
Skelton TS12 125 D3
Thornaby-on-T TS17 138 D6
Avon Cres DH4 26 A8
Avon Ct DL5 96 B8
Avon Dr TS14 143 D3
Avon Gr TS22 102 A6
Avon Rd
Hurworth-on-T DL2 168 B8
Peterlee SR8 49 C5
Redcar TS10 107 A4
Stanley DH9 13 F5
Stockton-on-T TS20 118 C7
Avon St Easington SR8 39 E4
Saltburn-by-t-S TS12 125 C6
Avon Way DL1 152 A6
Avoncroft Cl SR7 28 D8
Avondale Cl TS6 121 D4
Avondale Gdns TS24 77 B8
Avondale Ho DH2 15 F8
Avondale Rd 2 DH8 10 F3
Avondale Terr DH3 16 C3
Avondene Flats 4 TS24 77 C6
Avro Cl
Marske-by-t-S TS11 108 B1
Stockton-on-T TS18 137 E6
Axbridge Ct TS23 102 D7
Axford Terr NE17 4 B6
Axminster Rd TS8 139 F2
Axton Cl TS17 138 B3
Axwell View NE21 2 C8
Aycliffe Cl TS19 117 A3
Aycliffe Gates DL5 96 E3
Aycliffe Ind Pk DL5 96 C3
Aycliffe La
Brafferton DL1 113 A7
Mordon TS21 84 B1
Aycliffe Rd TS7 140 D3
Aycliffe Village Prim Sch DL5 96 E2
Aycliffe Young Peoples Ctr DL5 97 A7
Aykley Ct DH1 34 A4
Aykley Gn DH1 34 A4
Aykley Heads Bsns Ctr DH1 34 B4
Aykley Heads Sports Gd DH1 34 C4
Aykley Rd DH1 34 B6
Aykley Vale DH1 34 B5
Aylesbury Dr SR3 18 A5
Aylmer Gr DL5 96 C7
Aylsham Cl TS17 157 C8
Aylsham Ct SR3 18 A4
Aylton Dr TS5 139 C3
Aylward Pl DH9 14 B5
Aynsley Terr DH8 10 F3
Ayr Gr TS25 77 A1
Ayresome Grange Rd TS5 214 A1
Ayresome Green La TS5 119 D2
Ayresome Park Rd TS5 119 D2
Ayresome Prim Sch TS1 214 B1
Ayresome Rd TS5 119 B4
Ayresome St TS1 214 B1
Ayresome Way DL1 133 D3
Aysdalegate TS12 145 A2
Aysgarth Cl DL5 96 B7
Aysgarth Rd
Darlington DL1 152 B8
Middlesbrough TS5 119 C1
Stockton-on-T TS18 212 A3
Ayton Cres TS6 121 E1
Ayton Ct
Guisborough TS14 143 D6
Redcar TS10 107 B3
Ayton Dr Darlington DL3 151 D7
Redcar TS10 107 C3
Ayton Pl TS20 118 B5
Ayton Prim Sch NE38 9 F3
Ayton Rd
Thornaby-on-T TS17 138 C6
Washington NE38 9 F4
Azalea Ave 6 SR8 50 B6
Azalia Gr 5 TS10 107 E1
Azalia Rd TS19 118 A5

B

Babbacombe Dr DL17 70 C5
Back Child St TS12 126 B4

Bee – Bod 221

Beeches The TS6 ... 121 C3
Beechfield
Mount Pleasant TS8 ... 159 B8
Newton Aycliffe DL5 ... 96 B6
Beechfield Rise DH6 ... 58 A5
Beechgrove La DH2,DH7 ... 14 F2
Beechgrove Terr DH9 ... 14 E1
Beechside DL2 ... 200 F7
Beechtree Ct TS15 ... 156 B7
Beechways DH1 ... 33 F3
Beechwood NE39 ... 1 A2
Beechwood Ave
Darlington DL3 ... 132 E1
Middlesbrough TS4 ... 140 A8
Saltburn-by-t-S TS12 ... 125 C6
Beechwood Dr DL14 ... 80 C5
Beechwood Prim Sch
TS4 ... 140 A8
Beechwood Rd
Eaglescliffe TS16 ... 137 C4
Fishburn TS21 ... 72 C4
Thornaby-on-T TS17 ... 138 C7
Beechwoods DH2 ... 16 B5
Beeford Cl TS23 ... 88 E1
Beeford Dr TS5 ... 139 E6
Beehive Workshops DH1 ... 35 B2
Bek Rd Durham DH1 ... 34 C6
Newton Aycliffe DL5 ... 96 E7
Belasis Ave TS23 ... 103 A2
Belasis Ct TS23 ... 103 A3
Belasis Hall Tech Pk
TS23 ... 103 B3
Belford Cl TS19 ... 117 C4
Belford Gdns DL1 ... 133 C6
Belford St SR8 ... 39 F1
Belford Way DL5 ... 95 F7
Belgrave Ave DH6 ... 58 A3
Belgrave Ct Coxhoe DH6 ... 58 A3
Hartlepool TS25 ... 90 E8
Belgrave Dr TS6 ... 141 C7
Belgrave St DL1 ... 152 B8
Belgrave Terr DL2 ... 168 A8
Belk Cl TS6 ... 121 D5
Belk St Hartlepool TS24 ... 77 B7
Middlesbrough TS1 ... 214 C1
Bell Cl TS18 ... 212 C2
Bell Mdw DH7 ... 43 A3
Bell Sq TS21 ... 99 E3
Bell St
Bishop Auckland DL14 ... 80 B6
Cornforth DL17 ... 57 D1
Crook DL15 ... 52 F3
Middlesbrough TS5 ... 214 A1
9 Stockton-on-T TS20 ... 118 B5
Bell Wlk DL5 ... 96 F6
Bell's Folly DH1 ... 44 A7
Bell's Pl DL3 ... 132 F2
Bellamy Ct TS3 ... 120 D3
Bellasis Cl DL5 ... 96 E7
Bellasis Gr TS27 ... 63 D3
Bellburn La DL3 ... 132 E5
Belle St DH9 ... 13 F6
Belle View Dr 2 DH8 ... 177 A3
Belle Vue Crook DL15 ... 52 F3
Eggleston DL12 ... 193 E2
Frosterley DL13 ... 188 A7
Quarrington Hill DH6 ... 58 D8
Belle Vue Ct Durham DH1 ... 35 B3
Stockton-on-T TS20 ... 118 B6
Belle Vue Gdns 7 DH8 ... 10 F3
Belle Vue Gr TS4 ... 120 B1
Belle Vue Ho 11 TS20 ... 118 B6
Belle Vue Rd TS5 ... 119 D2
Belle Vue St DL16 ... 68 E7
Belle Vue Terr
Carlin How TS13 ... 126 F3
Durham DH1 ... 35 B3
Hunwick DL15 ... 66 E6
1 Middleton St George
DL2 ... 153 F7
Willington DL15 ... 53 F3
Belle Vue Way TS25 ... 77 C3
Bellerby Dr DL2 ... 8 E2
Bellerby Rd TS18 ... 117 B1
Bellister Pk SR8 ... 49 E4
Bellows Burn La TS27 ... 62 B5
Bells Bldgs 6 DH9 ... 12 F5
Bells Pl 4 DH9 ... 12 F5
Bells Wood Ct DH8 ... 10 D4
Bells' Ville DH1 ... 35 A2
Bellwood Ave TS12 ... 145 D6
Bellwood Terr DH8 ... 11 D3
Belmangate TS14 ... 143 F3
Belmont Ave
Billingham TS22 ... 102 C5
Eston TS6 ... 121 B3
Hawthorn SR7 ... 39 B8
Middlesbrough TS5 ... 139 D3
Stockton-on-T TS19 ... 117 F5
Belmont Bsns Pk DH1 ... 35 B4
Belmont CE Jun Sch
DH1 ... 35 C3
Belmont Cheveley Park Prim
Sch DH1 ... 35 E4
Belmont Comp Sch DH1 ... 35 C3
Belmont Gdns TS26 ... 77 A5
Belmont Ho DH1 ... 35 C3
Belmont Ind Est DH1 ... 35 B4
Belmont Inf Sch DH1 ... 35 C3
Belmont Prim Sch TS14 ... 143 F3
Belmont Rise DH5 ... 27 A1
Belmont St TS6 ... 121 F2
Belmont Terr TS14 ... 143 F4
Belmont Villa DH1 ... 35 C3
Belmonte Ave TS27 ... 50 F2
Belsay NE38 ... 9 F4
Belsay Ave SR8 ... 49 F8
Belsay Cl Ferryhill DL17 ... 70 B6
Belsay Cl *continued*
Stockton-on-T TS19 ... 117 C4
Belsay Ct TS21 ... 85 A7
Belsay Wlk DL1 ... 133 C6
Belton Dr TS5 ... 139 E6
Belvedere Rd
Darlington DL1 ... 152 A8
6 Middlesbrough TS4 ... 120 A1
11 Thornaby-on-T TS17 ... 138 D8
Belverdere Gdns DH6 ... 48 B7
Belvoir Gr DL14 ... 80 A6
Benbow Wlk DL14 ... 81 B8
Bendle Terr DL12 ... 193 B2
Benedict St TS3 ... 215 C2
Benevente St 2 SR7 ... 29 D6
Benfield Cl DH8 ... 10 D6
Benfieldside Prim Sch
DH8 ... 10 C5
Benfieldside Rd DH8 ... 10 C6
Beningborough Gdns
TS17 ... 138 B1
Benmore Rd TS25 ... 90 A8
Bennett Rd TS25 ... 76 D3
Bennison Cres TS10 ... 106 F4
Bennison St TS14 ... 143 E5
Benridge Bank DH4 ... 26 A2
Benridge Cl TS5 ... 139 B5
Bensham Rd DL1 ... 133 B7
Benson St
Chester le Street DH3 ... 16 C2
4 Hartlepool TS26 ... 77 A5
Middlesbrough TS5 ... 119 E2
Stanley DH9 ... 13 E7
Stockton-on-T TS20 ... 118 B8
Bent House La DH1 ... 45 A8
Bentick St TS26 ... 77 A6
Bentinck Ave TS5 ... 139 E8
Bentinck Rd TS19 ... 117 B3
Bentley Ave TS23 ... 103 B5
Bentley St 5 TS26 ... 77 A5
Bentley Wynd TS15 ... 156 B6
Benton Cl TS23 ... 102 E8
Benton Rd TS5 ... 139 E7
Benton Terr DH9 ... 13 F7
Bents La DL13 ... 179 B2
Benville Terr DH7 ... 42 E8
Benwell Cl TS19 ... 117 C4
Berberis Gr TS19 ... 117 C3
Beresford Cres TS3 ... 120 F3
Beresford St DL4 ... 95 A7
Berkeley Ave TS25 ... 90 A7
Berkeley Cl TS23 ... 102 D5
Berkeley Dr TS10 ... 107 E3
Berkeley Gr DL14 ... 80 A6
Berkeley Rd DL1 ... 152 A7
Berkley Dr TS14 ... 143 F2
Berkshire Cl DH1 ... 35 C3
Berkshire Ho TS6 ... 121 E3
Berkshire Rd Peterlee SR8 ... 49 C8
Stockton-on-T TS20 ... 118 C7
Berksyde DH8 ... 11 A1
Bernaldby Ave TS14 ... 143 C3
Bernard Gilpin Prim Sch
DH5 ... 26 E8
Bernard Shaw St 8 DH4 ... 26 D8
Bernard St DH4 ... 26 D8
Bernard Terr DH2 ... 15 E5
Berner St TS5 ... 119 D2
Bernera Ct DL1 ... 133 D7
Bernica Gr TS17 ... 157 A7
Berriedale Dr DL1 ... 133 B7
Berrington Gdns 2
TS17 ... 157 B8
Berry Ave TS29 ... 59 E4
Berry Bank DL11,DL2 ... 201 A2
Berry Edge Factories
DH8 ... 10 E2
Berry Edge Rd DH8 ... 10 F2
Berry Edge View DH8 ... 10 E3
Berrybank Crest DL3 ... 132 B4
Berryfield Cl SR3 ... 18 A5
Bertha St Consett DH8 ... 10 F3
Ferryhill DL17 ... 70 A5
Hartlepool TS26 ... 77 C4
Bertie Rd DL5 ... 96 C7
Bertram St 3 DH3 ... 9 C4
Berwick NE38 ... 9 F4
Berwick Chase SR8 ... 49 B3
Berwick Ct TS29 ... 59 E4
Berwick Gr TS20 ... 102 A1
Berwick Hills Ave TS3 ... 120 F3
Berwick Hills Prim Sch
TS3 ... 120 C2
Berwick Rd DL3 ... 132 B5
Berwick St TS25 ... 90 E8
Berwick Wlk TS10 ... 107 E4
Bessemer Ct TS6 ... 121 D7
Bessemer Rd DH6 ... 37 F7
Bessemer St Consett DH8 ... 10 E3
Ferryhill DL17 ... 69 E5
Best's Yd DH7 ... 33 A8
Bethany Gdns DH9 ... 12 F5
Bethany Terr 1 DH9 ... 12 F5
Bethune Ave SR7 ... 29 A7
Bethune Rd TS5 ... 119 B2
Betjeman Cl
1 Billingham TS23 ... 102 E8
Stanley DH9 ... 14 A6
Bevan Ave SR2 ... 18 E6
Bevan Cres DH6 ... 47 E1
Bevan Gr Durham DH1 ... 35 B3
Shotton Colliery DH6 ... 48 C6
Bevan Sq SR7 ... 28 C4
Bevanlee Rd TS6 ... 121 B5
Beveridge Arc DL5 ... 96 D7
Beveridge Cl TS21 ... 72 C5
Beveridge Way DL5 ... 96 D7
Beverley Dr NE21 ... 1 F8
Beverley Gdns
Chester le Street DH3 ... 16 D2
Chilton DL17 ... 82 F8
4 Consett, Blackfyne DH8 ... 10 F3
Consett, Blackhill DH8 ... 10 D5
Beverley Rd
Billingham TS23 ... 102 F8
Middlesbrough TS4 ... 139 F7
Nunthorpe TS7 ... 141 B3
Redcar TS10 ... 107 F4
Beverley Sch TS4 ... 139 F7
Beverley Terr
Annfield Plain DH9 ... 12 E5
5 Consett DH8 ... 10 F3
Beverley Way SR8 ... 49 C7
Bevin Gr TS27 ... 50 F2
Bevin Sq DH6 ... 38 B7
Bewholme Cl TS23 ... 88 E1
Bewick Cl DH2 ... 24 A8
Bewick Cres DL5 ... 96 D6
Bewicke Maine Cvn Site
DH2 ... 8 E5
Bewicke View DH3 ... 9 D5
Bewley Gr
Middlesbrough TS5 ... 139 C6
Peterlee SR8 ... 49 A3
Bewley Inf Sch TS23 ... 103 A7
Bewley Jun Sch TS23 ... 103 A7
Bewley Terr DH7 ... 42 E8
Bexley Cl TS4 ... 140 B6
Bexley Dr Hartlepool TS25 ... 77 B2
Normanby TS6 ... 141 D7
Bglws The DL15 ... 52 E4
Bickersteth Cl TS18 ... 213 A1
Bickersteth Wlk TS18 ... 213 A1
Bickford Terr DL5 ... 96 E2
Bickley Cl TS22 ... 102 A5
Bickley Way TS8 ... 140 B2
Biddick Cl TS19 ... 117 C4
Biddick La NE38 ... 17 D8
Bielby Ave TS23 ... 102 E8
Biggin Cl TS5 ... 139 E6
Bigland Terr DL14 ... 80 D5
Billingham Bank TS23 ... 102 D1
Billingham Beck Valley
Country Pk* TS23 ... 118 D8
Billingham Beck Valley Ctry
Pk* TS23 ... 102 C2
Billingham Beck Valley Ctry
Pk Visitor Ctr* TS23 ... 102 C2
Billingham Campus Sch
TS23 ... 102 F7
Billingham Halt TS23 ... 102 F4
Billingham Rd TS20 ... 102 C1
Billingham South Com Prim
Sch TS23 ... 102 E2
Billy Hall Farm DL15 ... 52 F6
Billy Hill DL15 ... 52 E8
Billy La DL12 ... 194 C2
Billy Row Gn DL15 ... 52 E7
Bilsdale Ave TS10 ... 107 A4
Bilsdale Rd
Hartlepool TS25 ... 90 D7
Middlesbrough TS4 ... 215 C1
Stockton-on-T TS19 ... 212 B4
Binchester Croft DL5 ... 95 F4
Bingfield Ct TS23 ... 102 E8
Binks St TS5 ... 119 E2
Birch Ave
Bishop Auckland DL14 ... 80 B5
Shildon DL4 ... 81 A1
Birch Cl TS15 ... 172 D8
Birch Cres NE16 ... 6 A6
Birch Dr DL15 ... 54 C2
Birch Gr 5 Consett DH8 ... 177 E4
Stockton-on-T TS19 ... 117 E7
Birch Mdws DL15 ... 66 D7
Birch Mews NE16 ... 5 F6
Birch Pl DH7 ... 41 D8
Birch Rd
Barnard Castle DL12 ... 209 C5
Cornforth DL17 ... 57 E1
Darlington DL1 ... 133 B8
Birch St DH8 ... 10 F2
Birch Tree Cl 9 TS7 ... 141 B7
Birch Wlk TS24 ... 77 A8
Bircham St DH9 ... 13 D5
Birches The
Coulby Newham TS8 ... 140 A1
Hurworth-on-T DL2 ... 152 E1
Stanley DH9 ... 13 F8
Birchfield Cl 1 TS16 ... 137 B1
Birchfield Dr TS16 ... 137 B1
Birchgate Rd TS5 ... 139 D8
Birchgrove Ave DH1 ... 35 B3
Birchill Gdns TS26 ... 76 E7
Birchington Ave TS6 ... 121 F4
Birchmere DL16 ... 55 E2
Birchwood Ave TS4 ... 120 A1
Birchwood Cl DH9 ... 14 E8
Birchwood Dr DH6 ... 48 F5
Birchwood Rd TS7 ... 140 F4
Birdsall Brow TS20 ... 101 F1
Birdsall Row TS10 ... 107 C6
Biretta Cl TS19 ... 117 A4
Birk Brow Rd TS14 ... 145 B3
Birkdale Cl 6 TS27 ... 63 C4
Birkdale Dr Eston TS6 ... 121 E1
Shiney Row DH4 ... 17 F4
Birkdale Gdns DH1 ... 35 D3
Birkdale Rd
Darlington DL3 ... 132 B3
New Marske TS11 ... 124 A6
Stockton-on-T TS18 ... 117 B1
Birkhall Rd TS3 ... 121 A2
Birkhead Cotts NE11 ... 7 E6
Birkheads La NE11 ... 7 E6
Birkland La DH9,NE11,NE16 ... 7 E7
Birkley Rd TS20 ... 118 B6
Birtley Ave TS5 ... 139 C5
Birtley East Com Prim Sch
DH3 ... 9 C6
Birtley La DH3 ... 9 D3
Birtley Villas 1 DH3 ... 9 C5
Biscop Cres DL5 ... 96 E7
Bisham Ave TS5 ... 119 C1
Bishop Auckland Coll
DL14 ... 79 F5
Bishop Cl DL1 ... 133 D5
Bishop Ian Ramsey CE Prim
Sch DH8 ... 4 C1
Bishop Middleham CE Prim
Sch DL17 ... 71 C3
Bishop St
7 Bishop Auckland DL14 ... 80 B8
Middlesbrough TS5 ... 119 B3
Stockton-on-T TS18 ... 213 B3
Bishop's Cl DL16 ... 68 F8
Bishopdale DH4 ... 17 E8
Bishopgarth DL17 ... 71 B3
Bishops Ct
Bishop Middleham DL17 ... 71 C4
High Shincliffe DH1 ... 44 F6
Bishops Mill TS20 ... 102 B1
Bishops Way Durham DH1 ... 34 B7
Stockton-on-T TS19 ... 117 A5
Bishops Wynd DH5 ... 26 E7
Bishopsgarth Sch TS19 ... 117 A6
Bishopton Ave TS19 ... 117 E5
Bishopton Ct TS19 ... 117 B3
Bishopton Ctr The TS19 ... 212 C4
Bishopton La
Bishopton DL1,DL2,TS21 ... 114 D2
Stockton-on-T TS18 ... 213 A3
Bishopton Rd
Middlesbrough TS4 ... 119 F1
Stockton-on-T TS18,TS19 ... 212 C4
Bishopton Rd W TS19 ... 117 B4
Bishopton Redmarshall CE
Prim Sch TS21 ... 115 D7
Bisley Ct DL1 ... 133 F4
Black Boy Rd
Fence Houses DH4 ... 26 A7
Great Lumley DH4 ... 25 E7
Black Diamond Way
TS16 ... 137 B2
Black Dr DH3 ... 17 B5
Black Hall DL15 ... 189 F5
Black Horse Terr DL13 ... 194 E5
Black House La DH7 ... 22 F8
Black La DH6 ... 47 F3
Black Path The TS18,
TS20 ... 213 B4
Black Rd Billy Row DL15 ... 52 F7
Brandon DH7 ... 43 E6
Ryhope SR2 ... 18 F7
Black Squares Dr TS21,
TS22 ... 86 F3
Black Thorn Cl DH7 ... 43 A3
Blackburn Cl
Bearpark DH7 ... 33 A4
Stockton-on-T TS19 ... 117 C3
Blackburn Gr TS11 ... 108 A2
Blackbush Wlk TS17 ... 138 C3
Blackcap Cl NE38 ... 9 F3
Blackcliffe Way DH7 ... 33 A4
Blackdown Cl SR8 ... 49 B5
Blackett Ave TS20 ... 118 B6
Blackett Hutton Ind Est
TS14 ... 143 E3
Blackett Rd DL1 ... 133 C4
Blackett St
Annfield Plain DH9 ... 12 E4
Bishop Auckland DL14 ... 80 C7
Blackfell Rd NE37 ... 9 F6
Blackfriars TS15 ... 156 C5
Blackfyne Com Sch DH8 ... 10 F4
Blackgate E 6 DH6 ... 58 A4
Blackgate W 5 DH6 ... 58 A4
Blackhall Colliery Ind Est
TS27 ... 50 D4
Blackhall Colliery Prim Sch
TS27 ... 50 D4
Blackhall Sands TS5 ... 139 B3
Blackhills Rd SR8 ... 50 A7
Blackhills Terr SR8 ... 50 A7
Blackling Hole* DL13 ... 194 D6
Blackmore Cl TS14 ... 143 F2
Blackmore Wlk TS25 ... 76 D2
Blacksail Cl TS19 ... 212 C3
Blacksmiths Cl TS6 ... 121 E2
Blackthorn TS8 ... 159 C8
Blackthorn Cl TS10 ... 107 E2
Blackthorn Gr TS19 ... 117 C3
Blackthorne Ave 9 SR8 ... 50 B6
Blackton Cl DL5 ... 96 A7
Blackton Rd TS26 ... 76 C6
Blackwater Ho 7 SR3 ... 18 A6
Blackwell DL3 ... 151 C6
Blackwell Cl
Billingham TS23 ... 103 A6
Darlington DL3 ... 151 D7
Blackwell Gr DL3 ... 151 C7
Blackwell La DL3 ... 151 D7
Blackwell Scar DL3 ... 151 C7
Blackwellgate 13 DL1 ... 132 F1
Blackwood Cl TS27 ... 63 C4
Bladeside DL15 ... 52 F3
Bladon Dr TS11 ... 108 C2
Blagden Gr DL14 ... 79 E5
Blaidwood Dr DH1 ... 44 A5
Blair Ave
Ingleby Barwick TS17 ... 156 F8
Spennymoor DL16 ... 69 A8
Blair Cl DH6 ... 35 F1
Blair Ct DH7 ... 43 E5
Blair Gr DL14 ... 80 B6
Blairgowrie TS8 ... 140 E2
Blairgowrie Gr TS25 ... 89 F8
Blairmore Gdns TS16 ... 137 C1
Blaise Garden Village
TS26 ... 76 D6
Blake Cl Billingham TS23 ... 102 E8
Stanley DH9 ... 14 A6
Blake St Hartlepool TS26 ... 77 A7
8 Shildon DL4 ... 95 A8
Blake Wlk 8 TS26 ... 77 A7
Blakelock Gdns TS25 ... 77 A4
Blakelock Rd TS25 ... 76 F3
Blakeston Com Sch
TS19 ... 101 C1
Blakeston Ct TS19 ... 101 D1
Blakeston La
Stockton-on-T TS19,TS21 ... 101 C2
Wynyard Village TS21 ... 100 F4
Blakeston Rd TS23 ... 102 F6
Blakey Cl TS10 ... 107 C2
Blakey Wlk TS6 ... 122 A3
Blakiston Ct DL5 ... 82 C2
Blanche Gr SR8 ... 49 D5
Blanche Terr DH9 ... 6 B2
Blanchland Ave DH1 ... 34 E6
Blanchland Gn DL3 ... 132 A5
Blanchland Rd TS3 ... 140 E8
Bland Wlk DL5 ... 96 F7
Blandford Pl SR7 ... 29 D7
Blandford St DL17 ... 69 E5
Blanford Cl TS20 ... 102 B1
Blankney Cl TS14 ... 143 D3
Blantyre Rd TS6 ... 121 C1
Blatchford Rd TS6 ... 120 F5
Blaxton Pl NE16 ... 2 F5
Blayberry Cl TS10 ... 107 C2
Blaykeston Cl SR7 ... 18 E1
Bleach House Bank TS21 ... 99 A3
Bleak Terr 4 DL13 ... 195 E3
Blenavon Ct TS15 ... 156 B6
Blencathra Cres DL15 ... 52 F2
Blencathra Way NE21 ... 2 C8
Blenheim Ave TS11 ... 108 C2
Blenheim Cl TS11 ... 108 C2
Blenheim Ct TS17 ... 156 F7
Blenheim Mews TS10 ... 107 B6
Blenheim Rd TS4 ... 215 B2
Blenheim Rd S TS4 ... 215 B1
Blenheim Terr TS10 ... 107 B7
Blenkinsopp Ct SR8 ... 49 B2
Blessed John Ducket RC
Prim Sch DL13 ... 183 E2
Bletchley Cl TS19 ... 117 C4
Blind La
Chester le Street DH3 ... 16 D6
Easington SR8 ... 39 C5
Guisborough TS14 ... 142 E3
Hurworth-on-T DL2 ... 168 C8
New Silksworth SR3 ... 18 B7
Summerhouse DL2 ... 110 B6
Blindy La DH5 ... 27 C1
Bliss Cl DL3 ... 132 D4
Bloemfontein Pl DH9 ... 14 B3
Bloemfontein Prim Sch
DH9 ... 14 A3
Bloom Ave DH9 ... 13 E6
Bloomesley Cl DL5 ... 82 C2
Bloomfield Dr DH5 ... 26 D3
Bloomfield Rd DL3 ... 132 D3
Blorenge Ct TS17 ... 156 F7
Blossom Cl DL3 ... 132 D4
Blossomfield Way DH6 ... 37 F3
Blue Barn La TS15 ... 173 F3
Blue Bell Gr
Middlesbrough TS5 ... 139 E4
Stockton-on-T TS19 ... 117 C3
Blue Coat CE Jun Sch
DH1 ... 34 C6
Blue Coat Ct DH1 ... 211 A3
Blue House Bldgs DH1 ... 35 C4
Blue House Est DL16 ... 69 A3
Blue House Point Rd
TS18 ... 118 F4
Blue Post Yd TS18 ... 213 A2
Bluebell Cl
Bishop Auckland DL14 ... 79 E7
Blackhall Colliery TS27 ... 50 D3
Darlington DL3 ... 132 D4
Leadgate DH8 ... 11 C3
Newton Aycliffe DL5 ... 96 B8
Bluebell Dr DL16 ... 68 D7
Bluebell Mdw DL5 ... 96 B8
Bluebell Way
Hartlepool TS26 ... 63 D2
Newton Aycliffe DL5 ... 96 B8
Skelton TS12 ... 125 E1
Bluehouse Bank DH2,DH9 ... 15 A3
Blumer St DH4 ... 26 A8
Blyth Terr DH3 ... 9 B4
Blythe Ave DL14 ... 79 D3
Blythport Cl TS18 ... 213 C4
Blyton Ave SR2 ... 18 E6
Boagey Wlk TS24 ... 64 A2
Boar La TS17 ... 138 C1
Boat La DL11,DL2 ... 201 D2
Boathouse La
Cleasby DL2 ... 150 D7
Stockton-on-T TS18 ... 213 B1
Bob Hardisty Dr DL14 ... 80 B7
Bob Harrison Ct DL1 ... 133 A5
Bobby Shafto Cvn Pk DH9 ... 8 A1
Boddy St DL14 ... 80 A3
Bodiam Dr TS10 ... 107 F3

Bodmin Gr
Darlington DL3 ....132 F8
Hartlepool TS26 ....76 D8
Boeing Way TS18 ....137 F7
Boghouse La TS13 ....166 F5
Bogma Ave DH6 ....57 F3
Bolam NE38 ....9 F4
Bolam Gr TS23 ....102 E7
Bolam St SR8 ....39 F4
Bolam's Bldgs NE16 ....5 A6
Bolckow Rd TS6 ....121 D6
Bolckow St Eston TS6 ...121 F1
Guisborough TS14 ....143 E5
Middlesbrough TS1 ....214 C4
Skelton TS12 ....125 F1
Boldron Cl TS18 ....137 A8
Boldron La DL12 ....209 A5
Bollihope Gr DL14 ....79 E5
Bollington Rd TS4 ....140 B6
Bolsover Rd TS20 ....118 B6
Boltby Cl TS5 ....139 E6
Boltby Way TS16 ....137 B2
Bolton Cl Darlington DL3 .132 B4
Durham DH1 ....34 C8
Redcar TS10 ....107 E4
Bolton Ct TS4 ....119 F1
Bolton Gr
Bishop Auckland DL14 ....80 A6
Seaton Carew TS25 ....90 E8
Bolton Way TS14 ....143 F4
Bolton's Bglws NE17 ....4 B8
Boltsburn Cres DL13 ...180 D5
Boltsburn Crescent Flats
DL13 ....180 D5
Boltsburn Terr DH8 ....174 F2
Bon Lea Trad Est TS17 .213 C1
Bond St TS24 ....77 F8
Bondene Gr TS19 ....117 A5
Bondfield Rd TS6 ....121 D3
Bondgate DL3 ....132 F2
Bondisle Terr DL13 ....206 D2
Bondisle Way DL13 ....206 D2
Bone Mill Bank DL14 ....80 E6
Bone St TS18 ....213 B4
Bonemill La
Chester le Street NE38 ....16 F8
Washington NE38 ....17 C8
Bonington Cres TS23 ..102 D8
Bonnie Gr DL16 ....54 E1
Bonny Gr TS8 ....140 F1
Bonnygrove Way
Coulby Newham TS8 ....140 C1
Mount Pleasant TS8 ....159 C8
Bonnyrigg Cl TS17 ....157 B7
Bonnyrigg Wlk TS25 ....90 A8
Boosbeck Rd TS12 ....145 B8
Booth Wlk DL5 ....96 C8
Bordesley Gn TS3 ....120 D3
Borough Rd
Darlington DL1 ....133 A2
Middlesbrough TS1 ....215 B2
Redcar TS10 ....107 E5
Borough Road Ind Est
DL1 ....133 A2
Borrowby Ct TS14 ....143 D5
Borrowby La TS13 ....149 B6
Borrowdale Birtley DH3 ....9 D1
Leadgate DH8 ....11 D4
Borrowdale Cl DH1 ....35 E4
Borrowdale Cres NE21 ....2 B8
Borrowdale Dr DH1 ....35 C4
Borrowdale Gr
Crook DL15 ....52 F2
Eaglescliffe TS16 ....156 C7
Middlesbrough TS5 ....139 C7
Borrowdale Rd TS6 ....121 F4
Borrowdale St
Hartlepool TS25 ....77 B3
Hetton-le-H DH5 ....27 A2
Borton Wlk TS19 ....212 C4
Boscombe Gdns TS8 ...139 F1
Boston Cl Darlington DL1 133 C6
Hartlepool TS25 ....89 F7
Boston Dr TS7 ....140 E2
Boston St SR8 ....39 F4
Boston Wlk TS20 ....118 C7
Boswell Gr TS25 ....76 E2
Boswell St TS1 ....215 A3
Bosworth Way TS23 ....102 F6
Botany Rd DL12 ....198 A8
Botany Way TS7 ....141 A2
Bothal Dr TS19 ....117 A5
Bothal Wlk TS19 ....117 A6
Botham Gr 3 DL3 ....133 A7
Bottle Works Rd SR7 ....29 E6
Bouch St DL4 ....95 A7
Boulby Bank TS13 ....128 D2
Boulby Barns Cotts
TS13 ....128 D3
Boulby Cl SR3 ....18 C7
Boulby Dr TS13 ....127 C1
Boulby Rd Redcar TS10 ....106 F5
Skinningrove TS13 ....127 A4
Boulby Wlk 7 TS6 ....121 F3
Boulmer Ct DH2 ....16 C2
Boundary Cl DH7 ....33 A1
Boundary La DH8 ....3 A3
Boundary Rd
Middlesbrough TS1 ....214 C4
Normanby TS6 ....141 C8
Bourne Ave DL1 ....133 C2
Bourne Ct Darlington DL1 133 C2
Stanley DH9 ....14 B7
Bourne Ho TS10 ....107 A6
Bourne St SR8 ....39 F4
Bourne Terr 4 DH9 ....12 F4
Bourne Way DL15 ....54 A3
Bournemouth Ave TS3 .140 F8
Bournemouth Dr
Hartlepool TS24 ....63 D4
Seaham SR7 ....28 F6
Bournemouth Rd TS3 ..140 F8
Bournmoor Prim Sch
DH4 ....17 E3
Bourton Ct TS3 ....140 D7
Bousfield Cres DL5 ....96 D8
Bow La DH1 ....210 C2
Bow Prep Sch DH1 ....210 C1
Bow St Bowburn DH6 ....45 D1
Guisborough TS14 ....143 F4
Middlesbrough TS1 ....214 C2
Thornley (nr Wheatley Hill)
DH6 ....47 D4
Bow St Ctr TS14 ....143 F4
Bowburn Inf Sch DH6 ...57 D8
Bowburn Jun Sch DH6 ..45 D1
Bowburn North Ind Est
DH6 ....45 C1
Bowburn South Ind Est
DH6 ....57 C8
Bowen Rd DL3 ....132 C5
Bowes Ave
Hetton-le-H DH5 ....27 B1
Seaham SR7 ....28 F6
Bowes Castle* DL12 ...203 D8
Bowes Cl DL17 ....70 B6
Bowes Cres NE16 ....6 D8
Bowes Ct Darlington DL1 .133 B3
Durham DH1 ....34 D7
Bowes Farm Cotts DH3 ..17 D5
Bowes Gn TS24 ....63 D4
Bowes Gr
Bishop Auckland DL14 ....80 A6
Spennymoor DL16 ....56 A2
Bowes Hill DL14 ....78 B3
Bowes Hutchinsons CE Aided
Prim Sch DL12 ....203 D8
Bowes Lea DH4 ....17 F4
Bowes Lyon Cl NE39 ....5 D8
Bowes Lyon Ho DL12 ...209 C5
Bowes Mus The* DL12 .209 D5
Bowes Rd
Barnard Castle DL12 ....209 A5
Billingham TS23 ....102 C6
Middlesbrough TS2 ....119 D7
Newton Aycliffe DL5 ....96 D6
Bowes Rly* NE9 ....9 E8
Bowes Terr DH9 ....12 D8
Bowesfield Cres TS18 ..138 B7
Bowesfield Ind Est The
TS18 ....138 A7
Bowesfield La TS18 ....138 A8
Bowesfield Prim Sch
TS18 ....213 A1
Bowesville NE16 ....6 B5
Bowfell Cl TS16 ....137 B2
Bowfell Rd TS3 ....120 C2
Bowhill Way TS23 ....103 A7
Bowland Cl TS7 ....140 F2
Bowlees Cotts DL12 ....192 A7
Bowlees Visitor Ctr
DL12 ....192 A7
Bowley Cl TS6 ....121 B1
Bowley Wlk TS1 ....214 B3
Bowline Ho TS24 ....77 C7
Bowman St DL3 ....133 A7
Bowmont Dr DH9 ....13 C8
Bowmont Wlk DH2 ....16 A1
Bowness Cl
Hartlepool TS25 ....77 B2
Peterlee SR8 ....49 E7
Bowness Gr Ferryhill DL17 69 F6
Redcar TS10 ....107 C5
Bowood Cl SR2 ....18 D6
Bowron St TS20 ....118 B5
Bowser St TS24 ....77 C5
Box Dr TS7 ....141 B2
Boxer Ct TS6 ....121 A5
Boyd St Consett DH8 ....11 A1
Durham DH1 ....211 A1
Easington SR8 ....39 F4
Boyd Terr DH9 ....13 D5
Boyden Cl DL14 ....79 C2
Boyden Ct DL5 ....96 E6
Boyes Hill Gr DL3 ....132 D2
Boyne Ct Brandon DH7 ...43 D5
Sedgefield TS21 ....85 A7
Boyne St DL15 ....54 A4
Boyne View Trimdon TS29 .59 E1
Trimdon TS29 ....72 E8
Boynston Gr TS21 ....85 B7
Boynton Rd TS4 ....120 A2
Boyntons DH2 ....23 F4
Brabazon Dr 6 TS11 ....108 B1
Brabourn Gdns TS8 ....139 F1
Brack's Rd DL14 ....80 E7
Bracken Cl DH9 ....13 E6
Bracken Cres TS14 ....143 B3
Bracken Ct DH7 ....33 A2
Bracken Field Rd DH1 ....34 B5
Bracken Hill SR8 ....48 F5
Bracken Hill Ind Pk SR8 .48 F4
Bracken Hill Rd DL15 ....66 C7
Bracken Rd
Darlington DL3 ....132 D3
Stockton-on-T TS19 ....117 E7
Brackenbeds Cl DH2 ....15 F6
Brackenbeds La DH2 ....15 F7
Brackenberry Cres
TS10 ....107 F3
Brackenberry Wlk 5
TS6 ....121 F3
Brackendale Ct TS28 ....60 F5
Brackendale Rd DH1 ....35 D4
Brackenfield Ct TS6 ....141 E8
Brackenhill Ave DH6 ....48 E6
Brackenhill Cl TS7 ....141 A1
Brackenhill Wlk TS9 ...159 A1
Brackenridge NE16 ....5 E6
Brackenthwaite TS5 ....139 B4
Bracknell Cl SR3 ....18 C8
Bracknell Rd TS17 ....138 E7
Bradbury Cl DH9 ....13 C8
Bradbury Rd
Newton Aycliffe DL5 ....96 D4
Stockton-on-T TS20 ....102 B1
Bradford Cl DL5 ....96 D5
Bradford Cres DH1 ....211 C4
Bradhope Rd TS3 ....120 B2
Bradley Ave DH5 ....26 E6
Bradley Bglws DH8 ....11 C6
Bradley Cl DH2 ....8 E2
Bradley Cotts DH8 ....11 C6
Bradley Ct TS23 ....102 F6
Bradley Lodge Dr DH9 ...12 E8
Bradley St Easington SR8 ..39 F4
Leadgate DH8 ....11 C4
Bradley Terr Dipton DH9 ..12 E7
Easington Lane DH5 ....27 C1
Bradley Workshops Ind Est
DH8 ....11 C4
Bradleys Terr TS9 ....161 A3
Bradman Dr DH3 ....16 E1
Bradshaw Ct TS24 ....63 F2
Brae Head TS16 ....137 C1
Braemar Ct Consett DH8 ..10 C3
Darlington DL1 ....133 E7
Braemar Gr TS6 ....121 B3
Braemar Rd
Billingham TS23 ....102 D6
Hartlepool TS25 ....90 A8
Middlesbrough TS5 ....139 B8
Braemar Terr 1 SR8 ....50 B6
Braeside Burnhope DH7 ...21 D4
Edmondsley DH7 ....23 B7
Kirklevington TS15 ....172 D8
Braeworth Cl TS15 ....156 F5
Brafferton Cl DL5 ....82 E1
Brafferton Dr TS23 ....102 F8
Brafferton La DL1 ....113 A6
Brafferton St 2 TS26 ....76 F6
Brafferton Wlk TS5 ....139 C5
Braid Cres TS23 ....102 D3
Braidwood Rd TS6 ....121 C1
Braithwaite Rd SR8 ....49 F6
Braithwaite St
9 Bishop Auckland DL14 ..80 B8
Shildon DL4 ....80 E1
Brakespeare Pl SR8 ....49 E5
Bramall La DL1 ....133 F3
Bramble Dykes 7 TS10 .107 E1
Bramble Rd TS19 ....117 E7
Brambles Prim Sch TS3 120 E3
Brambles The DH3 ....9 D6
Brambling Cl TS20 ....101 F1
Bramcote Way TS17 ...138 C3
Bramfield Way TS17 ...138 A3
Bramhall Dr NE38 ....17 B8
Bramham Chase DL5 ....95 F8
Bramham Down TS14 ..143 E3
Bramley Ct TS25 ....90 A8
Bramley Gr TS7 ....140 E4
Bramley Par TS18 ....213 A1
Brampton Cl TS8 ....139 E3
Brampton Ct SR8 ....39 B3
Bramwell Terr DH8 ....11 A4
Bramwith Ave TS3 ....140 D8
Brancepath Wlk TS24 ...63 F3
Brancepeth Ave TS3 ....140 C8
Brancepeth Chare SR8 ..49 B3
Brancepeth Cl
Durham DH1 ....34 E6
New Marske TS11 ....124 A6
Newton Aycliffe DL5 ....82 E1
Brancepeth Ct TS22 ....102 C6
Brancepeth Gr DL14 ....80 A6
Brancepeth Rd DL17 ....70 A6
Brancepeth Terr DL15 ...54 A4
Brancepeth View DH7 ...42 F3
Brancpeth Cl DH7 ....33 C1
Brandlings Way SR8 ....49 D6
Brandon Cl
Billingham TS23 ....102 D7
Blaydon NE21 ....2 A8
Chester le Street DH2 ....15 F1
Hartlepool TS25 ....89 D5
Houghton-le-S DH4 ....26 D7
Brandon Jun & Inf Sch
DH7 ....43 C4
Brandon La Brandon DH7 .43 C5
New Brancepeth DH7,DL15 .42 B5
Brandon Rd
Esh Winning DH7 ....41 E8
Middlesbrough TS3 ....120 F2
Brandon View DH7 ....43 C8
Brankin Ct TS12 ....125 F3
Brankin Dr DL1 ....152 C7
Brankin Rd DL1 ....152 C7
Branklyn Gdns TS17 ...157 B8
Branksome Ave TS5 ....139 E7
Branksome Gn DL3 ....131 F5
Branksome Gr TS18 ....137 C8
Branksome Hall Dr DL3 132 A5
Branksome Lodge DL3 .132 B5
Branksome Sch DL3 ....132 A4
Branksome Terr DL3 ....132 F3
Bransdale
Guisborough TS14 ....143 A3
Penshaw DH4 ....17 E8
Spennymoor DL16 ....55 E1
Bransdale Cl TS19 ....212 B4
Bransdale Gr
Hartlepool TS25 ....90 E8
Redcar TS10 ....106 F4
Bransdale Rd TS3 ....120 C2
Brantwood DH2 ....15 F2
Brantwood Cl TS17 ....157 C8
Brantwood Terr DL14 ....80 A3
Brass Castle La
Marton TS8 ....140 F1
Mount Pleasant TS8 ....159 E7
Brass Thill DH1 ....210 B2
Brass Wynd TS8 ....140 F1
Braunespath Est DH7 ....42 F8
Brawton Gr DL3 ....132 E4
Braygate TS12 ....126 E1
Breakhouse Bank DL2 ..169 C6
Breamish Dr NE38 ....16 F8
Brechin Dr TS17 ....138 D3
Brechin Gr TS25 ....90 A8
Breck Rd DL3 ....132 D2
Brecken Way DH7 ....43 C4
Breckland Wlk TS3 ....120 D1
Breckon Ct DL13 ....195 C4
Breckon Hill DL13 ....195 C4
Breckon Hill Prim Sch
TS4 ....215 B2
Breckon Hill Rd TS4 ...215 B2
Breckon Terr TS21 ....72 C5
Brecon Cl SR8 ....49 B5
Brecon Cres TS17 ....156 F8
Brecon Dr TS10 ....107 A3
Brecon Pl DH2 ....15 F8
Brecon Rd DH1 ....34 E7
Brecon Side DL1 ....133 E5
Brecongill Cl TS24 ....77 B8
Breen Cl TS3 ....215 C2
Brenda Rd TS25 ....90 C6
Brendon Cres TS23 ....102 E4
Brendon Gr TS17 ....157 B6
Brendon Pl SR8 ....49 B7
Brenkley Cl TS20 ....101 E1
Brent Ct TS23 ....102 C3
Brentford Ct TS12 ....126 C3
Brentford Rd TS20 ....118 B6
Brentnall St TS1 ....214 C3
Brentwood Ct DH9 ....14 C6
Brereton Rd TS4 ....140 A7
Bretby Cl TS4 ....140 A8
Brettenham Ave TS4 ....140 B6
Breward Wlk 2 TS24 ....77 B7
Brewer St DL14 ....80 B6
Brewer Terr SR2 ....19 A6
Brewery Sq DH9 ....13 F7
Brewery St 7 TS24 ....77 B5
Brewsdale Rd TS3 ....120 C5
Brian Rd DL1 ....133 A6
Briar Ave Brandon DH7 ...43 A3
2 Houghton-le-S DH4 ....26 D8
Briar Cl Darlington DL3 .151 C6
Great Lumley DH4 ....17 E1
Kimblesworth DH2 ....23 F3
Shiney Row DH4 ....17 F4
Spennymoor DL16 ....68 D6
Briar Dale DH8 ....177 E4
Briar Gdns DL15 ....52 D3
Briar Glen SR7 ....28 A3
Briar Gr Redcar TS10 ....107 C5
Trimdon TS29 ....72 D8
Briar Hill DL13 ....179 C1
Briar Lea
Witton Gilbert DH7 ....23 B1
Shiney Row DH4 ....17 F4
Briar Mews DH8 ....10 D5
Briar Rd Durham DH1 ....35 D4
Rowlands Gill NE39 ....1 D2
Thornaby-on-T TS17 ....138 C6
Briar Terr NE16 ....6 C6
Briar Wlk Darlington DL3 151 D6
Hartlepool TS26 ....77 A6
Stockton-on-T TS18 ....212 A1
Briardene Burnopfield NE16 .5 E6
Durham DH1 ....210 B2
Esh Winning DH7 ....31 C1
Lanchester DH7 ....20 E3
Briardene Ave TS5 ....139 E7
Briardene Ct TS19 ....117 A7
Briardene Way SR8 ....39 E4
Briardene Wlk TS19 ....117 A7
Briargate TS6 ....121 F2
Briarhill DH2 ....16 A5
Briarhill Gdns TS26 ....76 E7
Briarside DH8 ....10 D5
Briarsyde Cl NE16 ....2 E5
Briarvale Ave TS5 ....139 D8
Briarwood Ave DH2 ....15 E3
Briarwood St DH4 ....17 E1
Briary Gdns DH8 ....10 C6
Briary The DH8 ....10 D6
Brick Garth DH5 ....27 C1
Brick Row
Commondale YO21 ....164 C2
Ryhope SR2 ....18 E7
Brickton Rd TS5 ....119 B2
Bridge Ct Eston TS6 ....121 C1
Shadforth DH6 ....46 E7
Yarm TS15 ....156 B7
Bridge End Coxhoe DH6 ..57 F5
Frosterley DL13 ....188 A7
Piercebridge DL2 ....130 B4
Willington DL15 ....53 F3
Bridge House Est DL17 ..69 F5
Bridge Inn Yd DL12 ....209 B5
Bridge Island DH8 ....10 B6
Bridge Rd
Bishop Auckland DL14 ....80 A8
Cornforth DL17 ....57 E2
Darlington DL2,DL3 ....151 C6
Redcar TS10 ....107 A7
Bridge Rd *continued*
Shotton Colliery DH6 ....48 D6
Stockton-on-T TS18 ....213 B1
Bridge Rd Bglws DH6 ...48 D5
Bridge St
Bishop Auckland DL14 ....67 B1
Consett DH8 ....10 D3
Durham DH1 ....210 B3
Ferryhill DH6 ....57 B2
Great Ayton TS9 ....160 F2
Hartlepool TS24 ....77 D5
Howden-le-W DL15 ....65 E7
Langley Park DH7 ....32 C7
Middleton-In-T DL12 ....208 B5
Stanley DH9 ....13 E4
Stockton-on-T TS20 ....118 B5
Thornaby-on-T TS17 ....213 C1
Tow Law DL13 ....183 E1
Willington DL15 ....53 E1
Yarm TS15 ....156 B7
Bridge St E TS2 ....215 A4
Bridge St W TS2 ....214 C4
Bridge Terr
Darlington DL1 ....133 B1
Station Town TS28 ....60 F5
Bridge View TS21 ....72 D4
Bridge Way DH7 ....32 D6
Bridgefield Ct DL15 ....65 E7
Bridgegate DL12 ....209 B5
Bridgemere Dr DH1 ....34 A6
Bridgend Cl TS6 ....121 E5
Bridgepool Cl TS24 ....64 C2
Bridle The DL5 ....82 D2
Bridnor Rd TS3 ....140 C8
Bridport Cl TS18 ....118 D4
Bridport Gr TS8 ....139 F1
Brier Ave SR8 ....49 F8
Brierley Dr TS21,TS22 ...86 D3
Brierley Gn TS7 ....140 E2
Brierton Com Sch TS25 ..76 E1
Brierton La TS25 ....76 C1
Brierville DH1 ....210 B2
Brierville Rd TS19 ....117 F5
Brig Open TS24 ....77 F8
Brigandine Cl TS25 ....90 D8
Briggs Ave TS6 ....121 A5
Brigham Rd TS3 ....120 C1
Brighouse Bsns Village
TS2 ....119 C8
Brighouse Ct DL5 ....96 D3
Bright St Consett DH8 ....10 F4
Darlington DL1 ....133 C1
Hartlepool TS26 ....76 F6
Middlesbrough TS1 ....215 B3
Stockton-on-T TS18 ....213 A3
Brightlea DH3 ....9 E5
Brighton Cl TS17 ....138 B4
Brighton Rd DL1 ....152 B8
Brighton Terr DH6 ....36 D1
Brignall Cl DH3 ....25 B7
Brignall La DL12 ....204 E7
Brignall Moor Cres DL1 152 D8
Brignall Rd TS18 ....137 F8
Brignell Rd TS2 ....119 D7
Brimham Cl TS17 ....138 C1
Brimham Ct TS10 ....107 B4
Brimston Cl TS26 ....76 D7
Brindle Cl TS7 ....140 E2
Brindley Rd SR8 ....48 F6
Brine St TS4 ....215 B2
Brinewells Gn TS4 ....215 C1
Brinkburn DH2 ....16 A3
Brinkburn Ave DL3 ....132 D4
Brinkburn Cl
Bishop Auckland DL14 ....79 E5
Blaydon NE21 ....2 A8
Brinkburn Ct TS25 ....76 F4
Brinkburn Dr DL3 ....132 D5
Brinkburn Rd
Darlington DL3 ....132 E4
Hartlepool TS25 ....77 A4
Stockton-on-T TS20 ....118 A6
Brinsley Ct DL14 ....81 B8
Briony Cl DL16 ....56 B3
Brisbane Cres TS17 ....138 C5
Brisbane Gr TS18 ....212 A1
Briscoe La DL12 ....198 B6
Briscoe Way TS8 ....139 C1
Bristol Ave TS12 ....125 C7
Bristol Wlk TS26 ....76 E8
Bristow Rd TS4 ....120 B1
Bristow St TS3 ....120 C4
Britain Ave TS5 ....139 C7
Britannia Cl 7 TS24 ....77 C6
Britannia Pl TS10 ....106 E4
Britannia Rd
New Silksworth SR3 ....18 A7
Stockton-on-T TS19 ....212 C3
Britannia Terr
Brotton TS12 ....126 B4
Fence Houses DH4 ....26 A8
British Steel Redcar Halt
TS10 ....106 C5
Britten Cl DH9 ....14 A5
Brixham Cl SR7 ....29 A6
Broad Cl TS8 ....139 B1
Broad Field Rd TS24 ....64 F1
Broad Gates 9 DL12 ....209 C5
Broad Rd TS27 ....50 F2
Broadbent St TS12 ....126 B3
Broadgate Gdns TS5 ..139 C8
Broadgate Rd
Langley Park DH7 ....32 C3
Middlesbrough TS5 ....139 C8
Broadhaven Cl TS6 ....121 E3
Broadlands TS17 ....138 A2
Broadmeadows
Bowburn DH6 ....45 E1

Corn Cl DL12 209 A5
Corn Mill Dr DH5 26 D6
Cornbank Cl SR3 18 A5
Corncroft Mews TS6 121 E6
Cornelia Cl 7 SR3 18 A7
Cornelia Terr SR7 29 D7
Corner Bank La DL2 94 E4
Cornfield Garth SR8 49 F5
Cornfield Rd
Middlesbrough TS5 119 E1
Stockton-on-T TS19 117 A3
Thornaby-on-T TS17 138 B8
Cornforth Ave TS3 140 D8
Cornforth Cl TS19 117 B6
Cornforth Gr TS23 102 F7
Cornforth La
Cornforth DH6 57 F2
Coxhoe DH6 57 F3
Corngrave Cl TS11 108 E1
Cornhill Wlk TS7 141 A7
Cornmill Ctr 12 DL1 132 F2
Cornmoor DH2 15 F2
Cornriggs DL13 179 A4
Cornriggs Wlk 4 TS19 117 B7
Cornsay Cl
Middlesbrough TS5 139 B6
Stockton-on-T TS19 117 B6
Cornsay La DH7 30 B5
Cornwall Ave DL1 133 C4
Cornwall Cl TS7 141 A3
Cornwall Cres TS23 102 F3
Cornwall Ct SR7 28 D3
Cornwall Gr TS20 118 C7
Cornwall Pl DL14 80 B5
Cornwall Rd TS14 143 D3
Cornwall St Easington SR8 39 F4
Hartlepool TS25 77 A3
Cornwall Wlk DH1 35 D3
Cornwallis Cl TS12 126 C5
Coronation Ave
Blackhall Colliery TS27 50 E3
Durham DH1 35 D4
Fishburn TS21 72 C4
Hinderwell TS13 149 E5
2 Peterlee SR8 50 A6
6 Ryhope SR2 18 F6
Shildon DL4 81 B1
Stanhope DL13 206 E2
Tow Law DL13 183 D2
Coronation Cotts DH6 48 C6
Coronation Cres
High Pittington DH6 36 B6
Yarm TS15 156 A4
Coronation Ct 1 TS6 121 D1
Coronation Dr TS25 77 D3
Coronation Gdns 6 DL2 200 E7
Coronation Gn
Easington Lane DH5 37 D8
Middlesbrough TS3 140 F8
Coronation Homes DH7 41 F8
Coronation Rd
Chilton DL17 83 A8
Loftus TS13 127 B1
Wingate TS28 60 D8
Coronation Sq DH6 38 B7
Coronation St
Barnard Castle DL12 209 C7
Carlin How TS13 126 F3
Chester le Street DH3 16 D1
Crook DL15 52 E4
1 Darlington DL3 132 E4
Middlesbrough TS3 120 C4
Coronation St S SR7 28 D2
Coronation Terr
Annfield Plain DH9 13 B4
Chester le Street DH3 16 C2
18 Cockfield DL13 195 E3
Cornforth DL17 57 D1
Coxhoe DH6 57 F5
Durham DH1 35 C1
Fir Tree DL15 52 A1
Hetton-le-H DH5 27 A2
Hunwick DL15 66 D7
Kibblesworth NE11 8 C6
Kirk Merrington DL16 69 A3
Trimdon TS29 59 E1
West Pelton DH2 15 B4
Willington DL15 53 C3
Wingate TS29 59 F6
Corporation Rd
Darlington DL3 132 F3
Hartlepool TS24 64 E1
Middlesbrough TS1 215 A3
Redcar TS10 107 B6
Corporation Road Com Prim Sch DL3 132 F3
Corporation St TS18 213 A3
Corpus Christi RC Prim Sch TS3 120 E3
Corriedale Cl DH1 34 C8
Corrighan Terr DH5 26 C4
Corry Cl TS27 50 E3
Corsair NE16 2 F6
Corscombe Cl DL17 70 C5
Corsham Wlk 4 TS3 140 D8
Cort St DH8 10 E3
Cortland Rd Consett DH8 10 C4
Nunthorpe TS7 141 C3
Corvan Terr DH9 6 A2
Coryton Wlk 3 TS3 140 D8
Cosgrove Ave DL14 80 A4
Cosin Cl DL5 96 E5
Costa St
Middlesbrough TS1 214 B1
South Bank TS6 121 A6
Costain Gr TS20 102 C1
Cote House Rd DL12 208 D2
Cotgarth Way TS19 117 A6
Cotherstone Cl
2 Consett DH8 10 F1
Eaglescliffe TS16 136 F1
Cotherstone Dr TS5 139 C4
Cotherstone Moor Dr DL1 152 D7
Cotherstone Prim Sch DL12 198 F6
Cotherstone Rd
Durham DH1 34 D5
Stockton-on-T TS18 137 F8
Cotsford Cres 3 SR8 50 A6
Cotsford Inf Sch SR8 50 B6
Cotsford Jun Sch SR8 50 B7
Cotsford La SR8 50 B6
Cotsford Park Est SR8 50 B6
Cotswold Ave
Chester le Street DH2 16 B1
Middlesbrough TS3 120 E3
Cotswold Cl DL14 81 C8
Cotswold Cres TS23 102 D3
Cotswold Dr
Redcar TS10 107 B4
Skelton TS12 125 C3
Cotswold Pl SR8 49 B6
Cotswold Terr DH9 14 A5
Cotswolds The DL17 82 F7
Cottage Farm TS19 212 A2
Cottage Mews DL1 133 D4
Cottage Rd 8 DL4 80 F1
Cottages Rd SR7 29 D6
Cottages The Chilton DL17 82 E6
Coatham Mundeville DL1 112 F6
Heighington DL5 95 D1
Cottersloe Rd TS20 102 B1
Cottingham Cl SR8 49 B7
Cottingham Ct DL3 132 B4
Cottingham Dr TS3 120 D3
Cottonwood
Middlesbrough TS3 120 F2
Shiney Row DH4 17 F6
Coulby Farm Way
Coulby Newham TS8 140 B1
Mount Pleasant TS8 159 B8
Coulby Manor Farm TS8 140 A2
Coulby Manor Way TS8 139 F3
Coulby Newham Sch TS8 140 B2
Coulson Cl TS15 156 B3
Coulson St DL16 69 B8
Coulthard Ct 9 TS6 121 A6
Coulton Gr TS22 102 A5
Coulton Terr DL16 69 A3
Council Of Europe Bvd TS17 213 B3
Coundon Gn 2 TS19 117 B6
Coundon Ind Est DL14 81 C6
Coundon Prim Sch DL14 81 C8
Countess Cl SR7 29 C8
Countisbury Rd TS20 101 E2
County Hospl DH1 210 B3
Courageous Cl TS25 77 D1
Court La DH1 211 A2
Court Rd TS4 120 A1
Court St SR8 39 F4
Courtine The DL5 95 D1
Courtlands Rd DL3 132 D4
Courtney Dr
1 New Silksworth SR3 18 A7
Pelton DH2 15 F7
Courtney Wlk TS3 120 E3
Courtyard The
Middleton St George DL2 153 E5
Tanfield Lea DH9 13 C8
Covent Cl TS6 141 C7
Coventry Rd DH1 34 E7
Coverdale TS8 139 D1
Coverdale Bldgs TS12 126 C4
Coverdale Ct DL5 96 B8
Coverdale Rd TS19 117 C2
Coverley DH3 25 A8
Covert The DL5 95 F8
Cow Close La TS12 165 C8
Cow Green Resr Nature Trail★ DL12 184 D1
Cowclose La DL11 204 E5
Cowdray Cl
Guisborough TS14 143 F2
Newton Aycliffe DL5 82 F2
Cowell Gr NE39 1 C2
Cowell St SR8 49 F7
Cowen St NE21 2 B8
Cowen Terr NE39 1 F3
Cowfold La DL2 111 B5
Cowgarth Hill DL13 206 C3
Cowley Cl
Eaglescliffe TS16 137 D5
Seaton Carew TS25 77 E2
Cowley Cres DH5 26 C4
Cowley La DL13 194 E4
Cowley Rd TS5 139 D6
Cowley St DH6 48 D6
Cowpen Bewley Rd TS23 103 C4
Cowpen Bewley Woodland Ctry Pk★ TS23 103 C7
Cowpen Bewley Woodland Ctry Pk Visitor Ctr★ TS23 103 C7
Cowpen Cres TS19 117 B6
Cowpen La TS23 103 A5
Cowpen Lane Ind Est TS23 103 B4
Cowper Gr TS25 76 D2
Cowper Rd TS20 118 C5
Cowscote Cres TS13 127 A2
Cowshill Gn 7 TS19 117 B6
Cowsley La DH7 30 A1
Cowton Way TS16 137 B3
Coxgreen Cl TS19 117 B6
Coxhoe Prim Sch DH6 57 F3
Coxhoe Rd TS23 102 F5
Coxmoor Way TS11 123 F6
Coxwold Cl TS5 139 E6
Coxwold Dr DL1 152 C7
Coxwold Ho 9 DL1 152 C8
Coxwold Rd TS18 212 A2
Coxwold Way TS23 103 B3
Craddock St DL16 68 E8
Cradley Dr TS5 139 C3
Cradoc Gr TS17 156 F8
Cradock St DL14 80 C6
Crag La DL2 93 F3
Crag Works DH8 11 C6
Cragdale Gdns DH5 26 F2
Cragdale Rd TS3 120 C2
Cragg View DL12 208 F2
Craggs St
Middlesbrough TS4 215 B3
Stockton-on-T TS19 213 A4
Craggyknowe NE37 9 F6
Craghead La DH9 14 E3
Craghead Rd DH2 15 E4
Cragleas NE16 6 A4
Cragside Brotton TS12 126 C4
Chester le Street DH2 16 A4
Chilton DL17 83 A8
Sedgefield TS21 85 A5
Witton Gilbert DH7 33 B8
Cragside Cl DL16 68 F7
Cragside Ct
Annfield Plain DH9 12 F3
Consett DH8 10 C4
4 Houghton-le-S DH5 26 F8
Ingleby Barwick TS17 138 B1
Cragston Cl TS26 76 D7
Cragston Ct 2 TS10 107 E1
Cragwellside DL1 133 C5
Craig Lea Rd DL15 52 A6
Craig Miller Pk DL3 131 F1
Craig St 2 Birtley DH3 9 C4
Darlington DL3 132 E3
Craig Terr Easington SR8 39 B3
Wolsingham DL13 207 E5
Craigearn Rd TS6 121 C2
Craigland Villas DH7 23 C2
Craigton Ho TS10 107 C7
Craigweil Cres TS19 117 F5
Craigwell Dr SR3 18 A4
Crail Gdns DL1 133 C7
Crail Wlk TS25 89 F8
Craister Rd TS20 213 C4
Crake Way NE38 9 F2
Cramlington Cl TS8 139 E2
Cramond Cl DL3 132 A1
Cranage Cl TS5 139 B8
Cranberry TS8 140 D1
Cranbourne Dr TS10 107 F1
Cranbourne Terr TS18 212 C1
Cranbrook TS8 140 E1
Crane Row La DL13 195 C6
Cranfield Ave TS3 120 F4
Cranford Ave TS6 121 B4
Cranford Cl TS6 121 B4
Cranford Gdns TS5 139 B7
Cranford Terr SR8 39 B4
Cranleigh DH3 25 A7
Cranleigh Rd TS18 212 B2
Cranmore Rd TS3 120 D3
Cranstock Cl TS22 102 A5
Cranston Pl SR2 19 A6
Cranswick Cl TS23 102 F8
Cranswick Dr TS5 139 E6
Cranwell Gr TS17 138 D3
Cranwell Rd TS25 89 E7
Cranworth Gn TS17 118 D1
Cranworth St TS17 213 C1
Craster Cl DH2 15 F1
Crathie DH3 9 C7
Crathorne Cres TS5 119 B2
Crathorne Ct NE16 5 F6
Crathorne Pk Eston TS6 121 C1
Normanby TS6 141 C8
Crathorne Rd TS20 118 B8
Craven St TS1 214 B2
Craven Vale TS14 143 E3
Craven's Bldgs TS28 60 F5
Crawcrook Wlk TS19 117 B6
Crawford Ave SR8 49 D8
Crawford Avenue W SR8 49 C8
Crawford Cl
Bishop Auckland DL14 80 A4
Sherburn DH6 35 F1
Crawford Rd DL5 96 E6
Crawford St TS25 90 E8
Crawlaw Bglws SR8 39 E5
Crawlaw Rd SR8 39 E5
Crawley Rd TS17 138 E7
Crawleyside Bank DL13 206 C5
Crayke Rd TS18 212 A1
Creekwood TS3 120 F2
Creighton Rd DL5 96 E6
Cremorne Cl TS7 140 C4
Crescent Ave TS23 102 E1
Crescent Cl DH6 35 F1
Crescent Lodge TS5 119 D1
Crescent Rd TS1 214 B1
Crescent The
3 Blackhall Colliery TS27 50 D3
Carlton TS21 116 C8
Chester le Street DH2 16 B3
Chilton DL17 82 F8
Consett, Benfieldside DH8 10 C6
Consett, Blackfyne DH8 10 F4
Crescent The *continued*
Consett, Bridgehill DH8 10 C4
Coundon DL14 81 C8
Durham DH1 210 B4
Eaglescliffe TS16 156 B8
Easington SR8 39 E5
Hartlepool TS26 76 F6
Hetton-le-H DH5 27 A3
High Etherley DL14 78 F5
Kibblesworth NE11 8 C6
Kimblesworth DH2 23 F4
Langley Park DH7 32 A6
Maiden Law DH7 21 A8
2 Marske-by-t-S TS11 108 D1
Middlesbrough TS5 119 D1
Middleton St George DL2 154 C7
Nunthorpe TS7 141 C2
Ormesby TS7 140 F7
Redcar TS10 107 E6
Rowlands Gill NE39 1 F2
Saltburn-by-t-S TS12 125 C6
Sherburn DH6 35 F1
Stainton Grove DL12 209 F8
Tanfield Lea DH9 13 D8
Thornaby-on-T TS17 138 C7
Waldridge DH2 24 A7
West Rainton DH4 25 F2
Witton Gilbert DH7 23 B1
Cresswell Ave SR8 50 A6
Cresswell Cl Blaydon NE21 2 A8
Hemlington TS8 139 E2
Cresswell Ct TS26 76 D6
Cresswell Dr TS26 76 E6
Cresswell Rd Eston TS6 121 E6
Hartlepool TS26 76 E6
Crest The TS26 76 D6
Crestwood
Middlesbrough TS3 120 F2
Redcar TS10 107 D1
Crewe Ave DH1 35 B1
Crewe Rd DL5 96 E6
Cribyn Cl TS17 156 F8
Crichton Ave DH3 16 D1
Cricket Field Row DL3 132 F5
Cricket La TS6 141 C8
Cricket Terr NE16 6 A6
Crieff Wlk TS25 89 F8
Crimdon Cl TS8 139 E2
Crimdon Gr DH4 26 C7
Crimdon Terr TS27 51 A1
Crimdon Wlk TS19 117 A7
Crime Rigg Bank DH6 46 D8
Crinklewood TS3 120 F1
Crispin Ct Brotton TS12 126 C4
Sedgefield TS21 85 B6
Croft Ave Crook DL15 52 E3
Middlesbrough TS5 139 B7
Croft Ct DH7 20 E4
Croft Dr TS7 141 B2
Croft Gdns DL17 70 C4
Croft Rd Darlington DL2 151 D3
Eaglescliffe TS16 156 B8
Hurworth-on-T DL2 152 B1
Croft Rigg DH7 43 A3
Croft Side DL14 79 D6
Croft St Crook DL15 52 E3
Sacriston DH7 23 C3
Croft Terr
Annfield Plain DH9 13 A4
Coundon DL14 81 B8
Hartlepool TS24 77 F8
Croft Terr (E) DL13 188 A7
Croft Terr (W) DL13 188 A7
Croft The
Kirk Merrington DL16 68 F3
Marton TS7 140 E3
Newton Aycliffe DL5 82 E2
Sherburn Hill DH6 36 D1
Croft View
Cotherstone DL12 198 F6
Lanchester DH7 20 E4
Croft Way DL15 54 B4
Croft Yoke La DL12 193 C2
Crofton Ave 2 TS4 119 F1
Crofton Ct TS18 118 D4
Crofton Rd TS18 118 D4
Crofts The Stillington TS21 99 F3
Wolsingham DL13 207 C5
Croftside DH3 9 C5
Cromarty DH2 8 F2
Cromarty Cl DL1 133 E7
Cromer Ct TS16 156 C8
Cromer Lea DL13 188 A7
Cromer St TS4 215 B2
Cromer Wlk TS25 89 E7
Cromore Cl TS17 138 C4
Crompton Ct DL17 69 E5
Cromwell Ave
Loftus TS13 127 D1
Stockton-on-T TS18 213 B4
Cromwell Gn TS18 213 B3
Cromwell Rd TS6 121 A5
Cromwell Road Prim Sch TS6 121 A5
Cromwell St
Hartlepool TS26 77 C4
Middlesbrough TS3 215 C2
Cromwell Terr TS17 138 C8
Cronniewell NE17 4 B5
Crook (Beechburn) Ind Est DL15 52 E2
Crook Bsns Ctr DL15 52 E3
Crook Hall★ DH1 210 C4
Crook La DL12 209 D5
Crook Prim Sch DL15 52 E3
Crook St TS20 102 A1
Crookers Hill Cl TS7 141 A1
Crookhall La DH8 11 C3
Crookhall Rd DH8 11 A3
Crookhall Wlk 6 TS19 117 B6
Crooks Barn La TS20 102 B2
Crooksbarn Prim Sch TS20 102 A2
Cropton Cl TS10 107 B2
Cropton Way TS8 140 A8
Crosby Ct TS16 137 D1
Crosby Ho TS3 120 D3
Crosby Rd DL5 96 C5
Crosby St Darlington DL3 133 A6
10 Stockton-on-T TS20 118 B5
Crosby Wlk 8 TS17 138 C8
Cross Fell TS10 107 B4
Cross Hill DL13 206 C3
Cross La Cowshill DL13 179 B4
Great Ayton TS9 161 B1
Loftus TS13 127 C3
Sacriston DH7 23 C4
Cross Lanes DL2 111 B7
Cross Row
Boosbeck TS12 145 B6
Durham DH1 34 C7
Hunwick DL15 66 D5
Cross St
Bishop Auckland DL14 79 D2
Consett DH8 10 D4
Crook DL15 53 B3
Darlington DL3 132 F5
Easington SR8 39 F4
8 Fence Houses DH4 26 A8
Guisborough TS14 143 E4
High Pittington DH6 36 D3
Sedgefield TS21 85 B6
Shildon DL4 95 A8
Stanhope DL13 206 C3
Stockton-on-T TS20 118 B8
Sunderland Bridge DH6 56 B7
4 Eston TS6 121 F2
Cross Terr NE39 1 D1
Cross Valley Ct DH1 210 A2
Cross View Terr DH1 210 A1
Crossbeck Terr 4 TS6 121 D1
Crossbeck Way TS7 141 B7
Crosscliff TS8 139 E2
Crossfell Rd TS3 120 C1
Crossfield DH7 23 C2
Crossfield Cl DL2 152 D1
Crossfield Cres DH6 48 C7
Crossfield Rd DL3 132 C5
Crossfields TS8 159 B8
Crossgate DH1 210 C2
Crossgate Moor Gdns DH1 33 F3
Crossgate Peth DH1 210 B2
Crossgate Rd DH5 27 A2
Crossleas DH7 23 C3
Crosslet La DL13 186 A8
Crossway The DL1 133 D2
Crossways
Langley Park DH7 32 C6
Sacriston DH7 23 C2
Crosswell Pk TS17 156 F7
Crosthwaite Ave 1 TS4 139 F8
Crow La TS6 122 B3
Crow Trees La DH6 57 D8
Crowhurst Cl TS14 143 E3
Crowland Ave
Middlesbrough TS3 120 F1
Middlesbrough TS3 121 A1
Crowland Rd TS25 89 E6
Crowley Pl DL5 96 D7
Crown St
Bishop Auckland DL14 80 D5
Darlington DL1 133 A2
7 Darlington DL3 132 F2
Crowther Ind Est
Birtley NE38 9 F4
Washington NE38 9 F5
Crowther Rd NE38 9 F5
Croxdale Gr
Bishop Auckland DL14 79 E5
Stockton-on-T TS19 117 B2
Croxdale Rd TS23 102 E5
Croxden Gr 7 TS3 140 E8
Croxton Ave TS25 89 F6
Croxton Cl TS19 116 F3
Croydon Rd TS1 215 B1
Crummackdale TS17 157 B6
Crummock Rd TS10 107 C5
Crystal Cl DL17 82 F8
Culgaith Ave TS3 120 C2
Cullen Cl DL1 133 D6
Cullen Rd TS25 89 F8
Culloden Terr SR8 39 F3
Culloden Way TS23 103 A6
Culross Gr TS19 116 F3
Culzean Ct DH8 10 D4
Cumberland Cres TS23 102 D2
Cumberland Gr TS20 101 F1
Cumberland Pl DH3 9 D1
Cumberland Rd
Consett DH8 177 A4
Middlesbrough TS5 119 E2
New Silksworth SR3 18 A8
Cumberland St
Coundon Grange DL14 80 F5
Darlington DL3 133 A5
Cumberland Terr DL15 53 F3
Cumbernauld Rd TS17 138 E7
Cumbie Way DL5 96 D2
Cumbria Pl DH9 14 A7
Cumbria Wlk 11 TS25 77 B4
Cumbrian Ave DH2 16 C2
Cumbrian Way SR8 49 E6

Cumby Rd DL5 96 C5
Cummings Ave DH6 35 F2
Cummings Sq TS28 60 D8
Cumnor Wlk TS3 120 D3
Cundall Rd TS26 76 F6
Cunningham Cl TS12 126 B5
Cunningham Dr TS17 138 D3
Cunningham Pl DH1 211 C4
Cunningham St TS5 214 A1
Curlew Cl DL3 132 C6
Curlew La TS20 102 A2
Curran Ave TS5 119 B1
Curson St 1 TS6 121 F1
Curtain La DL11 201 D1
Curthwaite TS5 139 B4
Cut Throat La NE17,NE39 4 C4
Cuthbert Ave DH1 35 B1
Cuthbert Cl Durham DH1 35 B1
  Thornaby-on-T TS17 138 C8
Cuthbert Rd DL17 57 E1
Cuthbert St DL16 56 A2
Cutler Cl TS7 140 E4
Cutler's Ave DH8 10 C5
Cutlers' Hall Rd DH8 10 C5
Cutting St 3 SR7 18 F1
Cyclamen Gr DL1 133 C1
Cypress Cl DL3 151 C7
Cypress Ct DH7 43 B3
Cypress Gr Durham DH1 35 A3
  Newton Aycliffe DL5 96 A3
Cypress Pk DH7 41 D8
Cypress Rd Marton TS7 140 E4
  Redcar TS10 107 F5
Cypress Sq 12 SR3 18 A8
Cypress View DH6 47 E3
Cyril St DH8 10 F4

D

D'Arcy Sq SR7 28 E4
D'Arcy St DH7 32 C7
Dabble Duck Ind Est DL4 95 A8
Dacre Cl TS17 138 C6
Dacre Gdns DH8 11 A2
Daffodil Ave SR8 49 F7
Daffodil Cl TS27 50 D3
Dahlia Cres SR8 39 D3
Daimler Dr TS23 103 B5
Dairy La DH4 26 C8
Daisy Cotts 10 DH3 9 C4
Daisy Ct TS19 117 C5
Daisy Hill DH8 10 F8
Dalby Cl Billingham TS22 102 A5
  Redcar TS10 107 C2
Dalby Ct TS8 140 C2
Dalby View TS8 140 B1
Dalby Way TS8 140 B1
Dalcross Ct TS8 139 E1
Dalden Gr SR7 29 D8
Dale Cl
  Hurworth-on-T DL2 152 D1
  Stockton-on-T TS19 117 A6
Dale Garth TS11 124 D8
Dale Gr Shildon DL4 95 B7
  Stockton-on-T TS19 117 B2
Dale Rd
  Barnard Castle DL12 209 D6
  Darlington DL3 132 D2
  Sadberge DL2 134 F7
  Shildon DL4 95 B7
Dale Road Ind Est DL4 95 B8
Dale St
  Bishop Auckland DL14 79 E3
  Chilton DL17 82 F8
  Consett DH8 10 D3
  Langley Park DH7 32 C7
  Middlesbrough TS1 214 C3
  New Marske TS11 124 A7
  Ushaw Moor DH7 32 F2
Dale Terr Billy Row DL15 52 D6
  Dalton-le-D SR7 29 A5
  Lingdale TS12 145 E5
  Woodland DL13 194 D4
Dale View Crook DL15 53 A3
  High Etherley DL14 78 E6
  Mickleton DL12 208 F2
  Middleton-In-T DL12 208 C5
Dalehouse TS13 149 B8
Dales Park Rd TS8 139 D1
Dales St DL13 206 D3
Dales Terr DL13 206 D2
Daleside DH7 23 C5
Daleston Ave TS5 139 D8
Daleston Cl TS26 76 C7
Daleville Cl TS4 140 A8
Dalkeith Cl DL3 132 A1
Dalkeith Cres TS8 139 E3
Dalkeith Rd TS25 76 E1
Dallas Ct TS8 139 E1
Dallas Rd TS25 76 E1
Dallymore Dr DH6 45 C2
Dalmuir Cl TS16 137 C1
Dalry Gr TS25 89 E8
Dalston Ct 12 TS7 141 B7
Dalsy La TS7 141 B7
Dalton Ave
  Bishop Auckland DL14 79 E3
  Seaham SR7 29 B7
Dalton Back La
  Dalton Piercy TS27 75 E1
  Hartlepool TS22,TS27 89 A7
Dalton Cl DL14 79 E3
Dalton Cotts DL4 95 A7
Dalton Cres DL4 95 A8
Dalton Ct TS10 107 F1
Dalton Gr
  Billingham TS23 102 E7
  Stockton-on-T TS20 118 A6
Dalton Hts
  Dalton Piercy TS27 75 E3
  Seaham SR7 28 E6
Dalton Pk SR7 28 E2
Dalton St Darlington DL1 133 A2
  Hartlepool TS26 77 A5
Dalton Terr Chopwell NE17 4 B8
  Murton SR7 28 D2
  Wheatley Hill DH6 47 E1
Dalton Way DL5 96 D7
Daltry Cl TS15 156 E4
Dalwood Ct TS8 139 E1
Dam St TS13 127 C1
Damson Ct DL3 132 E3
Damson Way DH1 35 B2
Dan's Castle DL13 183 D2
Danby Cl
  New Silksworth SR3 18 B6
  Washington NE38 16 F8
Danby Ct Darlington DL1 133 C5
  1 Stockton-on-T TS20 118 B5
Danby Dale Ave TS10 107 A4
Danby Gr Hartlepool TS25 90 E8
  Thornaby-on-T TS17 138 D7
Danby Rd Eston TS6 121 F3
  Stockton-on-T TS20 118 B5
Danby Wlk TS23 102 C5
Danby Wynd TS15 156 B6
Danelaw DH3 25 A8
Danesbrook Ct TS17 157 B6
Danesfort Ave TS14 143 D4
Danesmoor Cres DL3 132 C2
Daniel Ct TS4 215 B1
Daniel La DL13,DL14 195 E8
Dante Rd TS7 140 B4
Daphne Cres SR7 29 C5
Daphne Rd TS19 118 A5
Darcy Cl TS15 156 A3
Darenth Cres TS3 120 D1
Dark La
  Barnard Castle DL12 209 A5
  Newsham DL11 205 C4
Darley Ct DH2 24 A5
Darling Pl DH9 14 B5
Darlington Arts Ctr* DL3 132 E2
Darlington Ave SR8 49 F7
Darlington Back La
  Longnewton DL2,TS21 115 E1
  Stockton-on-T TS19,TS21 116 C4
Darlington Coll of Tech DL3 132 D2
Darlington Golf Course DL1 133 D8
Darlington La
  Stockton-on-T TS20 117 F7
  Stockton-on-T, Bishopsgarth TS19 117 D6
Darlington Locomotive Sculpture* DL1 134 B1
Darlington Meml Hospl DL3 132 E3
Darlington Mus* DL1 133 A1
Darlington Railway Athletic Gd DL3 132 D4
Darlington Railway Ctr & Mus* DL3 132 F4
Darlington Rd
  Barnard Castle DL12 209 E7
  Bishop Auckland DL14 79 C1
  Durham DH1 210 A1
  Ferryhill DL17 69 F5
  Heighington DL5 95 D1
  Longnewton TS21 136 A5
  Sadberge DL2 134 E6
  Stockton-on-T TS18 137 C8
  Whorlton DL2 200 B3
Darlington Ret Pk The DL1 133 E1
Darlington St TS24 77 F8
Darlington Sta DL1 133 A1
Darnbrook Way TS7 140 F2
Darnell Gn TS4 140 B6
Darnton Dr TS4 140 B6
Darras Wlk TS3 120 D3
Darrowby Dr DL3 132 E4
Dart Rd SR8 49 C5
Dartmouth Cl SR7 29 A6
Dartmouth Gr TS10 107 D3
Darvel Rd TS25 76 E1
Darwen Ct TS8 139 E1
Darwin Gr Darlington DL1 152 C7
  Hartlepool TS25 76 D3
Darygton Cl DL1 133 D6
Dauntless Cl TS25 77 E1
Davenport Rd TS15 156 B3
Daventry Ave TS19 117 E6
David Rd TS20 118 C6
David Terr Bowburn DH6 45 D2
  Eldon Lane DL14 80 E4
  Quarrington Hill DH6 58 D7
Davis Ave DL14 79 E3
Davis Cres DH7 32 A7
Davis Terr SR8 39 D4
Davis Wlk SR8 49 E8
Davison Ave SR3 18 B7
Davison Cres SR7 28 B4
Davison Dr TS24 63 F2
Davison Rd DL1 133 B7
Davison Sq DH8 176 F3
Davison St Lingdale TS12 145 E5
  Middlesbrough TS1 214 C3
Davison Terr DH7 23 B4
Davisons Ct DL2 201 D3
Davy Dr SR8 48 F8
Davy Rd TS6 120 F5
Davy St DL17 69 E6
Dawdon Cl TS19 117 B7
Dawdon Cres SR7 29 D6
Dawdon Ind Est SR7 29 E4
Dawley Cl TS17 138 E7
Dawlish Cl SR7 28 F6
Dawlish Dr TS25 90 A7
Dawlish Gn TS4 140 B6
Dawn Cl TS20 102 A2
Dawson Ho TS23 102 D4
Dawson Rd
  Barnard Castle DL12 209 D6
  Wingate TS28 60 E8
Dawson Sq TS5 119 B2
Dawson St DL15 52 F3
Dawsons Wharf Ind Est TS5 119 E7
Day St TS12 126 B3
Daylesford Gr DL3 132 C7
Daylight Rd TS19 117 E5
Days Terr TS12 126 B4
De Brus Ct 4 TS12 125 C8
De Brus Pk TS8 159 E6
De Brus Way TS14 143 E5
De Havilland Dr TS11 108 B2
De La Mare Dr TS23 102 E8
Deacon Gdns TS25 90 E7
Deacon St TS3 120 C4
Deaf Hill Prim Sch TS29 59 F6
Deaf Hill Terr TS29 59 F6
Deal Cl TS19 117 E6
Deal Ct TS4 120 A1
Deal Rd Billingham TS23 102 D6
  Redcar TS10 107 E3
Dean & Chapter Ind Est DL17 69 E6
Dean Bank Grange DL17 69 E5
Dean Bank Prim Sch DL17 69 E6
Dean Cl Peterlee SR8 49 F5
  Shildon DL4 80 F2
Dean Gdns DL4 80 F2
Dean Pk DL17 70 A5
Dean Rd DL17 70 A5
Dean St Langley Park DH7 32 D8
  Shildon DL4 80 F2
  Stockton-on-T TS18 213 A2
Deanery Ct DL14 80 F4
Deanery View DH7 20 F4
Deans' Wlk DH1 211 C4
Deansgate TS6 122 A2
Debruse Ave TS15 156 A4
Dee Rd TS6 121 D3
Deepdale
  Guisborough TS14 143 A3
  Hutton Rudby TS15 173 F1
Deepdale Ave Eston TS6 121 F4
  Middlesbrough TS4 119 F1
  Middlesbrough, Beechwood TS4 140 A8
Deepdale Cl NE16 2 F4
Deepdale La TS13 127 A3
Deepdale Rd TS13 127 A1
Deepdale St DH5 27 A2
Deepdale Way DL1 133 F3
Deepdene Gr TS10 107 F2
Deepgrove Wlk 3 TS6 121 F3
Deerbolt Bank DL12 209 B5
Deerness Ct DH7 43 C4
Deerness Est DL13 183 E2
Deerness Estate Bglws DL13 183 E2
Deerness Gr DH7 31 D2
Deerness Hts DH7 43 B5
Deerness Rd DL14 80 A6
Deerness Valley Comp Sch DH7 33 A3
Deerness View
  East Hedleyhope DL13 40 D5
  Ushaw Moor DH7 32 D2
Deerpool Cl TS24 64 C1
Defoe Cres DL5 96 E8
Deighton Gr TS23 102 D6
Deighton Rd TS4 140 B5
Del'strother Ave TS19 212 B4
Delamere Cl NE38 17 B7
Delamere Ct 8 SR3 18 A6
Delamere Dr TS11 124 B8
Delamere Gdns SR8 39 D4
Delamere Rd TS3 140 D8
Delarden Rd TS3 120 D3
Delaval DH2 16 A3
Delaval Rd TS23 102 F5
Delavale Cl SR8 49 F5
Delaware Ave DL14 92 C7
Deleval Cl DL5 82 C1
Delight Bank DH9 12 D7
Delight Ct DH9 12 D8
Delight Row DH9 12 D8
Dell Cl TS7 140 C3
Dell Side DL15 54 B2
Dell The DL14 80 C8
Dellfield Cl TS3 140 D8
Delvedere DH8 11 B1
Delves Cotts DH8 177 D4
Delves La DH8 11 A1
Delves Lane Ind Est DH8 177 D4
Delves Lane Inf Sch DH8 177 D4
Delves Lane Jun Sch DH8 177 D4
Demesne Ct DL13 207 D5
Demesne La DL12 198 F6
Denbigh Rd TS23 102 E6
Dene Ave Easington SR8 39 E6
Dene Ave *continued*
  Houghton-le-S DH5 27 A7
  Rowlands Gill NE39 1 D1
  Shotton Colliery DH6 48 D6
Dene Bank DH7 33 B8
Dene Bank Ave SR8 50 B6
Dene Bridge DL15 65 E8
Dene Bridge Row DL17 69 D1
Dene Cl TS17 138 E7
Dene Com Sch of Tech SR8 50 A6
Dene Com Tech Sch SR8 49 F5
Dene Cotts DH2 15 D1
Dene Cres
  Rowlands Gill NE39 1 D1
  Sacriston DH7 23 D3
  Shotton Colliery DH6 48 D6
Dene Ct Birtley DH3 9 C7
  Hamsterley NE17 4 B6
  Shadforth DH6 46 E6
  Witton Gilbert DH7 23 B1
Dene Dr DH1 35 D5
Dene Garth TS27 75 E3
Dene Gdns DH5 26 F7
Dene Gr
  Bishop Auckland DL14 80 C7
  Darlington DL3 132 D3
  Redcar TS10 107 D6
Dene Hall Dr DL14 79 F7
Dene Hill DL13 188 A7
Dene House Prim Sch SR8 49 F5
Dene House Rd SR7 29 C8
Dene Park Ct 4 DL3 132 F3
Dene Pk DH7 41 D8
Dene Rd
  Barnard Castle DL12 209 B6
  Blackhall Rocks TS27 50 E3
  Middlesbrough TS4 120 A2
  Rowlands Gill NE39 1 D1
  Seaham SR7 29 B5
Dene St Esh DH7 31 D3
  Hetton-le-H DH5 27 B6
  Peterlee SR8 50 A7
  Stanley DH9 13 D5
Dene Terr Chilton DL17 82 E8
  Peterlee SR8 50 A6
  Seaham SR7 29 D8
  Shotton Colliery DH6 48 D6
Dene The
  Chester le Street DH2 24 B8
  Medomsley DH8 4 A2
  West Rainton DH4 26 A2
Dene Valley Prim Sch DL14 81 A5
Dene View
  Burnopfield NE16 6 A6
  Cassop DH6 46 F2
  Castle Eden TS27 61 D7
  Hesleden TS27 50 C1
  High Spen NE39 1 A3
  Rowlands Gill NE39 1 C2
  Stanley DH9 14 C7
  Willington DL15 53 E3
Dene Villas
  Chester le Street DH3 16 D1
  Kirk Merrington DL16 69 C1
  Peterlee SR8 50 B6
Dene Way SR7 29 C8
Dene Wlk TS11 108 B1
Deneburn Terr DH8 177 B4
Denecrest DH8 4 A2
Deneholme Terr DH7 22 D7
Deneside
  Bishop Auckland DL14 80 C6
  Howden-le-W DL15 65 E8
  Lanchester DH7 21 A3
  Sacriston DH7 23 C4
  Spennymoor DL16 55 F1
  Witton Gilbert DH7 33 B8
Deneside Cl TS15 156 D5
Deneside Jun & Inf Schs SR7 29 A6
Deneside Rd DL3 132 D3
Denesyde DH8 4 A2
Denevale TS15 156 D5
Deneway NE39 2 A4
Denewood Cl DL15 53 F3
Denewood Ct DH9 14 B4
Denewood Terr DL17 82 F8
Denham Gn TS3 120 D3
Denham Gr NE21 1 F8
Denham Pl DL5 96 E7
Denholme Ave TS18 137 E8
Denmark St
  Darlington DL3 133 A5
  Middlesbrough TS2 214 B4
Dennis St DH6 47 F3
Dennison Cres DH3 9 C6
Dennison St TS18 212 C1
Dennison Terr DL17 70 C4
Denshaw Cl TS19 117 A3
Dent Bank DL12 192 D5
Dent Cl DH6 37 E3
Dent Gate La
  Barnard Castle DL12 199 E7
  Copley DL12,DL13 195 A3
Dent St
  Bishop Auckland DL14 80 A3
  Hartlepool TS26 77 B6
  Shildon DL4 81 A2
Dent Wlk DL5 96 D7
Dent's Villas DL14 79 B8
Dentdale DH4 17 E8
Dentdale Cl TS15 156 C3
Denton Cl Darlington DL3 132 B4
  Middlesbrough TS5 139 B4
  Stockton-on-T TS19 117 B7
Denton Cross Roads DL2 110 B2
Denton Hall Cotts DL2 110 D2
Denver Dr DL2 154 B8
Denwick Cl DH2 24 A8
Deorna Ct DL1 133 B5
Depot Rd TS2 119 E7
Derby Ave TS5 139 A8
Derby Cl 3 TS17 138 D8
Derby Cres 5 DH8 177 A4
Derby Dr DH8 177 A4
Derby Rd
  Guisborough TS14 143 D3
  Stanley DH9 13 E5
Derby St Darlington DL3 132 F5
  Hartlepool TS25 77 B3
  Stockton-on-T TS18 213 A3
Derby Terr TS17 118 D1
Derby The TS7 140 C4
Derbyshire Dr DH1 35 D2
Dere Ave DL14 80 A3
Dere Pk DH8 11 C4
Dere Rd DH8 11 B1
Derwent Ave
  Bishop Auckland DL14 79 B1
  Crook DL15 52 F3
  Guisborough TS14 143 C3
  Rowlands Gill NE39 1 E1
Derwent Cl
  Redmarshall TS21 116 B7
  Sacriston DH7 23 B3
  Seaham SR7 29 C8
Derwent Cote NE17 4 B5
Derwent Cres
  Great Lumley DH3 25 B7
  Hamsterley NE17 4 B5
  Leadgate DH8 11 D5
Derwent Ctr The 14 DH8 10 F2
Derwent Dale DH8 10 C6
Derwent Haven NE17 4 B5
Derwent Ho TS23 103 A7
Derwent Mews DH8 10 D4
Derwent Pk TS13 127 D1
Derwent Pl Consett DH8 10 C6
  Newton Aycliffe DL5 96 A7
Derwent Rd Ferryhill DL17 69 F6
  Peterlee SR8 49 E7
  Redcar TS10 107 A5
  Skelton TS12 125 B3
  Thornaby-on-T TS17 138 D6
Derwent St
  Blackhall Mill NE17 4 C6
  Consett DH8 10 D4
  7 Darlington DL3 132 F3
  Hartlepool TS26 77 B6
  Hetton-le-H DH5 27 B2
  Middlesbrough TS1 214 B2
  Middlesbrough, North Ormesby TS3 120 C4
  Stockton-on-T TS20 118 A6
  Tanfield Lea DH9 13 E8
Derwent Terr
  Annfield Plain DH9 12 E4
  Burnopfield NE16 6 B7
  South Hetton DH6 37 E8
  Spennymoor DL16 56 A1
Derwent Valley Cotts NE39 1 F1
Derwent Valley Villas NE17 4 A6
Derwent View
  Blanchland DH8 175 A5
  Burnopfield NE16 6 B6
  Dipton DH9 12 C7
  Blaydon NE21 2 B8
Derwent View Terr DH9 5 D1
Derwent Walk Cty Pk* NE16,NE21,NE39 2 C5
Derwentcote Steel Furnace* NE17 4 E6
Derwentdale Ct DH8 10 D3
Derwentdale Ind Est DH8 10 D3
Derwentside Bsns Ctr DH8 11 B4
Derwentside Coll
  Consett DH8 10 F2
  Lanchester DH7 20 F4
  Stanley DH9 13 E6
Derwentwater Ave
  1 Chester le Street DH2 16 B1
  Middlesbrough TS5 139 C7
Derwentwater Rd TS6 121 F4
Desford Gn TS3 120 D2
Desmond Rd DL2 153 F6
Deva Cl TS4 120 B1
Devon Cl TS10 107 B4
Devon Cres
  Billingham TS23 102 F3
  Birtley DH3 9 B6
  Consett DH8 177 A4
  Skelton TS12 125 A2
Devon Dr
  New Silksworth SR3 18 A8
  Willington DL15 54 A3
Devon Pl DL14 80 C5
Devon Rd Eston TS6 121 E4
  Guisborough TS14 143 D3
Devon St Hartlepool TS25 77 B3
  Hetton-le-H DH5 26 F4
Devonport Gdns DL2 154 A5
Devonport Rd
  Middlesbrough TS5 119 F1
  Stockton-on-T TS18 213 C4
Devonshire Rd
  Darlington DL1 133 C4
  Durham DH1 35 C2
  Middlesbrough TS5 119 D2

E

Easington St SR8 ... 39 D4
Easson Rd Darlington DL3 132 F3
Redcar TS10 ... 107 C6
Easson St TS4 ... 120 A2
East Atherton St DH1 .. 210 B2
East Ave Billingham TS23 . 102 D1
Coundon DL14 ... 81 B8
Waldridge DH2 ... 24 A7
Washington NE38 ... 17 B8
East Blackdene DL13 ... 179 E1
East Block DH7 ... 33 A8
East Bridge St DL15 ... 52 F4
East Butsfield La DL13 . 183 D7
East Cl DL2 ... 134 E6
East Clere DH7 ... 32 C6
East Cliff Rd SR7 ... 29 F4
East Coronation St SR7 . 28 D3
East Cres Loftus TS13 ... 127 D1
Middlesbrough TS5 ... 119 B1
East Dr TS17 ... 118 D2
East Durham & Houghall Com Coll
Durham DH1 ... 44 E7
Seaham SR7 ... 29 C8
East Durham & Houghall Com Coll (Burnhope Way Ctr) SR8 ... 49 D6
East Durham & Houghall Com Coll (Howletch Ctr) SR8 ... 49 C7
East Ellen St SR7 ... 28 D2
East End Sedgefield TS21 .. 85 B6
Stanhope DL13 ... 206 E2
Wolsingham DL13 ... 207 D5
East Farm Cl TS6 ... 141 D8
East Gn
Bishop Auckland DL14 ... 79 C1
Heighington DL5 ... 95 E1
Shotton Colliery DH6 ... 48 D6
East Grange Ct SR8 ... 39 B3
East Haswicks DL13 ... 186 A8
East Hetton Aged Workmen's Homes DH6 ... 58 E5
East La DL13 ... 206 E3
East Law DH8 ... 3 D1
East Lea Blaydon NE21 ... 2 C8
Thornley (nr Wheatley Hill) DH6 ... 47 C5
East Lodge Gdns TS10 . 107 C1
East Mdws TS11 ... 108 D1
East Middlesbrough Ind Est TS3 ... 120 E5
East Mount Rd DL1 ... 133 A3
East Par
Bishop Auckland DL14 ... 80 B8
Consett DH8 ... 11 A2
Hartlepool TS24 ... 64 D2
Kimblesworth DH2 ... 23 F3
Sedgefield TS21 ... 85 B6
Skelton TS12 ... 125 B2
Stanley DH9 ... 14 A7
East Prec TS23 ... 102 D4
East Raby St 1 DL3 ... 132 F1
East Rainton Prim Sch DH5 ... 26 C4
East Row
8 Darlington DL1 ... 132 F1
3 Eston TS6 ... 121 F2
Middlesbrough TS5 ... 119 B1
East Scar TS10 ... 107 E3
East Side TS7 ... 160 C7
East Side Ave DH7 ... 33 A3
East St
Blackhall Colliery TS27 ... 50 D4
Consett DH8 ... 11 A2
Consett, Crookhall DH8 ... 11 B2
Darlington DL1 ... 133 A2
Gayles DL11 ... 205 E2
Hett DH6 ... 56 E6
Loftus TS13 ... 127 C1
Marske-by-t-S TS11 ... 108 D1
Middlesbrough TS2 ... 119 F7
Sacriston DH7 ... 23 B4
Shotton Colliery DH6 ... 48 D6
Stanley DH9 ... 14 B7
Thornley (nr Wheatley Hill) DH6 ... 47 E4
West Pelton DH2 ... 15 A5
East Stanley Sch DH9 ... 14 A7
East Tanfield Sta★ DH9 ... 6 E2
East Terr Billy Row DL15 .. 52 D6
Chopwell NE17 ... 4 C7
Coundon DL14 ... 67 F1
Hesleden TS27 ... 50 A1
Skelton TS12 ... 125 B2
East View
Annfield Plain DH9 ... 12 E6
Brandon DH7 ... 43 C3
Burnopfield NE16 ... 6 A6
Consett DH8 ... 10 F4
Dipton DH9 ... 12 D8
Easington SR8 ... 39 E5
8 Ferryhill DL17 ... 70 A6
Fishburn TS21 ... 72 D5
Kimblesworth DH2 ... 23 F2
Middleton St George DL2 . 154 A5
Murton SR7 ... 28 D2
1 Peterlee SR8 ... 50 A7
Rowlands Gill NE39 ... 1 C2
Ryhope SR2 ... 18 E6
Sadberge DL2 ... 134 E6
1 Seaham SR7 ... 18 F1
Sherburn Hill DH6 ... 36 D1
Stanley DH9 ... 13 E4
East View *continued*
Thornley (nr Wheatley Hill) DH6 ... 47 C4
Trimdon TS29 ... 59 D3
Wheatley Hill DH6 ... 47 F1
Willington DL15 ... 53 C3
East View Terr
Middlesbrough TS4 ... 120 A2
Seaton Carew TS25 ... 77 E1
Shildon DL4 ... 80 F2
East Villas DH6 ... 37 F4
Eastbank Rd TS7 ... 141 B6
Eastbourne Ave TS16 ... 156 C7
Eastbourne Comp Sch DL1 ... 133 C2
Eastbourne Gdns TS3 ... 140 F8
Eastbourne Rd
Darlington DL1 ... 133 C1
Middlesbrough TS5 ... 119 E1
Stockton-on-T TS19 ... 118 A5
Eastbury Cl TS17 ... 157 C8
Eastcroft
2 Middlesbrough TS3 ... 120 C2
Stanhope DL13 ... 206 C3
Eastcroft Rd TS6 ... 121 E6
Eastdene Rd SR7 ... 28 F7
Eastdene Way SR8 ... 49 F5
Easter Pk TS17 ... 138 D2
Eastern Ave DH7 ... 32 C6
Easterside Prim Sch TS4 ... 140 B5
Easterside Rd TS4 ... 140 B6
Eastfield SR8 ... 49 F5
Eastfield Rd TS11 ... 108 B1
Eastfields DH9 ... 13 E5
Eastfields Rd DL5 ... 95 F4
Eastgate Rd TS5 ... 139 D8
Eastham Sands TS5 ... 139 B3
Eastland Ave TS26 ... 76 F4
Eastland View TS3 ... 120 E3
Eastlands NE38 ... 16 E7
Eastlea Ave DL14 ... 80 C6
Eastlea Cres SR7 ... 29 A7
Eastlea Rd SR7 ... 28 F7
Eastleigh TS17 ... 138 E5
Eastlowthian St TS2 ... 119 F8
Easton St TS17 ... 138 D8
Eastpoint Rd DL1 ... 133 F2
Eastport Rd TS18 ... 213 C4
Eastwell Cl TS21 ... 85 B6
Eastwood DH7 ... 23 C2
Eastwood Rd TS3 ... 121 A1
Eaton Cl NE38 ... 17 B8
Ebba Cl DL5 ... 96 C6
Ebberston Ct DL16 ... 55 E3
Ebchester CE Prim Sch DH8 ... 3 E3
Ebchester Cl TS19 ... 117 B8
Ebchester Hill DH8 ... 3 F2
Ebchester Roman Fort★ DH8 ... 3 E4
Eccleston Wlk TS4 ... 140 B6
Eckert Ave TS5 ... 119 A1
Eckford Wlk TS25 ... 76 E1
Eddison Way TS8 ... 139 E1
Eddleston Wlk TS25 ... 76 D1
Eden Ave Burnopfield NE16 . 6 A6
Leadgate DH8 ... 11 D5
Eden Cl Coundon DL14 ... 81 C8
Heighington DL5 ... 95 C1
Hurworth-on-T DL2 ... 152 A1
Eden Com Prim Sch SR8 49 D7
Eden Cotts Hesleden TS27 . 50 A1
Leadgate DH8 ... 11 C5
Eden Cres DL1 ... 151 F7
Eden Crest DL2 ... 201 D3
Eden Croft DH9 ... 15 A6
Eden Ct 5 DL14 ... 80 B8
Eden Dr TS21 ... 85 B5
Eden Gdns DL17 ... 82 E6
Eden Gr
Bishop Auckland DL14 ... 79 B1
Middridge DL5 ... 81 E1
Eden La Gainford DL2 ... 201 D4
Peterlee SR8 ... 49 E8
Eden Pk DL2 ... 201 D3
Eden Rd Durham DH1 ... 34 C6
Middlesbrough TS4 ... 119 F2
Newton Aycliffe DL5 ... 96 E7
Skelton TS12 ... 125 C3
Spennymoor DL16 ... 68 F7
Eden St Hartlepool TS24 ... 77 B5
Peterlee SR8 ... 50 A7
Saltburn-by-t-S TS12 ... 125 C7
Spennymoor DL16 ... 68 E7
Eden Terr Chilton DL17 ... 82 F8
Coundon DL14 ... 81 F8
Durham DH1 ... 35 B3
Kirk Merrington DL14 ... 68 F3
Stanley DH9 ... 13 D5
Willington DL15 ... 54 A2
Eden Vale SR8 ... 49 F6
Eden View Coundon DL14 ... 68 E3
Shotton Colliery DH6 ... 48 D6
Eden Way TS22 ... 102 A6
Edendale Cres DL15 ... 65 D7
Edendale Terr SR8 ... 49 F6
Edenfield DH9 ... 15 A7
Edenhall Gr TS10 ... 107 C3
Edenhill Rd SR8 ... 49 E7
Eder Rd TS20 ... 118 B6
Edgar Gr DL14 ... 80 B8
Edgar St Hartlepool TS25 ... 77 B3
6 Stockton-on-T TS20 ... 118 B6
Edge Ct DH1 ... 211 C3
Edge Hill DL14 ... 80 B8
Edge La DH7 ... 21 B6
Edge The DL13 ... 194 F5
Edgecombe Dr DL3 ... 132 A3
Edgecombe Gr DL3 ... 132 A3
Edgehill Way TS23 ... 103 A6
Edgemoor Rd DL1 ... 152 D6
Edgewood Ct DH7 ... 23 B4
Edgeworth Ct TS8 ... 139 F1
Edgley Rd TS18 ... 117 B1
Edgmond Ct SR2 ... 18 E8
Edinburgh Ave TS5 ... 139 D8
Edinburgh Cl TS7 ... 141 A3
Edinburgh Dr DL3 ... 132 A1
Edinburgh Gr TS25 ... 90 B8
Ediscum Garth DL14 ... 79 F6
Edison St SR7 ... 28 D3
Edith St Consett DH8 ... 10 F2
Middlesbrough TS5 ... 119 B4
Seaham SR7 ... 29 E5
Edith Terr DL14 ... 79 B1
Edlingham Ct 6 DH5 ... 26 F8
Edlingham Rd DH1 ... 34 C5
Edmondbyers Rd TS19 . 117 B8
Edmondsley La DH7 ... 23 B5
Edmondsley Prim Sch DH7 ... 23 B7
Edmondsley Wlk 2 TS19 ... 117 C8
Edmund Ct DH7 ... 33 A4
Edmund St DL1 ... 133 A4
Edmundsbury Rd TS5 ... 119 F2
Edna St DH6 ... 57 D8
Ednam Gr TS25 ... 76 E1
Edridge Gn TS3 ... 120 E3
Edston Dr TS14 ... 143 F6
Edward Ave Bowburn DH6 45 D1
Peterlee SR8 ... 49 F6
Edward Cain Ct 9 SR8 .. 50 A7
Edward Kitching Terr TS9 ... 161 A3
Edward Rd DH3 ... 9 B5
Edward St
Bishop Auckland DL14 ... 80 B8
Burnopfield NE16 ... 6 A4
Chester le Street DH3 ... 16 C3
Craghead DH9 ... 14 C2
Darlington DL1 ... 133 B4
Durham DH1 ... 211 C3
Eldon Lane DL14 ... 80 F4
Esh Winning DH7 ... 41 E8
Hetton-le-H DH5 ... 27 A4
Middlesbrough TS3 ... 120 C4
New Silksworth SR3 ... 18 A7
6 Seaham SR7 ... 29 D6
South Bank TS6 ... 121 A5
Spennymoor DL16 ... 68 E8
Edward Street Ind Est DL1 ... 133 B4
Edward Terr
Annfield Plain DH9 ... 13 B4
New Brancepeth DH7 ... 42 F8
Pelton DH2 ... 15 C6
Edwardia Ct DH8 ... 10 E2
Edwards St Eston TS6 ... 121 F1
Stockton-on-T TS18 ... 213 A1
Edwards Wlk DH7 ... 21 E6
Edwardson Rd DH7 ... 43 D4
Edzell Wlk TS25 ... 76 D1
Egerton Cl TS20 ... 101 E1
Egerton Gr DL5 ... 82 D1
Egerton Rd TS26 ... 76 D5
Egerton St TS1 ... 215 A2
Egerton Terr TS25 ... 89 E4
Egglescliffe CE Prim Sch TS16 ... 156 C7
Egglescliffe Cl 1 TS19 . 117 C8
Egglescliffe Sch TS16 ... 156 A8
Eggleston Cl Durham DH1 . 34 E6
Great Lumley DH3 ... 25 B7
Eggleston Ct TS2 ... 119 C7
Eggleston Dr DH8 ... 10 F1
Eggleston Hall Gdns★ DL12 ... 193 D2
Eggleston La DL12 ... 193 D1
Eggleston Rd TS10 ... 107 C1
Eggleston View DL3 ... 132 A4
Egglestone Abbey★ DL12 ... 209 E3
Egglestone Ct
Billingham TS23 ... 102 E5
Skelton TS12 ... 125 D2
Egglestone Dr
Consett DH8 ... 11 A1
Eaglescliffe TS16 ... 137 A1
Egglestone Terr TS18 .. 212 C2
Egglestone Wlk DL14 ... 79 D2
Eglington Ave TS14 ... 143 E3
Eglington Rd TS6 ... 121 E6
Egmont Rd TS4 ... 215 B1
Egremont Gr SR8 ... 49 A3
Egton Ave TS7 ... 140 F2
Egton Cl TS10 ... 107 C2
Egton Dr TS25 ... 90 D7
Egton Rd TS20 ... 118 B6
Egton Terr DH3 ... 9 C5
Egton Way DL1 ... 133 E6
Eider Cl Hartlepool TS26 .. 76 D8
Ingleby Barwick TS17 ... 138 B1
Eight Houses TS27 ... 61 C5
Eighth Ave DH2 ... 16 B3
Eighth St
Blackhall Colliery TS27 ... 50 D4
Peterlee SR8 ... 50 A7
Elcho St TS26 ... 77 A6
Elcoat Rd TS20 ... 102 B1
Elcoat Terr DL15 ... 53 A2
Elder Cl DH7 ... 33 C1
Elder Ct TS1 ... 215 A3
Elder Gr Redcar TS10 ... 107 F2
Stockton-on-T TS19 ... 117 E7
Elderberry Mews TS21 .. 72 C5
Elderslie Wlk TS25 ... 76 D1
Elderwood Ct 5 TS4 ... 139 F8
Eldon Bank DL4,DL14 ... 81 A3
Eldon Bank Top DL4 ... 81 A3
Eldon Cl Langley Park DH7 . 32 A6
Newton Aycliffe DL5 ... 96 E7
Eldon Gr TS26 ... 76 F5
Eldon Grove Prim Sch TS26 ... 76 F4
Eldon Lane Prim Sch DL14 ... 80 E4
Eldon Pl DL3 ... 132 F5
Eldon Rd DL5 ... 96 D4
Eldon St Darlington DL3 .. 132 F5
Thornaby-on-T TS17 ... 138 C8
Eldon Terr Ferryhill DL17 .. 70 C4
Fishburn TS21 ... 72 C4
Eldon Wlk 1 TS17 ... 138 D8
Eleanor Pl TS18 ... 213 A1
Elemere Ct TS23 ... 102 E6
Elemore Cl DH7 ... 32 B6
Elemore Hall Sch DH6 ... 37 A5
Elemore La
Easington Lane DH5 ... 37 A7
High Pittington DH6 ... 36 E6
Elemore Pl DL5 ... 82 C1
Elemore St DH6 ... 36 B5
Elemore View DH6 ... 37 F7
Eleventh Ave DH2 ... 16 B3
Eleventh St
Blackhall Colliery TS27 ... 50 C4
Blackhall Colliery TS27 ... 50 D4
8 Peterlee SR8 ... 50 A7
Elgar Cl DH9 ... 14 A5
Elgin Ave Eston TS6 ... 121 D6
Middlesbrough TS3 ... 140 D8
Seaham SR7 ... 28 F7
Elgin Ct DL1 ... 133 E7
Elgin Gr DH9 ... 14 B6
Elgin Pl DH3 ... 9 D2
Elgin Rd Hartlepool TS25 .. 76 E1
Thornaby-on-T TS17 ... 138 D3
Eliot Ct TS23 ... 102 D7
Elisabeth Ave DH3 ... 9 B6
Elishaw Gn 4 TS17 ... 157 A7
Elite Bldgs DH9 ... 13 F7
Eliza La DH8 ... 177 C1
Eliza St DH7 ... 23 B2
Elizabeth Barrett Wlk DL5 ... 96 D5
Elizabeth Ct DH6 ... 36 C5
Elizabeth Pl DL1 ... 133 A4
Elizabeth St
Annfield Plain DH9 ... 13 A4
Blackhall Rocks TS27 ... 50 E2
Seaham SR7 ... 29 C7
2 Thornaby-on-T TS17 ... 138 D8
Elizabeth Terr TS3 ... 215 C2
Elizabeth Way TS25 ... 90 E7
Elkington Wlk TS3 ... 121 A1
Ellam Ave DH1 ... 210 A1
Elland Ave TS4 ... 140 B6
Elland Ct DL1 ... 133 F3
Ellary Wlk TS25 ... 76 D1
Ellen Ave TS18 ... 212 C1
Ellenport Ct 5 TS18 ... 213 C4
Ellerbeck Way TS7 ... 141 B8
Ellerbourne Terr TS28 ... 60 F5
Ellerburne St 7 TS17 ... 138 D8
Ellerby Bank TS13 ... 149 F1
Ellerby Cl TS10 ... 107 C3
Ellerby Gn TS3 ... 120 C2
Ellerby La TS13 ... 149 F2
Ellerby Rd TS6 ... 121 F3
Ellers Bank TS14 ... 124 C1
Ellerton Cl
Darlington DL3 ... 132 A5
Middlesbrough TS5 ... 139 E6
Ellerton Rd TS18 ... 137 B8
Ellesmere
Bournmoor DH3,DH4 ... 17 D3
Spennymoor DL16 ... 55 E2
Ellesmere Dr SR7 ... 28 F7
Ellesmere Wlk TS3 ... 120 E3
Ellett Ct TS24 ... 63 F2
Ellicott Wlk TS18 ... 213 A1
Ellington Cl Ryhope SR2 .. 18 F5
Urpeth DH2 ... 8 E2
Elliot St
Middlesbrough TS1 ... 215 A3
Redcar TS10 ... 107 B7
Skelton TS12 ... 125 B1
Thornley (nr Wheatley Hill) DH6 ... 47 D4
Elliott Rd SR8 ... 49 D7
Elliott St Crook DL15 ... 52 E4
Hartlepool TS26 ... 77 B6
Sacriston DH7 ... 23 C3
Elliott Terr
Annfield Plain DH9 ... 13 A3
Eldon Lane DL14 ... 80 F4
Ellis Gdns TS8 ... 139 E1
Ellis Leazes DH1 ... 211 B3
Ellison Rd SR8 ... 49 E7
Ellison St TS26 ... 77 A4
Elm Ave
Blackhall Rocks TS27 ... 50 F2
Brandon DH7 ... 43 B3
Pelton DH2 ... 15 C6
Sedgefield TS21 ... 85 B7
Elm Cl Eston TS6 ... 121 C3
Saltburn-by-t-S TS12 ... 125 A7
Spennymoor DL16 ... 56 A3
Willington DL15 ... 53 E2
Elm Cres DH2 ... 23 F3
Elm Ct DH7 ... 23 C3
Elm Dr Marton TS7 ... 140 D4
Elm Dr *continued*
Shildon DL4 ... 80 E2
Elm Gdns DL15 ... 52 D7
Elm Gr Burnopfield NE16 ... 5 F6
Hartlepool TS26 ... 76 F6
Thornaby-on-T TS17 ... 138 C7
Ushaw Moor DH7 ... 33 B1
Elm Park Rd DH8 ... 10 F7
Elm Park Terr
Consett DH8 ... 10 E7
Tow Law DL13 ... 183 E1
Elm Rd Cornforth DL17 ... 57 E1
Ferryhill DL17 ... 70 A5
Guisborough TS14 ... 143 E5
Redcar TS10 ... 107 E6
Shildon DL4 ... 80 E2
Elm St Billingham TS23 ... 103 E2
Chester le Street DH3 ... 16 C3
Consett DH8 ... 10 F4
Langley Park DH7 ... 32 C7
Middlesbrough TS1 ... 215 A3
South Bank TS6 ... 121 A6
Stanley DH9 ... 13 D4
Elm Terr
Annfield Plain DH9 ... 12 E5
Birtley DH3 ... 9 B5
Bishop Auckland DL14 ... 80 C6
Eldon Lane DL14 ... 80 F4
Leadgate DH8 ... 11 D4
Peterlee SR8 ... 50 A6
Tantobie DH9 ... 6 B2
The Middles DH9 ... 14 B3
Elm Tree Ave TS19 ... 117 B4
Elm Tree Ctr TS19 ... 117 C5
Elm Wlk TS13 ... 127 B2
Elmcroft DL1 ... 133 B7
Elmdale Rd DH8 ... 11 A3
Elmfield
Houghton-le-S DH5 ... 27 A6
Lanchester DH7 ... 20 E4
Elmfield Ave DH1 ... 35 B3
Elmfield Gdns TS25 ... 76 F1
Elmfield Pl DL5 ... 96 B5
Elmfield Prim Sch DL5 .. 96 B6
Elmfield Rd Consett DH8 .. 10 F4
Hurworth-on-T DL2 ... 168 B8
Elmfield St DL3 ... 132 F3
Elmfield Terr
Darlington DL3 ... 132 F3
Shildon DL4 ... 80 E2
Elmhurst Gdns TS8 ... 139 E1
Elms Rd DL3 ... 132 E2
Elms The Consett DH8 ... 10 E7
Easington Lane DH5 ... 37 D8
Hesleden TS27 ... 50 D1
Elmstone Gdns TS8 ... 139 E1
Elmtree Ct SR7 ... 29 C5
Elmtree Gdns SR8 ... 49 F6
Elmtree St DL3 ... 132 F6
Elmway DH2 ... 16 A5
Elmwood
Chester le Street DH2 ... 15 F2
Coulby Newham TS8 ... 140 B3
Elmwood Gr TS19 ... 212 A4
Elmwood Pl TS26 ... 76 E7
Elmwood Rd
Eaglescliffe TS16 ... 137 C4
Hartlepool TS26 ... 76 E7
Elmwood St DH4 ... 17 E1
Elphin Wlk TS25 ... 76 D1
Elsdon Cl
Chester le Street DH2 ... 15 F1
Peterlee SR8 ... 49 C3
Elsdon Gdns Consett DH8 . 10 F5
Ingleby Barwick TS17 ... 157 A7
Elsdon Rd DH1 ... 34 D6
Elsdon St TS18 ... 212 C2
Elstob Cl
Newton Aycliffe DL5 ... 96 D8
Stockton-on-T TS19 ... 117 B8
Elstob La TS21 ... 98 C4
Elstob Rd DL5 ... 96 E3
Elstone Rd TS4 ... 215 B2
Elterwater Cl TS10 ... 107 B5
Elterwater Rd DH2 ... 16 B1
Eltham Cres TS17 ... 138 E3
Eltisley Gn TS3 ... 120 E3
Elton Cl TS19 ... 117 C8
Elton Gr Darlington DL3 .. 132 D1
Stockton-on-T TS19 ... 117 A2
Elton Home Pk TS21 ... 116 A2
Elton La TS16 ... 156 B8
Elton Par DL3 ... 151 D8
Elton Rd Billingham TS22 . 102 B6
Darlington DL3 ... 132 D1
Elton St TS10 ... 107 C6
Eltringham Rd TS26 ... 77 A5
Elvan Gr TS25 ... 76 E1
Elvet Bridge DH1 ... 211 A2
Elvet Cl DL17 ... 57 D1
Elvet Cres DH1 ... 211 A2
Elvet Gn
Chester le Street DH2 ... 16 C2
Hetton-le-H DH5 ... 27 A1
Elvet Hill Rd DH1 ... 44 C7
Elvet Hill, East Asian Studies (Univ of Durham) DH1 . 44 B7
Elvet Moor DH1 ... 44 A7
Elvet Pl DL3 ... 132 B4
Elvet Waterside DH1 ... 211 A2
Elvington Cl TS23 ... 88 F1
Elvington Gn TS3 ... 120 E2
Elwick Ave
Middlesbrough TS5 ... 139 C6
Newton Aycliffe DL5 ... 82 A1
Elwick Cl TS19 ... 117 B8
Elwick Ct 3 TS26 ... 77 A4
Elwick Gdns TS19 ... 117 B8

Fern Rd DH7 .23 D3
Fern St Consett DH8 .10 F3
Middlesbrough TS1 .215 A2
Fern Terr DH9 .5 F1
Fern Valley DL15 .52 D2
Ferndale Durham DH1 .35 D4
Stockton-on-T TS19 .117 C5
Wolsingham DL13 .207 E5
Ferndale Ave TS3 .120 E4
Ferndale Cl
9 New Marske TS11 .124 A6
Station Town TS28 .60 F5
Ferndale Ct TS3 .120 F3
Ferndene Ave DH2 .15 E3
Fernhill Rd TS6 .121 F1
Fernie Rd
Guisborough TS14 .143 E2
Stockton-on-T TS20 .102 B1
Fernlea Ct DL1 .152 B7
Fernleigh DH3 .25 A7
Fernwood
Mount Pleasant TS8 .159 B7
Redcar TS10 .107 D2
Sacriston DH7 .23 B2
Fernwood Ave TS25 .77 A3
Fernwood Cl SR3 .18 A5
Fernwood Gr NE39 .4 F5
Ferrand Dr DH4 .26 D8
Ferry Rd Hartlepool TS24 .77 E8
Middlesbrough TS2 .119 F7
Ferryhill Bus Ent Coll
DL17 .69 C5
Ferryhill Station Prim Sch
DL17 .70 C3
Feversham Terr DL17 .70 C3
Festival Villas DL13 .194 F5
Festival Wlk DL16 .68 F8
Feversham St TS2 .215 A4
Fewston Cl
Hartlepool TS26 .76 C6
Middlesbrough TS3 .120 C2
Newton Aycliffe DL5 .95 F7
Field Cl TS17 .138 E7
Field Head TS10 .107 B4
Field Ho 3 SR3 .18 A5
Field Hos DH9 .13 A3
Field House Farm SR7 .18 F1
Field House Terr DH6 .37 F3
Field St DL1 .133 A4
Field View Terr DH7 .33 B3
Fieldfare Cl 2 NE38 .9 F3
Fieldfare Ct NE16 .6 C5
Fieldfare La
Stockton-on-T TS20 .102 B1
Stockton-on-T TS20 .102 B2
Fieldfare Rd TS26 .63 E1
Fieldhouse La DH1 .210 A4
Fieldhouse Terr DH1 .210 B4
Fielding Ct
Billingham TS23 .102 D7
Crook DL15 .52 C3
Fieldon Dr DL14 .79 C2
Fieldside East Rainton DH5 26 C3
Pelton DH2 .15 E7
Fieldview Cl TS2 .103 E1
Fiennes Rd SR8 .48 F7
Fife Ave DH2 .16 C3
Fife Cove DL3 .132 E1
Fife Gr TS25 .89 D8
Fife Rd
Barnard Castle DL12 .209 C7
Darlington DL3 .132 E1
Stockton-on-T TS20 .102 A1
Fife St Middlesbrough TS1 215 B3
Murton SR7 .28 D2
Fife Terr NE17 .4 B6
Fifth Ave DH2 .16 B3
Fifth St
Blackhall Colliery TS27 .50 D4
Consett DH8 .11 B2
Peterlee SR8 .50 A7
Filby Dr DH1 .35 D5
Filey Cl TS10 .107 F3
Fillpoke La TS27 .63 A8
Finchale Ave
Billingham TS23 .102 D5
Durham DH1 .34 F8
Middlesbrough TS3 .140 E8
Finchale Cl DH4 .26 D8
Finchale Cres DL3 .132 A4
Finchale Ct DH4 .25 F2
Finchale Prim Sch DH1 .34 E7
Finchale Priory* DH1 .25 B3
Finchale Rd Durham DH1 .34 D8
Durham, Framwellgate Moor
DH1 .34 B5
Newton Aycliffe DL5 .96 D5
Finchale Sq DL14 .79 D3
Finchale Terr DH4 .17 E1
Finchale Training Coll
DH1 .24 D1
Finchale View
Durham DH1 .34 B7
West Rainton DH4 .25 E2
Fincham Cl TS20 .117 E8
Finchdale Cl 6 TS10 .107 E1
Finchdale Terr 2 DH3 .16 C3
Finchfield Cl TS16 .137 B1
Finchley Ct TS5 .139 E3
Finchley Rd TS20 .102 B1
Findlay Gr TS25 .89 E8
Findon Ave Sacriston DH7 .23 C3
Witton Gilbert DH7 .23 B1
Findon Hill DH7 .23 C2
Fine La DH8 .3 B3
Fines Pk DH9 .12 F5
Fines Rd DH8 .4 B1
Fines Terr 5 DH9 .12 F4
Finings Ave
Langley Park DH7 .32 A6
Langley Park DH7 .32 B6
Finings St DH7 .32 B6
Finkle St
Bishop Auckland DL14 .67 B1
Stockton-on-T TS18 .213 B2
Finney Terr DH1 .211 A3
Finsbury St TS1 .214 B2
Fir Ave Brandon DH7 .43 B3
Durham DH1 .35 A1
Fir Gr Redcar TS10 .107 A2
Thornaby-on-T TS17 .138 C7
Fir Pk DH7 .33 B2
Fir Rigg Dr TS11 .108 C1
Fir Terr NE16 .6 B6
Fir Terraces DH7 .31 D1
Fir Tree Cl Durham DH1 .35 A3
Hilton TS15 .157 F3
Firbank Ho TS9 .161 A2
Firbeck Wlk TS17 .138 C3
Firby Cl Hartlepool TS24 .64 C1
Stockton-on-T TS20 .101 E1
Fire & Rescue Station Cotts
DL15 .52 E6
Firlands The TS11 .108 D2
Firs Terr DH7 .32 D7
Firs The DL1 .133 D6
Firsby Ct TS8 .139 E1
Firsby Wlk 2 TS3 .120 D2
First Ave DH2 .16 B8
First St
Blackhall Colliery TS27 .50 D3
Consett DH8 .11 B2
Leadgate DH8 .11 C5
Leadgate DH8 .11 C6
Peterlee SR8 .50 A7
Wheatley Hill DH6 .47 F3
Firthmoor Cres DL1 .152 E8
Firthmoor Prim Sch
DL2 .152 E7
Firtree DL4 .81 A1
Firtree Ave TS6 .141 D8
Firtree Dr
Howden-le-W DL15 .65 D7
Normanby TS6 .141 C8
Firtree Rd TS19 .117 E5
Firtrees DH2 .16 B5
Firwood Cres NE39 .1 A3
Firwood Gr DL15 .66 E6
Firwood Terr DL17 .70 C2
Fishburn Ind Est TS21 .72 C5
Fishburn Prim Sch TS21 .72 D5
Fishburn Terr TS21 .72 B5
Fishermans Sq TS10 .107 D6
Fishponds Rd TS10 .123 B7
Fiske Ct TS5 .139 C3
Fitzhugh Ct DL12 .198 F6
Fitzwilliam Cl 3 TS11 .108 D1
Fitzwilliam Dr DL1 .133 B6
Fitzwilliam St TS10 .107 D6
Five Hos DL15 .52 B3
Flag Terr DL13 .183 F1
Flambard Ct DL17 .71 C4
Flambard Dr DL14 .80 E7
Flambard Rd DH1 .34 B5
Flamborough 2 TS4 .120 B1
Flamingo Cl DL1 .133 E1
Flanders Way DL15 .52 E4
Flass Ave DH7 .33 A2
Flass St DH1 .210 B3
Flass Terr
Esh Winning DH7 .32 A2
6 Ushaw Moor DH7 .32 F2
Flassburn Rd DH1 .210 A4
Flasshall La DH7 .32 B2
Flats Bank DL11 .205 F2
Flatts Farm DL14 .67 B2
Flatts La Eston TS6 .121 D1
Normanby TS6 .141 E6
Ormesby TS7 .141 C5
Flatts Lane Ctry Pk*
TS6 .141 E6
Flatts Lane Dr TS6 .141 D7
Flatts Rd DL12 .209 B6
Flaxfield DL12 .209 B6
Flaxmill Cl DL11 .205 C5
Flaxton Ct 2 TS26 .77 A4
Flaxton St TS26 .77 A4
Fleck Way TS17 .138 E1
Fleece Cotts DH7 .23 B6
Fleece Terr DH7 .23 B7
Fleet Ave TS24 .77 D6
Fleet Bridge Rd TS18,
TS20 .118 D6
Fleet Ho Hartlepool TS24 .77 D6
Middlesbrough TS3 .120 F2
Fleet Rd TS18,TS23 .118 C8
Fleet St DL14 .80 B6
Fleet The Redcar TS10 .106 E4
Thornaby-on-T TS17 .138 F7
Fleetham Cl DH2 .15 F1
Fleetham Gr TS18 .117 B1
Fleetham St
Middlesbrough TS1 .214 B3
Middlesbrough TS1 .214 C2
Fleming Ct DH6 .48 B7
Fleming Pl SR8 .49 D6
Fleming Rd TS6 .121 A4
Fleming St TS10 .107 B7
Fletcher St TS1 .215 A3
Fletcher Wlk TS25 .76 D2
Flexley Ave TS3 .140 F8
Flint Hill Bank DH9 .5 E1
Flint Wlk TS26 .76 D8
Flintoff St 8 DL14 .80 C8
Flixton Gr TS22 .102 B5
Flodden Cl DH2 .15 F1
Flodden Way TS23 .103 A7
Flora Ave DL3 .151 D8
Flora St Eston TS6 .121 E2
Spennymoor DL16 .68 E8
Floralia Ave SR2 .19 A6
Florence Ct 4 TS17 .157 B8
Florence St TS2 .214 C4
Florida Gdns TS5 .139 D7
Flottila Ho TS24 .77 D6
Flounders Ho TS16 .156 B7
Flounders Rd TS15 .156 A4
Flynn Ct DL5 .96 E6
Fold DH7 .31 C4
Fold The Burnopfield NE16 .6 A7
New Silksworth SR3 .18 B5
Folds The
East Rainton DH5 .26 D4
Fence Houses DH4 .26 B8
Folkestone Cl TS8 .139 E1
Folland Dr TS11 .108 B2
Folly Bank
Bishopton TS21 .115 C6
Eggleston DL12 .193 E2
Folly Terr DH1 .34 A7
Folly View DL13 .195 C4
Fondlyset La DH9 .12 D7
Fonteyn Ct TS8 .139 E1
Fonteyn Pl DH9 .14 B5
Fontwell Cl TS19 .117 A5
Forber Rd TS4 .139 F7
Forbes Ave TS5 .119 B1
Forbes Bldg TS1 .214 C1
Forbes Terr SR2 .18 E6
Forcett Cl TS5 .139 C4
Forcett St DL3 .132 C4
Ford Cres DH7 .20 F2
Ford Dike La DL2 .201 D5
Ford Pl TS18 .213 A4
Ford Rd Durham DH1 .34 D7
Lanchester DH7 .20 F2
Ford St 8 Consett DH8 .177 D4
Lanchester DH7 .20 F3
Ford Terr DL17 .82 E8
Ford Way DL14 .80 A4
Fordham Dr DH7 .23 B4
Fordham Rd DH1 .34 C6
Fordon Pl TS4 .140 A7
Fordwell Rd TS19 .117 A4
Fordy Gr TS17 .138 C6
Fordyce Rd
Hartlepool TS25 .89 E8
Hemlington TS8 .139 D1
Hemlington TS8 .139 E1
Fore Bondgate DL14 .67 B1
Foreland Point TS17 .157 A6
Forest Dr Ormesby TS7 .141 B5
Washington NE38 .16 F8
Forest Gate TS28 .60 D8
Forest La TS15 .172 C8
Forest Mews TS17 .138 D4
Forest Moor Rd DL1 .152 D7
Forest of Teesdale Prim Sch
DL12 .191 C8
Forest View DH7 .42 F3
Forester Cl TS25 .77 D1
Foresters Cl TS22 .101 E8
Forfar Ave TS4 .140 B5
Forfar Cl DL1 .133 D7
Forfar Rd TS25 .89 D8
Forge Cl NE17 .4 B6
Forge La Bournmoor DH3 .17 B2
Hamsterley Mill NE17 .4 E5
Forge The DH1 .34 A8
Forge Way DL1 .133 B4
Forget Me Not Dr TS19 117 D5
Formby Cl 7 TS27 .63 C4
Formby Gn TS4 .140 A7
Formby Gr TS27 .63 D4
Formby Wlk TS16 .137 C2
Forres Ct DH9 .14 B6
Forres Wlk 7 TS25 .89 D8
Forresters Path DL5 .95 F4
Forster Ave
Cold Hesledon SR7 .28 E1
Sherburn DH6 .36 A2
Forster Cl DL5 .82 B2
Forster Cres DH6 .38 B6
Forster Ho TS1 .215 A3
Forster Sq TS28 .60 D8
Forster St Consett DH8 .11 A2
Darlington DL3 .132 F3
Fort Rose Cl TS16 .156 C8
Forth Cl SR8 .49 D5
Forth Gr TS25 .89 E8
Forth Rd TS10 .107 A5
Forty Foot Rd TS2 .119 D7
Forum Ct TS3 .215 C2
Fosdyke Gn TS3 .121 A1
Foss Way DH8 .3 E3
Fossfeld TS19 .117 A5
Foster St TS12 .126 A3
Foster Terr DH6 .56 B6
Foston Cl TS20 .101 F1
Fotheringhay Dr DL1 .133 E7
Foumarts La DL17 .71 B3
Foundary TS27 .61 C7
Founders Ct TS25 .89 E4
Foundry Fields DL15 .52 E4
Foundry Rd SR7 .29 E7
Foundry St DL4 .81 A2
Fountain St TS14 .143 E4
Fountains Ave TS17 .138 C1
Fountains Cl
Guisborough TS14 .143 E4
Guisborough TS14 .143 F4
Fountains Cres TS6 .121 D2
Fountains Ct TS12 .125 E2
Fountains Dr TS5 .139 E7
Fountains Sq DL14 .79 D2
Fountains View DL3 .132 B4
Four Lane Ends
Consett DH8 .177 A3
Escomb DL14 .79 D6
Hetton-le-H DH5 .27 B2
Houghton-le-S DH5 .26 D6
St John's Chapel DL13 .179 E1
Four Riggs DL3 .132 F2
Four Winds Ct TS26 .76 D6
Fourth Ave DH2 .16 B3
Fourth St
Blackhall Colliery TS27 .50 D4
Consett DH8 .11 B2
Leadgate DH8 .11 C5
Leadgate DH8 .11 C6
Peterlee SR8 .50 A7
Quaking Houses DH9 .13 D2
Fourway Ct TS28 .48 E1
Fowler Cl TS15 .156 E4
Fowler Rd DL5 .96 E7
Fowlers Yd DH1 .210 C3
Fox Almshouses 1
TS20 .118 B8
Fox Cl Hurworth-on-T DL2 168 B8
Ingleby Barwick TS17 .138 C2
Fox Cover Ct SR7 .29 C5
Fox Cover Ind Est SR7 .29 E4
Fox Covert DL16 .56 C3
Fox Covert Gr DL15 .65 D8
Fox Hills Cres DH7 .20 D3
Fox Ho SR3 .18 A4
Fox Howe TS8 .140 B3
Fox Pl DL5 .96 C8
Fox St Seaham SR7 .29 D6
Stockton-on-T TS20 .118 B7
Foxberry Ave TS5 .139 B4
Foxes Row DH7 .54 E8
Foxglove DH4 .17 F5
Foxglove Cl
Hartlepool TS26 .63 D1
Newton Aycliffe DL5 .82 B1
Stockton-on-T TS19 .117 C5
Foxglove Dr DL14 .79 E7
Foxgloves
Coulby Newham TS8 .140 C1
Mount Pleasant TS8 .159 C8
Foxgrove DH2 .15 F2
Foxheads Ct TS1 .214 B3
Foxhills Covert NE16 .2 E5
Foxhills The NE16 .2 E6
Foxlair Cl SR3 .18 A4
Foxrush Cl TS10 .107 C2
Foxton Cl
Newton Aycliffe DL5 .96 D8
Yarm TS15 .156 E5
Foxton Dr TS23 .102 E8
Foxton La TS21 .99 B7
Foxton Way DH1 .45 B5
Foxwood Dr TS19 .117 C5
Frampton Gn TS3 .140 D7
Framwelgate DH1 .210 C3
Framwelgate Bridge
DH1 .210 C2
Framwelgate Peth DH1 .210 B4
Framwelgate Waterside
DH1 .210 C3
Framwellgate Moor Prim Sch
DH1 .34 B6
Framwellgate Sch Durham
DH1 .34 B6
France St TS10 .107 D7
Frances St 9 SR3 .18 A7
Frances Terr DL14 .80 B6
Francis St Beamish DH9 .7 D1
Stanley Crook DL15 .52 F8
Francis Wlk 5 TS17 .138 C8
Frank Ave SR7 .29 B7
Frank St DH1 .35 A2
Frankfield Mews TS9 .161 A3
Frankfield Pl TS9 .161 A2
Frankland La DH1 .211 A4
Frankland Rd DH1 .34 B5
Franklin Cl TS18 .117 B1
Franklin Ct TS17 .138 D4
Franklyn Rd SR8 .49 C7
Fransham Rd TS3 .120 D2
Fraser Ct 8 Coundon DL14 81 B8
Hartlepool TS25 .89 D8
Fraser Gr TS25 .89 D8
Fraser Rd TS18 .137 D8
Fred Peart Sq DH6 .47 F2
Frederic St TS24 .64 E1
Frederick Nattrass Prim Sch
TS20 .118 A8
Frederick St Chopwell NE17 4 B8
Coundon DL14 .68 B1
Middlesbrough TS3 .120 C4
Seaham SR7 .29 D7
Stockton-on-T TS18 .213 A4
Thornaby-on-T TS17 .213 C1
Frederick St N DH7 .43 C4
Frederick St S DH7 .43 D4
Frederick Terr
Hetton-le-H DH5 .27 B1
South Hetton DH6 .37 F7
Fredric Terr TS23 .103 D2
Freebrough Rd TS12 .165 B7
Freeman's Pl
Darlington DL1 .133 A2
Durham DH1 .210 C3
Freemantle Gr TS25 .90 B8
Fremantle Cres TS4 .140 A8
Fremington Wlk TS4 .140 B5
Frensham Dr TS25 .77 B2
Frensham Way DH7 .43 C4
Freshingham Cl TS8 .139 E1
Freville Gr DL3 .132 A2
Freville St Hartlepool TS24 77 C5
Shildon DL4 .80 E1
Friar St Hartlepool TS24 .77 F8
Shotton Colliery DH6 .48 D6
Friar Terr TS24 .77 F8
Friar's Row NE16 .5 F5
Friarage Gdns TS24 .77 F8
Friars Pardon DL2 .152 C1
Friars' Row DH1 .211 C4
Friarside DH7 .33 B8
Friarside Cres NE39 .5 D8
Friarside Gdns NE16 .5 F6
Friarswood Cl TS15 .156 E5
Friendship La TS24 .77 F8
Frimley Ave TS3 .120 D2
Frobisher Cl TS11 .124 F8
Frobisher Rd TS17 .138 D4
Frome Ho 11 TS4 .139 F8
Frome Rd TS20 .118 B6
Front Rd NE39 .1 A5
Front Row DL14 .81 A4
Front St Annfield Plain DH9 12 F4
5 Annfield Plain DH9 .12 F5
Bishop Auckland DL14 .79 C1
Bishop Middleham DL17 .71 B3
Brandon DH7 .43 E6
Burnopfield NE16 .6 B6
Burnopfield, Lintz NE16 .5 E6
Carlin How TS13 .126 F3
Castleside DH8 .176 F3
Chester le Street DH3 .16 C3
Cockfield DL13 .195 E3
Consett DH8 .10 C6
Consett, Templetown DH8 .10 F2
Coxhoe DH6 .58 A3
Craghead DH9 .14 C3
Dipton DH9 .12 C8
Durham,Gilesgate DH1 .35 B1
Durham,Pity Me DH1 .34 A7
Ebchester DH8 .3 E3
Edmondsley DH7 .23 B7
Esh DH7 .31 F5
Fence Houses DH4 .26 A8
Fishburn TS21 .72 C5
Frosterley DL13 .188 A7
Great Lumley DH3 .25 A7
Greatham TS25 .89 E4
Hart TS27 .63 A2
Haswell DH6 .37 E1
Hesleden TS27 .50 A1
Hetton-le-H DH5 .27 A3
Hetton-le-H, Low Moorsley
DH5 .26 E1
High Pittington DH6 .36 B6
Hunwick DL15 .66 D7
Hutton Henry TS27 .61 C5
Ingleton DL2 .201 D7
Kelloe DH6 .58 D5
Kelloe DH6 .58 E5
Kirk Merrington DL16 .69 A3
Lanchester DH7 .20 E4
Langley Park DH7 .32 B5
Leadgate DH8 .11 C4
Pelton DH2 .15 D7
Pelton,Pelton Fell DH2 .15 D5
Pelton,Perkinsville DH2 .15 F8
Quarrington Hill DH6 .58 D8
Quebec DH7 .31 B4
Rookhope DL13 .180 E5
Sacriston DH7 .23 B3
Sedgefield TS21 .85 B6
Sherburn DH6 .36 A1
Sherburn Hill DH6 .36 D1
Shotton Colliery DH6 .48 D7
South Hetton DH6 .37 F7
Spennymoor DL16 .56 B4
Spennymoor, Merrington Lane
DL16 .69 A8
St John's Chapel DL13 .185 F8
Staindrop DL2 .200 E7
Stanhope DL13 .206 D3
Stanley DH9 .13 E6
Stanley, East Stanley DH9 .14 B7
Station Town TS28 .60 F5
Sunderland Bridge DH6 .56 B6
Tanfield DH9 .6 D3
Tantobie DH9 .6 B2
Tantobie, Pickering Nook
NE16 .6 A4
Tow Law DL13 .40 A1
Trimdon TS29 .59 F5
Ushaw Moor DH7 .43 C8
Wearhead DL13 .179 C1
Westgate DL13 .180 A1
Wheatley Hill DH6 .47 F3
Willington,Helmington Row
DL15 .53 C3
Willington,Sunnybrow DL15 .53 F1
Wingate TS28 .60 E6
Witton Gilbert DH7 .33 A8
Wolsingham DL13 .207 C5
Front St E Coxhoe DH6 .58 A4
Haswell DH6 .37 F3
Sunderland Bridge DH6 .56 B6
Front St N TS29 .59 E1
Front St S
Quarrington Hill DH6 .58 D7
Trimdon TS29 .59 D1
Trimdon TS29 .59 E1
Front Street Ind Est DH6 .47 F3
Front The Hartlepool TS25 .90 F8
Middleton St George DL2 .154 A5
Frosterley Cl Durham DH1 34 D6
Easington Lane DH5 .37 D8
Great Lumley DH3 .25 B7

Frosterley Com Sch
DL13 ....188 A7
Frosterley Gdns DH9 ....12 F4
Frosterley Gr TS23 ....102 F7
Frosterley Sta* DL13 ..188 A7
Fry St TS1 ....215 A3
Fryer Cres DL1 ....133 E5
Fryup Cres TS14 ....143 D2
Fuchsia Rd TS19 ....117 C3
Fudan Way TS17 ....213 C2
Fulbeck Cl TS25 ....76 F1
Fulbeck Ct TS23 ....102 F4
Fulbeck Ho TS3 ....121 A1
Fulbeck Rd
Middlesbrough TS3 ....141 A8
Newton Aycliffe DL5 ....96 D3
Fulford Gr TS11 ....123 F6
Fulford Pl DL3 ....133 A6
Fulford Way TS8 ....140 F1
Fulforth Cl DH7 ....33 A4
Fulforth Way DH7 ....23 B4
Fuller Cres TS20 ....117 F8
Fulmar Dr NE38 ....9 F3
Fulmar Head TS14 ....143 B4
Fulmar Ho TS24 ....77 D6
Fulmar Rd TS20 ....102 A2
Fulmerton Cres TS10 ..107 C1
Fulthorp Ave TS24 ....63 E3
Fulthorpe Ave DL3 ....132 B2
Fulthorpe Cl DL3 ....132 B2
Fulthorpe Gr
Darlington DL3 ....132 A2
Wynyard Village TS22 ....101 D8
Fulton Ct DL4 ....80 F2
Fulwell Rd SR8 ....49 F5
Fulwood Ave TS4 ....140 A8
Furlongs The TS10 ....107 D5
Furnace Pit Ind Est DL4 .94 F8
Furness Cl
Bishop Auckland DL14 ....79 E5
Peterlee SR8 ....49 B6
Furness St
2 Darlington DL1 ....133 C6
Hartlepool TS24 ....77 B7
Fylingdale Dr SR3 ....18 C7
Fyndoune DH7 ....23 C2
Fyndoune Community Coll
DH7 ....23 C2
Fyndoune Way DH7 ....23 B1
Fynes Cl SR8 ....49 D8
Fynway DH7 ....23 C2

G

Gable Terr DH6 ....47 F2
Gables The Burnhope DH7 .21 D4
Hurworth-on-T DL2 ....152 D1
Marton TS7 ....140 D3
Redcar TS10 ....107 B7
Sedgefield TS21 ....85 A8
Thornley (nr Wheatley Hill)
DH6 ....47 C4
Gadwall Rd DH4 ....26 B6
Gainford DH2 ....16 A3
Gainford Ave TS5 ....139 E8
Gainford CE Prim Sch
DL2 ....201 C3
Gainford Rd
Billingham TS23 ....102 F5
Ingleton DL2 ....201 D7
Stockton-on-T TS19 ....117 C2
Gainford St 4 TS24 ....77 B5
Gainsborough Cl TS6 ..141 D7
Gainsborough Cres
Billingham TS23 ....102 D7
1 Shiney Row DH4 ....17 F5
Gainsborough Ct
Bishop Auckland DL14 ....67 B1
Darlington DL1 ....152 A8
Gainsborough Rd
Marton TS7 ....140 C4
Stanley DH9 ....13 F5
Gair Ct DH2 ....23 F4
Gairloch Dr DH2 ....15 F7
Gairsay Cl 5 SR2 ....18 E8
Gaisgill Cl TS7 ....141 B7
Gala Cl TS25 ....77 E2
Galbraith Terr TS29 ....59 E4
Gale St DH9 ....13 D5
Galfrid Cl SR7 ....28 F6
Galgate DL12 ....209 C6
Galgate Cl TS7 ....140 E3
Gallagher Cres SR8 ....49 F6
Galley Hill Prim Sch
TS14 ....143 B3
Galleys Field Ct TS24 ....64 F1
Gallow Hill DL12 ....204 B8
Galloway DL1 ....133 E7
Galloway Rd SR8 ....49 D7
Galloway Sands TS5 ....139 B3
Galsworthy Rd TS25 ....76 D3
Galt St DH6 ....47 D4
Gamul Cl DL5 ....82 B1
Ganstead Way TS23 ....102 F8
Ganton Cl
Billingham TS22 ....102 A5
New Marske TS11 ....124 A7
Garburn Pl DL5 ....96 B7
Garbutt Cl DL4 ....80 E2
Garbutt Sq DL1 ....133 B1
Garbutt St Shildon DL4 ....80 E2
Stockton-on-T TS18 ....213 B4
Garbutts La TS15 ....173 D1
Garden Ave Durham DH1 ..34 A6
Langley Park DH7 ....32 B6
Garden Cl 11 Consett DH8 .10 F3
Stanhope DL13 ....206 D3
Garden Cl *continued*
Thornaby-on-T TS17 ....138 B8
Garden Cres DH8 ....3 F4
Garden Est DH5 ....27 B4
Garden House La DL13 .195 E3
Garden Pl 12 Consett DH8 .10 F3
Crook DL15 ....52 F4
7 Darlington DL3 ....133 A7
Eston TS6 ....121 D1
Leadgate DH8 ....11 C4
Garden St Darlington DL1 133 A2
Newfield DL14 ....67 B7
Garden Terr Coxhoe DH6 ..57 F3
Leadgate DH8 ....11 C4
Middleton-In-T DL12 ....208 C5
Stanley DH9 ....13 E5
The Middles DH9 ....14 B3
Thornley (nr Wheatley Hill)
DH6 ....47 D4
Tow Law DL13 ....40 A1
Garden View DL13 ....195 C4
Garden Villas
3 Annfield Plain DH9 ....12 F5
Willington DL15 ....53 F3
Gardens The
Chester le Street DH2 ....16 B3
Crook DL15 ....52 F4
Hunwick DL15 ....66 D5
Middlesbrough TS4 ....140 A8
Gardiner Cres DH2 ....15 E4
Gardiner Sq NE11 ....8 C6
Gardner Ave DL15 ....53 F2
Gardners Pl DH7 ....43 D5
Garesfield Gdns
Burnopfield NE16 ....5 F6
Rowlands Gill NE39 ....1 E3
Garesfield La NE21,NE39 ...1 E6
Garforth Cl TS20 ....101 F1
Garland Terr 6 DH4 ....26 A8
Garmon Cl TS17 ....156 F8
Garmondsway Rd DL17 ..70 F8
Garnet Rd TS17 ....138 D7
Garnet St
Middlesbrough TS1 ....214 C2
Saltburn-by-t-S TS12 ....125 C8
Garrett Wlk TS1 ....214 B2
Garrick Ct 17 DL1 ....133 B1
Garrick Gr TS25 ....76 E2
Garron St SR7 ....29 D6
Garrowby Rd TS3 ....120 C1
Garsbeck Way TS7 ....141 B7
Garsdale DH3 ....9 E1
Garsdale Cl TS15 ....156 B3
Garsdale Ct 2 DL3 ....132 F1
Garsdale Gn 5 TS3 ....120 D2
Garside Ave DH3 ....9 C6
Garside Dr TS24 ....64 A2
Garside Gr SR8 ....49 B8
Garstang Cl TS7 ....140 F3
Garston Gr TS25 ....90 B8
Garth Cl TS21 ....116 C8
Garth Mdws 1 DL14 ....78 F5
Garth The Brotton TS12 .126 C4
Ferryhill DL17 ....69 F6
Ingleton DL2 ....201 D7
Marske-by-t-S TS11 ....108 C2
Medomsley DH8 ....4 C2
Mount Pleasant TS8 ....159 B8
Pelton DH2 ....15 E7
School Aycliffe DL5 ....95 F4
Sedgefield TS21 ....85 B7
Spennymoor DL16 ....56 B1
Stockton-on-T TS20 ....118 A8
Wolsingham DL13 ....207 D5
Garth Wlk TS3 ....120 C1
Garthlands DL5 ....95 D1
Garthlands Rd DL3 ....132 C4
Garthorne Ave DL3 ....132 A2
Garths The DH7 ....20 F3
Garvin Cl TS3 ....120 C1
Gas La DL12 ....208 C5
Gascoyne Cl TS7 ....140 E4
Gaskell La TS13 ....127 B1
Gaskell Way DL15 ....52 C3
Gatcombe Cl DL5 ....82 F1
Gate La DL2 ....150 D8
Gatehouse Cl DL1 ....133 E6
Gatehouse Factories 13
DH8 ....10 F2
Gatehouse Farm Cvn Pk
DL13 ....179 C1
Gatenby Dr TS5 ....139 C4
Gatesgarth Cl TS24 ....64 B1
Gateway The DL1 ....133 B6
Gateways DL13 ....207 D6
Gatley Wlk TS16 ....137 D4
Gatwick Gn 4 TS3 ....120 D2
Gaunless Lead Mill*
DL13 ....195 A3
Gaunless Terr
1 Bishop Auckland DL14 ..80 C8
Bishop Auckland, South Church
DL14 ....80 D5
Copley DL13 ....195 A4
Gayfield Terr SR8 ....39 F3
Gayhurst Cres SR3 ....18 B6
Gayton Sands TS5 ....139 B3
Gedney Ave TS3 ....140 D7
Gelt Cres DH5 ....27 B2
Geltsdale TS5 ....139 C4
General Bucher Ct DL14 .80 C7
General Hospl The DL14 .80 B6
General's Wood The
NE38 ....17 B8
Genesis Way DH8 ....10 E2
Geneva Cres DL1 ....152 B7
Geneva Dr
Darlington DL1 ....152 B7
Geneva Dr *continued*
Redcar TS10 ....107 C5
Geneva Gdns DL1 ....152 B7
Geneva La DL1 ....152 B7
Geneva Rd DL1 ....152 C7
Geneva Terr DL1 ....152 A8
Gent Rd DL14 ....80 C6
Gentian Way TS19 ....117 C5
Geoffrey Ave DH1 ....210 A1
Geoffrey Terr DH9 ....13 D5
George Ave SR8 ....39 E5
George Parkinson Meml
Homes DH6 ....35 F1
George Pit La DH3,DH4 ..25 C6
George Reynolds Ind Est
DL4 ....95 B6
George Short Cl DL1 ...133 A4
George Sq Shadforth DH6 .46 E6
Shotton Colliery DH6 ....48 D6
George St
1 Barnard Castle DL12 ..209 C5
Birtley DH3 ....9 B4
2 Bishop Auckland DL14 ..80 B8
Bishop Auckland,West Auckland
DL14 ....79 B1
Bowburn DH6 ....45 D2
Chester le Street DH3 ....16 D2
Consett DH8 ....10 F3
Consett, Blackhill DH8 ....10 D4
Craghead DH9 ....14 C2
8 Darlington DL1 ....133 A1
Dipton DH9 ....12 D8
Durham DH1 ....210 A2
Esh Winning DH7 ....41 E8
Ferryhill DL17 ....70 C2
Hartlepool TS24 ....77 C6
Haswell DH6 ....37 F3
Hetton-le-H DH5 ....27 A5
Langley Park DH7 ....32 C7
Murton SR7 ....28 D2
Redcar TS10 ....107 D6
Ryhope SR2 ....19 A6
Seaham SR7 ....29 D7
Sherburn DH6 ....36 A1
Sherburn Hill DH6 ....46 E8
Shildon DL4 ....80 E1
Thornaby-on-T TS17 ....213 C1
Trimdon TS29 ....59 F5
George St E SR3 ....18 A8
George St W 10 SR3 ....18 A8
George Street Ind Est
SR7 ....29 C7
George Terr
Bearpark DH7 ....33 C3
Brotton TS12 ....126 B3
Crook DL15 ....52 F4
Willington DL15 ....53 E3
Georgia Ct DH8 ....10 E2
Georgian Theatre TS18 .213 B3
Georgiana Cl TS17 ....213 C1
Gerard St DL16 ....56 A1
Gerrick La TS12 ....165 E5
Gerrie St TS12 ....145 B6
Gervaulx Ct DL16 ....55 E3
Ghent St DL16 ....67 E8
Ghyll Field Rd DH1 ....34 B5
Gib Chare DL14 ....80 C8
Gibb Sq TS24 ....64 F1
Gibbon St
Bishop Auckland DL14 ....80 B8
Spennymoor DL16 ....68 C5
Gibbs Ct 3 DH2 ....16 C2
Gibside DH2 ....16 A3
Gibside Chapel* NE16 ....2 A1
Gibside Cl DH9 ....14 B7
Gibside Cres NE16 ....6 D8
Gibside Ct NE16 ....6 B6
Gibside Terr NE16 ....6 B6
Gibside View NE21 ....2 B8
Gibson Gr TS24 ....63 D4
Gibson Row DL12 ....208 C5
Gibson St
Close House DL14 ....81 A4
Consett DH8 ....10 F3
Gifford St TS5 ....119 E2
Gilbert Rd SR8 ....49 C7
Gilberti Pl TS24 ....63 F3
Gilderdale DH4 ....17 E8
Gilderdale Cl DL3 ....132 C7
Gilesgate DH1 ....211 B3
Gilesgate Cl DH1 ....211 A3
Gilesgate Rd DH5 ....27 B1
Gilkes St TS1 ....214 C3
Gill Burn NE39 ....1 E3
Gill Crescent N DH4 ....17 E1
Gill Crescent S DH4 ....17 E1
Gill Croft DH2 ....15 F2
Gill La DL12 ....209 B5
Gill Side View DH8 ....10 C5
Gill St Consett DH8 ....11 A2
Guisborough TS14 ....143 E5
5 Hartlepool TS24 ....77 B5
Saltburn-by-t-S TS12 ....125 C6
Gill-lands La DL12 ....198 A6
Gillas La DH5 ....27 A7
Gillas La E DH5 ....26 F7
Gillas La W DH5 ....26 E6
Gillas Lane Prim Sch
DH5 ....26 F7
Gillbrook Tech Coll TS6 121 C3
Gillercomb TS10 ....107 C1
Gilliland Cres DH3 ....9 C6
Gilling Cres
Darlington DL1 ....152 C8
Spennymoor DL16 ....69 A8
Gilling Rd TS19 ....117 B3
Gilling Way TS10 ....107 E3
Gilling Wlk 3 TS3 ....120 C2
Gillpark Gr TS25 ....90 D8
Gilmonby Rd TS3 ....140 D7
Gilmour Garth DL12 ....198 F6
Gilmour St TS17 ....138 C8
Gilpin Ct DL5 ....96 E5
Gilpin Ho 1 TS20 ....118 A8
Gilpin Rd
Newton Aycliffe DL5 ....96 E5
Thornaby-on-T TS17 ....138 C7
Gilpin Sq TS19 ....117 F5
Gilpin St DH4 ....26 D8
Gilside Rd TS23 ....102 F5
Gilsland Cl TS5 ....139 B4
Gilsland Cres DL1 ....133 C6
Gilsland Gr TS6 ....121 D1
Gilwern Ct TS17 ....156 F7
Gipsy La DL17 ....83 E7
Girlington Bank
Hutton Magna DL11 ....205 F8
Ovington DL11 ....200 F1
Girrick Cl TS8 ....139 C1
Girton Ave TS3 ....140 D7
Girton Cl SR8 ....49 B5
Girton Wlk DL1 ....133 B5
Girvan Cl DH9 ....14 B6
Girvan Terr DH5 ....27 B1
Girvan Terr W DH5 ....27 B1
Gisborne Gr 2 TS18 ....117 C1
Gisburn Ave TS3 ....140 D8
Gisburn Rd TS23 ....102 F5
Gladesfield Rd TS20 ....118 B6
Gladstone Gdns DH8 ....11 A3
Gladstone Ind Est TS17 .213 C1
Gladstone St
Brotton TS12 ....126 A3
Carlin How TS13 ....126 F3
Consett DH8 ....11 A3
Crook DL15 ....52 E4
Darlington DL3 ....132 F2
Eston TS6 ....121 F2
Fence Houses DH4 ....26 B8
Hartlepool TS24 ....77 F8
Loftus TS13 ....127 C1
Stanley DH9 ....14 D7
Stanley, Oxhill DH9 ....13 D5
Stockton-on-T TS18 ....213 A1
Gladstone Terr
Binchester DL14 ....68 A4
Birtley DH3 ....9 B4
Coxhoe DH6 ....57 F3
9 Ferryhill DL17 ....70 B5
Penshaw DH4 ....17 F8
Tow Law DL13 ....40 A2
Wingate TS28 ....60 E6
Gladstone Villas DL17 ...70 B4
Glaisdale DL16 ....55 E1
Glaisdale Ave
Middlesbrough TS5 ....139 E7
Redcar TS10 ....106 F4
Stockton-on-T TS19 ....117 E5
Glaisdale Cl TS6 ....122 A3
Glaisdale Gdns DL4 ....81 B1
Glaisdale Gr TS25 ....90 E8
Glaisdale Rd Eston TS6 ..122 A3
Yarm TS15 ....156 F5
Glamis Cres NE39 ....2 B4
Glamis Ct DH4 ....17 D1
Glamis Gr TS4 ....140 A8
Glamis Rd
Billingham TS23 ....102 C5
Darlington DL1 ....133 D6
Glamis Terr DL14 ....92 C7
Glamis Villas DH3 ....9 C6
Glamis Wlk TS25 ....89 D8
Glamorgan Gr TS26 ....76 D8
Glanton Cl DH2 ....16 A2
Glanton Ct DL3 ....132 C7
Glanton Terr 2 SR8 ....50 B6
Glasgow St TS17 ....213 C1
Glastonbury Ave TS6 ...121 E2
Glastonbury Cl DL16 ....55 E3
Glastonbury Ho 8 TS3 .140 E8
Glastonbury Rd TS12 ...125 D2
Glastonbury Wlk TS26 ....76 E8
Gleaston Cres TS4 ....140 A7
Gleaston Ct SR8 ....49 B3
Gleaston Wlk TS4 ....140 A7
Glebe Ave SR8 ....39 D4
Glebe Dr SR7 ....18 F2
Glebe Est SR7 ....18 F2
Glebe Gdns Loftus TS13 .148 A8
Stainton TS8 ....139 C1
Glebe Houses DL17 ....69 F6
Glebe Prim Sch The
TS20 ....117 F8
Glebe Rd Darlington DL1 .133 B8
Great Stainton TS21 ....98 D1
Middlesbrough TS1 ....214 B2
Glebe Terr SR8 ....39 D4
Glebe The TS20 ....101 E1
Glebe View
Frosterley DL13 ....188 A7
Murton SR7 ....28 E4
Glebe Villas DL17 ....57 E1
Glebeside Satley DL13 ..183 D6
Witton Gilbert DH7 ....33 B8
Gledstone TS22 ....87 A4
Glen Barr DH2 ....16 B4
Glen Cl NE39 ....1 E3
Glen Ct TS5 ....139 E7
Glen Terr DH2 ....16 A4
Glen The TS16 ....156 C7
Glen's Flats DH6 ....36 B5
Glenavon Ave DH2 ....16 B4
Glenburn Cl NE38 ....9 F3
Glenbury Gr TS10 ....107 F1
Glencairn Gr 5 TS25 ....89 D8
Glencoe Ave DH2 ....16 B4
Glencoe Rise NE39 ....1 C1
Glencoe Terr NE39 ....1 C1
Glencot Gr SR7 ....39 A7
Glendale
Guisborough TS14 ....143 A2
Hutton Rudby TS15 ....173 E1
Glendale Ave TS26 ....76 F5
Glendale Cl NE21 ....1 F8
Glendale Dr DL3 ....151 D7
Glendale Rd TS5 ....139 E7
Glendene Sch SR8 ....39 D5
Glendue Cl TS7 ....141 A2
Gleneagles Cl TS22 ....102 A5
Gleneagles Ct TS4 ....140 A7
Gleneagles Rd
Darlington DL1 ....133 E7
8 Hartlepool TS27 ....63 C4
Middlesbrough TS4 ....140 A7
New Marske TS11 ....124 A6
Glenfall Cl TS22 ....102 A5
Glenfield Cl TS19 ....117 A3
Glenfield Dr TS5 ....139 E7
Glenfield Rd
Darlington DL3 ....151 D7
Stockton-on-T TS19 ....117 A3
Glenholme Cl 7 NE38 ....9 F3
Glenholme Dr DL15 ....52 F3
Glenholme Terr TS27 ....50 E3
Glenhow 7 TS12 ....125 C7
Glenhurst Cotts SR8 ....39 D4
Glenhurst Dr NE16 ....2 F4
Glenhurst Rd SR8 ....39 D4
Glenhurst Terr SR7 ....28 D3
Glenluce DH3 ....9 E3
Glenluce Cl TS16 ....137 C1
Glenluce Ct DH8 ....10 C3
Glenmeads DH2 ....23 F4
Glenmere DL16 ....55 E2
Glenmor Gr TS6 ....121 C2
Glenmore DH8 ....177 E4
Glenmore Ave DH2 ....16 C4
Glenn Cres TS7 ....140 D3
Glenroy Gdns DH2 ....16 B4
Glenside Consett DH8 ....10 D6
Saltburn-by-t-S TS12 ....125 D7
Glenside Terr DH2 ....15 F4
Glenston Cl TS26 ....76 C7
Glentower Gr TS25 ....90 D8
Glentworth Ave TS3 ....121 A1
Glentworth Ho TS3 ....121 A1
Globe Cl 19 DL1 ....133 B1
Gloucester Cl
Great Lumley DH3 ....25 A6
Nunthorpe TS7 ....141 A3
Gloucester Pl
5 Barnard Castle DL12 ..209 C5
Darlington DL1 ....133 C4
Peterlee SR8 ....49 B7
Gloucester Rd
Consett DH8 ....11 B1
Guisborough TS14 ....143 D2
Gloucester St TS25 ....77 A3
Gloucester Terr
Billingham TS23 ....102 F3
Haswell DH6 ....37 E1
Gloucestershire Dr DH1 .35 C3
Glue Garth DH1 ....211 C3
Glyder Ct TS17 ....156 F8
Goatbeck Terr DH7 ....43 D5
Goathland Cl SR3 ....18 C7
Goathland Dr
Hartlepool TS25 ....90 D7
New Silksworth SR3 ....18 B6
Goathland Gr TS14 ....143 D2
Goathland Rd TS6 ....121 F3
Gofton Pl TS6 ....121 D4
Gold Crest TS14 ....143 B4
Goldcrest Cl
Hartlepool TS26 ....63 D1
1 Ingleby Barwick TS17 ..138 B1
Goldcrest Rd NE38 ....9 F3
Golden Acre DH8 ....10 D5
Golden Flatts Prim Sch
TS25 ....90 B7
Golden Gr DL17 ....82 F8
Goldfinch Rd TS26 ....76 D8
Goldhill La DH8 ....176 D2
Goldsborough Ct TS28 ...48 E1
Goldsmith Ave TS24 ....63 E4
Goldsmith Cl TS23 ....102 D7
Golf Course Rd 3 DH4 ...17 F5
Gomer Terr DL14 ....67 B1
Gonville Ct DL1 ....133 B6
Good Ave TS29 ....59 E4
Good St DH9 ....13 E8
Goodburn Pl DL12 ....208 B5
Goodison Way DL1 ....133 E3
Goods Sta DL15 ....52 E3
Goodwell Lea DH7 ....42 E1
Goodwin Cl TS10 ....107 B1
Goodwin Wlk 15 TS24 ....77 C5
Goodwood Cl Consett DH8 10 E6
Sadberge DL2 ....134 E7
Goodwood Rd TS10 ....107 D3
Goodwood Sq TS17 ....119 A1
Goodyear Cres DH1 ....35 B1
Goose Garth TS16 ....156 B8
Goosepastures TS15 ....156 C5
Gooseport Rd TS18 ....213 C4
Gordon Ave SR8 ....49 F7
Gordon Bank DL12 ....193 D3
Gordon Cl DL1 ....133 E7
Gordon Cres TS6 ....121 E5
Gordon La DL14 ....92 B8
Gordon Rd TS10 ....107 A5

Gordon St 4 TS26 ....76 F6
Gordon Terr
3 Bishop Auckland DL14 ..80 B8
Ferryhill DL17 ....70 A5
Ryhope SR2 ....19 A6
Stanley DH9 ....13 F8
Wolsingham DL13 ....207 D5
Gore Hill Est DH6 ....47 C4
Gore Sands TS5 ....139 A3
Gorecock La DH8,DH9 ....20 B8
Gorleston Way SR3 ....18 A4
Gorman Rd TS5 ....119 D2
Gorsedale Gr DH1 ....35 D3
Gorsefields Ct TS6 ....141 E8
Gort Pl DH1 ....211 C4
Gort Rd DL5 ....96 D7
Gorton Cl TS23 ....102 C6
Gosford Mews TS2 ....214 C4
Gosford St TS2 ....215 A4
Gosforth Ave TS10 ....107 D6
Goshawk Rd TS26 ....63 D1
Gough Cl TS1 ....214 B2
Gouldsmith Gdns DL1 ..133 E5
Goulton Cl TS15 ....156 F5
Goundry Ave SR2 ....19 A6
Gower Cl TS1 ....214 B3
Gower Wlk TS26 ....63 E1
Gowland Sq SR7 ....28 B3
Grace Cl TS25 ....90 E7
Grace Ct
Annfield Plain DH9 ....12 E3
2 Darlington DL3 ....132 F2
Graffenberg St TS10 ..107 D7
Grafton Cl TS14 ....143 E3
Graham Ct
1 Darlington DL1 ....133 B1
Sacriston DH7 ....23 C3
Graham Sports Ctr The (Univ of Durham) DH1 ....44 E7
Graham St Hartlepool TS24 64 E1
Liverton TS13 ....127 A1
Stanhope DL13 ....206 D3
Graham Terr DH6 ....36 B5
Graham Way The SR7 ..29 B6
Grainger Cl TS16 ....137 B2
Grainger St
Bishop Auckland DL14 ....67 B1
Darlington DL1 ....152 A8
Hartlepool TS24 ....77 B7
Spennymoor DL16 ....56 B1
Grammar School La TS15 ....156 B5
Grampian Ave DH2 ....16 B2
Grampian Ct DH9 ....12 E3
Grampian Dr SR8 ....49 B5
Grampian Rd
Billingham TS23 ....102 D4
Skelton TS12 ....125 C3
Grampian Way DL17 ....83 A8
Granaries The DH4 ....26 B8
Granary Ct DH8 ....11 B3
Granary The TS22 ....87 C2
Granby Terr TS28 ....48 E1
Grand View DH6 ....45 F8
Grange Ave
Auckland Park DL14 ....80 E6
Billingham TS23 ....102 E1
Easington SR8 ....39 B3
Hartlepool TS26 ....76 F6
Hurworth-on-T DL2 ....168 A8
Stockton-on-T TS18 ....212 B4
Grange Bank DL15 ....66 A4
Grange Bsns Ctr The TS23 ....102 F2
Grange Cl Eston TS6 ....121 E5
Hartlepool TS26 ....76 E6
Peterlee SR8 ....49 D8
Grange Cotts DL12 ....200 C2
Grange Cres Coxhoe DH6 .58 A4
Marton TS7 ....140 D2
Grange Ct
Newton Aycliffe DL5 ....96 E8
West Pelton DH2 ....15 B5
Grange Est
Kibblesworth NE11 ....8 C6
Lazenby TS6 ....122 C4
Grange Farm TS8 ....140 B3
Grange Farm Rd TS6 ..121 E5
Grange Hill DL14 ....81 A7
Grange La TS13 ....127 E3
Grange Park Cres DH6 ..57 E8
Grange Prim Sch TS25 ..89 D7
Grange Rd
Darlington DL1,DL3 ....151 E7
Durham DH1 ....35 C4
Hartlepool TS26 ....76 F6
Middlesbrough TS1 ....214 C3
Middlesbrough TS1 ....215 A3
Stanley DH9 ....13 D6
Stockton-on-T TS20 ....118 B7
Thornaby-on-T TS17 ....138 C8
Grange St
9 Consett DH8 ....177 D4
Pelton DH2 ....15 E7
Grange Terr
Chester le Street DH2 ....15 D4
Kibblesworth NE11 ....8 C6
Medomsley DH8 ....4 B1
Shotton Colliery DH6 ....48 C7
Trimdon TS29 ....59 D3
Whorlton DL12 ....200 C2
Grange The
Newton Aycliffe DL5 ....82 D2
Summerhouse DL2 ....110 A3
Tanfield Lea DH9 ....13 C8
Grange View
Billingham TS23 ....102 C7
Coundongate DL14 ....80 F8
East Rainton DH5 ....26 D5
Grange Wood TS8 ....139 F3
Grangefield Rd TS18 ..212 B3
Grangefield Sch TS18 ..212 A3
Grangefields TS12 ....126 A4
Grangeside
Darlington DL3 ....151 D7
Redworth DL5 ....95 C4
Grangetown Prim Sch TS6 ....121 E5
Grangetown Station Rd TS6 ....121 E8
Grangeville Ave TS19 ..117 A3
Grant Bank DL2 ....201 B4
Grant St Peterlee SR8 ....50 A7
Redcar TS10 ....107 C7
Grantham Ave
Hartlepool TS26 ....77 A5
Seaham SR7 ....29 B6
Grantham Gn TS4 ....140 B5
Grantham Rd TS20 ....101 F1
Grantley Ave TS3 ....121 A3
Grantly DL3 ....132 C3
Granton Cl DL3 ....132 B1
Grants Cres SR7 ....29 D7
Granville Ave
Annfield Plain DH9 ....12 F4
Hartlepool TS26 ....76 F6
3 Shildon DL4 ....80 F1
Granville Cl DL4 ....80 F1
Granville Dr DL17 ....83 A8
Granville Gr TS20 ....118 B6
Granville Rd
Bishop Auckland DL14 ....80 A6
Eston TS6 ....121 D5
Middlesbrough TS1 ....214 C1
Peterlee SR8 ....49 F5
Granville Terr
Binchester DL14 ....67 F5
Redcar TS10 ....107 E7
Wheatley Hill DH6 ....47 F3
Granwood Rd TS6 ....121 F1
Grape La DH1 ....210 C2
Grasby Cl TS3 ....121 A1
Grasmere Birtley DH3 ....9 E2
Spennymoor DL16 ....55 E2
Grasmere Ave
Bishop Auckland DL14 ....79 B1
Easington Lane DH5 ....37 C8
Middlesbrough TS5 ....139 C6
Grasmere Cres
Blaydon NE21 ....2 B8
Skelton TS12 ....125 B2
Grasmere Dr TS6 ....121 C2
Grasmere Gr DL15 ....52 F3
Grasmere Rd
Chester le Street DH2 ....16 B1
Darlington DL1 ....152 B8
Ferryhill DL17 ....69 F5
Peterlee SR8 ....49 E7
Redcar TS10 ....107 C5
Stockton-on-T TS18 ....212 B3
Grasmere St 4 TS26 ....77 A4
Grasmere Terr
Murton SR7 ....28 D2
South Hetton DH6 ....38 B7
Stanley DH9 ....13 D4
Grass Croft TS21 ....136 A5
Grass St DL1 ....133 A4
Grassdale DH1 ....35 D3
Grasshill Cswy DL13 ....185 A8
Grassholm Rd TS20 ....118 B7
Grassholme 12 DL1 ....152 C8
Grassholme Cl DH8 ....11 A1
Grassholme La DL12 ....197 C8
Grassholme Pl 3 DL5 ....96 A7
Grassholme Rd TS26 ....76 C6
Grassholme Way TS16 ..137 A1
Grassington Gn TS17 ....157 B6
Grassington Rd TS4 ....140 A8
Grasslees NE38 ....16 F8
Grassmere Mews DH8 ....11 D4
Gravel Wlks 1 DH5 ....26 F8
Gray Ave
Chester le Street DH2 ....16 B2
Durham DH1 ....34 B5
Murton SR7 ....28 C3
Sherburn DH6 ....35 F2
Gray Ct SR8 ....39 D4
Gray La DL12 ....209 C5
Gray Sq TS28 ....60 E8
Gray St Consett DH8 ....10 E3
Eldon Lane DL14 ....80 F4
Hartlepool TS24 ....77 A7
Middlesbrough TS2 ....215 A4
Gray Terr DH9 ....13 C5
Gray's Rd TS18 ....212 B3
Gray's Terr DH1 ....210 A2
Graygarth Rd TS3 ....120 C2
Graylands NE38 ....16 E8
Grayson Rd DL16 ....68 D6
Graythorp Ind Est TS25 ..90 D4
Graythwaite DH2 ....15 F3
Great Auk TS14 ....143 B4
Great Ayton Sta TS9 ..161 C2
Great Gates DL14 ....80 C8
Greatham CE Prim Sch TS25 ....89 E3
Greatham Cl TS5 ....139 D4
Greatham Hospl Almshouses TS25 ....89 E4
Greatham St TS25 ....77 C3
Greathead Cres DL5 ....96 E6
Green Bank Terr TS12 ..145 C7
Green Cl TS7 ....141 A2
Green Cres DH6 ....58 A4
Green Ct Durham DH1 ..211 C3
Esh DH7 ....31 F4
Green Dragon Mus* TS18 ....213 B3
Green Gates Prim Sch TS10 ....107 B2
Green Head DL15 ....52 B1
Green La
Barnard Castle DL12 ....209 D6
Bishop Auckland DL14 ....80 B3
Darlington DL1 ....133 B8
Darlington DL1 ....133 C7
Durham DH1 ....211 B2
Durham,Gilesgate DH1 ..211 C3
Eldon Lane DL14 ....80 F4
Haswell DH6 ....37 D4
Holmside DH7 ....21 E7
Hunwick DL15 ....66 B5
Hutton Magna DL12 ....205 D8
Marske-by-t-S TS11 ....108 A3
Middlesbrough TS5 ....139 C8
Newby TS7,TS8 ....160 B4
Newton Aycliffe DL5 ....97 A2
Redcar TS10 ....107 F2
Satley DL13 ....183 C7
Satley DL8,DL13 ....183 C8
Seaton SR7 ....27 F6
Shildon DL4 ....81 A2
Spennymoor DL16 ....56 C1
Stockton-on-T TS19 ....117 E6
Thornaby-on-T TS17 ....138 C6
Wingate DH6,TS29 ....59 E8
Yarm TS15 ....156 C3
Green Lane Cvn Site DL14 ....80 B3
Green Lane Ind Est DL16 56 C2
Green Lane Prim Sch TS5 ....139 D8
Green Lea DH7 ....23 B1
Green Leas TS21 ....116 C8
Green Rd TS12 ....125 B2
Green Rise DL16 ....54 E1
Green Rising DL15 ....66 D5
Green Scar TS10 ....107 E2
Green St Consett DH8 ....10 F3
Consett, Shotley Bridge DH8 ....10 C7
Darlington DL1 ....133 B1
Hartlepool TS25 ....77 C4
Leadgate DH8 ....11 C4
Seaham SR7 ....29 D7
Green Terr TS25 ....90 E8
Green The
Barnard Castle DL12 ....199 F4
Billingham TS23 ....102 D1
Bishop Middleham DL17 ..71 C4
Bishopton TS21 ....115 C7
Brafferton DL1 ....113 A7
Chester le Street DH2 ....16 B3
Chopwell NE17 ....4 B8
Cleasby DL2 ....150 E7
Cockfield DL13 ....195 E3
Cornforth DL17 ....57 E2
Dalton-on-T DL2 ....168 B5
Eggleston DL12 ....193 E2
Elwick TS27 ....75 D5
Evenwood DL14 ....92 D6
Frosterley DL13 ....188 A7
Greatham TS25 ....89 E4
Hawthorn SR7 ....39 B7
Headlam DL2 ....201 D6
Hett DH6 ....56 E6
High Coniscliffe DL2 ....130 F3
High Shincliffe DH1 ....45 B4
2 Houghton-le-S DH5 ....26 F8
Hurworth-on-T DL2 ....152 D1
Kimblesworth DH2 ....23 F4
Kirklevington TS15 ....172 D8
Longnewton TS21 ....136 A5
Newton Aycliffe DL5 ....96 E1
Peterlee SR8 ....49 A4
Piercebridge DL2 ....130 B4
Redcar TS10 ....106 E4
Rowlands Gill NE39 ....1 C2
Saltburn-by-t-S TS12 ....125 B5
Seamer TS9 ....158 F1
Seaton Carew TS25 ....77 E1
Spennymoor,Tudhoe DL16 ..56 A3
Spennymoor,Tudhoe Village DL16 ....55 F4
Stapleton DL2 ....151 A5
Stockton-on-T TS20 ....102 B1
Stockton-on-T TS20 ....118 A8
Thornaby-on-T TS17 ....138 C5
Thornaby-on-T TS17 ....138 C6
Trimdon TS29 ....59 E1
Witton Park DL14 ....66 A1
Wolviston TS22 ....102 C8
Green Vale Gr TS19 ....117 A2
Green Way TS7 ....141 A2
Green's Bank DH9 ....15 A7
Green's Beck Rd TS18 ..117 C1
Green's La TS18 ....117 C1
Greenacre Cl TS9 ....160 F1
Greenacres Pelton DH2 ..15 D7
Stainton TS8 ....139 B1
Greenacres Cl 3 TS11 .108 C1
Greenacres Rd DH8 ....10 D5
Greenbank DL12 ....193 E2
Greenbank Ave TS5 ....119 B2
Greenbank Cl TS29 ....72 D8
Greenbank Ct
Darlington DL3 ....132 E3
Hartlepool TS26 ....76 E6
Greenbank Rd DL3 ....132 E3
Greenbank St 4 DH3 ....16 D4
Greenbank Terr TS15 ..173 F1
Greencroft Redcar TS10 .107 A2
South Hetton DH6 ....38 B7
Greencroft Cl DL3 ....132 D1
Greencroft Ct DL3 ....151 E8
Greencroft Ind Est DH9 ..12 E2
Greencroft Ind Pk DH9 ..12 E2
Greencroft Parkway DH9 12 F2
Greencroft Rd DH8 ....177 E4
Greencroft Sch DH9 ....12 E4
Greencroft Terr DH9 ....12 E3
Greencroft Wlk TS3 ....140 E8
Greendale Gdns DH5 ....26 F2
Greenfield Cl DL2 ....152 C2
Greenfield Cotts DL15 ..52 F4
Greenfield Dr TS16 ....137 B1
Greenfield Sch Comm & Arts Coll DL5 ....95 F7
Greenfield St DL16 ....54 E1
Greenfield Terr DH9 ....12 F4
Greenfield Way DL5 ....95 F7
Greenfields
Bishop Auckland DL14 ....79 A4
Cotherstone DL12 ....198 F6
7 Ferryhill DL17 ....70 A6
Ouston DH2 ....9 A2
Greenfields Ind Est DL14 .79 F4
Greenfields Rd DL14 ....79 D5
Greenfields Way TS18 ..117 A2
Greenfinch Cl
Hartlepool TS26 ....63 E1
Washington NE38 ....9 F3
Greenfoot Cvn Site DL13 ....206 A3
Greenford NE11 ....8 D6
Greenford La DH2,NE11 ..8 F6
Greenford Wlk TS3 ....121 A1
Greengates La DL12 ....193 B3
Greenham Cl TS3 ....121 A1
Greenhead Crook DL15 ..52 E1
Washington NE38 ....9 F4
Greenhead Cl TS8 ....139 E3
Greenhill Rd DL5 ....95 C1
Greenhills DL16 ....54 E1
Greenhills Est TS28 ....48 E1
Greenhills Terr DH6 ....47 F3
Greenhow Cl SR2 ....18 F5
Greenhow Gr TS25 ....90 E8
Greenhow Rd TS3 ....120 C2
Greenhow Wlk TS10 ....107 C3
Greenland Ave TS5 ....119 A1
Greenland Jun & Inf Schs DH9 ....13 D4
Greenland Rd Esh DH7 ..31 D4
Hartlepool TS24 ....77 C8
Greenlands
Hutton Rudby TS15 ....173 F3
Stanley DH9 ....13 D4
Greenlands Rd TS10 ..107 E5
Greenlea TS27 ....75 C5
Greenlea Cl NE39 ....1 A3
Greenlee Cl 5 TS17 ....157 A7
Greenlee Garth DL5 ....96 A8
Greenmount Rd DL3 ....151 E8
Greenock Cl TS11 ....123 F6
Greenock Rd TS25 ....89 E8
Greenrigg Cl DL3 ....132 C7
Greenrigg La DL12 ....193 A1
Greens Gr TS18 ....117 C1
Greens Valley Dr TS18 ..117 C1
Greensfield Cl DL3 ....132 C7
Greenshank Cl TS26 ....63 D1
Greenside Greatham TS25 .89 E4
Ingleby Barwick TS17 ....138 B1
Normanby TS6 ....141 C7
Greenside Ave SR8 ....49 F7
Greenside Cl TS21 ....72 D5
Greenside Ct DL2 ....152 C1
Greenside Pl DL15 ....53 A2
Greenstones Rd TS10 ..107 E3
Greentree La DH9 ....12 E5
Greenway Eston TS6 ....121 E2
Ingleby Barwick TS17 ....138 B1
Greenway Ct TS3 ....120 F3
Greenway The
Middlesbrough TS3 ....121 A2
Middleton St George DL2 .153 E7
Greenways Consett DH8 .177 E4
Willington DL15 ....53 E2
Wolsingham DL13 ....207 D6
Greenways Ct 2 DH8 ..177 E4
Greenwell Rd DL5 ....96 D7
Greenwell St DL1 ....152 A8
Greenwell Terr DL13 ..188 A7
Greenwells Garth DL14 ..81 C8
Greenwood Ave
Burnhope DH7 ....21 D4
Houghton-le-S DH4 ....26 C8
Middlesbrough TS5 ....139 D8
Greenwood Cl DH6 ....48 A3
Greenwood Cotts DH6 ..47 C4
Greenwood Rd
Billingham TS23 ....103 A3
Hartlepool TS24 ....77 B7
Stockton-on-T TS18 ....117 C1
Gregory Ct DL5 ....96 D5
Gregory Terr
4 Fence Houses DH4 ....26 A8
10 Ferryhill DL17 ....70 A6
Gregson St DH7 ....23 C3
Gregson Terr Seaham SR7 .18 F1
South Hetton DH6 ....38 B6
Grendale Ct TS13 ....127 D1
Grendon Gdns DL2 ....153 E8
Grenville Cl TS11 ....124 E8
Grenville Rd TS17 ....138 D4
Gresham Cl DL1 ....133 B5
Gresham Rd TS1 ....214 C2
Gresley Rd SR8 ....49 A6
Greta Ave TS25 ....77 A2
Greta Bridge Bank DL12 ....205 A8
Greta Pl DH7 ....20 F3
Greta Rd
Barnard Castle DL12 ....209 D6
Redcar TS10 ....107 A5
Skelton TS12 ....125 D3
Stockton-on-T TS20 ....118 A7
Greta St
Middlesbrough TS1 ....214 B2
Saltburn-by-t-S TS12 ....125 C6
Greta St N DH2 ....15 C6
Greta St S DH2 ....15 C6
Gretton Ave TS4 ....140 B6
Greville Way DL5 ....96 E6
Grewburn La DL13 ....195 B4
Grewgrass La
New Marske TS11 ....123 E7
Redcar TS10 ....107 E1
Grey Coll (Univ of Durham) DH1 ....44 C7
Grey Gables DH7 ....43 C5
Grey Gdns DL14 ....81 B8
Grey Ridges DH7 ....43 C4
Grey St
Bishop Auckland DL14 ....80 B8
Crook DL15 ....52 F4
Darlington DL1 ....133 B3
Newfield DL14 ....67 B7
4 Stockton-on-T TS20 ..118 B6
Grey Terr 3 Ferryhill DL17 70 B5
10 Ryhope SR2 ....18 F6
Grey Towers Dr TS7 ....141 A1
Greyfriars Cl DL3 ....132 A1
Greylands Ave TS20 ....118 B7
Greylingstadt Terr DH9 ..14 A3
Greymouth Cl TS18 ....117 C1
Greys Ct TS17 ....157 B8
Greystoke Gr TS10 ....107 C2
Greystoke Rd TS10 ....107 C2
Greystoke Wlk TS10 ....107 C2
Greystone Rd TS6 ....122 A4
Greystones DH6 ....47 C7
Greystones Dr DL3 ....132 C3
Greywood Cl TS27 ....63 C5
Gribdale Rd TS3 ....120 D2
Gribdale Terr TS9 ....161 F3
Grice Ct DL2 ....200 F7
Griffin Rd TS4 ....120 A2
Griffiths Cl TS15 ....156 B3
Griffiths Rd TS6 ....121 E4
Grimston Wlk TS3 ....120 B2
Grimwood Ave TS3 ....120 E4
Grindon Ct DL5 ....82 E1
Grindon Way DL5 ....96 D1
Grinkle Ave TS3 ....140 D8
Grinkle Ct TS14 ....143 E5
Grinkle La Liverton TS13 .147 F2
Loftus TS13 ....148 A6
Grinkle Park Cotts TS13 ....148 A4
Grinkle Rd TS10 ....106 F5
Grinstead Way DH1 ....35 D5
Grinton Park Way 4 DL1 ....152 C7
Grinton Rd TS18 ....137 B8
Grisedale Cl TS5 ....139 C4
Grisedale Cres
Egglescliffe TS16 ....156 C8
Eston TS6 ....121 F4
Grisedale Rd SR8 ....49 E6
Gritten Sq TS24 ....64 C2
Groat Ave DL5 ....96 E4
Groat Dr DL5 ....96 E5
Groat Rd DL5 ....96 E4
Groat Way DL5 ....96 E4
Grosmont DH3 ....25 A7
Grosmont Cl TS10 ....107 C2
Grosmont Dr TS23 ....102 C5
Grosmont Pl TS6 ....121 F3
Grosmont Rd Eston TS6 .121 F3
Hartlepool TS25 ....90 E8
Gross St TS23 ....103 D2
Grosvenor Cl DL13 ....206 C3
Grosvenor Ct TS17 ....157 B7
Grosvenor Gdns
Eston TS6 ....121 D1
13 Hartlepool TS26 ....77 A6
Grosvenor Pl TS14 ....143 D4
Grosvenor Rd
Billingham TS22 ....102 C5
Middlesbrough TS5 ....119 C1
Stockton-on-T TS19 ....117 C2
Grosvenor Sq TS14 ....143 D4
Grosvenor St
Darlington DL1 ....152 A8
5 Hartlepool TS26 ....77 A6
Grosvenor Terr
Carlin How TS13 ....126 F3
Consett DH8 ....11 A3
Trimdon TS29 ....59 F5
Grove Bank TS15 ....172 C8
Grove Cl TS26 ....76 F5
Grove Cotts 9 DH3 ....9 C4
Grove Ct Hett DH6 ....56 E5
Shotton Colliery DH6 ....48 C5
Grove Hill TS13 ....127 A4
Grove Pk DL12 ....209 C6
Grove Prim Sch The DH8 10 C1
Grove Rd
Bishop Auckland DL14 ....80 A7
Brandon DH7 ....43 A3
Middlesbrough TS3 ....215 C2
Redcar TS10 ....107 D6
Skinningrove TS13 ....127 A4
Tow Law DL13 ....183 D2
Grove St Durham DH1 ..210 B2

Grove St *continued*
Stockton-on-T TS18 212 C1
Grove Terr
Brandon DH1,DH7 43 E6
Burnopfield NE16 6 B6
Stockton-on-T TS20 118 B6
Grove The Burnhope DH7 21 D4
Chilton DL17 82 F7
Cornforth DL17 57 E1
Coxhoe DH6 58 A3
Durham DH1 210 A4
Easington SR8 39 A4
Fir Tree DL15 52 A1
Greatham TS25 89 E4
Guisborough TS14 143 B2
Hartlepool TS26 76 F5
Houghton-le-S DH5 26 D6
Marton TS7 140 E5
Middlesbrough TS5 139 D3
Rowlands Gill NE39 1 F1
Ryhope SR2 18 F6
★ Woodland DL13 194 E8
Yarm TS15 156 C4
Groves St TS24 77 F8
Groves The TS18 212 C1
Grundales Dr TS11 108 C1
Gudmunsen Ave DL14 80 A4
Guernsey Wlk TS14 143 D3
Guildford Cl DL1 133 E5
Guildford Ct TS6 141 D7
Guildford Rd
Billingham TS23 102 C5
Normanby TS6 141 D7
Guillemot Cl TS26 63 D1
Guisborough 8 TS4 120 B1
Guisborough Ct 9 TS6 121 F2
Guisborough Forest Visitor Ctr★ TS14 142 E3
Guisborough General & Maternity Hospl TS14 143 E5
Guisborough Mus★ TS14 143 E5
Guisborough Priory★ TS14 143 F5
Guisborough Rd
Great Ayton TS9 160 F3
Moorsholm TS12 146 B1
Nunthorpe TS7 141 B2
Saltburn-by-t-S TS12 125 B6
Thornaby-on-T TS17 138 D7
Guisborough Sports Ctr TS14 143 F6
Guisborough St TS6 121 F2
Guiseley Way TS16 137 B3
Gullane Cl DH9 14 B6
Gulliver Rd TS25 76 D2
Gully Rd TS28 60 E8
Gunn La DL5 96 F6
Gunnergate Cl TS12 125 A7
Gunnergate La TS7, TS8 140 C2
Gunners Vale TS22 87 A3
Gunnerside Rd TS19 117 A3
Gunnerton Cl DL3 132 C7
Gurlish Terr DL14 68 B1
Gurney Pease Prim Sch DL1 133 B4
Gurney St Darlington DL1 133 A4
Middlesbrough TS1 215 A3
New Marske TS11 124 A7
Gurney Terr DL14 81 A5
Gurney Valley DL14 81 A5
Gurney Way DL5 96 D4
Guthire Wlk 6 TS25 89 D8
Guthrie Ave TS5 139 A8
Guthrum Pl DL5 82 C1
Gwynn Cl TS19 117 A4
Gypsy La Marton TS7 140 E3
Nunthorpe TS7 141 B4
Gypsy Lane Halt TS7 141 A4

H

Habgood Dr DH1 35 A1
Hackforth Rd TS18 137 B8
Hackness Wlk TS5 139 E6
Hackworth Cl
Ferryhill DL17 69 E5
Newton Aycliffe DL5 96 E5
Shildon DL4 95 A8
Hackworth Ct TS18 213 A4
Hackworth Ind Pk DL4 94 F8
Hackworth Rd
Blackhall Colliery TS27 50 D4
Easington SR8 38 F1
Hackworth St
Ferryhill DL17 69 E5
Shildon DL4 81 A1
Hadasia Gdns TS19 117 C3
Haddon Rd TS23 102 C5
Haddon St TS1 215 A2
Hadleigh Cl TS21 85 A5
Hadleigh Cres TS4 120 A1
Hadlow Wlk 1 TS3 120 D2
Hadnall Cl TS5 139 A6
Hadrian Ave DH3 16 D5
Hadrian Ct
Darlington DL3 151 E8
Station Town TS28 60 E6
Hadrians Way DH8 3 E3
Hadston Cl TS10 107 D2
Haffron Ave TS18 213 B4
Hag Bridge Cvn Site DL13 180 F1
Hagg La Byers Green DL16 55 A1
Byers Green DL14 54 F1
Hagg Rd DL16 67 F8
Haggitt Hill La TS15 172 E1
Haggs La DL14 94 B8
Haig Cres DH1 35 A1
Haig St Darlington DL3 132 F5
Ferryhill DL17 70 C4
Haig Terr DL17 69 E6
Haigh Terr DH1 35 A1
Hailsham Ave TS17 138 D1
Haldane Gr TS25 89 E8
Haldon Pl SR8 49 B5
Hale Rd TS23 102 E6
Hale Rise SR8 49 E6
Half Moon La
Spennymoor DL16 56 C1
Spennymoor DL16 69 B8
Halidon Way TS23 102 F6
Halifax Cl TS11 108 B1
Halifax Pl 9 SR2 18 F6
Halifax Rd TS17 138 D4
Hall Ave DH7 33 A2
Hall Cl Carlton TS21 116 C8
Marske-by-t-S TS11 108 C1
Seaton SR7 18 D1
West Rainton DH4 26 A2
Hall Cl The TS7 141 A7
Hall Cres SR8 39 F1
Hall Dene Way SR7 18 F2
Hall Dr TS5 139 D6
Hall Farm DH1 44 F6
Hall Farm Ct TS29 59 D1
Hall Farm Rd SR3 18 A5
Hall Garth Comp Sch TS5 139 D6
Hall Gdns DH6 36 A1
Hall Grounds TS13 127 C1
Hall Hill Farm★ DH7 183 E6
Hall La Haswell DH6 37 F3
Heighington DL5 95 D2
High Shincliffe DH1 44 F5
Houghton-le-S DH5 26 F7
West Rainton DH4 26 A2
Hall Lane Est DL15 53 F2
Hall Lea TS21 85 A7
Hall Moor Cl TS15 172 D8
Hall Rd Consett DH8 10 C2
Esh DH7 31 F4
Hall St DL12 209 C5
Hall Terr DL15 54 A2
Hall View DL15 66 D7
Hall View Gdns DL15 65 D8
Hall View Gr DL3 132 A3
Hall Wlks SR8 39 A3
Hall's Bldgs DH9 14 E1
Hallam Rd SR8 49 D7
Hallcroft Cl TS23 102 D1
Hallfield Cl SR3 18 A5
Hallfield Dr SR8 39 A3
Hallgarth Consett DH8 10 C1
Kirk Merrington DL16 69 A3
Hallgarth Cl TS5 139 C4
Hallgarth La DH6 36 B5
Hallgarth Rd TS29 72 D8
Hallgarth St
Durham DH1 211 A1
Sherburn DH6 35 F1
Hallgarth Terr
Ferryhill DL17 70 A6
Lanchester DH7 20 F3
Hallgarth The DH1 211 A1
Hallgarth View
Durham DH1 211 A1
High Pittington DH6 36 C5
Hallgarth Villas DH6 36 A1
Hallgate Cl TS18 137 B8
Halliday Gr DH7 43 D5
Hallifield St TS20 118 B6
Hallimond Rd DL14 79 D7
Hallington Head DL5 95 F7
Halls Cl TS27 50 D3
Halnaby Ave DL3 131 F2
Halton Cl TS23 102 E8
Halton Ct
6 Billingham TS23 102 E8
Middlesbrough TS3 121 A3
Halton Rd DH1 34 D5
Halyard The TS3 215 C4
Hambledon Ave DH2 16 B2
Hambledon Cres 3 TS12 125 C3
Hambledon Pl SR8 49 A5
Hambledon Rd TS5 119 C1
Hambleton Ave TS10 107 B3
Hambleton Cres TS11 124 E8
Hambleton Ct DL5 96 A8
Hambleton Dr SR7 29 B8
Hambleton Gr 4 DL1 133 C6
Hambleton Rd
Coundon DL14 81 C8
Nunthorpe TS7 141 B3
Hambleton Sq TS23 102 C4
Hambleton Way DL17 83 A8
Hambletonian Yd TS18 213 A2
Hamilton Ct
Shotton Colliery DH6 48 C6
Thorpe Thewles TS21 100 E3
Hamilton Dr DL1 133 C7
Hamilton Gr Eston TS6 121 B3
Redcar TS10 107 A6
Hamilton Rd
Hartlepool TS25 89 E8
Stockton-on-T TS19 117 F5
Hamilton Row DH7 41 B6
Hamilton St SR8 49 F7
Hamilton Terr DH7 23 B6
Hammer Square Bank DH9 7 F1
Hammermill La DH8 176 E8
Hammond Cl TS7 140 C3
Hammond Dr DL1 151 F6
Hampden St TS6 121 A5
Hampden Way TS17 138 D4
Hampshire Gn TS20 118 C7
Hampshire Pl
Bishop Auckland DL14 80 C5
Peterlee SR8 49 B7
Hampshire Rd DH1 35 C3
Hampstead Gdns TS26 76 E6
Hampstead Gr TS6 141 C7
Hampstead Rd TS6 141 C7
Hampstead The TS10 107 E3
Hampton Cl
Annfield Plain DH9 12 E4
Nunthorpe TS7 141 A3
Hampton Ct DH3 16 D7
Hampton Gr TS10 107 F5
Hampton Rd TS18 212 B2
Hamsteels Bank DH7 31 A6
Hamsteels La DH7 31 B6
Hamsteels Prim Sch DH7 31 C1
Hamsterley Cl DH3 25 B7
Hamsterley Cres DH1 34 D6
Hamsterley Ct 6 SR3 18 A6
Hamsterley Dr DL15 52 D3
Hamsterley Forest North Forest Dr★ DL13 189 A1
Hamsterley Forest S★ DL13 194 D7
Hamsterley Forest Visitor Ctr★ DL13 189 B2
Hamsterley Forest, Forest Wlk★ DL13 189 A1
Hamsterley Gdns DH9 12 F4
Hamsterley Prim Sch DL13 189 D2
Hamsterley Rd
Newton Aycliffe DL5 96 B8
Stockton-on-T TS19 117 C6
Hamsterley St DL3 132 E4
Hamsterley Way TS12 125 C3
Hanbury Cl TS17 138 B1
Handale Cl TS14 144 A4
Handel Terr DH6 47 E2
Handley Cl TS18 137 F5
Handley Cres DH5 26 C4
Handley Cross DH8 4 C2
Handley St SR8 49 F7
Hangingstone La DH8, DH9 12 C3
Hankin Rd TS3 215 C2
Hannah's Meadow Nature Reserve★ DL12 197 D5
Hanover Cl DL3 132 A1
Hanover Ct
Bishop Auckland DL14 80 C6
Durham DH1 210 B2
Stockton-on-T TS20 117 F8
Hanover Gdns
Bishop Auckland DL14 80 C6
Crook DL15 53 A3
Middlesbrough TS5 119 C1
Hanover Ho 5 TS12 125 C8
Hanover Par TS20 117 F8
Hanover Point TS20 117 F8
Hanover Wlk NE21 2 A8
Hansard Cl DL5 95 F4
Hanson Ct TS10 107 C6
Hanson Gr TS3 120 F3
Hanson St TS10 107 C6
Hansons Bldgs 6 DL2 153 F8
Harap Rd
Fishburn TS21,TS29 72 B7
Kelloe DL17 71 E8
Harbinson Cl TS21 72 C5
Harborne Gdns TS5 139 D4
Harbottle Cl TS17 157 A7
Harbour Wlk
Hartlepool TS24 77 C7
Seaham SR7 29 C7
Harcourt Rd TS6 121 A5
Harcourt St
Darlington DL3 132 F4
Hartlepool TS26 76 F6
Hardale Gr TS10 107 A4
Harding Row TS20 118 B7
Harding Terr DL3 132 E4
Hardinge Rd DL5 96 D8
Hardings DL12 198 D7
Hardisty Cres DL14 80 A5
Hardknott Gr TS10 107 B5
Hardwick Ave TS5 139 C7
Hardwick Cl DL1 133 D6
Hardwick Ct
Hartlepool TS26 76 C4
Newton Aycliffe DL5 96 D8
Hardwick Hall Ctry Pk★ TS21 84 F7
Hardwick Prim Sch TS19 117 B8
Hardwick Rd
Billingham TS23 102 F5
Sedgefield TS21 85 A7
South Bank TS6 121 A6
Stockton-on-T TS19 117 C7
Hardwick St
Blackhall Colliery TS27 50 C3
Peterlee SR8 50 A6
Hardy Gr TS23 102 D7
Hardy St SR7 29 D7
Hardy Terr
Annfield Plain DH9 13 C4
Crook DL15 52 E4
Hare Law Sch DH9 12 E6
Hare's Bldgs DH2 15 C5
Harebell Cl
Ingleby Barwick TS17 138 B2
Skelton TS12 125 E2
Spennymoor DL16 56 B3
Harebell Mdws DL5 82 D2
Harehills Rd TS5 119 B1
Harelaw DH2 15 D6
Harelaw Gdns DH9 12 E6
Harelaw Ind Est DH9 12 E7
Haresfield Way TS17 157 B8
Hareshaw Cl TS17 157 A7
Hareson Rd DL5 96 A8
Harestones TS22 87 B3
Harewood 9 TS4 120 B1
Harewood Cres TS19 117 B5
Harewood Gr DL3 151 E8
Harewood Hill DL3 151 E8
Harewood Jun Sch TS17 138 D8
Harewood Rd TS17 118 D1
Harewood St TS1 214 C1
Harewood Terr DL3 151 E8
Harewood Way TS10 107 E3
Harford St TS1 214 B1
Hargill Dr NE38 17 A8
Hargill Gr DL15 65 D7
Hargill Haven DL15 65 E7
Hargill Rd DL15 65 D7
Hargreave Terr DL1 133 A1
Harker Cl TS15 156 B4
Harker St 5 DL4 80 F1
Harland Pl 1 TS20 118 B7
Harle St DH7 43 D3
Harlech Cl TS6 121 E3
Harlech Ct TS17 156 F8
Harlech Gr TS11 124 A6
Harlech Wlk TS26 76 E8
Harley Gr DL1 133 E6
Harley Terr DH6 35 F2
Harlow Cres TS17 138 E6
Harlsey Cres TS18 137 C8
Harlsey Gr TS18 137 C8
Harlsey Rd TS18 137 C8
Harmire Cl DL12 209 C7
Harmire Ent Pk DL12 209 C8
Harmire Rd DL12 209 C7
Harold Wilson Dr TS27 49 F1
Harpenden Wlk TS3 120 D2
Harper Bglws DH6 47 E1
Harper Par TS18 137 D8
Harper Terr TS18 137 D8
Harperley Gdns DH9 12 E5
Harperley La DH9 13 B7
Harperley Rd DH9 12 F5
Harperley Terr DL15 52 A1
Harpers Terr DL2 134 E1
Harpington View TS21 84 C1
Harras Bank DH3 9 C3
Harraton Terr
15 Birtley DH3 9 C4
Bournmoor DH3 17 C7
Harrier Cl Hartlepool TS26 76 D8
Thornaby-on-T TS17 138 C5
Harringay Cres DL1 133 E3
Harris Gr TS25 89 E8
Harris St Darlington DL1 152 D8
Middlesbrough TS1 214 C3
Harris Wlk TS14 143 D3
Harrison Cl Peterlee SR8 49 E5
Shildon DL4 95 A7
Harrison Cres DL14 79 F4
Harrison Ct DH3 9 C3
Harrison Garth DH6 35 F2
Harrison Ho DH1 210 B2
Harrison Pl TS24 63 F2
Harrison St
Middlesbrough TS3 120 C4
Tow Law DL13 183 D1
Harrison Terr
Darlington DL3 132 E4
Easington SR8 39 D4
Harrogate Cres TS5 119 E2
Harrogate Terr SR7 28 C3
Harrow Gate Prim Sch TS19 117 C7
Harrow Rd
Middlesbrough TS5 139 D8
Stockton-on-T TS18 212 B2
Harrow St TS25 77 A3
Harrowgate Hill Inf Sch DL3 133 A6
Harrowgate Hill Jun Sch
Darlington DL3 132 F6
Darlington DL3 133 A6
Harrowgate La TS19 117 A7
Harrowgate Village DL1 133 A8
Harry Dack Inf Sch TS13 127 B1
Harry St DL3 132 F5
Harsley Wlk TS3 120 D2
Hart Ave TS26 76 E7
Hart Cl TS19 117 D6
Hart Cres TS27 50 F1
Hart La TS26 76 E7
Hart Lane Cotts TS26 76 F7
Hart Pastures TS27 63 A2
Hart Prim Sch TS27 62 F3
Hart Rd TS27 63 D3
Hart View TS29 72 E8
Hartbrigg La DL14 78 E3
Hartburn Ave TS18 212 B1
Hartburn Ct TS5 139 C5
Hartburn La TS18 212 B1
Hartburn Prim Sch TS18 212 A1
Hartburn Village TS18 137 D8
Hartbushes TS28 61 A4
Harter Cl TS7 141 A2
Hartford Rd DL3 151 D8
Hartforth Ave TS5 139 C4
Harthope Cl NE38 16 F8
Harthope Gr DL14 79 F5
Harthope Rd DL13 185 E8
Hartington Cl TS17 138 C8
Hartington Rd
Middlesbrough TS1 214 C3
Stockton-on-T TS18 213 A2
Hartington St
Consett DH8 11 A3
Loftus TS13 127 A1
7 Thornaby-on-T TS17 138 C8
Hartington Way DL3 132 E5
Hartland Dr DH3 9 D3
Hartland Gr TS3 140 E8
Hartlea Ave DL1 113 A2
Hartlepool TS25 76 F3
Hartlepool Ave SR8 49 F8
Hartlepool Cl TS19 117 D6
Hartlepool Coll of F Ed TS24 77 C5
Hartlepool General Hospl TS24 63 F1
Hartlepool Historic Quay & Heritage Ctr★ TS24 77 C7
Hartlepool Ind Est TS24 64 B1
Hartlepool Power Sta Visitor Ctr★ TS25 90 F3
Hartlepool Rd
Elwick TS21,TS22 87 C3
Sedgefield TS21 86 D6
Hartlepool Sixth Form Coll TS25 76 F4
Hartlepool St DH6 47 D4
Hartlepool Sta TS24 77 C6
Hartlepool Utd FC (Victoria Pk) TS24 77 B6
Hartlepool-Middleton Grange Sh Ctr TS24 77 B5
Hartley Ave DL14 68 C1
Hartley Cl
11 Hartlepool TS26 77 A6
Staindrop DL2 200 F7
Hartley Rd DL5 96 D7
Hartley St 10 TS26 77 A6
Hartley Terr DL16 56 A1
Harton Ave TS22 102 B5
Harts Bldgs 1 DL2 153 F8
Hartsbourne Cres TS11 123 F6
Hartside Birtley DH3 9 D1
Crook DL15 52 D4
Hartside Cl DL15 52 E4
Hartside Cotts DH9 12 F4
Hartside Cres NE21 2 A8
Hartside Gdns
Easington Lane DH5 27 C1
Hartlepool TS26 76 D7
Hartside Gr TS19 117 E6
Hartside Prim Sch DL15 52 D4
Hartside View
Bearpark DH7 33 A4
Durham DH1 34 A7
Hartville Rd TS24 63 C5
Hartwith Dr TS19 117 B8
Harvard Ave TS17 213 C2
Harvester Cl TS25 77 D2
Harvester Ct TS7 140 B5
Harvey Cl Peterlee SR8 49 D7
Washington NE38 9 F5
Harvey Ct Consett DH8 11 A3
Redcar TS10 106 F4
Willington DL15 54 B4
Harvey Wlk TS25 76 D2
Harwal Rd TS10 107 A6
Harwell Cl TS4 140 A8
Harwell Dr TS19 117 B5
Harwich Cl TS10 107 F3
Harwich Gr TS25 90 B8
Harwick Ct DH9 14 C6
Harwood Ct
Middlesbrough TS2 119 D7
Trimdon TS29 59 E4
Harwood St TS24 77 A7
Haselrigg Cl DL5 95 F4
Hasguard Way TS17 156 E7
Hasledon Gr TS21 85 A5
Haslewood Rd DL5 82 C2
Hastings Ave DH1 44 A7
Hastings Cl
Nunthorpe TS7 141 A3
Thornaby-on-T TS17 138 C3
Hastings Pl TS24 63 F2
Hastings Way TS23 103 A6
Haswell Ave TS25 77 B2
Haswell Ct 3 TS20 118 B5
Haswell Prim Sch DH6 37 E3
Hatfield Ave TS5 139 C7
Hatfield Cl Durham DH1 34 A6
Eaglescliffe TS16 137 A1
Hatfield Coll (Univ of Durham) DH1 211 A2
Hatfield Pl SR8 49 E5
Hatfield Rd
Billingham TS23 102 F4
Newton Aycliffe DL5 96 E7
Hatfield Way DL14 80 D4
Hatherley Ct TS3 120 F3
Hatherley Sq 6 TS27 50 D3
Hatterall Ct TS17 156 F7
Haughton Com Sch DL1 133 D5
Haughton Gn DL1 133 E4
Haughton Rd DL1 133 C3
Hauxley Cl TS10 107 F3
Hauxley Dr DH2 23 F8
Hauxwell's Bldg TS15 156 B6
Havelock Cl DL5 96 E6

Langdale Wlk DL14 ...79 F4
Langdon Gdns DH9 ...12 E5
Langdon Sq TS8 ...140 B3
Langdon Way TS16 ...137 A1
Langham Wlk TS19 ...117 A3
Langholm Cres DL3 ...132 E1
Langhurst SR2 ...18 E8
Langleeford Way TS17 .157 A7
Langley Ave
Burnhope DH7 ...21 D4
Thornaby-on-T TS17 ...138 D8
Langley Cl TS10 ...107 C2
Langley Cres DH7 ...43 D5
Langley Ct [13] TS3 ...140 D8
Langley Garth DL2 ...200 F7
Langley Gr
Bishop Auckland DL14 ...80 A6
Peterlee SR8 ...49 A4
Langley La DH7 ...22 B2
Langley Moor Ind Est DH7 ...43 E5
Langley Moor Prim Sch DH7 ...43 E6
Langley Park Ind Est DH7 ...32 C8
Langley Park Prim Sch DH7 ...32 C6
Langley Rd Durham DH1 ..34 C6
Newton Aycliffe DL5 ...96 E7
Langley St DH7 ...32 C7
Langley Terr
Annfield Plain DH9 ...13 A4
Burnhope DH7 ...21 D5
Langley View DH9 ...13 C3
Langmere DL16 ...55 E2
Langridge Cres TS3 ...120 D1
Langsett Ave [1] TS3 ...120 C1
Langthorne Ave [10] SR8 ..50 B6
Langthorne Gr TS18 ...117 A1
Langthorpe TS7 ...140 F3
Langthwaite Wlk TS10 .107 C2
Langton DL2 ...201 D6
Langton Ave TS22 ...102 B5
Langton Cl TS4 ...119 F2
Langton Lea DH1 ...45 C5
Langton Terr DH4 ...17 E2
Langton Wlk [11] DL1 ...152 C8
Lanivet Cl [4] SR2 ...18 F8
Lanrood Gn TS4 ...120 B2
Lansbury Cl Birtley DH3 ...9 B6
South Bank TS6 ...121 A5
Lansbury Dr Birtley DH3 ..9 B5
Murton SR7 ...28 C3
Lansbury Gr TS24 ...77 B7
Lansdown Way
Billingham TS23 ...103 A6
Willington DL15 ...53 E1
Lansdowne SR2 ...18 E7
Lansdowne Rd
Brotton TS12 ...126 C3
Hartlepool TS26 ...77 A5
Middlesbrough TS4 ...120 B2
Thornaby-on-T TS17 ...138 E7
Yarm TS15 ...156 D5
Lansdowne St DL3 ...133 A5
Lanshaw Gn TS4 ...120 B2
Lantsbery Dr TS13 ...147 A8
Lanyard The TS24 ...77 C6
Lapwing Cl NE38 ...9 F3
Lapwing Ct NE16 ...6 C5
Lapwing La TS20 ...102 A2
Lapwing Rd TS26 ...76 D8
Larch Ave
[2] Houghton-le-S DH4 ...26 C8
Shildon DL4 ...81 B1
Larch Cl TS7 ...140 F4
Larch Cres TS16 ...137 D4
Larch Gr TS24 ...64 A1
Larch Rd
Guisborough TS14 ...143 D5
Stockton-on-T TS19 ...118 A5
Larch St DH8 ...10 F3
Larch Terr
Billingham TS2 ...119 F8
Tantobie DH9 ...6 A1
The Middles DH9 ...14 B3
[13] Langley Park DH7 ...32 C6
Larches Rd DH1 ...210 A4
Larches The
Burnopfield NE16 ...6 B7
Esh Winning DH7 ...41 D8
Eston TS6 ...121 B3
Ormesby TS7 ...141 B6
Redcar TS10 ...107 E5
Stockton-on-T TS19 ...117 C5
Larchfield Gdns DL15 ...52 D4
Larchfield Ho [17] DL3 ...132 F1
Larchfield St DL3 ...132 F1
Largo Gdns DL1 ...133 C7
Lark Dr TS14 ...143 A4
Larkhall Sq TS20 ...118 B6
Larkhill SR2 ...18 F7
Larkspur Cl
Hartlepool TS26 ...63 D2
Tanfield Lea DH9 ...13 D8
Larkspur Ct DL14 ...79 F6
Larkspur Dr DL1 ...133 C2
Larkspur Rd TS7 ...140 C4
Larkswood Rd TS10 ...107 C1
Lartington Ct DH3 ...25 B6
Lartington Green La DL12 ...198 E4
Lartington La DL12 ...199 B4
Larun Beat The TS15 ...156 C4
Larvik Ct TS13 ...127 A4
Larwood Ct
Annfield Plain DH9 ...12 E3
Chester le Street DH3 ...16 E1
Lascelles Ave DL5 ...96 A8
Lastingham Ave TS6 ...121 E2
Latham Rd TS5 ...119 D2
Latimer Cl TS15 ...156 A3
Latimer La TS14 ...143 C3
Latimer Rd DL1 ...133 D5
Laude Bank DH7 ...31 D4
Lauder Cl TS19 ...117 B4
Lauder Ho [1] TS19 ...117 B4
Lauder St TS24 ...77 B6
Lauderdale Dr TS14 ...143 F3
Launceston DH3 ...25 A7
Laura St
Middlesbrough TS1 ...215 A1
Seaham SR7 ...29 D6
Laurel Ave Durham DH1 ..35 A1
Middlesbrough TS4 ...140 A8
Seaham SR7 ...29 B7
Thornaby-on-T TS17 ...138 C6
Laurel Avenue Com Prim Sch DH1 ...211 C2
Laurel Cl TS12 ...125 C6
Laurel Cres Beamish DH2 .15 B7
Brotton TS12 ...126 A4
Thornley (nr Wheatley Hill) DH6 ...47 C3
Trimdon TS29 ...59 F5
Laurel Ct
Chester le Street DH2 ...16 B5
Shildon DL4 ...95 B8
Laurel Dr DH8 ...11 D3
Laurel Gdns DL15 ...52 D4
Laurel Pk TS13 ...127 B1
Laurel Rd Chilton DL17 ...70 C2
Eaglescliffe TS16 ...137 C4
Marton TS7 ...140 D3
Redcar TS10 ...107 F5
Saltburn-by-t-S TS12 ...125 C6
Stockton-on-T TS19 ...117 F5
Laurel St Darlington DL3 .132 E3
Middlesbrough TS1 ...215 A2
Laurel Terr
Burnopfield NE16 ...5 F6
Langley Park DH7 ...32 D6
Sadberge DL2 ...134 E6
Laurel Way [10] DL14 ...80 C8
Laurels The [13] SR3 ...18 A8
Lauren Ct SR8 ...39 C4
Laurence Jackson Sch TS14 ...143 F6
Lauriston Cl DL3 ...132 A1
Lavan Ct TS10 ...107 E2
Lavan Sands TS5 ...139 B3
Lavender Ct TS11 ...124 D8
Lavender Dr DL14 ...79 E7
Lavender Gdns DH7 ...23 D3
Lavender Rd TS3 ...120 C3
Lavender Way TS20 ...118 A7
Laverick Terr DH9 ...13 A3
Lavernock Cl TS10 ...107 E3
Lavers Rd DH3 ...9 C5
Lawnhead Sq SR3 ...18 B6
Lawns Gill [4] TS12 ...125 A2
Lawns The
Easington Lane DH5 ...27 C1
Hartlepool TS24 ...77 F8
Seaham SR7 ...29 A6
Lawnswood DH5 ...26 F7
Lawnswood Rd TS3 ...121 A2
Lawrence Rd TS17 ...138 B6
Lawrence St
Darlington DL1 ...133 B1
Redcar TS10 ...107 D6
Stockton-on-T TS18 ...213 A2
Lawrenny Gr TS17 ...156 F7
Lawson Cl
Middlesbrough TS3 ...120 C5
South Bank TS6 ...121 B5
Lawson Ct [6] DH2 ...16 C2
Lawson Ind Est TS3 ...120 C5
Lawson Rd Bowburn DH6 .45 D1
Seaton Carew TS25 ...77 E1
Lawson St TS18 ...213 A2
Lawson Terr
Durham DH1 ...210 B2
Hetton-le-H DH5 ...27 B1
Lawson Way TS3 ...120 C5
Lawson Wlk TS18 ...213 A2
Lawson's St TS29 ...60 A4
Lax Terr Crook DL15 ...52 D3
Wolviston TS22 ...102 C8
Laxford DH3 ...9 D2
Laxford Ct SR3 ...18 A5
Laxton Cl TS23 ...102 D6
Layburn Pl SR8 ...49 C7
Laycock St TS1 ...214 A2
Layfield Prim Sch TS15 .156 B3
Layland Rd TS12 ...125 E2
Layton Ct DL1 ...82 D1
Lazenby Bank★ TS6 ...122 C2
Lazenby Bank Rd TS6 ...122 C3
Lazenby Cl DL3 ...132 B3
Lazenby Cres DL3 ...132 B3
Lazenby Gr DL3 ...132 B3
Lazenby Rd TS24 ...63 E4
Lea Gn Birtley DH3 ...9 E1
Wolsingham DL13 ...207 C5
Lea La SR8 ...39 B6
Lea Riggs DH4 ...26 A2
Lea Side DH8 ...177 D4
Lea Terr NE47 ...179 C8
Leach Gr DL3 ...132 C5
Lead La DH8 ...3 C6
Leadenhall St DL1 ...133 A3
Leadgate Com Jun Sch DH8 ...11 D3
Leadgate Ind Est DH8 ...11 E2
Leadgate Inf Sch DH8 ...11 C3
Leadgate Rd Consett DH8 .11 B4
Leadgate DH8 ...11 B4
Leadgate Terr DL13 ...207 E5
Leadpipe La DL12 ...198 E6
Leafield Cl DH3 ...9 D6
Leafield Rd DL1 ...152 A8
Leaholme Terr TS27 ...50 E2
Leahope Ct TS17 ...138 E4
Lealholm Cres TS3 ...140 E7
Lealholm Rd TS25 ...90 A8
Lealholm Way TS14 ...143 D2
Lealholm Wlk [2] TS6 ...121 F3
Lealholme Gr TS19 ...117 B2
Leam La TS19 ...117 A5
Leamington Dr [2] TS25 ..77 B3
Leamington Gr TS3 ...140 F8
Leamington Par TS25 ...77 B3
Leander Ave DH3 ...16 D7
Leas Gr TS24 ...64 D2
Leas The Darlington DL1 .133 A6
Redcar TS10 ...107 E3
Sedgefield TS21 ...85 B5
Leas Wlk TS24 ...64 D2
Leases The DH6 ...57 D8
Leaside DL5 ...96 D4
Leaside N DL5 ...96 D4
Leasyde Wlk NE16 ...2 F5
Leatham SR2 ...18 E8
Leazes Ct DH1 ...211 A3
Leazes La
Bishop Auckland DL14 ...79 C3
Durham DH1 ...211 B3
Wolsingham DL13 ...207 B5
Leazes Pl DH1 ...211 A3
Leazes Rd DH1 ...211 A3
Leazes Rise SR8 ...49 F5
Leazes The NE16 ...5 F6
Leazes View
Rowlands Gill NE39 ...1 D2
Wolsingham DL13 ...207 B5
Leazes Villas NE16 ...6 A6
Leazon Hill TS17 ...138 A2
Leckfell Cl TS7 ...140 F2
Leconfield TS9 ...158 F1
Ledbury Dr
Middlesbrough TS5 ...139 D3
Thornaby-on-T TS17 ...138 C4
Ledbury Way TS14 ...143 D2
Lee Gn DL5 ...96 D5
Lee Hill Ct DH7 ...20 E3
Lee Rd TS6 ...121 E6
Lee Terr Easington SR8 ...39 C4
Hetton-le-H DH5 ...27 B2
Shotton Colliery DH6 ...48 C6
Leech Ct SR8 ...39 F4
Leechmere Cres SR7 ...18 F1
Leechmere Ind Est SR2 ..18 F8
Leechmere View [5] SR2 ..18 F8
Leechmere Way SR2 ...18 F8
Leechmire Terr TS27 ...61 C5
Leeds St TS18 ...213 A3
Leehall La DL5,TS21 ...97 E4
Leeholme DH5 ...26 F7
Leeholme Ct DH9 ...13 A3
Leeholme Rd
Billingham TS23 ...102 F4
Coundon DL14 ...81 D8
Leekworth Gdns DL12 ..208 C5
Leekworth La DL12 ...208 C5
Leeman's La DH6 ...56 F5
Leeming Rd TS5 ...119 C1
Lees Rd TS1 ...214 B2
Lees St DH9 ...13 F7
Leesfield Dr DH7 ...43 C3
Leesfield Gdns DH7 ...43 C3
Leesfield Rd DH7 ...43 C3
Leeway The TS3 ...215 C3
Leicester Gr DL1 ...133 E5
Leicester Rd TS20 ...118 C7
Leicester Way TS16 ...156 A7
Leicester Wlk SR8 ...49 C8
Leicestershire Dr DH1 ..35 D3
Leighton Rd Eston TS6 ..121 E6
Stockton-on-T TS18 ...137 A8
Leighton Terr Birtley DH3 ..9 B5
Hartlepool TS27 ...63 D3
Leinster Rd TS1 ...214 A1
Leith Gdns DH9 ...6 D1
Leith Rd DL3 ...132 B1
Leith Wlk TS17 ...138 D3
Lendings The DL12 ...209 C4
Lenham Cl TS22 ...102 A5
Lenin Terr Chopwell NE17 ..4 C8
Stanley DH9 ...13 F5
Lennox Cres TS23 ...102 D3
Lennox Wlk TS25 ...89 D8
Leonard Ropner Dr TS19 ...117 A4
Leonard St DL1 ...152 B8
Leopold Pl DL14 ...80 C7
Lerwick Cl TS19 ...116 F3
Lesbury Cl DH2 ...15 F1
Lesbury Terr NE17 ...4 B8
Leslie St DL14 ...79 D2
Leslie Villas DH6 ...58 A4
Letch Ave SR7 ...39 B8
Letch La Carlton TS21 ...116 E8
Stockton-on-T TS21 ...117 A8
Letch Rd TS20 ...102 B1
Letitia Ind Est TS5 ...119 B4
Leuchars Ct DH3 ...9 C3
Leven Ave DH2 ...16 B1
Leven Bank Rd TS15 ...157 A4
Leven Camping Site TS17 ...157 A6
Leven Cl TS16 ...156 B7
Leven Ct TS9 ...161 B1
Leven Gdns DL1 ...133 C7
Leven Gr Hartlepool TS25 .89 D8
Thornaby-on-T TS17 ...138 D6
Leven Ho [10] SR3 ...18 A6
Leven Rd
Bishop Auckland DL14 ...79 B1
Guisborough TS14 ...143 D3
Middlesbrough TS3 ...120 C4
Stockton-on-T TS20 ...118 A8
Yarm TS15 ...156 D5
Leven St Billingham TS23 .103 D2
Middlesbrough TS1 ...214 A2
Saltburn-by-t-S TS12 ...125 C7
South Bank TS6 ...121 A6
Leven Wlk SR8 ...49 C4
Levendale TS15 ...173 E1
Levendale Cl TS15 ...156 E5
Levendale Prim Sch TS15 ...156 E5
Levens Wlk TS10 ...107 C4
Levenside TS9 ...160 F2
Leveret Cl TS17 ...138 C2
Levick Cres TS5 ...139 B7
Levington Wynd TS7 ...141 A2
Levisham Cl
Middlesbrough TS5 ...139 E7
New Silksworth SR3 ...18 C7
Stockton-on-T TS18 ...212 A1
Lewes Rd DL1 ...152 B8
Lewes Way TS23 ...103 A7
Lewis Gr TS25 ...76 D2
Lewis Rd TS5 ...119 D2
Lewis Wlk TS14 ...143 D3
Lexden Ave TS5 ...139 B7
Lexington Ct Brandon DH7 43 A2
[8] Stockton-on-T TS20 ...118 B6
Leybourne Hold DH3 ...9 C6
Leybourne Terr TS18 ...212 C2
Leyburn Cl DH2 ...8 D1
Leyburn Gr TS18 ...137 B8
Leyburn Pl DH3 ...9 B6
Leyburn Rd DL1 ...133 A6
Leyburn St TS26 ...77 A4
Leyfield Cl SR3 ...18 B5
Leyland Cl DH6 ...45 E2
Libanus Ct TS17 ...156 F8
Liberty Terr DH9 ...6 B2
Library Terr DH9 ...12 F4
Library Wlk DH9 ...12 F4
Lichfield Ave
Eaglescliffe TS16 ...137 A1
Eston TS6 ...121 E3
Lichfield Cl DH3 ...25 A6
Lichfield Rd
Cornforth DL17 ...70 F8
Middlesbrough TS5 ...119 F1
Lidcombe Cl SR3 ...18 C7
Liddel Ct TS24 ...64 A2
Liddell Cl DL5 ...96 F6
Liddell Terr NE11 ...8 C6
Liddle Ave
Butterknowle DL13 ...195 C4
Sherburn DH6 ...35 F1
Liddle Cl SR8 ...49 B8
Lidell Terr DH6 ...47 E1
Light Pipe Hall Rd TS18 212 C2
Lightfoot Cres TS24 ...63 F2
Lightfoot Gr TS18 ...213 A2
Lightfoot Rd DL5 ...96 C7
Lightfoot Terr DL17 ...69 E5
Lilac Ave
Blackhall Rocks TS27 ...50 F2
Durham DH1 ...34 B5
[12] Houghton-le-S DH5 ...26 E8
New Silksworth SR3 ...18 B8
Sacriston DH7 ...23 C3
Sedgefield TS21 ...85 B7
Thornaby-on-T TS17 ...138 C6
Lilac Cl Carlton TS21 ...100 D1
Lazenby TS6 ...122 C4
Saltburn-by-t-S TS12 ...125 A6
Spennymoor DL16 ...68 D7
Lilac Cres Brotton TS12 ..126 A4
Burnopfield NE16 ...6 A6
Wingate TS29 ...60 B5
Lilac Ct DL4 ...95 B8
Lilac Gdns Beamish DH2 ..15 B7
Crook DL15 ...52 D3
Lilac Gr
Chester le Street DH2 ...16 A5
Middlesbrough TS3 ...120 E3
Redcar TS10 ...107 E5
Trimdon TS29 ...59 D1
Lilac Pk DH7 ...33 A1
Lilac Pl DH8 ...11 D3
Lilac Rd Chilton DL17 ...70 C2
Eaglescliffe TS16 ...137 C4
Eston TS6 ...121 C3
Ormesby TS7 ...141 B6
Stockton-on-T TS19 ...117 F5
Lilac Sq DH4 ...17 E3
Lilac Terr
Annfield Plain DH9 ...12 E5
Shotton Colliery DH6 ...48 C6
Lilac Way DL14 ...78 E5
Lilburn Cl
Chester le Street DH2 ...24 A8
[9] Shildon DL4 ...80 F1
Lilburne Cres DL5 ...96 D7
Lile Gdns TS21 ...85 B6
Lilian Ave SR2 ...18 E8
Lilian Terr [4] DH7 ...32 C6
Lilley Terr NE39 ...1 F3
Lilleycroft NE39 ...1 F2
Lillie Terr TS29 ...59 D3
Lily Bglws DH9 ...12 E8
Lily Gdns DH9 ...12 E8
Lilywhite Terr DH5 ...27 B1
Limber Gn TS3 ...141 A8
Limbrick Ave TS19 ...117 A3
Limbrick Ct TS19 ...117 B3
Lime Ave
Blackhall Rocks TS27 ...50 E3
Darlington DL1 ...133 A8
Houghton-le-S DH4 ...26 C8
Lime Cl TS7 ...140 D4
Lime Cres Eston TS6 ...121 C2
Hartlepool TS24 ...77 A8
Lime Gr
Bishop Auckland DL14 ...80 B4
Shildon DL4 ...81 B1
Stockton-on-T TS19 ...117 B3
Lime La Mordon DL1 ...97 C1
Newton Aycliffe DL5 ...112 F8
Lime Pk DH7 ...43 B4
Lime Rd Eaglescliffe TS16 137 D4
Eston TS6 ...121 C2
Ferryhill DL17 ...69 F6
Guisborough TS14 ...143 D5
Redcar TS10 ...107 E6
Lime St Stanley DH9 ...13 D4
Waldridge DH2 ...15 E1
Lime Terr Eldon Lane DL14 .80 F4
Langley Park DH7 ...32 D6
Lime Tree Cl TS2 ...103 E1
Lime Tree Wlk DL13 ...206 D3
Lime Wlk TS13 ...127 B2
Limecragg Ave DH1 ...35 B3
Limehurst Rd DL3 ...132 E3
Limeoak Way TS18 ...213 C4
Limerick Rd TS10 ...106 D4
Limes Cres TS11 ...124 D8
Limes Rd TS5 ...119 E1
Limetree Ct [7] TS4 ...139 F8
Limpton Gate TS15 ...156 C4
Linacre Ct SR8 ...49 B5
Linacre Way DL1 ...133 B6
Linburn NE38 ...17 B8
Linburn Dr DL14 ...79 F5
Linby Ave TS3 ...140 C8
Lincoln Ave SR3 ...18 A8
Lincoln Cl DL5 ...96 C7
Lincoln Cres
Billingham TS23 ...102 F3
Hetton-le-H DH5 ...26 F4
Lincoln Ct DL1 ...133 E4
Lincoln Dr DL15 ...53 F2
Lincoln Gr TS20 ...118 C7
Lincoln Pl
[6] Consett DH8 ...177 A4
Thornaby-on-T TS17 ...138 C7
Lincoln Rd Consett DH8 .177 A4
Durham DH1 ...34 D7
Guisborough TS14 ...143 D3
Hartlepool TS25 ...89 D7
Redcar TS10 ...107 F4
Lincoln St DL14 ...81 D8
Lincoln Wlk
Great Lumley DH3 ...25 A7
Peterlee SR8 ...49 C8
Lincolnshire Cl DH1 ...35 C3
Lincombe Dr TS5 ...139 D3
Linden Ave
Darlington DL3 ...151 D8
Great Ayton TS9 ...160 F2
Stockton-on-T TS18 ...137 E8
Linden Cl
Great Ayton TS9 ...160 F3
Shildon DL4 ...95 B8
Linden Cres
Great Ayton TS9 ...160 F2
Marton TS7 ...140 C3
Linden Ct
Spennymoor DL16 ...69 A8
Thornaby-on-T TS17 ...138 C7
Linden Dr Darlington DL3 151 D8
Hurworth-on-T DL2 ...168 A8
Linden Gr Coxhoe DH6 ...57 F4
Great Ayton TS9 ...160 F3
Hartlepool TS26 ...76 F5
Houghton-le-S DH4 ...26 D8
Leadgate DH8 ...11 D3
Middlesbrough TS5 ...119 D1
Thornaby-on-T TS17 ...138 C7
Linden Ho TS12 ...126 A4
Linden Lo DL3 ...151 D8
Linden Mews DH7 ...32 C6
Linden Pk DH7 ...43 B4
Linden Pl DL5 ...96 A6
Linden Rd Bearpark DH7 ..33 B3
Bishop Auckland DL14 ...80 C6
Brotton TS12 ...126 A4
Cornforth DL17 ...70 E8
Ferryhill DL17 ...70 B5
Great Ayton TS9 ...160 F2
Linden Terr Coxhoe DH6 ..57 F4
Ferryhill DL17 ...70 C3
Linden Way DH8 ...10 E4
Lindisfarne
High Shincliffe DH1 ...45 B5
Peterlee SR8 ...49 D4
Ryhope SR2 ...18 E6
Lindisfarne Ave DH3 ...16 D3
Lindisfarne Cl
Bishop Auckland DL14 ...79 E6
Chester le Street DH2 ...16 A1
Hartlepool TS27 ...63 D3
Lindisfarne Rd
Durham DH1 ...34 D5
Middlesbrough TS3 ...140 F8
Lindom Ave DH3 ...16 D3
Lindon Rd DH9 ...13 E5

Meadow Dale Ct TS12 ..145 E5
Meadow Dr
Chester le Street DH2 .....15 F2
Hartlepool TS26 ....76 D5
Ormesby TS7 ....141 B6
Meadow End TS16 .....137 B2
Meadow Gn DL16 ....56 C3
Meadow Grange DH4 ....17 E2
Meadow Hill TS21 ......72 A1
Meadow Ho 4 SR3 .....18 A5
Meadow Rd
Marske-by-t-S TS11 .....124 D8
Stockton-on-T TS19 ......117 C3
Trimdon TS29 ....72 D7
Meadow Rise Consett DH8 11 A3
Darlington DL3 ....132 B2
Meadow St DH5 ....26 C3
Meadow The TS25 ......77 A2
Meadow View
Bishop Auckland DL14 .....79 C2
Consett DH8 ....177 E4
Coxhoe DH6 ....57 F3
Dipton DH9 ....5 E1
Eggleston DL12 ....193 E2
Sacriston DH7 ....23 C3
Stanhope DL13 ....206 D2
Meadow View Rd TS5 ..119 B2
Meadow Way DH7 ....20 E3
Meadow Wlk TS21 .....116 C8
Meadowbank DH7 ......32 B6
Meadowbank Rd TS7 ...141 B6
Meadowcroft Rd TS6 ...121 B1
Meadowdale DL17 ....82 F7
Meadowdale Cl TS2 .....103 E1
Meadowfield DH8 ....10 D3
Meadowfield Ave
Middlesbrough TS4 ......139 F8
Spennymoor DL16 ....56 D2
Meadowfield Dr TS16 ..137 B2
Meadowfield Ind Est
DH7 ....43 D3
Meadowfield Rd DL3 ...132 B5
Meadowfield Way
Newton Aycliffe DL5 ......96 A8
Tanfield Lea DH9 ....13 C8
Meadowgate TS6 ....122 A2
Meadowgate Dr TS26 ...76 E7
Meadowings The TS15 ..156 B4
Meadowlands Cl TS13 ..148 A8
Meadows Edge DL13 ...181 C7
Meadows La DH4,DH5 ....26 B3
Meadows The
Bournmoor DH4 ....17 D3
Burnopfield NE16 ....6 A4
Coulby Newham TS8 ......140 C1
Middleton St George DL2 .153 F7
Middridge DL5 ....81 E1
Redcar TS10 ....107 B4
Sedgefield TS21 ....85 B6
West Rainton DH4 ....26 A3
Meadowsweet Cl DH8 ...11 A2
Meadway TS10 ....107 B2
Measham Cl TS20 ......117 F8
Meath St TS1 ....214 A1
Meath Way TS14 ....143 D3
Meatlesburn Cl DL5 .....95 F4
Medbourne Cl 4 TS6 ..121 F1
Medbourne Gdns TS5 ..139 D4
Medina Cl TS19 ....117 B4
Medina Gdns TS5 ......139 E4
Medlar Cl DH4 ....17 F6
Medomsley Cross Rds
DH8 ....11 A8
Medomsley Rd DH8 .....10 F4
Medway DH3 ....25 A7
Medway Cl Peterlee SR8 ..49 C4
Skelton TS12 ....125 C4
Medway Gdns DH9 ......13 E4
Medway Ho TS23 ......102 D1
Medwin Cl TS12 ....126 A5
Medwyn Cl DH4 ....17 E3
Meet The DL5 ....95 F8
Meeting Ho The 6
DL12 ....209 C5
Megarth Rd TS5 ....119 D2
Meggitts Ave TS10 .....106 E3
Melbeck Dr DH2 ....8 E2
Melbourne Cl TS7 .....140 E3
Melbourne Pl DL13 ....207 D5
Melbourne St TS18 ....213 A3
Melbourne Terr DH7 .....23 B5
Melbreak Gr TS5 ....139 B6
Melbury St SR7 ....29 E5
Meldon Ave DH6 ....36 A1
Meldon Cl DL1 ....133 D5
Meldon Way
Annfield Plain DH9 ....13 B4
Blaydon NE21 ....1 F8
High Shincliffe DH1 ....45 B5
Meldrum Sq 9 TS19 ...117 B4
Meldyke La TS8 ....139 C1
Meldyke Pl TS8 ....139 C1
Melford Gr TS17 ....157 B8
Melgrove Way TS21 .....85 A5
Melksham Sq 6 TS19 ..117 B4
Mellanby Cres DL5 ......96 F7
Mellanby La TS25 ....89 E4
Melland Ct DL1 ....133 A1
Melland St DL1 ....133 A1
Mellbutts Bank DL13 ...188 A7
Mellor Ct DL3 ....133 A5
Mellor St TS19 ....212 C4
Melrose Ave
Billingham TS23 ....102 E5
Darlington DL3 ....133 A7
Middlesbrough TS5 ......139 C8
Murton SR7 ....28 A3
Melrose Cres
Guisborough TS14 ....144 A4
Seaham SR7 ....28 F8
Melrose Ct DH8 ....10 C4
Melrose Dr
Bishop Auckland DL14 .....79 D3
Stockton-on-T TS18 ......137 E8
Melrose St
Hartlepool TS25 ....77 A3
Middlesbrough TS1 ......215 A3
Melsanby Ct TS23 .....103 A7
Melsonby Ave TS3 .....140 E8
Melsonby Cres DL1 ....152 C8
Melsonby Gr TS18 .....117 A1
Melton Rd TS19 ....117 B4
Melton Wlk TS8 ....139 D2
Melville St
Chester le Street DH3 .....16 C2
2 Darlington DL1 ....132 F3
Melville Wlk TS20 .....118 C5
Memorial Ave SR8 ....39 E4
Memorial Cotts DL13 ..195 C4
Memorial Dr TS7 ......140 D4
Memorial Homes DH9 ...13 D8
Menceforth Cotts DH2 ...16 B4
Mendip Ave
Chester le Street DH2 .....16 C2
5 Skelton TS12 ....125 C3
Mendip Cl SR8 ....49 B6
Mendip Dr TS10 ....107 A3
Mendip Gn DL17 ....82 F8
Mendip Gr DL1 ....133 C5
Mendip Rd TS23 ....102 D4
Mendip Terr DH9 ....14 A5
Mendip Wlk DL14 ....81 C8
Menom Rd DL5 ....96 D2
Menville Cl DL5 ....95 F4
Mercantile Rd DH4 .....26 C7
Merchant Ho TS24 ......77 D6
Mercia Ct DL3 ....132 F2
Mercia Ret Pk DH1 .....34 C8
Mere Dr DH1 ....34 B7
Meredith Ave TS6 .....141 C8
Mereston Cl TS26 ......76 C7
Merganser Rd TS26 .....63 D1
Merion Dr TS11 ....123 F6
Merioneth Cl TS17 ....156 E8
Merlay Cl TS15 ....156 A3
Merlin Cl
Guisborough TS14 ....143 A4
Seaham SR7 ....29 C8
Merlin Ct DH7 ....41 C8
Merlin Dr DH3 ....16 D7
Merlin Rd
Middlesbrough TS3 ......120 E4
Stockton-on-T TS19 ......117 B4
Merlin Way TS26 ....63 D1
Merriman Gn TS24 ......63 D3
Merring Cl TS18 ....117 A2
Merrington Ave TS5 ...139 B4
Merrington Cl DL16 ....69 A3
Merrington Hts DL16 ...68 F3
Merrington Lane Ind Est
DL16 ....69 B7
Merrington Rd
Ferryhill DL16,DL17 ....69 C5
Kirk Merrington DL17 ......69 C5
Merrington View DL16 ..69 A8
Merrybent DL2 ....131 C2
Merrybent Dr DL2 .....131 D1
Merryweather Ct TS15 .156 C6
Mersehead Sands TS5 ..139 B4
Mersey Rd TS10 ....107 B5
Mersey St DH8 ....11 D5
Merton Cl DL1 ....133 B6
Merville Ave TS19 .....117 C2
Meryl Gdns TS25 ....90 A7
Merz Rd DL5 ....96 D6
Messenger Bank DH8 ...10 C6
Messines La TS21 ......99 E3
Metcalfe Cl TS15 .....156 B3
Metcalfe Cres SR7 ......28 B3
Metcalfe Rd Consett DH8 .11 B1
South Bank TS6 ....120 F5
Method Ho DH9 ....14 E8
Metz Bridge Rd TS2 ...214 B4
Mewburn Ct DL3 ......132 F7
Mewburn Rd DL3 ......132 F7
Mews Ct DH5 ....26 E8
Mews The
Fence Houses DH4 ....26 A7
High Shincliffe DH1 ....44 F6
Kimblesworth DH2 ....24 A4
Marske-by-t-S TS11 ......108 C1
Mexborough Cl TS19 ..117 D5
Meynell Ave TS14 .....143 B3
Meynell Ho TS16 ......156 B7
Meynell Rd DL3 ....132 F5
Meynell's Wlk TS15 ...156 B4
Michael Terr DL16 ......67 E7
Mickle Gr DL14 ....81 C8
Mickle Hill Rd TS27 ....50 D1
Mickleby Cl TS7 ....140 F2
Mickledales Dr TS11 ..108 C1
Micklemire La TS25 .....89 F3
Mickleton Cl Consett DH8 .10 F1
Great Lumley DH3 ....25 B7
Mickleton Cl CL DH8 ....10 F1
Mickleton Rd TS2 .....119 C8
Micklow Cl TS10 ......107 C2
Micklow La TS13 ......127 D2
Micklow Terr TS13 ....127 D1
Midbourne Rd TS19 ...118 A5
Middle Ave TS23 ......102 D1
Middle Bank TS21 .....100 E3
Middle Bank Rd TS7 ...141 B6
Middle Blackdene DL13 179 E1
Middle Chare DH3 ......16 D3
Middle Farm DL12 .....199 F5
Middle Gr DH7 ....43 A3
Middle Rd TS17 ....138 B1
Middle Row DH4 ....17 E1
Middle St
Blackhall Colliery TS27 ....50 D4
Consett DH8 ....10 F2
Gayles DL11 ....205 E2
Stockton-on-T TS18 ......213 A3
Middlefield DH2 ....15 E7
Middlefield Rd
Marske-by-t-S TS11 ......108 B1
Stockton-on-T TS19 ......117 C6
Middlefield Terr DH7 ....32 F1
Middlegate TS24 ....77 F8
Middleham Cl DH2 ....8 E1
Middleham Rd
Cornforth DL17 ....57 E1
Darlington DL1 ....133 B7
Durham DH1 ....34 D7
Stockton-on-T TS19 ......117 C2
Middleham Way
Newton Aycliffe DL5 ......82 E1
Redcar TS10 ....107 F4
Middleham Wk DL16 .....55 F1
Middleham Wlk DL16 ....56 A2
Middlehope Gr DL14 ....79 E5
Middles Rd DH9 ....14 B3
Middlesbrough Coll
Middlesbrough, Acklam
TS5 ....139 D6
Middlesbrough,Beechwood
TS4 ....140 C7
Middlesbrough,Linthorpe
TS5 ....119 D1
Middlesbrough Rd
Guisborough TS7, TS14 ..142 D4
South Bank TS6 ....120 F6
South Bank TS6 ....121 A6
Thornaby-on-T TS17 .....118 E1
Middlesbrough Rd E
TS6 ....121 B7
Middlesbrough Road E 5
TS6 ....121 A6
Middlesbrough Sta TS1 215 A4
Middlesbrough Wharf Trad
Est TS2 ....119 E8
Middlestone Moor Prim Sch
DL16 ....68 E7
Middleton Ave
Billingham TS22 ....102 B5
Middlesbrough TS5 ......139 B8
Rowlands Gill NE39 ....1 F1
Thornaby-on-T TS17 .....138 C3
Middleton Cl Consett DH8 11 A1
Eaglescliffe TS16 ....136 F1
Seaham SR7 ....18 E1
Middleton Ct
Darlington DL1 ....133 A2
Yarm TS15 ....156 C4
Middleton Dr TS14 ....143 F3
Middleton Grange La 2
TS24 ....77 B6
Middleton La DL2 .....153 F6
Middleton Rd
Hartlepool TS24 ....77 B7
Sadberge DL2 ....134 E6
Shildon DL4 ....94 F8
Woodland DL13 ....194 E5
Middleton St DL1 .....133 A2
Middleton St George CE Prim
Sch DL2 ....153 E7
Middleton Wlk TS18 ...212 C2
Middleton-in-Teesdale Prim
Sch DL12 ....208 C5
Middleway TS17 ....213 C1
Middlewood DH7 ....33 A2
Middlewood Ave DL14 ..79 D2
Middlewood Cl 3 TS27 ..63 C4
Middlewood Rd DH7 ....20 E3
Middridge Farms DL5 ...95 E8
Middridge Gr TS23 ....102 F7
Middridge La DL4,DL5 ...81 C1
Middridge Rd
Langley Park DH7 ....32 B6
Middridge DL5 ....82 A1
Newton Aycliffe DL17,DL5 ..82 C4
Midfield The TS5 ......214 B1
Midfield View 3 TS19 ..117 B4
Midfields DL5 ....95 F4
Midhill Cl Brandon DH7 ...43 B5
7 Langley Park DH7 ......32 C6
Midhurst Rd TS3 ......121 A2
Midlothian Rd TS25 ....89 C8
Midvill Wlk TS3 ....121 A1
Midville Wlk TS3 ......141 A8
Miers Ave TS24 ....64 A2
Milbank Cres DL3 .....132 D2
Milbank Ct
Darlington DL3 ....132 C2
Stockton-on-T TS18 ......213 A3
Milbank Rd
Darlington DL3 ....132 D2
Hartlepool TS24 ....77 B8
Milbank St
3 South Bank TS6 ....121 A6
Stockton-on-T TS18 ......213 A3
Milbank Terr
Redcar TS10 ....107 C7
Shotton Colliery DH6 ......48 D6
Station Town TS28 ....60 F5
Milbanke Cl DH2 ....8 F1
Milbanke St DH2 ....8 F1
Milbourne Ct TS21 ......85 A8
Milburn Cl DH3 ....16 E2
Milburn Cres TS20 ....118 A6
Milburn St DL15 ....52 E4
Milburn Way DL15 ......65 E7
Mildenhall Cl TS25 .....89 E6
Mildred St
Darlington DL3 ....132 F3
Hartlepool TS26 ....77 A7
Miles St TS6 ....121 A6
Milfoil Cl TS7 ....140 B4
Milford Ho TS3 ....120 D4
Milford Mdw DL14 ......80 D4
Milford Terr 9 DL17 ....70 A6
Milkwood Ct DL3 ......132 E4
Mill Bank TS13 ....126 F2
Mill Cl DL11 ....205 F2
Mill Cotts DL17 ....82 C6
Mill Ct Billingham TS23 ..118 D8
Bournmoor DH4 ....17 E2
Hamsterley NE17 ....4 B6
Mill Farm Rd NE39 ....5 A5
Mill Hill Easington SR8 ...39 A1
Houghton-le-S DH5 ....26 D6
Peterlee SR8 ....49 A8
Mill Hill Prim Sch SR3 ..18 A5
Mill Hill Rd SR3 ....18 A6
Mill House Ct DH1 .....35 A2
Mill La Billingham TS23 ..102 E1
Bishop Auckland DL14 .....80 D5
Bishopton TS21 ....115 E8
Carlin How TS13 ....126 F2
Darlington DL1 ....133 E4
Durham DH1 ....35 A2
Ebchester DH8 ....3 E4
Frosterley DL13 ....188 A7
High Coniscliffe DL2 .....130 F3
Kimblesworth DH2,DH3 ....24 B4
Longnewton DL2,TS21 ...135 D3
Mickleton DL12 ....193 B3
New Brancepeth DH7 ......43 A8
Redworth DL4,DL5 ....95 C4
Sherburn DH6 ....36 A1
Shincliffe DH1 ....45 A7
Skinningrove TS13 ....127 A3
Spennymoor DL16 ....55 E4
Stockton-on-T TS20 ......102 B1
Urpeth DH2 ....8 D1
Winlaton Mill NE21 ....2 B7
Wolviston TS22 ....102 B7
Mill Lane Prim Sch
TS18 ....213 A3
Mill Meadow Ct 10
TS20 ....118 B8
Mill Race Cl NE17 ....4 B6
Mill Rd Brandon DH7 .....43 E5
Chopwell NE17 ....4 B8
Seaham SR7 ....28 F8
Mill St Consett DH8 ....177 D4
Crook DL15 ....52 F4
Guisborough TS14 ....143 E4
Shildon DL4 ....95 A8
Stockton-on-T TS20 ......118 A8
Willington DL15 ....53 F3
Mill St E TS18 ....213 B3
Mill St W TS18 ....213 A3
Mill Terr Easington SR8 ..39 A4
Great Ayton TS9 ....160 F2
Houghton-le-S DH5 ....26 D6
Thorpe Thewles TS21 ....100 D3
Mill The Blanchland DH8 .174 F2
Great Ayton TS9 ....161 A2
Mill View TS13 ....127 B1
Mill Wynd Staindrop DL2 .200 E7
Yarm TS15 ....156 B6
Millais Gr TS23 ....102 D8
Millbank DL5 ....95 D1
Millbank Cl
Bishop Auckland DL14 .....79 C1
Hart TS27 ....63 A3
Millbank Ct DH1 ......210 B4
Millbank La TS17 .....138 C5
Millbank Terr
Eldon Lane DL14 ....80 F4
Stillington TS21 ....100 A2
Millbeck Gr DH5 ....26 D6
Millbeck Way TS7 .....141 B7
Millbrook Ave TS3 ....120 F4
Millburngate DH1 .....210 C3
Millburngate Sh Ctr
DH1 ....210 C3
Millclose Wlk TS21 .....72 B1
Milldale SR7 ....28 F8
Millennium Pl DH1 ....210 C3
Millennium Way DL5 ...112 D8
Miller Cl TS15 ....156 D4
Miller Cres TS24 ....63 D3
Miller Gdns DH2 ....15 D4
Miller Terr SR3 ....18 A8
Millers La TS12 ....145 E3
Millershill La DH8 ....177 C1
Millfield DH7 ....20 E4
Millfield Cl
Chester le Street DH2 .....16 A1
Eaglescliffe TS16 ....156 B8
Thornaby-on-T TS17 .....138 E8
Millfield Ct DH8 ....10 C3
Millfield Gr DL15 ......52 E4
Millfield Rd Fishburn TS21 72 D4
Middlesbrough TS3 ......120 C3
Millfield Road W TS21 ..72 D4
Millfields DL5 ....96 F2
Millford Rd TS20 ......117 F7
Millford Way DH6 ......45 E1
Millgin Ct TS17 ....138 A2
Millhill La DH1 ....44 B7
Millholme Cl TS12 ....126 A3
Millholme Dr TS12 ....126 A3
Millholme Terr TS12 ...126 A3
Milliington Cl TS23 .....88 F1
Millom Ct SR8 ....49 A3
Millpool Cl TS24 ....64 C2
Millrace DL13 ....207 C5
Millrace Cl DL1 ....133 F6
Mills Bldgs DL17 ....70 C4
Mills Cl DL5 ....96 C6
Mills St TS1 ....214 A2
Millston Cl TS26 ....76 C8
Millstone Cl 3 TS10 ...107 E1
Millstone Pl DL13 .....207 D5
Millwood DL17 ....82 E8
Milne Wlk TS25 ....89 C8
Milner Gr TS24 ....77 B7
Milner Rd Darlington DL1 152 A8
Stockton-on-T TS20 ......102 A1
Milton Ave
Bishop Auckland DL14 .....80 B6
Blackhall Colliery TS27 ....50 C5
Houghton-le-S DH5 ....26 F7
Milton Cl Brotton TS12 ..126 A5
Seaham SR7 ....29 B7
Stanley DH9 ....14 B6
Milton Ct TS1 ....214 B3
Milton Gr DH6 ....48 D6
Milton La SR8 ....39 C4
Milton Rd TS26 ....77 A6
Milton St Crook DL15 ....52 E5
Darlington DL1 ....152 C8
Saltburn-by-t-S TS12 .....125 C7
Milton Terr DH2 ....15 E3
Minch Rd TS25 ....89 D7
Minehead Gdns 9 SR3 ..18 A8
Miners Homes DL14 .....79 E3
Miners' Bglws 12 DL13 .195 E3
Miners' Homes DL15 ....54 A2
Mingarry DH3 ....9 E2
Mingary Cl DH5 ....26 C4
Miniott Wlk TS8 ....139 D2
Minors Cres DL3 ......132 B5
Minstarley DH3 ....25 A7
Minster Ct Durham DH1 ..35 C3
Willington DL15 ....54 A3
Minster Wlk DL2 ......152 D1
Minsterley Dr TS5 .....139 A6
Mire La DL12 ....198 F6
Miry La DL12 ....192 B6
Missenden Gr TS3 .....140 F8
Mission Pl DL16 ....69 A3
Mistletoe St DH1 ......210 B2
Mistral Dr DL1 ....133 B7
Mitchell Ave TS17 .....138 E6
Mitchell Cl SR8 ....49 B8
Mitchell St
Annfield Plain DH9 ....13 A4
Birtley DH3 ....9 C4
Durham DH1 ....210 B3
1 Hartlepool TS26 ....77 A5
Stanley DH9 ....13 D4
Mitchell Terr DH9 ....6 B2
Mitford Cl
Chester le Street DH3 .....16 D8
High Shincliffe DH1 ....45 B5
Ormesby TS7 ....141 B7
Mitford Cres TS19 .....117 A6
Mitford Ct Peterlee SR8 ..49 D4
Sedgefield TS21 ....85 A8
Mitford Dr DH6 ....36 A2
Moat The TS23 ....103 B3
Moatside Mews DH1 ...210 C2
Model Pl 4 DL1 ....133 A1
Model Terr 17 DL13 ....195 E3
Moffat Cl DL1 ....133 D7
Moffat Rd TS25 ....89 D7
Moir Terr SR2 ....19 A6
Mona St DH9 ....13 F7
Monach Rd TS25 ....89 D7
Monarch Gn DL1 ......133 B7
Monarch Gr TS7 ......140 E4
Moncreiff Terr SR8 .....39 D4
Mond Cres TS23 ......118 D8
Mond Ho TS3 ....120 D1
Money Slack DH1 ....44 B5
Monk Ct SR8 ....49 B3
Monkland Cl TS1 ......214 C3
Monks End DL5 ....96 F2
Monks' Cres DH1 ......211 C4
Monkseaton Dr TS22 ...102 C5
Monkswood Sq SR3 .....18 B6
Monkton Rd TS25 ....89 C7
Monkton Rise TS14 ....143 F6
Monmouth Dr TS16 ....137 C1
Monmouth Gr TS26 .....63 E1
Monmouth Rd TS6 .....121 E4
Monreith Ave TS16 ....137 C1
Montagu Ct DL1 ......151 E8
Montagu's Harrier TS14 143 B4
Montague Ho 2 DH1 ....35 A2
Montague St TS24 ......64 F1
Montalbo Prim Sch
DL12 ....209 C7
Montalbo Rd DL12 .....209 C7
Monteith Cl DL14 ....79 C1
Montfalcon Cl SR8 .....49 C6
Montgomery Gr TS26 ....76 E8
Montgomery Rd
Barnard Castle DL12 .....209 B7
Durham DH1 ....211 C4
Montreal Pl TS4 ....120 A2
Montrose Cl TS7 ......140 C3
Montrose St
Darlington DL1 ....133 B3
Middlesbrough TS1 ......215 A3
Saltburn-by-t-S TS12 .....125 C7
Monument Terr 11 DH3 ...9 C4
Moor Cl
Kirklevington TS15 ......172 D8
Moorsholm TS12 ....146 B1
Moor Cres Durham DH1 ..35 B3

Newgale Cl TS17 ....156 E7
Newgate
Barnard Castle DL12 .....209 C5
Eston TS6 ....121 F2
Newgate St DL14 ....80 C8
Newham Ave TS5 ......139 E7
Newham Bridge Prim Sch
TS5 ....139 E7
Newham Cres TS7 .....140 D3
Newham Grange Ave
TS19 ....212 B4
Newham Grange Leisure
Farm* TS8 ....140 A3
Newham Way TS8 ......140 B3
Newhaven Cl TS8 ......139 D2
Newhaven Ct 3 TS24 ...77 C5
Newholm Ct TS25 ....90 A8
Newholm Way TS10 ....107 C3
Newholme Cres DL14 ....92 C7
Newholme Ct TS14 .....143 D5
Newholme Est TS28 .....60 F5
Newhouse Ave DH7 .....31 D1
Newhouse Rd DH7 ......41 E8
Newick Ave TS3 ....120 D2
Newington Rd TS4 .....140 A7
Newker Prim Sch DH2 ...16 B2
Newlands DH8 ....10 D4
Newlands Ave
Bishop Auckland DL14 .....80 B6
Hartlepool TS26 ....76 F5
Stockton-on-T TS20 ......118 B7
Newlands Gr TS10 .....107 B5
Newlands RC Sch The
TS4 ....139 F6
Newlands Rd
Darlington DL3 ....132 D4
Durham DH1 ....35 C4
Eaglescliffe TS16 ....156 B8
Middlesbrough TS1 ......215 B2
Skelton TS12 ....145 B8
Trimdon TS29 ....72 D8
Newlands Rd E SR7 .....29 B8
Newlands Rd W SR7 .....29 A8
Newlands View DL15 ....52 F2
Newley Ct TS3 ....121 A1
Newlyn Dr DL3 ....132 F8
Newlyn Gn TS3 ....140 E8
Newlyn Way TS10 ......107 F2
Newmarket Ave TS17 ...118 F1
Newmarket Rd TS10 ....107 D4
Newmarket St DH8 ......10 F3
Newmin Way NE16 ....2 F5
Newport Cl TS17 ....156 E7
Newport Cres TS1 .....214 C3
Newport Ct DL1 ....133 E4
Newport Gr 6 SR3 ......18 A8
Newport Prim Sch TS1 .214 B2
Newport Rd TS1, TS5 ..214 B3
Newport Way TS1 .....214 A3
Newquay Cl
Darlington DL3 ....132 F8
Hartlepool TS26 ....76 E7
Hemlington TS8 ....139 D2
Newsam Cres 4 TS16 ..156 B8
Newsam Rd TS16 ......156 B8
Newsham Hill DL11 ....205 E6
Newstead Ave TS19 ....117 D5
Newstead Rd TS4 ......215 B1
Newstead Rise DH8 .....10 C5
Newstead Sq SR3 ....18 A6
Newton Aycliffe Sta DL5 .96 B5
Newton Cap Bank DL14 ..67 B1
Newton Cl TS6 ....121 F1
Newton Dr Durham DH1 ..34 B6
Thornaby-on-T TS17 .....138 C4
Newton Gr TS22 ....102 B5
Newton Hanzard Long Dr
TS22 ....87 B4
Newton Hanzard Short Dr
TS22 ....87 C4
Newton La
Darlington DL2,DL3 .....132 A5
Newton Mulgrave TS13 ...149 E3
Walworth DL2 ....131 F7
Newton Mall TS1 ......214 C3
Newton Rd
Great Ayton TS9 ....161 A4
Redcar TS10 ....107 B3
Newton St Ferryhill DL17 ..69 E6
Witton Gilbert DH7 ....33 A8
Newton Villas DH6 .....57 E6
Newton Wlk 7 TS20 ...118 B5
Newtondale TS14 ......143 A3
Newtown DL12 ....208 B5
Newtown Ave TS19 ....212 C4
Newtown Ind Est DH3 ....9 C2
Newtown Villas DH7 ....23 C3
Nicholas St DH5 ....27 B5
Nicholson Terr DL12 ...198 F6
Nicholson Way TS24 ....63 E3
Nicholson's Terr DH9 ...14 F8
Nicklaus Dr TS16 .....137 D1
Nickleby Chare DH1 ....44 B7
Nickleby Cl DL12 ......209 D7
Nickstream La DL3 ....132 B5
Nidderdale TS12 ......125 B4
Nidderdale Ave DH5 .....26 F2
Nightingale Ave DL1 ...133 D6
Nightingale Cl TS26 .....63 C1
Nightingale Pl DH9 ......14 B5
Nightingale Rd TS6 ....121 E3
Nightingale Wlk TS20 ..102 A1
Nile St Consett DH8 .....10 F2
Middlesbrough TS2 ......214 C4
Nimbus Cl TS7 ....140 C4
Nimbus Ct 13 SR3 ......18 A6
Nine Acres TS27 ....62 E2
Nine Lands DH4 ....26 C8
Ninefields DL14 ....80 B8
Ninian Terr DH9 ....12 C7
Ninth Ave DH2 ....16 B3
Ninth St
Blackhall Colliery TS27 ....50 D4
6 Peterlee SR8 ....50 A7
Noble St SR8 ....39 E5
Noel Ave NE21 ....2 C6
Noel St DH9 ....14 B7
Noel Terr NE21 ....2 D7
Nolan Ho TS18 ....213 A4
Nolan Pl TS18 ....213 A4
Nolton Ct TS17 ....156 F7
Nook La DL12 ....192 D1
Nookston Cl TS26 ....76 D8
Norbeck Bank DL11 ....205 A5
Norburn La DH7 ....22 F2
Norburn Pk DH7 ....23 A1
Norcliffe St TS3 ......120 C4
Norfolk Ave Birtley DH3 ...9 D1
8 New Silksworth SR3 ....18 A8
Norfolk Cl Hartlepool TS25 77 B3
Redcar TS10 ....107 B4
Seaham SR7 ....19 A1
Skelton TS12 ....125 A2
Norfolk Cres TS3 .....140 F7
Norfolk Pl Birtley DH3 .....9 D1
Bishop Auckland DL14 .....80 C5
Middlesbrough TS3 ......120 D2
Norfolk Rd DH8 ....177 A4
Norfolk St Hetton-le-H DH5 26 F4
Stockton-on-T TS18 ......212 C2
Norfolk Terr TS23 .....102 F3
Norfolk Wlk SR8 ....49 C8
Norham Ct DH4 ....17 D1
Norham Dr SR8 ....49 C3
Norham Rd DH1 ....34 D7
Norham Wlk TS7 ....141 A7
Norhurst NE16 ....2 E5
Norman Ave SR3 ....18 B7
Norman Rd NE39 ....1 F1
Norman Terr Chilton DL17 .82 F8
Consett DH8 ....10 E3
High Pittington DH6 ......36 C5
South Bank TS6 ....120 F6
Norman's Bldgs DL15 ...66 D7
Normanby Cl SR7 ....19 A1
Normanby Ct TS7 ......140 C3
Normanby Hall Pk TS6 .141 C8
Normanby Prim Sch
TS6 ....141 D8
Normanby Rd Eston TS6 .121 B4
Ormesby TS7 ....141 B8
Normandy Cres DH5 .....26 F8
North Albert Rd TS20 ..102 A1
North App DH2 ....16 B4
North Ave Peterlee SR8 ...49 F7
Saltburn-by-t-S TS12 .....125 B7
North Bailey DH1 ......210 C2
North Bank Cres TS7 ...141 B6
North Bitchburn Bank
DL15 ....65 F7
North Bitchburn Terr
DL15 ....66 A6
North Bondgate DL14 ...67 B1
North Brancepeth Cl
DH7 ....43 E6
North Burns DH3 ....16 C4
North Cl Elwick TS27 .....75 C5
Thorpe Thewles TS21 .....100 E4
North Close Rd
Kirk Merrington DL16 .....69 A4
Spennymoor DL16 ....68 F5
North Coronation St SR7 28 D3
North Cotts DL5 ....96 A4
North Cres Durham DH1 .210 B4
Easington SR8 ....39 C3
North Cross St DH8 .....11 C4
North Dene DH3 ....9 C7
North Dr
Chester le Street NE38 .....16 E7
Hartlepool TS26 ....76 E6
Ormesby TS7 ....141 A7
Spennymoor DL16 ....68 D6
North East Ind Est SR8 ..39 D1
North Eastern Terr 3
DL1 ....133 A1
North End Brandon DH7 ..43 A5
Durham DH1 ....210 A4
Hutton Rudby TS15 ....173 F2
Sedgefield TS21 ....85 B7
North End Gdns DL14 ...80 D6
North End Villas DL15 ..189 F5
North Fen TS10 ....107 B4
North Field DL12 ......209 D7
North Gn
4 Staindrop DL2 ....200 E7
Stockton-on-T TS18 ......213 A1
North Haven SR7 ....29 B8
North Holm DH8 ....11 C4
North La Elwick TS27 .....75 C6
Gainford DL2 ....201 D4
Hetton-le-H DH5 ....27 E5
Killerby DL2 ....201 F7
Tow Law DL13,DL15 ....40 C1
Willington DL15 ....53 C6
North Leigh DH9 ....6 D1
North Lodge DH3 ....16 D7
North Lodge Terr DL3 ..132 F3
North Magdalene DH8 ....4 B1
North Mdw TS15 ......173 F2
North Moor Ave TS29 ....59 F4
North Mount Pleasant St 9
TS20 ....118 B6
North Ormesby Prim Sch
TS3 ....120 C4
North Ormesby Rd TS1,
TS4 ....215 B3
North Park Prim Sch
DL16 ....56 A1
North Park Rd TS21 .....85 A7
North Railway St SR7 ...29 D7
North Rd
Annfield Plain DH9 ....12 E6
Chester le Street DH3 .....16 C7
Darlington DL1 ....133 A6
Durham DH1 ....210 B3
Hetton-le-H DH5 ....26 E4
Houghton-le-S DH5 ....26 E4
Loftus TS13 ....127 C1
Middlesbrough TS2 ......214 B4
Seaham SR7 ....29 D8
Seaton Carew TS25 ....77 E1
Spennymoor DL16 ....56 B1
Tow Law DL13 ....183 D2
Wingate TS28 ....60 E8
North Rd E TS28 ....60 E8
North Rd W TS28 ....60 E7
North Rise DL3 ....133 A5
North Road Ind Est DL3 132 F4
North Road Prim Sch
DL1 ....133 A5
North Road Sta DL3 ...132 F4
North Row TS6 ....122 C4
North Side
Hutton Rudby TS15 ......173 F1
Middridge DL5 ....81 E1
Shadforth DH6 ....46 E7
North St Birtley DH3 ......9 E3
Blackhall Colliery TS27 ....50 D3
Byers Green DL16 ....54 E1
Consett DH8 ....11 B2
East Rainton DH5 ....26 D4
Ferryhill DL17 ....69 F6
Hett DH6 ....56 E6
Middlesbrough TS2 ......119 F7
New Silksworth SR3 ....18 A8
South Bank TS6 ....121 A7
Spennymoor DL16 ....68 F8
Stockton-on-T TS18 ......213 A3
West Rainton DH4 ....26 C2
North Stead Dr DH8 .....10 C5
North Tees Ind Est
Middlesbrough TS18 .....119 A5
Stockton-on-T TS18 ......118 F5
North Terr
Annfield Plain DH9 ....13 C5
Crook DL15 ....52 F4
Durham DH1 ....34 A6
Easington SR8 ....39 B4
Gainford DL2 ....201 D4
Loftus TS13 ....127 C3
11 New Silksworth SR3 ....18 A8
Newton Aycliffe DL5 ......96 E2
Redcar TS10 ....107 C7
Seaham SR7 ....29 D8
1 Skelton TS12 ....125 A2
Willington DL15 ....54 A2
Witton Gilbert DH7 ....33 A8
North Thorn DH9 ....13 F7
North View
Barnard Castle DL12 .....209 C5
Bearpark DH7 ....33 A3
Bishop Middleham DL17 ...71 C4
Bournmoor DH4 ....17 E2
Brandon DH7 ....43 C3
Castle Eden TS27 ....49 B1
Consett DH8 ....10 D4
Dalton Piercy TS27 ....75 F3
1 Durham DH1 ....35 A2
Easington SR8 ....39 E5
Easington Lane DH5 ......27 C1
Haswell DH6 ....37 E1
Hunwick DL15 ....66 D5
Langley Park DH7 ....32 B6
Ludworth DH6 ....47 C7
Medomsley DH8 ....4 B1
Murton SR7 ....28 D2
Ouston DH2 ....8 F1
Pelton DH2 ....15 D5
Rowlands Gill NE39 ....1 C2
Sherburn Hill DH6 ....36 D1
The Middles DH9 ....14 B3
North View Terr DH4 ....26 B8
North View W NE39 ......1 C2
North West Ind Est
Easington SR8 ....39 A1
Peterlee SR8 ....49 A8
Shotton Colliery SR8 ......48 F7
North Wood TS5 ....139 D6
Northallerton Rd
Dalton-on-T DL2 ....168 C3
Thornaby-on-T TS17 ......138 D7
Northampton Rd SR8 ....49 C8
Northampton Wlk 9
TS25 ....77 B4
Northamptonshire Dr
DH1 ....35 D3
Northbourne Rd TS19 ..117 F5
Northbrook Ct TS26 .....76 E6
Northburn Gr DL15 .....65 D8
Northcliffe Gr TS15 ....173 F2
Northcote St TS18 .....213 A1
Northcote Terr DL3 ....132 E4
Northdale Ct TS3 ......120 E2
Northdene Ave SR7 .....29 D8
Northern Rd TS5 ......119 B2
Northfield Cl NE16 ......2 F5
Northfield Rd
Billingham TS22 ....102 C5
2 Marske-by-t-S TS11 ....108 B1
Northfield Sch & Sports Coll
TS22 ....102 B6
Northfield View DH8 ....11 A3
Northfield Way DL5 .....96 C5
Northfields TS15 ......173 F2
Northfleet Ave TS3 ....120 E4
Northgate
Annfield Plain DH9 ....12 F3
Darlington DL1 ....133 A3
Guisborough TS14 ....143 E5
Hartlepool TS24 ....64 E1
Northgate Jun Sch
TS14 ....143 E6
Northgate Rd TS5 .....139 D8
Northgrain DL13 ......179 B2
Northiam Cl TS8 ......139 D2
Northland Ave TS26 .....76 F5
Northlands DH3 ....16 C5
Northlands Pk TS29 .....59 E4
Northlea Rd SR7 ....29 A8
Northleach Dr TS8 .....139 D2
Northpark TS23 ....102 E8
Northport Rd TS18 ....213 C4
Northrop Cl DL15 ....53 E2
Northside Birtley DH3 .....9 D6
Trimdon TS29 ....59 E3
Northside Cl DL5 ....81 E1
Northside Ct DL5 ....81 E1
Northside Terr TS29 ....59 E3
Northumberland Ave
Bishop Auckland DL14 .....80 B6
Willington DL15 ....54 A3
Northumberland Gr
12 Hartlepool TS25 ....77 B4
Stockton-on-T TS20 ......101 F2
Northumberland Pl
Birtley DH3 ....9 D1
Peterlee SR8 ....49 B8
Northumberland Rd
TS17 ....138 C7
Northumberland St
19 Darlington DL3 ....132 F1
Peterlee SR8 ....49 F8
Northumberland Wlk 13
TS25 ....77 B4
Northumbria Pl DH9 ....14 B7
Northwold Cl TS25 .....89 E6
Northwood Rd SR7 ......29 B8
Norton Ave Bowburn DH6 .45 D1
Seaham SR7 ....19 A1
Stockton-on-T TS20 ......118 A7
Norton Back La DL2 ...135 A8
Norton Cl
Auckland Park DL14 ....80 F6
Chester le Street DH2 .....15 F1
Norton Cres DL2 ......134 E7
Norton Ct 12 TS20 .....118 B6
Norton Dr TS19 ....117 A5
Norton Hall TS20 ......102 B1
Norton Junction Cotts
TS20 ....101 D1
Norton Prim Sch TS20 .118 C6
Norton Rd
Billingham TS20,TS23 ....102 C1
Sadberge DL2 ....134 E7
Stockton-on-T TS20 ......118 B6
Norton Sch The TS20 ...118 C6
Norwich Ave TS19 .....117 C5
Norwich Cl DH3 ....25 B7
Norwich Gdns DL15 .....53 F2
Norwich Gr DL1 ....133 E5
Norwich Rd Durham DH1 .34 D7
Middlesbrough TS5 ......119 E2
Redcar TS10 ....107 F4
Norwood Cl TS19 ......117 B5
Norwood Cres NE39 ......1 F2
Norwood Rd TS3 ....121 A2
Nottingham Dr TS10 ...107 E4
Nottingham Pl SR8 .....49 B8
Nottingham St DL14 ....68 C1
Nottingham Wlk 10 TS25 .77 B4
Nottinghamshire Rd DH1 35 C3
Nuffield Ct DL1 ....133 B6
Nuffield Rd TS23 ......103 A4
Nugent Ave TS1 ....214 A2
Number One Ind Est DH8 11 A4
Nuneaton Dr TS8 ......139 D2
Nunnery Cl DL3 ....132 B2
Nunnery La DL3 ....132 C2
Nunnington Cl TS17 ...138 B1
Nuns Cl DL14 ....80 D5
Nuns St TS24 ....77 F8
Nuns' Row DH1 ....211 C4
Nunthorpe Gdns TS7 ...141 B2
Nunthorpe Prim Sch
TS7 ....141 C3
Nunthorpe Sch TS7 ....141 C3
Nunthorpe Sta TS7 ....141 B3
Nursery Ct NE17 ....4 B6
Nursery Dr TS21,TS22 ...86 F3
Nursery End DL2 ......201 D7
Nursery Gdns
Easington SR8 ....39 B3
Yarm TS15 ....156 D4
Nursery La
Middlesbrough TS5 ......119 C2
Stockton-on-T TS18 ......212 B2
Nursery The DL14 ....79 C1
Nut La TS4 ....120 A2
Nutfield Cl TS8 ....139 D2
Nuthatch Cl TS26 ....76 D8
Nutley Rd TS23 ....102 F5

O

O' Hanlan St 4 DL16 ....55 F1
O'Neil Dr SR8 ....49 E5
Oak Ave
Blackhall Rocks TS27 ......50 E3
Durham DH1 ....35 A1
5 Houghton-le-S DH4 ......26 D8
Marton TS7 ....140 E3
Oak Ave continued
Willington DL15 ....54 B2
Oak Cres DH2 ....24 A3
Oak Ct DH7 ....23 C3
Oak Gdns DL15 ....52 D6
Oak Gr TS24 ....76 F8
Oak Hill TS8 ....140 C2
Oak La DH8 ....10 C7
Oak Lea Shildon DL4 .....81 B1
Witton Gilbert DH7 ....23 B1
Oak Leaf Cvn Pk DL13 ..207 D4
Oak Rd Brotton TS12 ....126 A5
Eaglescliffe TS16 ....137 D4
Easington SR8 ....39 D3
Guisborough TS14 ....143 E5
Redcar TS10 ....107 F5
Oak St Billingham TS23 ..103 E2
10 Consett DH8 ....10 F2
Eldon Lane DL14 ....80 F4
Great Lumley DH4 ....17 E1
Langley Park DH7 ....32 C7
Middlesbrough TS1 ......215 A3
South Bank TS6 ....121 A6
Waldridge DH2 ....15 E1
Oak Terr
Annfield Plain DH9 ....12 E5
Bishop Auckland DL14 .....80 C7
Burnopfield NE16 ....6 C6
Cornforth DL17 ....70 E8
Holmside DH7 ....22 D7
Leadgate DH8 ....11 D4
Murton SR7 ....28 D2
Pelton DH2 ....15 C7
Peterlee SR8 ....50 A6
Spennymoor DL16 ....68 E8
Tantobie DH9 ....6 B2
The Middles DH9 ....14 B3
Oak Tree Cl DL2 ....154 C7
Oak Tree Cres TS21 .....85 B7
Oak Tree Prim Sch The
TS19 ....212 B4
Oak Wlk TS13 ....127 B2
Oakdale TS7 ....141 B7
Oakdale Rd Consett DH8 ..11 A3
New Marske TS11 ....123 F6
Oakdale Terr DH3 ......16 C2
Oakdene Ave
Darlington DL3 ....151 E8
Stockton-on-T TS18 ......137 E8
Oakdene Cl TS6 ....121 D1
Oakdene Prim Sch TS23 102 F6
Oakdene Rd TS21 ....72 D4
Oakdene Terr DL16 .....68 C5
Oakenshaw Dr TS5 ....139 C5
Oakenshaw Wildlife
Reserve* DL15 ....54 B7
Oakerside Dr SR8 ....49 C4
Oakesway TS24 ....64 B1
Oakeys Rd DH9 ....13 F8
Oakfield
Chester le Street DH2 .....15 F2
Newton Aycliffe DL5 ......96 B6
Oakfield Ave TS16 ....137 B2
Oakfield Cl TS16 ......137 B2
Oakfield Cres DH6 ......45 E1
Oakfield Gdns TS7 ....121 B1
Oakfield La DH8 ....10 C1
Oakfield Rd
Middlesbrough TS3 ......215 C2
Whickham NE16 ....2 F5
Oakfields Burnopfield NE16 .6 B7
Hunwick DL15 ....66 D7
Oakgreen Flats DH7 ....43 B4
Oakham Ave NE16 ....2 F6
Oakham Dr DH1 ....35 D5
Oakham Gn TS20 ......118 C7
Oakhurst Cl 5 TS17 ...138 C1
Oakhurst Rd DL3 ......132 E3
Oakland Ave TS25 ......77 A2
Oakland Gdns DL1 ....133 B7
Oaklands TS9 ....161 A3
Oaklands Ave 6 TS20 ..118 B7
Oaklands Rd TS6 ......141 E8
Oaklands Terr 6 DL3 ..132 F3
Oaklands The DL2 .....154 A5
Oaklea
Chester le Street DH2 .....16 A5
Shiney Row DH4 ....17 F4
Oaklea Cl TS20 ....118 A8
Oaklea Ct 24 DL1 .....132 F1
Oaklea Mews DL5 ....96 E1
Oaklea Terr 2 DL14 .....80 B6
Oakley Cl
Guisborough TS14 ....143 F2
Hemlington TS8 ....139 D2
Oakley Cross Prim Sch
DL14 ....79 C1
Oakley Gdns TS24 ......77 A7
Oakley Gn DL14 ....79 D1
Oakley Rd TS12 ....145 C6
Oakley Wlk Eston TS6 ..121 E1
Normanby TS6 ....141 E8
Oakridge
1 Ormesby TS7 ....141 B7
Whickham NE16 ....2 F6
Oakridge Com Prim Sch
TS13 ....149 E5
Oakridge Rd DH7 ....33 A1
Oakrise TS7 ....141 B7
Oaks Bank DL14 ....92 C8
Oaks Ho DL14 ....92 C8
Oaks The Cornforth DL17 ..57 D1
Darlington DL3 ....132 D3
Esh Winning DH7 ....41 D7
Hemlington TS8 ....139 D2

Parklands Ave TS23 ....102 D2
Parklands Cl TS3 ......120 D2
Parklands Gr DH6 ....38 B6
Parklands Way TS26 ....76 C5
Parks The DH3 ....16 E1
Parkside Burnhope DH7 ...21 E5
Consett DH8 ....10 E3
Darlington DL1 ....152 A7
Guisborough TS14 ....143 E5
Howden-le-W DL15 ....65 E8
Longnewton TS21 ....135 F5
Middlesbrough TS3 ......140 E7
Sacriston DH7 ....23 C3
Spennymoor DL16 ....55 E1
Tanfield Lea DH9 ....6 C1
Parkside Comp Sch DL15 54 A2
Parkside Cotts DH9 ......6 C1
Parkside Cres SR7 ......29 C6
Parkside Inf Sch SR7 ...29 C5
Parkston Ho TS23 .....102 D2
Parkstone Cl TS11 .....124 A6
Parkstone Gr TS24 ......63 D4
Parkstone Pl TS16 .....156 C8
Parkview Rd E TS25 .....90 C8
Parkview Rd W TS25 ....90 B8
Parkway NE16 ....2 E6
Parkway Ctr TS8 ....140 B2
Parkway Dr TS6 ....141 D8
Parkway Gr TS3 ....120 D2
Parkway The TS12 .....125 A7
Parkwood Dr TS18 .....137 D8
Parliament Cl TS18 .....213 A1
Parliament Rd TS1 .....214 B2
Parliament St
Consett DH8 ....10 F2
Stockton-on-T TS18 ......213 A1
Parliament Wlk TS18 ...213 A1
Parmeter St DH9 ....13 E4
Parnaby St DH8 ....10 F2
Parnell St DH4 ....26 B8
Parracombe Cl TS17 ...157 B6
Parrington Pl TS6 .....122 C4
Parsons Ct Ferryhill DL17 .69 E5
South Bank TS6 ....121 A4
Parsons Lonnen DL12 ..209 C5
Parsons Rd SR8 ....39 D1
Partnership Ct SR7 ......18 E2
Parton St TS24 ....77 B8
Partridge Ave TS5 .....139 C4
Partridge Cl
3 Ingleby Barwick TS17 .138 B1
Washington NE38 ....9 F4
Partridge Terr TS28 .....60 E8
Passfield Cres TS6 .....121 B6
Passfield Sq
Easington SR8 ....39 C3
Thornley (nr Wheatley Hill)
DH6 ....47 D4
Passfield Way SR8 ......49 B4
Pasteur Rd DH6 ....37 F7
Pasture Cl TS11 ....108 A1
Pasture Field TS21 ......72 B1
Pasture La TS6 ....122 C4
Pasture Rows DL14 ......81 B4
Pasture The TS17 ......138 A2
Pastures The TS8 ......140 C1
Patches La DL3 ....112 E3
Pateley Moor Cres DL1 .152 C7
Patenson Ct DL5 ....82 B2
Patrick Cres DH6 ....37 E8
Patten La TS14 ....143 E5
Patten St 3 TS6 ....121 D1
Patterdale Ave
Middlesbrough TS5 ......139 C7
Stockton-on-T TS19 ......212 B4
Patterdale Cl Crook DL15 .52 F2
Durham DH1 ....35 E4
Patterdale Mews DH8 ...11 D4
Patterdale St
Hartlepool TS25 ....77 B3
Hetton-le-H DH5 ....27 A2
Pattison Cres TS27 ......50 F2
Pattison Gdns TS27 .....50 F2
Pattison St 22 DL1 ......133 B1
Patton Wlk DH6 ....48 A3
Paulinus Rd DL5 ....96 C6
Pauls Gn DH5 ....27 A6
Pauntley Dr TS5 ....139 C3
Pavilion Cl TS25 ....90 E7
Pavilion Terr DH7 ....21 D5
Pawston Rd NE21,NE39 ....1 B5
Paxton Cl
Newton Aycliffe DL5 ......96 B8
Stockton-on-T TS18 ......213 B4
Paxton St DL17 ....69 D5
Pea Flatts La DH3 ....25 C7
Pea Rd DH9 ....13 D6
Peabody St DL3 ....133 A6
Peace Haven 4 DL17 ....70 B5
Peaceful Valley DL2 ....168 A8
Peakston Cl TS26 ....76 D7
Pear Lea DH7 ....43 A4
Pear Tree Cotts TS8 ....157 F7
Pear Tree Ct TS11 .....124 A7
Pear Tree Terr
Chopwell NE17 ....4 B8
Great Lumley DH3 ....17 B1
Peareth Terr DH3 ....9 C3
Pearl Cl DL17 ....82 F8
Pearl Rd TS17 ....138 D7
Pearl St
Middlesbrough TS1 ......214 C2
Saltburn-by-t-S TS12 .....125 C8
Shildon DL4 ....80 F1
Pears' Terr 6 DL4 ....95 A8
Pearson Cl TS18 ....213 A1
Pearson St
Middlesbrough TS1 ......214 A3

Pearson St *continued*
Spennymoor DL16 ....69 C8
Stanley DH9 ....13 F8
Pearson Terr DL12 .....209 C6
Pearson Ville TS9 ......161 A2
Pearson Way TS17 .....213 C2
Pearson Wlk TS18 .....213 A1
Peart Cl DH6 ....36 A1
Peartree Bglws NE17 .....4 C6
Peartree Ct NE17 ....4 C6
Peartree Terr DH7 ....22 B6
Pease Cotts DL1 ....132 F1
Pease Ct
Eaglescliffe TS16 ....137 B2
Guisborough TS14 ....143 B2
Lingdale TS12 ....145 E5
Pease Rd SR8 ....48 F8
Pease St Darlington DL1 .133 C1
Lingdale TS12 ....145 E5
Pease Way DL5 ....96 C6
Peaseholm Bglws DL15 ..52 D4
Peases Row DL14 ....79 F3
Peases W DL15 ....52 E7
Peases West Prim Sch
DL15 ....52 D7
Peaton St TS3 ....120 C4
Peebles Ave TS25 ....77 A3
Peebles Cl DL1 ....133 E7
Peel Ave Durham DH1 ....35 B3
Trimdon TS29 ....59 E4
Peel Pl DL14 ....66 F2
Peel St Binchester DL14 ...68 A5
Bishop Auckland DL14 .....80 C7
8 Darlington DL1 ....133 B1
Middlesbrough TS1 ......214 C2
Thornaby-on-T TS17 .....138 C8
Peelers Ct TS14 ....143 E6
Peggy's Wicket DH9 .....14 F8
Pegman Cl TS14 ....143 F6
Peile Ct DH8 ....10 C6
Peile Pk DH8 ....10 C6
Peirse Cl TS4 ....215 B3
Peirson Ct TS10 ....107 B7
Peirson St TS10 ....107 B7
Pelaw Ave
Chester le Street DH2 .....16 C5
Stanley DH9 ....14 A8
Pelaw Bank DH3 ....16 C4
Pelaw Cres DH2 ....16 B5
Pelaw Grange Ct DH3 ....16 C8
Pelaw Leazes La DH1 ...211 A3
Pelaw Pl DH2 ....16 C5
Pelaw Rd DH2 ....16 C5
Pelaw Sq DH2 ....16 B5
Pelham Ct DH6 ....58 A3
Pelham St Hartlepool TS24 77 A8
Middlesbrough TS1 ......214 C2
Pelton Cl TS23 ....102 D8
Pelton Com Prim Sch
DH2 ....15 F7
Pelton Fell Rd DH2 ......16 B4
Pelton House Farm Est
DH2 ....15 E6
Pelton La
Chester le Street DH2 .....16 B5
Pelton DH2 ....15 C5
Pelton Mews DH2 ....15 C6
Pemberton Ave DH8 ...177 B4
Pemberton Bank DH5 ....27 C1
Pemberton Cres TS4 ...140 A8
Pemberton Rd
Consett DH8 ....10 B2
Newton Aycliffe DL5 ......82 D2
Pemberton St DH5 ......27 A4
Pemberton Terr 2 DL2 .153 F8
Pemberton Terr N DH9 ...14 B3
Pemberton Terr S DH9 ...14 B3
Pembroke Ave Birtley DH3 .9 D1
New Silksworth SR3 ....18 A6
Pembroke Ct 15 DL1 ...133 B1
Pembroke Dr TS17 .....157 A6
Pembroke Gr TS26 ......63 E1
Pembroke Pl SR8 ....49 B8
Pembroke Rd TS20 .....118 A7
Pembroke St DL14 ....81 D8
Pembroke Way TS10 ...107 E5
Penarth Wlk TS26 ....76 D8
Penberry Gdns TS17 ...156 F7
Pendeen Gr DL3 ....132 F8
Penders La TS15 ....172 E8
Penderyn Cres TS17 ...156 F7
Pendle Cl Peterlee SR8 ...49 B5
Skelton TS12 ....125 B3
Pendle Cres TS23 ......102 E4
Pendleton Rd
Darlington DL1 ....133 A5
Darlington DL1 ....133 A6
Pendleton Rd S DL1 ....133 A5
Pendock Cl TS5 ....139 D4
Pendower St DL3 ....132 F3
Pendragon DH3 ....25 A8
Penhale Dr SR2 ....18 F7
Penhill Cl
Middlesbrough TS3 ......120 C2
Urpeth DH2 ....8 F1
Penhill Rd TS18 ....117 B1
Penistone Rd TS3 ......140 E7
Penllyn Way TS8 ....139 E3
Pennal Gr TS17 ....156 E8
Pennard Gn TS3 ....120 E2
Pennine Ave
Chester le Street DH2 .....16 B2
Stockton-on-T TS18 ......118 F5
Pennine Cl DL3 ....132 C3
Pennine Cres TS10 .....107 B4
Pennine Ct
Annfield Plain DH9 ....12 F3
Fir Tree DL15 ....52 A2

Pennine Dr SR8 ....49 A5
Pennine Gdns DH9 ......14 A5
Pennine View
Chopwell NE17 ....4 B8
Tow Law DL13 ....183 D2
Pennine Way Chilton DL17 83 A8
Ingleby Barwick TS17 ....157 B7
1 Skelton TS12 ....125 C3
Pennington Cl TS23 ....102 E6
Penny La TS18 ....213 A1
Pennyman Cl TS6 ......121 C1
Pennyman Ct TS3 ......140 F7
Pennyman Gn TS8 .....157 F7
Pennyman Prim Sch
TS3 ....141 A8
Pennyman St TS3 ......215 C3
Pennyman Way TS8 ....139 C1
Pennyman Wlk TS11 ....108 D1
Pennypot La TS16 ......137 D5
Penrhyn St TS26 ....77 B4
Penrith Cl TS10 ....107 C4
Penrith Rd TS3 ....120 D1
Penrith St TS24 ....64 D2
Penryn Ave SR7 ....28 D3
Penryn Cl Darlington DL3 132 F8
Skelton TS12 ....125 D3
Penryn Way DH7 ....43 C4
Pensbury St DL1 ....133 A1
Pensby Ave TS4 ....140 B5
Penshaw Cl
3 Ingleby Barwick TS17 .138 C1
Langley Park DH7 ....32 B6
Penshaw Ct TS23 ......102 E8
Penshaw Gdns DH9 .....14 B7
Penshaw View Birtley DH3 .9 E3
Sacriston DH7 ....23 D2
Penshaw Way DH3 ....9 E4
Penshurst Pl TS23 .....102 F5
Pentilly St TS24 ....64 F1
Pentland Ave
Billingham TS23 ....102 D4
Redcar TS10 ....107 A3
6 Skelton TS12 ....125 C3
Pentland Cl SR8 ....49 A5
Pentland Ct 5 DH2 ......16 C2
Pentland Gr DL3 ....132 B1
Pentland Prim Sch
TS23 ....102 D3
Pentlands Terr DH9 .....14 A5
Pentlands The DL17 .....82 F8
Penton Ct TS23 ....102 E7
Penwick Cl TS15 ....156 B4
Penyghent Way TS17 ...157 B6
Penzance Ct SR7 ....28 D4
Peppermires DH7 ....43 A1
Percy Ave DH9 ....12 E5
Percy Cres DH7 ....20 F3
Percy Cross Rigg YO21 .162 E3
Percy Gdns Consett DH8 ..11 B1
1 Consett DH8 ....177 D4
Percy La DH1 ....210 A2
Percy Rd DL3 ....132 F6
Percy Sq DH1 ....44 A7
Percy St
Bishop Auckland DL14 .....80 B5
Crook DL15 ....52 E5
Hartlepool TS26 ....76 F7
Hetton-le-H DH5 ....27 B4
Middlesbrough TS1 ......214 C2
Stanley DH9 ....13 D5
Thornley (nr Wheatley Hill)
DH6 ....47 D4
Wheatley Hill DH6 ....47 F3
Percy Terr
Annfield Plain DH9 ....13 B4
Consett DH8 ....11 B1
Durham DH1 ....210 A2
Peregrine Ct TS14 ......143 B4
Perm Terr DL17 ....71 C4
Perry Ave TS17 ....138 D2
Perrycrofts SR3 ....18 A4
Pert Rd TS24 ....63 E4
Perth Cres TS7 ....140 D3
Perth Gr Darlington DL1 .133 F7
Stockton-on-T TS18 ......212 A1
Perth St TS24 ....77 A7
Pesspool Ave DH6 ....37 F3
Pesspool Bglws DH6 .....37 F3
Pesspool La
Easington DH6,SR8 ....38 C4
Haswell DH6 ....37 F3
Pesspool Terr DH6 ......37 F3
Petch Cl TS1 ....214 B2
Petch St TS18 ....213 A3
Peter Lee Cotts DH6 .....47 E2
Peter's Bank DH9 ....13 A7
Peterborough Rd DH1 ...34 E7
Peterhouse Cl DL1 .....133 B5
Peterlee Cl SR8 ....49 C7
Peterlee Com Hospl SR8 49 E5
Peth Gn DH5 ....27 B1
Peth La DH7 ....21 B3
Pethside DH7 ....21 A3
Petrel Cres TS20 ....102 A2
Petterson Dale DH6 .....58 A4
Petwell Cres SR8 ....39 C4
Petwell La SR8 ....39 C5
Petworth Cres TS17 ....157 B8
Pevensey Cl TS4 ....140 A7
Peverell St DL14 ....80 D5
Peveril Rd TS23 ....102 D5
Pexton Cl TS8 ....139 C2
Phalp St DH6 ....38 B6
Pheasant Cl 2 TS17 ....138 B1
Pheonix Ct DH8 ....10 C3
Philip Ave DH6 ....45 D2
Phillida Terr TS5 ....119 F2
Phillips Ave TS5 ....139 E8

Phillips Cl DH6 ....37 E3
Phillips Ho TS1 ....215 A3
Philpotts Wlk DL5 ....96 E8
Phoenix Cl
Hartlepool TS25 ....89 E7
Langley Park DH7 ....32 B6
Phoenix Ct DL1 ....133 D1
Phoenix Gdns TS18 ....212 A2
Phoenix Pk TS8 ....139 E3
Phoenix Pl
Newton Aycliffe DL5 ......82 C1
3 Shildon DL4 ....81 A2
Phoenix Rd NE38 ....9 E6
Phoenix Row DL14 ......78 F7
Phoenix Sidings TS19 ..213 A3
Phoenix Way DH4 ....26 C7
Phoenix Wlk TS18 .....212 A2
Phoenix Workshops
TS19 ....213 A3
Phyllis Mohan Ct 10
TS3 ....140 D8
Pickard Cl SR8 ....49 E7
Pickering Gr TS25 ....90 A8
Pickering Ho 13 TS4 ....139 F8
Pickering Rd TS17 .....138 E7
Pickering St TS28 ....60 D6
Picktree Cotts 2 DH3 ....16 D4
Picktree Cotts E 3 DH3 .16 D4
Picktree Farm Cotts
NE38 ....16 E7
Picktree Gdns TS25 .....76 F1
Picktree La
Chester le Street DH3 .....16 D4
Chester le Street,Rickleton
DH3,NE38 ....16 E7
Picktree Lodge Birtley DH3 9 E1
Chester le Street DH3 .....16 D8
Picktree Mews DH3 .....16 D4
Picktree Terr 1 DH3 .....16 D4
Pickwick Cl DH1 ....44 B7
Pickwick Ind Est DL14 ...79 C2
Picton Ave
Billingham TS22 ....102 B6
Middlesbrough TS5 ......139 B8
Picton Cres TS17 ......138 B4
Picton Pl 2 TS20 ....118 B8
Picture House Bldgs
TS23 ....102 D1
Piercebridge Cl TS19 ..117 C5
Pierremont Cres DL3 ..132 D3
Pierremont Dr DL3 ....132 D3
Pierremont Gdns DL3 ..132 D2
Pierremont Rd DL3 ....132 D3
Piersburgh La TS15 ....171 D8
Piggy La DL2 ....201 C3
Pike Hill DH8 ....176 F8
Pikeston Cl TS26 ....76 D7
Pikesyde DH9 ....12 B7
Pilgrim St TS24 ....77 C5
Pilgrims' Way DH1 .....211 C4
Pilkington St TS3 ......120 C4
Pilkington Way DL14 ....80 E6
Pilkingtons Bldgs TS5 ..119 D1
Pilmoor Gn DL1 ....152 C7
Pilot Ho TS24 ....77 D6
Pimlico DH1 ....210 C1
Pimlico Rd DH5 ....27 B1
Pinder Cl TS20 ....118 A8
Pinders Way DH6 ....36 D1
Pine Ave Burnopfield NE16 ..5 F6
Durham DH1 ....35 A1
3 Houghton-le-S DH4 .....26 D8
Pine Ct TS19 ....117 C5
Pine Gr Darlington DL3 ..151 C8
Hartlepool TS24 ....76 F8
Pine Hill TS8 ....140 C2
Pine Lea DH7 ....43 A4
Pine Pk DH7 ....33 B1
Pine Rd Ferryhill DL17 ....57 B1
Guisborough TS14 ....143 E5
Ormesby TS7 ....141 B7
Pine Ridge Ave TS21 ....85 B8
Pine St Beamish DH2 .....15 B7
Birtley DH3 ....9 C5
4 Chester le Street DH3 ..16 C3
Langley Park DH7 ....32 D7
Middlesbrough TS1 ......215 A3
Middlesbrough, Cargo Fleet
TS3 ....120 D5
Stanley DH9 ....13 D4
Stockton-on-T TS20 ......118 B8
Waldridge DH2 ....15 E1
West Pelton DH2 ....15 A5
Pine Terr DH9 ....12 E5
Pine Tree Cres DL4 ......81 B1
Pine View DH9 ....13 A8
Pine View Villas DH7 ....41 F8
Pine Wlk TS13 ....127 B2
Pineda Cl TS5 ....139 D3
Pinedale Dr DH6 ....37 F7
Pinehurst Way TS11 ....123 F6
Pinero Gr TS25 ....76 D2
Pines The TS15 ....156 C5
Pinetree DH7 ....41 D8
Pinetree Gdns DL15 .....52 D3
Pinetree Gr DL2 ....153 F7
Pinewood Ave TS4 .....139 F8
Pinewood Cl
Hartlepool TS27 ....63 C4
Loftus TS13 ....148 A8
Newton Aycliffe DL5 ......82 B1
Pinewood Cres DL5 .....95 C1
Pinewood Rd
Eaglescliffe TS16 ....137 C4
Marton TS7 ....140 F4
Pinewood St DH4 ....17 E1
Pinfold La DL13 ....195 C4
Pinfold St TS18 ....213 B4

Pintail Cl TS26 ....76 D8
Piper Knowle Rd TS19 .117 B8
Pipershaw NE37 ....9 F6
Pipit Cl TS17 ....138 A1
Pippins The TS22 ......102 C8
Pirbright Gr TS8 ....139 E2
Pirnmill View TS19 .....117 B5
Pit La Brandon DH7 ......42 E5
Durham DH1 ....34 C7
Pithouse La
Medomsley DH8 ....11 B8
West Rainton DH4 ....25 E3
Pitt St Binchester DL14 ...68 A4
Consett DH8 ....10 F2
Pittington La DH1,DH6 ...35 F5
Pittington Prim Sch DH6 36 B5
Pittington Rd DH5,DH6 ..36 A7
Pixley Dell DH8 ....177 E4
Plane St DH8 ....11 A2
Planetree Ct TS7 ....140 E4
Plantagenet Ave DH3 ....16 D2
Plantation Ave DH6 ......36 E3
Plantation Cotts TS12 ..145 F4
Plantation Rd TS10 .....107 C1
Plantation St DH8 ....11 D4
Plantation Terr
Fir Tree DL15 ....52 A1
Howden-le-W DL15 ....65 E8
Plantation View
Howden-le-W DL15 ....65 E8
West Pelton DH9 ....14 F6
Plantation Wlk DH6 .....37 F7
Plantations TS22 ....87 A3
Plawsworth Rd DH7 .....23 C3
Plawsworth Road Inf Sch
DH7 ....23 C3
Player Ct TS16 ....137 C1
Playlin Cl TS15 ....156 E4
Pleasant Pl 5 DH3 ....9 C5
Pleasant View
Burnhope DH7 ....21 D4
Consett DH8 ....10 B4
Darlington DL3 ....133 A6
Leadgate DH8 ....11 B6
Plover Cl 5 NE38 ....9 F3
Plover Dr NE16 ....6 C5
Plover Lodge DH3 ....9 C6
Plumer Dr TS20 ....118 A8
Plunkett Rd DH9 ....5 E1
Plunkett Terr DH2 ....15 D4
Plymouth Cl SR7 ....28 F6
Plymouth Gr TS26 ....76 E8
Plymouth Wlk TS26 ......76 E8
Pochin Rd Eston TS6 ....121 D6
Eston TS6 ....121 E6
Polam Hall Jun Sch
DL1 ....151 E8
Polam Hall Sch DL1 ....151 F8
Polam La DL1 ....151 F8
Polam Rd DL1 ....151 F8
Polden Cl SR8 ....49 A5
Poldon Terr TS23 ......102 E3
Polemarch St 4 SR7 .....29 D6
Police Hos DL15 ....189 E5
Police Houses SR8 ......49 C6
Pollard's Dr DL14 ....80 A7
Polpero Cl DH3 ....9 D3
Polperro Cl 6 SR2 ....18 F8
Polperro Gr DL3 ....133 A8
Pond Farm Cl TS13 .....149 F6
Pond Field Cl DL3 ......151 B8
Pond St DH1 ....45 B4
Pond View DL1 ....133 C2
Ponds Court Bsns Pk
DH8 ....10 E2
Ponds Ct DH8 ....10 E2
Pont Bglws DH8 ....11 B6
Pont La DH8 ....11 C6
Pont Rd DH8 ....11 D5
Pont Terr DH8 ....11 C4
Pont View DH8 ....11 B5
Pontac Rd TS11 ....124 A6
Ponteland Cl NE38 ....9 F4
Ponthaugh NE39 ....1 F3
Ponthead Mews DH8 ....11 D4
Pontop Ct 8 DH9 ....12 F4
Pontop Pike La DH9 .....12 C6
Pontop St DH5 ....26 C4
Pontop Terr DH9 ....12 E3
Pontop View Consett DH8 .11 B1
Dipton DH9 ....12 B7
Rowlands Gill NE39 ....1 D2
Pontopsyde DH9 ....12 C7
Poole Terr TS7 ....160 B8
Pope Gr TS25 ....76 D3
Poplar Ave
Burnopfield NE16 ....5 F6
1 Houghton-le-S DH4 .....26 D8
Hutton Rudby TS15 ......173 F1
Poplar Cres Birtley DH3 ...9 B5
Fishburn TS21 ....72 D5
Poplar Dr Durham DH1 ...35 A3
Spennymoor DL16 ....68 F7
Poplar Gr Brotton TS12 .126 A4
Darlington DL1 ....133 C2
Dipton DH9 ....12 E8
Redcar TS10 ....107 E6
South Bank TS6 ....121 B4
Stockton-on-T TS18 ......212 C1
7 Sunderland SR2 ....18 E8
Poplar Lea DH7 ....43 A4
Poplar Pl TS14 ....143 C5
Poplar Rd Durham DH1 ...35 D4
Eaglescliffe TS16 ....156 B8
Thornaby-on-T TS17 .....138 C7

Q

R

Rookery The NE16 5 F6
Rookhope NE38 16 F8
Rookhope Gr DL14 79 E5
Rookhope Prim Sch DL13 180 D5
Rookhope Walks* DL13 180 D5
Rookswood Gdns NE39 1 E3
Rookwood Hunt DL5 96 A8
Rookwood Rd TS7 141 B3
Roosevelt Rd DH1 211 C4
Roper's Terr TS29 59 D3
Ropery La Bournmoor DH3 16 F3
Chester le Street DH3 16 D2
Ropery Rd TS24 64 C2
Ropery St TS18 213 A3
Ropery Walk Prim Sch SR7 29 E6
Ropery Wlk SR7 29 E6
Ropner Ave TS18 212 B1
Ropner Gdns DL2 153 F5
Rosa St DL16 68 E8
Rosa Street Prim Sch DL16 68 E8
Roscoe Rd TS23 102 E1
Roscoe St TS1 215 B2
Rose Acre DH1 45 A6
Rose Ave
Marske-by-t-S TS11 108 A1
Stanley DH9 13 D5
Rose Cotts Burnopfield NE16 5 E5
Shotton Colliery SR8 48 E7
South Hetton DH6 38 A7
Rose Cres Bournmoor DH4 17 D3
Sacriston DH7 23 D3
Rose Ct Esh Winning DH7 31 C2
Peterlee SR8 49 B3
Rose Gdns NE11 8 C6
Rose Hill TS15 156 C5
Rose La DL1 133 E5
Rose Lea DH7 23 B1
Rose St
7 Houghton-le-S DH4 26 D8
Middlesbrough TS1 214 C3
Trimdon TS29 59 E4
Rose Terr
Eaglescliffe TS16 156 C7
East Hedleyhope DH7 40 E6
6 Langley Park DH7 32 C6
Middleton-In-T DL12 208 B6
Pelton DH2 15 E5
Stanhope DL13 206 C3
Rose Wood Prim Sch TS8 159 B8
Rosebank TS26 76 F4
Rosebank Cl SR2 18 E8
Rosebank Sch DL17 70 A5
Rosebay Ct
Darlington DL3 132 E3
Guisborough TS14 143 B3
Rosebay Rd DH7 43 E4
Roseberry Ave TS9 161 B3
Roseberry Com Prim Sch TS9 161 B3
Roseberry Cres
Crook DL15 52 D4
Eston TS6 122 A3
Great Ayton TS9 161 B3
Stockton-on-T TS20 102 B1
Thornley (nr Wheatley Hill) DH6 47 C4
Roseberry Ct TS9 161 A3
Roseberry Dr
Great Ayton TS9 161 A3
Stainton TS8 139 C1
Roseberry Flats TS23 102 D4
Roseberry Inf Sch TS23 102 E4
Roseberry Jun Sch TS23 102 E5
Roseberry La TS9 161 C6
Roseberry Mews 1 TS26 76 F6
Roseberry Mount TS14 143 C4
Roseberry Prim Sch DH2 15 C5
Roseberry Rd
Billingham TS23 102 C4
Great Ayton TS9 161 A3
Middlesbrough TS4 120 B2
Middlesbrough TS4 215 B1
Redcar TS10 107 B3
Stockton-on-T TS20 102 B1
Trimdon TS29 72 D8
Roseberry Sports & Com Coll DH2 15 C6
Roseberry Sq TS10 107 B3
Roseberry St DH9 14 D7
Roseberry View
Great Ayton TS9 161 C7
Thornaby-on-T TS17 138 C8
Roseberry Villas DH2 15 C5
Rosebery Rd TS26 76 F6
Rosebery St DL3 132 E3
Rosebery Terr
6 Consett DH8 10 F2
4 Shildon DL4 81 A2
Roseby Rd SR8 49 F6
Rosecroft Ave
Loftus TS13 147 B8
4 Middlesbrough TS4 119 F1
Rosecroft La TS13 147 B7
Rosedale DL16 55 E1
Rosedale Ave
Consett DH8 10 D5
Hartlepool TS26 76 F5
Middlesbrough TS4 119 F2
Rosedale Cl TS21 85 B7
Rosedale Cres
Darlington DL3 132 B4
Guisborough TS14 143 B3
Loftus TS13 127 B2
Shildon DL4 81 B1
Rosedale Gdns
Billingham TS23 102 D6
Edmondsley DH7 23 B7
Lingdale TS12 145 E5
3 Stockton-on-T TS19 117 D8
Rosedale Gr TS10 106 F4
Rosedale La TS13 149 E7
Rosedale Rd Durham DH1 35 D4
Nunthorpe TS7 141 B3
Rosedale St DH5 26 E1
Rosedale Terr
Peterlee SR8 49 F7
Willington DL15 54 A3
Rosehill Great Ayton TS9 161 A2
Hinderwell TS13 149 E6
Rosehill Inf Sch TS19 117 B2
Roseland Cres TS7 140 E5
Roseland Dr TS7 140 E5
Roselea Ave SR2 18 F7
Rosemary Cotts TS11 124 D8
Rosemary Ct 7 DL1 152 C8
Rosemary La SR8 39 B4
Rosemead Ave DL15 54 A3
Rosemoor Cl TS7 140 C3
Rosemount Beamish DH9 15 A7
Durham DH1 34 D8
Rosemount Ct DL14 80 D5
Rosemount Rd
Bishop Auckland DL14 80 D5
New Marske TS11 123 F6
Rosemount Terr DL15 52 E4
Roseneath Ave TS19 101 D1
Rosetown Ave SR8 50 A6
Roseway The TS12 125 C6
Rosewood DL17 82 E8
Rosewood Cl
Ormesby TS7 141 B7
Sacriston DH7 23 C3
Rosewood Ct TS7 140 E4
Rosewood Gdns DH2 16 B5
Rosewood Terr DH3 9 B5
Roseworth Prim Sch TS19 117 C8
Rosgill TS10 107 B4
Rosiere Gr TS10 107 C5
Roslin Terr DL13 189 D2
Roslyn Ave TS3 120 D1
Roslyn St DL1 152 A8
Ross DH2 9 A1
Ross Gr TS25 90 B8
Ross St
Middlesbrough TS1 214 B2
11 Seaham SR7 29 D7
Ross Terr 3 DL17 70 A5
Ross Wlk DL5 96 F7
Rossall St TS25 77 A3
Rossendale Cl 1 TS11 124 C8
Rossett Wlk
2 Middlesbrough TS3 120 C1
Middlesbrough TS3 140 C8
Rossetti Way TS23 102 D7
Rosslare Rd TS19 117 C8
Rosslyn Ave SR2 18 F7
Rosslyn Ct TS18 137 E8
Rosslyn Pl DH3 9 D2
Rossmere DL16 55 E2
Rossmere Prim Sch TS25 89 F8
Rossmere Way TS25 89 F8
Rossway DL1 133 E7
Rosthwaite TS5 139 B4
Rosthwaite Ave TS19 117 E8
Rosthwaite Cl TS24 64 B1
Rostrevor Ave TS19 101 D1
Rothbury SR2 18 D6
Rothbury Ave
Peterlee SR8 49 F8
Stockton-on-T TS19 117 D8
Rothbury Cl
Chester le Street DH2 16 A1
Ingleby Barwick TS17 157 B7
Trimdon TS29 59 E4
Rothbury Dr DL3 132 B5
Rothbury Rd Durham DH1 34 D7
Middlesbrough TS3 120 C1
Rothbury St TS23 102 D4
Rotherham Ave TS19 117 D7
Rotherham Cl DH5 26 D6
Rothesay DH2 8 F1
Rothesay Dr TS10 107 E3
Rothesay Gr TS7 141 B4
Rothley Ave SR8 49 F8
Rothley Terr DH8 4 B1
Rothman Cl DL16 56 B3
Rothwell Cres TS19 117 D7
Rothwell Mews TS6 121 F2
Rottingdean Cl TS19 117 D8
Rough Lea Colliery DL15 66 E8
Rough Lea La DL15 66 E7
Rough Lea Terr DL15 66 D7
Roundhay Dr TS16 137 C1
Roundhill Ave TS17 156 F7
Roundhill Cl
Hartlepool TS26 76 C6
Hurworth-on-T DL2 152 C1
Roundhill Rd DL2 152 C3
Roundhill Way DL15 54 B4
Roundway TS7 140 E4
Rounton Gn TS3 120 C1
Rounton Gr TS19 117 B2
Routledge Ct TS24 64 A1
Routledge Rd TS20 118 C5
Row The CA9 178 A6
Rowallane Gdns TS17 157 B7
Rowan Ave
Guisborough TS14 143 B3
Shildon DL4 81 B1
Rowan Ct Burnopfield NE16 6 B6
Darlington DL3 132 C1
Esh Winning DH7 41 C7
Spennymoor DL16 69 A8
Rowan Dr Durham DH1 34 E8
Great Ayton TS9 161 A3
Hetton-le-H DH5 26 F4
Rowan Gr TS8 139 B1
Rowan Lea DH7 43 B4
Rowan Oval TS21 85 B7
Rowan Pl DL5 96 B6
Rowan Rd
Eaglescliffe TS16 156 B8
Stockton-on-T TS19 118 A5
Rowan Tree Ave DH1 35 A4
Rowanwood Ct TS5 139 E4
Rowell Cl SR2 18 C6
Rowell St TS24 64 G8
Rowen Cl TS17 156 F8
Rowland Cres TS27 49 A1
Rowland Keld TS14 143 B2
Rowlands Gill Inf Sch NE39 1 F3
Rowlands Gill Jun Sch NE39 1 F3
Rowlands Gr TS23 103 A8
Rowlands Terr TS28 60 E6
Rowlandson Terr 5 DL17 70 B5
Rowley Bank DH8 176 F3
Rowley Cl DH7 42 E7
Rowley Cres DH7 31 D1
Rowley Dr DH7 33 B1
Rowley Link DH7 31 D1
Roworth Rd TS3 121 A1
Roxburgh Cl Blaydon NE21 2 A8
Eston TS6 121 B3
Roxby Ave
Guisborough TS14 143 D2
Middlesbrough TS3 140 E7
Roxby Cl Hartlepool TS25 90 D7
Redcar TS10 107 C3
Stockton-on-T TS19 117 F7
Roxby La TS13 148 F6
Roxby Moor Ave DL1 152 D7
Roxby Wynd TS28 48 E1
Royal George Cl DL4 95 A7
Royal George Dr TS16 137 B2
Royal Gr DL15 52 E4
Royal Oak Cotts DL13 206 C5
Royal Oak Yd DL3 132 F2
Royal Rd DH9 13 F7
Royal Yd DL13 195 E3
Royce Ave TS23 103 B5
Royce Ct TS23 103 B5
Royd The TS15 156 B4
Royston Ave TS3 140 E7
Royston Cl TS19 117 F7
Royston Gr TS25 89 D6
Ruberry Ave 8 TS19 117 C8
Ruby Ave DL17 82 F8
Ruby Rd TS17 138 D7
Ruby St Darlington DL3 133 A6
Middlesbrough TS1 214 C2
Saltburn-by-t-S TS12 125 C8
Shildon DL4 80 F1
Rudby Cl TS15 156 E5
Rudd's Pl TS5 119 E2
Ruddock Ave DL14 80 A5
Ruddock's Wynd 8 DL2 200 E7
Rudds Hill DL17 70 C5
Rudland Way DL14 78 F6
Rudland Wlk 1 TS6 121 F3
Rudston Ave TS22 102 B6
Rudston Cl TS17 138 B4
Rudyard Ave TS19 117 C8
Ruff Tail TS14 143 B4
Rufford Cl
Guisborough TS14 143 E2
Ingleby Barwick TS17 138 C1
1 Marton TS7 140 F3
Ruffside DH8 175 D6
Rufus Gn 2 DL5 96 F8
Rugby Rd TS18 212 C2
Rugby St TS25 77 A3
Rugby Terr TS2 103 E1
Rugeley Cl 4 TS19 117 D7
Ruislip Cl TS19 117 D7
Rumby Hill DL15 52 F1
Rumby Hill Bank DL15 65 F8
Rumby Hill La DL15 53 A2
Runcie Rd DH6 57 D8
Runciman Rd TS24 63 F2
Runcorn SR2 18 C7
Runcorn Ave TS19 117 D7
Runfold Cl TS19 101 D1
Runnymead Gn TS3 140 E7
Runnymede
Great Lumley DH3 25 A8
Nunthorpe TS7 141 A2
Ryhope SR2 18 D7
Runnymede Cl TS19 117 D8
Runnymede Ct 6 DL14 80 C8
Runnymede Gdns NE17 4 B7
Runswick Ave
Middlesbrough TS5 139 C4
Redcar TS10 107 A5
Stockton-on-T TS19 117 D7
Runswick Cl SR3 18 C7
Runswick Dr SR7 19 D1
Runswick Ho TS1 214 C3
Runswick La TS13 149 F5
Runswick Rd TS6 121 F2
Rupert St TS18 213 B4
Rush Pk DL14 79 E6
Rushey Gill DH7 43 A4
Rushford SR2 18 D6
Rushleigh Ave TS5 139 B6
Rushmere TS8 140 E1
Rushmere Heath TS16 156 C8
Rushmoor DL16 69 B8
Rushpool Cl TS10 107 B3
Rushsyde Cl NE16 2 E5
Rushy Lea La DL13 207 B2
Rushyford Ave TS19 117 D7
Rushyford Ct 1 DL5 96 D8
Ruskin Ave
Chester le Street DH2 15 E3
Easington Lane DH5 37 D8
Middlesbrough TS5 139 B7
Saltburn-by-t-S TS12 125 B7
1 Shildon DL4 80 F1
Ruskin Cl
Dalton-on-T DL2 168 B5
Stanley DH9 14 B7
Ruskin Cres DH6 47 C4
Ruskin Gr TS25 76 F3
Ruskin Rd Birtley DH3 9 C4
Darlington DL1 152 A6
Russ St DL15 53 C3
Russell Cl DH8 11 A3
Russell Cres TS29 60 B5
Russell Ct DL5 96 A8
Russell Pl DL15 54 A3
Russell St
Bishop Auckland DL14 80 B8
Darlington DL1 133 A2
Esh Winning DH7 41 C6
Hartlepool TS24 64 F1
Middlesbrough TS1 215 A3
Stockton-on-T TS18 213 A3
Russell Terr DH3 9 B6
Russell Wlk
8 Hartlepool TS25 77 B4
4 Thornaby-on-T TS17 138 C8
Russell's Yd DL15 53 F3
Rustington Cl TS19 117 D8
Rustland Dr DL3 151 D8
Ruswarp Ave 1 TS19 117 D7
Ruswarp Cl 1 TS6 121 F2
Ruswarp Dr SR3 18 B6
Ruswarp Gr TS25 90 E7
Ruswarp Rd TS6 121 F2
Ruth Ave TS3 120 E2
Rutherford Ave SR7 28 F8
Rutherford Ct DH7 32 B7
Rutherford Ho SR8 39 D4
Rutherford La DL12 204 B6
Rutherford Terr 2 DL17 70 A5
Rutherglen Wlk TS16 156 C8
Ruthin Cl TS19 117 E8
Rutland Ave
Bishop Auckland DL14 80 B6
Marton TS7 140 C3
3 New Silksworth SR3 18 A7
Rutland Cl TS19 117 E8
Rutland Ct TS1 215 A3
Rutland Dr DL15 54 A3
Rutland Pl 7 DH8 177 A4
Rutland Rd DH8 177 A4
Rutland Sq DH3 9 B5
Rutland St Coundon DL14 81 D8
Hetton-le-H DH5 26 F4
Seaham SR7 29 B8
Rutland Terr DH6 37 E1
Rutland Wlk SR8 49 C8
Rutter St DH7 43 E5
Ryan Ave TS18 213 B4
Ryan Terr DH6 47 E1
Ryan Wlk TS18 213 B4
Ryan's Row TS11 108 B1
Rydal Ave
Billingham TS23 102 E1
Easington Lane DH5 37 C8
Eston TS6 121 F4
Middlesbrough TS5 139 C7
Redcar TS10 107 C5
Stanley DH9 13 D4
Rydal Cl DH7 23 B3
Rydal Cres Blaydon NE21 2 B8
Peterlee SR8 49 E6
Rydal Dr DL15 53 A3
Rydal Gr DL14 79 A1
Rydal Mews DH8 11 D4
Rydal Mount SR8 39 D4
Rydal Rd
Chester le Street DH2 16 C1
Darlington DL1 152 B8
Ferryhill DL17 69 F5
Skelton TS12 125 B3
Stockton-on-T TS18 212 B3
Rydal St TS26 77 A4
Rydal Way TS21 116 B7
Rydale Ct TS29 60 A5
Ryde Rd TS19 117 E7
Ryde Terr DH9 12 F5
Ryde Terrace Bglws 8 DH9 12 F5
Ryder Cl TS11 123 F6
Ryder Ct DL5 82 C3
Rye Cl TS16 156 B7
Rye Hill DL3 132 D4
Rye Hill Way TS8 159 C7
Rye Hills Sch TS10 107 D4
Rye View SR2 18 F7
Ryedale Durham DH1 35 D3
Guisborough TS14 143 B2
Ryedale Cl TS15 156 B3
Ryedale St TS3 120 C4
Ryehill Cl TS7 141 A1
Ryehill Gdns TS26 76 E7
Ryehill View DH5 26 C5
Ryehills Dr TS11 108 E1
Ryelands Pk TS13 148 A8
Ryelands Way DH1 34 C8
Ryemount Rd SR2 18 D7
Ryhill Wlk TS7 141 A7
Ryhope Ave 2 TS19 117 D8
Ryhope Engine Mus* SR2 18 E5
Ryhope General Hospl SR2 18 F5
Ryhope Inf Sch SR2 18 E7
Ryhope Jun Sch SR2 18 E7
Ryhope Rd SR2 19 A8
Ryhope St
Houghton-le-S DH5 26 F8
Ryhope SR2 18 E7
Ryhope St S SR2 18 F7
Ryhope Village CE Prim Sch SR2 18 F6
Rylstone Cl DL5 96 B8
Rylstone Ct TS4 140 A8
Rymers Cl SR8 39 A3
Ryton Cl TS17 138 B4
Ryton Cres Seaham SR7 29 A7
Stanley DH9 14 A8

S

Sabatier Cl TS17 213 C2
Sabin Terr DH9 13 B4
Sacred Heart RC Comp Sch TS10 107 B6
Sacred Heart RC Prim Sch
Byermoor NE16 6 D7
Hartlepool TS26 76 F7
Middlesbrough TS1 214 B1
Sacriston Cl TS23 102 C6
Sacriston Ind Est DH7 23 C3
Sacriston Jun & Inf Schs DH7 23 C2
Sacriston La DH7 23 B1
Sadberge CE Prim Sch DL2 134 E7
Sadberge Gr TS19 117 A2
Sadberge Rd
Middleton St George DL2 134 E2
Stockton-on-T TS18 138 A8
Sadberge St TS3 120 C4
Saddler Cl 4 TS17 138 B1
Saddler St
Bishop Auckland DL14 80 B8
Durham DH1 210 C2
Ferryhill DL17 69 F6
Saddlers La DH1 210 C2
Saddlery The DL5 95 F8
Saddleston Cl TS26 76 D7
Sadler Dr TS7 140 C3
Sadler Forster Way TS17 138 D1
Sadler La Evenwood DL14 92 D6
Kinninvie DL12 194 E1
Saffron Wlk TS25 77 E1
Sailport Ind Est TS17 138 B7
Saint Ct SR3 18 A5
St Abbs Wlk 7 TS24 77 C5
St Adens Way SR8 49 D5
St Agathas Cl DH7 43 C5
St Aidan Cres DH6 47 C3
St Aidan's Ave DH1 34 B5
St Aidan's CE Meml Prim Sch TS25 77 B2
St Aidan's Coll (Univ of Durham) DH1 44 B7
St Aidan's Cres
Billingham TS22 102 C3
Durham DH1 210 A3
St Aidan's Pl DH8 10 E4
St Aidan's St Consett DH8 10 E4
1 Hartlepool TS25 77 B3
Middlesbrough TS1 214 C2
St Aidan's Terr TS29 59 F6
St Aidan's Wlk
Bishop Auckland DL14 80 C5
3 Newton Aycliffe DL5 96 F8
St Aidans Cres DH9 13 A3
St Aidans Dr TS1 214 C3
St Alban's Cl DH3 25 B6
St Alban's Gn DL1 133 F5
St Alban's RC Prim Sch TS10 107 B2
St Alban's St DL13 183 E1
St Alban's Terr TS29 59 E3
St Aldwyn Rd SR7 29 B8
St Alphonsus' RC Prim Sch TS3 120 C4
St Andrew's Cl
Consett DH8 10 D4
Newton Aycliffe DL5 96 E1
St Andrew's Cres DH8 10 D4
St Andrew's Crest DL14 80 C7
St Andrew's Gdns DH8 10 D4
St Andrew's La DL16 56 A1
St Andrew's Pl
Bishop Auckland DL14 80 C7
Westgate DL13 180 A1
St Andrew's Prim Sch DL14 80 C5
St Andrew's RC Prim Sch TS6 121 B4
St Andrew's Rd
Bishop Auckland DL14 80 C5
Bishop Auckland DL14 80 D5
Consett DH8 10 D4
2 New Marske TS11 124 A6
Spennymoor DL16 56 A1
Tanfield Lea DH9 6 F1
St Andrew's Rd E TS6 121 E5
St Andrew's Rd W TS6 121 E5

Sanderson St
3 Coxhoe DH6 ....58 A4
Darlington DL1 ....133 A2
Sandford Cl TS4 ....140 A7
Sandford Rd DH8 ....10 B4
Sandgate DH9 ....13 B4
Sandgate Ind Est TS25 ..77 D4
Sandhall Cl 4 TS23 ....102 E8
Sandhill Bank YO21 ....164 D2
Sandlewood Wlk DH9 ...14 A7
Sandling Ct TS7 ....140 E4
Sandmartin La TS20 ....102 B2
Sandmoor Cl TS6 ....121 E1
Sandmoor Rd TS11 .....123 F6
Sandown Dr DL5 ....82 E2
Sandown Pk TS10 ......107 D4
Sandown Rd TS23 .....102 D6
Sandown Way TS17 ....118 F1
Sandpiper Cl
Redcar TS10 ....107 E2
Washington NE38 ....9 F2
Sandport Wlk 9 TS18 ..213 C4
Sandray Cl DH3 ....9 D1
Sandriggs DL3 ....132 C5
Sandringham Cres 11
SR8 ....50 B6
Sandringham Ct DL3 ...132 A2
Sandringham Dr 2 DH9 .12 F5
Sandringham Rd
Crook DL15 ....52 F4
Eston TS6 ....121 E4
Hartlepool TS26 ....77 A6
Lingdale TS12 ....145 F5
Middlesbrough TS3 ....140 E8
Redcar TS10 ....107 C6
Stockton-on-T TS18 ....212 C2
10 Thornaby-on-T TS17 ...138 D8
Sandringham Terr DL14 .68 D1
Sands The DH1 ....211 A3
Sandsay Cl SR2 ....18 D8
Sandsend Rd Eston TS6 .121 F3
Redcar TS10 ....107 A5
Sandwell Ave TS3 ....140 F8
Sandwell Chare TS24 ....77 F8
Sandwell Dr DH4 ....17 F8
Sandwich Gr TS27 ....63 D4
Sandwick Terr DH6 ....47 E1
Sandwood Pk TS14 ....143 B2
Sandy Bank TS21 ....84 D5
Sandy Flatts Ct TS5 ....139 E4
Sandy Flatts La TS5 ....139 E4
Sandy Gate DH1 ....210 A4
Sandy La Billingham TS22 102 B4
New Marske TS11,TS14 ..123 E4
Wynyard Village TS22 ....101 F7
Sandy Lane W TS22 ....102 A6
Sandy Leas La TS21 ....116 B2
Sandy Lonnen DL15 .....41 C3
Sandyford DH2 ....15 F7
Sandyford Pl DH2 ....15 E7
Sandypath La NE16 ....6 A7
Sapley Cl TS17 ....138 C4
Sapper's Cnr TS25 ....89 E5
Sarah St TS25 ....77 C3
Sark Wlk TS14 ....143 D3
Satley Cl DL15 ....52 D3
Satley Plough DL13 ....183 D5
Satley Rd TS23 ....102 F8
Saturn Cl SR8 ....39 C4
Saturn St SR7 ....29 A7
Saunders Ave DL13 ....189 D2
Saunton Ave TS10 ....107 E2
Saunton Rd TS23 ....102 F4
Sawley Cl DL3 ....131 F5
Sawley Gr TS18 ....117 A1
Sawmill Ave TS27 ....63 B8
Sawmill Cotts DH9 ....5 E1
Sawmill La DH7 ....43 B4
Sawtry Rd 3 TS3 ....140 F8
Saxby Dr DL15 ....53 E1
Saxby Rd TS20 ....118 B6
Saxon Gn DL14 ....66 D1
Saxon Terr DH8 ....10 E3
Saxonfield TS8 ....140 B2
Sayer Wlk SR8 ....49 E5
Scafell DH3 ....9 D1
Scafell Cl SR8 ....49 E6
Scafell Ct DH9 ....12 E3
Scafell Gdns DL15 ....52 F2
Scalby Gr Redcar TS10 ..107 E3
Stockton-on-T TS19 ....117 A3
Scalby Rd TS3 ....120 B2
Scalby Sq TS17 ....138 D7
Scaling Ct TS14 ....143 D5
Scampton Cl TS17 ....138 B4
Scanbeck Dr TS11 ....108 D1
Scarbeck Bank DL11 ...205 D3
Scarborough St
5 Hartlepool TS24 ....77 C6
Loftus TS13 ....127 A1
South Bank TS6 ....121 A5
10 Thornaby-on-T TS17 ...138 C8
Scardale Way DH1 ....35 E4
Scargill DL1 ....152 C8
Scargill Ct 14 DL1 ....152 C8
Scargill Dr DL16 ....55 F2
Scarteen Cl TS14 ....143 D3
Scarth Cl TS12 ....145 E5
Scarth St DL3 ....132 E1
Scarth Wlk TS18 ....213 A3
Scarthwood Cl 2 TS17 .138 C1
Scawfell Gr TS25 ....77 B3
Sch of Education (Univ of
Durham) DH1 ....211 A3
Scholar's Path DL5 .....96 A7
Scholars Gate TS14 ....143 D2
School Ave
1 Blackhall Colliery TS27 ..50 D3
Coxhoe DH6 ....57 F3
Kelloe DH6 ....58 E6
Middlesbrough TS5 ....119 B1
West Rainton DH4 ....25 F2
School Aycliffe La DL5 ..95 E3
School Cl
Marske-by-t-S TS11 .....108 D1
Spennymoor DL16 ....56 B1
St John's Chapel DL13 ...179 E1
Stockton-on-T TS18 ....213 A1
Thorpe Thewles TS21 ....100 D3
School Croft TS1 ....215 A4
School Ct DH6 ....35 F1
School Gn DH6 ....47 D4
School Hill DL13 ....179 A4
School Hos NE39 ....5 B8
School La
Great Ayton TS9 ....161 A2
High Spen NE39 ....1 A3
Liverton TS13 ....147 A8
Stanley DH9 ....13 D5
School Rd DH5 ....26 C4
School Row DL15 ....54 A6
School St Bowburn DH6 ..57 C4
Darlington DL3 ....132 C4
Easington SR8 ....39 E4
Howden-le-W DL15 ....65 E7
Seaham SR7 ....29 D5
Witton-le-W DL14 ....65 B3
School Terr
Great Lumley DH4 ....17 E1
Stanley DH9 ....13 D5
School View Dipton DH9 ..12 C8
Easington Lane DH5 ....37 D8
West Rainton DH4 ....25 F1
School Wlk TS18 ....213 A1
Schoolhouse La NE16 .....6 E7
Schooner Ct TS24 ....77 D6
Scira Ct DL1 ....133 B5
Scorer's La DH3 ....25 B8
Scotforth Cl 4 TS7 .....140 F3
Scotland Head NE21 .....2 A8
Scotland La DL13 ....195 D2
Scotland St SR2 ....19 A6
Scotney Rd TS23 ....102 D5
Scott Ct DH3 ....25 A7
Scott Dr TS20 ....117 F8
Scott Gr TS25 ....76 D2
Scott Pl DL5 ....96 C8
Scott Rd
Bishop Auckland DL14 .....80 B4
Eston TS6 ....121 B1
Scott St
6 Houghton-le-S DH4 ....26 E8
Redcar TS10 ....107 D6
Shildon DL4 ....94 F8
Stanley DH9 ....13 E6
Scott's Rd TS2 ....215 B4
Scott's Terr
Darlington DL3 ....133 A6
Hetton-le-H DH5 ....27 A4
Scotton Cl TS18 ....137 A8
Scotton Ct TS3 ....121 A1
Scrafton Pl TS11 ....108 D1
Scripton Gill DH7 ....43 A4
Scripton Gill Rd DH7 ....42 F3
Scripton La DH7 ....55 C7
Scruton Cl TS18 ....117 B1
Scugdale Cl TS15 ....156 B3
Scurfield Rd TS19 ....117 B7
Scutterhill Bank DL13 ..180 A1
Sea View
Blackhall Rocks TS27 ....50 F2
Easington SR8 ....39 B3
Ryhope SR2 ....19 A6
Sea View Cotts TS27 .....49 F1
Sea View Gdns SR8 ....50 A8
Sea View Ind Est SR8 ....39 F1
Sea View Terr TS24 ....64 F1
Sea View Wlk SR7 ....28 E4
Seaburn Dr 1 DH4 ....26 C8
Seaford Cl TS10 ....107 E2
Seaham Cl Redcar TS10 ..107 F2
Stockton-on-T TS20 ....101 E1
Seaham Grange Ind Est
SR7 ....18 E2
Seaham Kingfisher Ind Est
SR7 ....29 A8
Seaham Rd
Houghton-le-S DH5 ....27 A8
Ryhope SR2 ....19 A6
Seaham Sch of Technology
SR7 ....19 A1
Seaham St
New Silksworth SR3 ....18 A7
Seaham SR7 ....29 E5
Stockton-on-T TS20 ....213 B4
Seaham Sta SR7 ....29 C8
Sealand Cl TS17 ....138 D3
Seamer Cl TS5 ....139 E7
Seamer Gr TS18 ....212 A1
Seamer Rd Hilton TS15 ..157 F3
Thornton TS8 ....158 C6
Seaside La SR8 ....39 D4
Seaside La S SR8 ....39 E4
Seathwaite TS5 ....139 B3
Seaton Ave DH5 ....27 A7
Seaton Carew Rd TS2 ..104 B4
Seaton Carew Sta TS25 ..90 D8
Seaton Cl Redcar TS10 ..107 F3
Stockton-on-T TS19 ....117 A3
Seaton Cres SR7 ....18 E1
Seaton Gr SR7 ....28 D8
Seaton Holme Discovery
Ctr★ SR8 ....39 A4
Seaton La Hartlepool TS25 .90 C8
Seaham SR7 ....18 E1
Seaton Pk SR7 ....28 F8
Seaton St TS1 ....215 A2
Seaton Terr TS12 ....145 E4
Seatonport Ct 6 TS18 .213 C4
Secker Pl DL5 ....96 F7
Second Ave
Chester le Street DH2 .....16 B2
Chester le Street,South Pelaw
DH2 ....16 B8
Second St
Blackhall Colliery TS27 ....50 D3
Consett DH8 ....11 B2
Leadgate DH8 ....11 C5
Leadgate DH8 ....11 C6
Peterlee SR8 ....50 A7
Quaking Houses DH9 .....13 D2
Sedgebrook Gdns TS3 .141 A8
Sedgefield Com Coll
TS21 ....85 B7
Sedgefield Com Hospl
TS21 ....85 B8
Sedgefield Enterprise Ctr
DL16 ....56 D2
Sedgefield Hardwick Prim
Sch TS21 ....85 B7
Sedgefield Prim Sch
TS21 ....85 B6
Sedgefield Racecourse★
TS21 ....84 E5
Sedgefield Rd TS5 .....139 C4
Sedgefield Terr TS21 ....72 B5
Sedgefield Way TS18 ..118 E5
Sedgeletch Rd 5 DH4 ...26 A8
Sedgemoor Rd TS6 ....141 E8
Sedgemoor Way TS23 ..103 A7
Sedgewick Cl TS24 ....64 A3
Sedgwick St 3 DL3 .....132 E4
Seeingsike Rd DL13 ....179 F3
Sefton Rd TS3 ....121 A2
Sefton Way TS15 ....156 A4
Selaby Ct DL2 ....201 C4
Selaby La DL2 ....201 B5
Selborne Gdns DH8 ....10 E6
Selbourne St TS1 ....214 B2
Selbourne Terr DL3 ....132 F3
Selby Cl DL14 ....79 D2
Selby Cres DL3 ....132 A5
Selby Gdns DH8 ....10 C1
Selby Gr TS25 ....77 B1
Selby Rd TS7 ....141 B3
Selby's Grave NE21 ....1 F8
Selkirk Cl TS4 ....139 F7
Selkirk Cres DH3 ....9 C6
Selset Ave TS3 ....140 E7
Selset Cl Darlington DL1 .152 C7
Hartlepool TS26 ....76 C6
Selwood Cl TS17 ....138 D4
Selworthy Gn TS17 .....157 B6
Selwyn Dr TS19 ....117 A6
Semmerwater Gr TS10 .107 C5
Senhouse Rd DL1 ....152 F8
Sennings La DL12 ....193 D1
Sennybridge Gr TS17 ...156 F7
Serpentine Gdns TS26 ...76 E7
Serpentine Rd
Hartlepool TS26 ....76 E6
Hartlepool TS26 ....76 E7
Seton Com Prim Sch
TS13 ....129 C1
Seton Wlk DL5 ....96 E5
Setting Stones NE38 .....17 A8
Seven Hills Ct DL16 ....56 B2
Sevenacres DH3 ....25 B7
Seventh Ave DH2 ....16 B4
Seventh St
Blackhall Colliery TS27 ....50 D4
Peterlee SR8 ....50 A6
Peterlee SR8 ....50 A7
Severn Cl SR8 ....49 C4
Severn Cres DH9 ....13 E5
Severn Dr TS14 ....143 C3
Severn Gr Billingham TS22 102 A6
Skelton TS12 ....125 D3
Severn Rd TS10 ....107 A6
Severn St TS1 ....215 B2
Severn Way DL1 ....152 A6
Severs Dr TS8 ....139 C1
Sexhow La TS15 ....173 F1
Seymour Ave TS16 ....156 A7
Seymour Cl TS11 ....124 F8
Seymour Cres TS16 ....156 A8
Seymour Dr TS16 ....156 A8
Seymour Gr TS16 ....156 B8
Seymour Hill Terr TS13 .127 C1
Seymour St
Bishop Auckland DL14 .....80 B6
Consett DH8 ....11 A2
Peterlee SR8 ....50 B6
Seymour Terr DH5 ....27 B1
Shackleton Cl TS17 ....138 D4
Shadforth Cl SR8 ....49 A4
Shadforth Dr TS23 ....102 F7
Shadon Way DH3 ....9 E3
Shadwell Cl TS6 ....141 C7
Shaftesbury Ave
Blackhall Colliery TS27 ....50 D4
Ryhope SR2 ....18 E7
Shaftesbury Cres TS27 ..50 C4
Shaftesbury Rd
Blackhall Colliery TS27 ....50 C5
Eston TS6 ....121 D3
Shaftesbury St TS18 ...213 A2
Shafto Cl 4 DH8 ....177 D4
Shafto St Byers Green DL16 54 E1
Shafto St *continued*
Spennymoor DL16 ....68 F7
Shafto Terr Craghead DH9 .14 D2
Stanley DH9 ....13 F8
Shafto Way DL5 ....96 E6
Shaftsbury Dr DH7 ....43 A2
Shakespeare Ave
Blackhall Colliery TS27 ....50 C5
Eston TS6 ....121 F4
Hartlepool TS25 ....77 A3
Shakespeare Cl DH9 ....14 B7
Shakespeare Rd DL1 ...152 A7
Shakespeare St
Houghton-le-S DH5 ....26 E7
9 Seaham SR7 ....29 D7
Thornley (nr Wheatley Hill)
DH6 ....47 F2
Shakespeare Terr
Chester le Street DH2 .....15 E3
Easington SR8 ....39 C4
Shalcombe Cl SR3 ....18 A6
Shaldon Cl TS10 ....107 F2
Shallow Ford DL13 .....186 A8
Shandon Pk TS8 ....140 E1
Shannon Cres TS19 ....117 A4
Shannon Ct TS25 ....89 E4
Shannon Lea DL2 ....154 A8
Shannon Way DL1 ....151 F6
Sharon Ave DH6 ....58 D5
Sharp Cres Durham DH1 ..35 A3
Hartlepool TS24 ....64 A2
Sharp Rd DL5 ....96 D6
Sharpley Dr SR7 ....28 E8
Sharrock Cl TS3 ....215 C2
Shaw Cres Eston TS6 ....121 F4
Middleton-In-T DL12 .....208 B6
Shaw Gr TS25 ....76 D2
Shaw La
Barningham DL11 ....205 A5
Ebchester DH8,NE17 ....3 F4
Shaw St Seaham SR7 .....29 D7
Spennymoor DL16 ....68 F8
Shaw Wood Cl DH1 ....210 A4
Shawbrow View
Bishop Auckland DL14 .....80 B4
Darlington DL3 ....131 F2
Shawcross Ave TS6 ....121 D5
Shearwater Ave DL1 ...133 D2
Shearwater La TS20 ...102 A2
Sheelin Ave DH2 ....16 C1
Sheen Cl DH4 ....26 A2
Sheep Hill NE16 ....6 B6
Sheepdene TS22 ....87 A3
Sheepfoote Hill TS15 ..156 B4
Sheerness Gr TS24 ....77 C5
Sheerness Way TS10 ...107 E2
Shellbark DH4 ....17 F6
Shelley Ave DH5 ....37 D8
Shelley Cl
Billingham TS23 ....102 D8
Crook DL15 ....52 C2
Stanley DH9 ....14 A6
Shelley Cres TS6 ....121 C3
Shelley Ct DH2 ....15 E3
Shelley Gdns DH2 ....15 E3
Shelley Gr TS25 ....76 F3
Shelley Rd
Darlington DL1 ....133 C3
Middlesbrough TS4 ....139 F8
Shelley Sq SR8 ....39 C3
Shelley St SR7 ....29 D7
Shelley Terr DL17 ....82 F7
Shelton Ct TS3 ....121 A1
Shepherd Cl TS17 ....138 B6
Shepherd Ct TS12 ....145 C6
Shepherdson Ct 8 TS6 .121 A6
Shepherdson Way TS3 .215 C3
Sheppards Croft DL5 .....95 F4
Sheppey Ct SR3 ....18 A6
Shepton Cl TS17 ....138 E6
Sheraton Bank TS27 .....61 F3
Sheraton Cl DL5 ....96 E6
Sheraton Hall Est TS27 ..61 F3
Sheraton Pk TS19 ....117 E6
Sheraton Rd DL5 ....96 E6
Sheraton St
Darlington DL3 ....132 F5
Stockton-on-T TS18 ....212 C2
Sherborne DH3 ....25 B8
Sherborne Cl DL3 ....131 F4
Sherborne Ho DL3 ....131 F4
Sherburn Ave TS23 .....102 F7
Sherburn Cl TS5 ....139 C4
Sherburn Gn NE39 ....1 F3
Sherburn Hill Prim Sch
DH6 ....36 D1
Sherburn Park Dr NE39 ...1 F3
Sherburn Rd Durham DH1 35 A2
Durham DH1 ....211 C3
Sherburn Road Flats
DH1 ....211 C3
Sherburn Sta DH6 ....35 E1
Sherburn Terr
Consett DH8 ....11 A2
Hamsterley NE17 ....3 F5
Sherburn Village Prim Sch
DH6 ....36 A2
Sherburn Villas 19 DH8 ..10 F3
Sheridan Dr Crook DL15 ..52 C2
Stanley DH9 ....14 B6
Sheridan Gr TS25 ....76 F3
Sheriff St TS26 ....77 A6
Sheriff's Moor Ave DH5 .37 C8
Sheringham Cl SR3 ....18 A4
Sheringham Ct TS10 ...107 F2
Sheriton Ho TS20 ....102 B1
Sherwood Cl
Barnard Castle DL12 ....209 D6
Sherwood Cl *continued*
Consett DH8 ....10 E7
Ormesby TS7 ....141 B5
Sherwood Ct
5 Silksworth SR3 ....18 A6
Toronto DL14 ....66 F2
Sherwood Dr TS11 ....124 C8
Sherwood Rd TS17 .....138 C4
Shetland Cl TS5 ....139 D3
Shetland Ct 1 SR3 ....18 A6
Shetland Dr DL1 ....133 D7
Shevington Gr TS7 .....140 E3
Shibden Rd TS3 ....120 C3
Shield Row Gdns DH9 ...13 F8
Shield Row Prim Sch
DH9 ....14 A8
Shield Wlk DL5 ....96 E7
Shieldrow La
Annfield Plain DH9 ....13 A3
Annfield Plain, New Kyo
DH9 ....13 B4
Shields Rd DH3 ....16 D5
Shields Terr TS24 ....64 C2
Shildon Bsns Ctr DL4 ...95 A8
Shildon Cl TS23 ....102 D6
Shildon Ct 4 DL4 ....95 A8
Shildon Prim Sch DL4 ...80 E2
Shildon Rd
Blanchland DH8 ....175 A5
Redworth DL5 ....95 B4
Shildon St DL1 ....133 A5
Shildon Sta DL4 ....95 B8
Shillmoor Cl DH2 ....15 F1
Shincliffe CE Prim Sch
DH1 ....45 B5
Shincliffe La Cassop DH1 .45 C7
High Shincliffe DH1 ....45 C7
Sherburn DH1 ....45 D7
Shincliffe Rd TS23 .....102 F7
Shinwell Cres
South Bank TS6 ....121 A5
Thornley (nr Wheatley Hill)
DH6 ....47 C4
Shinwell Terr Murton SR7 .28 B3
Wheatley Hill DH6 ....47 E2
Ship Inn Yd TS18 ....213 A2
Shipham Cl TS10 ....107 E2
Shipley Gr DL14 ....79 F5
Shipley Terr
Cotherstone DL12 ....198 F6
Crook DL15 ....53 A3
Shire Chase DH1 ....34 D8
Shirley Ave TS5 ....119 B1
Shirley Cl DL14 ....92 D7
Shirley Terr DL14 ....92 C7
Shoreham Cl TS10 ....107 F2
Shoreswood Dr 3 SR3 ...18 B7
Shoreswood Wlk TS5 ..139 D4
Short Cl TS18 ....137 F7
Short Gr SR7 ....28 A3
Short St DL14 ....80 B5
Shotley Bridge Hospl
DH8 ....10 E6
Shotley Bridge Inf Sch
DH8 ....10 D6
Shotley Bridge Jun Sch
DH8 ....10 C7
Shotley Cl TS23 ....102 D6
Shotley Grove Rd DH8 ..10 B5
Shotton Bank SR8 ....48 F3
Shotton Colliery Ind Est
DH6 ....48 D7
Shotton Ct TS23 ....102 F5
Shotton Hall Inf Sch SR8 49 B4
Shotton Hall Jun Sch
SR8 ....49 B4
Shotton Hall Sch SR8 ...49 B4
Shotton La DH6,SR8 .....48 E5
Shotton Prim Sch DH6 ..48 C7
Shotton Rd Peterlee SR8 ..49 F7
Shotton Colliery DH6,SR8 ..48 E7
Shrewsbury Cl SR8 ....49 B5
Shrewsbury Rd TS3 ....121 A1
Shrewsbury St
Hartlepool TS25 ....77 A3
Seaham SR7 ....29 D5
Shrigley Cl NE38 ....17 B8
Shropshire Dr DH1 ....35 C2
Shropshire Wlk 15 TS25 .77 B4
Shull Bank DL13 ....189 B3
Shummard Cl DH4 ....17 F5
Sid Chaplin Dr DL5 .....96 C8
Sidcup Ave TS3 ....140 E7
Siddington Wlk TS3 ...120 D1
Sidegate DH1 ....210 C3
Sideling Tails TS15 ....156 C4
Sidings The DH1 ....211 B3
Sidlaw Ave
Chester le Street DH2 .....16 A2
2 Skelton TS12 ....125 C3
Sidlaw Rd TS23 ....102 C5
Sidmouth Cl
Middlesbrough TS8 ....140 B5
Seaham SR7 ....28 F6
Sidney Cl DH9 ....14 B6
Sidney Terr DH9 ....13 D8
Siemans St DL17 ....69 E6
Sildale Cl DL3 ....132 E4
Silent Bank DH6 ....46 E4
Silkin Way DL5 ....96 C7
Silkstun Ct 8 SR3 ....18 A7
Silksworth Rd SR3 ....18 A7
Silksworth Terr SR3 .....18 A7
Silkworth La 1 SR3 .....18 A8
Sills The DL12 ....209 B5
Silton Cl TS10 ....106 F4
Silton Gr TS18 ....212 A1
Silver Cts DH7 ....43 B4

Silver Pl DL1 ... 133 B1
Silver St
Bishop Auckland DL14 ... 67 C1
Consett DH8 ... 10 D4
Durham DH1 ... 210 C2
Hartlepool TS24 ... 77 B5
Middlesbrough TS2 ... 119 E7
4 Spennymoor DL16 ... 68 F8
Stockton-on-T TS18 ... 213 B3
Wolsingham DL13 ... 207 D5
Yarm TS15 ... 156 B6
Silverdale Nunthorpe TS7 140 F2
Silksworth SR3 ... 18 A4
Silverdale Dr NE21 ... 2 A8
Silverdale Pl DL5 ... 96 A7
Silverdale Way NE16 ... 2 F4
Silverton Rd TS14 ... 143 F2
Silverwood Cl TS27 ... 63 C4
Silverwood Ct 11 TS17 ... 138 C8
Simcox Ct TS2 ... 214 A4
Simonburn NE38 ... 9 F4
Simonside Gr TS17 ... 157 B7
Simonside Wlk TS3 ... 141 A8
Simpasture Ct DL5 ... 96 C5
Simpasture Gate DL5 ... 96 D5
Simpson Ave DL14 ... 79 E3
Simpson Cl TS6 ... 121 B5
Simpson Gn TS6 ... 121 A5
Simpson Rd DL14 ... 93 B8
Simpson St
Middlesbrough TS5 ... 119 E2
Stanley DH9 ... 13 F7
Sinclair Dr DH3 ... 16 D8
Sinclair Rd TS25 ... 76 D2
Sinderby Cl TS23 ... 102 E6
Sinnington Cl TS14 ... 143 E3
Sinnington Rd TS17 ... 138 C4
Sir Douglas Pk TS17 ... 138 C5
Sir E D Walker Homes
DL3 ... 151 D8
Sir Hugh Bell Ct TS10 ... 106 E7
Sir William Turner's Homes
TS10 ... 123 A8
Siskin Cl Hartlepool TS26 ... 76 D8
Stockton-on-T TS20 ... 102 A2
Sitwell Wlk TS25 ... 76 E2
Sixth Ave DH2 ... 16 B3
Sixth St
Blackhall Colliery TS27 ... 50 D4
Consett DH8 ... 11 B2
Peterlee SR8 ... 50 A7
Skeeby Cl TS18 ... 137 B8
Skeeby Rd DL1 ... 152 B8
Skel ton Ct TS14 ... 143 E6
Skeldale Gr DL3 ... 132 E4
Skelton Dr
Marske-by-t-S TS11 ... 108 E1
Redcar TS10 ... 107 E4
Skelton Ellers TS14 ... 144 A7
Skelton Ind Est TS12 ... 125 E3
Skelton Prim Sch TS12 ... 125 D3
Skelton Rd Brotton TS12 ... 126 A3
Thornaby-on-T TS17 ... 138 D7
Skelton St TS24 ... 63 F3
Skelwith Rd TS3 ... 120 C1
Skerne Ave TS29 ... 59 C1
Skerne Cl SR8 ... 49 C4
Skerne Gr DH8 ... 11 D5
Skerne Park Prim Sch
DL1 ... 152 A7
Skerne Rd Hartlepool TS24 64 A2
Newton Aycliffe DL5 ... 96 E4
Stockton-on-T TS20 ... 118 B7
Skerries Cres TS10 ... 107 B2
Skerries Wlk DL1 ... 133 D7
Skiddaw Cl
Eaglescliffe TS16 ... 137 B2
Peterlee SR8 ... 49 E6
Skiddaw Ct
Annfield Plain DH9 ... 12 F3
Nunthorpe TS7 ... 140 F2
Skinner St TS18 ... 213 A2
Skinnergate DL3 ... 132 F1
Skinningrove Bank Rd
TS13 ... 127 B4
Skinningrove Rd TS13 ... 127 A2
Skiplam Cl TS8 ... 139 C2
Skipper's La Eston TS6 ... 121 B2
South Bank TS6 ... 121 A4
Skipper's La Ind Est
TS6 ... 121 A4
Skipper's Lane Ind Est
TS6 ... 120 F5
Skippers Mdw DH7 ... 33 B1
Skipsea View SR2 ... 18 D7
Skipton Cl Ferryhill DL17 ... 70 B5
1 Newton Aycliffe DL5 ... 96 B7
Skipton Gr DL14 ... 80 A6
Skipton Moor Cl DL1 ... 152 D7
Skipton Rd TS23 ... 102 E5
Skirbeck Ave TS3 ... 141 A8
Skirlaw Cl DL17 ... 83 A8
Skirlaw Rd
Newton Aycliffe DL5 ... 96 E6
Yarm TS15 ... 156 B4
Skomer Ct TS10 ... 107 E2
Skottowe Cres TS9 ... 160 F3
Skottowe Dr TS9 ... 160 F3
Skripka Dr TS22 ... 102 A5
Skye Ct 2 SR3 ... 18 A6
Skye Wlk Darlington DL1 ... 133 D7
Guisborough TS14 ... 143 C2
Skylark Cl TS26 ... 63 E1
Slack The DL13 ... 195 D4
Slaidburn Rd DH9 ... 13 F7
Slake Terr Hartlepool TS24 ... 77 D6
Hartlepool, Middleton TS24 ... 77 D7
Slaley Cl TS11 ... 123 F6
Slaley Ct 4 SR3 ... 18 A6
Slater Pl DH6 ... 57 D8
Slater Rd TS6 ... 121 F4
Slater St 1 TS26 ... 77 A6
Slater Wlk TS6 ... 121 F4
Slayde The TS15 ... 156 C4
Sledmere Cl
Billingham TS23 ... 102 F8
Peterlee SR8 ... 49 D8
Sledmere Dr TS5 ... 139 E7
Sledwich Cotts DL12 ... 200 B2
Sledwick Rd TS23 ... 102 F5
Sleightholme Moor Rd
DL11,DL12 ... 202 E3
Sleights Cres TS6 ... 121 F3
Sleights Ct TS14 ... 143 E5
Slingley Cl SR7 ... 28 E8
Slingsby Cl TS5 ... 139 E6
Slip Inn Bank DL11 ... 205 E2
Sloshes La DL14 ... 78 C7
Smailes La NE39 ... 1 C2
Smailes St DH9 ... 13 E5
Smallhope Dr DH7 ... 20 F3
Smeathorns Rd TS12 ... 164 E7
Smillie Cl SR8 ... 49 D7
Smillie Rd SR8 ... 39 E1
Smirks Yd 7 TS20 ... 118 B8
Smith Cl DH6 ... 35 F1
Smith Gr SR2 ... 18 E6
Smith St
Middlesbrough TS1 ... 214 C3
Ryhope SR2 ... 18 F6
Stockton-on-T TS18 ... 213 A3
Tow Law DL13 ... 183 E2
Smith St S SR2 ... 18 F6
Smith Wlk DL5 ... 96 E7
Smith's Dock Park Rd
TS6 ... 121 C1
Smith's Dock Rd TS6 ... 121 A7
Smith's Terr DH5 ... 27 B1
Smithfield DH1 ... 34 B8
Smithfield Rd DL1 ... 152 B8
Smithy Gn DL11 ... 205 C4
Smithy La NE11 ... 8 E8
Smyth Pl TS24 ... 64 A3
Smythsons Cl DL5 ... 95 F4
Snackgate La DL5 ... 95 D1
Snaith Terr TS28 ... 60 D8
Sneck Gate La TS8 ... 159 B4
Snipe La Darlington DL2 ... 152 B6
Darlington, Blackwell DL2 ... 151 E6
Hurworth-on-T DL2 ... 152 A4
Loftus TS13 ... 148 A4
Snipe St TS10 ... 106 F7
Sniperley Gr DH1 ... 33 F5
Snipes Dene NE39 ... 1 E3
Snotterton La DL2 ... 200 D7
Snow Hall DL2 ... 201 E3
Snow's Green Rd DH8 ... 10 C7
Snowball Cl DL15 ... 52 D3
Snowberry Cl TS20 ... 118 A7
Snowden St TS6 ... 121 D2
Snowden Terr DL15 ... 54 A2
Snowdon Cres TS10 ... 107 B4
Snowdon Ct DH9 ... 12 E3
Snowdon Gr
Hartlepool TS24 ... 63 D4
Ingleby Barwick TS17 ... 156 F8
Snowdon Pl SR8 ... 49 A5
Snowdon Rd TS2 ... 119 E7
Snowdrop Ave SR8 ... 49 F7
Snowdrop Cl TS19 ... 117 C5
Snowdrop Way DL14 ... 79 F6
Sober Hall Ave TS17 ... 157 A6
Sockburn La DL2 ... 169 E7
Soho St DL4 ... 95 A8
Somerby Terr TS3 ... 120 D2
Somersby Cl TS24 ... 64 C2
Somerset Cotts 4 SR3 ... 18 A8
Somerset Cres TS12 ... 125 A2
Somerset Gr DL1 ... 133 C4
Somerset Rd
2 Consett DH8 ... 177 A4
Eston TS6 ... 121 E4
Guisborough TS14 ... 143 D3
Stockton-on-T TS20 ... 118 A7
Somerset St
Middlesbrough TS1 ... 215 B3
New Silksworth SR3 ... 18 A8
Somerset Terr TS23 ... 102 F3
Somerville Ave 7 TS3 ... 140 F8
Somerville Ct 1 DL1 ... 133 B6
Sophia SR7 ... 29 D7
Sophia St SR7 ... 29 D7
Soppett St TS10 ... 107 C6
Sopwith Cl TS18 ... 137 F7
Sorbonne Cl TS17 ... 213 B2
Sorrel Cl TS19 ... 117 B5
Sorrel Ct TS7 ... 140 C5
Sorrel Wynd DL5 ... 82 D2
Sorrell Gr TS14 ... 143 B3
Sotherby Rd
Middlesbrough TS3 ... 120 E4
South Bank TS6 ... 121 A5
South Acre DL15 ... 54 A6
South App DH2 ... 16 C2
South Arden St 21 DL1 ... 132 F1
South Ave
Billingham TS23 ... 118 D8
Redcar TS10 ... 106 E4
Shadforth DH6 ... 46 E7
Stillington TS21 ... 99 E3
South Bailey DH1 ... 210 C1
South Bank Bsns Ctr
TS6 ... 121 A6
South Bank Rd TS3 ... 120 E5
South Bank Sta TS6 ... 121 A7
South Burns DH3 ... 16 C4
South Church Ent Pk
DL14 ... 80 C4
South Church Rd DL14 ... 80 C7
South Cl DH5 ... 37 D8
South Cleatlam DL2 ... 200 E5
South Cotts DL5 ... 96 A4
South Cres Durham DH1 ... 210 B4
Great Lumley DH4 ... 17 F1
Hartlepool TS24 ... 64 G8
Peterlee SR8 ... 39 E1
Seaham SR7 ... 29 E7
Washington NE38 ... 17 B8
South Cross St DH8 ... 11 C4
South Ct
12 South Bank TS6 ... 121 A6
Spennymoor DL16 ... 68 D5
South Downs DL17 ... 82 F8
South Dr Hartlepool TS26 ... 76 F6
Marton TS7 ... 140 D4
Ormesby TS7 ... 141 A7
South End DH6 ... 36 C5
South End Villas DL15 ... 52 E3
South Farm SR2 ... 19 A6
South Fields DH9 ... 13 E4
South Gn Hett DH6 ... 56 E5
Staindrop DL2 ... 200 E7
Stockton-on-T TS18 ... 213 A1
South Gr DL5 ... 96 F1
South Grange Pk SR7 ... 18 F2
South Hetton Ind Est
DH6 ... 37 F7
South Hetton Prim Sch
DH6 ... 37 F7
South Hetton Rd DH5,
DH6 ... 37 D8
South Lackenby TS6 ... 122 A3
South Lea DH7 ... 23 B1
South Leigh DH9 ... 6 D1
South Lotus TS13 ... 147 C8
South Magdalene DH8 ... 4 B1
South Market St DH5 ... 27 B4
South Mdws DH9 ... 12 D8
South Moor Hospl
Stanley DH9 ... 13 F4
The Middles DH9 ... 14 A4
South Moor Rd DH9 ... 13 E3
South Mount Pleasant St 10
TS20 ... 118 B6
South Par Hartlepool TS25 ... 77 B3
Thornley (nr Wheatley Hill)
DH6 ... 47 D4
South Park Ave TS6 ... 141 D8
South Pelaw Inf Sch DH2 16 B5
South Railway St SR7 ... 29 D7
South Rd Durham DH1 ... 44 C6
Hartlepool TS24 ... 77 B5
High Etherley DL14 ... 78 F4
Stockton-on-T TS20 ... 118 C7
South Row DL14 ... 81 A4
South Sherburn NE39 ... 1 E1
South Side
Butterknowle DL13 ... 195 C5
Easington SR8 ... 39 B3
Hutton Rudby TS15 ... 173 F1
Middridge DL5 ... 81 E1
Shadforth DH6 ... 46 E6
South Side (Dean Rd)
DL17 ... 69 F5
South St
Chester le Street DH2 ... 16 B4
Consett DH8 ... 11 B2
Crook DL15 ... 52 E3
Darlington DL3 ... 132 F4
Durham DH1 ... 210 C2
East Rainton DH5 ... 26 C4
Eston TS6 ... 121 F1
9 Fence Houses DH4 ... 26 A8
Guisborough TS14 ... 143 D4
Sherburn DH6 ... 36 A1
Shildon DL4 ... 94 F8
Spennymoor DL16 ... 68 F8
Stillington TS21 ... 99 E3
West Rainton DH4 ... 26 A2
Willington DL15 ... 53 F3
Willington,Sunnybrow DL15 ... 53 F1
South Stanley Inf Sch
DH9 ... 13 E5
South Stanley Jun Sch
DH9 ... 13 E5
South Tees Bsns Ctr
TS6 ... 121 B7
South Terr
Bishop Auckland DL14 ... 80 C8
Chopwell NE17 ... 4 B8
Crook DL15 ... 53 A4
Darlington DL1 ... 132 F1
Durham DH1 ... 34 A5
Eggleston DL12 ... 193 D3
Esh Winning DH7 ... 31 F1
Esh Winning, Cornsay Colliery
DH7 ... 31 A2
Peterlee SR8 ... 50 A7
Redcar TS10 ... 107 E6
Seaham SR7 ... 29 E7
Shildon DL4 ... 94 C8
2 Skelton TS12 ... 125 A2
Skelton TS12 ... 125 B2
South Bank TS6 ... 121 A6
Spennymoor DL16 ... 56 A1
7 Staindrop DL2 ... 200 E7
South Thorn DH9 ... 13 F8
South Town La TS13 ... 147 E6
South View
Annfield Plain DH9 ... 13 A3
Beamish DH2 ... 15 A7
Billingham TS23 ... 102 D1
Birtley DH3 ... 9 D4
Bishop Auckland DL14 ... 80 C7
South View *continued*
Bishop Auckland, St Helen
Auckland DL14 ... 79 D2
Bishop Middleham DL17 ... 71 C4
Brandon DH7 ... 43 C3
Burnhope DH7 ... 21 D5
Castle Eden TS27 ... 49 B1
Chilton DL17 ... 82 F7
Chopwell NE17 ... 4 A8
Consett DH8 ... 177 C4
Consett, Bridgehill DH8 ... 10 C4
Coundon DL14 ... 81 B7
Durham DH1 ... 211 C3
Eaglescliffe TS16 ... 156 B8
Easington Lane DH5 ... 37 D8
Evenwood DL14 ... 92 C6
1 Ferryhill DL17 ... 70 A6
Fishburn TS21 ... 72 C5
Gainford DL2 ... 201 D4
Hart TS27 ... 62 F2
Heighington DL5 ... 95 D1
Hett DH6 ... 56 E6
Hunwick DL15 ... 66 D5
Hutton Rudby TS15 ... 173 F1
Kimblesworth DH2 ... 23 F3
Kirk Merrington DL16 ... 69 A3
Langley Park DH7 ... 32 C6
Murton SR7 ... 28 D2
Newfield DL14 ... 67 A7
Pelton DH2 ... 15 E7
Pelton,Newfield DH2 ... 15 C5
Sacriston DH7 ... 23 B4
Seaham SR7 ... 28 F5
Sherburn Hill DH6 ... 36 D1
Shildon DL4 ... 81 A2
Spennymoor DL16 ... 68 D6
Tantobie DH9 ... 6 B2
The Middles DH9 ... 14 B3
Trimdon TS29 ... 59 E3
Wearhead DL13 ... 179 B2
Wheatley Hill DH6 ... 47 E1
South View E NE39 ... 1 C2
South View Gdns DH9 ... 13 A3
South View Terr
Bearpark DH7 ... 33 B3
Fence Houses DH4 ... 26 B8
Middlesbrough TS3 ... 120 C4
South View W NE39 ... 1 C2
South Way TS20 ... 118 C7
South West Ind Est SR8 ... 48 F6
Southampton St
Darlington DL1 ... 133 A4
Redcar TS10 ... 107 D6
Southbrooke Ave TS25 ... 76 F2
Southburn Cl DH4 ... 26 C8
Southburn Gr DL15 ... 65 D7
Southburn Terr TS25 ... 77 B4
Southdean Cl TS8 ... 139 E2
Southdean Dr TS8 ... 139 F3
Southdowns DH2 ... 16 C2
Southend Ave DL1 ... 151 E8
Southend Pl DL3 ... 132 F1
Southfield DH2 ... 15 E7
Southfield Cl DL2 ... 152 D1
Southfield Cres TS20 ... 118 C6
Southfield Dr DL14 ... 78 E5
Southfield La
Middlesbrough TS1 ... 214 C2
Middlesbrough TS1 ... 215 A2
Southfield Rd
Marske-by-t-S TS11 ... 108 D1
Middlesbrough TS1 ... 215 A2
Stockton-on-T TS20 ... 118 B6
Southfield Terr TS9 ... 161 A3
Southfield Way DH1 ... 34 A4
Southgate Eston TS6 ... 122 A2
Hartlepool TS24 ... 77 F8
Southgate St 7 DL14 ... 80 C7
Southland Ave TS26 ... 76 F5
Southland Cvn Site
TS21 ... 137 A8
Southlands DH6 ... 57 E7
Southlands Cvn Site★
TS21 ... 137 A8
Southlands Dr TS7 ... 141 B4
Southlands Gdns DL4 ... 80 F2
Southmead Ave TS3 ... 140 E7
Southport Cl TS18 ... 118 D4
Southwark Cl TS6 ... 141 C7
Southway Lanchester DH7 ... 20 E4
Peterlee SR8 ... 49 C5
Southwell Gn DL1 ... 133 E4
Southwell Rd TS5 ... 119 F2
Southwell Sq TS5 ... 119 F1
Southwick Ave TS4 ... 140 B5
Southwood TS8 ... 159 B7
Southwood Cres NE39 ... 1 F2
Sowerby St DH7 ... 23 B2
Sowerby Way TS16 ... 137 B3
Spa Dr DH8 ... 10 C7
Spa Rd DL2 ... 201 C3
Spa Well Cl NE21 ... 2 B8
Spa Well Turn NE21 ... 2 E7
Spain Hill TS11 ... 108 D1
Spalding Rd TS25 ... 89 E6
Spalding Wlk TS20 ... 118 C7
Spark Sq TS19 ... 117 D5
Sparrow Hall Dr DL1 ... 133 D7
Sparrow La TS14 ... 143 F2
Spaunton Cl TS8 ... 139 C2
Spawood Cotts TS14 ... 144 C4
Spearman Wlk TS27 ... 63 D3
Speeding Dr TS24 ... 63 E4
Speedwell Cl DL1 ... 133 C1
Speeton Ave TS5 ... 139 E6
Speeton Cl TS23 ... 102 E8
Spell Cl TS15 ... 156 F5
Spellman Gr TS10 ... 106 E3
Spen Burn NE39 ... 1 A4
Spen La NE39 ... 1 B3
Spen St DH9 ... 13 E5
Spenborough Rd TS19 ... 117 D5
Spence Ct TS9 ... 161 A3
Spencely St DL4 ... 80 F2
Spencer Cl
Marske-by-t-S TS11 ... 108 C2
Stanley DH9 ... 14 B6
Spencer Gr DL1 ... 152 C7
Spencer Rd TS6 ... 121 D3
Spencer St Consett DH8 ... 10 F3
Eldon Lane DL14 ... 80 F4
Spencerbeck Farm TS7 141 B8
Spencerbeck Farm Cotts
TS7 ... 141 B8
Spencerfield Cres TS3 ... 121 A3
Spennithorne Rd TS18 ... 212 B3
Spennymoor Comp Sch
DL16 ... 68 E7
Spenser Gr TS25 ... 76 F3
Spilsby Cl TS25 ... 89 E6
Spinnaker Ho TS24 ... 77 D6
Spinney The
Darlington DL3 ... 151 D6
Easington SR8 ... 39 A4
Hartlepool TS26 ... 76 C5
Middleton St George DL2 ... 154 B8
Newton Aycliffe DL5 ... 82 D2
Spennymoor DL16 ... 56 C1
Stockton-on-T TS18 ... 137 D8
Spire Hollin SR8 ... 49 C6
Spital Gate TS15 ... 156 C4
Spital The TS15 ... 156 C5
Spitalfields TS15 ... 156 C5
Spitfire Cl 8 TS11 ... 108 B1
Spooner Cl DL5 ... 82 B1
Spout Bank DL12 ... 198 E7
Spout La DL4 ... 81 C1
Spring Bank Wood TS22 ... 87 B3
Spring Cl
Annfield Plain DH9 ... 13 A3
Ebchester DH8 ... 3 E2
Thornaby-on-T TS17 ... 138 C8
Spring Ct DL3 ... 132 C5
Spring Garden Cl TS7 ... 141 B5
Spring Garden La TS7 ... 141 B5
Spring Garden Rd TS25 ... 77 B3
Spring Gdns DL14 ... 79 A2
Spring Head Terr TS13 ... 127 C1
Spring Hill DL3 ... 132 F6
Spring La TS21 ... 85 A3
Spring Rd DL5 ... 96 C2
Spring Rise TS6 ... 141 C7
Spring St
Middlesbrough TS2 ... 215 A4
Stockton-on-T TS18 ... 212 C1
Spring Way TS18 ... 137 E8
Spring Wood Rd TS14 ... 143 E4
Springbank Rd
Newfield DL14 ... 67 B7
Ormesby TS7 ... 141 B6
Springdale Ave TS29 ... 60 B5
Springfell DH3 ... 9 D3
Springfield Ave
Brotton TS12 ... 126 B3
Stockton-on-T TS18 ... 137 E8
Springfield Cl TS16 ... 137 B1
Springfield Cres SR7 ... 29 C7
Springfield Gdns DH3 ... 16 C5
Springfield Gr TS15 ... 156 E1
Springfield Pk DH1 ... 210 A4
Springfield Prim Sch
DL1 ... 133 C5
Springfield Rd
Darlington DL1 ... 133 C6
Fishburn TS21 ... 72 C4
Middlesbrough TS5 ... 119 B2
Springfield Terr
Pelton DH2 ... 15 E5
Peterlee SR8 ... 39 F3
Willington DL15 ... 53 E3
Springfields DL15 ... 95 F4
Springhill 2 TS7 ... 141 B7
Springhill Gr TS17 ... 157 B7
Springholme
3 Ormesby TS7 ... 141 B7
Stockton-on-T TS18 ... 212 C1
Springholme Yd TS18 ... 212 C1
Springhouse La DH8 ... 3 E2
Springlea 6 TS7 ... 141 B7
Springmead 5 TS7 ... 141 B7
Springs The DH3 ... 9 E3
Springside DH7 ... 23 C3
Springston Rd TS26 ... 76 D7
Springsyde Cl NE16 ... 2 E5
Springvale Terr TS5 ... 119 B1
Springwalk 4 TS7 ... 141 B7
Springwell DL2 ... 201 D7
Springwell Ave
Durham DH1 ... 210 A4
Langley Park DH7 ... 32 C6
Trimdon TS29 ... 59 E1
Springwell Cl
Billingham TS23 ... 102 F8
9 Langley Park DH7 ... 32 C6
Springwell Flatlets TS26 ... 76 E8
Springwell Rd
Durham DH1 ... 210 A4
Springwell NE9 ... 9 F8
Springwell Sch TS26 ... 76 E8
Springwell Terr
Darlington DL1 ... 133 D5
Hetton-le-H DH5 ... 27 A2
Spruce Ct Shildon DL4 ... 95 B8

Name and Address	Telephone	Page	Grid reference

Addresses

Name and Address	Telephone	Page	Grid reference

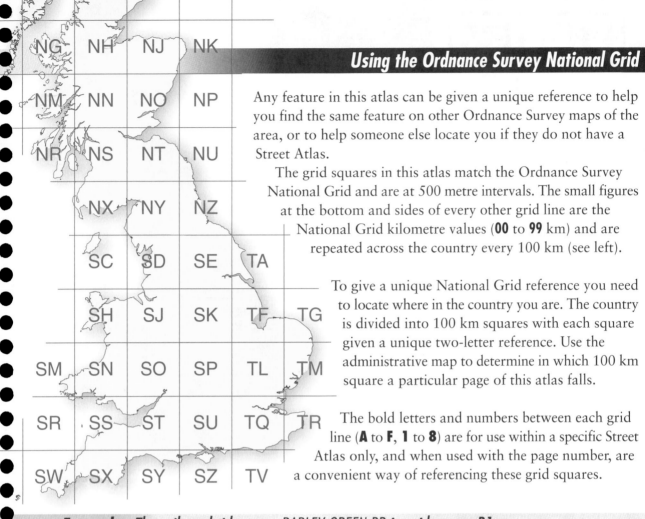

Any feature in this atlas can be given a unique reference to help you find the same feature on other Ordnance Survey maps of the area, or to help someone else locate you if they do not have a Street Atlas.

The grid squares in this atlas match the Ordnance Survey National Grid and are at 500 metre intervals. The small figures at the bottom and sides of every other grid line are the National Grid kilometre values (**00** to **99** km) and are repeated across the country every 100 km (see left).

To give a unique National Grid reference you need to locate where in the country you are. The country is divided into 100 km squares with each square given a unique two-letter reference. Use the administrative map to determine in which 100 km square a particular page of this atlas falls.

The bold letters and numbers between each grid line (**A** to **F**, **1** to **8**) are for use within a specific Street Atlas only, and when used with the page number, are a convenient way of referencing these grid squares.

Example   The railway bridge over DARLEY GREEN RD in grid square B1

Step 1: Identify the two-letter reference, in this example the page is in **SP**

Step 2: Identify the 1 km square in which the railway bridge falls. Use the figures in the southwest corner of this square: Eastings **17**, Northings **74**. This gives a unique reference: **SP 17 74**, accurate to 1 km.

Step 3: To give a more precise reference accurate to 100 m you need to estimate how many tenths along and how many tenths up this 1 km square the feature is (to help with this the 1 km square is divided into four 500 m squares). This makes the bridge about **8** tenths along and about **1** tenth up from the southwest corner.

This gives a unique reference: **SP 178 741**, accurate to 100 m.

Eastings (read from left to right along the bottom) come before Northings (read from bottom to top). If you have trouble remembering say to yourself "Along the hall, THEN up the stairs"!

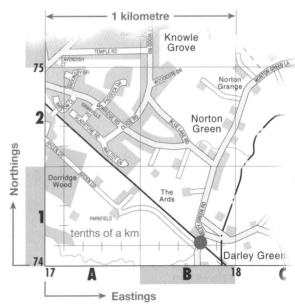

PHILIP'S MAPS

the Gold Standard for serious driving

◆ Philip's street atlases cover every county in England, plus much of Wales and Scotland.

◆ All our atlases use the same style of mapping, with the same colours and symbols, so you can move with confidence from one atlas to the next

◆ Widely used by the emergency services, transport companies and local authorities.

◆ Created from the most up-to-date and detailed information available from Ordnance Survey

◆ Based on the National Grid

BEST BUY • BEST BUY
Auto EXPRESS
BEST BUY • BEST BUY

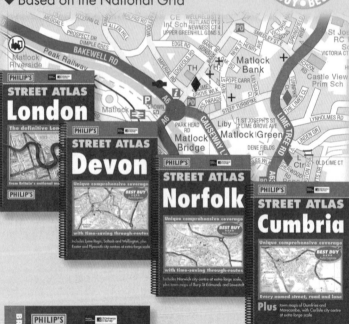

England

Bedfordshire
Berkshire
Birmingham and West Midlands
Bristol and Bath
Buckinghamshire
Cambridgeshire
Cheshire
Cornwall
Cumbria
Derbyshire
Devon
Dorset
County Durham and Teesside
Essex
North Essex
South Essex
Gloucestershire
North Hampshire
South Hampshire
Herefordshire Monmouthshire
Hertfordshire
Isle of Wight
East Kent
West Kent
Lancashire
Leicestershire and Rutland
Lincolnshire
London
Greater Manchester
Merseyside
Norfolk
Northamptonshire
Nottinghamshire
Oxfordshire
Shropshire
Somerset

All-England coverage

Staffordshire
Suffolk
Surrey
East Sussex
West Sussex
Tyne and Wear Northumberland
Warwickshire
Birmingham and West Midlands
Wiltshire and Swindon
Worcestershire
East Yorkshire Northern Lincolnshire
North Yorkshire
South Yorkshire
West Yorkshire

Wales

Anglesey, Conwy and Gwynedd
Cardiff, Swansea and The Valleys
Denbighshire, Flintshire, Wrexham
Herefordshire Monmouthshire

Scotland

Aberdeenshire
Edinburgh and East Central Scotland
Fife and Tayside
Glasgow and West Central Scotland
Inverness and Moray

For national mapping, choose **Philip's Navigator Britain** – the most detailed road atlas available of England, Wales and Scotland. Hailed by Auto Express as 'the ultimate road atlas', this is the only one-volume atlas to show every road and lane in Britain.